Deviance, Crime, and Control

Third Edition

Deviance, Crime, and Control

Beyond the Straight and Narrow

Lorne Tepperman and Alex Tepperman

OXFORD
UNIVERSITY PRESS

OXFORD
UNIVERSITY PRESS

Oxford University Press is a department of the University of Oxford. It furthers the University's objective of excellence in research, scholarship, and education by publishing worldwide. Oxford is a registered trade mark of Oxford University Press in the UK and in certain other countries.

Published in Canada by
Oxford University Press
8 Sampson Mews, Suite 204,
Don Mills, Ontario M3C 0H5 Canada

www.oupcanada.com

First Edition published in 2006
Second Edition published in 2010

Library and Archives Canada Cataloguing in Publication
Tepperman, Lorne, 1943-
Deviance, crime, and control : beyond the straight and narrow /
Lorne Tepperman and Alex Tepperman. -- 3rd ed.

Includes bibliographical references and index.
ISBN 978-0-19-544743-9

1. Deviant behavior---Textbooks. 2. Social control--Textbooks.
3. Criminology--Textbooks. I. Tepperman, Alex II. Title.

HM811.T45 2013 302.5'42 C2012-906115-8

Cover image: Grove Pashley/Photographer's Cloud/Getty Images

This book is printed on permanent (acid-free) paper ♾.

Printed and bound in the USA

1 2 3 4 — 16 15 14 13

Contents

Preface x
Acknowledgements xvii

Part I Introduction

1 Sociological Approaches to Deviance 2
Learning Objectives 2
Introduction 3
A Sociological Approach to Crime and Deviance 4
Sociological Approaches 4
Social Policy Implications 28
Conclusion 29
Questions for Critical Thought 29
Recommended Readings 30
Recommended Websites 30
Recommended Movies 31

Part II Deviant Activities

2 Appearance Issues 34
Learning Objectives 34
Introduction 35
Appearance Norms 35
Appearance: Its Social Meaning 39
Appearance Issues and the Fashion Industry 42
Communities and Subcultures of Appearance 44
Punk Appearance 46
Eating Issues and Appearance Norms 49
Theories about Appearance Issues 54
Consequences of Appearance Issues 59
Social Policy Implications 61
Economic Consequences 62
Conclusion 63
Questions for Critical Thought 64
Recommended Readings 64
Recommended Websites 65
Recommended Movies 66

3 Mental Illness 67
Learning Objectives 67
Introduction 68
The History of Mental Illness and Public Reactions 69
The Characteristics of Mental Illness and Mentally Ill People 74
Communities and Subcultures of the Mentally Ill 83
Media Depictions of Mental Illness 84
Theories about Mental Illness 86
Consequences of Mental Illness 90
Social Policy Implications 93
Conclusion 96
Questions for Critical Thought 97
Recommended Readings 97
Recommended Websites 98
Recommended Movies 99

4 **Sexual Deviance 101**
Learning Objectives 101
Introduction 102
The History of Sexual Deviance and Public Reactions 105
Prostitution 106
Pornography 110
Other Forms of Sexual Deviation 111
Anti-Homosexuality as a Form of Sexual Deviance 117
Media Depictions of Sexual Deviance 118
Theories about Sexual Deviance 119
Consequences of Sexual Deviance 127
Social Policy Implications 129
Conclusion 130
Questions for Critical Thought 131
Recommended Readings 131
Recommended Websites 132
Recommended Movies 133

5 **Substance Abuse 135**
Learning Objectives 135
Introduction 136
The Social Role of Intoxication 137
The History of Drug and Alcohol Abuse and Public Reactions 139
The Activities and Characteristics of Substance Abusers 144
Communities and Subcultures of Drug Users 151
Media Depictions of Substance Abuse 153
Theories about Drug and Alcohol Abuse 154
Consequences of Drug and Alcohol Abuse 157
Social Policy Implications 161
Conclusion 164
Questions for Critical Thought 165
Recommended Readings 166
Recommended Websites 166
Recommended Movies 167

Part III Delinquency and Crime

6 **Risky Behaviours and Delinquency 170**
Learning Objectives 170
Introduction 171
A Snapshot of Risky Behaviour: The Case of Ontario 172
The Developmental Course of Risk-Taking 173
The Gendering of Delinquency and Crime 174
Bullying 175
Adolescent Risk-Taking 177
The Influence of Family and Peers 180
The Activities of Juvenile Delinquents 182
Coexisting Problems 185
Communities and Subcultures of Delinquency 185
Media Depictions of Delinquency 190
Theories about Juvenile Delinquency 191
Consequences of Juvenile Delinquency 193
Social Policy Implications 195
Future Trends 198
Conclusion 198
Questions for Critical Thought 199

Recommended Readings 199
Recommended Websites 200
Recommended Movies 201

7 **Violent Crimes 202**
Learning Objectives 202
Introduction 203
The History of Violent Crime and Public Reactions 207
Defining Crimes of Violence 209
The Social Characteristics of Violent Criminals 213
Communities and Subcultures of Violence 213
Family Violence 214
Media Depictions of Violent Crime 220
Theories about Violent Crime 221
Consequences of Violent Crime 225
Social Policy Implications 228
Conclusion 229
Questions for Critical Thought 231
Recommended Readings 231
Recommended Websites 232
Recommended Movies 233

8 **Non-Violent Crimes 234**
Learning Objectives 234
Introduction 235
Non-Violent Crime: Its Types and Variety 236
The Demographic and Social Characteristics of Criminals 245
Media Depictions of Non-Violent Crime 254
Theories about Non-Violent Crime 255
Consequences of Non-Violent Crime 258
Fear of Crime 260
Social Policy Implications 263
Future Trends 263
Conclusion 265
Questions for Critical Thought 266
Recommended Readings 266
Recommended Websites 267
Recommended Movies 268

9 **Political Crimes 269**
Learning Objectives 269
Introduction 270
Corruption 270
Treason 273
Riots and Collective Protests 276
Torture 277
The History of Protest, War, and Rebellion and Public Reactions 278
Communities and Subcultures of Protest, War, and Rebellion 283
Media Depictions of Political Crime 286
Theories about Protest, War, and Rebellion 288
Consequences of Protest, War, and Rebellion 292
The Dominant Ideology as Normative System 297
Social Policy Implications 298
Conclusion 299
Questions for Critical Thought 299
Recommended Readings 300

Recommended Websites 301
Recommended Movies 302

10 **Victims of Crime and Victims of Conscience 303**
Learning Objectives 303
Introduction 304
Theories about Victims and Victimization 306
Victimization and the Case of Sex Workers 315
The Victimization of Aboriginal People 315
Victims of Conscience 319
Religion as a Source of Control and Deviance 320
Media Depictions of Victimization 324
Economic Consequences of Human Trafficking 325
Social Policy Implications of Victimization 326
Conclusion 327
Questions for Critical Thought 328
Recommended Readings 328
Recommended Websites 329
Recommended Movies 330

Part IV What Comes Next?

11 **Social Control 334**
Learning Objectives 334
Introduction 335
How Groups Protect Themselves 337
Managing Social Rewards 337
Strategies of Social Control 339
Media Depictions of Informal Control 359
Consequences of Social Control 360
Conclusion 360
Questions for Critical Thought 363
Recommended Readings 363
Recommended Websites 364
Recommended Movies 365

12 **Formal Punishment 366**
Learning Objectives 366
Introduction 367
Definition of Punishment 367
Goals of Punishment 367
Punishment in Canada 369
The Types and Characteristics of Punishment 371
Media Depictions of Formal Punishment 392
Consequences of Imprisonment 393
Social Policy Implications 396
Conclusion 397
Questions for Critical Thought 397
Recommended Readings 398
Recommended Websites 399
Recommended Movies 400

Glossary 401
References 410
Index 427

I

Enter ye in at the strait gate: for wide is the gate, and broad is the way,
that leadeth to destruction, and many there be which go in thereat:
Because strait is the gate, and narrow is the way, which leadeth unto life,
and few there be that find it.

The Holy Bible, King James Version (Matt. 7: 13–14)

II

Loving Shepherd, ever near,
Teach Thy lamb Thy voice to hear;
Suffer not my steps to stray
From the straight and narrow way.

J.E. Leeson, *Hymns & Scenes of Childhood* (1842)

III

Friendship loves a free air, and will not be fenced up
in straight and narrow enclosures.

William Penn,
Some Fruits of Solitude (1691)

IV

It's only the fear of pregnancy which keeps girls
on the straight and narrow.

F. Weldon,
Praxis (1978)

V

Take heed, never take advantage of the things you need,
never let yourself be overcome by greed,
walk the straight and narrow and you shall succeed.

***Shaggy*, "Why Me Lord?"** (2000)

Preface

Why do people depart from the straight and narrow path? This is an important question—one that invokes centuries-old religious, moral, and philosophical concerns. It is a societal question, of great interest to the upholders of social order, and it is also a sociological question, at least since the time of Émile Durkheim. Given the importance of this question's implications, it is fitting to ask, once more, why people depart from the straight and narrow path. Why do societies make rules? Why do people break those rules? Does the making and breaking of rules really matter? These are the fundamental sociological questions we consider in this book. Answering them will teach something about both how societies work and how sociology works.

Rule-breaking and rule-making activities surround us. Consider something we are all familiar with: traffic rules and violations. Driving in traffic is something most people experience and, even if you don't drive, you know how stressful it can be just sitting in traffic. But how many of us have made theories about—or even seriously thought about—the circumstances under which drivers make eye contact, honk their horn, exceed the speed limit, or stop for jaywalking pedestrians? Some of these behaviours—for example, making eye contact with other drivers—are just wise precautions; others show a concern for good manners (e.g., stopping for jaywalkers) or an eagerness to obey the law (e.g., staying below the speed limit).

When we drive a car, we have the opportunity to obey or violate social rules. Some of these rules are written as formal laws; others are unwritten rules of etiquette and good manners, but we know them nonetheless. When other people violate these rules, we get confused, upset, or even outraged. The apoplectic fits shown by some motorists—termed *road rage*—are an increasingly common form of vigilantism designed by individual drivers to punish other motorists for breaking the rules of the road. As we can see, in driving, there are rules and rule violators; there are also numerous measures we take to prevent or punish rule violation on the road.

This speaks to a broader truth, that every aspect of our social lives involves rules, rule enforcement, rule violation, and punishment. To lead normal lives, we all rely on social order, and social order depends on rules and rule enforcement. Situations differ as to whether the rules and rule-enforcement strategies are written or unwritten, formal or informal, regularly or irregularly enforced. But these differences are relatively minor and do not undermine our one overarching observation: people in societies make and enforce rules. This book is about a variety of the situations that involve rules and rule-breaking, or deviance.

Deviance, Crime, and Control: Beyond the Straight and Narrow will build on the assumption that deviance and conformity are both normal and socially constructed. Social order is a moving target and the mere existence of the idea of deviance, and the "discovery" of deviance in our midst, tells us a great deal about a society's control over individuals and tolerance for rule-breaking. The struggle to achieve order and uniformity—that is, an absence of intolerable difference—is an unending effort that cannot succeed, indeed, has never succeeded. The benchmarks for what makes up deviance are constantly changing, as are the limits of tolerable difference. These benchmarks vary both over time and from one place to another.

They also tell us about the oppressiveness of rules that other people make and enforce over us. As this book will show, we are all (from time to time) victims of rule-breakers and also victims of rule-makers. Thus, this book is ultimately about social organization and sociology's most central concerns—social structure, how it arises, and how it is preserved. In this way, the book is a logical secondary introduction to the field of sociology.

Deviance is an indicator of social order, or what sociologists usually call *social structure*. Deviance demonstrates the failure to make everyone behave the same way in a given situation or to adapt in expected ways as they pass from one situation to another. By this reckoning, "deviance" is not the breakdown or moral lapse of particular individuals; it is the failure of social controls to enforce an expected degree of conformity. Looking at it this way, the study of deviance repeatedly returns us to questions such as: "Why do we make the rules and laws we do and enforce them more or less loosely?"

Viewed from a critical perspective, the enforcement of laws and norms is, at base, the exercise of power by socially dominant groups. Thus, changes in norms, laws, and rule enforcement reflect the changing interests of dominant social groups and their changing wishes to control certain behaviours. What makes up deviance and crime differs from one society to another—for example, from a feudal agricultural society to a corporate capitalist society—because in each there are different ruling classes, different possibilities for deviance and crime, and different interests at stake.

Passing from the topic of norms to that of laws, and from the idea of informal control to formal control, we move into the domain of criminology. Criminology is concerned with why people act in ways that are widely perceived to be criminal, and why society and its agents of formal control—police officers and judges, for example—respond to criminal acts as they do. Viewed this way, criminology is a subtype of the sociology of deviance, and the sociology of deviance is a subtype of general sociology. This is not a criminology textbook, however. It is much more general than that, as we will look at crime as only one species of deviant behaviour among many.

The reader is advised to consult a book specifically focused on crime and delinquency for more comprehensive theorizing about these behaviours. In this book we will ask: What price do individual members of society pay—in control and repression—to be accepted as members of society? What are the social and emotional costs of conforming to the rules? What are the costs of breaking them? How do we get the kind of society we want to live in—where we are secure but respectful of differences—and are we moving in that general direction?

What, then, makes this book distinctive? First, *Deviance, Crime, and Control* discusses various forms of deviance and conformity against the backdrop of sociology's most general questions: Why do some societies require some kinds of behaviours, while other societies do not? How do socially required behaviours change over time? What social changes produce what kinds of change in the behaviours we require and the strictness with which we enforce our rules? We will keep the historical context in mind in this book, even as we focus on contemporary notions of right and wrong, deviant and conforming behaviour.

Second, *Deviance, Crime, and Control* takes a broadly theoretical approach. We will link theories and facts about deviance to broader sociological issues about social organization, social control, cultural change, and social inequality. In this respect, the book is a logical extension to what students have already learned, should they have taken an Introduction to Sociology course. As in that course, in this book theories of deviance and control are organized into three main categories—functionalist, symbolic interactionist (or social constructionist), and critical. This book shows how each category or approach makes a valuable contribution to understanding varieties of deviance and control, stressing that all of these approaches are useful. They serve, as needed, as the philosophical backdrop against which we examine "middle-range" theories about deviance, crime, and control.

Finally, this book puts a premium on learning aids: objectives, current events boxes, chapter reviews and summaries, discussion questions, recommended readings and websites, and a glossary. We think this will help students grasp theoretical arguments more readily and will help them understand that much of what we see today in Canada has been seen and thought about at other times, and in many other societies.

Organization of the Book

Deviance, Crime, and Control is comprised of 12 chapters. Following a general outline chapter that will introduce the student to various theoretical approaches, or models, of sociology, subsequent chapters discuss common and general types of deviance (appearance issues), slightly less common and more specific types of deviance (mental illness, sexual deviance, substance abuse), and, finally, criminal forms of deviance (violent, non-violent, political).

The chapters are loosely organized according to the "seriousness" of the impact of a deviant act and its harmful impact on society. Thus, Chapters 2 through 5 are about deviant acts that do not break the law; Chapters 6 through 9 are about delinquent and criminal acts that do. It should be noted that Chapter 6 is about delinquent behaviours whereas Chapters 7 through 9 are about criminal behaviours. Chapters 6 and 7 are about crimes that arguably hurt the fewest people in the least hurtful way, and Chapters 8 and 9 are about (violent) crimes that hurt a few people in extreme ways or (political) crimes that hurt many people less extremely. Chapter 10, a new chapter, discusses two aspects of victimization: specifically, it examines the victims of rule-breakers (especially, criminals) and the victims of rule-makers. Chapters 11 and 12 are about (informal) social control and formal punishment, respectively. In an important sense, they complete this book's general discussions about deviance and crime and their place in the social order.

By the book's end, we will find that there is much more to say—we have really only begun—and we are far from being able to predict the future of deviance, crime, or control in Canadian society. We have developed some insights and tools that will help us think about the present and future, however.

Each chapter is organized in roughly the same way. First comes a discussion of the background of a problem: the nature of the activity or behaviour in question (e.g., drug abuse) and public reactions to it. This is followed by a brief history of that activity. The largest part of the chapter is taken up with a discussion of the current state of that behaviour. This includes the demographic and social characteristics of people in this domain, theories about this activity (according to the different approaches of sociology), effects of the activity, and policies and theory applications to control this activity. The chapter ends with a brief discussion of future prospects. Chapters will vary somewhat in their organization and coverage of these issues, however, as we allow the book to wander into important related issues when warranted.

The "Funnel"—A Central Feature of Deviance and Crime

In every chapter, we will see that the greatest part of deviance and crime is hidden. It comes into view only when we look for it, and most of the time we aren't looking very hard. Most of the deviance and crime we *do* see is the result of special efforts made by rule-enforcers—paid and unpaid—to root out rule-breaking.

What that means is that for every counted or documented act of rule-breaking, there are likely tens, hundreds, or even thousands of undocumented, comparable acts. Deviance and crime are really common, yet rarely noted. This is most easily seen in connection with crime; here we at least *try* to keep systematic records of rule-breaking. Yet, even with crime, it is evident that rule-breaking is funnelled through a system of partial observation, enforcement, reporting, and conviction that, in the end, produces statistics on relatively few rule-breakers.

If we start with the reports of victims of crimes, for example—and consider these the best estimate of crimes actually committed—we see that relatively few are reported to the police. The fraction reported depends on the crime: most homicides, attempted homicides, and major property losses are reported; by comparison, few thefts, threats, and minor assaults are reported. There is much debate about what fraction of sexual assaults is reported, but the number is thought to be low.

So, we find a decrease as we move from crimes committed to crimes reported and then another decline as we move from crimes reported to crimes recorded by the police. The police have their own professional and institutional reasons for recording or not recording what people tell them. Of all recorded crimes, the police will investigate some and not others. While a portion of these criminal investigations will turn up suspects, many others will not. The police will then file charges against some of these suspects, while they will choose not to charge others. Of those charged, some will be convicted of that crime in court or submit a plea bargain while others will not. Lastly, some of these convictions will result in dispositions, or what we will later call *punishments*, while others will not.

At each stage, the numbers get smaller—like a funnel, the scope is wide up above and narrow down below. Nowhere is this more clearly drawn than in a *New York Times* article reporting that 35 million crimes at the top end of the US funnel result in a mere 500,000 convicted prisoners at the bottom end (Anderson, 1994), in other words, one conviction for every 70 crimes committed. We see similar patterns of crime and delinquency in Canada, though the specific numbers vary from one crime to another and one jurisdiction to another.

By studying the processes of deviance, crime, and control, we learn a great deal about exclusion and inclusion. On the one hand, we learn about the relatively few people who—at the bottom end of the funnel—are labelled, processed, punished, and stigmatized as rule-breakers and wrongdoers. We also learn about the many people who are not, and we discover a lot about the social institutions that undertake this sorting and funnelling process. We get behind the scenes and see how the proverbial sausage gets made. Specifically, we will see how social order is really maintained.

Sociological versus Other Explanations

The topics of deviance, crime, and control are not the exclusive domain of sociologists. In fact, both the natural and the social sciences have contributed their own unique understandings and perspectives to the study of deviance and control.

That is one of the reasons we decided to make this new edition of the book a father–son collaboration between a sociologist (father) and historian-criminologist (son). Everyone gains by bringing multiple perspectives to the table, especially if these perspectives are compatible. Happily, sociological, criminological, and historical approaches were perfectly compatible in this instance. As well, the historian-criminologist son brings an understanding of popular culture that, we think, enriches the book's content even more.

This is to say that, where truth-finding is concerned, disciplines need not be in competition with each other. For example, the contributions made by psychologists are not "right" and those by anthropologists "wrong"; both are correct, according to their own designs and self-imposed limits. Each approach can further our understanding of the problems we are considering. The study of deviance and control is best undertaken as a complementary, multi-levelled co-operative action in which the findings of one field corroborate the research and theories of the others. This is not to suggest an absence of conflicting data or results in areas of study. Contradictory findings usually suggest a flaw in one theory or another, calling for closer scrutiny and the need to further refine the theory used.

That said, in this book we focus on sociological, criminological, and historical explanations of deviance and crime. Biological and psychological explanations, when offered, are brief and necessarily tentative. Because this book is small and the topic is large, we keep a clear focus on what concerns us most centrally, namely, the role of social factors in deviance and control.

Often, *psychological perspectives* differ importantly from sociological perspectives. The former centre on individuals and are concerned mainly with cognitive and perceptual processes. Much of psychology's contribution to understanding deviance has come from social psychologists who study the ways in which social and mental forces influence action. Social psychologists distinguish themselves conceptually from sociologists by limiting their research to the thoughts and personalities of individuals as they are influenced by, and represented in, a social context.

For example, a social-psychological approach to the Holocaust might focus on how a charismatic authority can create unwavering obedience among subordinates as a way of explaining why Nazi soldiers would carry out the concentration camp atrocities ordered by Adolf Hitler against the Jews and other marginalized groups. Notice how this perspective stresses the individual soldier and his cognitions, rather than the entire National Socialist (Nazi) party as a social group or the political ideology of German society.

With respect to the topics we will discuss, the stance of sociology is as follows, depending on the particular theory in question:

- Deviance is the unusual (i.e., occasional) behaviour of normal people.
- Deviance is the usual behaviour of normal people in deviant roles.
- Deviance is the usual behaviour of normal people in abnormal situations.
- Deviance is the usual behaviour of people who violate unreasonable rules.
- Deviance is the usual result of unequal opportunities to conform to rules.
- Deviance is the usual result of deviant learning (e.g., imitation of criminals).
- Deviance is the usual result of defective social connection (e.g., lack of control).

Thus, the goal of sociology is often to make the unfamiliar familiar and to normalize the seemingly abnormal. Historically, sociology has sought to understand the underdogs and the rule-breakers from their own point of view.

In doing so, sociologists have challenged the powerful who, almost invariably, have sought to dominate (or governmentalize), vilify, pathologize, or medicalize the unfamiliar, the strange, and the deviant.

This distinction is important to bear in mind throughout this book, as it explains why we have taken pains to emphasize sociological explanations and ignore psychological ones. Psychology, because of its essential focus on the individual, looks for answers *inside* the individual actors; it wants to "cure" their deviance. The sociological stance looks for answers *outside* the individual actors. It wants to "cure" problems in society; to understand why society is pathological and inhuman; and to improve societies, not individuals.

In short, the sociological enterprise is different from the psychological enterprise in its goals, methods, theories, and social aims. We stress that it is *different*, but not *better* or *worse*. Any reader interested in the psychology of deviance is urged to read one of the many fine works on that topic. This book, however, focuses on the sociological approach.

Solutions to Problems of Deviance and Crime

Each chapter in this book suggests potential solutions to the problems under discussion, solutions that Canadians have tried with varying degrees of vigour and success. We need to be careful to attend to solutions of two broad types: *individual solutions* and *group-based* or *organization-based solutions*. We will see examples of each of these types of solutions as we move through the chapters that follow.

C. Wright Mills (1959) famously described "the sociological imagination" by noting that "knowledge can be power," but only if individuals choose to act on it. When we know what is going on in society, we can then act accordingly and in our best interests and we stand some chance of increasing our opportunities. Under individual-level solutions, we can act to "work the system" to our benefit.

The analyses to come will indicate that dominant groups often oppose certain solutions to certain social problems because they are not particularly in their interests. As Karl Marx and Max Weber, along with other scholars, have emphasized, such groups will have considerable organizational and ideological power. Nonetheless, many political struggles to change the rules actually succeed. In Canada and the United States alone, we see many examples of successful protest movements by subordinate groups: the Aboriginal rights movement in Canada, the civil rights movement in the United States, and the women's and gay rights movements in both countries, to name only a few. Another important example is the success of the labour movement in Canada and the United States, fighting over many decades to secure better wages and job conditions for workers.

We will have occasion to discuss some of these group-based strategies for solving social problems, including some initiated by government agencies. Such developments should give us hope when we consider the possibilities of political action to resolve social problems. Many problems are formidable, but there is room to effect change.

A Book of Ideas

For various reasons, this is not primarily a fact book or almanac about crime and deviance—it is a theory book, a book of ideas about deviance and control, and about the reasons people conform or do not conform to societal norms. Our approach reflects the view that we need to examine the basic ideas before we can make good use of facts. It is also an attempt to distinguish social science from journalism, which is heavy with current facts and usually light on ideas. Third, it reflects the fact that this is a book; facts change quickly whereas ideas (and books, for that matter) do not.

Finally, and equally important, for reasons that will become clear in the course of this book, we do not have good estimates, let alone secure facts, about many—perhaps most—of the deviant behaviours discussed in this book. For example, estimates vary widely on how many homosexuals, sex workers, delinquents, drug users, anorexics, mentally ill, or obese people there are in Canada. Figures on convicted criminals of various kinds are somewhat more precise, but even these are often incomplete or heavily flawed.

Typically, facts about deviant acts and actors come from sources that are limited, biased, and contradictory. These include self-reports of deviant behaviour, victimization reports, and institutional reports (e.g., reports by hospitals, police forces, courts, prisons, and so on). Self-reports suffer from frequent falsification: people often lie about themselves to feel or appear better or worse than they actually are, or because they cannot always remember what they have done. Victimization reports also suffer from exaggeration and forgetting. Beyond that, many kinds of deviance—drug abuse, obesity, or unsafe sex, for example—do not have "victims" in the usual sense other than the actors themselves. Institutional reports describe only the deviants who have been apprehended by the institution—arrested, tried, convicted, and so on. This represents only a small fraction of the entire deviant population, however.

So, in most instances, we have a very incomplete and imperfect knowledge about deviant people and their actions, let alone the reasons for their actions. We do have a good set of sociological questions and debates and interesting speculation about the answers, however. This book, for better or worse, is about what we *do* have.

Acknowledgements

This book took a year to revise, and, as with the writing of the first two editions, a lot has been learned from the exercise. Many people have helped to make this book what it is now, and we want to thank them all.

Since it is impossible to allot credit in precisely correct proportions, we will hand out laurels chronologically. In the fall of 2010, Mark Thompson and Lisa Peterson, acquisitions editor and developmental editor, respectively, got the ball rolling by soliciting and summarizing anonymous reviews. Together, we then worked out a revision plan. As always, length was a problem: there was too much worth saying and too few pages to say it in.

In the winter of 2011, undergraduate assistants Anita Feher and Brianna Sykes pulled together a great deal of valuable information on victimization; and much of this material, significantly reworked, found its way into the new chapter on victimization. Then, in the summer of 2011, Elena Tepperman updated a lot of statistics in the book and suggested some new boxed inserts. We are grateful to Anita, Brianna, and Elena for their excellent work.

In January of 2012 we turned in the revised manuscript and Richard and Laurna Tallman took over as copy editors. Thank you, Richard and Laurna, for a thorough and astute reading of the manuscript; you both have been thoughtful and thought-provoking, and we have profited from your advice.

As always we have been tremendously gratified by the support and professionalism of the people at Oxford University Press. They have made writing and publishing this book almost easy. So, we share credit with our helpers and advisers for what is good about this book; but, as usual, we take responsibility for what we have failed to do well or do at all. Perhaps these flaws can be remedied in yet another edition. We will look forward to receiving advice from our readers.

The authors and publisher would like to thank the following reviewers, along with those reviewers who wish to remain anonymous, whose insightful comments have helped shape this third edition.

Ronald McGivern, Thompson Rivers University
Deborah Boutilier, Niagara College
Cheryl Mitchell, Heritage College

PART I

Introduction

1 Sociological Approaches to Deviance

Learning Objectives

- To identify three major sociological approaches for the study of deviance and control
- To consider debates within and between approaches
- To describe key theorists and major ideas in deviance and control
- To see how Durkheim and Merton proved the normality of deviance
- To understand the role of learning in the development of deviance
- To note how control and labelling can create deviant identities

Introduction

This book is about deviant behaviour, the sort of behaviour that breaks rules or violates people's expectations. There are a great many topics we might have discussed but some selection was needed; and the deviance we discuss in this book primarily relates to appearance and sexuality, mental illness, adolescent risk-taking, street crime, terrorism, corporate theft, and political protest. The rules these behaviours violate may be either formal criminal laws or informal social rules and expectations.

In this book, we take the perspective that deviance and crime are "social constructions"—activities deemed to be undesirable in a particular time and place, but rooted in culture and, for that reason, infinitely changeable. We also note that "deviance" and "crime," though related, are different. All of us break social rules at one time or another, though not all of us break the criminal laws. We also repeatedly note that not all rule-breaking is harmful. Much of it is quite harmless to others, even if it brings negative consequences upon the rule-breaker. Some deviance may, in fact, be beneficial to society, as we will see.

This book is mainly about social responses to crime and deviance, for there is no deviance without a social response to behaviour. The social responses include formal attempts at control by the state (such as the arrest, trial, and punishment of criminal offenders) and informal attempts at control (such as ridicule, **social exclusion**, and bullying).

Ideas about rules and rule-breaking are fundamental to our culture and social order. Consider the root of the English word "dignity." We usually consider "dignity" a good thing, often saying we believe that all people should be treated with the dignity they deserve. However, consider the roots of this common idea. The word "dignity" is of Latin origin, from *dignitas*, meaning rank, status, merit, worth, excellence, or fitness; and from the Latin word *dignus*, meaning appropriate, suitable, or worthy. Here we can see that the two original notions underlying dignity are that everyone has a position or role in society and that dignity (as well as worth and respectability) consists of playing your assigned role in a suitable, proper, or worthy manner. That is, conformity to social expectations is considered good, while rule-breaking—improper or unsuitable behaviour—is bad because it is "undignified."

But is *conformity* really good and *deviance* really bad? Do we still think that everyone has a role to play and each of us is responsible for playing his or her role "appropriately"? And if we think this, how can we explain the large amount of deviant, undignified behaviour that goes on in every society? Sociologists think about these matters all the time, and they think about them differently from other people.

Why people break rules—a central topic of this book—is the flip side of the equally compelling question of why people obey or conform to the rules in the first place. Paradoxically, many social commentators view conformity—however necessary for the preservation of order—as the result of an individual's weak thinking, social mediocrity, and susceptibility to relentless social pressures. Philosopher Bertrand Russell put the matter this way: "Conventional people are roused to fury by departure from convention, largely because they regard such departure as criticism of themselves." We must ask, "Under what conditions do people deviate or conform and with what consequences for society? How *should* we think about these questions today, and how have sociologists thought about these questions in the past?"

This book will give short, introductory answers to these difficult and twisty questions. As we will see, there are no simple answers.

A Sociological Approach to Crime and Deviance

Sociological approaches to deviance are different from psychological approaches, as we will repeatedly see in the chapters that follow. The role of the three Cs—careers, cultures, and communities—are key in understanding the differences between psychological and sociological approaches to deviance and control.

- *Careers* are sequences of activities that characterize a person's life course. Most people have educational careers and occupational careers, and sociologists argue that some people also have deviant or criminal careers.
- *Cultures* are sets of ideas, beliefs, practices, and values that members of a group share. An important part of the sociological approach to crime and deviance is the identification and analysis of deviant cultures and subcultures.
- *Communities* are social groups formed around common activities and a shared culture. Sociologists argue that people involved in deviant careers and cultures are often members of a broader deviant community that supports deviant careers and cultures.

These three Cs are essential features of *social structure* and *social interaction*—the central concerns of sociology as a discipline. They offer sociologists a unique framework through which to examine deviance and control.

Sociological Approaches

As you have learned throughout your studies, sociologists approach issues from varying viewpoints and within different theoretical frameworks. When sociologists analyze reality, whether consciously or not they tend to use one of three major approaches: **functionalism, symbolic interactionism**, and **critical or conflict theories** (Table 1.1). Each approach

TABLE 1.1 Three Main Sociological Approaches

Functionalism
Elements in society are interconnected and interrelated.
Well-functioning societies require value consensus, social cohesion, and social control.
Social change or inequality may create social disorganization and strain, sometimes leading to deviance and crime.
Crime strengthens social cohesion by renewing the public's commitment to social boundaries.
Symbolic Interactionism
Society is a product of continuous face-to-face interactions.
Deviance is a social accomplishment and rarely is practised solo.
Socialization and labelling shape deviant identities and subcultures.
Social problems are socially constructed.
Critical Theories
Conflict and change are basic features of social life.
Crime is a response to conflict, change, and inequality.
Conflicting groups promote contesting notions of "deviance" and "crime" to impose control on others, often resulting in intensified conflict.
Social inequality increases the likelihood of self-interested crime.

contributes to a fuller understanding of deviance, crime, control, and conformity. This book intends to help students connect new materials on crime and deviance to familiar materials from their introductory sociology courses, where these approaches were systematically examined.

Functionalism

The first approach we discuss has the longest history. Functionalism (sometimes called *structural functionalism*) arose two centuries ago from the writings of early Western European social philosophers. These social thinkers investigated the ways in which various elements of society are interconnected and interdependent. The result of this thinking is what we today call *functionalism*.

Early functionalists applied ideas from the natural sciences to the social world, hoping for the same success as the natural sciences enjoyed. In particular, they compared society to an organism, asserting that each institution has a function or role to perform in society, much like each body part has a function to perform in keeping a body healthy. Working together like a body's organs, social institutions achieve a rough balance or equilibrium in functioning society.

One of sociology's founders, Émile Durkheim, was the primary inspiration for functionalism. An early essay by Durkheim(1938 [1895])stressed the "normality of crime," a notion we will consider at length in Chapter 10. Functionalists like Durkheim typically label universal features of social life (such as crime) "normal" and they look for ways in which these universal features contribute to the social order. Durkheim argued that crime is "normal" in several senses. First, it is universal and unavoidable, no matter what form society or its laws take. Second, by violating social boundaries, criminals—and deviants more generally—help renew a commitment to those social boundaries. Violations bring community members together in outrage, and, for this reason, crime strengthens social cohesion. Furthermore, the punishment of crime strengthens social bonds and reminds people of the need to obey the rules.

Throughout the twentieth century, functionalist sociologists examined the impact of large social and economic forces on crime and deviance that appeared to threaten the social equilibrium—forces such as industrialization, urbanization, immigration, and unequal opportunity. Functionalists also analyzed how strong social bonds could be created and maintained—and equilibrium restored—in the face of these changes.

Early Functional Theories

Durkheim: Social Change and "Anomie"

According to functionalists, people usually play their learned, necessary social roles in all of a society's key institutions. This reproduces social life and keeps individuals socially stable and mentally healthy (two ideas that go together, in Durkheim's theory). In turn, these social institutions—family, economy, government, education, and others—contribute to the survival of society. For instance, the family functions to reproduce, regulate, and nurture members of society, while the economy functions to regulate the production, distribution, and consumption of goods and services among members of society.

A number of factors, including rapid social change, tend to upset these processes, however. The consequences are many and varied, including crime, addiction, and even suicide. In his classic work, *Suicide* (1966 [1897]), Durkheim offered a sociological explanation for a type of deviant behaviour—suicide—that is usually understood in purely psychological terms. By doing so, he showed that sociology could make a unique contribution to our understanding of deviant behaviour.

Durkheim insisted that we cannot fully understand suicidal behaviour if we concentrate on the psychology of isolated individuals, who may be ignorant of the causes of their own behaviour. We must learn the laws of societies, and of social life, to understand the behaviour of individuals. This we do by studying *rates* of behaviour—in this case, rates of suicide—not individual behaviours.

Durkheim argued that suicide rates increase with sudden social, cultural, political, or economic shifts, such as an economic depression. These changes disrupt traditional norms and values, leading to a gap between peoples' goals or expectations and their means of achieving them. This gap produces stress, often giving rise to deviant behaviours like suicide, mental illness, drunkenness, and a host of other things. Durkheim claimed that when rapid changes make norms and values weak or unclear, the result is "anomie," a state of alienated "normlessness." When they suffer anomie, people are not tied to the social order as securely as usual and feel released from the normal controls on their behaviour.

The Chicago School: Social Change and "Disorganization"

Early functional theorists, like Durkheim, largely ignored historical evidence, choosing instead to look at the interconnections among present-day social institutions. The ahistorical tendencies eventually resulted in a new school of functionalism, the study of "social ecology." Social ecologists examined the distribution of social activities across both space and time. The ecology of crime and deviance approach was very important in early twentieth-century American sociology.

Nearly a century ago, University of Chicago sociologists applied functionalism to studying city life, focusing particularly on the ways urban communities differ from one another. Between the 1920s and 1940s, Chicago sociologists geographically mapped out rates of crime and deviance in different areas of their city. (For the classic description of Chicago's "zones," and crime within them, see Burgess, 1967 [1925]; Shaw et al., 1929; Shaw and McKay, 1942.)

The Chicago School scholars ultimately proposed a **social disorganization theory** to explain the higher rates of crime and deviance in urban versus rural areas. Most importantly, they noted that crime and deviance rates were highest in the "transitional" inner-city neighbourhoods, those being the poor neighbourhoods with significant population turnover and heavy immigration. Like Durkheim, the Chicago School functionalists believed the forces of modernization (industrialization, immigration, and urbanization) disrupted traditional patterns of social and economic life, loosened social control, and eventually led to increased deviance and crime.

Some of the Chicago School sociologists went a step further in examining the high-crime neighbourhoods of the inner city. They undertook ethnographic studies in which they closely studied the workings of these neighbourhoods. The results of these studies led some sociologists to conclude that neighbourhoods with high rates of crime and deviance were not disorganized, just "differently disorganized" (see, e.g., Sellin, 1938). They claimed that inner-city neighbourhoods were structured around cultural values and norms that were in conflict with society at large, but were still capable of being learned and passed on from one generation to the next. This "differential organization" theory does not assume that deviance and crime result from a lack of rules, or "normlessness." Rather, it assumes the existence and persistence of criminal or deviant subcultures that compete, and may be in conflict, with the dominant culture.

Some neighbourhoods also experience higher crime rates simply because they provide better space for deviant and criminal activities. Though secrecy exists everywhere, it thrives in large and relatively anonymous spaces, like the modern metropolises. Parts of the inner city often provide *deviant service centres* for drugs, prostitutes, gambling, and other secret deviant pursuits. Georg Simmel, one of the earliest sociological investigators of metropolitanism, was especially interested in the role and organization of secrecy in social life (Box 1.1). Later sociologists added detail to these insights by examining deviant and criminal subcultures, which flourish best in the darkness of secrecy.

Classic Works

BOX 1.1

Georg Simmel and the Study of Secrecy

Over a century ago, Simmel (1906 [1902]) first offered us sociological insight into the importance of secrecy. Indirectly, he asserted the normality of deviance and the universal need for secrecy among those performing deviance. His argument also provides one basis for a functionalist understanding of crime and deviance.

Simmel suggests we all live in two worlds. Our "first world" is the openly recognized world of socially acceptable activities. Our "second world" includes hidden deviant activities—sexual affairs, drug addictions, violent acts, etc.—that other people (especially, outsiders) cannot see most of the time. According to Simmel, everyone uses secrets to furnish and occupy these second worlds. People can only control their social relations by controlling other people's knowledge and ignorance, so they all practise some degree of secrecy in their everyday lives.

Secrecy, then, is a normal part of our social relations: a functional necessity for the operation of complex societies. Cities are especially useful since they allow us much more secrecy than small communities. In cities, we all—especially strangers—gain freedom, though at the expense of inclusion. In Simmel's view, however, both secrecy and a lack of secrecy can be harmful. Consider the role of lies. Lies are potentially harmful because people may base important decisions on false assumptions. Yet, sometimes lies are helpful. People may use *white lies* to avoid speaking the unspeakable. In practice, every relationship has its own notions—stated and unstated—about lies, truth-telling, and secrecy. Every relationship also has its own tolerable limit of deviation and secrecy.

Some communities are built on secrecy and lies. These "secret societies" hold particular importance for religion and politics. Political secret societies, for example, often form under dangerous conditions of political oppression. With the greatest secrecy, they plot to carry out secret political goals (see, e.g., Erickson, 1981). Simmel defines a *secret society* as any group or community governed by secrecy. To protect their most important ideas, sentiments, and information, members of this community control the publication or spread of truthful information. To promote bonding and build on elaborate hierarchies of authority, these groups often rely on ritual. Such ritual activity helps to preserve group cohesion, a sense of belonging, and a greater willingness to obey the leader's authority.

Robert Merton: Structural Inequality and Anomie

Sociologist Robert Merton's (1957 [1938]) **anomie theory**, sometimes called **strain theory**, provides an important variation on Durkheim's original conception of anomie. Merton's theory holds that crime and other forms of deviance increase when the social structure prevents people from achieving culturally defined goals (e.g., getting money) by legitimate means (e.g., through a job). He called this gap between goals and means *anomie*, after Durkheim's concept.

According to Merton, it is not a sudden social change that causes deviance, as Durkheim believed, but rather a persisting social structural gap that pushes people to break rules. This gap, Merton believed, is unavoidable in modern, capitalist societies like the United States, which strongly promote material success but provide unequal opportunities for achieving this success. People who accept culturally defined goals, but are unable to achieve them by following the rules, are caught in a permanent conflict. They adapt to this conflict in different ways: some conform to the rules and accept their lack of success; others turn to alternatives, which are sometimes deviant or criminal.

Merton describes five ways an individual may respond to conflict and strain: conformity, innovation, ritualism, retreatism, and rebellion. An individual who *conforms* accepts both the goals and the means for achieving culturally acceptable goals. An individual who *innovates* accepts the goals but not the means for achieving these goals. For example, drug dealers may accept materialist values but reject conventional means for attaining them. *Ritualists* reject the goals but accept the means. *Retreatists* reject both the goals and the means. *Rebels* not only reject both the goals and means but also substitute the rejected goals with another set of goals.

According to Merton's theory, (1) strain (or anomie) is normal and inescapable, (2) the adaptations to strain are normal and inescapable, and (3) the adaptations described above make possible the persistence of an unequal, acquisitive society—that is, they help capitalism and inequality to survive. Thus, crime and deviance are normal, even necessary, under conditions of social inequality.

There exists an important likeness between Merton's theory of anomie and Robert Park's earlier theory of "marginal men." In his 1937 essay, "Cultural Conflict and the Marginal Man," Park—speaking about immigrant minorities—writes, "The marginal man . . . is one whom fate has condemned to live in two societies and in two, not merely different but antagonistic cultures . . . his mind is the crucible in which two different and refractory cultures may be said to melt and, either wholly or in part, fuse" (Park, 1937: iii). Like Merton's condition of "anomie," Park's condition of "marginality," common to many North Americans, describes the problem faced by people who are simultaneously lured in two directions. For Park, this "marginality" is a source of frustration and stress; for Merton, it is (sometimes) a source of creative adaptation.

Merton's anomie theory is the most commonly cited theory in crime and deviance and—perhaps—in all of sociology. It cleverly combines a great many social causes and effects in a tidy package. As a result, sociologists have made many efforts to improve and refine it. Robert Agnew (2001), for example, is well known as a modern developer of strain theory. He claims that strains are most likely to result in crime when they (1) are seen as unjust, (2) are seen as high in magnitude, (3) are associated with low social control, and (4) create some pressure or incentive to engage in criminal coping.

Cloward and Ohlin (1960) extended Merton's theory by developing the idea of **differential illegitimate opportunity**. They agreed with Merton that people are driven to deviate whenever a particular success goal is emphasized but the legitimate means of reaching this goal are limited. However, Cloward and Ohlin also point out that many poor people not only lack access to socially *legitimate* ways of reaching the desired goals, but they may also lack access to socially *illegitimate* ways of reaching these goals. Thus, in studying crime and deviance, we have to look at both kinds of opportunity structures: law-abiding and criminal.

Delinquent behaviours, according to Cloward and Ohlin, flourish among poor people when *illegitimate* opportunities for success are more readily available than *legitimate* opportunities. Often, these illegitimate "adaptive" behaviours support criminal subcultures. In turn, the types of criminal subculture that flourish—sometimes, in the form of gangs—depend on the area in which they develop. For example, "criminal gangs" emerge in areas where unconventional modes of behaviour are closely tied to business opportunities. In this circumstance, the criminal gang is more stable than other gangs: it has clear goals and is well integrated with the community. Another type of gang, "the conflict or violent gang," is much less integrated into the community, or into professional crime. Its lack of integration and criminal organization results in instability. Members of these violent gangs are double failures—integrated into neither a stable criminal gang nor into the greater society—and often they retreat into a world of sex, drugs, and alcohol.

Social Control Theories

Functionalists are also concerned with explaining why most people conform to the rules and do *not* become deviant or criminal. "Social disorganization," for example, may explain what predisposes a group to deviance or crime, but it cannot explain why only *some* members of that group become deviant. The functionalist approach to this question examines how mechanisms of social control keep certain people tied to the social order, even if their friends or family deviate from it.

Durkheim and "Egoism"

Functionalism's concern with social control is obvious in Durkheim's early work on suicide. In explaining variations in suicide rates, Durkheim not only looked at the impact of large social changes, but he also considered how suicide rates were affected by social bonds and institutions on an ongoing basis.

What he found was that people who were well integrated into social life, and had strong ties to the social order (e.g., married people, women with children, and the deeply religious), were least likely to commit suicide. According to Durkheim, these ties to family and religious institutions not only provide clear rules for conforming behaviour, but they also instil a sense of social responsibility that militates against suicide. Durkheim found much higher suicide rates for unmarried men and explained this by their weak ties to others and to the social order. He called this form of suicide *egoistic*, that is, suicide because of excessive individualism (or lack of integration).

Social Networks and Deviant Careers

Social control theory assumes that anyone may have deviant impulses, but the question is why these impulses are not acted upon, or why people do *not* break the rules.

Social control theorists believe that people conform to the rules when they develop a "stake in conformity," thinking they will benefit by doing what is expected of them. As people get older and set up long-term social relationships with friends, spouses, neighbours, and workmates, they find themselves locked into networks of reciprocal duty. People continue to conform because they want and need the rewards conformity brings and fear or dislike the punishments for deviance. They feel secure and socially connected and are not motivated to deviate.

At the same time, other people can get locked into deviant or criminal "careers." Sampson and Laub (2002) show that a process of cumulative disadvantage can cause long-term stability in deviant behaviour. Early involvement in crime weakens social bonds to significant others and conventional institutions. The early life failure to build social networks outside of crime can keep people locked in a criminal lifestyle. These researchers also argue, however, that people may transition out of this lifestyle by undergoing a key life-event, such as marrying or entering the labour force. These events can lead to the formation of new social bonds that impose controls on behaviour and reduce the risk of further criminal behaviour.

Family Bonds and Delinquency

In the 1920s, the Chicago School sociologists noted that "social disorganization" in the inner cities often led to "broken families" and that this in turn led to unsupervised children and increased juvenile delinquency. It was not until the 1950s, however, that sociologists examined the role of the family more closely. Then, social control theorists began to challenge the prevailing view that juvenile delinquency was mainly the product of gang associations and deviant socialization. They argued that juvenile delinquency could be better explained by the failure of families to provide their children with appropriate controls on their behaviour (see, e.g., Toby, 1957; Nye, 1958; Sykes and Matza, 1957).

Hirschi's *Causes of Delinquency* (1969) is perhaps the most influential early statement of social control theory. To develop his theory, Hirschi gathered information from a large sample of juvenile delinquents, asking them about their activities, family life, friendships, attitudes, and beliefs. From this data, Hirschi concluded that a child's relationship with parents is the most important factor in determining his or her involvement in delinquent activities. Children weakly bonded to their parents were most likely to commit delinquent acts. Hirschi went on to state a more general theory—that social control works through the "social bond" developed between an individual and the larger society and that this bond has four elements: *belief* (in conventional values), *attachment* (to others and a sensitivity to their opinions), *commitment* (to the social rewards of conformity), and *involvement* (in conventional activities).

Along similar lines, Hagan et al. (1985) later developed a variant of social control theory to explain the higher rates of delinquency among boys than among girls. Hagan and his colleagues argued that the gender difference in delinquency reflects the gendering of socialization experiences within families—also, the gendering of social bonds. The traditional "patriarchal" family exerts much more control over the behaviour of girls than of boys. As a result, boys are relatively "free to deviate" and get comfortable with taking risks. Girls, on the other hand, tend to be kept under close supervision and develop an aversion to risk. Of course, we can expect to see this change as families change—as family relationships become more egalitarian. Then, these gender differences in delinquency will lessen; but for the time being there are still strong gender differences in delinquency and crime, as well as in child socialization.

Time to Reflect: What is there about "bad parenting" that leads children to turn to delinquency and even crime? And does "bad parenting" have the same meaning and same effects in all cultures?

Attachment and Parenting

Hirschi's **social bond theory** stresses the importance of attachment to friends and family, as well as to society as a whole, as an important foundation for conforming behaviour. This points to the importance of a stable, supportive family life.

"Good parents" provide their children with love and attachment, emotional stability, protection and control, and fair and moderate discipline. Research on parenting shows that the three strongest influences on feelings of attachment are supervision, identity support, and instrumental communication (Cernkovich and Giordano, 1987). The result is a sense of attachment and relatedness among members of a family, preserved and represented by shared activities, self-identification as a family member, and signs of familiarity and liking.

Family rituals are as important for family stability and cohesion as religious or patriotic rituals are for communities. Even small rituals matter: for example, researchers report that children who live in families that have sit-down meals together at least three times a week are much less likely to become delinquents in their adolescence or to turn to crime in adulthood. Family dinners are a sign of family cohesion and stability, which contribute to the healthy emotional development of children. Also, families that have recreational activities together are much less likely to produce delinquent children.

No less important than love and stability is parental control—how firmly, consistently, and fairly parents make and enforce rules for the child. Good rules guide and protect the child, showing parents' concern and attachment to the child. As functionalists would predict, it is the quality of family relationships and family dynamics that count in forming and socializing children. Youths who are supported at home develop identities conducive to school success, while youths deprived of support form identities that make school success much less likely.

Rule enforcement is another type of attachment between parents and their children—a way that parents show concern for their children. Family researchers have identified four parenting styles—authoritative, authoritarian, unengaged, and permissive—distinguished by their degree of acceptance (the amount parents like and respect their children) and control of the child's behaviour.

The "authoritative" parenting style (high acceptance, high control) produces children who achieve the highest levels of academic performance and mental well-being. Adolescents raised by authoritative parents are more likely than other adolescents to have a strong community orientation, less likely to be self-centred, and less likely to engage in deviant behaviour (Radziszewska et al., 1996).

"Authoritarian" parenting (low acceptance, high control), on the other hand, produces undesirable outcomes. This parenting style hinders the development of expressiveness and independence. Authoritarian parenting also increases the risk of drug use in adolescent children. Children with authoritarian parents are more likely to become delinquents (see, e.g., Man, 2001), to become depressed, and to fail in school (Radziszewska et al., 1996).

"Unengaged" parenting (low acceptance, low control) can also be harmful. It amounts to little more than negligence and, at worst, amounts to abuse. Permissive parenting at the extreme can shade into neglectful parenting.

A study of high school students in the San Francisco Bay area found that "permissive" parenting (high acceptance, low control) produces poor grades (Vergun et al., 1996). Poor students are more likely to come from families with permissive parenting styles (Bronstein et al., 1996; Radziszewska et al., 1996). Furthermore, parenting failures build up over time, and with increases in problem behaviour, internal distress, and poor school performance (Steinberg et al., 1994).

Recent research continues to confirm the superiority of authoritative parenting, compared to the other methods. For example, a longitudinal study of eighth grade children found that having two authoritative parents produces the most positive outcomes in adolescents. Failing that, even just one authoritative parent can, in most cases, buffer a child from the harmful consequences associated with less ideal styles of parenting (Simons and Conger, 2007).

Parental control is related, for obvious reasons, to parental discipline. A desire for control leads to the creation of rules, with discipline serving to enforce these rules. Parents can, however, exercise too much control, just as they can exercise too little. Overzealous or inattentive discipline may greatly diminish or totally eliminate the benefits of control. As well, the type of discipline technique used also makes a difference.

Hoffman (1979) distinguishes between three basic types of disciplining techniques: power assertion, love withdrawal, and induction.

Love withdrawal, as the name suggests, means threatening or actually reducing signs of affection to the child, in the event of non-compliance. *Induction* means showing the child good behaviour by example and explaining its value. *Power assertion* means threatening a child with punishment for non-compliance. In the short term, power assertion may work. The threatened child may change his or her behaviour to avoid punishment; however, the child does not base compliance on moral learning. The compliant behaviour is driven by external threats, not internal conviction. When not being watched, such children often return to misbehaving. However, physical punishments, love withdrawal, and power assertion all appeal to parents who lack the knowledge, time, patience, energy, or inclination to teach rules inductively.

Self-Control: "A General Theory of Crime"

One of the most significant variants of functionalist theory today is Gottfredson and Hirschi's **general theory of crime** (1990). This theory proposes that we can organize all of the known facts about crime and criminals around the general concept of self-control.

Low self-control explains an individual's inclination to commit (or inability to refrain from committing) crimes, just as high self-control explains an individual's likelihood of conforming to social norms and laws. People with low self-control are unable to defer gratification; they lack diligence and tenacity; and they are usually risk-seeking, impulsive, self-centred, and insensitive to the needs of others. These characteristics, the researchers argue, are established in childhood (by age seven or eight). The result of a lack of socialization, discipline, and training on the part of parents, these characteristics do not change much in adulthood.

Gottfredson and Hirschi also argue that crime itself has certain notable characteristics: it is often unplanned, unskilled, and unspecialized; results in little to gain when there is no substantial risk involved; occurs whenever and wherever the offender sees an opportunity for immediate gain or gratification; and is indifferent to the costs to others. In other words, much (if not all) criminal activity is the kind of activity people with low self-control are likely to carry out.

To sum up, functionalists stress the importance of value consensus, value stability, social cohesion, social involvement, social control, and the internalization of morality as factors determining deviant and conforming behaviours. These principles work at every level of society: families, communities, classrooms, or businesses.

Symbolic Interactionism

Like functionalism, symbolic interactionism has a long history in sociology. In the early twentieth century, Charles Cooley at the University of Michigan and George Herbert Mead at the University of Chicago first developed the ideas behind symbolic interactionism as a sociological perspective.

When naming the approach *symbolic interactionism* in 1937, Herbert Blumer described the basic elements of the approach in three propositions: "human beings act toward things on the basis of the meanings that things have for them," these meanings "arise out of social interaction," and social action results from a "fitting together of personal lines of action."

Unlike functionalism, symbolic interactionism does not ask what is required to create and preserve a well-functioning "society." Rather, it focuses on the processes by which people interpret and respond to the actions of others and the way social definitions of "reality" and social structures arise naturally out of these processes. Symbolic interactionism is an inherently micro-sociological perspective, explaining society from the "bottom-up." In effect, social structure emerges automatically, and continuously, from the actions of people interacting with one another.

In short, symbolic interactionists stress the importance of interaction, negotiation, symbolic meanings, stigmatization, and the effects of external labelling on sense of self as factors determining deviant and conforming behaviours. Underlying all this behaviour is the human need to make sense of life, self, and society.

By virtue of its approach, symbolic interactionism naturally encourages ethnographic studies of deviant or criminal subcultures that directly observe the social interactions within those communities. Symbolic interactionism also, unsurprisingly, has had an important influence on the development of socialization theories. A key concern for sociologists of deviance is why, and how, people take on a deviant identity or "become deviant." This question has had a great appeal for symbolic interactionists, for whom the "self" is an important topic of inquiry.

Symbolic interactionists in the 1950s and 1960s also started asking new questions about how deviance was defined and who got to make the decisions about what was defined as "deviant." These sociologists concluded that "deviance" was a social label that some groups used to describe and stigmatize the behaviour of other groups. **Labelling theory**, as it came to be called, concluded that being fixed with a deviant label may even *increase* deviant behaviour due to the label's negative impacts on one's social status, "life chances," and sense of self.

Labelling theory has had a major impact on Canadian social policy in two areas related to deviance: that is, in respect to juvenile delinquency and mental illness. Regarding juvenile delinquency, policy-makers in the 1960s and 1970s became concerned about young people being "labelled" criminal by being charged and tried in the criminal justice system. Canada's 1984 Young Offenders Act (now the Youth Criminal Justice Act) addressed these concerns by, among other things, providing for "alternative measures" to divert young offenders from the court system whenever possible.

Similar concerns supported the massive deinstitutionalization of mental patients in Canada between 1965 and 1985, though new means of chemical control also permitted that deinstitutionalization. Once again, policy-makers had concerns that exposure to institutional life was both creating and reinforcing negative self-images among patients and slowing down recovery and reintegration into the community. We will further discuss these (and other) social policy initiatives related to the symbolic interactionist approach in subsequent chapters of this book.

The Development of Self and Socialization

Like the other approaches we discuss, symbolic interactionism has its own set of research interests and approaches. Symbolic interactionists are interested in two questions: how people become the people they are—that is, how the "self" (and self-control) develop—and how people reach new understandings about a situation and proper behaviour in that situation.

All sociologists view socialization as a social process, but symbolic interactionists are most concerned with understanding *how socialization works*. How—specifically—do people come to take on the norms, values, attitudes, beliefs, and behaviour patterns of the people around them? A related but more general question is: How do people come to be themselves? By "self" we mean a person's experience and awareness of having a personal identity that is separate from that of other people. Sociologists believe that the process by which people develop this sense of self is the same as the process by which they internalize their culture.

As psychologist Jean Piaget (1932) showed in his research, young children are egocentric; they have no sense of self as distinct from other people. Children only become aware of themselves as they become aware that other people (such as their parents or siblings) are distinct from them. This means the self is a social product. It emerges as people interact (or imagine interacting) with others, even with people they hate or admire from afar (such as movie stars or heroic ancestors). The person's experiences in life, the groups to which he or she belongs, and the socio-historical settings of those groups all shape a person's sense of self. Further, because the self is a social product, it changes throughout life.

Piaget spent a great deal of time studying children, watching how they learn to play together. In his research, Piaget (1954 [1937]) identified three stages of play: practice play, symbolic or make-believe play, and games with rules. He finds that play develops in stages, in step with social and cognitive development. At first, a child's play is solitary. Then comes parallel play, where children play independently in each other's company. Socially, the final stage is co-operative play, which consists of organized activities characterized by social roles. This phase, what we might call the *game phase*, involves an even higher level of social behaviour, because it means co-ordinating social roles. For symbolic interactionists, social life is like a game, and we learn how to participate in society—to play social games by taking co-ordinated roles and anticipating the role play of others—while we are children.

This approach leads naturally into a focus on cultural socialization and, here, Edwin Sutherland (1939) was one of the first sociologists to apply a symbolic interactionist approach to the study of deviant subcultures. Consistent with symbolic interactionism, Sutherland proposed that deviance—even crime—was learned through a process of socialization. Specifically, he maintained that:

- deviant behaviour is learned in association with others in intimate social relationships;
- views about deviance are learned through communication with others who share the cultural meanings ("definitions") of particular deviant behaviour; and
- deviant behaviour occurs when people share an excess of favourable definitions of deviance, compared to unfavourable ones.

Sutherland called this **differential association theory**, following the Chicago School's observation that deviant (or criminal) communities were "differentially organized" subcultures with their own values, traditions, and norms for behaviour. According to this theory, members of a deviant community—for example, a delinquent gang—would interact regularly, participating in and communicating about delinquent acts. They would hold and express positive views of these acts, contrary to people outside the gang, and deny their activities were harmful or unworthy.

Sutherland was not the first criminologist to argue that deviant and criminal behaviours have cultural rather than individual (psychological or biological) roots. Many others have known that people value and imitate what they see other people doing. In communities where crime is common, accepted, and even highly organized—like the Neapolitan Camorra about which Gabriel Tarde (1903) wrote—ordinary people engage in crime because that is a "normal" activity in that place. What political theorist Hannah Arendt (1963) wrote in the mid-twentieth century about Nazism holds true for many other harmful and criminal activities: we are shocked to learn just how banal and ordinary it can become.

Symbolic interactionist theories continue to influence the study of deviant and criminal socialization and to emphasize its ordinariness. For example, symbolic interactionists Prus and Grills (2003) define "deviance" as a label referring to *any* activity, actor, idea, or humanly produced situation that an "audience" labels as being "threatening, disturbing, offensive, immoral, evil, disreputable or negative in some way." The authors assert that their work reflects the notion that nothing is inherently good or bad and that "deviance" only exists when someone chooses to define something as being deviant.

Some sociologists have criticized the symbolic interactionist approach, however, turning to more instrumental theories to explain deviant socialization. For example, Akers (1985) has argued that although deviant socialization does occur in association with others, the key to this socialization is not so much "favourable definitions" of deviance as favourable outcomes. In other words, people learn to be deviant through a system of rewards and punishments. They make a "rational choice" to deviate when it brings them more rewards than conventional behaviour, not merely to imitate other people. This view is based on a view common in psychology and economics that all behaviour is motivated by hedonism ("what's in it for me?").

Symbolic interactionist theories about deviant socialization also do not mesh well with social control theories, developed within the functionalist perspective. For social control theorists, people break the rules because the usual socialization processes have failed to produce people with meaningful social bonds and strong attachment to the social order. For symbolic interactionists, as we have seen, people break the rules because they have learned from others to do so.

Social Reaction and Labelling

Social theorists differ in their accounts of the growth of "the self," but they agree on one thing: social interaction is central to this growth. American sociologist Charles Cooley (1902) was the first to stress the importance of the self in the process of socialization, emphasizing the role of the social environment in the development of a self-concept. According to Cooley, people form concepts of themselves according to how they experience other people reacting to them. He called this the *looking glass self*. The labelling theory of deviance comes directly out of this idea.

Sociologists regard Edwin Lemert (1951) as a pioneer in the development of labelling theory for his work on societal reaction theory. He emphasizes **secondary deviance**—rule-breaking acts that follow from, and react to, the imposition of a deviant label. Lemert's theory, contrary to what we might expect, holds that people labelled as deviant are *more likely* to engage in deviant behaviour because that fits in with their new self-image and their new, even more restricted social opportunities. Thus, labelling someone deviant doesn't discourage or correct a tendency to deviant behaviour: it cements the tendency.

Howard Becker (1963), another symbolic interactionist trained in the Chicago School, stressed that everyone is capable of deviant behaviour and that everyone fails to conform to social rules from time to time. Becker's work examined how people come to attract a "deviant" label, the process by which they learn to participate in deviant subcultures, and how they adjust to the label of "deviant." In Becker's view, deviant subcultures not only socialize people into deviant behaviour and values, but they are also products of social labelling and exclusion.

Becker analyzed the ways that people move into (and out of) the recreational use of marijuana. He emphasized that deviance is rarely practised solo; rather, it is a social accomplishment. For example, people need others to help them recognize and enjoy the chemical effects of marijuana. Without such help, they are unlikely to enjoy or repeat the experience. Also, smoking marijuana often becomes a valued social activity in its own right, as enjoyable for its sociability as for its chemical effects. So, we cannot understand deviance outside a social context.

The Definition of the Situation

Labelling theory turns our attention away from the deviant behaviour itself towards the question of how deviance comes to be defined and who is targeted to be labelled "deviant." Symbolic interactionists want to understand how new meanings and new relationships arise as people interact with one another in a state of conflict or confusion. The meanings are social because, through interaction, people create the meanings, share them, learn them, and often pass them down to the next generation. Sociologists capture this idea in another important concept: the **definition of the situation**. We must understand an actor's definition of the situation because people will act meaningfully in relation to their definition of reality, not ours.

The Construction of Social Problems

Symbolic interactionists typically examine how larger social problems are "constructed" through interactive social processes. Blumer (1971) proposed that all social problems develop in stages. The first stage is "social recognition," the point at which a given condition or behaviour (e.g., drug use) is first identified as a potential social concern. Second, "social legitimating" takes place—society and its various institutional elements formally recognize the social problem as a serious threat to social stability. At both stages, many people are involved in discussing, defining, and building a shared sense of "the problem."

Symbolic interactionism, therefore, also provides an insight into the ways that social issues or behaviours designated as "social problems" develop. Take the rise in public concern over sex-offending. During the 1980s and 1990s, the media and policy-makers alike denounced a perceived increase in sex-offending, especially against children. Images of sex offenders as compulsive recidivists whose behaviour often turned violent dominated news outlets. However, law enforcement data show that sex crimes against children merely remained stable over this period and that sex crimes against adults declined. In short, there was no correlation between public concern over the crime and the incidence of the crime.

Thus, sex-offender legislation did not arise because of a growing, objective risk of sex-offending. Rather, it was the result of a socially constructed panic stimulated by media depictions and used by policy-makers to successfully promote sex-offending as a menacing social problem meriting costly and sweeping legislation. Or consider another example: the debate about the ethics of Insite. Political debate has swirled around this clinic in Vancouver where people can inject previously acquired illegal drugs under the supervision of medical staff, showing how an issue can be portrayed as either highly negative or very positive, depending on the perspective we take (Box 1.2).

Time to Reflect: Why do the media and political leaders have so much influence over the construction of social problems? That is, why are we so ready to accept their interpretation of what is and what is not a social problem?

Current Events

BOX 1.2

Debates around Vancouver's Insite

A great deal of controversy has developed around Insite, a supervised injection site in Vancouver. Many note that the site has saved the lives of many injection drug users (IDUs). There hasn't been a single death from drug overdose at the facility, thanks to interventions by staff. In fact, there were over 200 such interventions last year, providing drugs and oxygen to users who risked overdosing.

Insite has also reduced the spread of disease and infection. Visitors to the site are discouraged from borrowing and sharing syringes, thus cutting down on the spread of infections such as HIV. By contrast, such borrowing and sharing are common on the streets. As well, Insite staff teach drug users hygienic injection practices that can prevent the spread of disease—practices unknown to most users before they visit Insite. At the facility, detox and treatment programs are also promoted; and other treatments—medical care and addiction counselling, for example—are offered on site. In these and other ways, Insite helps to create a safer community and improve public health. Drug-related crime has not increased since the clinic was established and there has been a decline in injections performed in public places, such as back alleys and doorways. People trying to stop using drugs have not been dissuaded by the facility's presence.

On the other hand, some oppose Insite. For example, some argue that the government is essentially encouraging and facilitating illegal drug use by providing addicts with a place to shoot up. Some also feel that the efforts and money going towards Insite should be directed towards discouraging drug use and helping drug addicts quit. Some have suggested that the clinic merely perpetuates the injection of illegal drugs at the expense of the taxpayers who fund the clinic. Others believe that Insite creates a sense that drug use is a normal activity, rather than showing it to be it an unsafe, dangerous one. The result, they say, is that Insite attracts drug dealers; and for the sake of public safety, illegal drugs should be discouraged at all cost.

The Supreme Court has recently come down on the side of Insite supporters, finding that the federal government has no right to close down Insite. Doing so would infringe the rights of drug users to secure safe treatment of the kind Insite offers, thus discriminating unfairly against them.

Sources: Wendy Stueck, "The Arguments for and against Vancouver's Supervised Injection Site," *Globe and Mail*, 11 May 2011; Susan Martinuk, "Supervised Injection Site Nothing More than State-Sponsored Addiction," *The Province*, 17 Sept. 2003, 20; Evan Wood, Thomas Kerr, Elisa Lloyd-Smith, Chris Buchner, David C. Marsh, Julio S.G. Montaner, and Mark W. Tyndall, "Methodology for Evaluating Insite: Canada's First Medically Supervised Safer Injection Facility for Injection Drug Users," *Harm Reduction Journal* 1 (2004).

In other words, social problems are socially created or "constructed." The social construction approach examines *how* social problems come to be defined as such: that is, why some potential problems are defined as problems and many others are not. No problem, no matter how important, is self-sufficient in gaining widespread attention and concern without social construction. Even the most catastrophic social acts—genocide, for example—need to be propelled into public visibility and "constructed" as problems. Legal interpretations and understandings of moral responsibility all have a social history. From the smallest issue in a single community to the biggest issue on the world stage, social problems are rooted in a particular time and place, with a particular social meaning that some group has constructed.

In practice, this means we cannot easily interpret data showing changes in rates of crime or deviance. Do statistical increases prove real increases in behavioural incidence, or do they merely reflect an increased tendency to outlaw, arrest, prosecute, and convict certain kinds of activities—showing social construction and moral entrepreneurship by the powerful? As we see in Figure 1.1, there has been little increase in society's most serious and unambiguous offences—violent crimes—since 1962. Less serious, more ambiguous offences—property crimes, for example—fluctuate widely during this period. Is this a fluctuation in criminality or in punitiveness? A variation in the extent of crime or a variation in the perception of a "crime problem"?

The victim rights movement has been extremely successful in promoting legislative changes regarding victim restitution. This, too, has required social construction. The rights movement has used various devices to socially construct victim rights issues, employing victim imagery and horror stories to do so. This has also meant making skilful use of the media to disseminate their claims, framing victims' needs as rights, and aligning

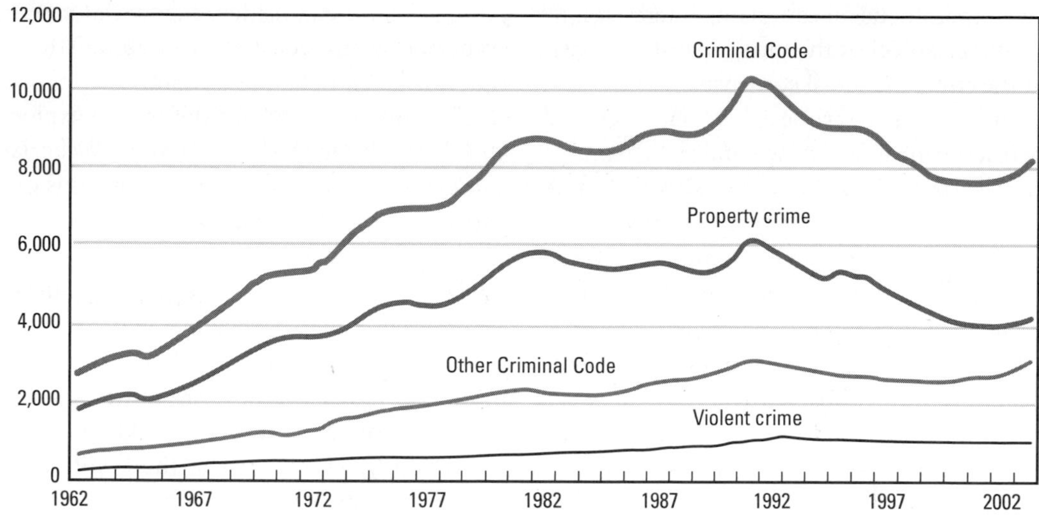

FIGURE 1.1 Rates of Criminal Code incidents in Canada, 1962 to 2003

Source: Statistics Canada: 2005. "Exploring Crime Patterns in Canada," Figure 1, Page 8, Catalogue no. 85-561-MIE2005005.

the group with public officials and private interest groups.

Successful construction of a social problem often also relies on the creation of a "moral panic." British sociologist Stanley Cohen (1972) defined the notion of "moral panic," an important concept in understanding how social problems develop. The mass media provide, preserve, and "police" popular conceptions of deviance, shaping public awareness of and attitudes towards social problems. During a moral panic, a certain group becomes the focus of widespread public attention. Moral panics feature stereotypical representations by the mass media and a tendency for those "in power" to pronounce moral judgement.

Over time there have been many panics about various issues ranging from crime to juvenile delinquency to drugs and sexual freedom, each considered a threat to the moral fibre of society at that particular time. Today, there is much less public anxiety about or anger directed towards people who smoke marijuana, engage in sex outside of marriage, watch pornographic films, or curse in public, as compared to 50 years ago; however, new moral panics always surface. Research finds that moral panics often develop when society has trouble adapting to dramatic social changes and when such changes lead those concerned to fear a loss of social control. In 2012, we saw some signs of this in connection with the Quebec students' strike over tuition increases.

Critical Theories

Critical theorists stress conflict and change as basic features of social life. They argue that conflict and change are unavoidable because society is composed of groups with different amounts of power, status, and influence. These groups invariably try to seize power in society, including the power to make and enforce rules. Given their focus on competing interests, conflict theorists reject the functionalist emphasis on the coherent social consensus.

In the study of crime and deviance, critical theories came to be known under the name of *critical criminology*. Since the 1970s, they have developed in various directions, embracing feminist and postmodern, as well as Marxist and Weberian, approaches. From Marx, critical theorists took the idea of conflict arising from a class structure in which capitalists control the means of production and the workers must sell their labour to survive. The ruling class makes laws to help dominate the workers; the subordinate classes develop strategies and practices of resistance. Workers and unemployed people often lack a deep commitment to the prevailing social order, owing to its exploitive nature. This reduces the legitimacy of the laws and law enforcers that control social behaviour.

From Weber, critical theorists took the idea of conflict arising from non-class-based hierarchical relations of dominance and subordination, and also from horizontal status structures in which groups compete to capture and protect their resources. Competing status groups—which may include ethnic, religious, linguistic, regional, gender, or even age groups—use both social closure and usurpation (or seizure) to advance their interests. To do so, they set up group boundaries and promote group cohesion. To achieve and keep dominance, they capture and protect necessary resources for the group; this process is called *usurpation*. Within this context, crime and deviance may arise out of inter-group conflict (e.g., gang fights over turf) or group subordination to a stronger, more effective, or more "institutionally complete" status group.

Weber's conflict analysis is more powerful than Marx's because it is more general. Some might even argue that Marxian class analysis—with classes viewed as status groups—can be considered a special case of Weberian group conflict: the capitalist class is set on social closure—forming a "power elite"—and seizure of wealth through exploitative labour practices. What's more, Weberian conflict analysis is not limited to groups of a particular size. It can be used to analyze conflict between nations and empires, and it can be used to analyze conflict between peer groups—for example, bullying by cliques in high school.

Out of the works of Marx and Weber comes modern critical theory, transformed and nourished by the so-called Frankfurt School of sociology, which arose at the Institute for Social Research, affiliated with the University of Frankfurt, in 1923. Marxist scholars there, believing that Marxist theory had become too closely aligned to the workings of Communist parties, tried to develop a brand of theory that was distinct from political practice. Prominent sociologists associated with the Institute have included Max Horkheimer, Karl Wittfogel, Leo Lowenthal, Herbert Marcuse, Theodor Adorno, Walter Benjamin, and Jürgen Habermas. Many of these scholars fled Germany during the Nazi era and made major contributions to American sociology.

Horkheimer (1937) has contrasted modern critical theory with earlier Marxist theory by pointing to some important differences. The more traditional version, steeped in nineteenth-century positivism, used scientific and historical methods to formulate general "laws" about society. By contrast, the twentieth-century (and beyond) version has taken a more subjective, less dogmatic approach to shed light on society and bring about change. This less scientific approach, Horkheimer has argued, is necessary, because of the distinction between social science and natural science. Horkheimer, like Weber, claims that observations about society can rarely be fully objective.

A researcher inevitably shapes the observations according to his or her own ideology. As a result, the researcher's conclusion is likely to confirm what he or she already believes to be true. The only apparent way out of this dilemma is to acknowledge one's biases at the outset, while continuing the search for a truly scientific basis for the study of human behaviour in social contexts.

Whether a Marxist, a Weberian, or a follower of the Frankfurt School, the critical theorist invariably asks who benefits and who suffers from the existing social order. Conflict invariably develops between groups whose goals oppose each other—for example, the rich and the poor, workers and management, or (often) husbands and wives. These people differ from each other in at least one social characteristic, respectively: their wealth, their relationship to power at work, or their power in the household. The critical theorist never supposes that any behaviour or relationship will benefit everyone and does not look for such a universal benefit. Instead, the critical theorist looks for particular groups that will benefit most and that have the power to seize this benefit.

In any society, the battle for people's minds is critical, since people are easier to control if they believe inequality is unavoidable or that they deserve their station in life. This means making and enforcing laws is an ideologically and politically significant activity, for laws serve to legitimate the prevailing inequality. For example, laws about ownership, inheritance, consumer liability, price setting, and corporate liability—the great mass of corporate, commercial, and property laws in our society—best serve the interests of people with the most wealth or investments. The question, of course, is whether criminal laws are written specifically to benefit these people.

Conflict theorists are inclined to think that powerful members of society make and enforce the laws to their advantage; and that less powerful members of society break laws when it is to their advantage. By this logic, rule-making and rule-breaking are simply aimed at gaining material benefits (property, money, or power). Sometimes, however, rule-making and rule-breaking are symbolic—aimed at increasing a group's, or person's, social status and respectability—or lashing out against an unfair society. Within the context of conflict and social inequality, rule-breaking is rational, given most people's limited opportunities and a societal goal of material success. From this standpoint, Merton's famous "strain theory" has connections to the critical approach, since it contends that criminal behaviour is a result of the lack of opportunities combined with a wish for material success.

Critical theories also highlight groups with opposing interests and, often, opposing values that reflect their opposing interests. For this reason, we can see the beginnings of critical theory in the early work of Thorsten Sellin, who wrote about culture conflict in the late 1930s.

Sellin's Theory of Culture Conflict

In general, critical theory focuses on social and political factors as the reasons for crime; psychological motives are secondary. From this standpoint, deviant or criminal acts are conflicts between norms and between the groups that hold those norms. For every group, and therefore every person, there is a right and wrong way of acting in a specific situation. Often, groups re-conceive these behaviour codes or conduct norms as statements of normality and abnormality, of morality and immorality. People who fail to change their behaviour in keeping with the new norms are considered deviant.

Sociologists like Thorsten Sellin (1938) and Edwin Sutherland (1927, 1934) believed that the children of immigrants were caught in a conflict between the conduct norms that immigrants brought with them and those they encountered in North America. When different cultural groups come into contact, conflict is likely to result. The conflict is greatest if (at least) one group's conduct norms have been institutionalized in the criminal code, making that group's point of view dominant in the society.

For Sellin, criminal law embodies the conduct norms of the dominant social group: in the US, native-born white Anglo-Saxon Protestants. This dominant group writes its norms and values into the criminal law and tries, through law enforcement, to impose its conduct norms—and, more generally, its cultural values—on weaker groups. It does this by designating and treating the less powerful group as deviant or criminal for following a different set of conduct norms.

This cultural conflict between conduct norms opens the door to crime and deviance. Members of the subordinate culture have only two options: to assimilate and adapt to the dominant culture or to maintain their culture and undergo continued conflict. At their worst, these conflicts set off power struggles over the right to define "good" and "bad" behaviour. Such a culture conflict was evident during Prohibition in the US, a topic we will discuss in Chapter 5.

> **Time to Reflect:** What are the social factors that contribute to culture conflict over "right" and "wrong" behaviour? After all, don't all cultures agree that criminal acts are bad and should be punished?

Critical Criminology

Crime is just one type of conduct norm violation, and it may occur because the prevailing conduct norms lack legitimacy or because the norms of one group are being imposed on another. The outcome of this conflict will depend on the power of the dominant group to enforce its views. In the end, deviance and crime must be viewed as the outcome of a social and political struggle, the result of intergroup competition for power rather than a result of individual abnormality.

Most important, the extent of this conflict will determine the extent of crime. More severe conflicts produce both more *actual* crime and more *apparent* crime. Sociologist Austin Turk (1969) elaborated on this theme by connecting it to Weberian theories about social inequality. He said that cultural conflicts have their roots in the unequal distribution of resources—especially the unequal distribution of authority. In his general critical theory of crime, Turk drew on the analysis of modern society presented by Ralf Dahrendorf (1959) and connected it to the earlier work of Sellin.

Dahrendorf, following Weber, had focused on the struggle in modern societies for status and authority. In modern societies, power is embedded in the structural relations between competing institutions and between competing groups. Not only do we see struggles between native-born groups and immigrant groups, as Sellin had noted; nor do we only see struggles between Protestants and Catholics, whites and blacks, or Irish-Americans and Italian-Americans living in densely populated urban neighbourhoods. We also see competitions between the key social institutions that dominate everyday life, institutions that control central positions in religious, educational, governmental, and even family relations. This institutional authority is sometimes linked to economic position (i.e., social class), but it is not necessarily dependent on it.

In his analysis, Turk focused on legal conflict and criminalization. Specifically, he asked the following two questions: Under what conditions are cultural and behavioural differences transformed into legal conflict, and under what conditions do people who violate the written laws (i.e., the norms of the authorities) become criminalized? In other words, under what circumstances are laws likely to be enforced, and against whom?

Turk posited that the conflict between "authorities" and "subjects" (i.e., dominant and subordinate groups in society) is sharpest when the power differences between them are compounded by cultural differences. The sharper the cultural differences, the sharper the subsequent conflict, he asserted. This conflict sharpens further when people with an illegal attribute, or engaged in an illegal act, become organized. The more organized the subjects become, the more likely is an outbreak of conflict. This likelihood of conflict especially exists when subjects are relatively unsophisticated, perhaps because less sophisticated subjects have fewer resources and negotiation skills. Said otherwise, they lack established mechanisms for bargaining with those in authority.

Turk posits that the probability of law enforcement will increase with decreases in the power of norm violators (or resisters) and with decreases in the norm violators' willingness to negotiate. That is, law enforcers will dig in their heels when the norm violators are powerless or unwilling to change. Finally, the enforcement of legal norms is most probable when people in positions of authority are in consensus—that is, hold similar views. Conversely, when they hold different views, enforcement of the criminal laws will be weakened, even undermined.

Sociologist Richard Quinney (1974) proposed another form of critical theory around the same time. He was interested in studying which factors dictate how values and behaviour patterns are "enshrined" in law and held up as the "standard" by which individual or group behaviours are to be evaluated. The following are his six propositions:

- Crime is a definition of human conduct created by authorized agents in a politically organized society.
- Criminal definitions describe behaviours that conflict with the interests of the segments of society with the power to shape public policy.
- Criminal definitions are applied by the segments of society that have the power to shape the enforcement and administration of criminal law.
- Behaviour patterns are structured in segmentally organized society in relation to criminal definitions, and within this context persons engage in actions that have relative probabilities of being defined as criminal.
- Conceptions of crime are constructed and diffused in the segments of society by various means of communication.
- The social reality of crime is constructed by the formulation and application of criminal definitions, the development of behaviour patterns related to criminal definitions, and the construction of criminal conceptions.

As is evident from these propositions, crime and law are profoundly political issues for Quinney. He conceives of the study of crime as a study of larger political issues and argues that studying the "political reality of crime" is essential for developing a greater understanding of criminal behaviour. For Quinney, crime must be understood within the context of a political process that allows people in powerful positions to maintain their dominance over people in less powerful positions.

Feminist Approaches

Feminist theory is also a branch of critical theory, as it also focuses on relations of inequality—in this case, relations of dominance and subordination between men and women.

As the name implies, the feminist approach is about gender inequality. Feminist theory especially focuses on the ways that women's lives differ from men's due to gender-based inequality. The first wave of feminism occurred between the middle of the nineteenth century and the early twentieth century. By the early twentieth century, the movement culminated in women gaining the right to vote in many Western countries. Feminism today is obviously far beyond its early concerns with political and legal equality.

Feminist sociology today aims to amend the androcentric (male-dominated) history of sociological thinking. Feminist sociologists highlight the experiences of women because there can be no sociological generalizations about human beings as long as half of all such beings—women—are systematically excluded or ignored. In sociological practice, feminist research is a mixture of symbolic interactionist and critical approaches. However, a unique set of assumptions about reality informs feminist research:

- All personal life has a political dimension.
- Both the public and the private spheres of life are gendered (i.e., unequal for men and women).
- Women's social experience routinely differs from men's.
- **Patriarchy**—or male control—structures the way most societies work.
- Because of routinely different experiences and differences in power, women's and men's views of reality differ.

For example, men and women typically have different views about divorce, since each experiences divorce very differently. For men, it means a brief drop in the standard of living, if any decline at all, and a huge drop in parenting responsibilities. For women, it usually means a dramatic, long-term loss in both income and standard of living. Single mothers and their children often find themselves impoverished and burdened by greater parental responsibilities, since mothers usually keep custody of the children.

To be a woman in our society (and many others) is to act out a role that others have defined. For centuries, the "feminine" role in our society has placed women in a subservient role to men, in which they sometimes are degraded or victimized. Like children, women generally are less powerful than men and are sometimes in physical danger. There is no denying that both men and women abuse one another in emotional and physical ways. However, the statistics show that men tend to abuse women more viciously—for example, men tend to kill women far more often than women kill men. We will say more about this in later discussions of victimization and domestic violence. Thus, women's acceptance of the female role is far more costly—even dangerous—than men's acceptance of the male role.

Feminists stress that our notions of what it means to be male or female, and our dealings with one another as male or female, are a result of the social arrangements prevalent in our society. They do not arise naturally out of mere physiological differences. Accordingly, achieving gender equality will mean cultural and social change. Feminism is therefore a form of political activism that attempts to change the circumstances within which men and women lead their lives.

Several prominent ideas one finds in the literature on deviance and control have their roots in feminist research. First, feminist research pays the greatest attention to gendered influences on social life, or *the gendering of experiences*. Contrary to prevailing views, some of women's experiences of the world are vastly different from men's. Some experiences are specifically female or male, not generalizable to both sexes. Here, certain topics receive a great deal of attention, including violence against women, women's economic vulnerability, and women's vulnerability to male-dominated standards of attractiveness and social worth.

Yet, also contrary to prevailing views, some experiences are actually the same for both men and women. In such instances, it is necessary to clear away historic misrepresentations of women and their preconceived weaknesses or strengths—for example, the traditional male view of women as especially emotional and irrational.

The *problem of victimization* is also a central concern of feminist sociology. Since women have often been victimized, feminists have been especially interested in victimization and the experiences of other victimized groups (e.g., poor people, racial minorities, disabled people, and people of alternative sexual orientations). Following from this, feminists have been especially interested in "intersectionality"—the interaction of gender with other victimizing social characteristics, such as class and race, to produce particular combinations of disadvantage.

Furthermore, feminists are concerned with *the problem of truth-finding*. Since powerful men have often misrepresented women's lives and interests, feminists have tended to suspect theories and (supposed) facts promoted by people in positions of authority, treating these ideas as social constructions or ideologies instead of facts. Feminists have also shown distrust for traditional views of science—including social science—and traditional methods of gathering and analyzing information. Related to this, they have distrusted "generalization"—preferring the study of individual cases and life histories—and have tended to stress not the average experience in a population but the varieties of experience in that same population.

Given these starting points, feminists—not surprisingly—stress the gendered nature of both deviance and control. They call our attention to the relationship between events in the private sphere (e.g., domestic violence) and events in the public sphere (e.g., the cultural and legal tolerance of domestic violence). They note the gendering of law enforcement practices—for example, how the police treat prostitutes compared with how they treat prostitutes' customers. They note evidence of patriarchal values in the legal system—for example, centuries of the failure to concede that husbands might be guilty of raping their wives. Here, as in other areas of sociology, feminist research combines macro-sociological and micro-sociological perspectives, showing how personal lives and political issues are intertwined.

For example, male and female victims of violent attacks use different strategies for seeking help. Victims who seek help from family and friends, and who use mental health services, social services, and self-help groups, tend to be female. In contrast, most male victims do not seek help at all. When men do seek help, they are more likely to call the police than to call on family and friends. Shelters and services for battered males are in short supply. And when men do congregate for self-help they are derided for showing insufficient "manliness" because such behaviours are perceived as feminine. Finally, help-seeking strategies are unique to particular gender/victim–offender relationship categories. Women victimized by known offenders rely on family and friends, whereas men are unlikely to.

As we will see repeatedly in this book, risk-taking, delinquency, violence, and crime are largely male activities. The gender–delinquency relationship is one of the strongest relationships in delinquency research, and gender differences in both the experience of, and response to, family related strain may largely account for the delinquency gender gap.

Hagan et al. (2002) pay particular attention to gender-linked differences in delinquent aggression, as well as to the links between these forms of delinquent aggression, depression, and substance abuse. Their power-control theory of the gender–delinquency relationship draws attention to differences in family control practices that are linked to gendered variations in the expression of delinquency and despair. We will have more to say about this theory later.

Postmodern Approaches

Postmodernism can be considered another prominent form of critical theory. This approach is especially interested in unmasking ideologies that protect the dominant social order and its ideologies. According to postmodern views, reality itself is fragmentary; all we have are personal, biased, often conflicting, accounts. Any claims that there is a single knowable and known truth, or that any account can be The Truth, are false and illusory from this perspective.

Postmodernists tend to view science, including social science, as prescriptive rather than descriptive, and normative rather than value-neutral. Its effect, whether intended or not, is to impose beliefs about "normality": to discover and dictate what is normal to the non-scientific public. Accordingly, the job of *applied* science is to establish norms that, through surveillance and control, turn abnormal people into normal people. From a postmodern perspective, such an undertaking raises several questions: Is there any such thing as "normality" and, if there is, what makes it "good"? Within our current context, is deviance abnormal or normal? In either event, should social control be used to wipe out abnormality and to enforce a current view of "normality"?

The notion that there is a consistent, knowable reality and that we can understand it unambiguously by using reason and science, is the foundation of what we call Enlightenment thinking. This belief in reason, science, freedom, and progress was central to the attack on traditional restrictions based in religious belief and to the rise of modern societies. Yet the twentieth century, with its many horrors, demonstrated that we cannot *rely* on reason and science to give us freedom and progress. As we have seen, reason and science can also readily produce oppression, violence, and mass death. One case in point was the Holocaust; another, the dropping of atomic bombs on Japan. Neither would have been possible without science, reason, and the belief in human perfectibility through progress. In the twenty-first century, it remains difficult to retain a nineteenth- or twentieth-century confidence in science and its role in society.

An influential example of postmodern research is Michel Foucault's analysis of prisons and imprisonment, *Discipline and Punish* (1975), a text in which science plays a key role. For Foucault, all of modern society is a prison—indeed a Panopticon, as Jeremy Bentham (1995 [1787–91]) had named a prison in which guards could constantly watch their prisoners without being seen. Foucault's interest in prisons—in discipline and punishment—was part of his effort to frame a general understanding of power in modern societies. Foucault, leaving Marxism behind, aimed at uncovering a new type of domination in modern society that operates through "technologies of power."

Foucault's approach represented a radical repudiation of the Enlightenment tradition, in which knowledge was considered the basis of progress, citizenship, and good government. Faced with the horrors of twentieth-century totalitarian governments, which had used knowledge to oppress and kill millions, Foucault saw knowledge as being as fully oppressive as ignorance and twice as effective. He noted that modern society relies on structures of dominance, control, and surveillance that, in turn, rely on expertise. Power in modern society is exercised through a variety of institutions of social control—prisons, schools, clinics, and hospitals, among others—which apply the expert discourses of control.

Foucault links the birth of the modern prison in the nineteenth century to a general history of institutions. He argues that *all* modern institutions—including the army, the factory, and the school—discipline the bodies of their subjects through techniques of surveillance and control. Thus, he notes the rise of a disciplinary society with new means of enforcing power. Power in modern societies is diffuse and internalized; it "doesn't only weigh on us as a force that says no," he says, "it induces pleasure, forms knowledge, produces discourse" (Foucault, 1980: 119).

Thus, power and knowledge are inextricably linked. Control is achieved more by the internal monitoring of those who are controlled than by heavy physical constraints. The principle of the Panopticon—the all-seeing, internal and external authority—can be applied not only to prisons but to any system of disciplinary power: for example, the university or community college. According to Foucault, surveillance is the instrument through which modern discipline has replaced pre-modern sovereignty (kings, judges) as the fundamental power relation.

At the core of Foucault's picture of a modern "disciplinary" society are three primary techniques of control: hierarchical observation, normalizing judgement, and examination. To a great extent, control over people (power) can be achieved merely by watching them. A distinctive feature of modern power (disciplinary control) is its concern with what people have *not* done—for example, that person's failure to reach required standards. This concern shows the primary role of modern disciplinary systems: to correct deviant behaviour. The goal of discipline is not revenge but reform, where reform means forcing people to live by society's standards or norms. Science and technology serve the interests of power in carrying out regimentation ever more effectively than in the past.

Rational Choice Theories

Another critical approach, *rational choice theory*, focuses on the reasons individuals might purposely set out to commit criminal acts. We group rational choice explanations here because they assume that, under some circumstances, individuals are motivated to maximize their own welfare at the expense of social order.

"Rational choice" is a general theoretical perspective—or family of theories—that explains social outcomes by setting up models of individual action and social context. Like the critical approach more generally, rational choice theory assumes that people are competing—indeed, in conflict—over desired social and economic resources. Unlike functionalists, rational choice theorists do not assume consensus and stability in a society—only individuals chasing their own goals as effectively as they can.

From the rational choice standpoint, illegal work (crime) and legal work are mere points on a continuum of income-generating activities. The choices between illegal work and legal work involve assessments of likely returns, costs of reward and punishment, opportunity costs (i.e., opportunities forgone), and tastes and preferences about both types of work. Often, ordinarily law-abiding people engage in illegal work because of the low wages and harsh conditions they find in legal work. Many criminal offenders engage in both legal work and crime at the same time or sequentially. This overlap suggests a fluid relationship between legal and illegal work.

Businesses as well as individuals behave rationally where crime is concerned, weighing the benefits and costs of criminal activity. Corporate crime is similar to street crime in that sense, as we will see in Chapter 8. Though street crimes are a primary concern of most people (and criminologists), in recent years the public has paid a great deal more attention to crimes committed by corporations. The factors encouraging corporate crime include the failure of government to control illegal business practices, lack of corporate self-regulation, and a lack of public concern about corporate crime.

In rational choice theory, what matters most for controlling crime is the swiftness and certainty of deterrence. Since potential rule-breakers often are controlled only by external sanctions—by the threat of detection, arrest, and punishment—a get-tough-with-offenders policy should work well to prevent crime. However, stiffer penalties are usually inadequate. The only sure deterrent would be swift and certain punishment; yet, as we know, the probability of a crime resulting in arrest, prosecution, conviction, and punishment is usually quite low (i.e., the so-called funnel effect we discussed earlier).

> **Time to Reflect:** What kinds of crimes are least likely to be the result of "rational choice," and how can our society prevent and discourage such "irrational" crimes?

Social Policy Implications

We will discuss the social policy implications of different theoretical approaches chapter by chapter. It may be useful, however, to start with some general points on this topic. After all, every sociological approach implies a certain set of preferred social policies. We will discuss these here in the most general terms.

The structural functionalist approach to deviance and crime, as noted, focuses on social cohesion. Where deviant or criminal acts disrupt society or undermine social cohesion, and there is a clear consensus about the harmfulness of these acts, policies will typically aim to control or eliminate these acts. In some instances, the public will seek particularly harsh punishments—for example, capital punishment, the implications of which we will discuss in Chapter 12 . When consensus is not quite as great, governments may take other, less sweeping actions, including so-called "harm-reduction strategies." These have as their goal the control of unwanted activities that people feel cannot reasonably be eliminated.

The interactionist approach to social policy typically focuses on issues of labelling and the effects of law enforcement on rule-breaking and recidivism (i.e., repeated deviance or crime). The underlying theory that labelling will perpetuate deviance leads interactionists to advocate against labelling people who are already disadvantaged or whose identities are particularly fragile (e.g., addicts and mentally ill people) or incompletely formed (e.g., juveniles).

The critical approach to social policy typically focuses on inequalities of power in the shaping of public policy. It may seek to reduce inequalities as a way of reducing deviance and crime, or it may urge preventive measures (e.g., a war on poverty, better schools, a job program, or more public information campaigns) to influence the root causes of deviance or crime. Policies flowing from the critical approach will be concerned with helping both perpetrators and their targets—each of whom is viewed as a victim in his or her own way.

Conclusion

The study of deviance and control is wide-ranging, marked by a variety of theories and approaches. The single most familiar theory in the study of deviance is credited to Robert Merton, who argued that we are encouraged, through the socialization process, to want certain things in life (for example, the "American Dream" of independent economic prosperity). Social inequality, however, makes some people less able than others to achieve these cultural goals (not to mention the essential biological needs for survival). Some of these become criminals, some deviate in non-criminal ways, and others continue to obey the rules. That is, they adapt by devising different deviant strategies. This theory has continued to influence sociologists with a variety of perspectives, showing just how fertile Merton's insight really is.

As we have seen, consensus and cohesion are key concerns for functionalists, whereas power and inequality are key concerns of critical theorists. In the eyes of functionalists, socialization and formal laws are necessary for social organization. By contrast, critical theorists argue that, because social constructs work to preserve the ruling class's view of deviant and undesirable behaviours, formal laws work to oppress society rather than improve (or protect) it.

Symbolic interactionists largely focus on socialization, starting with the work of George Herbert Mead. In their studies of deviance, symbolic interactionists analyze the ways that certain behaviours and conditions become defined as deviant and the ways some people come to be seen as, and see others as, deviant. Thus, labelling and social construction are key in this approach.

The critical approaches to deviance focus on inequality and power, as already noted. A related approach—feminism—interrogates the gendered nature of deviance and control. In certain respects, the feminist approach is an amalgam of conflict and interactionist perspectives. Finally, we referred to postmodernism and related it to the concerns of its most famous protagonist, Michel Foucault. Here, the central organizing concept is normality, which links knowledge and power in a structure that invisibly controls us, even as it persuades us to change.

Questions for Critical Thought

1. Why is adopting a sociological approach useful when considering issues of crime and punishment?
2. What problems are likely to occur if we adhere strictly to one sociological approach when examining particular issues of crime and deviance?
3. Which approach to crime and deviance would likely be most attentive to the problems and concerns of marginalized (minority) groups?

4. Should we blame criminals for their acts? Isn't society to blame when people decide to break the rules?
5. Why would a critical theorist be interested in cybercrime? Be sure to include motivation and opportunity in your discussion.
6. What type of deviance is least well analyzed by the three main sociological frameworks we have discussed? Does this suggest other ways of analyzing crime and deviance?

Recommended Readings

Abramsky, Sasha. 2008. *American Furies: Crime, Punishment, and Vengeance in the Age of Mass Imprisonment*. Boston: Beacon Press.

Abramsky examines the recent growth of, and violence in, American prisons. He criticizes mandatory sentencing laws and notes that law and order wins political races, and jails provide jobs in places where industry has dried up. The book makes good use of on-the-ground reporting with prisoners, corrections officials, and scholars.

Britt, Chester L., and Michael R. Gottfredson, eds. 2003. *Control Theories of Crime and Delinquency*. New Brunswick, NJ: Transaction.

In this book, contributors discuss the notion of learning, or socialization, in the context of control theory and the effects that families, peers, and criminal justice have on self-control, social ties, and criminal behaviour. Part 3 looks at crime cross-nationally.

Hagan, John, and Wenona Rymond-Richmond. 2009. *Darfur and the Crime of Genocide*. New York: Cambridge University Press.

Besides tracing the intellectual history of competing approaches to genocide, the authors make excellent use of interviews with more than 1,000 Darfuris that were conducted as part of a study launched by the US State Department in 2004.

Grisso, Thomas. 2004. *Double Jeopardy: Adolescent Offenders with Mental Disorders*. Chicago: University of Chicago Press.

What are the duties of our juvenile justice system when facing delinquent youth with mental disabilities? How do issues of adolescent development complicate the court's response to delinquents with special mental health needs? The author considers how the juvenile justice system can best respond to the needs of children.

Recommended Websites

Canadian Centre for Justice Statistics (CCJS)

www.statcan.ca/bsolc/english/bsolc?catno=85F0033MWE

Not as interactive or as diverse in scope as many other websites, this Statistics Canada site is an important official government resource nonetheless. All recent issues of the Canadian Centre for Justice Statistics Profile Series are available for free download.

Canadian Centre on Substance Abuse

www.ccsa.ca/Eng/Pages/Home.aspx

The Canadian Centre on Substance Abuse provides one of the most generous offerings of links and free online publications related to substance abuse issues in Canada. Also provided here are links to Canadian drug treatment centres and college and university substance abuse programs.

Canadian Department of Justice

www.canada.justice.gc.ca

The Canadian Department of Justice website is a great starting point for deviation research. It contains up-to-date information on laws and policies. The website also provides various publications such as reports, working documents, and policy papers.

Statistics Canada

www.statcan.gc.ca

The Statistics Canada website is a comprehensive site that releases various studies, surveys, and documents daily. It contains plenty of relevant information to help Canadians and policy-makers better understand Canada.

Recommended Movies

***Do the Right Thing*, Dir. Spike Lee (1989)**

On the hottest day of the year, racial animosity breaks out in a Brooklyn neighbourhood in which blacks, whites, and Asians had been living in a fragile state of peace. Directed by one of cinema's most influential African-American provocateurs, Spike Lee's breakthrough film explores the ways in which social tensions compound, much to the detriment of society.

***Short Cuts*, Dir. Robert Altman (1993)**

A series of intertwining stories, linking the lives of 22 Los Angelinos over the course of a few days. In exploring all manner of human relationships, Altman—an icon of American cinéma-vérité—shows the multitude of ways in which real-life concerns clash with societal expectations and create feelings of alienation, anger, and despondency.

***Fast, Cheap, and Out of Control*, Dir. Errol Morris (1997)**

This film, directed by one of the world's foremost documentarians, investigates, in Morris's words, "four versions of the myth of Sisyphus," exploring the lives of four men living decidedly outside of the societal mainstream. These men are lion tamer Dave Hoover, topiary gardener George Mendo, mole-rat specialist Ray Mendez, and robotics scientist Rodney Brooks.

***The Conformist* (Italian: *Il conformista*), Dir. Bernardo Bertolucci (1970)**

Based on a 1951 political novel by **Alberto Moravia**, the film is a story of seduction, betrayal, and murder, all under the guise of conformity to the rule of Italian Fascism under Mussolini. A use of 1930s art and décor helps to evoke the stylish yet suffocating mentality that allowed respectable people to co-operate with thugs and ruffians.

***Babies*, Dir. Thomas Balme (2010)**

This documentary film provides a fascinating comparative study of the first year of life for four unrelated children. Taking his subjects from Namibia, Mongolia, Japan, and the United States, Balme implicitly emphasizes the fundamental biological similarities of his subjects, noting the importance of culture and parenting in shaping children's identities.

PART II

Deviant Activities

2 Appearance Issues

Learning Objectives

- To identify the characteristics of people who have appearance issues
- To understand the sociological perspectives used to explain appearance deviance
- To see the role that societal reaction plays in shaping the deviant's behaviour
- To learn how fashion communities project image standards
- To understand the social and health consequences of appearance deviance issues
- To examine policies proposed to control appearance issues

Introduction

As we see in this chapter about appearance, it is very easy to break society's rules—to become a deviant—even if you don't mean to do so. This chapter is about less acceptable or usual ways of dressing and takes us into a discussion of punk culture, tattooing, and piercing as means of deviating from conventional **appearance norms**. And it is also about obesity, anorexia, and other kinds of disapproved appearance.

Though forms of appearance deviation vary widely, they have a few features in common. First, they all violate prevailing cultural standards. Second, they are all social in their effects, if not their causes, for they all lead to labelling and even stigmatization or exclusion. Third, appearance deviations often give rise to deviant communities and subcultures, as responses to this stigmatization.

This chapter will outline the differences between deviant appearances that *intentionally* carry cultural meanings—as high-fashion clothing, tattoos, and punk dress do—and *unintentionally* convey cultural meanings—as severely overweight and underweight bodies do. Finally, we consider the consequences of appearance deviation, noting that sometimes people harm their health by deviating from the appearance norms. In other cases, they harm themselves by conforming. Moreover, deviance and conformity in appearance often have no health effect whatsoever. What all these behaviours have in common, though, is that they violate social expectations and, in that sense, they are all deviant appearances.

Appearance Norms

Appearance norms affect everyone, but women feel them most keenly since, historically, women have been most valued (by men) for their perceived beauty and supposed fertility. No wonder, then, that women fear aging more than men; aging brings with it a natural reduction of what our popular media-driven culture considers attractive.

That is, aging pushes women, most dramatically, across the normative boundaries from attractiveness to unattractiveness, if youthful standards are applied. For that reason, some women, more so than men, feel pushed to counter the natural process of aging. The cosmetics, fashion, and cosmetic surgery industries are founded on, and drive, this desire to attain an imagined "normalcy" and even "perfection." When people, especially women, succumb to the siren call of an "ideal" image, they are taking a position about our society's most important appearance norms.

Canadian researchers Laura Hurd Clarke and Meredith Griffin (2007) examined "older women's perceptions of natural and unnatural aging in relation to the use of beauty work interventions, including anti-wrinkle creams, cosmetics, hair dyes, cosmetic surgeries, and non-surgical cosmetic procedures." In a sample of Canadian women aged 50–70, they found that:

> the women tended to define natural aging as a lack of beauty work intervention and argued that this was a commendable goal. However, the majority engaged in beauty work and many articulated the importance of producing a "natural look" through their beauty practices. While some women argued for an acceptance of the physical realities of growing older, others asserted that an aged appearance should be fought against using whatever beauty work interventions were required and available. (ibid. 187)

In short, these women—like all of us—know our society's appearance norms and how important it is to obey them.

In judging appearance, people often look for points of likeness and familiarity that make them feel secure. They also compare other people (however unconsciously) to the cultural ideal. We generally admire and feel attracted to others who look prosperous, fit, and healthy, according to society's standards. Appearance features that approximate the ideal—not merely the familiar—are important because everyone wants to be admired and accepted. Such ideal features, though rare in real life, frame what we consider "appearance norms." Most people prefer others who approximate these appearance expectations; and they criticize people who seem unconcerned about meeting the appearance norms of their own culture.

Appearance norms are often measurable, in body size and shape, dress, and other adornment. And since these norms are measurable, it is easy to see deviations from the expected. We look at deviations from appearance norms for signs of rebellion, carelessness, or ignorance.

Some physical attributes—for example, a perfect nose or flawless white teeth—are valued because they are scarce; but this is far from the whole story. Abundant photos and images glorify ideal men and women in the mass media, and since these images of perfection vary in interesting ways, we can see various ways to meet the culture's appearance norms. In general, however, our culture idealizes youth; a slender, toned body; and symmetrical, delicate facial features. Extreme departures from these norms suggest poor genes, poor grooming, or a lack of self-discipline and self-worth. Many people—especially younger people—are able to approximate the cultural expectations; however, few can meet the cultural ideals. And satisfying the appearance norms gets harder the older (or poorer) a person gets. In fact, meeting the appearance norms is getting harder for everyone, as a careful study of "beautiful people" has shown.

Using data from 11 national health surveys in Canada and the US, Spiter et al (1999) compared the body standards of North Americans aged 18–24 with data on *Playboy* centrefold models, Miss America Pageant winners, and *Playgirl* models. Doing so, the researchers found a growing, startling inconsistency between real bodies and ideal bodies in North America.

They found that, since the 1950s, the body sizes of Miss America Pageant winners have *decreased* noticeably and those of *Playboy* centrefold models have remained below normal body weight. Ideal women have remained or become lighter and more slender than the average for "real people." Over the same period, the body sizes of average young North American women and men have *increased* considerably—mainly because of an increase in body fat and growing obesity in the general population.

In short, since the 1950s, the body sizes and shapes of real North American women have increasingly deviated from those of idealized women. Further, male and female body images changed in opposite ways over this period, drawing a stronger contrast between ideal males and females. As ideal *women* (in the mass media) became smaller, more toned, and physically fit, ideal *men* bulked up through increased muscularity. Thus, in photos at least, ideal men and women became more and more different. This difference between ideal men and women played to a (very old) stereotype that men should be the muscular protectors and possessors of petite women. By contrast, the difference between real men and women remained small, as both men and women gained more body fat. In this respect, actual men became less masculine and actual women less feminine than

MACHINE MEASURES BEAUTY OF FACE

EVEN beauty may now be reduced to cold, hard figures, according to the inventors of a device that is said to record the contours of a face with thousandth-of-an-inch accuracy. Beauty shops might use the device, the inventors say, to learn how to change their customers' features. In the inventors' opinion, the following measurements are ideal: *nose*, same length as the height of forehead; *eyes*, separated by a space the width of one eye.

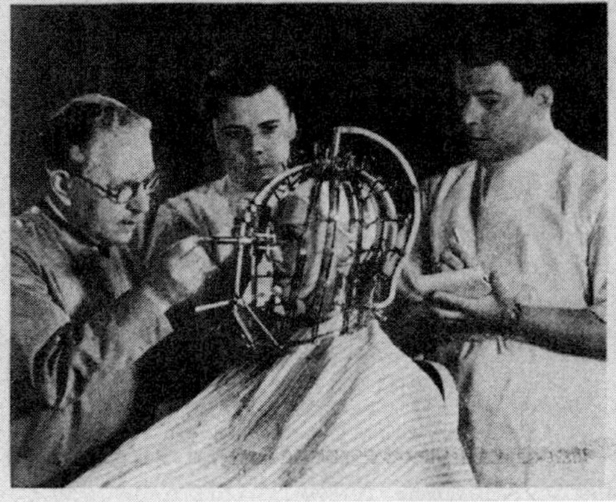

FIGURE 2.1 Measuring the Beauty of a Face

Source: This article originally appeared in the February 1933 issue of *Popular Science*®. Copyright 2009. Permission licence #58830-WR-MO.

the cultural ideas had come to require. In short, more and more people were deviating from the appearance norms.

We know these things without measuring them scientifically, but careful measurement confirms our suspicions. Some early efforts to measure appearance are depicted in Figures 2.1 and 2.2. We can choose to laugh at the crude efforts scientists made to measure facial beauty, but billion-dollar industries are built on "beautifying" women's and, increasingly, men's faces. Scientists also continue to measure body characteristics, partly to find out and record bodily norms and partly for ergonomic purposes. Here, their goal is to devise body-friendly clothing, furniture, automobiles, and other "body containers," and to ensure that workspaces reflect the needs of "normal" people's body shapes.

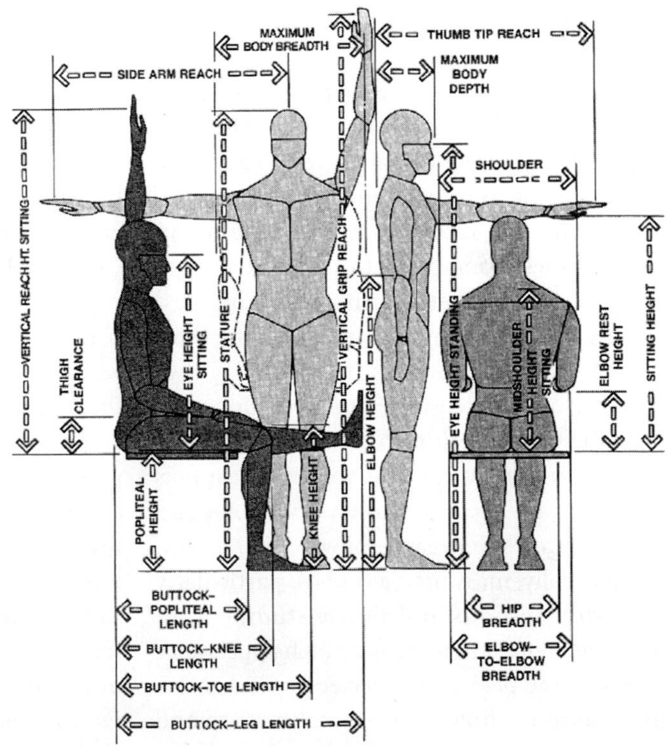

FIGURE 2.2 Normal Body Shapes and Movements

Source: Available at: <http://www.k-state.edu/udlearnsite/img/L4-bodymeasurementsgif.gif>.

The inconsistencies between actual bodies and ideal (media) bodies may account for the increased dissatisfaction people express about their bodies. Eating disorders, which we discuss shortly, are one result of this dissatisfaction. However, there are other sources and other consequences. In a society like ours, with growing numbers of elderly, disabled, and chronically ill people, we are bound to see more and more people wrestling with image issues.

As we know from Merton's (1957 [1938]) classic study of anomie, a gap between cultural ideals and real-world possibilities can have at least two results. One is acceptance of the norms and an effort to reproduce them—what Merton called *conformity* or, where the effort is doomed to fail, *ritualism*. An alternative is rejection of the norms, sometimes accompanied by attempts to live by new appearance rules—*innovation*—or establish new appearance norms—what Merton called *rebellion*. Rebellion, as we will see, may lead to the spread of deviant styles and trends (such as tattooing and piercings) that purposefully violate prevailing appearance norms.

In hopes of crafting a more acceptable appearance, North Americans have shown great ingenuity. Many have employed surgery to pare away, or drain away, excess fat; erase lines and wrinkles; and refashion facial features (especially noses, chins, and eyes). They have used clothing and makeup to hide or accentuate body and face features, depending on whether these conformed to, or violated, society's appearance norms. And they have used dieting and exercise to shape and tone their bodies. At no time in human history have people pursued physical fitness so doggedly or with such devotion to appearance norms. The pursuit and display of youthful beauty is evident in almost every Hollywood movie and major network television show.

Generally, mass media outlets, particularly television stations and movie studios, have remained reluctant to depict much appearance diversity, and people are selected for on-camera jobs based on how photogenic they are and how well their appearance matches the "norms" of attractiveness. A homely, overweight TV "weather girl," for instance, is practically unimaginable. Obesity—or heftiness—has become one of the more common deviant appearances on television—although it did not begin that way, with earlier TV performers such as Kate Smith, Jonathan Winters, Raymond Burr, and William Conrad having their own shows without reference to their size. More recently, Roseanne Barr, John Goodman, Rosie O'Donnell, and, of course, the yo-yoing maven of weight consciousness, Oprah Winfrey, have had shows in which their size, in one way or another, became part of the performance. Television executives have used a "fat, lovable man with an attractive wife" formula to create popular series like *The Honeymooners* (1955–6), *Family Matters* (1989–98), and *The King of Queens* (1998–2007). Rarely is a husband's size a cause for genuine concern or empathy in these shows, however, usually being played for laughs.

Filmmakers are more likely than television producers to depict deviant appearances empathetically. In David Lynch's *The Elephant Man* (1979) and Peter Bogdanovich's *Mask* (1985), the principal characters' facial deformities are the main focus of their respective stories. Current Hollywood films rarely if ever depict characters with noticeable physical disabilities—paraplegics or amputees, for instance—whose lives do not revolve principally around these physical abnormalities.

In real life, however, for some unfortunate people they do. David Merrick, the subject of *The Elephant Man*, was labelled "deviant" for his physical appearance when, in fact, he was an intelligent, sensitive man who sought to maintain his dignity in the face of public scorn and ridicule. The same theme is played out in the Lasse Hallström–directed *What's Eating Gilbert Grape* (1993), in which the title character, played by Johnny Depp, after his morbidly obese mother has died, empties the family home of all belongings and then torches the house—the only way to have removed her body from the upstairs bedroom would have been by crane, and he didn't want his mother, even in death, or his siblings to face further ridicule.

Race concerns have been at the heart of the most hotly contested battle over so-called appearance deviance over the last few decades. Rankled by a study of *TV Guide* magazine that depicted 91 per cent of all characters on new American shows as white-skinned, black, Hispanic, and Asian communities called for change (Greenberg et al., 1997: 225–47). This resulted in a number of telling studies on the depiction of racial diversity on television.

According to one study administered by the organization Children Now, 76 per cent of all characters on television during the 2000–1 season were white, 18 per cent black, 2 per cent Latino/Hispanic, 2 per cent Asian, and 0.2 per cent Native American (ibid.). This study showed, perhaps unexpectedly, a slight over-representation of blacks and a vast under-representation of Hispanics and Asians on American television. While we will explore race to a greater degree later in the book, it is important to note that the mass media outlets may depict even as fundamental an appearance trait as skin colour as deviant.

Systematic studies of this issue are rare, but an analysis of American prime-time television conducted and published in 2009 found that out of 90 hours of primetime programming per week, fully 32.5 hours were dedicated to reality TV, news, or Sunday night movies. Of the remaining 57.5 hours of scripted series, only 13.5 hours of programming (e.g., *Law and Order*) contained *any* minority primary characters, 6.5 hours (e.g., *ER*) contained *multiple* minority primary characters, and only 3 hours contained a *lead* minority character or one labelled as "different"—i.e., *Ugly Betty*, *The Unit*, *Everybody Hates Chris*, and *The Game*). Conceivably, the results are slightly different in multicultural Canada, but that remains to be seen (freshisback.com/2009/02/11/diversity-tv/).

Appearance: Its Social Meaning

In his classic sociological work *Asylums*, Erving Goffman (1961) notes that the first step a total institution—for example, a prison or mental hospital—takes to re-socialize an inmate is to separate the inmate from old identities by changing his or her appearance.

Usually this process, which Goffman calls a **degradation ceremony**, begins with changes to the inmate's clothing and adornment—for example, forcing the inmate to wear an institutional uniform and removing individual identifiers such as jewellery. Often, the inmate is also forced to wear a generic hairstyle—for men, often a shaved head—erasing all signs of individuality. Being forced in this way to give up their own clothing and personal style signifies an inmate's loss of identity and social status. Being forced to take on an institutional uniform signifies entry into a low-status community of apparently identical, subordinate inmates. So, in total institutions, the old maxim is true that "clothes make the man" (or woman). Humble clothes make humble people. Defeated people are forced to wear the signs of their defeat.

The connection between appearance, clothing, and self has been known and commented on for a long time. For example, nineteenth-century Scottish novelist and essayist Thomas Carlyle wrote about clothing, metaphorically, in his comic work *Sartor Resartus* (1846). There he used clothing to stand in for all symbols of self. He noted that all people use clothing and other appearance items to declare and confirm their personal identities in everyday life.

Increasingly, then as now, the symbols become the social reality.

Present-day sociologists would agree with this view. Through clothing, we link our personal identities to shared social identities. Clothes are like roles we play: we put them on to signify who we think we are and who we want to be. They are part of the "script" we follow when we enter a social situation. Clothes define our place, role, and position in the social order. Carlyle believed that "clothes present us to ourselves and to the world" as we express our freedom in socially acceptable ways. We are free to choose the clothing we wear, insofar as we have the money to afford it; but we do so knowing that we may be judged and treated accordingly.

At the same time, society affects both what we reveal and hide of our bodies. Social pressures constantly limit our range of choice here, and reduce the basic right of self-expression. Nowhere was this more evident than in recent "slut" protests where young women—through signs and provocative clothing—proclaimed their right to dress as they wished without giving up any rights to protection against sexual assault. Sometimes, however, we choose to hide more of our bodies than usual, believing this will be considered more proper or, perhaps, more seductive. Clothes never reveal the whole self, any more than they reveal the whole body; clothes are both adornments and disguises. Remember, here, the importance of secrecy in social life that we discussed in the last chapter.

Not surprisingly, appearance norms are gendered. Not only are men and women judged by different appearance standards, but they also wear different kinds of clothing, connoting their different social roles and statuses. Take pockets: historically, pockets on women's clothing have been smaller and fewer than pockets on men's clothing. For women, pockets have been decorative; for men, practical. Even today, men and women use their pockets differently (that's why women carry purses, but most men don't), and pockets play a part in constructing gender. A man who wears pants (or worse, a suit) without any pockets is making a very strong statement about his self-image and, indirectly, about his gender.

Time to Reflect: Given what you understand about gender and lifestyle, what do you imagine men and women will be wearing 50 years from now? For example, will they be dressed similarly or differently, and why?

All fashion, including clothing fashion, is intended to reveal a person's taste. This is made amply clear in a classic work, *Distinction: A Social Critique of the Judgement of Taste* (1984 [1979]), by French sociologist Pierre Bourdieu. In this imposing book, Bourdieu shows how relations of dominance in society are maintained through the exercise and display of "taste" under conditions of (supposed) free choice. Indeed, preferences for food, books, singers, painters, films, radio, television, and leisure activities are all indicators of taste, as data from over 50 surveys and opinion polls proved to Bourdieu.

Bourdieu concludes that what we call "taste" and imagine to be an inborn personal quality is actually determined by society. In large part, our taste reflects the class we are born into, the family experiences we have, and the schooling we receive. Bourdieu calls the connection between a person's social position and his taste *habitus*. "Habitus"—a poorly defined and elusive term in *Distinction*—embodies the preferences and mannerism of any given actor and the required preferences and mannerisms of a position in Social Space. More often than not, an actor acquires the habitus of his position. So, for example, in the 1960s people in high social positions tended to incorporate (i.e., learn) fine etiquette, golf, bridge, and horseback riding, among other things. By similar means, they came to speak, act, and pursue activities markedly different from people lower in the Social Space whose activities included football, beer drinking, and fishing, among others.

The main, and paradoxical, point is that these tastes are considered extremely personal choices, by almost everyone. Yet they are socially structured in the sense that they are learned, shared, and earmarked for particular groups. Only some people will learn to value golf, bridge, and wine-drinking; while other people will learn to value football, fishing, and beer-drinking; and socio-economic background features will (largely) predict which group a person will fall into. Yet, though these differences in taste are largely determined by social class membership, they are not always accompanied by class consciousness. People in the same class will often be alike due to the closeness of their habitus, but they may not be aware that class membership produced this similarity.

People only become aware of class differences when choice is denied—that is, when they can't get what they need to meet our culture's appearance norms. The teenaged girl, unemployed single mother, and 20-year-old single male who can't afford clothes that would make them look great are all on the verge of asking sociological questions about inequality. Likewise, for people who have been disempowered: as noted earlier, appearance sometimes is used to dramatize inequality, not merely enact it. With degradation ceremonies in total institutions, when people in authority want to control people, they try to control their modes of dress. This has been obvious in the history of fashion in fascist countries.

For example, Italy's government under the Fascist dictator Mussolini used fashion to discipline the social body—especially women's bodies—and to create an identifiable national style (Paulicelli, 2002). Similarly, in the most repressive Islamic countries today—for example, Iran and Saudi Arabia—women, when they go out in public, are expected to dress in ways that limit the colour, adornment, and sensuousness of their clothing.

In our own and other societies, some children are obliged to wear school uniforms to limit their show of individuality and independence. In general, dress codes for children and other subordinates limit people's self-expression and raise questions about freedom and equality. Left on their own, and unless forced to wear uniforms, young people develop clothing ambitions early in life. Even before adolescence, children begin making style decisions and building knowledge about different products and brands. As these pre-adolescents grow older, they learn more of the norms and information needed to make fashion-conscious clothing decisions and crave more independence in shopping for clothes. They want to be free to dress in a way that gains them admission to the desired peer group, and also to declare their independence from the world of parents and other adults.

Yet, paradoxically, given a choice in how they dress, people usually choose to conform to prevailing appearance norms. In particular, they try to dress like their peers; so even if a school does not have a specific dress code or uniform, the vast majority of students dress similarly. Variations in dress reflect different group (or clique) memberships. Eliminating dress codes at school allows pupils to use their clothing to gain recognition, forge bonds with their friends, and develop peer subcultures. It also helps to distinguish and separate those who fit in with social expectations of dressing in popular fashions and those who do not. Certain items and brand names or fashion accessories (such as tattoos and piercings) acquire specific, symbolic value for purposes of rebellion.

In short, our tendency to conform to appearance norms, learned from childhood onward, separates us into different and sometimes opposing groups. Nowhere is this more evident than in the realm of fashion, which is a social institution in its own right.

Appearance Issues and the Fashion Industry

The earliest sociological works on clothing and fashion were by Thorstein Veblen and Georg Simmel.

In his classic work, *Theory of the Leisure Class* (1979 [1899]), published at the end of a decade in American cultural and economic history when the materialism, self-indulgence, and frivolity of the wealthier classes were seemingly boundless, Veblen stressed that rich people use fashion—whether new dances, vacation spots, or modes of dress—as means of "conspicuous consumption," to distinguish themselves from their social inferiors. Therefore, fashions—to be "fashionable"—have to be costly, perhaps foolish, and generally short-lived. It is precisely their conspicuous (or glaring) wastefulness that makes these fashions "status markers"—a means of distinguishing the rich from the thrifty middle class or the abject poor.

Veblen claimed that fashionability is an elite concern that trickles down to lower classes; typically, a new fashion is created as soon as the old fashion has diffused to a large portion of common society. When a new fashion or appearance norm has been widely adopted by the middle class, it is no longer "fashionable" to the wealthy. The rich will have long since moved on to a new fashion. This explains the high turnover rate in the fashion industry where new trends are adopted first by the wealthy, then by the rest of society.

Imitation, therefore, is as central to fashion and fashionableness as is innovation, a fact we can see in all hierarchical societies. For example, in colonial societies, the native peoples often imitate the clothing of colonizers, to represent their identification with the colonial rulers. All consumption in colonial or post-colonial societies—including styles of dress—reflects a system of social values and categories imposed or imported from the outside. In the Congo, for example, the practice of *la sape* (meaning "to dress elegantly") is even considered a means of gaining power over the (European) life force, whose form is wealth, health, whiteness, and status (Thomas, 2003). In short, *la sape*—a type of social imitation—is a means of amassing what sociologists call **social capital** and **cultural capital**.

However, colonial and post-colonial people do not all copy their colonizers to the same degree. Some resist the colonizers' norms. In Hong Kong, over the past 150 years, both nationalism and colonialism have affected styles of dress. Chinese men adopted Westernized dress earlier than women—perhaps because they had more social or business contact with Westerners—and working-class Chinese women moved away from the traditional *cheongsam* earlier than middle-class women—perhaps for similar reasons.

Veblen's theory of fashion reflects a long history of so-called sumptuary laws in Europe. These laws, dating back to medieval European society, were used to regulate which types of people were permitted to wear which kinds of clothing and fabrics. Sumptuary laws were intended to prevent low-status people from representing themselves above their station by dress, speech, or otherwise. People were expected to dress for the part they played in society—not the part to which they aspired. To keep the lower classes from copying the clothing of the upper class, most European countries passed sumptuary laws to regulate dress. Clothing was thought to offer a window into people and societies alike. It told the careful observer about the general prosperity of a population and about the society's degree and extent of social differentiation.

During the seventeenth and eighteenth centuries, with the end of sumptuary laws but before industrialization, high fashion was largely restricted to prosperous, educated people. Yet gradually, in the middle and upper classes, new forms of thinking about fashion emerged. Educated people came to see fashion as important and as a sign of cultivation—not merely a form of conspicuous consumption by the rich. People of "taste" were increasingly celebrated for their subtlety and worldliness.

Gradually, both the French and English clothing industries expanded at this time, largely because of a growing demand by the working classes and the rise of industrialism, which allowed for the cheap replication of upper-class fashions. The influence of fashion filtered down to the middle class and then even to the working class. In England, the dress of the common people changed over the eighteenth century. Efforts to prevent the lower classes from wearing fashionable-looking clothes—cheap knock-offs, then as now—increasingly failed. The fashion floodgates were opened even wider by the French Revolution, which encouraged every citizen to dress as he or she chose, in praise of individuality and against hierarchy.

Increasingly, two linked social processes—the imitation of social superiors and the effort to distinguish oneself from one's equals or inferiors—became central to the evolution of lifestyles, fashions, and consumption patterns. With the continued mass production of clothing in the nineteenth and twentieth centuries, fashions trickled down from the richest to poorest classes, and fashions continued to change.

It was sociologist Georg Simmel (1906 [1902]) who fully grasped the complexity of fashion and its inner irony. On the one hand, all items of appearance are individual—expressions of the self, as Carlyle had pointed out. On the other hand, ironically, all items of appearance are also social—a means of identifying with particular social groups or communities, as Veblen had pointed out.

Fashion—whether in clothing, body shape, body adornment, or otherwise—must be viewed as a process of constant negotiation between these two levels of reality: between self and society. Simmel highlighted this when he tried to explain the rapid diffusion and decline of fashion. He hypothesized that the instability of fashion results from the combined action of imitation (of those of higher social status) and distinction (from those belonging to lower statuses). This process—in earlier days, highly controlled and centralized by sumptuary laws—was gradually replaced by a fluid system in which fashion designers around the world create designs for small publics in global markets. Often, these designers are in the "fashion business," more generally, and not merely the clothing business; mainly, they make their profits from luxury products other than clothing (e.g., perfumes, jewellery, leather goods).

Today, many fashion trends continue to trickle down from the rich and the aristocracy—the social and cultural elites; however, other fashion trends emerge from the "streets." Often, rich people seek to emulate the fashion of people who are young and innovative, even if they are poor. More often than not, the fashion industry drives the engines of fashion, defining new appearance norms and promoting them in magazines, movies, and on television. From the costliest design houses emerge fashions that, within days or hours, are available in cheaper versions, under cheaper labels, throughout the major cities of the world.

Clothing designers and cosmetic manufacturers constantly produce new things for us to want and need. Consumerism drives the modern global capitalist economy. In turn, promoting dissatisfaction with appearance drives consumerism. Thus, for the past 100 years at least, the spread of fashion has gone hand in hand with mass advertising—and with the mass production of appearance discontent.

Communities and Subcultures of Appearance

Some people break the appearance rules, however, and form communities of like-minded individuals. Often, these communities or subcultures are committed to achieving beauty and distinctiveness in unconventional ways that deviate from the mainstream. Some do so through unconventional beauty: the world of high-fashion modelling, for example, attempts to set the publicized (commercial) trends and, eventually, the standards of appearance for women who follow these trends.

Deviant communities, however, such as the world of tattooing and body piercing, present alternative visions of dress and body adornment through engagement in distinctive lifestyles and ideas. It is to tattooing and body piercing as signifiers of these communities that we now turn.

Tattooing and Body Piercing

People decorate their bodies in all kinds of ways. Throughout the centuries, people have relied on clothing, jewellery, hairstyles, and makeup to decorate and beautify themselves. Increasingly, in recent years, people in our society have used tattoos and body piercings for this purpose.

Before the invention of the tattooing machine, tattoos were costly, dangerous, and hard to apply. They were often seen in the higher ranks of European society, such as the aristocracy. Among upper-class German men attending university, duelling scars served a similar purpose of showing class and courage. Gradually, like other fashions, tattoos moved down the social hierarchy. The first professional tattoo artist in the United States—a man named Martin Hildebrandt—opened the first tattoo parlour in New York City in 1846.

However, despite the commercial availability, tattoos and piercings have always been connected to certain groups and their members. Tattoos and piercings have always made the identification of group membership easier and, in doing so, have also promoted self-identification for members of marginalized groups. As with some forms of dress, tattoos also can function as the self-marginalization of those who otherwise would not be seen as different. It is deviance by choice. In the past, many tattoo wearers were likely to have spent much time in the presence of other men: in gangs or prisons, on ships or military bases. For gang members and prisoners, the layers of tattoos recorded important personal events. For people in prison, they expressed a convict's wish to remember his loved ones or his own identity.

Tattoos, in this way, told the story of people's lives, ambitions, and group affiliations. They also symbolized the toughness or "manliness" involved in undergoing what can be a lengthy, painful procedure: for example, members of the Japanese Yakuza, one of the world's oldest and largest transnational crime gangs, are known for their nearly full-body tattooing (see Knight and Keating, 2010: 291).

Public views about tattooing have changed over the years. The increased presence and visibility of trained, "fine art," or "custom" tattoo artists has led many to view tattoos as artistic products, not just bodily adornment. Nor are tattoos now limited to a small group of people, as in the past; or even limited to men. In the last 20 years, Canadian women have taken to tattoos in record numbers. Like men, these women use tattoos to send various personal and cultural messages, challenging the long-standing association between tattooing and masculinity.

In these ways, the social and cultural meanings of tattooing have changed. Having shifted from being considered a mark of elitism to being considered lower-class or dangerous symbols, tattoos began to be defined as hip, trendy, and glamorous in the 1990s. Like all fashions they will go into decline, if they have not already done so. But in the meantime, tattoos have lost their stigma as the indicator of a peculiar, esoteric, or despised group membership.

This shift in opinions about tattooing shows how a deviant act can lose its stigma. The process starts with people trying to justify or legitimate their tattoos in interactions with others. In the 1990s, people who got their first tattoos served as "agents of change," caught between multiple symbolic orders, old and new. Gradually, those in the middle class overcame the negative meanings of tattoos (e.g., the associations with biker gangs and convicts) by getting body art that conformed to core, mainstream norms and values.

Though tattooing is much less limited to men than it was in the past, it remains largely a young person's adornment. Young people are far more likely than older people to get tattoos and body piercings and to experiment with a variety of other modes of dress, jewellery, and hairstyle. In recent decades, tattoos and piercings have been especially popular among people aged 18–22, and the number of women with tattoos reportedly quadrupled between 1960 and 1980. In response to the new demand, the number of tattooing and piercing shops has also increased dramatically.

So, today, tattoos are more widespread than in the past. They are not restricted to men or men who spend a lot of time in the company of other males. Yet, one thing has not changed: the tattooed body remains a distinctively communicative body. Ordinary people are finding more ways to use tattoos to make creative, imaginative, and even humorous statements about the world and their place in it.

Wearing a tattoo may increase a person's acceptance in a deviant community but also increase the likelihood of rejection in a conventional community. According to the Health Canada (2001) report on youth tattooing and piercing, body piercings and tattoos are intended to suggest that a teen wants to be associated with an experimental, risk-taking community. As a result, the tattooed and pierced teen sets himself apart from the conventional teen. The tattooed teen (and to a lesser extent, the pierced teen) is more prone to risky behaviour and more likely to use drugs and alcohol.

Does this differential still persist, now that tattooing and piercing have become so much more common than a decade or two ago? Reliable data on this are hard to come by, but a Texas study suggests that, at least in some places, the difference has remained. Koch, Roberts, Armstrong, and Owen (2007) collected data from a sample of 450 college students to examine the association between having a tattoo and engaging in premarital sexual intercourse. Their data showed that tattooed respondents were significantly more likely to be sexually active than non-tattooed college students. As well, tattooed men had become sexually active at a significantly earlier age than non-tattooed men; however, no such difference was found between tattooed and non-tattooed women in the sample.

Punk Appearance

Another violation of the mainstream appearance norm was the adoption of punk-oriented dress and behaviour; like other fashions, it was associated with its own community and subculture. The pure punk style has now largely receded into fashion history, though it has fertilized other protest-oriented styles of dress and adornment. Punk is worth mentioning here because it is relatively recent, yet it is old enough for us to have seen it come full circle—from fashion innovation to mainstream youth fashion, to outmoded fashion (with some lingering and residual influence).

Punk started in Britain with the appearance of punk bands in mainstream rock music. There, the punk subculture and its music helped change the way people talked about social inequality in the late 1970s. Punk music, and the musicians who made it popular, reintroduced working-class and youth values of rebellion into British culture, exposing the wider public to the privations of poverty during an era of economic recession. The punk songs had promoted punk values through a repeated emphasis on anarchy and violent revolt, and, notably, the repetitious "no future" lyric at the end of the Sex Pistols' 1977 parody anthem, "God Save the Queen." It was a nasty, in-your-face, aggressive style of music, dance, talk, and adornment.

Punk is a term usually applied to music. However, it is also used to describe the subculture that grew up around the music. In addition, some fans created shrines, set up concerts, and spent their free time celebrating punk ideals. The influence of punk style peaked in the 1990s, and today it has a marginal but continued status in the youth culture as part of a rebellious repertoire of clothing and behaviour styles.

At its peak, the punk style of dress was aggressively poor and openly opposed to conventional middle-class dress. It combined various appearance traits—dress, makeup, hairstyle, body language, and body adornment (tattoos, piercings, and jewellery)—in particularly non-conventional ways. These unconventional fashion statements were as central to the punk persona as "rude" and unconventional ways of acting and speaking. In punk communities, punk music was a central symbol around which punk socializing could take place. Drug-taking and drinking were central activities of these groups.

In short, the punk culture was rebellious, a collection of related subcultures, each with its own slightly distinctive language, style, and dress code. It offered people who appreciated those standards and who, for various economic-related reasons, were already marginalized an attainable model of appearance, correlated with a shared value system and sense of belonging. The codes of appearance, such as raggedy mismatched clothing and black leather, enabled members to find each other and form subcultures on the outskirts of mainstream culture. What the punk phenomenon showed is that cultural, social, and political ideas, expressed musically and in other ways (e.g., through drug use and drinking), could be associated with particular styles of dress and appearance.

Time to Reflect: Do you suppose there has always been, and will always be, one or more groups in society who dress in a manner intended to shock people and aggravate parents? Or are people really becoming more individualistic and unconventional in their dress?

However, this was certainly not the first group to do so—or the last. Hippies linked a particular style of dress and music in the 1960s, as did their immediate precursors, the beatniks of the late 1940s and 1950s. Zoot suiters did the same in the 1930s and 1940s. The easily identifiable "zoot suit" first gained popularity in New York's Harlem jazz culture in the late 1930s. There, they were initially called *drapes*. Quickly, these zoot suits were widely adopted by young Hispanic-Americans, Italian-Americans, and Filipino-Americans, as well as African-Americans. In the 1940s, wearing a zoot suit was a way to declare identification with jazz and swing, drugs, and marginal (urban, non–white Anglo-Saxon Protestant) social groups. During World War II, riots erupted in Los Angeles between off-duty soldiers and sailors and zoot-suit-wearing Mexican-Americans and African-Americans. Here, as elsewhere, style of dress was used to draw group boundaries for the purpose of inclusion and exclusion.

In the 1990s, loose connections formed between punk and rave cultures. Like punk culture, rave culture developed in an urban environment as part of the urban lifestyle. Drug use in the rave culture, as in the punk culture, focused on music and dance as well as aesthetics (e.g., clothing and adornment). Members of rave culture were particular about which substances were used where and how. Hard drug use was usually restricted to parties and weekends. This is because, even though the culture was founded on (mild) deviance, its members shared some of the values held by conventional society, such as employment and (even) success. Rave culture also embodied values prominent in Western capitalist societies, such as individuality, a faith in technology, and a need for new experience.

When discussing particular subcultures and their appearance styles, bear in mind that groups and fashions come and go, often rapidly. Yet even fads can make a big splash, changing the ways we dress and adorn ourselves. Sometimes they make a lasting impression; at least, we remember them fondly because we associate them with formative periods of our lives and, often, with people we knew then.

Fashion Models

One might think that people who embody the cultural ideal are conformists, but in fact they are not. They are more deviant than anyone, in the same sense that Mother Teresa—though saintly—was "deviant."

The community of high-fashion models is deviant in its excessive devotion to the "ideal" body and face. Thus, fashion models are to appearance norms as saints are to everyday morality. In both instances, segments of mainstream society seek to emulate the extra-normal represented: in the case of Mother Teresa, a greater sense and action of selfless giving and sacrifice; in the case of the runway supermodel, an overly thin, assertive, yet helplessly pouty appearance that might lead some women down a path of anorexia and bulimia.

Fashion models: the very words cause people to conjure up images of runways, beautiful clothes, foreign travel, glamour, and fame. Models are meant to represent the ideal woman or man. The projected image captures the attention of fashion-conscious people everywhere. Over time, the modelling industry has become more inclusive by widening the range of qualifications that models may possess in different types of modelling. Older people, stouter people, and members of racial minorities are among the types who are more often seen modelling today.

Plus-size and petite-size models, as their names imply, are hired to sell products designed to meet the needs of larger-than-average and smaller-than-average people, respectively.

However, tall, slim, and waiflike runway and high-fashion models continue to generate the greatest media attention. Runway and high-fashion modelling has very specific requirements, and at times models can face as great problems as wrestlers, boxers, and weightlifters in trying to make a prescribed weight for competition. Recently, for example, a Dutch-Canadian model won a lawsuit against the agency that dropped her and failed to fulfill her contract—because of a couple of extra centimetres—after the agency insisted that its models' hip measurement could be no more than 90 centimetres (www.cbc.ca/news/world/story/2012/03/08/dutch-model-wins-lawsuit.html).

As well, top models are expected to display confidence, independence, discipline, intelligence, and stamina. No wonder there are only a few top models in the world, and they are certainly not representative of most women! Yet, in a society like ours that places enormous value on physical beauty, this elite group exerts great influence on the average woman's self-image. Some researchers suggest that this influence is a factor in the widespread development of anorexia, especially among women.

Unintended Deviance: Anorexia, Bulimia, and Obesity

Like fashions in clothing and adornment, fashions in how body size and shape are viewed or valuated have changed over time. For centuries, eating disorders among women have been discussed and debated. What we now call *anorexia* has its roots as far back as the thirteenth century. Then, some religious women were canonized as saints for their rigorous fasting practices—part of their religious devotion and self-denial. Scholars today sometimes call these women *holy anorexics.*

Over 70 years ago, Wallis Simpson—the woman for whom King Edward VIII gave up his throne—declared that "No woman can be too rich or too thin." Today, people would likely disagree with the second part of that statement. Increasingly, people consider thinness, to the degree that bones show through skin—whatever its merits for fashion modelling or ballet—unhealthy and unattractive. More than that, excessive thinness is often linked to disordered eating. In the 1970s and 1980s, eating disorders finally received media attention with the death of singer Karen Carpenter from cardiac complications because of anorexia nervosa. This was the first time the media focused attention on the life-threatening effects of eating disorders and stopped viewing them as simply a group of relatively benign psychiatric illnesses.

At the other end of the continuum, we find the result of excessive eating: obesity. Today, people increasingly recognize the health problems associated with too much weight, and a media-driven moral panic, which often fails to account for different body types and different metabolic rates, has ensued. *Obesity* is excessive body weight, given the person's age, sex, and height, and the weight norms that prevail in a given culture or subculture. Where anorexia tends to be found among young middle- and upper-middle-class women, obesity is found among both men and women, disproportionately in the poorer parts of the population. Less educated and rural people are also more likely to be obese.

Like excessive thinness, obesity can reduce the length and quality of life. It is associated with health problems such as diabetes, back pain, and even smoking and drinking. Typically, people who are obese eat badly and abuse their bodies in other ways as well—for example, by not getting enough sleep, exercise, or fresh vegetables. So, like thinness caused by anorexia, obesity is thought by some to be the result of a faulty lifestyle and, sometimes, a troubled psychological state. In fact, it may be caused by any of various physiological factors—genetic, viral, hormonal/glandular, or chemical—or by environmental factors reaching back to infancy and early childhood. In addition, medications, including anti-depressants and neuroleptics, cause excessive weight gain for some people.

Nonetheless, obesity carries symbolic and moral meanings in our society as many consider it a violation of appearance norms. Earlier, most people thought obesity revealed a hearty, healthy appetite; a lust for living; and a good sense of humour (think of Shakespeare's Falstaff or of Santa Claus, for example). This cultural viewpoint was reflected in William Sheldon's "constitutional psychology," a theory developed in 1940 that equated human body shape with personality and behaviour. Sheldon classified human body types into different groups, called *somatotypes*, and proposed that one could predict personality traits based on a person's somatotype. Those who were obese fell under the "endomorph" somatotype, which he said was linked to having an easygoing personality. While interesting and representative of earlier societal viewpoints on obesity, this theory holds little validity in behavioural sciences today, particularly as Sheldon was never able to generate a personality test to statistically verify his theories.

Today, people are more likely to shun and/or criticize those who are obese or even slightly overweight. Like racial slurs, such behaviour can be profoundly harmful. A huge industry devoted to dieting, exercise, and "weight-watching" has developed to encourage people to lose weight and keep it off, and since dieting strategies usually fail over the long term, this industry has a perpetual supply of customers. Most of those who turn to the dieting industry are women. They continue to be more concerned about their appearance than men, since they are more likely than men to view their appearance as a major asset in mating and interpersonal relations.

Eating Issues and Appearance Norms

Many different disorders involve food, eating, and weight. However, in everyday conversation, the term *eating disorder* has come to mean anorexia nervosa, bulimia, binge-eating, and obesity. All these disorders (except obesity) are more common among women than men. However, men are also starting to come forward with problems of body image, thinness concerns, and eating disorders.

Anorexia nervosa, one of the most common eating disorders, is characterized by a relentless pursuit of thinness and a refusal to preserve "normal" body weight, given the person's age and height. The characteristics of anorexia nervosa include a 15 per cent or more loss of body weight, the use of various strategies to lose weight, a weight phobia, body image disturbances, amenorrhea (i.e., the end of menstruation for at least three consecutive cycles), and a constant preoccupation with food.

Researchers are convinced that this eating disorder is part of a more general psychological disorder. For example, anorexia nervosa often includes symptoms of depression, irritability, and withdrawal. About 95 per cent of anorexics are women. Though only 1 per cent of female adolescents have anorexia, certain attachment problems and anxiety disorders may put adolescents at risk of developing the illness. Young females, who feel more anxious and concerned with their body image, shape, and size, often seek a smaller body size and experience more concern with their appearance if they gain weight. Generally, anxiety about weight and a negative body image are strong predictors of the development of eating disorders.

Women with a related illness, bulimia nervosa, throw up their food after eating. Like an anorexic, a bulimic believes attractiveness depends on being thin. Typically, bulimics consume large amounts of food in a short time. Their binges often occur in secret and usually involve high-calorie, high-carbohydrate foods they can eat quickly, such as ice cream, doughnuts, candy, popcorn, and cookies. Like anorexia, bulimia can be lethal. As well, the two diseases are connected; about 50 per cent of people who have been anorexic develop bulimia or bulimic patterns. Research suggests that about one out of every 25 college-aged women has had bulimia. However, because people with bulimia are secretive, it is hard to know how many older people remain affected.

Obesity

Overall, a person is judged obese if her or his weight is at least 20 per cent above the statistical norm for that person's sex, age, height, and skeletal frame. That said, however, statistical norms are not widely used. Rather, the Body Mass Index (BMI), a numerical tool—weight multiplied by height squared—has become the standard. It was developed by the insurance industry for measuring large populations instead of individual people. This actuarial tool, based on insurance company mortality tables, was created with artificially low weight standards to maximize life insurance costs, and has become an improper standard that has been picked up by physicians and health institutes. The National Institutes of Health in the US, for example, began using the BMI in its studies and definitions in 1985, although it fails, among other things, to account for age as a variable (see, e.g., Kite, 2011a, 2011b).

Given women's preoccupation with thinness, it is no surprise that men are more likely than women to be deemed obese; and many are relatively unconcerned about their weight. Current concerns about obesity are only partly driven by concerns about appearance and appearance norms; health concerns are equally important. Yet, as Figure 2.3 shows, people haven't come any closer to meeting their appearance norms. If anything, they have fallen

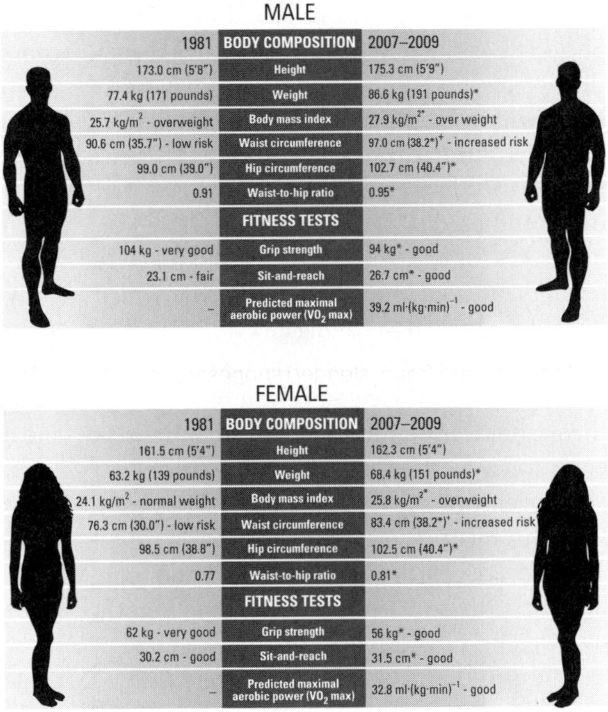

MALE

1981	BODY COMPOSITION	2007–2009
173.0 cm (5'8")	Height	175.3 cm (5'9")
77.4 kg (171 pounds)	Weight	86.6 kg (191 pounds)*
25.7 kg/m^2 - overweight	Body mass index	27.9 kg/m^{2*} - over weight
90.6 cm (35.7") - low risk	Waist circumference	97.0 cm (38.2*)$^+$ - increased risk
99.0 cm (39.0")	Hip circumference	102.7 cm (40.4")*
0.91	Waist-to-hip ratio	0.95*
	FITNESS TESTS	
104 kg - very good	Grip strength	94 kg* - good
23.1 cm - fair	Sit-and-reach	26.7 cm* - good
–	Predicted maximal aerobic power (VO_2 max)	39.2 ml·(kg·min)$^{-1}$ - good

FEMALE

1981	BODY COMPOSITION	2007–2009
161.5 cm (5'4")	Height	162.3 cm (5'4")
63.2 kg (139 pounds)	Weight	68.4 kg (151 pounds)*
24.1 kg/m^2 - normal weight	Body mass index	25.8 kg/m^{2*} - overweight
76.3 cm (30.0") - low risk	Waist circumference	83.4 cm (38.2*)$^+$ - increased risk
98.5 cm (38.8")	Hip circumference	102.5 cm (40.4")*
0.77	Waist-to-hip ratio	0.81*
	FITNESS TESTS	
62 kg - very good	Grip strength	56 kg* - good
30.2 cm - good	Sit-and-reach	31.5 cm* - good
–	Predicted maximal aerobic power (VO_2 max)	32.8 ml·(kg·min)$^{-1}$ - good

FIGURE 2.3 Portrait of Typical 45-Year-Old Male and Female, 1981 and 2007–9

*Significantly different from estimate for 1981 ($p < 0.05$).

Note: To make estimates more comparable, Canadian Health Measures Survey estimates for flexibility and muscular strength exclude respondents screened out of aerobic fitness test.

Source: Margot Shields et al., "Fitness of Canadian Adults: Results from the 2007–2009 Canadian Health Measures Survey," Figure 3, at: <www.statcan.gc.ca/pub/82-003-x/2010001/article/11064/figures/fig3-eng.htm>.

further short of them. Over the last 30 years, middle-aged (45-year-old) Canadian men and women have become heavier, wider, and thicker—though also slightly taller.

Obese people—especially obese children—are often treated like deviants, ridiculed, and stigmatized. A recent example demonstrating the extent of "fat-phobia" is the offensive blog post that appeared on the *Marie Claire* website last October (Box 2.1). Obese people are often the targets of teasing and exclusion, and this may lead to heightened psychological stress and lower self-esteem. Obese people are more likely to suffer rejection by others and develop

Current Events

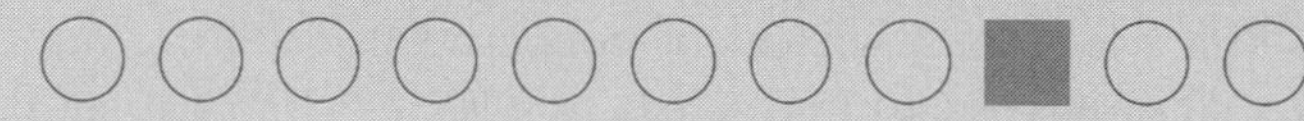

BOX 2.1

Consider the Rights of Obese People

In October 2010, the blog post "Should 'fatties' get a room? (Even on TV?)"appeared on the *Marie Claire* website. The author, Maura Kelly, wrote that she's "grossed out" when fat television characters kiss on screen. The post created a great deal of controversy, with the magazine soon receiving 28,000 e-mails and lots of criticism. Kelly responded by apologizing, while also admitting that her comments could have been a product of her own battle with anorexia.

However, the personal is also public. Her negative conception of fat people is becoming increasingly common. Obesity has come to be seen as a disease, and the growing portion of society deemed to be overweight suggests this supposed disease has turned into an epidemic, a boon perhaps for the medical business and for the diet and nutrition industry but a bane for those who struggle with weight problems or who, regardless of size, are comfortable in their own bodies. Further, many people have come to believe that weight is an indicator of character: looking good (read: slender) supposedly reflects hard work and dedication to fitness and dieting, for example. This moralistic view is perpetuated by books, magazines, and advertisements that promote workouts, diets, and other products that supposedly will allow people to attain a fit body.

Dr Howard Steiger, chief of the eating disorders program at the Douglas Institute in Montreal, believes that this highly negative attitude towards fat people could be changed if the media presented a broader assortment of body types. The *Marie Claire* website and magazine is therefore in a perfect position to initiate change and promote the acceptance of a wider range of body types (rather than supporting the notion that a skinny body is the only acceptable one).

Steiger also suggests that moderate eating (rather than obsessive dieting) and a healthy body image both contribute to good health. This view opposes the popular belief that a person's shape and weight are the most accurate indicator of personal health. Many skinny women look the way they do because they follow unhealthily strict diets and exercise routines, and smoke cigarettes, too, in their efforts to stay thin. These thin-obsessed women face much worse health risks than overweight women who exercise regularly and eat well—a fact we might all keep in mind when we turn down that second piece of cheesecake.

Sources: Annemarie Jutel, "Weighing Health: The Moral Burden of Obesity," *Social Semiotics* (2006): 113–25; Jessica Murphy, "Fat-Phobic Blog Post Forces Apology," QMI Agency, 27 Oct. 2010, at: <lifewise.canoe.ca/Beauty/2010/10/27/15854511.html>.

a fear of interacting with peers, leading to social isolation, and they often experience hardships related to employment, intimacy, and family relations. Stereotyping and social exclusion can lead to the development of a persisting negative self-image that may begin in children as young as five.

People abuse and exclude obese people because they assume obesity connotes laziness and a lack of discipline or concern for personal appearance. And while this belief may not be warranted, often there are connections between obesity and lifestyle. Activity patterns, for example, play an important part in the development and avoidance of obesity. Obese children typically spend fewer hours in active physical play, take part in fewer extracurricular activities, and watch more television than other children. Not only do sedentary activities displace physical activity, but they also promote overeating. Children who spend a lot of time watching television tend to gorge on calorie-rich food and often ignore cues from their bodies that they have eaten enough.

Most scientists believe the main factors affecting obesity are environmental, not genetic. In over-nourished countries like ours, prosperity and plenty are at the root of the obesity problem. In these societies, even poor families, who can hardly afford "lean cuisine," develop weight problems because cheap and packaged foods are high in carbohydrates, which are poorly metabolized. Reportedly, children from low-income, ethnic minority families have experienced the greatest increase in child obesity over the past 20 years (prevention.stanford.edu/word-pdf/youth.pdf).

Fitness and leanness are far more common in the prosperous upper-middle class. Sudden changes in lifestyle and diet in a population also can lead to obesity and related problems, such as diabetes and heart disease. This has occurred in Canada's North over the past two or three generations as Aboriginal populations were moved into permanent settlements to allow for more centralized and accessible social services, such as health care and education. But the people became much less active, and their diet changed dramatically, from largely country food (wild game, fish, berries, etc.) to store-bought foods, packaged junk food, and soft drinks. A similar problem with obesity and attendant health problems has occurred among native Hawaiians and other Pacific Islanders with the introduction to their diets, especially since World War II, of canned meats and other processed foods, such as white flour and white sugar. Obesity has followed in both cases.

> **Time to Reflect:** Recent research has found a strong connection between obesity and lack of sleep. How do you account for this connection (i.e., state your theory about the linkage) and how might it be related to social class, if at all?

As the 2010 data in Figure 2.4 show, there are wide regional variations in rates of obesity among major cities of Canada. Likely, this reflects provincial variations in average income and education, eating practices, and exercise (or lack of it).

The problem of obesity often starts at birth, with both genetic and environmental influences. Early childhood nutrition influences the number of adipose (fat-holding) cells, for example. By early childhood, eating and activity patterns are well established. And among children, eating attitudes, obesity, physical activity, and body image are all interrelated. Although genetic makeup is important, dietary and physical factors play a key role.

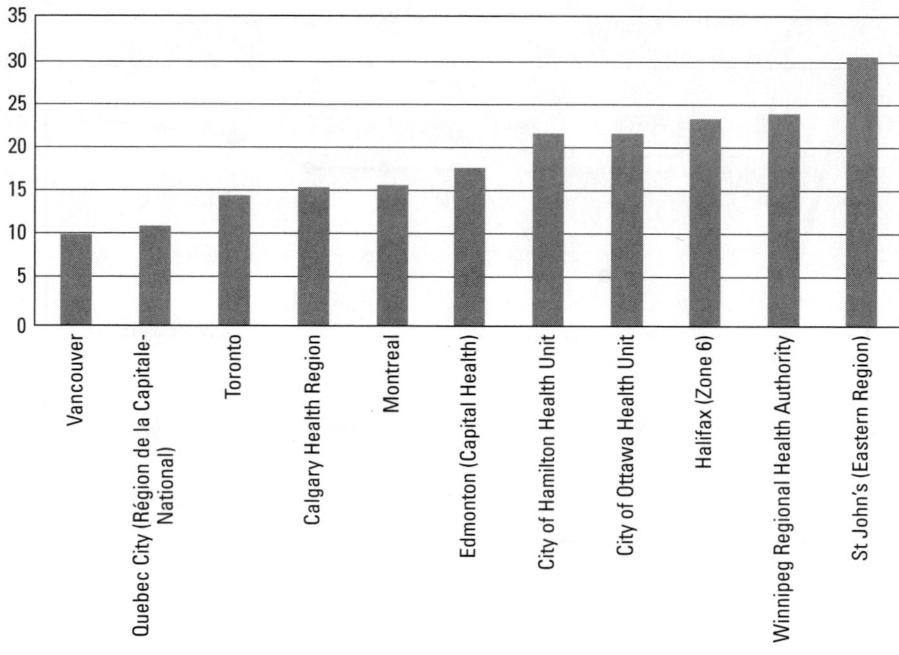

FIGURE 2.4 Obesity Rates (age 18 and over) in Major CMAs, 2010

Source: Canadian Institute for Health Information, "Canada's Vital Signs 2011: Research Findings," Figure 2, at: <www.vitalsignscanada.ca/2011_2health-e.html>.

Certain types of behaviour are likely to increase the risk of obesity from childhood on. They include poor nutritional practices—for example, a tendency to eat junk foods or binge eat and an absence of exercise, practices usually acquired in the family home. They also include poor adaptations to mental stress. Females, young and old, are more likely than males to overeat in response to negative emotions such as anger, anxiety, and depression. Such binge eating is typically triggered by troublesome or stressful events occurring on the binge days.

As the data in Figure 2.5 show, rates of obesity vary widely from one nation to another. Likely, they reflect important differences in lifestyle and eating behaviour. They also appear to reflect differences in physical activity: the least obese populations are those where most people walk, cycle, or use public transportation in preference to using their automobiles, as North Americans do.

Does obesity make a difference to people's attractiveness—especially to women's attractiveness? A study of young college men (Swami et al., 2008) finds that BMI is a key predictor of women's perceived sexual attractiveness, with men's assessment of a woman's sexual attractiveness peaking at a BMI level of about 19. At the extremes, it drops sharply for especially thin women (with BMI values less than 17) and drops gradually for stout women (with BMI values over 25). Though tolerance for obesity may be growing, with the growing prevalence of obesity many still consider it to be a health problem and a sexual turnoff.

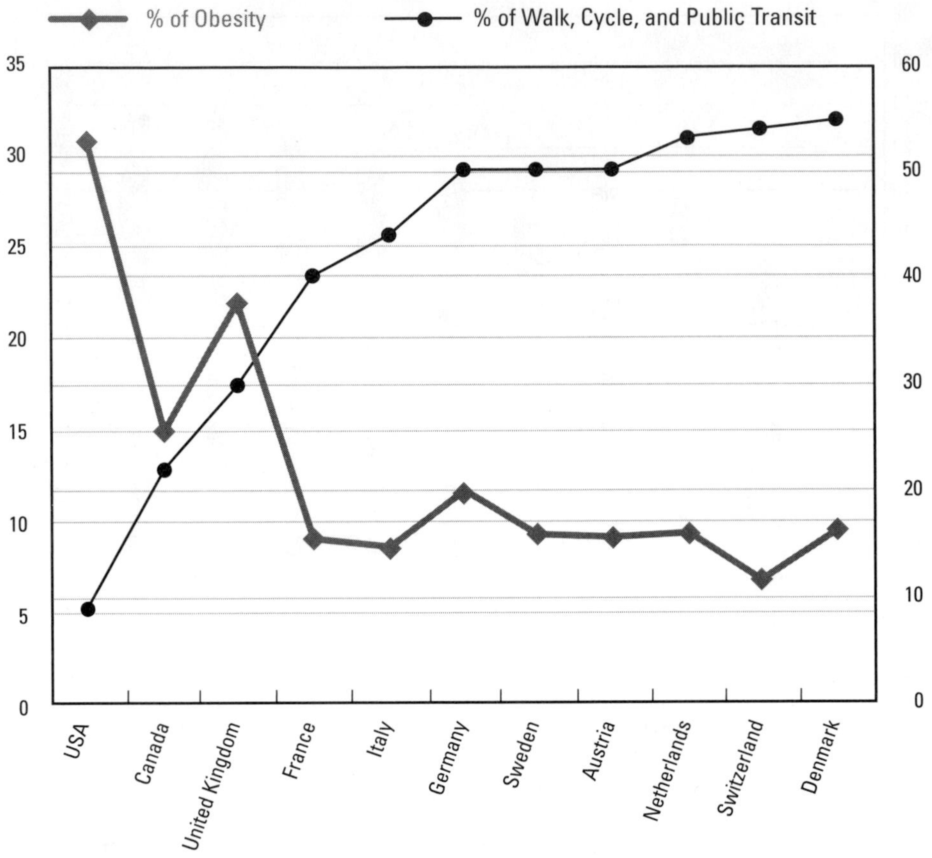

FIGURE 2.5 Obesity Rates and Transportation Patterns in Selected Countries

Source: "Supplementary Memorandum from Professor John Whitelegg, Liverpool John Moores University (RS 73)," House of Commons (UK), 2008, at: <www.publications.parliament.uk/pa/cm200708/cmselect/cmtran/460/460we80.htm>.

Theories about Appearance Issues

Psychological theories about appearance issues tend to argue that deviants are reacting against figures of authority, or against conformity itself, or that deviance shows self-hate and self-negation. In contrast, sociologists note that deviant appearance is largely a social phenomenon and occurs in groups, as part of a communal lifestyle. Therefore, we need sociological theories to explain the role of the social groups that encourage and support a deviant appearance. With this goal in mind, sociologists have developed various perspectives on how deviant appearances emerge.

Functionalist Theories

The main functionalist approaches to understanding a deviant appearance are structural. Recall Merton's (1957 [1938]) theory of adaptations to anomie, in which certain deviant types of conduct arise out of the gap between culturally prescribed ideals and access to the socially accepted methods for reaching them. This approach may apply to appearance norms as well.

Bodily beauty as a cultural goal presents a strong risk of anomie (in Merton's terms) because beauty is largely an innate physical feature. Likewise, people appear to have an innate preference for symmetrical (facial) features. Evolutionary psychologists think this is because such symmetry denotes health and good genes, hence helps to identify a suitable mate for the procreation and protection of offspring (Rhodes, 2006).

People born without symmetrical, regular features can do little to change this, so they are limited in the degree to which they can approximate the ideal—or even average—appearance. Even with exercise and plastic surgery, we cannot all achieve the ideal appearance. So people who are not thin, beautiful, or wealthy enough to afford a makeover are caught in a dilemma. They may try to reject the beauty goals of our culture, but this is hard to do in a society so immersed in media images of conventional beauty. Like the *rebels* in Merton's model of anomie, they can join a group that substitutes different, attainable norms of dress and appearance for the conventional ones.

However, the rebellious adaptation to anomie takes a lot of work. For example, preserving a rebellious community means recruiting new members. Like any community, it must grow or die. Learning and practising a deviant appearance code, the way of entry into the subculture, also takes a lot of work. Piercings, tattoos, unnatural colours of hair (e.g., blue, green), and a distinct manner of dress, though they take work, may all help to recruit members and maintain group cohesion.

First, they give people membership in the deviant subculture. Second, they signal what is acceptable and what is not: conventional appearance norms are most definitely not acceptable. Without such visible boundaries—group-specific appearance norms—it is harder to enforce behaviour in such a community. Thus, deviant items of appearance help strengthen social cohesion by drawing a clearer line between the people who honour the appearance norms and people who do not.

Symbolic Interactionist Theories

Symbolic interactionist theories, as we have seen, focus on the ways people interpret behaviour (whether deviant or not) and the ways these interpretations help to construct the social world. Most important, symbolic interactionist theories, by focusing on socialization, remind us that deviants are made, not born.

The values we learn—from family, friends, co-workers, and others—either oppose or support different kinds of deviant behaviour. Differential association theory suggests that eating disorders, for example, are behaviours often learned directly from more powerful family members. Girls with eating disorders are disproportionately likely to have mothers with eating disorders. Many adolescents also grow up with a distorted view of food and its social value. For example, they may grow up associating food, food preparation, and eating with their mother's role in the family. In some families, to eat a lot is to honour your mother—to give her your love and approval.

Differential association theory can also be used to explain punk culture. Tattooing, piercing, and the other deviant behaviours associated with punk culture are learned from members of the punk subculture. People identify with the culture itself and with other members by "marking" themselves so other people can also identify their membership. The specific meaning of a tattoo, or appearance trait, is less important than the fact that it is shared with other members of the group.

Appearance and Stigmatization

Nowhere is the role of appearance more important—as an expression of conformity or deviance—than it is in the dramaturgical approach to social life developed by sociologist Erving Goffman. In his classic work, *The Presentation of Self in Everyday Life* (1959), Goffman uses the theatrical metaphors of stage, actors, and audiences to examine the complexities of social interaction. Appearance issues are especially well suited to this approach because physical attractiveness—like theatre—relies so much on what we can and can't see.

Here, Goffman notes that—like actors—we bring social expectations to any situation, and these serve as scripts we feel obliged to follow. We are motivated to give believable performances, but our performances and their credibility are put at risk by **discrediting or discreditable features**. Of these, a flawed or deviant appearance is the most immediately visible, and therefore dangerous, to our successful performance.

For example, a prominent black eye or facial scar invites staring, curiosity, and potentially unpleasant questions. These responses undermine the actors' performances and impede social interaction. A person who has been physically deformed may even be excluded or targeted because of his deformities. He may be reduced in our minds from a whole and usual person to a tainted and discounted one—in part because his appearance interrupts the smooth, easy, and conventional flow of interaction.

Any feature that has such a discrediting effect may be called a *failing*, a *flaw*, or a *handicap*. Goffman calls it a **stigma**—a brand or mark that brings disgrace. Such a mark reveals a gap between virtual and actual social identity—between the person I am pretending to be and the person I actually am (Box 2.2). In its most general meaning, a stigma is any characteristic, behaviour, or experience that may cause the "branded" person to be rejected by others. The stigma spoils that person's social identity and interferes with his or her social life.

Goffman specifically mentions two types of stigmatized people: the discredited and the discreditable. The discredited are those who visibly vary from ideal humans. They are appearance deviants, as we are calling them in this chapter: the very fat or very thin, the very tall or very short, the scarred or disabled, and so on. They have to manage their social interactions in spite of discredited, or visibly deviant, features.

The discreditable, by contrast, vary from ideal humans in covert ways. They have secret deformities and "scars" such as a history of sexual abuse, imprisonment, or expulsion from university. If their secrets were known, they would be discredited—rejected—by other people. The discreditable have an interest in managing their social interactions to keep their stigmatizing qualities hidden.

Discredited people may try to compensate for their status-losing flaw by developing superior features in another area. Discreditable people try to hide their shame, pass for "normal," and worry about their secret getting out.

In the end, Goffman is talking about everyone. Everyone reading this book varies from the ideal (or "average") human—both visibly and secretly—so everyone is both discredited and discreditable to some extent. The appearance of "normalcy" is always staged—always a social accomplishment achieved only by people committed to preserving the illusion of normality.

What we learn from studying appearance norms is that social norms can have unintended consequences. Norms that are meant to uphold the social order and include people in the community also punish and exclude people who deviate.

Classic Works

BOX 2.2

Erving Goffman's *Stigma*

In *Stigma: Notes on the Management of Spoiled Identity* (1963), American sociologist Erving Goffman examined the many people not commonly perceived as "normal"—people who are stigmatized for their appearance or other potentially discrediting features—and the ways the label "normal" affects their social interactions and sense of self. The reasons for stigma can include anything that distinguishes a person from the norm, from physical or mental defects to ethnicity and religion. When Goffman was writing 50 years ago, white, heterosexual, Protestant males were considered the norm in most of Canada and the United States. This definition excluded the vast majority from being categorized as "normal," and it does so even more today.

Still, in any social interaction, people want to present themselves *and* others involved as "normal." *Stigma* explores how stigmatized people manage their interactions to appear "normal," or at least normal enough. To appear normal, people try to hide their discreditable features with strategies of "passing" and "covering." "Passing" is the effort to disguise discreditable facts about one's identity by appearing (and behaving) as normally as possible. Ex-mental patients, for example, can usually disguise their history or labelled identity because their stigma isn't readily visible. However, some potentially discrediting features, such as facial scars or racial background, are harder to disguise, so "passing" is not always an option, although in America many lighter-skinned people of mixed African-American and European heritage passed as white. An alternative, "covering," is used by people who are already discredited, often because their stigma is highly visible. Their goal is to manage tension in interaction, which they do by deflecting attention away from the stigmatized feature so the interaction can proceed as if they were "normal."

An example of "covering" is the practice by some members of ethnic minorities who adopt names used by the majority—for example, Tenenbaum becomes Thompson, Janowsky becomes Jefferson. Another way of avoiding the pains of stigma is to associate with other people who are similarly stigmatized.

In short, the pressures on people to seem normal force stigmatized people to act in accordance with fixed, unsatisfiable norms. But since most people, in reality, deviate from the norm in some way or other, the concerns and techniques discussed in Goffman's book apply to all of us. The people Goffman describes merely bear more visible marks of disrepute than the rest of us.

As noted, symbolic interactionists are particularly interested in the ways we learn deviant values and behaviours. First, they are interested in the means of transmission—in how people learn to conform and deviate. For example, *how* do people learn to identify and copy a punk style of dress? Second, symbolic interactionists are interested in secondary deviation: What happens to people *after* they have deviated, and how do reactions to their deviance strengthen their deviant identity?

So, for example, where eating disorders are concerned, symbolic interactionists would be interested in knowing how people learn to binge and purge. What skills and drugs are used and how do people share this information? They would be interested in knowing whether anorexic people feel a kinship with other anorexic people and whether they express and enact this kinship through association and conversation. Likewise, do obese people feel a kinship with other obese people, or merely a sense that they are violating the weight norms of society? To take another example: Do people with freckles, gaps between their front teeth, or premature baldness share a sense of community with one another, and how do they communicate this?

Finally, symbolic interactionists would be interested in knowing whether (and how) anorexic, obese, punk, or tattooed and pierced people are stigmatized for their deviant appearance. They might study the form this stigmatization takes, be it ridicule, exclusion, social distance, or job discrimination, for example. They would also be interested in knowing how people who suffer these reactions "make sense" of their experience and what effect it has, if any, on their social life, social behaviour, and self-esteem. Does the stigmatized appearance feature become a "master status" in the person's life—a central feature of their identity?

Time to Reflect: If almost everyone deviates from the media-created ideal in appearance, why do people still ridicule or stigmatize people who deviate, as though appearance deviation is important or meaningful?

Critical Theories

Critical theories propose that deviance is the result of a clash between competing value systems or lifestyles. Unequal power determines who has the right to declare what is normal and abnormal, proper and deviant. People with less power use deviant acts to challenge and rebel against the norms instituted by those in power.

Who benefits from promoting strong appearance norms? In our society, the answer is simple: people who make their living by capitalizing on other people's sense of inadequacy. This would include the fashion industry, the dieting industry, the medical profession, the exercise and sporting goods industry, the cosmetic industry, and—above all—the advertising industry. Body image has become an enormous source of concern in North America. Both men and women spend a lot of money on plastic surgery to achieve the appearance they are taught to desire by mass media advertisers.

Our consumerist society is geared to making people hate themselves and feel discontented, making it easier for a plastic surgeon, fitness instructor, dietician, or other "expert" to sell a formula for happiness. As we see in Figure 2.6, hundreds of thousands of North Americans—especially in the US—use cosmetic surgery to alter their appearance.

Feminist Approaches

Feminists who study appearance tend to focus on issues having to do with female beauty. In their view, although women today enjoy more independence than they did in the past, they still rely largely on their physical beauty to attract and manage men.

Appearance, for women, is a weapon in the war between the sexes; to dominate men, or at least to escape domination by men, they need to optimize their physical appearance. The appearance industries encourage women to strive for features that are almost impossible to achieve—after all, even *Playboy* photos of alluring, naked women are known to have been airbrushed to remove imagined "imperfections." By failing to meet these impossible standards, women may feel they have failed in their role as women—whether as companions, lovers, or wives. This, in turn, has the effect of strengthening the power of men over women.

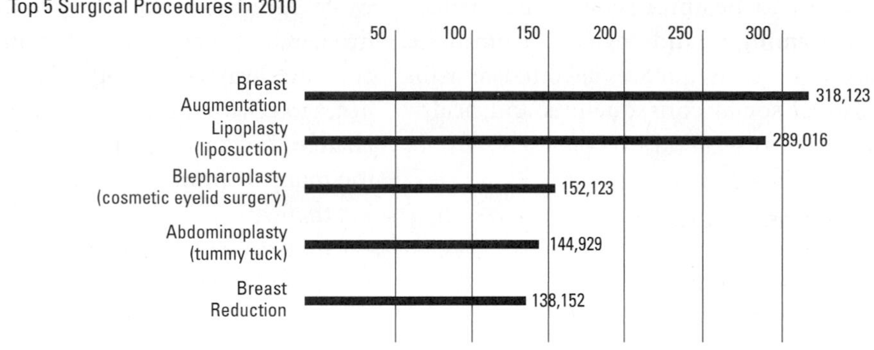

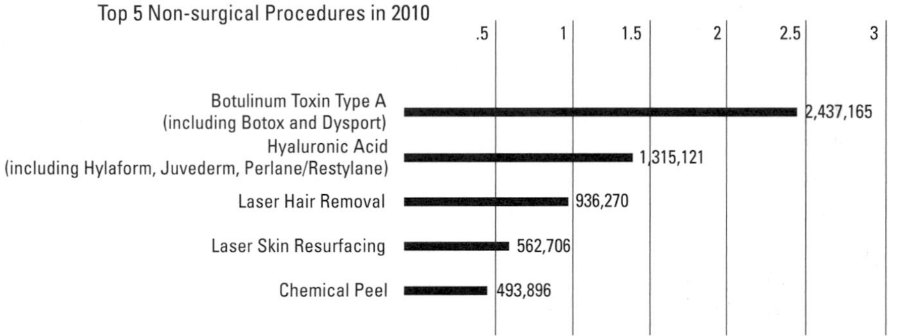

FIGURE 2.6 Top Five Surgical and Non-Surgical Procedures, 2010

Source: American Society for Aesthetic Plastic Surgery, at: <www.surgery.org/sites/default/files/2010-top5.pdf>.

Women are taught to be attuned to the **male gaze**, a concept that originates in film analysis because most directors controlling the camera's "eye" are male. As Schroeder notes, "Film has been called an instrument of the male gaze, producing representations of women, the good life, and sexual fantasy from a male point of view" (1998: 208). The notion may have gained wide currency because, like Michel Foucault's view of surveillance as power, it relates visibility to domination. The more a woman is subjected to the male gaze, the more she feels dominated by that gaze.

The male gaze invites women to enter a competition for physical perfection—a competition less often required of men. It invites women to be continually self-conscious about their bodies in comparison with other women and continuously conscious about how they are being judged. They are led to equate "looking good" with "feeling appreciated, loved, and admired."

In short: for women, there is still no simple way of dealing with our society's appearance norms.

Consequences of Appearance Issues

Conformity to and deviation from appearance norms are important issues because our society takes appearance very seriously. There are bound to be important consequences for conforming to and deviating from these norms. These consequences fall into two main categories: social consequences and health consequences.

Social Consequences

"Appearance Warfare"

By far the most important and enduring social consequence of "appearance warfare" is what social theorist Thorstein Veblen called *conspicuous waste.* This has financial implications for individuals and entire societies and, as we are increasingly aware, ecological implications for the world as a whole.

In his analysis of conspicuous consumption by the **leisure class**, Veblen (1979 [1899]), writing towards the end of a period noted for its decadence, suggests that both conspicuous leisure and consumption are notable as types of waste. One is a waste of time and effort, while the other is a waste of goods. Veblen hastens to explain that *waste*, in this sense, is a technical and not a moral term: "It is here called 'waste' because this expenditure does not serve human life or human well-being on the whole, not because it is waste or misdirection of effort or expenditure as viewed from the standpoint of the individual consumer who chooses it."

Likewise, he notes that a product or service that is conspicuously wasteful may also have usefulness, to some degree: "Even in articles which appear at first glance to serve for pure ostentation only, it is always possible to detect the presence of some, at least ostensible, useful purpose."

That said, the ongoing competitions for attractiveness, acceptance, and status that people conduct using fashion, cosmetic surgery, dieting, and various consumer products and services represent precisely what Veblen meant by conspicuous consumption and conspicuous waste. Almost all gains in this battle are short-lived, in large part because the markers of success are always changing. As Simmel pointed out, those with the most status and acceptance change the markers, and the rules, whenever too many "common people" succeed in imitating them.

So, the battle for appearance conformity, and social success by this means, is by its nature bound to fail. The net result is constant frustration and disappointment among many; a high rate of expenditure on what some would consider frivolous, "wasteful" goods and services; and devastation of the planet's raw materials for even rarer, more expensive items of distinction.

Health Consequences

Eating Disorders

Appearance issues interest sociologists because they shed so much light on the boundaries between deviant and conforming behaviour and the measures people take to control and shame other people. However, appearance deviance and conformity can have a significant impact on people's health as well.

Consider eating disorders: the health impact of eating disorders extends far beyond the costs of the health-care services for anorexic and bulimic people. Eating disorders tax the mental, social, and economic well-being of people with the illness, their family members, friends, and employers, the community, and the whole society. The costs include health services that are provided to the patients, family therapy, and prevention and educational programs, as well as time lost from work and other socially useful activities.

Anorexia is deviant because it exceeds, rather than falls short of, our society's appearance norms. It shows the terrible costs of over-conformity to cultural norms. Taken to this extreme, the dieting and exercise associated with anorexia can be fatal. Even after getting psychiatric help for their anorexic eating habits, many women continue to struggle with low body weight and a variety of mental problems. They remain more vulnerable than other women to major depression, alcohol dependence, and anxiety disorders at the time of their illness and later in life.

Sufferers of eating disorders often develop severe self-consciousness and think that other people are constantly watching and waiting to confront them or interfere in their lives. They also often harbour feelings of shame and guilt that prevent them from seeking help in a timely fashion. Time-consuming rituals govern the everyday lives of many eating-disordered people—a result of feeling helpless.

Tattooing and Body Piercing

Tattoos and piercings are less dangerous than eating disorders, but they are not without health consequences. The processes of body modification may be dangerous if unhygienic. Many tattoos are applied with electronically powered vibrating instruments that inject tattoo ink into the skin. However, some are still applied using pencils, pens, straight pins, or needles to inject ink, carbon, mascara, or charcoal. Tattoos applied in this traditional, less technologically advanced manner, usually to avoid the high costs of professional tattooing, increase the risk of dangerous diseases.

Body piercing also involves needles and, if unhygienic, can infect the part of the body that is being pierced. Inadequate care of the area pierced or tattooed raises the risk of infection. The diseases acquired from unsanitary tattooing and body-piercing practices include hepatitis, tetanus, HIV, and skin infections (Health Canada, 2001). People who get, or plan to get, tattoos and body piercings are often aware of the associated health risks. There is a potential for new risks as many attempt tattoo removal. For example, burns from defective machinery or unskilled technicians may occur, as well as infection of the treatment areas. Scarring is possible if severe burns occur. Also, some people may develop too much or too little melanin/colour in the treatment area. Non-white skins are at particular risk of discoloration from these tattoo-removal procedures.

Social Policy Implications

In a capitalist, consumer-driven society like ours, we will not soon see legislative measures taken to limit the harmful social or environmental consequences of appearance conformity or deviance. There is simply too much power and too much vested interest in the fashion, advertising, dieting, and other industries that vie for our bodies and their adornment.

The most we can hope for is social legislation to help prevent, avoid, or solve the health problems that come with appearance conformity and appearance deviance. Take the problem of obesity and its connection to bad eating and activity patterns in the family home. Some families have more difficulty than others providing good food and remaining physically active. Parents in poor families, for example, typically work long hours that leave them little time to prepare home-cooked meals or promote physical activity, and they hardly have the time or resources to allow their children to participate in organized, out-of-school activities like hockey. We need to develop new and better approaches to support these vulnerable families.

Schools are an ideal means of getting information to the family and the community because they can reach all parents through their children (and most adults in the community). Most children under the age of 16 are obliged to attend school, making them a captive audience for health promotion messages. Parents are sometimes interested in hearing what children are learning at school. Most important, teachers and educational institutions enjoy a high degree of trust and respectability in our society. However, most schools already suffer from stretched social and educational responsibilities and strained resources.

Research can play an important part, if the results are made widely available. For example, we need better information about the incidence of each eating disorder by sex, socio-economic status, education, and ethnicity. Too often, there is a major disconnect between researchers, health institutions, health professionals, the mass media, and the general public. We need more and better-focused research about appearance-related health problems and better ways to get this information into the hands (and minds) of people who need it. This, in turn, will require money for research and knowledge translation.

Leaving aside health issues, we still have to resolve some of the multicultural issues associated with appearance and "reasonable accommodation." Increasingly, in multicultural societies like Canada's, we encounter appearance issues—non-normative modes of dress or adornment—that violate our expectations. This has already become a problem in Quebec and in certain parts of Europe where multiculturalism is unfamiliar. Nowhere is the debate over school dress more active today than in France, in relation to the demands that children avoid wearing items of clothing—hijabs, large crosses, or yarmulkes (skullcaps)—that declare their religious affiliation.

In the Islamic tradition, both men and women are expected to dress modestly. Women traditionally cover their hair with a hijab (Islamic scarf) and, in some traditions, are expected to wear a burka—a shapeless, full-body cover—when in public. These practices have created a controversy in France in recent years. The image of the Muslim woman's veil acts as a symbol of Islamic oppression and violence in Western media.

As a result, Muslim women living in the West often suffer discrimination, harassment, even assault. In France, wearing the Islamic headscarf in school has resulted in dress code and discipline problems, with its underlying symbolism causing widespread arguments about religious freedom in a secular state, pluralism, and integration. Similar, though less intensely debated, issues have arisen in Canada in regard to the voting rights and courtroom testimony of women who commonly wear the burka. In Quebec, where Canadian multiculturalism has been recast as "interculturalism," the 2008 report of the government-appointed Bouchard-Taylor commission on reasonable accommodation, headed by two leading academics, received a cool reception after it called for greater understanding and accommodation between the majority and ethno-religious minorities.

Economic Consequences

The pursuit of beauty has enormous economic consequences, as both men and women feel constant societal pressure to invest in their appearance. In fact, enterprising entrepreneurs have built a multi-billion dollar "beauty industry" entirely on the advertising-driven pursuit of a particular form of bodily attractiveness. Consumers pursue beauty in many different ways, though the most pervasive of these are body alteration, dieting, and fashion.

Plastic surgery is the most costly and physically extreme form of pursuing an ideal of beauty. Consumers spend many thousands of dollars to permanently—and often drastically—change their bodies. While society might widely accept and practise some of these expensive procedures (such as orthodonture) and raise little fuss over less expensive, semi-invasive permanent procedures (laser eye surgery or botox injections, for instance), a host of other widely practised, expensive surgeries are available. Liposuction, stomach stapling, and breast augmentation are some of the more popular forms of extreme body alteration.

These more invasive surgeries often put major financial burdens on people who wish to be beautiful but may not have the disposable income to take time off work and pay for this non-insured surgery. Furthermore, doctors occasionally botch these surgeries, and the regulatory and licensing framework for these surgeries has been lax in some jurisdictions. The complications resulting from poorly delivered liposuctions, for instance, often result in substantial burdens on public health-care systems (Larcher et al., 2011), and in some instances have led to patients dying. Ultimately, a poorly delivered liposuction or chin lift may lead to both lost work time for the patient and avoidable costs for the public health system.

The culture of dieting continues to provide enormous money-making opportunities through dieting plans, aides, and medications. Popular diets, like the Atkins or South Beach programs, make their originators millions of dollars, promoting a culture of eating that revolves around the precepts of these diets. In the words of the social critic Mabel Gracia-Arnaiz (2010), the "relationship between diet, beauty and health has been appropriated and re-elaborated as a marketing strategy." People are not just "on" diets; they "live" diets. For this reason, the dieting industry remains immensely profitable.

The fashion industry is another important branch of the beauty industry. It is one of the least invasive and most expensive ways of pursuing beauty. The fashion industry successfully combines people's fundamental need for clothing with their desire to be attractive. By pricing commonplace items (dresses, shoes, or bags) as "luxury goods," fashion tastemakers can both craft popular understandings of what "beauty" is and provide the clothing that fits those definitions at exorbitant costs.

Conclusion

Most of us get at least some of our ideas about appearance from the mass media. Appearance norms portrayed by the mass media are nowhere near reality, however. Some people develop dangerous and sometimes life-threatening eating disorders to meet or even exceed the social norms. They engage in deviant behaviours such as starving themselves or purging the food they have eaten in hopes of turning themselves into a false ideal. Others dress up in dangerous-looking outfits, their bodies covered with studs and tattoos, perhaps to show that, with nothing to lose, they are strong survivors.

Often intentionally, behavioural innovations may seem threatening at first (as with punk culture). They incite members of the upstanding middle-aged middle class to try to control and stigmatize these new behaviours. In fact, it might be argued that some subcultural groups actively invite stigma and injustice. Some innovations (like eating disorders) are truly harmful and call attention to the social pathologies of our age. Others seem less harmful as time passes (as with tattooing and piercing), though we have yet to see how reversible (or removable) these adornments will prove to be in future.

As we have noted in this chapter, understanding eating disorders, punk culture, and deviant appearance requires understanding how and why these behaviours emerge. Some emerge to provoke a negative public reaction, while others arise from deep-seated psychological needs and may have dangerous health and social effects. All violate social norms and social expectations. Clearly, there are many ways to deviate in appearance. Some deviations are voluntary and intentional, and some are not. Though some kinds of appearance deviation are largely social in their origins, others are largely genetic or chemical. Finally, some kinds of appearance deviation violate deeply held ideals, while some merely violate common, current practices.

What many of these appearance deviations show is that people can become deviants—can be labelled and stigmatized and excluded as deviants—even if they don't want to do so. This is a central sociological observation and we will have occasion to revisit it throughout this book.

We are now ready to discuss mental illness in Chapter 3. Like appearance deviance, mental illness is unintentional, has multiple forms, causes, and consequences, and there are different approaches to understanding the phenomenon. These approaches tell us as much about currents of social thought as they do about deviance itself.

Questions for Critical Thought

1. In his classic work on anomie, Merton discusses various reactions to norms. Contrast Goth and haute couture purchasers' reactions to the norms.
2. Personal identities are linked to social identities. Illustrate this using any of the theorists discussed in this chapter.
3. Discuss Veblen's approach to fashion and how it has been applied to colonial discourse. How is this significant to the contemporary study of deviance?
4. Explain how a symbolic interactionist might view the mainstream popularity of tattoos.
5. How can appearance-deviant communities provide positive spaces for their members?
6. Discuss the ways sociologists might see anorexia as an attempt to satisfy appearance norms. How about obesity?

Recommended Readings

Black, Paula. 2004. *The Beauty Industry: Gender, Culture, Pleasure.* New York and London: Routledge.

Beauty salons are becoming the refuge of working mothers and female professionals, where they are pampered with facials and manicures. Interviews reported in this book—with beauty workers and their clients—help us rethink issues around the body, the maintenance of gender identity, and changing definitions of well-being.

Collins, Jane L. 2003. *Threads: Gender, Labor, and Power in the Global Apparel Industry.* Chicago: University of Chicago Press.

The author traces the links between First World and Third World producers and consumers, showing how the economics of the clothing industry allow firms to relocate their work anywhere in the world, making it harder for garment workers in North America to demand fair pay and good working conditions.

Foster, Helen Bradley, and Donald Clay Johnson. 2004. *Wedding Dress across Cultures.* Oxford: Berg.

This book reviews the evolution and ritual functions of wedding attire in the context of different cultures. Through the lens of wedding wear, it provides insights into various societies and their cultures. The discussion of ritual attire indicates the centrality of dress in shaping individual identity and reflecting cultural ideals.

Wolf, Naomi. 2002. *The Beauty Myth: How Images of Beauty Are Used against Women.* New York: Perennial.

In this classic feminist work, Naomi Wolf discusses how an ideal version of the modern woman has been constructed through marketing and extensive advertising. She looks at how women deal with an unhealthy obsession towards becoming the "ideal."

Recommended Websites

Body Piercing

www.pubmedcentral.nih.gov/articlerender.fcgi?artid=1127091

This is a link to a 1999 article from the *British Medical Journal* written by Henry Ferguson, the editor of *Body Art.* The article explores the idea of body art (piercings, tattoos, etc.) as being both a sign of personal expression and a sign of societal cohesion.

National Eating Disorder Information Centre

www.nedic.ca

The National Eating Disorder Information Centre provides important resources for those seeking any information about eating disorders or weight issues. The website contains numerous links to various other organizations and includes articles related to eating disorders.

Report of the APA Task Force on the Sexualization of Girls

www.apa.org/pi/women/programs/girls/report-full.pdf

Commissioned by the American Psychological Association, this report investigates the ways in which girls—often adolescent or younger—are culturally "sexualized" and provides insights into media and cultural understandings of female beauty, as well as the power of fetishes.

Beauty Check

www.uniregenburg.de/Fakultaeten/phil_Fak_II/Psychologie/Psy_II/beautycheck/english/index.htm

Run by Dr Martin Gruendl out of the University of Regensburg (Germany) Institute for Psychology, this website provides valuable scientific data on public understandings of facial attractiveness and attempts to explain—with some success—why people are considered "beautiful" and what role beauty plays in attaining social power.

Recommended Movies

***Angus*, Dir. Patrick Read Johnson (1995)**

Ostensibly a film about the struggle for status in high school, this film is fundamentally about the normality of "abnormal" appearance. Angus is a star lineman on the football team and a standout science student, as well as being ostracized by more popular kids for being obese. The movie shows Angus's struggles to appreciate himself, in spite of his appearance.

***Mask*, Dir. Peter Bogdanovich (1985)**

Bogdanovich, a filmmaker widely known for exploring themes of alienation and despair, helmed this outstanding *bildungsroman.* The film follows the life of Rocky Dennis, an intelligent and kind-hearted young man who suffers from lionitis, a disease that causes extreme facial disfigurement and, eventually, death. In spite of his unenviable position, Rocky retains a provisional optimism.

***Thin*, Dir. Lauren Greenfield (2006)**

This is an engrossing, feminist study of the way cultural expectations can damage and destroy women. Greenfield follows four women, aged 15 to 30, as they attend a Florida residential treatment centre for eating disorders. The director ably illustrates the harrowing effects of anorexia nervosa and the monumental challenges to overcoming this illness.

***Freaks*, Dir. Tod Browning (1932)**

Censored and banned for decades following its initial release, this off-beat morality tale is now considered a minor classic of American cinema. Browning explores the class and status divisions within a travelling circus, showing how the sideshow "freaks" (played by real-life circus and carnival performers) are bullied by "normal" performers, regardless of their obvious charms and intellect.

3 Mental Illness

Learning Objectives

- To understand the development of ideas about mental illness
- To identify the varieties of mental illness
- To understand the theories and perspectives that seek to explain mental illness
- To identify the social and health consequences of mental illness
- To be familiar with the policies aimed at helping and controlling mental illness
- To understand the reasons for the deinstitutionalization of mentally ill people

Introduction

In the last chapter, we discussed different kinds of appearance deviance. As we saw, some of this deviance—for example, obesity—is unintentional. In this chapter, we will discuss another kind of unintentional deviance—mental illness. People who suffer from mental illness are breaking rules and violating people's expectations without wishing to do so.

Though widespread, mental illness is also deviant in the sense that it is feared, stigmatized, and treated as though it is statistically unusual. Some behaviours associated with mental illness are "deviant" in the sense of being unexpected and (therefore) disruptive. Often, mentally ill people communicate differently from other people, and some severely mentally ill people cannot communicate verbally at all. Some mental illness also results from deviant behaviour—for example, from family violence or from substance abuse. So, there are many connections between deviance and mental illness, but some are indirect.

Horwitz (2007: 321) points out that:

> for millennia, students of mental health have debated the question of "what is a mental disorder?" Yet, it is impossible to answer this question without referring to some conception of what normal mental functioning involves. One [prominent view of normality], popular among sociologists, is that social values determine normality so that it is impossible to derive any universal standards of normal mental functioning. A second view equates what is normal with what is frequent so that normality is whatever falls inside the tails of a statistical distribution.

Because of these ambiguities, many prominent researchers today hold the view that "distress and disorder" are the best ways to determine if a person is mentally ill.

Diagnostically, what we call **mental illness** is characterized by changes in thinking, mood, or behaviour (or some combination of these) associated with significant distress and hindered functioning (i.e., disorder). Symptoms of mental illness vary, depending on the type of illness, the person, his or her family, and the socio-economic environment, and they fall on a spectrum from lesser to much more severe symptoms on an array of measures. Mental illnesses usually result from an interaction between social stresses and other predisposing factors that are psychological, chemical, physiological, or genetic in nature. So we cannot understand mental illness without a knowledge of the social context (including social responses); nor can we understand it without a knowledge of non-social factors (biochemical and physiological factors, for example) that we will discuss only briefly in this book.

Stated more formally, mental illness is a condition of distress and disorder that would permit the diagnosis of mental illness by mental health professionals. Thus, such a diagnosis also would permit the individual to take on the "sick role," with its various rights and responsibilities. The stigmatization of mental illness in our society, however, means that many mentally ill people are unable to access this role, even if they wanted to, and others never receive an appropriate diagnosis. Deviance from the sick role, when applied and accessed, could be viewed as a failure to meet the social responsibilities of mental illness—for example, to comply with treatment plans, take prescribed medications, and generally avoid situations that hinder recovery.

However, often the very conditions that lead to—or exacerbate—distress and disorder in individuals are hard to avoid and may systematically undermine people's efforts to abide by the "social rules" of mental illness. As well, some of the palliative and curative prescriptions, such as neuroleptic drugs and antidepressants, have been shown to exacerbate rather than ameliorate mental illness (see, e.g., Whitaker, 2010b). Historically, the methods used to treat mental illness have often been harmful, some cruelly so (Whitaker, 2010a).

The History of Mental Illness and Public Reactions

For most of human history, people lacked much understanding of mental illness and its causes. Early explanations of mental illness included notions of "evil spirits" and "demons." However, that doesn't mean all societies were hostile to mentally ill people. Some pre-industrial societies were gently tolerant of them, viewing the mentally ill as simpletons or holy fools. Others, however, believed that the strange, deviant behaviours associated with mental illness could only be due to the acts of hostile witches or devils, a result of spells, or as a punishment for wrongdoing. As a result, some people attempted to heal the mentally ill by "casting out demons" and other communities tortured people suffering from mental illnesses (e.g., from delusions) in efforts to drive out the demons.

Of course, torture usually failed to return people to sanity, although it sometimes drastically controlled their behaviour—as in the case of frontal lobotomies, which were performed in the mid-twentieth century on many thousands of patients who were unable or unwilling to give their consent to such a drastic procedure. In fact, there is a long human history of efforts—some more successful than others—to look for more effective treatments.

One long-lived treatment was hospitalization in mental hospitals—for example, in places like Bedlam. Founded in London in 1247 by Simon Fitz Mary, Bedlam—originally called the Hospital of St Mary of Bethlehem and eventually converted into a lunatic asylum—became infamous for its treatment of the mentally ill. There, mentally ill people were chained to walls so the rest of the world could forget they existed, except for those who wanted to visit to watch the suffering of the inmates as if they were animals in a zoo. In time, the name "Bedlam" came to be synonymous with the uproarious, confused behaviour of the inmates. To say that a place was "bedlam" was to say that it displayed the maximum chaos and madness. Bedlam was the earliest—but far from the last—attempt that people made to isolate and "warehouse" mentally ill people, supposedly for their own safety and that of others.

As time passed, hospitals and asylums began to attempt curing the mentally ill. They also began to treat mentally ill patients in almost the same way as other patients, providing cleaner surroundings, better care and nutrition, fresh air, and light. Nineteenth-century "moral treatment" advocates such as Dorothea Dix in the United States and Philippe Pinel in France fought successfully for more humane treatment of the mentally ill in mental institutions. Dix played a significant role in the opening of 30 mental hospitals and adamantly opposed what she felt were cruel and careless practices towards the mentally ill. These included caging, being incarcerated without clothing, and painful physical restraint.

This surge of compassion towards mentally ill people peaked with the development of professional nursing, a response to the surge in the number of war casualties during the Crimean War. In England, Florence Nightingale played an especially important role in the rise of nursing. However, it was later, during World War I, that medical caregivers gained their first systematical understanding of wartime mental illness. Specifically, they noted that emotional problems deriving from what was then called "shell shock" disabled many soldiers returning from the front. Many previously normal people fell into mental illness because of damage to their ears from the noise of weapons and their shocking experiences, not because of cowardice (as some alleged). We continue to see this problem today among soldiers returning from warfare (in Iraq and Afghanistan, for example) and call the illness **post-traumatic stress disorder (PTSD)**.

Caregivers reasoned that if a major trauma like combat could cause such widespread symptoms, then minor traumas, occurring more often, might produce similar effects. This was a crucial insight about the harmful effects of stress and trauma on human functioning. Generally, though we all live with some stress, we cannot live well with continued high levels of stress. Eventually, this insight would transform our understanding of mental illness.

However, popular opinion about mental illness was slow to change. Most people continued to view shell shock as a disgrace rather than an illness—a demonstration of cowardice and moral weakness—and some soldiers suffering from the trauma of warfare were executed for desertion or for refusing to return to the front lines. Many imagined that soldiers suffering from shell shock simply lacked the strength and conviction needed for combat. This, again, revealed a tendency to view mental illness as the result of a moral flaw: a spiritual and not a medical problem. Even today, many people view suicide as evidence of such moral weakness, leading families to hide the truth about suicides in their midst.

The modern approach to mental illness dates from World War II and the development of modern chemical treatments. In the 1940s and 1950s, researchers found medications that controlled the behaviour of the severely mentally ill. Doctors then reasoned that, if chemicals controlled mental illness, the causes might be chemical as well—not moral. However, as the International Coalition for Drug Awareness has pointed out, a growing body of data indicates that the same chemicals that sometimes control behaviour may also cause very severe losses of control, including suicide, homicide, and killing sprees (www.drugawareness.org/).

With the rise of modern social science in the latter half of the twentieth century, researchers also developed a better sense of the way social factors affect mental illness. We now know that some mental illnesses are more prevalent in some communities and some population groups than others.

For example, neighbourhood disadvantages—high rates of poverty, unemployment, and violence, for example—are associated with higher-than-average rates of depression and substance abuse. In low-income neighbourhoods, high rates of residential mobility—that is, high rates of people moving in and out of the neighbourhood—are also associated with higher-than-average rates of schizophrenia, major depression, and substance abuse. Of course, many people cannot afford to live in a safer and more stable neighbourhood with fewer stress factors, and the problems are not so much caused by the neighbourhood per se as by the lack of income and a sense of security.

Various theories have sought to link "social disorganization" and mental illness, and these have mainly focused on understanding the mechanisms that translate social inputs into psychological outcomes. Through research into the relationship between neighbourhood residence and schizophrenia, Robert Faris and H. Warren Dunham at the University of Chicago found that people who live in poverty are segregated from normal social contacts. For this reason, they argued, these people are more likely to develop a "seclusive personality," considered one of the main traits of schizophrenia. Faris and Dunham (1939) argued that prolonged social isolation would even cause people to experience hallucinations and delusions and to engage in inappropriate behaviours. They observed that the highest rates of schizophrenia were found in what they referred to as the slum neighbourhoods of the city.

They were right about one thing: there is indeed a statistical correlation between neighbourhood and mental illness. However, in this case, they had the causation wrong. Later research showed that it was not the social isolation that caused schizophrenia; rather, the schizophrenia led to social isolation. Schizophrenics tended to drift into poor, less organized parts of the city for social and economic reasons. Their inability to communicate normally resulted in exclusion and isolation, which, combined with unemployment, landed them in the slums.

Today, nearly 80 years after the research of these Chicago School theorists, we are less likely to reject and stereotype mentally ill people than in the past. Most people now understand that mental illness includes far more than psychotic (i.e., delusional) disorders. We are far more familiar with a wide variety of less dramatic, less visible forms of mental illness, especially milder mood disorders. However, reports of a few mentally ill people who are violent or frightening continue to surface, giving the impression that all mentally ill people are dangerous. As a result, many are still afraid to talk about their mental problems with family or friends, and are reluctant to seek professional treatment.

Suicide—while not necessarily a mental illness—is most often a consequence of mental illness or anomie, and often results from depression. Taking one's own life is particularly common among young people, especially young men, and among marginalized and oppressed groups such as Aboriginal people.

Though few mentally ill people are delusional or dangerous, many other mentally ill people suffer significant consequences. Consider the Canadian comedian Howie Mandel, who took a stand against the ignorance and stigma he feels are attached to mental disorders by coming clean about his own obsessive-compulsive disorder (OCD) and attention deficit hyperactivity disorder (ADHD) (see Box 3.1). The data in Table 3.1 show that, in any given year, over 12 per cent of Canadians suffer an anxiety disorder and over 4 per cent suffer from major depression.

Current Events

BOX 3.1

Howie Mandel: A Public Figure Speaks Out

Comedian and game-show host Howie Mandel has felt uncomfortable about his OCD and ADHD for most of his life, and until recently he hid these conditions from the public. But 10 years ago he revealed how intensely troubling they were for him while on Howard Stern's radio show. More recently, Mandel discussed his struggles with OCD and ADHD in his book, *Here's the Deal: Don't Touch Me* (2009).

Mandel admits that OCD disrupts his life on a regular basis, as is evident in his abnormal daily routine and his touring habits. His germophobia has driven him to take as many as 20 showers in one day. While touring and staying in bacteria-ridden hotels, Mandel refuses to let his feet touch the carpet, preferring instead to lay dozens of towels down. But because Mandel has been so open about his condition, people who interact with him have the opportunity to respect his dread of germs. For example, guests on his show courteously bump fists with him, instead of troubling Mandel with offers of bacteria-laden handshakes.

Through therapy and medication, Mandel claims he has been able to keep the OCD from interrupting his life as much as it has in the past. In addition, he credits his wife and three children with helping him handle his disorders. About the stigmatization that surrounds mental health problems such as OCD, Mandel says:

> I didn't even want to be public about it. The reason I'm doing that is because the issue of mental health is something of a stigma. Mental health care is not nearly equal to physical health care. People will go get regular medical and dental checkups, even if nothing hurts. But people don't regularly go to talk to a psychologist or psychiatrist to check on their mental well-being, to talk about their coping skills or depression issues. Is there anyone out there who at one point in their lives doesn't need to seek the help of a professional to talk about these issues?

Sources: Andy Smith, "Howie Mandel's Got a Good Deal Going," *Providence Journal*, 8 July 2006; Bill Brownstein, "Mandel's Disorder No Laughing Matter," *Montreal Gazette*, 14 May 2011, at: <www.montrealgazette.com/health/Mandel+disorder+laughing+matter/4783443/story.html>.

TABLE 3.1 Estimated One-Year Prevalence Rates of Mental Illness in Canada

Mental Illness	Estimates* of One-Year Prevalence
Mood disorders	4.1–4.6%
Major (unipolar) depression	0.2–0.6%
Bipolar disorder	0.8–3.1%
Dysthymia	
Schizophrenia	0.3%
Anxiety disorders	12.2%
Personality disorders	—
Eating disorders	
Anorexia	0.7% women 0.2% men
Bulimia	1.5% women 0.1% men
Deaths from suicide	12.2 per 100,000
	2% of all deaths
	24% of all deaths among those aged 15–24 years
	16% of all deaths among those aged 25–44 years

*Estimated percentage of the population who have the disorder during any one-year period, for most recent year for which data are available.
Source: Adapted from *A Report on Mental Illnesses in Canada* (Ottawa: Public Health Agency of Canada, 2002). Reproduced with the permission of the Minister of Public Works and Government Services Canada, 2009.

In other words, hundreds of thousands of Canadians are immobilized by their fear or sadness: unable to get out of bed, go to school or work, eat, sleep, or even see friends. Other illnesses—schizophrenia, bipolarity, and eating disorders, for example—are much less common, yet many thousands of cases have been reported. And they are particularly common in some groups—for example, eating disorders are particularly common among young women, as we saw in the last chapter.

In terms of the people it affects and the years of productive activity it takes away, mental illness—along with alcohol and drug addiction—is a leading social and health problem in Canada, the US, and Western Europe, even more so than a variety of other highly publicized, highly funded health problems such as cancer and heart disease (Figure 3.1). To a greater extent than these more socially acceptable diseases, mental illness robs people of years of "healthy life" and full, productive activity. Mental illness is a widespread, long-term affliction that significantly reduces participation in school, work, family, and social life, but most people do not seem to know or accept this fact. Perhaps that is because the moral explanation of mental illness still persists among many who feel that the victims of mental illness, or their families, are to blame.

Statistics tabulated in Table 3.2 show that about 20 per cent of all Canadians can expect to suffer some mental illness during their lifetime. Of these, 12 per cent will suffer an anxiety disorder and 8 per cent a major depression on one or more occasions or for extended periods. As many as 3 per cent of women will suffer an eating disorder—a risk 10 times greater for women than for men. Note that these lifetime prevalence rates are higher than the single-year rates, indicating that throughout life, people run a continuing risk of mental illness. For some people, episodes of mental illness—for example, depression—are recurrent.

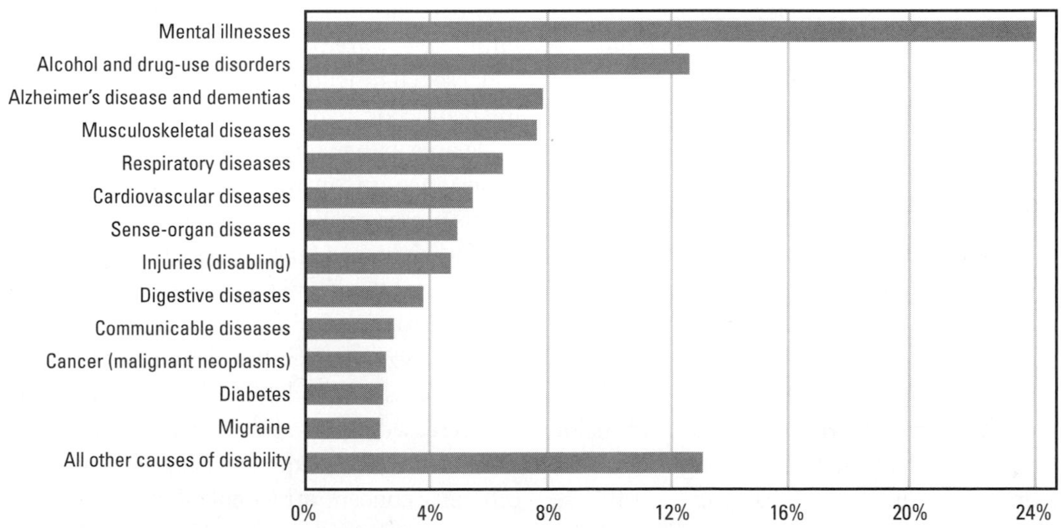

FIGURE 3.1 Causes of Disability*: United States, Canada, and Western Europe, 2000

* Causes of disability for all ages combined. Measures of disability are based on the number of years of "healthy" life lost with less than full health (i.e., years lost due to specified disability) for each incidence of disease, illness, or condition. All data shown add up to 100%.

Source: President's New Freedom: Commission on Mental Health, Figure 1.1, available at: <http://govinfo.library.unt.edu/ mentalhealthcommission/reports/FinalReport/FullReport-02.htm>.

TABLE 3.2 Lifetime Likelihood of Selected Mental Disorders, Canada (%)

Any mental illness	20*
Anxiety disorder	12
Major depression	8
Eating disorder:	
Women	3
Men	0.3
Bipolar disorder	1
Schizophrenia	1

* Including multiple illnesses.
Source: Mood Disorders Society of Canada, "Quick Facts: Mental Illness and Addictions in Canada," at: <www.mooddisorderscanada.ca/documents/Media%20Room/Quick%20Facts%203rd%20Edition%20Referenced%20Plain%20Text.pdf>. Reprinted by permission of the publisher.

Time to Reflect: If mental illness is so common, why is it so widely feared and stigmatized? Under what imaginable circumstances might the widespread negative viewpoint change?

The Characteristics of Mental Illness and Mentally Ill People

As we have said, mental illnesses vary, but overall they are characterized by changes in thinking, mood, or behaviour associated with major distress and weakened functioning over weeks or months. The symptoms of mental illness vary from mild to severe, depending on the type of illness, the person, the family, and the socio-economic environment. Different people run the risk of different disorders, resulting from different predisposing factors.

Mood Disorders

Mood disorders are among the most common mental illnesses in the general population. Canadian research has found that around 8 per cent of adults over 18 years of age and living in the community—that is, not institutionalized—meet the criteria for a diagnosis of major depression at some time in their lives.

By "depression" we are talking about one or more major episodes of incapacitating sadness and sensed isolation. Everyone feels sad sometimes. Most people experience a wide range of moods and emotional sensations; yet, usually, they regain control of their moods and emotions in a time frame considered "reasonable." It is normal for people to grieve following the death of a loved one, for example. That period of mourning normally decreases during the following months and years. However, people with diagnosable mood disorders experience profound distress and lose control of their life: they become unable to work, to relate to their families, to care for children, or to perform usual social functions such as shopping, meeting people, or focusing on tasks.

People with mania (i.e., heightened moods) experience uncontrollable streams of ideas, flights of imagination, an inability to sleep, and briefly heightened (and occasionally grandiose) self-esteem; that mania will usually be followed by depression, if it does not escalate into full-blown schizophrenia. People with depression (i.e., depressed moods) lose their appetite, suffer decreased energy and interest, isolate themselves from others, express feelings of guilt, have difficulty concentrating, and sometimes think obsessively about death or suicide. Other mood disorders include major (or clinical) depression, bipolar disorder (which alternates between episodes of mania and depression), and dysthymia (a chronic state of mild depression).

Mood disorders affect people of all ages; but often, the symptoms appear in adolescence or young adulthood. Some causes may be purely biochemical, physiological, or psychological. For example, the French clinician Guy Bérard reports having identified hearing deficiencies for certain frequencies of sound, usually in the left ear, for people suffering different levels of depression (Bérard, 1993: 42–8). Yet, though there are purely physiological and psychological causes of depression, research repeatedly finds social causes as well. Poverty and poor living conditions, danger, subordination, learned helplessness, and conflict are some of the social conditions that increase the likelihood and duration of depression. Often, they are factors that ignite or set off the inborn (genetic or physiological) predispositions.

Mood disorders—especially depression—are also more prevalent among women than men. In fact, women are about twice as likely as men to become clinically depressed. Women are also two to three times more likely than men to develop dysthymia—a persistent, low-level form of depression without major swings. It is not clear how much of the gender difference in mood disorders is because of differences in the life experiences of men and women—for example, due to the prevalence of gender inequality.

As the report in Box 3.2 suggests, some people fear there is a danger of over-diagnosing depression, mistaking it for mere temporary sadness, the "blues," or a moment of unhappiness. Of course, this risk exists. Like many other illnesses—especially those involving pains whose source is not immediately detectable with the naked eye or by replicable medical testing—depression can be easily ignored until it is incapacitating. On balance, over-diagnosis may be better than under-diagnosis if it serves a preventive or early warning function.

That said, we must be aware of the extent to which the medical profession and the pharmaceutical industry have sought to medicalize and control more and more aspects of human behaviour and function. Diagnosis of mood disorders, whether those disorders are truly debilitating or not, often results in doctors prescribing psychoactive drugs or antidepressants—e.g., children are given Ritalin, stay-at-home moms get Prozac, businessmen get Valium, and a panoply of SSRIs (selective serotonin reuptake inhibitors) and neuroleptic drugs are given to people for every small complaint from poor sleep and ennui to strange thoughts. These drugs mask symptoms at first, though they don't heal, and for many people the drugs become addictive and exacerbate symptoms.

Depression and mania cause significant distress and impairment in all the important areas of functioning: social, occupational, educational, and so on. Risk of suicide, loss of quality of life, and economic costs are the main health concerns for those with mood disorders. Among people with dysthymia, despite a high recovery rate, the risk of a relapse is great. People suffering from this disorder are also at high risk of experiencing episodes of major depression.

We are seeing intensified interest in solving the problems of depression and other mental illnesses, thanks to the efforts of leaders like ex-Senator Michael Kirby, the first Chair of the Mental Health Commission of Canada. A report by the Canadian Institute for Health Information (CIHI) concludes: "The majority of people with probable depression do not seek medical care for their depression, even though the vast majority are in contact with a doctor at least once a year for other reasons" (CIHI, 2008: 53). This report also noted, as sociologists have long argued, that "People with a weak sense of belonging and those who are single/never married are more likely to be admitted to acute care hospitals with a mental health related principal diagnosis, all else being equal" (ibid.).

Current Events

BOX 3.2

The Depression Epidemic

Rates of depression seem to have spiked in the last few years. Roughly one out of every five people is reported to be depressed at some point in his or her life, and in 2007, over 31 million prescriptions for anti-depressants were given in England—an all-time high. Comparable increases have been seen in Canada and the US. Because treatment is expensive, and because victims of depression tend to take time off work, this "epidemic" costs society billions of dollars.

However, some of this treatment may be excessive. Professor Gordon Parker of the University of New South Wales (Australia) suggests that the stated symptoms for depression are currently too broad and many people who aren't really depressed are getting treatment they don't need. Over three-quarters of the participants in a study he conducted were "depressed" according to the current definition of the term—a definition recently extended to include symptoms like sadness that virtually everyone experiences at some time or another.

But these less severe, "normal" cases of depression don't require treatment, says Parker. The extent to which diagnosis and treatment have taken over the lives of people is attested to by the various websites and chat rooms established by patients, former patients, and parents of patients to help others who are trying to withdraw from SSRIs, tranquilizers, and other psychoactive drugs because of the harm—addiction, exacerbated symptoms, suicide—they have done.

In contrast to those who speak out against over-diagnosis, Professor Ian Hickie of the University of Sydney in Australia claims that a diagnosis and treatment policy that addressed only the needs of the most severely depressed people would mean that many would die, when they could have been helped and potentially saved. According to Hickie, a broad definition of depression helps to lower the suicide rates; and the spike in diagnoses has helped to diminish the stigma attached to this disorder.

Others agree, including Marjorie Wallace, chief executive of the UK mental health charity, SANE. Wallace notes that depression encompasses a broad range of feelings and symptoms, from feeling sad to being completely unable to function. Because depression often leads to suicide, Wallace feels that over-diagnosing depression would be better than failing to provide people with the help they need.

Is the incidence of depression really rising? A 2006 study by Costello et al. revealed that the number of people who struggle with depression has not, in fact, risen in the past 30 years. The recent increase in diagnoses merely shows that the public has become more conscious of this condition; it also suggests a greater sensitivity to the condition among doctors and therapists.

Sources: E. Jane Costello, Alaattin Erkanli, and Adrian Angold, "Is There an Epidemic of Child or Adolescent Depression?" *Journal of Child Psychology and Psychiatry* (2006): 1263–71; BBC News, "Depression Is 'Over-diagnosed'," 17 Aug. 2007, at: <news.bbc.co.uk/2/hi/health/6950733.stm>.

Mood disorders such as depression and mania often accompany other mental illnesses, including anxiety disorders, personality disorders, substance abuse, and dependencies. We know that the presence of another mental illness—what is called "co-morbidity"—increases the severity of the original illness and results in a poorer prognosis. We also know that people suffering from mood disorders are at high risk of suicide. That said, there is still much to be learned about mood disorders and their treatment. According to the CIHI report: "The data currently available do not support any definitive results on the health outcomes actually achieved in Canada with regard to the treatment of Canadians with probable depression" (ibid.).

Schizophrenia

Schizophrenia is a less common disorder that causes people to have difficulty interpreting reality, and it is characterized by psychosis. "Schizophrenia" was named by an early twentieth-century psychiatrist, Paul Bleuler. The word means split mind; in other words, the two hemispheres of the brain lack integration and the right hemisphere—the seat of dreams, imagination, and desire—asserts dominance, and the left hemisphere—the location of rationality, self-control, and values—loses dominance.

Because of the stigmatizing nature of the term *schizophrenia*, patients' advocates in some countries, such as the UK, have sought to have this label dropped from medical and common usage, and in Japan psychiatrists and neurologists have replaced the "mind-split-disease" term ("Seishin Bunretsu Byo") with "integration disorder"("Togo Shitcho Sho") (Tallman, 2010: 369). With the onset of this illness, schizophrenics develop a marked change in their thinking, views, and behaviour. This shows itself in a variety of symptoms: hallucinations, delusions, paranoia, disorganized speech, disorganized behaviour, apathy, and social withdrawal.

People who imagine unlikely scenarios—that they are Jesus or Napoleon, or they are being pursued by people from outer space or the CIA, for example—fall into this category. Only if these symptoms last for at least six months and are associated with a significant decline in the person's ability to care for him/herself, or perform in social and work situations, are therapists likely to declare a diagnosis of schizophrenia. This suggests that many people experience occasional, brief delusions or manias in the course of their lives. For only a few does this become a continuing, incapacitating problem.

Many researchers today believe schizophrenia results from a biochemical disturbance in the "wiring" of the brain. What has been less clear is the extent to which genetics, substance abuse, traumatic brain injury, persisting traumatic stress, or other problems associated with severe abuse and neglect are involved. One recent intriguing theory regarding the cause of much mental illness and brain-related disability, supported by the research discoveries and clinical practice of two French otolaryngologists, Doctors Alfred Tomatis and Guy Bérard, points to an audio-processing deficit caused by the inability of the brain's left hemisphere to receive sufficient energizing high-frequency sound because a tiny muscle in the middle right ear has lost or lacks tonicity, a condition that can be ameliorated or healed (see Tallman, 2010, 2011; Tomatis, 1996, 2005; Bérard, 1993).

Schizophrenia is probably the most devastating mental illness when we consider how it affects the patients. The disease has a profound effect on people's ability to function effectively in all aspects of life. Functional impairment may occur in a person's family relationships, school, and employment—even one's ability to care for oneself. As mentioned earlier, schizophrenia normally sets in during the early adult years, at a time when most people are forming families, establishing careers, and building their lives.

Early in the course of the disease, people with schizophrenia may lose their ability to relax, concentrate, or sleep. Performance at work or school often suffers. Though some are able to maintain healthy relationships, the majority of people with this mental illness (60–70 per cent) do not marry, and most have limited social contacts. Another health risk arising from this mental illness is substance abuse. Up to 80 per cent of people with schizophrenia will abuse substances during their lifetime. Substance abuse is associated with poor functional recovery, suicide, and violence.

Overall, the level of mortality associated with schizophrenia is one of the most distressing consequences of the disorder. Roughly 40–60 per cent of people with schizophrenia attempt suicide, and schizophrenics are 15–25 times more likely than the general population to die of a suicide attempt. Approximately 10 per cent will die of suicide (Public Health Agency of Canada, 2002). However, the World Health Organization has reported that in Third World countries, such as India and Nigeria, where only 16 per cent of patients are regularly on anti-psychotic medications, the outcomes for schizophrenia are much better than in Canada, the US, and other rich countries (Whitaker, 2010b: x).

Anxiety Disorders

Anxiety disorders are mental illnesses that manifest as phobias, panic attacks, or obsessive-compulsive disorder. These disorders are not only distressing in themselves, but they also interfere with people's normal functioning at home, work, and in the company of other people. According to the Mood Disorder Society of Canada (2009), 9 per cent of men and 16 per cent of women experience anxiety disorders in a given year. These include social phobias (6.7 per cent), obsessive-compulsive disorder (or OCD) (1.8 per cent), and various other specific phobias (6.2–8 per cent).

These disorders are extremely disruptive. They interfere with a person's social relationships—the ability to fulfill the role of husband or wife; father or mother; son or daughter; friend, employee, or student. They can reduce people to tears and trembling and make them unable to leave the house, cook a meal, or carry out any of the usual activities of daily living (e.g., washing, dressing, toileting). In their effects, they are like the most profound physical handicap. The reality TV show *Hoarders* has shown glimpses of how these disorders are manifested.

Anxiety disorders and their symptoms develop during adolescence. Most people suffering from these disorders have only a mild impairment. People with severe symptoms of anxiety disorders are also more likely to have other problems—for example, major depression or dysthymia, alcohol or substance abuse, or a personality disorder (Eaton et al., 1994). Anxiety disorders can also affect the sufferer's health if treatment is not received on time. Many people, as mentioned before, do not seek treatment soon enough. Others are afraid to seek treatment, fearing the stigma that diagnosis may bring. Left untreated, anxiety disorders can affect the person's general health and quality of life.

Suicide

As we have mentioned several times in this book, suicide is the topic of one of sociology's classic works, by a founder of the discipline, Émile Durkheim.

We often like to think of suicide as a uniquely personal act—so personal and idiosyncratic that it cannot possibly have any connection to the larger society or a person's connection to the world around him. Indeed, it might seem strange that Durkheim chose such a seemingly individualistic phenomenon for what would become the prototypical work of sociology. Yet, since Durkheim's classic study, research has repeatedly shown that suicide is intensely social in its causes (as well as its consequences). As Durkheim said, suicide rates are social facts; they tell us a great deal about the cohesion of the society in which a person lives and a person's social connectedness within that society.

Yet suicides, however social, are immediately personal. Individual people think suicidal thoughts and some of them commit suicide. Typically, these are seriously depressed people; not surprisingly, there are strong connections between suicide and mental illness. An estimated 90 per cent of suicide victims have a diagnosable psychiatric illness. The same factors that predict and cause unhappiness and dissatisfaction with life, not to mention depression—isolation, loneliness, lack of purpose—predict (and cause) suicide (Tepperman and Weerasinghe, 1994). So, suicide is usually a result of depression and loss of meaning. In turn, depression and loss of meaning are usually results of social disruption and disconnectedness, as Durkheim argues in his classic theory on the topic (Box 3.3).

The evidence that social disruption causes suicide is supported in many particulars. For example, Durkheim shows that divorced people (especially men) without children are much more suicide-prone than married people (especially women) with children. Among many, marriage and divorce are social experiences that shape people's most important and personal actions.

Like other manifestations of mental illnesses, suicide is highly gendered (Figure 3.2; Table 3.3). Women are more likely than men to attempt suicide without succeeding, for example, which suggests that—for women—suicide attempts are often calls for help, not efforts to end one's life. This contrast again suggests the importance of gender as a form of social differentiation in human societies. Paradoxically, though women tend to be disadvantaged economically compared with men, they are typically advantaged by greater social connectedness. Gender-based disparities in suicide also result from differences in the ways men and women respond to the social relationships and mental health problems they experience (Lubell, 2001).

So much is suicide a social phenomenon that exposure to suicide through the media is associated with an increase in suicide rates. On at least one occasion, adolescent suicidal deaths increased shortly after media coverage of a prominent suicide or after television episodes featuring an adolescent suicide (Shaffer, 1988). This suicide **contagion** is known as the **Werther effect**, referring to a wave of suicides that swept through Germany and France after the 1774 publication of Goethe's wildly popular novel, *The Sorrows of Young Werther*, about a lovesick young man who kills himself.

Even today, stressful life events and hopelessness, as well as substance abuse and personality disorders, are all secondary risk factors associated with adolescent suicide. A troubled family history, poor family functioning, and conflictual parent–child relationships all increase the risks of youthful suicide. Two aspects of family history—a history of psychopathology and a history of suicides—are particularly relevant. In particular, a family history of psychiatric disorders predicts youth suicide.

Classic Works

BOX 3.3

Émile Durkheim on Suicide

Durkheim's book *Suicide* was written in part to establish sociology as a recognized academic discipline. Durkheim based his approach on what he called the sociological method, which emphasized that "social facts must be studied as things, as realities external to the individual." Specifically, Durkheim attempted to show the links between suicide and marriage, widowhood, family cohesion, and religion.

Accordingly, Durkheim discusses the "social causes and sociological types of suicide." He groups suicides into three types: egoistic, altruistic, and anomic. People commit suicide for different reasons, then: egoistic suicide because, once isolated, they see no reason for living; altruistic suicide because their life goal (e.g., protecting the community) requires their death; and anomic suicide because their activities, norms, and values have been thrown into confusion. By anomic suicide, Durkheim means "the suicides produced by any sudden social shock or disturbance, such as that due to economic disturbance."

By egoistic suicide, Durkheim means that individuals may be driven to commit suicide when they leave the social group they belong to or when its bonds are weakened. In this connection, he notes the importance of religion, education, and family, and how dissolving social bonds will increase the risk of suicide. Overall, Durkheim finds that rates of suicide fall as the degree of social integration rises; in short, groups with less social integration have more suicide. To support this, Durkheim uses statistics to compare Protestants and Catholics, showing that Protestants have a higher suicide rate. He theorizes that Protestants, compared to Catholics, lack "a sufficiently intense collective life." Their weaker association with religious values results in the weakening of social ties, which increases the tendency to commit suicide.

Along similar lines, married people have more immunity from suicide than divorced people, a phenomenon Durkheim calls the matrimonial selection. However, women benefit much less from marriage than men, except when children are present. Surprisingly, "widowhood diminishes but does not abolish the protection conferred by marriage." Interestingly, these findings about the protective features of marriage and parenthood—their effects on well-being and suicide risk, for example—still stand up well today, over a century later.

Less robust is Durkheim's conclusion regarding the difference in Protestant and Catholic suicide rates. His use of German data gave particular results that may be restricted to German-speaking Europe and thus may have been caused by other factors. For example, Catholic families and physicians, for doctrinal reasons, would have been more likely to report suicide deaths as accidents or of unknown cause (Pope and Danigelis, 1981).

Time to Reflect: What is there about marriage that reduces the risk of suicide? Can we gain that benefit outside marriage, in a cohabiting relationship or close friendship?

Social integration aside, social inequality also plays a part. Suicide risks are also clustered in vulnerable, at-risk populations where other stresses—such as poverty, unemployment, substance abuse, and hopelessness—are common. These are all found, for example,

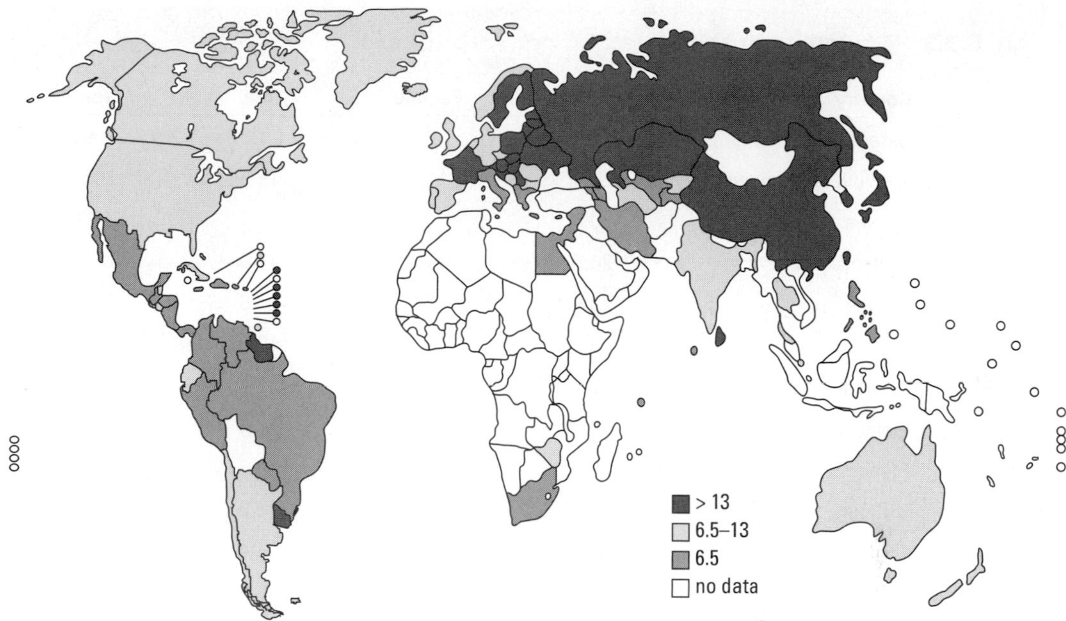

FIGURE 3.2 Suicide Rates per 100,000 Population (most recent year available as of 2011)

Source: World Health Organization, at: <www.who.int/mental_health/prevention/suicide/suicideprevent/en/index.html>.

TABLE 3.3 Forty Highest National Suicide Rates per 100,000 People, Various Years

Rank	Country	Male	Female	Total	Year
1	Lithuania	61.3	10.4	34.1	2009
2	South Korea	41.4	21.0	31.2	2010
3	Guyana	39.0	13.4	26.4	2006
4	Kazakhstan	43.0	9.4	25.6	2008
5	Belarus	n.a.	n.a.	25.3	2010
6	Hungary	40.0	10.6	24.6	2009
7	Japan	33.5	14.6	23.8	2011
8	Latvia	40.0	8.2	22.9	2009
9	People's Republic of China	n.a.	n.a.	22.2	2010
10	Slovenia	34.6	9.4	21.9	2009
11	Sri Lanka	n.a.	n.a.	21.6	1996
12	Russia	n.a.	n.a.	21.4	2011

TABLE 3.3 (continued)

Rank	Country	Male	Female	Total	Year
13	Ukraine	37.8	7.0	21.2	2009
14	Serbia & Montenegro	28.4	11.1	19.5	2006
15	Estonia	20.6	7.3	18.1	2008
16	Switzerland	24.8	11.4	18.0	2007
17	Croatia	28.9	7.5	17.8	2009
18	Belgium	26.5	9.3	17.6	2009
19	Finland	27.2	8.6	17.6	2010
20	Moldova	30.1	5.6	17.4	2008
21	France	26.4	7.2	16.2	2008
22	Uruguay	26.0	6.3	15.8	2004
23	South Africa	25.3	5.6	15.4	2005
24	Austria	23.8	7.1	15.2	2009
25	Poland	26.4	4.1	14.9	2008
26	Hong Kong	19.0	10.7	14.6	2009
27	Suriname	23.9	4.8	14.4	2005
28	Czech Republic	23.9	4.4	14.0	2009
29	New Zealand	20.3	6.5	13.2	2008
30	Sweden	18.7	6.8	12.7	2008
31	Cuba	19.0	5.5	12.3	2008
32	Bulgaria	18.8	6.2	12.3	2008
33	Romania	21.0	3.5	12.0	2009
34	Norway	17.3	6.5	11.9	2009
35	Denmark	17.5	6.4	11.9	2006
36	United States	19.0	4.9	11.8	2008
37	Ireland	19.0	4.7	11.8	2009
38	Bosnia & Herzegovina	20.3	3.3	11.8	1991
39	Canada	17.3	5.4	11.3	2004
40	Iceland	17.9	4.5	11.3	2009

n.a. = not available

Notes: Male and female suicide rates are based on the total male population and total female population, respectively (i.e., total number of male suicides divided by total male population). The total rate of suicides is based on the total number of suicides divided by the total population rather than merely the average of the male and female suicide rates because the gender ratio in many countries is not 1:1. "Year" refers to the most recent year that data were available.

Source: Adapted from Wikipedia, at: <en.wikipedia.org/wiki/List_of_countries_by_suicide_rate>. Original source for most entries is World Health Organization, *Country Report* (2010), at: <www.who.int/mental_health/prevention/suicide/country_reports/en/index.html>.

among Canada's Native people, with the result that suicide rates are exceptionally high in Aboriginal communities, especially among young people.

Family dysfunction of many kinds is associated with suicidal ideation (thoughts about suicide) and continued attempts following a suicidal episode, as we learn from accounts by people who have attempted suicide. Additionally, family structure affects the risk of suicide in adolescents particularly. A family environment disrupted by separation, divorce, widowhood, absence of the father in the home, or separation of the adolescent from parents increases the likelihood of suicide. A family history of attempted or completed suicide also increases the risk of adolescent suicide. Adolescents may learn from their families that suicide is not only a problem-solving strategy for dealing with difficulties or stressful life events but also that it is the only strategy.

Communities and Subcultures of the Mentally Ill

As we repeatedly see in this book, deviant people often form subcultures. This is just as true of mentally ill people, who, like other deviant people, often end up as members of communities with their own subculture.

Consider as an example the communities of homeless people in our large cities: they contain large fractions of mentally ill people. Often, they include deinstitutionalized mental patients who have gone off their medication. Generally, they are homeless because they lack the money, supportive kin, or social contacts that would keep them off the street. And, while mental illness increases the likelihood that a person will end up homeless, so homelessness increases the likelihood that a person will end up mentally ill. Conditions on the street are harsh, dangerous, and depriving.

Largely, these communities of the mentally ill are a result of recent **deinstitutionalization**, and it turns out that (unregulated) deinstitutionalization can cause as many problems as (unregulated) institutionalization. We mentioned earlier that, in the past, some communities ignored their mentally ill members. Other, larger communities increasingly institutionalized them, consigning them to hospitals or asylums. Whatever the original motives behind them, these asylums became warehouses for social outcasts. These institutions were mainly interested in controlling and isolating people who were potentially disruptive and socially inconvenient.

In his classic work ***Asylums*** (1961), sociologist Erving Goffman discussed the defining features of mental hospitals as social and cultural institutions. Goffman characterized mental institutions as belonging to a larger category of organizations he calls **total institutions**. He wrote: "A total institution may be defined as a place of residence and work where a large number of like-situated individuals, cut off from the wider society for an appreciable period of time, together lead an enclosed, formally administered round of life" (Goffman, 1961: xiii).

Mental hospitals, convents, prisons, and military installations have a lot in common as organizations. First, they all exercise total control over their inmates—whether mental patients, nuns, convicts, or soldiers in training. Total institutions—whatever their stated goal—tend to punish, brainwash, and re-socialize unco-operative citizens. The mechanisms for doing this are isolation, degradation, and re-education. All aspects of life in a mental hospital—or other total institution—are conducted in the same place and under the same single authority. Like Bentham's Panopticon, discussed in Chapter 1 and used by Foucault to exemplify the use of surveillance for social control, the mental hospital puts inmates under continuous view and supervision.

Thus, the secluded treatment of mentally ill people in institutions suggests low public regard and concern, an absence of trust, and a tendency to treat mentally ill people as dangerous or childlike. The result is often conflict and resentment, not rehabilitation.

Not surprisingly, after deinstitutionalization—release from a mental hospital—former patients often could not survive on their own. As it turned out, some of the needed supports were forthcoming, from family members and municipal governments. By and large, however, provincial and federal governments turned their backs on the problem. This made informal social supports, and mutual supports, all the more important for mentally ill people. So, for the last 40 years, former mental patients have struggled to build community supports for themselves.

Media Depictions of Mental Illness

You would not know much of this if you relied for your information on the mass media alone. Mass media depictions of mental illness generally tend to represent one of three dominant emotional arcs: tragedy, comedy, or patronizing sympathy. There have been a few exceptions. Recently, with the development of shows like *United States of Tara* and *In Treatment*, audiences have had an opportunity to watch programs in which people with mental health concerns are defined by more than their cognitive and emotional issues. By and large, however, producers and filmmakers have tended to focus, rather romantically, on how suffering with mental illness ennobles the soul and strengthens one's moral mettle.

One of the most historically common depictions of mental illness in Hollywood has been that of the "loveable simpleton." These are characters who, struggling with some mental difficulties, overcome their disabilities to live "normally," if only for a brief period. Oscar-nominated films often turn to this trope, using autism (*Rain Man*), schizophrenia (*A Beautiful Mind*), or general mental handicaps (*Charly*; *Forest Gump*; *I Am Sam*) to troll for best actor nominations.

Another common theme in the mass media is that of the "disabled-as-eccentric." In the movie *As Good As It Gets* and the long-running cable TV show, *Monk*, lead characters suffering from obsessive-compulsive disorder are neither mocked nor pitied, but are laughed *with*, as their illness is pitched as a mere personality quirk and not as deep-rooted anxiety and emotional tumult. While it is certainly a good thing for obsessive compulsives to feel good about themselves, very few sufferers of OCD consider the enormous emotional burden of their condition a cause for mirth.

The most common understanding of mental illness in the mass media is likely as tragedy. The stories of the mental illnesses that led to the deaths of River Phoenix, Karen Carpenter, and George Reeve were major news stories. Each of these events has been considered the tragic consequence of the subject's "personal demons," an idea that imbues a special stigma on them that does not exist for those who succumb to fatal illnesses or who are victims of murder. Of the latter, for example, the comic actor Phil Hartman was murdered by his wife, whose "demons" included addictions to cocaine and Zoloft, a popular SSRI, a category of prescription anti-depressant that has been implicated in numerous headline-grabbing tragedies, including the 1999 "Columbine massacre" at a Colorado high school.

Social Support Networks

As noted, outside mental institutions different types of support may be available to mentally ill people. They can include informal networks of other mentally ill (and often homeless) people; personal networks based on kin and friends; voluntary or charitable support groups; formal groups organized and funded by government; and groups of patients and patient advocates who challenge psychiatric treatment and the use of chemicals to control "different" behaviour.

These groups vary widely in size, composition, and activity. Medical professionals lead some; social service professionals and peers lead others; and academics who have personally experienced or who have known those with mental illness problems are at the forefront of others. They all share a desire to help patients and caregivers help themselves and one another. However, people get far more of the information and support they need from their personal networks than from special-purpose support groups. Hundreds of empirical studies show that personal social networks play a key role in helping troubled people deal effectively with their life stresses and misfortunes. Social relationships give people the sense they are supported, and this sensed social support is important for their well-being.

Beyond the emotional support they provide, social networks also provide instrumental support and social control. They get sick people to address their medical needs and use the health-care system wisely. Family and friends also intervene to increase compliance with treatment plans and to research the efficacy of proposed or ongoing treatment.

Generally, large, cohesive networks are best for people's health, encouraging a wise use of hospital and other health services. As the ill person's network size increases, outpatient service use increases and hospitalization decreases. In fact, the greater a mental patient's social and family resources—or *social capital*—the better his or her chances of avoiding hospitalization, especially commitment to a state institution.

Some people, however, do not have access to large or diverse social networks. As a result, they are more likely to rely on support groups. Increasingly, telephone- and computer-mediated support groups are gaining widespread use. Both telephone- and computer-mediated support groups have the potential to serve clients at a distance—people who are unable or unwilling to take part in traditional face-to-face support groups. Computer-mediated groups offer particular advantages: they eliminate time and distance barriers and limits on group size, like telephone groups, and they also provide more anonymity and more opportunity for expression through written communication.

As a result, health professionals have adapted computer technology to a variety of self-help/mutual-aid groups, including computer-based groups for problems with alcohol, narcotics, eating, gambling, compulsive sexuality, relationships, smoking, and others.

Treatment and Non-Compliance

A problem therapists and mental health professionals face with many mentally ill patients is their refusal to take their medication—that is, to comply with their treatment program.

Often, patients reject or suspend their medication treatment because they become disenchanted with the adverse physical, psychological, and behavioural side effects of the drugs. As noted above, besides physiological side effects ranging from weight gain, tremors, and mild insomnia to life-threatening conditions, the psychotropic medications prescribed for a wide variety of mental instabilities can worsen the conditions—sleep disorders, hallucinations, paranoia—they are intended to mask or alleviate. In addition, withdrawal from such drugs can be both difficult and dangerous.

Also, many patients are reluctant to enter a dependency on drugs to deal with their mental illness. Among other things, it involves the acceptance of a new definition of the "self" as mentally ill and dependent. According to sociologist David Karp (1996), a patient who starts taking medication trades emotional malaise for a biochemical one. During a mental illness, taking "medications involves a complex and emotionally charged interpretative process in which nothing less than one's view of self is at stake" (ibid., 102). Given the stigma associated with mental illness in our society, the patient who starts treatment by medication "officially" enters the world of the mentally ill. So, to reject medication treatment is to reject the stigmatizing label itself.

Theories about Mental Illness

All sociological theories of mental illness focus on social factors that may be associated with certain mental illnesses. Moreover, most sociologists agree that mental illness is usually a result of combined biological, psychological, and social factors. However, sociologists vary in where they put their emphasis.

Functionalist Theories

Durkheim (1951 [1897]) was the first sociologist to study mental illness from a functionalist perspective. As we said earlier, he studied suicide as a highly personal act that arose from two social, structurally induced conditions: inadequate moral control and inadequate social connectedness.

Durkheim's ideas, in time, produced the social disorganization approach to mental illness, as well as the ecological approach that dominated Chicago School studies of deviance in the first half of the twentieth century. At the University of Chicago, sociologists agreed that modern urban life produced rapid change, disrupted relationships, and caused social isolation. By causing anomie and egoism (a focus on one's self-interest), these conditions all lead to deviance, including mental illness and suicide.

Since that time, sociologists taking the functionalist approach have continued to study the importance of social organization and disorganization as sources of mental health and illness. They continue to find that people who are most securely rooted in stable, cohesive, and supportive communities are most likely to avoid mental illness or to recover from it.

Time to Reflect: Why are people with stable social relationships less likely than other people to become mentally ill and more likely to recover from mental illness? What, if anything, does it have to do with the role of families and friends?

Symbolic Interactionist Theories

The symbolic interactionist approach stresses that people with mental or physical problems are cast into a recognized, stigmatized social role. As with other kinds of deviance, symbolic interactionists are not so much interested in finding the original cause of the behaviour but rather in seeing the effects of labelling and stigmatization. That is to say, they are more interested in labelling as a source of secondary deviance.

To receive a label—for example, the label of patient or mentally ill person—means becoming an outsider in mainstream society. It is an isolating and exclusionary label. True, to be labelled mentally ill is to be freed of certain expectations and responsibilities, but this freedom comes at a high cost—specifically stigmatization. What's more, the labelling may itself complicate the illness and recovery from it. Often, mentally ill people avoid seeking help in fear of rejection. For example, only two in every five individuals experiencing a mood, anxiety, or substance abuse disorder report seeking help in the first year after the onset of the disease (WHO, 2001, 2004). This reluctance to seek help delays diagnosis and treatment and prolongs the painful effects of mental illness.

Deinstitutionalization was originally considered a triumph by symbolic interactionists, for several reasons. First, it reflected the influence of one of their own kind—Goffman—who helped promote this important social change with the publication of his classic book, *Asylums.* Second, deinstitutionalization appeared to demonstrate a public acceptance of the premise of labelling theory: namely, that the way we treat deviants can be as harmful as the conditions that give rise to deviance in the first place. Most important, deinstitutionalization seemed like a humane, progressive act that recognized the equal rights of the stigmatized to due consideration.

The changes were rapid and dramatic. During the first 20 years of deinstitutionalization (roughly 1965–85) in Canada, the number of beds in mental institutions was reduced by more than 60 per cent. One of the primary goals of deinstitutionalization was to integrate the mentally ill with other members of the community, to help them develop support systems and aid in "normalizing" their lives.

However, integrating the deinstitutionalized people into neighbourhoods proved more easily said than done. Just as many people opposed garbage dumps, halfway houses for convicts, and group homes for errant youth, property owners often opposed building facilities for the deinstitutionalized mentally ill in their neighbourhoods. Some feared an influx of dangerous strangers. Others feared an adverse effect on their property values. Empirical research has proved these fears unfounded. No negative effects on property values for people living near community mental health facilities, for example, have been identified. Nonetheless, many remained opposed to having former mental patients in the vicinity.

This proves more strongly than almost anything else that the symbolic interactionists were right: labelling and prejudice are indeed key problems to be solved in relation to mental illness.

Critical Theories

Critical theorists view mental illnesses as reflections of the unequal distribution of social stresses, vulnerabilities, and disadvantages in a society. They continue to expect, and find, higher-than-average rates of mental illness among the poorer, most vulnerable members of society because these people suffer the greatest deprivation of supportive family relationships, living and work conditions, and good health services.

Originally, critical theorists took a Marxist class-oriented approach and focused on poverty and economic inequality. While these factors remain important, today we recognize that other types of inequality can also cause stress and mental illness. Prejudice, discrimination, and abuse based on other factors such as race, ethnicity, gender, age, or sexual orientation can all play a role. As well, we recognize today the equally important role of social—as well as economic—capital in determining people's lives. As a result, inequalities in social capital—in social connectedness, for example—can also result in mental illness.

In critical theories, as in functionalist theories, neighbourhood characteristics play a role, too. However, critical theorists focus on social deprivation, not social disorganization. They note that socially deprived neighbourhoods—neighbourhoods with high unemployment, crime, and substance abuse, for example, as well as poor schools, transportation, and public facilities—experience a higher-than-average rate of mental illnesses. Because of such deprivation, mental illness—for example, depression—is more prevalent among poor people. Living in poor conditions, without easy access to satisfactory health care, contributes significantly to the onset of mental illness. Nowhere is this more evident than among Aboriginal people on reserves.

Still needed is a theory that examines the intersection of inequalities, to see how multiple inequalities interact and under what conditions these interacting inequalities produce the worst outcomes. A beginning in this regard, which examines numerous aspects of health in Canada, including mental health, is the edited volume, *Health Inequities in Canada: Intersectional Frameworks and Practices* (Hankivsky et al., 2011). In recent years, as Canada increasingly has become a nation of new immigrants, many people have grown concerned about the mental health of these newcomers, and for good reason. They may experience a combination of underemployment, racism, and social disconnectedness, all while they are grappling with assimilation into an alien culture.

- Likelihood women will develop depression in their lifetime: twice as likely as men.
- Percentage of women who will develop depression during pregnancy: 10 per cent.
- Percentage of women in the general population who will develop postpartum depression: 15–20 per cent.
- Percentage of women with a history of depression who will experience postpartum depression: 30 per cent.
- Percentage of women who have experienced a postpartum depression who are likely to re-experience it in a subsequent pregnancy: 50 per cent.
- Percentage of women who develop postpartum psychosis (depression accompanied by delusions and disordered thinking): 0.1–0.2 per cent.
- Percentage of women with bipolar disorder who develop postpartum psychosis: 50 per cent.
- In the world, 80 per cent of those most affected by violent conflict, war, disaster, and displacement are women and children.
- Percentage of women in the world who experience rape or attempted rape in their lifetime: 20 per cent.
- The country that ranks the highest in the world for gender equality: Canada.

FIGURE 3.3 Fact Sheet on Women's Mental Health

Sources: D. Stewart et al., "Women's Health Surveillance Report: Depression," at: <www.phac-aspc.gc.ca/publicat/ whsr-rssf/pdf/WHSR_Chap_18_e.pdf>; Canadian Mental Health Association, Ontario, "Women's Mental Health Fact Sheet," at: <www.ontario.cmha.ca/content/about_mental_illness/women.asp?cID=3974>; World Health Organization (WHO), "Gender and Women's Health," at: <www.who.int/mental_health/prevention/genderwomen/en/>; WHO, "Women's Mental Health: An Evidence-based Review" (2000), at: <www.who.int/mediacentre/factsheets/fs334/en/index.html>; Mood Disorders Society of Canada, at: <www.mooddisorderscanada.ca/documents/Media%20Room/Quick%20Facts%203rd%20Edition%20Referenced%20Plain%20Text.pdf>.

Postmodern Approaches

One of the great sociological works on mental illness is found in the postmodern tradition. *Madness and Unreason: History of Madness in the Classical Age* (2005 [1961]) originated from Michel Foucault's academic study of psychology and his work in a Parisian mental hospital. The book is an indictment of what Foucault considers the moral hypocrisy of modern psychiatry, a view perhaps related to his own experiences as a psychiatric patient.

Foucault studied the rise of the modern idea of "mental illness" in Europe. Conventional histories depict the nineteenth-century medical treatment of madness as far more enlightened and generous than treatment in earlier periods. After all, it was during this period that scientists moved from a focus on devils and moral transgressions to a focus on physical, biological causation. But Foucault claims the new idea that the mad were merely sick ("mentally" ill) and in need of medical treatment was not a clear improvement on earlier thinking. Moreover, this new treatment of the mentally ill was harsh and unsympathetic—as though a punishment for the incapacities of mental illness. Foucault writes:

> Madmen were included in the proscription of idleness. From [the asylum's] origin, they would have their place beside the poor, deserving or not, and the idle, voluntary or not. Like them, they would be subjects to the rules of forced labour. . . . In the workshops in which they were interned, they distinguished themselves by their inability to work and to follow the rhythms of collective life. The necessity, discovered in the eighteenth century, to provide a special regime for the insane, and the great crisis of confinement that shortly preceded the [French] Revolution, are linked to the experience of madness available in the universal necessity of labour. . . . In the Classical Age, for the first time, madness was perceived through a condemnation of illness and in a social immanence guaranteed by the community of labour. The community acquired an ethical power of segregation, which permitted it to eject, as into another world, all forms of social useless. (Foucault, 1967: 58)

In short, theories of madness came to reflect a bourgeois civilization's preoccupation with hard work and profitability. The supposed scientific neutrality of modern medical treatments merely disguised efforts to protect this bourgeois morality against attack. Foucault argues that the supposed scientific discovery that madness is mental illness is a questionable social belief based on ideological assumptions and vested interests. The point is, Foucault claimed that modern experts *created* the modern notion of madness as a category of knowledge—they established the relevant concepts and theories and then took control of the mad by putting them in asylums. Asylums of the modern type would not have existed without the invention of "modern" madness by experts and their ability to enact their expertise in institutional, regulatory forms.

From a postmodern perspective, what we believe about mental illness today—however apparently scientific its origins—is merely an ideological product. It reflects a particular time and place in history and satisfies particular institutional interests. From this standpoint, the *Diagnostic and Statistical Manual of Mental Disorders* (DSM)—the handbook in universal use among psychotherapists—is not a fact book like the *Farmers' Almanac* or even a set of scientific laws like Euclid's algebra; it is a compendium of cultural assumptions (considered "findings") that masks the biased methodology used to "discover" these "findings." In short, it is a written system of beliefs, like the Holy Bible or the Koran.

That the medical profession continues to add new "disorders" and categories of mental illness, it can be argued, suggests an attempt to extend its reach into and control over society, especially among weaker and marginalized groups such as children and women, at least as much as it is a testament to new medical breakthroughs and discoveries. That said, the DSM is a work in progress and, like Sigmund Freud's celebrated "case studies" in the last century, a cultural as much as medical artifact.

By this reckoning, the next version—DSM-V, expected out in 2012—will likely contain a somewhat different set of beliefs than in the past. Many forms of "illness" will have been added and some will have been removed, just as homosexuality was (mostly) removed from the manual in 1973. Symptoms of mental disorder—like language, fashion, or music—all have meaning only within a specified cultural framework. Likewise, "normal behaviours" can be judged only in relation to prevailing cultural norms. "Symptoms" are not direct indicators of underlying dysfunction. They merely suggest underlying vulnerabilities, or risks, framed to match current cultural understandings about the forms and causes of mental illness. In short, they are nothing more than educated guesses about the boundary line between "normality" and "abnormality."

The historical specificity of our knowledge about mental illness is obvious everywhere. Our concepts of good behaviour, and even "normality," for children change over time. As they change, we use new strategies to control "abnormality." The process of doing so starts with surveillance, assessment, classification, and streaming—just as Foucault said.

The growing medicalization of deviance, and the normalization of vice as disease, can be seen in a variety of situations. Take the current problematization of excessive gambling as a disease or addiction, like alcoholism. What the "discovery" and naming of new mental illnesses show is that, in our civilization, science serves the social order by defining "normality" in seemingly verifiable, value-neutral terms that are apparently non-ideological. The theories that result from this process may yield testable and even valid predictions. Yet, as Foucault said, they also support the social order and serve as another way of defining the line between good and bad, socially acceptable and socially unacceptable. Or, as we might say, they scientifically define "the straight and narrow" at a particular moment in time.

Consequences of Mental Illness

Social Consequences

Crime and Victimization

Many people who suffer from mental illness get into trouble with the police and courts. For this reason, there is a strong and continuing connection between mental health and crime. In recent years, diminished social supports—including limited access to medical and other services, deteriorating living conditions, increased reliance on psychiatric emergency ward consultations, and growing service demands on community resources—have made community care of the mentally ill more of an illusion than a reality.

Mentally ill people are not only likely to be involved in some type of public altercation or minor offence, but they are also at a higher risk of victimization than most other people. Given the lack of sufficient community supports and residences for mentally ill people, a great many of them end up in prison after committing an offence that might have gone unnoticed or unpunished if they were socially integrated people (or members of a higher economic class.)

As a result, a higher-than-average proportion of all people admitted to federal prisons are currently diagnosed with a mental illness or have been diagnosed with a mental illness in the past. A great many inmates have been hospitalized for a mental illness in the past or have been outpatients. As well, almost half are taking prescribed medications for a mental illness or have done so (Table 3.4). This does not even begin to count the others who medicate

TABLE 3.4 Prevalence of Mental Illness among Persons Admitted to Federal Prisons in Canada

Percentage of total offender population with a diagnosis of mental illness on admission				
Calendar year	**1997**	**1998**	**1999**	**2000**
Diagnosed current	7.8	8.3	9.3	9.7
Diagnosed past	11.4	12.3	14.0	14.7
Prescribed medication current	10.7	11.7	14.4	16.1
Prescribed medication past	23.3	25.0	29.6	31.7
Hospitalized current	2.0	2.3	2.4	2.3
Hospitalized past	17.4	17.9	19.1	19.8
Outpatient current	5.5	5.4	6.2	6.6
Outpatient past	17.6	18.0	21.2	21.9

Source: Roger Boe and Ben Vuong, "Mental Health Trends among Federal Inmates," *FORUM on Corrections Research* 14, 2 (2002): 1. Reproduced with the permission of the Minister of Public Works and Government Services Canada, 2009.

themselves against anxiety or depression using alcohol, other drugs, or over-the-counter pharmaceuticals.

Mentally ill people are likely to be victimized because of their illness. Severely ill people, especially those who experience delusional beliefs or hallucinations, often arouse negative responses in people around them who misunderstand their sometimes aggressive and impolite behaviours. Ex-mental patients under high levels of stress are more likely than other people to provoke verbal and physical conflicts, for example. Sometimes, this gets them injured. And, all too often, mentally ill people are killed by police because of disturbances and apparently threatening behaviour (www.thestar.com/news/article/1081174--siu-clears-officer-in-fatal-shooting-of-toronto-woman).

Mental illness not only increases victimization, but victimization can also cause certain types of mental illnesses. Bullying experiences, for example, can produce psychiatric consequences—stress reactions—and can also predict future psychiatric problems. Symptoms of PTSD among battered wives, soldiers returning from war, and even car crash victims illustrate this same point. Even indirectly, a wide variety of stressful events can lead to PTSD.

Stigma

As we have noted, many who suffer from a mental illness are stigmatized for it. A *stigma*, as the term is used in sociology, is a mark of shame, disgrace, or infamy. People who are socially disapproved for personal characteristics or beliefs that are against cultural norms are often stigmatized—in this way disgraced. They may suffer mere disapproval, ridicule, or even exclusion, discrimination, and ostracism.

Stigmas arise from superstition, lack of knowledge, old belief systems, and a tendency to fear and exclude people we perceive as different; and stigmas connected with mental illness have existed throughout history. The stigmatization of mental illness results in fear, embarrassment, and avoidance. It forces people to keep silent about their mental illnesses, often causing them to delay seeking health care and avoid sharing their concerns with family, friends, co-workers, employers, health service providers, and others in the community.

For instance, many women suffering from mental illnesses and addiction disorders are parents and caregivers, and they fear that by seeking help they may lose their children to relatives or the authorities. This apprehension not only delays their recovery, but it also puts their children in danger if the disorder is not under control.

Reducing the stigma associated with mental illness has recently become a priority in Canada. To be effective, it requires innovative and effective public mental health interventions informed by a clear understanding of what stigma means and how harmful it can be. Our society makes it hard for these suffering people. Not only do they have to deal with the illness and the treatment, but they also have to overcome the stigma attached to their mental disorder, an additional disadvantage not present in more socially acceptable illnesses.

Mental Illnesses and Work

Work is a central part of our society. Our occupational status is central to our assessment of our own and others' social value: "we are what we do" (Karp, 1996). A mental illness, however, can leave the individual incapable of regular, structured employment in the workforce or can lead to unemployment, and this is highly disruptive to an individual's self-concept and self-worth.

According to the Canadian Mental Health Association, 70–90 per cent of those suffering from mental illnesses are unemployed. On the one hand, the stigma associated with mental illness keeps these individuals from getting or holding a job. On the other hand, the condition itself may lessen the person's self-trust. These feelings may prompt the individual to leave the job and discourage him or her from seeking future employment.

Mood disorders and other psychiatric conditions translate into absenteeism, which can be expensive for organizations and limit productivity. In many companies, permanent staff are able to take time off in the event of mental illness so they can concentrate on recovering. In the short term, this is costly for the employer. In the long term, however, it is a wise strategy. It removes the need to hire and train replacement workers and improves the performance of the current workforce. More important, it strengthens employee morale and loyalty.

However, not all companies are so enlightened. Many fail to take a comprehensive approach to mental illness, and many others hire only temporary employees who do not qualify for long-term disability benefits in most cases. Temporary or part-time employees often do not have access to paid vacation time or leaves of absence in the event of a mental illness. This limits their immediate personnel costs but rules out the possibility of many individuals taking time off to relieve the stresses that lead to mental illnesses.

Time to Reflect: Would employers likely benefit from hiring people who are mentally ill? Would there be any likely disadvantages or costs, and if so, what would they be?

Economic Consequences

Much attention has recently been paid to the prevalence and the consequences of mental illness. However, public interest has largely been limited to the direct costs of mental illness: to losses of employment, earning, and productivity. WHO predicts that by the year 2020, depression will be the second leading cause of global disability burden in industrialized nations (2001, 2004). Already, mental illnesses like depression and anxiety affect Canadian society in terms of health-care costs, productivity losses, and lost taxes.

Estimates using data from the 1996–7 National Population Health Survey concluded that depression, distress, and health services use in connection with mental illness may cost Canada as much as $14.4 billion a year. However, more recent estimates suggest a much higher figure. For example, the Centre for Addiction and Mental Health (CAMH) in Toronto cites an estimate by Lim et al. (2008) that the cost to Canada of mental illness in terms of treatment and lost productivity is, in fact, $51 billion, the much higher estimate owing to continued increases in the prevalence of mental illness and the costliness of health services.

Like physical disabilities, mental illnesses (particularly depression and various anxiety disorders) make many potential workers unemployable or, at the very least, lose productivity through mental health-related absences. While these issues need not prevent sufferers from being productive employers or employees, those suffering from depression experience greater unemployment, more absences, and poorer work-based performance reviews (Lerner and Henke, 2008).

Another economic issue linked to mental illness is the enormous amount of money at stake. Pharmaceutical companies make billions of dollars a year manufacturing drugs for what have been defined as "mental illnesses," recouping the cost of developing and marketing the drugs many times over. Furthermore, these companies often fight to keep lower-cost generic versions of their medications off the market as a means of keeping their profits as high as possible, and encourage doctors to believe in and prescribe a "magic pill" for every imaginable symptom of human emotion and mental distress. The fact that the Canadian government does not cover prescription medications means that, even in a country with "universal health care," prescription medications are big business.

Even when generic medications do make it to the market, medication companies work hard to maintain "brand recognition" of the original version. Drug companies encourage the public to self-diagnose various mental illness symptoms and then ask their physician for the appropriate drug by brand name (you've likely heard of Prozac, for instance, but may not know that drug's generic name, Fluoxetine). A study of American prescription medication users found that respondents would need to save an average of $25.50 per prescription to choose a generic drug over its brand-name counterpart, and 13 per cent of anti-depressant users would reportedly ***never*** buy a generic drug (Shrank et al., 2011).

The lack of popularity of generic medications only serves to compound the financial problems that face people who use medications to treat cognitive or emotional issues. In fact, even generic medications often are too expensive for consumers. One study found that low-income people suffering from chronic health issues often underuse their medications as a means of saving money. This results in 32 per cent of these people experiencing "significant declines" in their overall health (Heisler et al., 2004) for financial reasons.

Social Policy Implications

Education

It is likely that the stigmatization of mentally ill people will decline in the future, as people become better informed. Research generally shows that people with a higher education express more positive attitudes towards the mentally ill. Less-educated respondents tend to be less tolerant.

Another problem leading to stigmatization is unfamiliarity. Many people have negative attitudes towards the mentally ill because they do not know any better. It is the "fear of the unknown" that provokes the stereotypes and stigma that many attach to the mentally ill. In the future, scholars, researchers, patient advocacy groups, and governments will have to provide the public with more information about mental illnesses, their causes, and how ordinary people can help. Such measures will inform the public that these illnesses affect many people and no one can be sure of avoiding them. Public awareness programs, by reducing the social stigma that many attach to the mentally ill, will help prevent an escalation of the symptoms and social isolation that many experience because of discrimination.

Likewise, we also need to do something about media depictions of mental illness, which can be so injurious and misleading.

Poverty Reduction

We have also mentioned in this chapter that there is a connection between mental illnesses and poorer, less socially integrated neighbourhoods. Governments should try to provide better services to the poor and ensure equal access to the scarce resources poor people need to maintain their health and a good quality of life.

We also need more education in these poorer areas to ensure that people who experience mental health problems are not afraid to seek help. We can effectively treat most mental illnesses (or at least their symptoms) if people in need ask for help soon enough, especially if they or those close to them are in a position to ask the right questions and to seek answers beyond those offered by the medical and pharmaceutical mainstream. Mental illness is debilitating, for sufferers and for those with whom they share their lives, but answers are being found.

Diagnosis

Mental illness professionals assess the existence of disorders by observing symptoms. Ideally, patients with the same diagnoses will show similar symptoms and respond to similar treatments.

The unreliability of psychiatric diagnoses is a serious problem for our society and, as noted earlier, some patients' groups advocate for an end to psychiatry and the solutions it proposes for mental illness. If mental health professionals cannot accurately detect and classify mental disorders, they are unlikely to be able to treat disorders effectively. Moreover, many people who need treatment are failing to receive it. At the same time, some people who are diagnosed and treated for a certain mental health condition are not suffering from the disorder. They are merely experiencing some symptoms of the illness but not the illness itself. So, while some people are being under-treated for mental illness, others are being over-treated.

Family-Based Care in Suicide Prevention

Families play an important role in alleviating and preventing various mental illness problems. Increasingly, families will need to play an even bigger role in the prevention and treatment of family members with a mental illness, a need that, arguably, is difficult to meet in a mobile society with increasing numbers of broken and dysfunctional families. Yet, in many ways, families are the best situated in our society to provide this assistance. That said, they will need public supports and services to carry out their job.

Consider the matter of suicide: family functioning is a mediator of adolescent suicide, and can act either as a buffer against suicide or a provocation to it. Given the family's role in producing, preventing, and treating adolescent suicide, parents are important targets of intervention. Therapists recognize the need to give family members new ways of understanding a suicidal episode and not allow it to reinforce negative family patterns. Treatment must be focused on the family to encourage protective factors such as family communication, cohesion, and effective problem-solving skills.

Evaluation research has demonstrated that, where mentally ill or suicidal family members are concerned, family-based treatment is typically better than non-family-based treatment, and some of these treatments are better than others. This is shown by the successes of three family-based programs directed at adolescents who have attempted suicide: each of these treatments focuses on the suicide attempter in the context of the individual's family and works to solve the problems within the context of family dynamics.

The Home-based Intervention Program (HBI), is set up to reduce the likelihood of further suicidal episodes. The aims of the program are to increase the family's acknowledgement and acceptance of the suicidal episode; to help the family improve its communication by focusing on expressiveness and openness; and, finally, to help the development of problem-solving skills among family members.

A second program, designed for in-patient treatment, is called Specialized Emergency Room Care. This program involves staff training, a structured family therapy session, and the presentation of a videotape to the family that outlines both the harmful effects of ignoring suicide attempts and the benefits that come from treatment.

A third program, called SNAP, is a six-session outpatient program for suicide attempters and their families. During these sessions, therapists set up a sympathetic family climate and then help people air their feelings, solve family problems, and help family members enjoy pleasant activities together. Various exercises such as role-playing give family members the opportunity to work together and to heighten family cohesion.

Deinstitutionalization

Despite the evident problems, with deinstitutionalization Western societies have taken the first step towards correcting the injustices historically done to many mentally ill people. Increasingly, since the 1950s, we have removed mentally ill people from institutional care. To an important degree, the deinstitutionalization movement reflects a belief in the human rights of mentally ill people, as well as skepticism about both the psychiatric profession and the therapeutic value of confinement.

Goffman and others writing in the mid-twentieth century viewed total institutions, including mental hospitals, as anti-therapeutic and ineffective in helping their patients. Instead of making inmates healthy and better adjusted to life in the outside world, total institutions made inmates sicker and more poorly adjusted. This insight provided the first line of argument in favour of releasing patients from mental hospitals.

Supporters believed that deinstitutionalization would be the first step in recreating social ties and social roles that existed before the patient's induction into total institutions. It would also allow patients to exercise initiative and learn skills associated with independent living. Finally, it would allow mental patients to escape the dangers (like physical and sexual assault) commonly associated with life in total institutions. So, outpatient care would be health-preserving and health-enhancing, as well as socially integrative.

As hoped, deinstitutionalization has had an enormous impact on the mentally ill, the community, family members, and taxpayers. There have been many success stories to celebrate. And despite persistent mental illness, many deinstitutionalized patients have developed new roles and new identities, a new sense of independence, new coping abilities, and a new capacity to voice future goals and desires.

However, we have come only part of the way. The rest of the way will demand more systematic and compassionate attempts to provide in-community supports for these deinstitutionalized patients. The social exclusion of former mental patients continues. For example, many people still express concern that deinstitutionalization and community-based programs will increase the likelihood that women with serious mental disorders will give birth to and raise troubled children. Others, expressing NIMBY ("not in my backyard") concerns, continue to argue for the safety of the community or about land values.

So far, the problems caused by deinstitutionalization have been largely economic. The move to deinstitutionalize mental patients coincided with major cuts in spending on health care and social services. Regrettably, the fight to deinstitutionalize mental patients had a negative goal—the virtual elimination of mental hospitals—but no positive goal. There was no standard plan for outpatient care and no funding provided to deliver that care. Still, many felt—and continue to feel—that community-based professionals (in clinics and halfway houses) would provide better care than mental patients received in institutions. We have yet to see the end of this story.

Conclusion

What we call "mental illnesses" are characterized by alterations in thinking, mood, or behaviour (or some combination of these) associated with significant distress and impaired functioning. The symptoms of mental illness vary greatly, depending on the type of mental illness, the person, the family, and the socio-economic environment.

Mental illnesses, though personal, are socially structured. Because mental illness is socially structured, it is of interest to sociologists. Social supports for the mentally ill are central to recovery. Among the elderly, more resource-rich and diversified networks (of friends and neighbours) lead to more social support and, as a result, less activity limitation and better health. However, as we have seen, providing support is stressful, increasing the risks of mental illness for the caregiver.

Considering the negative stereotypes evoked by the notion of mental illness, it is not surprising that many people have been opposed to the deinstitutionalization of the mentally ill and the idea of placing community-based mental health services near neighbourhood residents. People are more willing to accept help for psychological distress today because attitudes towards mental illness have changed; there is less shame attached to seeking mental health services. What remains is to create a society that is less stressful and more sympathetic, in this way preventing avoidable mental illnesses from developing, and to provide in-community help for people who succumb to unavoidable mental illnesses.

Questions for Critical Thought

1. In what sense is mental illness a social role? What are the pros and cons of playing that role if you are suffering mental distress?
2. Why did it take people so long to come to the conclusion that mental illness is an illness, not a form of immorality?
3. Judging from the current state of deinstitutionalization, what policy changes could ensure that deinstitutionalization benefits those suffering from mental illness?
4. Stigma and victimization of mental illness sufferers are still major problems in the community. As a policy-maker, what suggestions would you make to help the general population better empathize with mentally ill patients?
5. Is mental illness found in all societies? Is it possible that our own definitions of mental illness are culturally bound?
6. Based on the information provided in this chapter, what effect do families have on an individual's mental health?

Recommended Readings

Kadison, Richard, and Theresa Foy Digeronimo. 2004. *College of the Overwhelmed: The Campus Mental Health Crisis and What to Do about It*. San Francisco: Jossey-Bass.

This book documents the conditions that gave rise to the current mental health crisis on campuses and what colleges, parents, and students can do about it. The authors identify the stressors facing students. Unhealthy responses to these stressors include depression, sleep, anxiety, and eating disorders, substance abuse, and even suicide.

Mayes, Rick, Catherine Bagwell, and Jennifer Erkulwater. 2009. *Medicating Children: ADHD and Pediatric Mental Health*. Cambridge, Mass.: Harvard University Press.

The authors examine possible explanations for such rapid increases in stimulant medication use. As well, the authors consider the increase in medication treatment of ADHD in the context of the wider use of psychotropic medications for children generally. Finally, the authors consider why this disease has been so controversial, noting that an important distinction between ADHD and other diagnoses is the strong educational aspect of ADHD: that is, the first diagnosis is often made by a teacher.

Mirowsky, John, and Catherine E. Ross. 2003. *Social Causes of Psychological Distress*. New York: Aldine de Gruyter.

This book describes the relationship between social problems and psychological distress. It explains how patterns of social inequality influence various health outcomes.

Whitbeck, Les B. 2009. *Mental Health and Emerging Adulthood among Homeless Young People*. London: Psychology Press.

This book examines what happens to homeless and runaway adolescents when they become adults. The study on which it is based follows homeless youth into young adulthood and reviews the mental health consequences of runaway episodes and street life. The distress, including self-mutilation and suicidal behaviours, among this population is examined, as well as the impact street life has on future relationships, education, and employment.

Recommended Websites

Canadian Mental Health Association

www.cmha.ca/bins/index.asp

This section of the Canadian Mental Health Association provides links to different entities that deal with specific concerns related to mental health, such as suicide prevention and terminal illnesses, among others. Links to Canadian, American, and worldwide resources and information are also offered.

Centre for Addiction and Mental Health

www.camh.net/

The Centre for Addiction and Mental Health (CAMH) is the leading Canadian addiction and mental health teaching hospital. CAMH provides information, assistance, and treatment as well as mental health promotion programs across Ontario through its 26 branches.

Mood Disorders Association of Canada

www.mooddisorderscanada.ca/

This Canadian site offers a great deal of information about the different mood disorders and provides statistics and surveys of the state of mental health of the population. It also provides information on resources in the community to help individuals with mental health concerns.

National Institute of Mental Health

www.nimh.nih.gov/index.shtml

This is the mental health branch of the US National Institutes of Health system of institutions, themselves offshoots of the US Department of Health and Human Services. The National Institute of Mental Health provides useful information on mental health research, policy, and diagnostic tools.

National Center on Birth Defects and Developmental Disabilities

www.cdc.gov/ncbddd/index.html

Also American, the NCBDDD provides information on the causes of and accommodations for persons with birth defects and developmental disabilities. Run out of the Centers for Disease Control in Atlanta, this site provides data and research on the ways in which lifestyle, geography, and occupation can affect one's chances of birthing a child with cognitive issues.

World Health Organization—Mental Health Division

www.who.int/mental_health/en/

WHO's comprehensive website provides up-to-date statistics and information on general mental health matters around the world. It provides a good picture of the mental health crisis and what is being done on a global basis.

Recommended Movies

***Shine*, Dir. Scott Hicks (1996)**

Notable especially for its brilliant portrayal by Geoffrey Rush of a concert pianist with schizophrenia, this Australian film is based on the life of pianist David Helfgott, who suffered a mental breakdown and spent years in institutions. Eventually, the love of a devoted wife helped him to overcome a long struggle with mental illness so that he could again play for audiences.

***Charly*, Dir. Ralph Nelson (1968)**

Based on Daniel Keyes's successful novel, *Flowers for Algernon*, Nelson's film depicts the life of 30-year-old mentally handicapped baker, Charly. Taking part in an experiment, Charly is bequeathed genius-level intelligence, only to find the gift fleeting. Both Charly and those around him must ultimately come to terms with who Charly is and what, as an intellectual outsider, he has to offer society. Cliff Robertson won an Academy Award as best actor for his portrayal in the title role.

***One Flew Over the Cuckoo's Nest*, Dir. Milos Forman (1975)**

This culturally iconic film, based on Ken Kesey's 1962 novel, provides an interesting, at times darkly humorous, and ultimately bitter depiction of the psychiatric hospital as a total institution. In an attempt to avoid additional prison time, Randle McMurphy feigns insanity and is sent to a mental hospital for evaluation. There, McMurphy finds himself at odds with the harsh Nurse Ratched, who uses all her institutional power to extract obedience from the patients. This moving, satiric portrayal of asylum life was only the second film (after *It Happened One Night* in 1934) to win all five of the major Academy Awards—for best film, director, actor, actress, and screenplay. Kesey's novel drew on his earlier experience as a psychiatric hospital orderly, as well as on his experimentation with hallucinogenic drugs.

***Girl, Interrupted*, Dir. James Mangold (1999)**

Perhaps most famous for making Angelina Jolie a star, this film is a powerful historical look at the realities of mental health institutions. Susanna, a 19-year-old with borderline personality disorder, is committed to Claymore Psychiatric Hospital and immediately has trouble adapting. This movie is perhaps most valuable for its exploration of the difficulties in removing oneself from a total institution.

***Best Boy*, Dir. Ira Wohl (1979)**

This Oscar-winning documentary follows the everyday life of Philly Wohl, a developmentally disabled adult man who, at the age of 52, is still being taken care of by his aged parents. With the help of his cousin Ira, Philly is encouraged to live as an independent adult for the first time in his life. *Best Boy* is a serious-minded but good-natured work on the difficulties facing the developmentally disabled.

***The Soloist*, Dir. Joe Wright (2009)**

Cynical Los Angeles journalist Steve Lopez stumbles across Nathaniel Ayers, finding the schizophrenic homeless man is a gifted cellist. Ayres's battles with schizophrenia had limited his potential career as a Juilliard-trained musician, but Lopez makes an effort to get the musician back on his feet. This film provides an interesting depiction of the real-world effects of mental illness and the accompanying stigma.

4 Sexual Deviance

Learning Objectives

- To understand norms about sexual deviation
- To identify the demographic and social characteristics of sexual deviants
- To understand the theories that explain sexual deviations
- To identify the social and health effects of sexual deviance
- To become familiar with the policies that aim to control paraphilia
- To understand homophobia as a form of sexual deviance

Introduction

How differently we would behave in a society that assumed the purpose of sexual activity is pleasure, where different people take pleasure from different kinds of sexual activities and sexual partners.

Then, there would be no more reason for the idea of "sexual deviation" than there would be for sandwich preferences. (Obviously, some people like cheese sandwiches and others peanut butter. People who like roast beef are not labelled "sandwich deviants," except possibly in a vegan community.) Then, the traditional distinctions would make no sense and have no social acceptance. However, our society *does* make rigid distinctions of these kinds; as a result, many people are secretly, or publicly, sexual deviants. In some cases they deviate intentionally and in other cases they do so unintentionally—as with other types of deviant behaviour we have discussed so far.

In this chapter, we will discuss three types of non-normative sexuality that are especially common in our society: violations of the sexual double standard by women; violations of sexual fidelity by married people; and violations of heteronormativity. The chapter will also discuss **fetishism**, pornography, prostitution, and sexual deviations; some are judged criminal, while others are not.

Paraphilias, a name given to sexual deviations, are any sexual desires or activities that lie outside the cultural norm. Some are harmless; some risk harming the deviant; others risk harming other people. We will provide theoretical frameworks for understanding these sexual deviations. The chapter will briefly consider alternative sociological theories of sexual deviance to help us understand why we consider particular sexual behaviours deviant or not. The purpose of this chapter is not to argue for or against any particular sexual activities; rather, our intent is to examine the boundary line between conformity and deviance and see how it is managed.

The Double Standard and Romantic Love

Sexuality and responses to sexuality are almost always gendered. Sexual beliefs and practices, and deviations from them, are rooted in beliefs about men and women and the social roles that some people think men and women *should* occupy. This arbitrary set of distinctions results in what we call a *double standard*.

The most common form of sexual deviance, in our own and other societies, involves violating the so-called double standard: the assumption that women are supposed to behave differently from men where sexual matters are concerned. Specifically, men are supposed to want sex intensely—to be the sexual hunters—whereas women are supposed to be passive, almost asexual, when not in a monogamous relationship, and to prefer only traditional styles of sex when in a relationship (Lai and Hynie, 2010). In short, women are thought of as hunted sex objects—man's sexual prey.

This sexual objectification of women not only indicates gender inequality—it calls into question the possibility of true intimacy, passion, or **romantic love** between men and women. How can there be intimacy, passion, or love when one party—a male—is "the hunter" while the other party—a female—is "the prey"? This peculiar conception of sexuality is most marked in societies where women have the least social equality with men and, not accidentally, the highest rates of child-bearing. Child-bearing tends to increase gendered inequality within couples, just as high rates of fertility tend to increase gendered inequality within societies. Whatever lip service is paid to romantic love, the reality is a double standard that gives women much less sexual freedom than men.

In societies that value gender equality, however, sexual pleasure is equally accessible to and expected for both sexes, and in all economic and social classes; or at least, that is the norm. As a result, people—in Canada, Sweden, or Japan, for example—don't have to buy sex or marry for sex merely to satisfy their desires. Yet, even in egalitarian Scandinavia, a double standard persists. According to research on the topic, sex education there continues to characterize boys' sexual desires as instinctive and physical, without any connection to their emotion or awareness, and to characterize girls' desires as arising in their hearts and minds.

So, in some important respects, we find little difference between sexual standards in the global North and South, the developed and developing worlds. In both parts of the world, boys still have more sexual freedom. Girls still bear more responsibility for safe sex and chastity and are more controlled by gossip, rumours, and stigma. Despite liberalizing changes in the past 50 years, the double standard remains, even in economically developed countries.

That said, sexual liberation—an inevitable consequence of access to secure birth control and the economic independence of women—continues to spread around the world. More women are initiating sex and having sex outside of marriage, with multiple partners—just like their male counterparts.

Gradually, the extent of the double standard in the sexual behaviour of men and women is decreasing for younger generations, and the age of sexual initiation is decreasing as well. Throughout the industrialized West especially, more people are having more sex, with more people, at younger ages. Gradually, the double standard is growing fainter and will disappear.

Marital Infidelity

Another type of sexual deviance is marital infidelity, the intimate contact—whether sexual or emotional or both—with another partner to whom one is not married.

Estimates of the frequency of this behaviour range widely and no fully reliable data are available. The hallmark study of American sexual behaviour, by Laumann et al. (1994) at the National Opinion Research Center (NORC) in Chicago, found that about 3–4 per cent of currently married people have sexual partners besides their spouse in a given year. About 15–17 per cent of people who have been married say they have had a sexual partner other than their spouse while married.

According to Tom Smith (1998) at NORC, we have little reliable information about extramarital relations before 1988. Before then, indirect evidence suggested that extramarital relations may have been increasing over time. Seemingly, people born before about 1940 were less likely to engage in extramarital relations than married people born more recently. Current extramarital relations are seemingly more common among younger adults than among older ones.

Smith (ibid.) speculates that some recently married people may have trouble switching from a premarital pattern of multiple sexual partners to a monogamous partnership. Partly for this reason, recent marriages are more likely than long-term marriages to end in divorce. Husbands are about twice as likely as wives to engage in extramarital relations. Extramarital relations are also more common among people with lower incomes, people who attend church less often, and people who, after divorce or separation, have remarried. Not surprisingly, people who are unhappy with their marriage are also more likely to engage in extramarital relationships.

Other information about the prevalence of extramarital relations comes from family therapists, who see a lot of people for whom this has become a problem. Yet Meldrim (2005) reports that few studies have documented the impact of infidelity on the cheated spouse. The research shows that partners who have been cheated on, whether men or women, view the infidelity as a kind of abandonment; and for those with children, they view it as an abandonment of the children, too. In trying to cope with this, people turn to friends and family for support, seek professional counselling or the consolations of religion, or turn inward to focus more attention on the children.

The increase in cyberspace relationships has apparently increased the likelihood of marital infidelity at a distance. Whitty (2005), for example, studied instances of infidelity in cyberspace (i.e., through e-mail or social networking sites like Facebook or Myspace). He asked over 200 participants to write a story about infidelity on the Internet. As their stories showed, not all participants saw cyber-cheating as a real act of betrayal. However, the majority did see it as real infidelity, with as serious an impact on the couple's relationship as sexually physical infidelity. Most important of all, the *emotional* infidelity of such "cyber-affairs" was considered as important and harmful as *sexual* infidelity.

While there is much more to learn about this topic, clearly, many people think about or explore extramarital relationships, whether emotional or sexual or both, though these are deviant and violate the partner's expectations. Marital infidelity tends to be a sign of marital conflict, and when discovered, it contributes significantly to the extent of that conflict.

Heteronormativity

A third type of deviance is homosexuality, the clear violation of heteronormativity. Ironically, this type of deviance affirms what our own experiences and observations teach us is true, namely, that sexual tastes and desires vary.

In most spheres of life, we accept variations in tastes and desires. Yet this is often untrue about sexuality: we impose labels and constraints on people's tastes, designating some as normal and others as perverse. In particular, our society imposes the standard of heteronormativity. Under this standard, almost all aspects of social life are built on the assumption that all ("normal") people are heterosexual. Gradually, however, this view of sexuality has been changing.

Certain key figures in social and sexual thought have helped change Western thinking about sex over the past century. Sigmund Freud, the founder of psychoanalysis, produced a comprehensive theory of human development in which sexual development and sexual identity played a large part. He proposed that the development of a healthy adult personality depends on the successful passage through stages of psychosocial and psychosexual development. English author and scientist Henry Havelock Ellis (1859–1939), in his classic work *Psychopathia Sexualis*, also challenged accepted sexual norms in Victorian England (famous for its sexually repressive norms and abundance of secret erotic literature). He assured his readers that masturbation does *not* lead to illness and that homosexuality is *not* a disease but an innate variation from the norm, rather than a vice or amoral choice.

Far more influential was the American zoologist Alfred Kinsey, who carried out a statistical study of human sexuality. Kinsey (1894–1956) argued that human sexuality has goals other than reproduction—most especially, pleasure. He criticized biologists and psychologists who assumed that heterosexual responses are part of an animal's innate or instinctive equipment and especially the views that non-reproductive sexual activities (such as masturbation or foreplay) are abnormal. Kinsey was famous for arguing that homosexual and heterosexual inclinations are points on a continuum; sexual orientation is not either/or—heterosexual versus homosexual. Further, he declared that no position on the sexual continuum is intrinsically normal or abnormal.

Although the popular conception of human sexuality may rest on a distinction between heterosexuality and homosexuality, Kinsey was right to argue that this is far too limited a view of sexuality. Such a bipolar conception of human sexuality fails to account for the full spectrum of sexual tastes, which includes bisexuality and pansexuality. This dualism has impeded the acceptance of people who don't fit neatly into only the heterosexual or homosexual community. Certain myths—such as that bisexuals are confused about their sexuality or that bisexuality is merely a pit stop on the way to homosexuality—have forced many bisexuals and pansexuals to pass as one of the larger group in both the queer and straight communities.

Typically, this "passing" takes the form of a double life, where one acts straight around heterosexuals and queer around homosexuals. As a result, even after coming out, bisexuals and pansexuals may nevertheless feel closeted, as if they must conform to the sexual norms of both communities, yet are unable to openly act on their desires. The inability to properly tolerate bisexuals and pansexuals may represent a problem within the queer community, showing that it is as narrow-minded in its sexual focus as the heterosexual community it has criticized.

Recently, some efforts have been made to gain public acceptance for polyamorous relationships, in which people may have multiple partners of either sex. Whatever the outcome of these efforts, it is clear that we are surrounded by changes in public attitude towards sexuality and sexual variety. These changes signify a continued trend towards understanding sex as a form of intimate pleasure with numerous legitimate, idiosyncratic forms within a growing context of gender equality.

The History of Sexual Deviance and Public Reactions

Social views about sexuality are not static and Canadian public opinion about sexual topics has changed dramatically in the last three decades. Consider attitudes regarding same-sex intimacy and marriage: today, fewer Canadians view homosexuality as immoral or worthy of criminalization, as many did in the past.

Tolerance for homosexuality is widespread today, though the practice itself remains relatively rare. Recent surveys have gathered information about the prevalence of homosexuality in Canada, with relatively uniform results. The Canadian Community Health Survey, Cycle 2.1 (2004), was the first—and most recent—government survey to include a question on sexual orientation. In that survey, among Canadians aged 18–59, 1 per cent reported that they consider themselves to be homosexual and 0.7 per cent considered themselves to be bisexual. About 1.3 per cent of men considered themselves homosexual, about twice the proportion among women (0.7 per cent).

In the US, Smith (1998) reports that "few debates have been so contentious as the controversy over the sexual orientation of Americans." Though gay and lesbian communities sometimes assert that as much as 10 per cent of the population is homosexual, national surveys in the US and Canada suggest the true figure is closer to 2–3 per cent of sexually active men and 1–2 per cent of sexually active women. What's more, these findings are also consistent with findings in local communities, as well as statistics from several Western European countries including the United Kingdom, France, Norway, and Denmark.

Studies of male and female homosexuality both in North America and Europe regularly find a higher fraction of males who are gay than females who are lesbian. These figures, however, may vary depending on the *definition* of homosexuality: i.e., whether the definition includes people who had sex with a same-sex partner only once or twice or those who used to have same-sex relations but are now in long-term heterosexual relationships. In addition, some people may not feel comfortable identifying as homosexual or bisexual, even though they may not completely identify as heterosexual.

Despite the increased visibility and acceptance of homosexuals, some people still remain hostile to them, and we will discuss these people at greater length in this chapter. It is only through the survival of these anti-homosexuals that we can continue to view homosexuality as a deviant sexuality; for, as stated earlier, without labelling and stigmatization, deviance does not exist for sociologists. Yet, because of its transitional status, it is no longer possible to categorize homosexuality by traditional standards.

According to Gagnon and Simon (1967), sexual deviance can be broken down along three main dimensions: incidence or frequency; the level of invoked sanctions; and the existence of a specialized social structure that arises to support this type of sexual activity.

Using this classification scheme, we can identify a few major types of sexual deviance. First, there is behaviour that is relatively common but invites few sanctions despite receiving some public disapproval—for example, premarital sex and masturbation. Even in the 1960s, Gagnon and Simon found that almost all men and (at least) two-thirds of the female population engaged in masturbation, despite the stated taboos against it. This type of sexual deviance is so common it is referred to as "normal" deviance. There is no specialized community to support premarital sex or masturbation—perhaps a testimony to the lack of need for such community support.

The second category of sexual deviance is relatively rare and tends to violate both laws and public mores. It is deemed pathological deviance by most people and includes pedophilia, voyeurism, incest, exhibitionism, and aggressive sexual offences. There is some evidence of communities that support and practise these types of sexual deviance: for example, networks of people who exchange and sell sexually explicit pictures of children. However, if this is indeed a community, it is an underground community and we know little about its structure.

The third and final type of sexual deviance is relatively common and is widely disapproved, though widely practised. The best example is female prostitution—what has been called the world's oldest profession. Here, as with homosexuality, public norms and official sanctions are changing rapidly; and as with homosexuality, we see the growth of community structure to provide supports to people involved in this community. We will have more to say about homosexual neighbourhoods later in this chapter. We will note here that prostitutes have increasingly organized themselves to fight for better protection from the law.

Prostitution

Though prostitution is found everywhere, it is especially common among people who are impoverished and socially vulnerable. Women and children are more likely to enter into prostitution in many parts of the world: they are often simply considered less valuable than adult men. A sexual double standard, poverty, and an unequal labour market increase the frequency and likelihood of prostitution. Women and children sell sex when they have no other ways to get money, especially in societies without a strong social safety net.

Some families may even drive their members into prostitution. In poor countries where old people dominate the family, young people—male and female—may be forced into the sex trade and expected to turn over almost all of their earnings to the family elders. While despairing about their plight, the sex workers recognize and respond to these societal norms, and a continuing sense of filial duty often leads them to comply with their parents' wishes. Women who continue to practise prostitution suffer serious health risks (including sexually transmitted diseases or STDs, physical abuse, and homicide) and stigmatization. As well, "floating" sex workers, who return to their families after work, suffer from the sense of leading a discreditable double life.

How the Sex Trade Works

Throughout history, prostitutes have fallen into three classes, with the lowest being prostitutes of the streets. These women were originally slaves, and in later times were drawn from the ranks of the entrenched poor. The next class includes women who work in brothels or similar facilities; typically, they came from working-class backgrounds. The upper classes of prostitutes, historically, are the courtesans—providers of sex to the wealthiest and most aristocratic members of society, at the highest rates of payment. In every society, we can find a similar hierarchy of workers providing sex for money. In Canada, women who work for so-called escort services might be included in this upper category.

Classic Works

BOX 4.1

Kingsley Davis on "The Sociology of Prostitution" (1937)

Davis's classic paper tries to explain the seeming paradox that prostitution flourishes in our society even though many claim to despise it as a social evil. What's more, prostitution flourishes even though people claim to revere marriage. Marriage is widely respected as an institution because it ensures legitimate reproduction; it also encourages physical and emotional intimacy in exclusive relationships. By contrast, prostitution is disrespected because sexual relations with a prostitute are shallow and sterile.

Nonetheless, prostitution is universal and it persists. Why? Davis believes the persistence of prostitution is explained by human nature: in particular, people want and need sex. Marriage satisfies this need, but not for everyone and in many cases not well enough. Society places limits on "proper" sexuality, even for married couples, frowning on certain forms of sexual pleasure. This means the demand for "improper" sex has to be satisfied outside marriage.

Not only is there a persistent demand for sex outside marriage, but there is also a persistent supply. Invariably, some people—chiefly, women—will sell sex for money, at a price much cheaper than the cost of marrying and maintaining a wife. This holds true even as women's other job opportunities multiply and wage rates increase. As these alternate opportunities increase, fewer women may enter prostitution, but then the price of sex increases, bringing more women back into prostitution. Since prostitution, in Davis's words, "comes perilously near the situation of getting something for nothing" when compared to marriage (1937: 750), there will always be a financial incentive to become a prostitute and to use a prostitute.

For clients, prostitution takes care of the sexual needs that are not satisfied by other institutions. Historically, it also has provided a sexual outlet for armies of men away from home and country, and for the many people in society who, for various reasons, find it impossible to mate with a regular partner. Indeed, prostitution remains a threat to marriage because it provides some of the same benefits. However, marriage fulfills more social functions, so prostitution remains a social evil, if not a crime. No wonder prostitutes pay a steep price in social status. Sexual liberality—for example, premarital sex—may reduce the demand for prostitution, but limits on "proper" sexuality remain, preserving marriage and "normal" dating. In the end, prostitution is less of a threat to marriage than complete sexual liberty.

Time to Reflect: How might Kingsley Davis respond to the observation that a large fraction of prostitutes—perhaps a majority—begin their "profession" in their teens and have a history of psychological and sexual abuse?

In Canada, prostitution itself is not illegal. However, one could be arrested for prostitution-related offences such as solicitation, bawdy house offences, or procuring. These offences target those sex workers who are more visible to the public eye and thus easily targeted by authorities. As a result, the poorest paid, most socially vulnerable prostitutes—streetwalkers—are also the most liable to arrest. Even in areas where prostitution is illegal, well-known places to buy sex exist. On the street level, they are referred to as "tracks."

Sex work, as a business, is about relations of production—relations between a prostitute, her client, and, possibly, her pimp. Street-level prostitution includes both pimp-controlled prostitution and independent entrepreneurial prostitution. Pimp-related violence is common for women involved in pimp-controlled prostitution. Female prostitutes are, in many senses, often at the mercy of their pimps. More will be said about this in connection with the global sex trade.

Everywhere, the relationship between sex workers and their clients is unequal. And everywhere, sex work infiltrates the family life of sex workers. Whether in Uganda, India, or Mexico, most female sex workers must constantly switch between the respected role of mother and disrespected role of prostitute. In doing so, they face society's double standard for women daily. Often they must even hide their profession from their families to avoid punishment for breaching the ideal of female purity. As a result, they lead split lives, dividing their personalities between the mother/saint and prostitute/sinner roles.

Perhaps because of the disrespect and deprivation they suffer, prostitutes often have difficulty mobilizing for their own protection and advancement. Some sex workers have tried to improve their health and social standing by forming advocacy groups. In various locales, prostitutes have organized politically and expressed their grievances in the public debate about prostitution—a debate from which they have often been excluded.

Why People Enter the Sex Trade

Some prostitutes get their start as unwilling participants in a "slave trade" or as victims of someone who has forced them to sell their bodies for money. Although this is rife in some countries, in North America most prostitutes have chosen to sell sex for money, and no one has forced them to do so. One expert has estimated that no more than 4 per cent are pushed into the sex trade here (Thio, 1998).

However, in saying this we immediately confront definitional difficulties. What do we really mean by "choice" or "free choice"? Though few prostitutes in our society have been forced into prostitution, a high percentage has been physically or sexually abused in their youth. The resulting drop in their self-esteem may have contributed to their "choice" of occupation. In this sense, they were pushed into prostitution by their traumatic childhood experiences.

Usually, people enter the sex trade because they are desperate for money—they are desperately poor—or they are fleeing something worse than poverty. Since the average age at which a sex worker enters the sex trade is around 14, fleeing from abusive homes would translate directly into a need for money. However, at the age of 14, what kinds of potential work are available to them? For example, Alberta Children's Services states that 85 per cent of sex workers were sexually abused as children before entering the trade.

Some women become dependent on abusive men, relying on them either for practical or financial help as they struggle to move from welfare to work. Some disadvantaged and vulnerable women become enmeshed in even more dangerous dependencies as they lose their welfare eligibility and fall into drug addiction and sex work.

The survival of prostitution today depends on a continuing sexual double standard, widespread global poverty, dysfunctional families, and unequal opportunities for women in the labour market. People—usually women—drift into prostitution or sex work because they are poor, suffer from addiction, or have been abused. While in "the life," prostitutes risk physical abuse and contracting deadly diseases. These facts make it hard to insist that prostitution is a profession, career, or form of work in the same sense as—say—secretarial work, teaching, engineering, law, or sales. That doesn't mean, however, that we should fail to regulate prostitution in the interests of the prostitutes themselves.

The Traffic in Sex

Prostitutes from Eastern Europe, Asia, and Latin America are appearing everywhere in the prosperous West. The rapid expansion and diversification of an international sex trade can be attributed to the rise in service occupations and temporary work for women; to an increase in labour migration, tourism, and business travel; to the growth in transnational organized crime; and to the explosion of corporate–commercial wealth and conspicuous consumption by the very wealthy.

Throughout the world, young women suffer the assaults of war, and in addition face the escalating levels of sexual and domestic violence, poverty, and social dislocation that war brings. International criminal rackets exploit the invisibility of poor girls in war zones for illegal sexual, domestic, and industrial labour.

The creation of massive poverty and transience—by war and global economic dislocation, among other things—leaves tens of millions of young people looking for work of any kind, at almost any price. The result is a global trafficking of sex.

It is hard to regulate sexual trafficking largely because of the complex worldwide refugee issue. New government departments and multinational organizations have developed to handle the problem. Nonetheless, much difficulty remains in discovering which kinds of refugees are legitimate and should be allowed to enter the country.

The attempt by some to substitute "sex work" for "prostitution" serves to hide the harm and danger many prostitutes face. Prostitution is not just another kind of work, like waiting on tables or practising dentistry, and prostitutes don't represent a random sample of the working public. There is a growing recognition that they deserve more protection than they have received in the past—a recognition reflected in policies concerning the arrest of those suspected of prostitution-related offences. Previously, women were unfairly targeted in these offences, yet there has been a shift from the focus on prostitutes to the focus on their clients, the "johns" (Fischer et al., 2002).

This reflects the shift from seeing a prostitute as a deviant to seeing a prostitute as a victim. There has been a conscious effort in many jurisdictions to change the discourse on prostitution, as evident in a press release from the Vancouver police that stated: "The root cause of Vancouver's street prostitution trade is the men who purchase or who recruit and control (pimp) juvenile or adult sex workers. Our limited resources are focused on pimps and 'johns' and other abusers. . . . If we can reduce the demand, the supply will decrease" (Lowman, 1998: 943).

For the first time, prostitutes are engaging in a public discourse in which they previously had no voice. But, as with most stigmatized populations, their entry into the public debate faces many difficulties. For example, they are limited in what they can say openly about the world of prostitution—a largely hidden, competitive, and violent world with important links to organized crime.

Pornography

Another common form of sexual deviance is the production and consumption of pornography. This behaviour is not deviant because it is uncommon, but because it transgresses traditional norms about the depiction of sexual activities.

Pornography is the forthright description or exhibition of sexual activity in literature, films, or otherwise, intended to stimulate erotic rather than aesthetic feelings. There is a lot of debate over whether pornography is healthy or pathological and how it should be controlled. The issues are pressing. On the one hand, there are concerns about pornography's effects on children. On the other hand, a great deal of money is changing hands, and the people profiting want to prevent any serious controls on their profit-making.

Today, pornography is a multi-billion-dollar worldwide business with alleged links to organized crime. So-called soft-porn magazines are available at every convenience store, with rougher material widely available at adult entertainment outlets. Pornography's popularity is seemingly exploding as the legal restrictions on the depiction of sex (in movies, television, and magazines) continue to weaken.

The essence of pornography is *easy sex*: sex without limits or commitments. Heterosexual pornography creates utopias of sexual abundance—especially an abundance of attractive, naked, sexually obedient women for men who might otherwise have trouble (in reality) getting a date with one such woman, let alone several. No wonder the chief theme of pornography is profusion and gluttony—an unending, unquenchable desire for sex.

Though modern means of mass communication have made pornography more readily available than ever, pornography itself is nothing new. It emerged centuries ago with the growth of popular literacy. The increasing availability and development of a market for pornography went hand in hand with the expansion of print culture, as part of the private consumption of printed material for private pleasure. With the growth of photography, movies, and television, the (visual) media have played a key role in "sexualizing" modern life. Since the late nineteenth century, pornography has relocated from elite society to mass culture, and vast amounts of pornographic material can be accessed on the Internet.

The media are partly responsible for teaching understandings of sexuality, as well as reflecting them, and people partially learn their sexual roles and responsibilities through the media. Some believe that the spread of more tolerant sexual understanding through pornography should be viewed positively. In many respects, it is argued, pornography has benefited women's and gay rights movements, increased public awareness of certain health issues, challenged conventional notions of sexuality, and undermined patriarchal dominance in particular societies.

The social role of pornography—whether positive or negative—is of particular interest to feminist sociologists, since women are the "sex objects" or commodities portrayed in most pornography. As a result, feminist scholars were among the first to see the body as a legitimate area of sociological inquiry. Accordingly, they have produced a large literature that examines the link between the mass media commodification of women's bodies and various personal troubles such as low self-esteem, eating disorders, and the increasing use of cosmetic surgery.

An area of continuing concern is the display and consumption of pornography depicting children. While many view this pornography to be a form of child abuse, Ost (2002) wonders whether there has been a moral panic about child pornography and the mere possession of such material. More research is needed to establish the existence of a causal link between possessing child pornography and the act of committing child sexual abuse; also, research needs to show that criminalizing the possession of child pornography reduces the market for such material. The real issue, however, is that for child pornography to exist in the first place, children were exploited.

A new and growing problem is posed by the spread of Internet pornography and Internet communication for sexual purposes. Some efforts have been made in other societies to protect children from online predators, who use the Internet to lure children for sexual purposes.

Other Forms of Sexual Deviation

Paraphilia is a general name for any kind of sexual deviation or departure from the norm, such as any persistent, intense sexual interest, fantasy, or urge that may involve non-human objects, pain or humiliation, children, or non-consenting individuals. At the extremes, paraphilia may interfere with the capacity for sexual activity with consenting adult partners.

There is disagreement regarding which sexual interests should be deemed paraphilic disorders versus normal variants of sexual interest. The Diagnostic and Statistical Manual of Mental Disorders (DSM) provides clinical criteria for paraphilia and defines these behaviours as follows:

- *Exhibitionism*: the recurrent urge or behaviour to expose one's genitals to an unsuspecting person; or, the recurrent urge to perform sexual acts in a public place or in view of unsuspecting persons.
- *Frotteurism*: the recurrent urge or behaviour of touching or rubbing against a non-consenting person.
- *Pedophilia*: the sexual attraction to prepubescent or peripubescent children.
- *Sexual masochism*: the recurrent urge or behaviour of wanting to be humiliated, beaten, bound, or otherwise made to suffer for sexual pleasure.
- *Sexual sadism*: the recurrent urge or behaviour involving acts in which the pain or humiliation of a person is sexually exciting.
- *Voyeurism*: the recurrent urge or behaviour to observe an unsuspecting person who is naked, disrobing, or engaging in sexual activities, or may not be sexual in nature at all.
- *Fetishism*: the use of inanimate objects to gain sexual excitement.
- *Partialism*: refers to fetishes specifically involving non-sexual parts of the body.
- *Transvestic fetishism*: a sexual attraction to the clothing of the opposite gender. (American Psychiatric Association, 2004)

Psychoanalyst Sigmund Freud was among the first to describe **sexual fetishism**—a form of sexual deviance that focuses attention on a specific object or body part. Fetishism, like other forms of sexuality, can be extremely varied and affect almost any aspect of human behaviour. Almost anything can become a fetish, compulsion, obsession, or addiction. Like other compulsions, obsessions, and addictions, sexual fetishism is generally considered a problem when it causes distress or begins to interfere with social functioning.

Voyeurism is another type of sexual deviance that is non-criminal if it is a consensual act. Voyeurs seek sexual pleasure by viewing other people either in states of undress or having sex. Considered a deviant sexual act in most cultures, voyeurism is most frequently practised by males. Likely, male voyeurism is related to male dominance, the objectification of women in our society, and the **sexual gaze** that puts women under male scrutiny at all times.

Time to Reflect: What is the likely connection between voyeurism and pornography? And if voyeurism is considered deviant, why is pornography considered legal and socially permissible in many contexts?

Sadism is taking sexual pleasure from inflicting (physical) pain and suffering on another person. It takes its name from the Marquis de Sade, who wrote voluminously on sexual experimentation, pain, and pleasure in eighteenth-century France. Although the Marquis de Sade noted that many engaged in non-consenting practices, today consent is a tenet of the behaviour. The counterpart of sadism is masochism, named after the nineteenth-century Count von Masoch. Masochists take sexual pleasure from being beaten, humiliated, bound, tortured, or otherwise made to suffer. Sadists and masochists belong to the larger BDSM community.

The acronym BDSM is derived from three practices: bondage and discipline (B/D), dominance and submission (D/s), and sadism and masochism (S/M). Although the BDSM community includes these three practices it is not the case that each member necessarily practices all three of them (Lenius, 2001).

The BDSM community was originally a primarily gay male community; now it includes members of every sexuality and has been the most accepting of pansexuals. The main goal of BDSM is to create a safe place where people can test personal boundaries and redefine for themselves what constitutes sex and what is erotic. This often takes the form of role-playing. The willingness to experiment often creates an open, thoroughly pansexual environment.

According to some psychoanalytic accounts, masochists feel guilt about something and feel that they need to be punished for it. Such theories rest on popular myth about BDSM, which has generally been debunked. Those participating in BDSM are no more likely than the general public to suffer from anxiety, depression, obsessive-compulsive disorder, or psychological sadism or masochism, and men who participate in BDSM tend to score lower on tests of psychological distress (Richters et al., 2008; Connolly, 2006). People who report having practised BDSM tend to be a part of the queer community and are more likely to have watched pornography, used sex toys, participated in group sex, had sex with someone other than their regular partner, had phone sex, and had anal sex. Participation in BDSM is reportedly not related to age, education, or sexual dysfunction, and BDSM participants did not report having ever been coerced (Richters et al., 2008).

Criminal Paraphilia

So far, we have discussed paraphilia that is consensual and is not considered criminal. However, some paraphilia, such as pedophilia, is non-consensual and is therefore criminalized.

Pedophilia is probably one of the most common criminal paraphilias in our society today. Two-thirds of molested children are girls, usually between the ages of eight and 11. Most pedophiles are men, but there are cases of women having repeated sexual contact with children. Although uninformed people often cite pedophilia as a reason for excluding or mistreating homosexuals, pedophiles are rarely people who practise homosexuality with other consenting adults. Pedophiles, whether homosexual or heterosexual, are people who gain their sexual pleasure from people who are below the age of consent. While many pedophiles seduce and abuse strangers, they seduce and abuse the children of family members and friends far more commonly.

Sado-Masochistic Communities and Cultures

Deviants often build communities for support and protection; the gay and lesbian communities provide the best possible example. SM communities, or at least SM networks, also exist, not only for the obvious reason that people with shared interests group together but because, beyond the community, sado-masochists are often labelled as sexual perverts.

These communities provide support and protection. In many urban centres in Canada and elsewhere, there exists a lively subculture of sado-masochists. They are a varied group that includes people of different sexual orientations, religions, socio-economic classes, races, and ages. Though open to any individual, this community is usually composed of members over the age of 30. Estimates of community membership are few and unreliable.

Some would-be members of this community say they have trouble joining the lifestyle. Most sado-masochists have to take two steps before they can fully engage: admitting to themselves that they are interested in SM and accepting that SM is a natural or "normal" part of sexuality. Once they have entered, the community supports their desires, helping them overcome loneliness. The SM community provides structure and support through the formation of organizations and meeting places (ibid.). In other words, just like ethnic communities, sexually deviant communities provide "institutional completeness," which includes meeting places where members are introduced to each other and get support for what many label as their deviant behaviour.

Swingers, too, develop community ties and social institutions that help them come together for sexual purposes. Recently, the Supreme Court of Canada declared that swingers clubs are legal, thereby opening the door to other such institutions for varied sexual communities.

Homosexual Communities and Cultures

Homosexuality is a sexual orientation characterized by a sexual or romantic attraction to people of the same sex. For males, we use the term *gay*; for females, we use the term *lesbian*. For a long time, homosexuality was considered a form of paraphilia or sexual deviance.

So far as we know, people with homosexual desires constitute a small minority of the population—probably far less than 10 per cent, though the estimates are imprecise. As the data in Table 4.1 show, the true numbers are probably closer to 1–2 per cent, and these numbers vary slightly from one province to another.

In many communities, homosexuals are still stigmatized and may suffer discrimination at work, in school, and in the community. Canadians are becoming less tolerant of such exclusionary and discriminatory attitudes and treatment, but it still persists. Many Canadians feel there is no excuse for letting ignorance and intolerance damage the self-esteem of gay, lesbian, bisexual, transgender, and questioning people. Yet, our culture as a whole does not completely approve of homosexual behaviour. Some Canadians continue to display traditional cultural norms about love and sex, which, since they are rooted in the goal of child-bearing, are intrinsically heterosexual.

In response, homosexuals, pansexuals, and bisexuals manage stigma by forming supportive networks and communities. All non-heterosexuals are represented in the queer community, where the term *queer* has been reclaimed to describe any deviant sexual behaviour and where **queer theory** has risen to challenge the assumptions of male–female binary thinking about sexuality. Given the differences between gay men, lesbians, bisexuals, and pansexuals, each group tends to create its own subculture for support and friendship. These communities have a special "language" that helps to distinguish its members from the out-groups, and many have special meeting places where members can gather, usually at certain coffee shops, cafés, and clubs. Each community develops its own subcultural norms and values, a milieu in which their members can live safely and comfortably, and provide social support with an information medium for its members.

The problems homosexuals face when they are in a hostile subculture are well illustrated by the story in Box 4.2, on anti-homosexual attitudes in professional sport.

Like many minority groups, the queer community has sought to educate, form organizations, change laws, and build their own institutions in order to shed their caste-like status. John D'Emilio (1983) dates the beginning of the homosexual subculture, as we see it today, to World War II. That war separated the sexes somewhat and gave homosexuals more

Current Events

BOX 4.2

Sexual Orientation in the Big Leagues

In May 2011, Rick Welts, president and chief executive of the Phoenix Suns basketball team, openly discussed his homosexuality with the *New York Times*, effectively coming out in an industry that remains largely uncomfortable with the subject. However, Welts's co-worker, Alvin Gentry, head coach for the Suns, wasn't bothered at all by this admission, and fellow team member Steve Nash offered his support. Reactions to Welts's coming out therefore weren't unanimously negative.

Still, it's obvious that Welts took a great risk in opening up about his homosexuality, considering the anti-gay attitudes that pervade professional sports. Basketball superstar Kobe Bryant, for example, was fined $100,000 for calling a referee a "faggot" after the referee gave him a foul. Former Pittsburgh Steeler Joey Porter also used the slur against an opposing football player in 2006. And the Chicago Blackhawks devised a "gay distraction" plan as part of their strategy to win the NHL playoffs—the strategy entailed ridiculing Chris Pronger (of the Philadelphia Flyers) by showing images of him dressed in a skirt.

Evidently, anti-gay sentiments abound within the professional sports world. By coming out, Welts aims to challenge these attitudes. He says he wants to offer guidance to gay people who feel their homosexuality prevents them from pursuing careers in sports. However, he is not alone in his desire to change anti-homosexual attitudes. In an effort to discourage homophobia, the NBA has initiated a public service campaign called "Think B4 You Speak." The ads target adolescents, and use Phoenix Suns stars Jared Dudley and Grant Hill to discourage discriminatory language. In the ad, Hill says, "Using gay to mean dumb or stupid—not cool."

Reactions to this effort have been mixed. Some feel that the ad campaign and monetary punishments for anti-homosexual speech demonstrate the NBA's commitment to initiating change and developing a gay-safe environment. However, some players remain unfazed by these fines and continue to make their anti-gay sentiments clear. Some feel that these ads and fines haven't been very effective and much more needs to be done. An example is Toronto Maple Leafs GM Brian Burke, whose son Brendan came out of the closet shortly before he died in a car accident. Burke and his other son continue to make efforts to improve tolerance in sports. As Burke said in a 2010 interview with the *Toronto Star*, "Of course there are gay hockey players . . . [but] they don't feel it's a safe environment to come out."

Sources: Frank Cerabino, "Gay-Slur Fines Show Basketball Has Standards," *Palm Beach Post*, May 2011; Laura Dunhoff and Sue Kerr, "Yet Another Anti-Gay Rant; It's Time for the Steelers and Other Pro Sports Teams to Confront the Homophobia in Their Ranks," *Pittsburgh Post*, July 2011; Zosia Bielski, "What Happens When Gay Male Execs Come Out?" *Globe and Mail* blog, 16 May 2011, at: <www.theglobeandmail.com/life/the-hot-button/what-happens-when-gay-male-execs-come-out/article2024122/>.

access to other homosexuals. Later, cities like San Francisco and New York began to attract homosexuals to "the gay life." The growth of gay communities also coincided with reports by researchers such as Kinsey that challenged the accepted definitions of sexuality.

TABLE 4.1 Reported Sexual Orientation, Canada, 2003

	Homosexual or Bisexual	
	Number	**% of Total Population**
Total	316,800	1.7
Newfoundland and Labrador	4,100*	1.3*
Prince Edward Island	**	**
Nova Scotia	5,900*	1.1*
New Brunswick	7,200A	1.6*
Quebec	103,400	2.3
Ontario	107,200	1.5
Manitoba	9,600*	1.5*
Saskatchewan	6,600*	1.2*
Alberta	23,400*	1.2*
British Columbia	47,700	1.9
Male	172,600	1.8
Female	144,300	1.5
18–34	139,200	2.0
35–44	101,900	1.9
45–59	75,700	1.2

*Use with caution.

**Suppressed due to high sampling variability.

Source: Statistics Canada, "Canadian Community Health Survey," *The Daily*, 15 June 2004, at: <www.statcan.gc.ca/daily-quotidien/040615/dq040615b-eng.htm>.

Homosexuality came into sharper focus during the late 1950s and 1960s. Beginning in San Francisco, the gay and lesbian movement formed an identity around sexual orientation that gained attention throughout the United States. This residential clustering also meant that homosexuals could more freely meet and engage in the gay subculture.

Today, these communities have expanded to become more inclusive, and sizable queer communities exist in numerous North American cities, including Toronto. Not only are these communities and their members increasingly visible—they are increasingly celebrated. Work by geographer and policy researcher Richard Florida, for example, has argued that cities with large homosexual populations typically have high levels of artistic and intellectual creativity, which are key to the development of new knowledge-based economies. According to Florida's template for the "creative city," a high degree of innovativeness and economic growth in the service sector is one result, as is a high quality of life for city residents. So, in this case as in many others, human diversity is seen to pay off economically, as well as socially and culturally.

Anti-Homosexuality as a Form of Sexual Deviance

In North America, sexual minorities are finally receiving the legal rights and social acceptance they deserve as citizens. Yet, as we have noted, many people still fear and hate homosexuals. Such attitudes of fear and hate have traditionally been called **homophobia**. This type of behaviour creates conflict and occasionally violence; and, increasingly, it is becoming a form of deviance.

The idea of "homophobia" first came into use in the 1970s, when anti-homosexuality was viewed as an irrational and persistent fear of homosexuality—a psychopathology, like claustrophobia (fear of closed spaces) or ophidiophobia (fear of snakes). Over the years, however, popular thinking has changed. People today are more likely to think of hostility to homosexuals as something more akin to xenophobia—a fear of or hostility towards strangers—and not necessarily a psychopathology. It is a subcultural outlook, not a psychiatric condition. So, today, it is probably more common to speak about "heteronormativity" or "heterosexism" to emphasize that we are speaking about a preference that is culturally promoted in certain population subgroups. More simply, in this chapter we will refer to "anti-homosexuality," because it is a simple, learned cultural habit for most people. Perhaps only at the extremes can we still view anti-homosexuality as a psychiatric issue—that is, as homophobia. Adorno et al. (1950), in their study of the "authoritarian personality," found both xenophobia and homophobia to be related to each other and to other unhealthy and anti-social states of mind. However, that is an extreme version of the anti-homosexual trait.

Progress in the Canadian acceptance of homosexuals has been significant in the past few decades, perhaps dating to then Justice Minister Pierre Trudeau's famous remark in 1967 that "the state has no place in the bedrooms of the nation." This acceptance is especially marked among certain kinds of people. The ruling principle is that more sexual experience reduces fearfulness about sex. For example, childhood sex play predicts earlier non-marital sexual activity in adolescence and young adulthood. In turn, premarital experiences reduce marital fearfulness about sex. People with first- or second-hand knowledge of premarital sex, extramarital sex, or homosexuality are less hostile to homosexuals than people with more limited sexual knowledge and experience.

Another ruling principle is that familiarity breeds acceptance. People who know homosexuals personally are less often hostile to homosexuals than people who do not. Personal contact with homosexual friends and relatives has more influence on attitudes toward gays and lesbians than any other social or demographic variable.

In addition, class and education correlate with anti-homosexuality. In part, these factors may operate through the principle of familiarity: people from larger communities, with more education and higher class origins (therefore larger, more varied social networks), are more likely to know homosexual people. As well, higher social class and educational attainment may reduce anti-homosexuality by increasing a sense of self-worth. People with low status and a less secure position in society may have less self-worth; this may give them more reason to attack and oppose vulnerable groups like homosexuals.

Another social factor characterizing people hostile to homosexuals is their place of residence. Rural areas are especially problematic for homosexuals since few gay communities exist there. Living in a rural area seriously restricts their opportunities for help-seeking and help-giving. As well, rural attitudes and values often inhibit gays' use of available mental health services. In contrast to rural people, urban people are more tolerant of homosexuals, and this tolerance includes a willingness to protect the civil liberties of homosexuals. Moreover, they are willing to allow free expression to people with non-conformist political views.

Anti-homosexuality is more often found among men than among women. Study after study confirms this gender difference. Sex of the target is also important; typically, heterosexual men are more hostile to gay men than to lesbians. Gender-specific anti-homosexuality may be connected to male bonding. As well, research shows that anti-homosexuality is related to heterosexism—a belief in the moral superiority of heterosexual institutions and practices.

Learned attitudes also affect the probability of being hostile to homosexuals. The best single predictor of anti-gay sentiment is sex-role rigidity: a belief in the need to keep women "in their place." Sex-role confusion, too, may explain why men are more prejudiced against homosexuals than women and why gay men elicit more negative reactions than lesbians.

People committed to traditional sex roles tend to show high levels of anti-homosexuality and low levels of openness to intimacy. Likewise, male college students who endorse traditional sex roles are often hostile to homosexuals, avoid revealing their emotions to female (though not to male) friends, and favour unequal decision-making power in relations with their intimate partner.

Homosociality, a social preference for members of one's own gender, is also strongly correlated with anti-homosexuality. Since male homosocial groups exclude both women and gays, anti-homosexuality and anti-femininity—though distinct—are highly correlated. Both are also correlated with the inability to form intimate non-sexual relationships.

Finally, the literature continues to report that religiosity and social conservatism, variously measured, contribute to anti-homosexuality. This pattern may be rooted in a larger syndrome of traits that Adorno et al. (1950) refer to as the **authoritarian personality**. In this context, people who are hostile to homosexuals tend to be conservative, anti-democratic, racist, superstitious, and opposed to the inspection of their own or other people's feelings.

Media Depictions of Sexual Deviance

The Queercore filmmaking movement of the 1970s, 1980s, and 1990s resulted in a powerful presence of deviant sexual identities in American mass media. Beginning with the works of directors such as Kenneth Anger, Andy Warhol, and Gus Van Sant, American filmmakers began openly discussing homosexuality and bisexuality. The mass media's willingness to discuss homosexuality has been rather remarkable, as homosexuality went from existing on Hollywood's fringe in late 1960s movies such as *Scorpio Rising* to being the subject of Oscar-winning films such as *Philadelphia* in less than a generation.

Today, discussions of queer sexuality and the inclusion of queer characters are commonplace in movies and on television. While TV shows like *Barney Miller* and *Cheers* had dealt in passing with queer culture in the 1980s, it was with the enormously popular *Will and Grace* that the queer community gained greater visibility in television. The present popularity of *Glee*, Ellen Degeneres, *The L Word, Queer as*

Folk, and the Oscar-nominated film *The Kids Are Alright* are all a testament to an increasing tolerance in American media.

However, it would be folly to claim that the mass media deal in a particularly nuanced way with all deviant sexual identities. Many depictions of queer characters rely on stereotypes and myths. For example, gay men are often depicted as extremely effeminate in their mode of dress or speech. Further, subcultures within the queer community are rarely portrayed in the media. Rarely is bisexuality considered a natural sexual disposition, meaning it remains less accepted on television than homosexuality and is usually treated frivolously, as a fleeting interest of young people, as seen in the 2002 film, *The Rules of Attraction*, and on television shows like *House* and *The OC*.

Media depictions of bisexual characters, especially bisexual women, typically correspond to heterosexual male fantasies and are used to attract audiences. Kangasvuo (2007) describes the media's depiction of bisexual women as "pornification," that is, a popular concept from pornography has been incorporated by the media. As a result, rather than accurately depicting the lived experiences of bisexuals, the media tend to depict bisexuals as hypersexual females.

Similarly, other modes of sexual deviance are rarely depicted with accuracy on television and in movies, and when they are they often become central plot elements rather than simply being one characteristic of the character's personality (the movie ***Secretary*** [2002] is good example of this). **BDSM** has recently begun to enjoy a great deal more visibility in the media (e.g., Rihanna's music video for "S&M"). However, those who do not practice **BDSM** reported that increased media visibility has not made them any more tolerant or more understanding of the practices (Weiss, 2006). Rather, **BDSM**, as depicted by the media, is normalized to become more acceptable and pathologized to become more understandable. For example, the mainstream movie ***Secretary*** normalizes **BDSM** relationships by showing that sadists and masochists can lead "normal" lives. However, the film ultimately pathologizes the main character as she is defined essentially by her masochism, which springs from a depressed and damaged identity. The film relies on the popular myth that masochists feel like they need to be punished and will commonly self-harm when not in a **BDSM** relationship—this myth is not supported by empirical evidence. Thus, by using popular myth, media depictions of deviant sexualities tend to police the boundaries between normal and deviant sex—the depictions help to strengthen the notion of what is normal and abnormal. And in consuming the media's depiction of deviant sexualities, audiences come to tolerate deviant sex but only insofar as it takes a particular form and is understood as the main component of a deviant character.

Time to Reflect: Why do people (apparently) find sexual deviation fascinating and entertaining as a mass media topic? Are people vicariously enjoying the deviation (i.e., imagining themselves participating in it)?

Theories about Sexual Deviance

Functionalist Theories

As we mentioned in the first chapter, functionalists believe that society works like an organism, with each part having its own function. When it comes to sexual deviance, functionalists argue that, although people may claim to view them negatively, some sexual deviations—for example, prostitution and pornography—play a valuable role in our society. At the very least, they test the boundaries for socially acceptable behaviour, and in this way they help society celebrate and promote social cohesion.

Like other deviant sexual behaviours, prostitution establishes the boundaries of acceptable morality within our society. By calling prostitution immoral and by stigmatizing sex workers and their clients, our society is clarifying the boundaries between acceptable and unacceptable behaviour. This, it is claimed, increases social cohesion, which, from a functional standpoint, is valuable and desirable.

Similarly, it can be argued that by providing an outlet for the sexual frustration of some married people, prostitution also helps to maintain individual families and the institution of marriage; so, according to functionalists, prostitution serves society as a whole. This is, essentially, the argument that functionalist Kingsley Davis put forward in 1937. However, the same argument—originally an argument about the normality of crime—can be put forward about any sexual deviation. The same arguments proving the functional value of prostitution might be made to prove the functional value of pornography. Arguments about homosexuality, on the other hand, would be slightly different.

Albert Reiss's 1961 study of "queers and peers" illustrates functionalist views on homosexuality and shows how society at that time reinforced negative and positive stereotypes. Among homosexuals, "peers" were the young, masculine men who engaged in sexual relations with effeminate "queers." As long as the peers "never took it," i.e., were not the recipients of anal intercourse, then their sex with men was considered masculine and reinforced notions of masculinity, as was the case among the ancient Greeks. The position of the queers was degraded, not only because they played a submissive (feminine) role to the peers but also because they were paid for sex. Sometimes the peers got the sex without paying, an act regarded among the peers as a show of masculinity and dominance over the queers.

Reiss's study affirmed the dominant view that gender-deviant homosexuals were negative role models because in this study they were the submissive queer prostitutes—men who (deviantly) behaved like women (Murray, 1996). At the same time, the study shows people reinforcing traditional (i.e., heterosexual) gender roles even as they perform non-traditional (i.e., homosexual) acts. This suggests that, to maintain equilibrium and consensus, people maintain traditional rationales for their behaviour even as they enact deviant behaviour.

Symbolic Interactionist Theories

According to the interactionist approach, sexual deviants are different only because we have repressed, labelled, and stigmatized them as different. Thus, everything depends on how we view and label their activities. Accordingly, everything depends on changes in public opinion. As we recall from Gagnon and Simon's (1967) classification of sexual deviance, some deviant acts elicit widespread disapproval even if many other people engage in them. Some of this is value conflict and some is hypocrisy.

In the past 30 years, Canadian public opinion on sexual matters has become more liberal. People today are much more accepting of nudity in the media and of the marketing of magazines and films with pornographic content, for example. It's hard to know how to classify extramarital sex, however; though popular norms remain strongly opposed to it, extramarital sex is apparently common. *How common* is hard to tell because the behaviour is strongly disapproved, at least nominally, so people are likely to distort or withhold information on the topic.

An article in Wikipedia, based on various sources dating back to Alfred Kinsey's path-breaking research, gives the following estimates based mainly on peer-reviewed sources:

> American biologist Alfred Kinsey found in his 1950-era studies that 50 per cent of American males and 26 per cent of females had extramarital sex (Kinsey Institute, online). Depending on studies, it was estimated that 26–50 per cent of men and 21–38 per cent of women (Choi et al. 1994), or 22.7 per cent of men and 11.6 per cent of women had extramarital sex (Wiederman, 1997). Other authors say that between 20 per cent and 25 per cent of Americans had sex with someone other than their spouse (Atkins et al., 2001). Durex's Global Sex Survey has found that 44 per cent of adults worldwide have had one-night extramarital sex and 22 per cent have had an affair (Durex, 2004). According to a 2004 United States survey (American Sex Survey, 2004), 16 per cent of married partners have had extramarital sex, nearly twice as many men as women, while an additional 30 per cent have fantasized about extramarital sex. There were also studies that have shown rates of extramarital sex as low as 2.5 per cent (Choi et al., 1994).

Other reliable peer-reviewed estimates of marital infidelity in North America, also including the Kinsey findings, are cited in a research article by Sprecher et al. (1998):

Marital infidelity has a long history in human existence (Harvey, 1995). In US samples alone, the percentage of married men and women reporting at least one incidence of extramarital sex (ES) ranges from 13 per cent to 50 per cent or higher (e.g., Blumstein and Schwartz, 1983; Greeley et al., 1990; Hunt, 1974; Kinsey et al., 1948; Kinsey et al., 1953; Laumann et al., 1994). For example, a recent NORC study based on a representative sample of the US population indicates that approximately 25 per cent of married men and 15 per cent of married women reported having engaged in ES at least once (Laumann et al., 1994). Although marital infidelity is not uncommon, attitude surveys reveal that there is widespread disapproval of extramarital sexual relationships in the US (e.g., Davis and Smith, 1991; Glenn and Weaver, 1979; Laumann et al., 1994; Thompson, 1984; Weis and Slosnerick, 1981).

Sexual norms and values change over time for a variety of reasons, but for the most part they change by means of the social (and sexual) interaction between individuals. As more people come to know and accept varieties in the sexual behaviour of others, they come to admit the acceptability and "normality" of behaviours formerly considered abnormal. In this way, some kinds of sexual deviance—including homosexuality, prostitution, sex changes, cross-dressing, and fetishism—have become increasingly accepted sexual practices in the general population.

As we saw earlier, first-hand familiarity with a wide range of people and practices is the most common way in which people change their views about sexuality. In short, it is hard to consider as deviant something that is familiar, close at hand, and even personally experienced. So, as symbolic interactionists tell us, our perceptions and meanings change through interaction. In Canada, the gay movement—particularly, the "coming out" of gays and lesbians—has made many more people familiar with the extent and proximity of a sexual orientation that, when hidden, seemed odd and shameful. The same principle—namely, familiarity breeds acceptance (not, as the old adage claims, familiarity breeds contempt)—holds for a wide variety of other sexual practices.

For this reason, the symbolic interactionist approach is also useful for studying the socialization of prostitutes, their introduction to sex work, and how they develop strategies to deal with johns and pimps. Prostitution is characterized by its own language, professional ethics, ways of exercising control and working around formal authority, and so on. So, as symbolic interactionists, we come to understand prostitution as a lifestyle and an occupation, with occupational socialization similar to that for any other job.

Finally, the interactionist approach is useful in studying the social construction of sexual offences and "crime waves." When, as in Figure 4.1, there is a visible surge in reported sex offences, we cannot always be certain whether this shows an increased prevalence of criminal behaviour or an increased effort by the police to apprehend and document such offences.

The same is true of interprovincial variations in sexual offences, as shown in Figure 4.2. Do the higher recorded rates in Saskatchewan and Manitoba necessarily reflect higher rates of sexual crime or merely a stronger determination to apprehend and document these offences? In either instance, we must ask why these jurisdictions have higher reported rates of sexual offences.

Critical Theories

If we apply critical theory to sexual deviance, we see that more powerful people are more successful in labelling certain sexual activities or preferences as deviant. Current debates about homosexuality—for example, on the topic of same-sex marriage—result from conflicting beliefs about the purpose and meaning of marriage, as well as from more or less understanding of homosexuality itself.

Many types of sexual deviance—for example, prostitution—relate to social inequality and the exercise of power. Dominant groups in our society have the greatest influence over defining

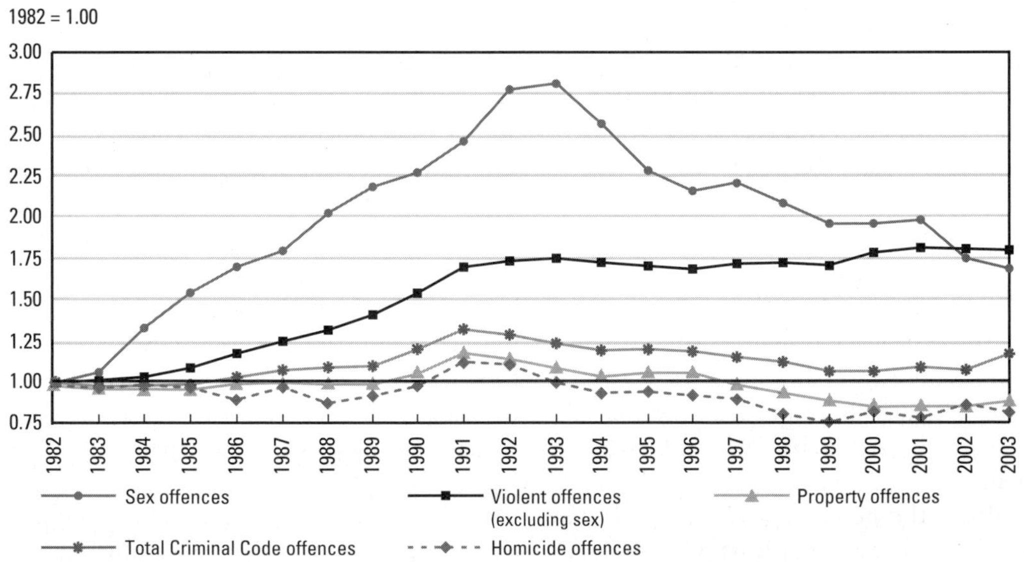

FIGURE 4.1 Police-Reported Criminal Offences in Canada, 1982–2003

Source: Statistics Canada. 2004. "Crime Statistics in Canada, 2003", Canadian Centre for Justice Statistics, *Juristat* 24, 6, at: <www.csc-scc.gc.ca/text/rsrch/safe_return2005/sr2005-eng.shtml>.

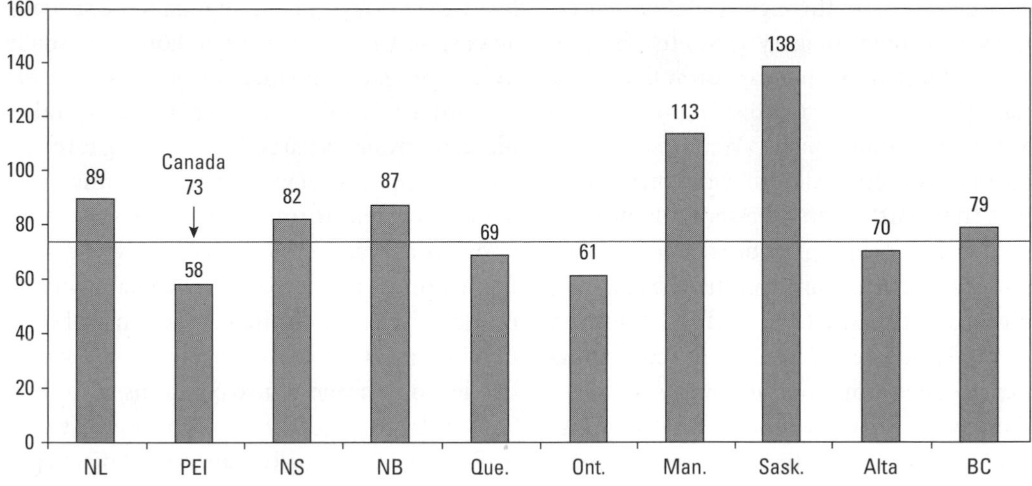

FIGURE 4.2 Provincial Rates of Police-Reported Sexual Offences, 2007

Source: Statistics Canada, at: <www.statcan.gc.ca/pub/85f0033m/2008019/charts-graphiques/c-g002-eng.htm>.

what kinds of sexual activities are to be considered normal and determine whether they will be legal or illegal. Consider the debates about the sex trade, which are certainly influenced by social inequality and the exercise of power: as we have seen, prostitution reflects gender inequality because it usually involves men gaining pleasure or income, or both, by exploiting women—often, women who are addicted or have been abused or trafficked. Whether the men are the owners and managers of an escort service, for example, or use the sexual services it provides, they are the main beneficiaries of this industry.

At another level, prostitution concerns poverty. Typically, women (and occasionally men) who resort to prostitution lack access to legitimate means of earning enough money. This is evident in the enormous numbers of prostitutes in economically less-developed countries; there, poverty marginalizes many women and forces them to earn money by selling their bodies. In our own society, prostitution tends to recruit its members from among less educated and socially disadvantaged women.

Feminist Approaches

Feminist theories usually argue that society is patriarchal: male dominated, oppressive, and exploitative of women and their bodies.

Sexual behaviour generally expresses or indicates the inequality in the roles of men and women. A given sexual encounter between a man and a woman may mean different things to the two participants, may have different consequences, or may be interpreted in different ways by members of the society. People typically condemn a sexually active teenage girl, for example, more strongly than they do a teenage boy. This reminds us that the foundation of all deviance—the application of stigma or condemnation—depends on whom we are stigmatizing or condemning. In turn, this evaluation may be based on the sex or gender of the person labelled deviant.

Many people regard the problems of teenage sex, pregnancy, and subsequent out-of-wedlock births as problems almost exclusively resulting from the behaviour of girls. Helen Boritch (1997) refers to the "fallen woman" as one who has shirked her gender role, losing her culturally required purity through sexual looseness. The fallen woman imagery serves to illustrate what can happen to a woman, or in this case a teenage girl, who does not display the supposedly innate feminine purity. We typically view female sex workers as deviant women, whereas we see their customers as essentially normal men. Thus, the criminal justice system unfairly targets the prostitute and not the client.

Prostitution has long divided feminist thinking. Some feminist thought condemns prostitution as a practice and wants to "save" individual prostitute women. Other feminist thought supports the legalization of prostitution and migration of foreign prostitutes. Certainly, feminists have very good reasons for criticizing the sex industry because of its inherent exploitation and objectification of women, generally for the advantage of men.

Most important, feminists remind us that women continue to be more likely than men to be victims of sexual crime. In Figure 4.3, we see that girls and young women are much more likely than boys and young men to be sexually abused within their Canadian homes—usually by parents, step-parents, or siblings.

Violence against women typically takes place in private, as part of a continuing intimate relationship. Sexual violence is a common and varied problem throughout the world, as we know from scattered studies and news reports. For example, in sub-Saharan Africa, women's refusal of sex is often cited as the cause of family violence. Fear of violence creates a major barrier for women to use condoms with their husbands for pregnancy prevention or as protection against sexually transmitted diseases.

In Central Asia, men have the choice of marrying the victims (through forced marriages) they sexually assaulted, raped, or abducted to reduce their punishment for this crime (Werner, 2009). Werner (ibid., 314) notes that:

> Discourses of shame are mobilized by local actors in support of the popular

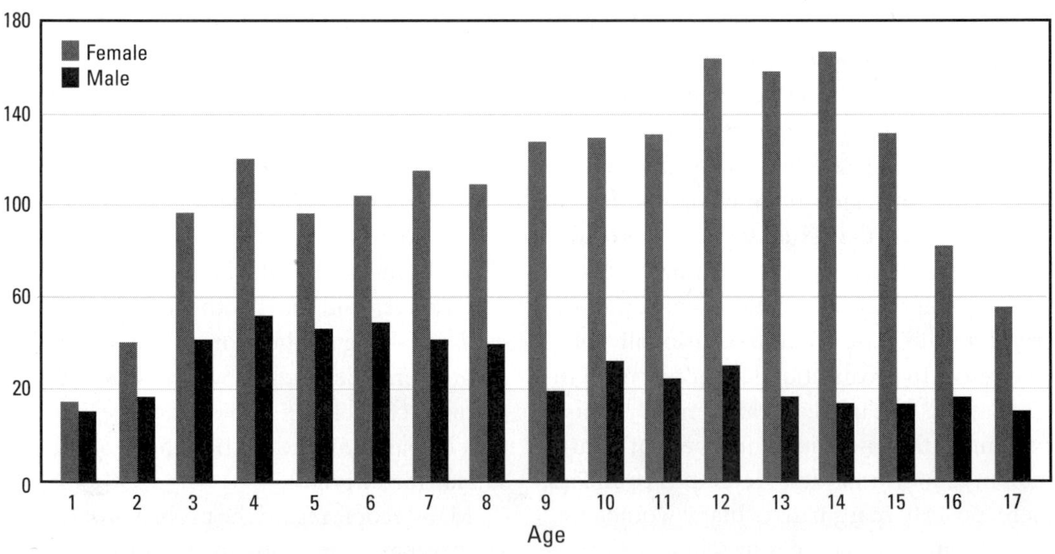

FIGURE 4.3 Family-Related Sexual Assault Rates per 100,000 Males and Females, Canada, 2005

Source: Statistics Canada, "Family Violence in Canada: a Statistical profile, 2005," in *Equality for Women: Beyond the Illusion* (Dec. 2005), at: <dsp-psd.pwgsc.gc.ca/Collection/SW21-134-2006E.pdf>.

view that a woman should "stay" after being abducted. Women can and do resist abductions, but they risk dealing with the burden of shame. Further, in Kyrgizstan, where bride abduction is increasingly re-imagined as a national tradition, women and activists who challenge this practice can be viewed as traitors to their ethnicity.

Sexual harassment is another form of sexual assault that is prevalent in schools and workplaces. Part of the problem, as with other types of intimate violence, is that views of sexual harassment vary by gender. Men are less likely than women to see a problem with it. This difference of views has to do with the history of patriarchy in our society: with "boys being boys," gendered workplaces and jobs, and the continued social acceptability of stereotypical locker room behaviour. Overall, women label more behaviours as harassing than men do, but this difference decreases with experience in the workforce, as women become used to "the norm."

In Figure 4.4, we see that young Canadian women are also likely to be victimized by criminal harassment (i.e., stalking). The rates of sexual assault and harassment are especially high in the youngest age ranges and are higher for stalking than for sexual assault. Stalking is, however, evidence of the attempt to exercise sexual control over a woman—treating a love object as though she is **sexual property**.

Postmodern Approaches

Postmodern approaches question our thinking about "normality"—what we think is normal and how we came to think that. A key figure in this project is postmodern sociologist Michel Foucault.

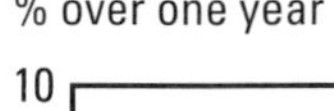
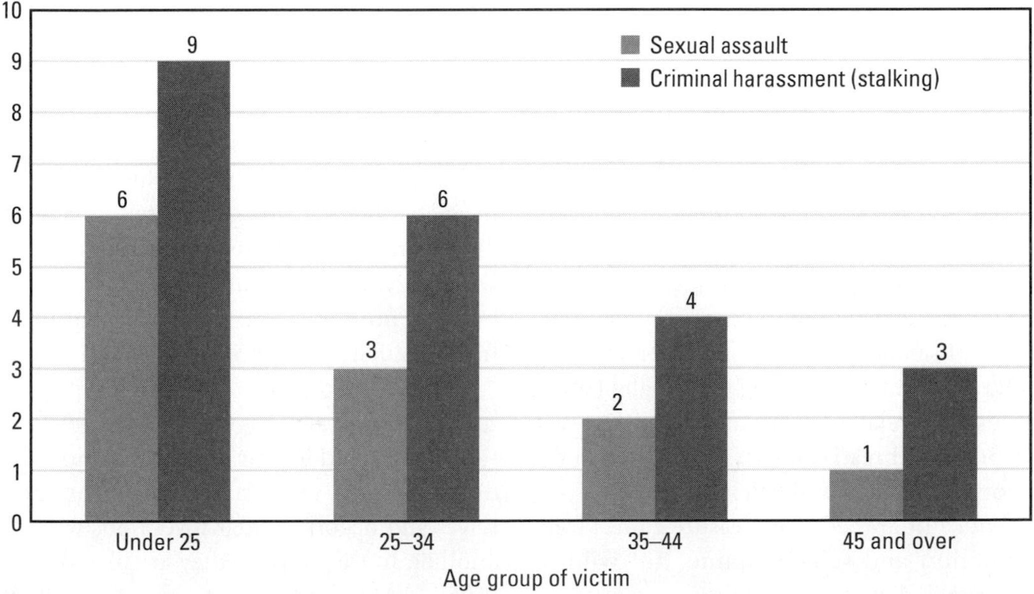

FIGURE 4.4 One-Year Rates of Sexual Assault and Criminal Harassment of Women, by Age, Canada

Source: Statistics Canada, General Social Survey (2004), at: <www.statcan.gc.ca/pub/85-570-x/2006001/figures/4054038-eng.htm>.

During the 1970s and 1980s, Foucault wrote three volumes of *The History of Sexuality*, a project he would never finish. His history of sexuality was originally projected as a fairly straightforward extension to the topic of sexuality of the genealogical approach taken in his *Discipline and Punish* (1975). As well, Foucault was gay and his experiences as a stigmatized sexual minority may have motivated him to undertake such a work and to arrive at some of his conclusions.

His goal was to trace the development of Christian ideas about sex to the present day, starting with pagan pre-Christian beliefs. Foucault believed that modern thinking about sexuality has an intimate association with the power structures of modern society. The Western (mainly Christian) understanding of humans as sexual beings, and the relation of this understanding to our moral and ethical lives, evolved over a long period to its current form.

In the pre-Christian Greek culture, sexual acts were good, natural, and necessary in moderation, though open to abuse. This changed under Christianity, when sexual pleasure became linked to unlawful conduct and rule-breaking. According to Foucault, in the Christian view, sexual acts were, on the whole, evil in themselves. Unlike the ancient Greeks, who emphasized the pursuit of pleasures, including a full range of sexual activities, the Judeo-Christian moral code forbade some forms of sexual activity (e.g., buggery, bestiality), perceived sex as being principally (if not exclusively) related to its biological procreative purpose, and restricted sexual activity to the union of husband and wife.

Foucault argued that pleasure comes from regulation and self-discipline, not wild or excessive behaviour, and that it is everyone's right and duty to pursue sexual pleasure without impediment by the state. However, the state comes to intervene nonetheless. The modern (state) control of sexuality parallels modern control of criminality by making sex—like crime—an object of allegedly scientific analyses, which offer both knowledge and domination of their objects.

The supposed sciences of sexuality exercise control via their study of individuals; they even attempt to tell people what to think about themselves. Internalizing the norms laid down by the sciences of sexuality, individuals try to conform to these norms. In the end, they are controlled not only as objects of disciplines but also as self-monitoring, self-forming subjects. For Foucault, as for a contemporary thinker, Herbert Marcuse (1955), the liberation of bodies and pleasures from their imprisonment in conventional sexuality should be our goal. What is needed is an escape from conventions—not the rejection of civilization, per se, as much as a new awareness, resistance, and re-evaluation of civilized sexuality.

Whether aware of Foucault's thinking or not, people have continued to rethink what is sexual "normality" and to reform their practices within sexually tolerant communities. Nowhere has this been more important than in the realm of physical disability. Erotic pleasure continues to extend far beyond the possibilities of an able-bodied, two-gender, two-sex society. Traditional conceptions have tended to leave the bodily impaired out of the sexual picture because notions of sexuality conventionally have postulated able-bodied men and women.

People who deviate from this physical norm—for example, who lack fully functional arms and legs or even conventional sex organs—must reinvent sexuality for themselves and negotiate their inventions with one another. In this respect, they are like Merton's (1957 [1938]) "adapters to anomie": unwilling to give up sex altogether, and unable to conform, they have to innovate. Physically handicapped people have gained an advantage from the development of new forms of cybersex that, in effect, level the playing field. They make sexual seduction and sexual pleasure much less dependent on physical location or mobility and enable people to interact sexually at a distance.

An even wider example of this rethinking process is the "discovery" of erectile dysfunction among older men and the provision of pharmaceuticals like Viagra and Cialis to treat it. As a result, a revolution in the thinking about age, ability, and sexual pleasure has been embraced by millions of middle-aged and elderly couples eager to continue their sexual practices with chemical assistance.

> **Time to Reflect:** Do you agree with Marcuse and Foucault that society needs the liberation of bodies and pleasures from their imprisonment in conventional sexuality? What do you suppose would happen if such a liberation took place? Would anyone lose by it?

Consequences of Sexual Deviance

Social Consequences

Prostitution

Throughout history, prostitution has aroused a wide range of social and moral reactions. However, no society has completely accepted prostitution as a valid and integral part of community life. This societal reaction is especially true of child prostitution. Sometimes, children sell sex, and this is rarely a free and conscious choice; more often, it is an activity forced upon them by older people or by extreme poverty. One source reports that "Migrant trafficking accounts for 8,000–16,000 illegal immigrants in Canada every year, many of them female youths and children who are forced to work in Canada's booming sex-trade industry. The same report estimates that those profiting from the illegal trafficking of children and women in Canada earn as much as $400 million annually" (Canada Women's Health Network, 2002).

The traffic in vulnerable children and young people violates their rights to an education, leisure, good health, a family life, and safety from exploitation. This traffic in children is not new, though we are still inexperienced in combatting it, just as we appear to be ineffective, as a global society, in alleviating the abject poverty that can lead young people and children to sell themselves for the sexual pleasure of others.

Homosexuality

Although there is increased awareness and acceptance of homosexuality, most people—especially those past middle age—still see heterosexuality as the ideal way of living. Parents of homosexual or bisexual children appear to have an especially hard time accepting their children's sexual orientation. They may be disappointed because their child's behaviour embarrasses them or because they wanted grandchildren, which they fear will be denied to them if their child is homosexual. Their reactions can lead to depression, harsh words, aggression, and broken relationships.

Also, because anti-homosexuality remains ingrained in some individuals and groups of people, homosexuals often have experienced ostracism and lost employment opportunities. In addition, **hate crimes** up to and including homicide have been perpetrated against them.

Pedophilia

Many of the children and teenagers who experience sexual harassment or sexual abuse suffer serious consequences, and some even become deviant adults. Pedophilia—though relatively uncommon—is much more dangerous than is often believed because it introduces many girls to the world of casual or even brutal sex. It is a form of sexual abuse, and as such, it lowers self-esteem and increases distrust. Male victims of pedophilia often experience confusion about their sexual identity in adulthood and are more likely than average to become pedophiles themselves.

Often, the victims of pedophilia inhabit a world of secret guilt, fear, and regret. They find it harder to trust others, including friends, family members, and adults in authority, and this inability to trust hinders the formation of close, stable relationships. Because of its effects on self-esteem and social relationships, pedophilia also contributes to the likelihood of juvenile delinquency and poor school performance. It interferes with the normal development of children and sets them apart from their peers.

Health Consequences

Prostitution and Homosexuality

The health problems associated with prostitution and, in some subcultures, homosexuality include violence, the risk of sexually transmitted diseases (STDs) such as HIV/AIDS, and the effects of drugs. Michel Foucault, for example, was among the many thousands in the gay community who died of AIDS at a relatively young age.

Mainly, the health risks have to do with unprotected sex. The poorest sex workers are usually unable to force their customers to use condoms, even though both their lives are at risk from unprotected sex. The use and non-use of condoms in sex work is an international health problem of staggering proportions. Largely, condom use depends on the balance of power between the sex worker and her client. When possible, female sex workers may employ condoms to maintain their emotional control over commercial sexual intercourse. Their use of contraceptives provides them the opportunity to construct working identities while preserving their emotional well-being.

The mental health consequences of prostitution include stress, depression, anxiety, self-medication through alcohol and drug abuse, eating disorders, and even suicide. The same is true of homosexuals, especially for those living in social circumstances that are neither accepting nor supportive.

For prostitutes, post-traumatic stress disorder may result from their work and lifestyle. PTSD sufferers experience fear and a sense of powerlessness. The severity of PTSD experienced by prostitutes is likened to that suffered by war veterans, rape survivors, and those seeking refuge from "state-organized torture," and the severity would increase with the increase of time (and thus the increase of served customers) spent in the sex trade. Farley and Barkan (1998) report that the probability of PTSD among prostitutes is strongly related to the total number of types of lifetime violence, such as childhood physical abuse and rape in adult prostitution, and the total number of times raped in prostitution.

Paraphilia

Many activities considered deviant and labelled paraphilia are without any observable health consequences. If a person receives sexual arousal from feet or certain types of fabric—frotteurism, for example—there are no visible health consequences.

However, some paraphilias are criminalized precisely because they cause harmful health or social consequences. Pedophilia, for example, causes problems in the development of the child because it affects self-image and how the child copes with difficult situations. Young girls who have been sexually abused are more likely to develop eating disorders during adolescence, and such abuse, regardless of the sex of the victim, can lead to a wide variety of personality and emotional disorders and can result in a diminished sense of self-worth leading to self-harm and suicide.

Other criminal paraphilias may have harmful and even fatal health consequences for the victim. In lust murders, where an individual derives sexual pleasure by committing a murder, health consequences for the victim are self-evident. Criminal paraphilias may also harm the perpetrator. One non-criminal type of paraphilia with adverse health consequences is coprophilia—sexual attraction to feces.

Social Policy Implications

Social policies concerning various types of sexual behaviour remain highly controversial. There is consensus, however, on one main point: in North America, people universally disapprove of sexual behaviour that involves the use of force or violence against an unwilling participant.

However, that's where the agreement ends; on most other issues, people disagree widely and often vigorously. For example, some believe that we should criminalize all forms of prostitution. They believe that prostitution has no intrinsic social value and can be completely eradicated through vigorous and uncompromising enforcement of the criminal law. However, other people believe the opposite and feel prostitution should be legalized, not to promote it but to regulate it and reduce the associated harm.

Today, Canadian policy provides a hybrid form of criminalization where sex is concerned. Although prostitution itself is theoretically legal, practising it is not. While the trend in other Western countries has been to move away from criminal sanctions for prostitution, Canada legislated a tougher anti-soliciting law in 1986. Various government committees and task forces have called for even tougher laws and more vigorous enforcement of the current legislation. In 1990, for example, the Standing Committee on Justice recommended strengthening the law to include fingerprinting and photographing prostitutes and removing drivers' licences from customers charged with communicating for the purpose of prostitution.

Recently, the laws around prostitution were thrown into uncertainty, due to a March 2012 Court of Appeal decision in Ontario. As CBC News reported:

> In response to a challenge from three sex-trade workers, the Ontario Court of Appeal released a decision on March 26 upholding an earlier ruling by Superior Court Judge Susan G. Himel that three provisions of the Criminal Code relating to prostitution should be struck because they are unconstitutional. The Appeal Court agreed with two-thirds of Himel's ruling, including that the provisions prohibiting common bawdy houses and living off the avails of prostitution are both unconstitutional in their current form. Ontario's top court struck down the ban on bawdy houses on the basis that it increased the dangers prostitutes face because they are forced to work on the streets. However, the Appeal Court affirmed the validity of the offence of communicating in public for the purpose of prostitution. (www.cbc.ca/news/canada/toronto/story/2012/04/25/ontario-federal-appeal-sex-trade.html)

The Supreme Court of Canada, in due course, will review this decision, following a request to do so by the federal Minister of Justice, Rob Nicholson, and Ontario's Attorney General, John Gerretsen.

In many other countries, prostitution is already legal and sometimes subject to government control to reduce health problems that may arise, such as the spread of disease. Some people support the decriminalization of prostitution in Canada because, despite enforcement efforts, prostitution will continue to exist. Governments, they reason, should reduce harm by ensuring adequate health-care services for sex workers, who are at risk of violence and sexually transmitted diseases. This was the logic behind the recent Ontario court decision by Justice Susan Himel.

As we have seen, prostitution flourishes wherever economic inequality limits the human rights of poor people, especially poor children and women. In some cases, people—usually women and children—are enslaved in the sex industry through physical and sexual violence, through forced or pre-existent addiction to drugs, or because of immigration and visa problems. By contrast, people with money and power find it easy to own or rent the bodies of refugees; the homeless; unemployed, undocumented, or unprotected immigrants; abandoned children; and those without economic rights and protection.

To deal with these human rights violations, we need policies that combat human trafficking. This will mean agreements at the international and national levels to achieve co-operation among various governments and branches of government. Some progress has been made in this direction. The International Labour Organization's Convention on the Worst of Forms of Child Labour (Convention 182), adopted in 1999, identifies the trafficking of children as a practice similar to slavery. The Convention calls for countries to take immediate action to secure the prohibition and elimination of all the worst forms of child labour. However, much remains to be done to bring this initiative to completion.

Conclusion

Most sexual deviation in Canada today is consensual and pleasure-seeking. As such, it does not pose a social problem for anyone who is able to tolerate sexual diversity. Over the last three or four decades, premarital sex and cohabitation have become common. Homosexuals have come out of the closet in large numbers. People in large and small communities use pornography for recreational purposes and engage in less-usual practices like BDSM, fetishism, and partner swapping. And, increasingly, the double sexual standard has started to disappear: women feel more secure than ever about initiating sex and openly enjoying it—just like men have (historically) been permitted to do—without any loss of their femininity.

However, other types of deviation remain unaccepted, shunned, and sometimes outlawed. Extramarital sex, though not uncommon, is widely disapproved. Child pornography is outlawed, as is sex with underage boys and girls. Non-consensual sex remains—rightly—disapproved and punishable by law, though often unreported. And, to the extent that pornography pairs sex with gendered violence, it is widely disapproved.

The topic of prostitution remains widely debated, since many people continue to view the sex trade as a form of traffic in virtually enslaved women and children. Much of the concern about prostitution grows out of the fact that many prostitutes have been, and continue to be, abused and/or deprived of free choice.

Gradually, throughout North America, gays and lesbians are receiving legal rights and social acceptance that they have not previously enjoyed in modern times, including the right to marry. Today, with a deeper and wider understanding of homosexuality, anti-homosexuality is becoming socially unacceptable—like racism or sexism. It may be time, therefore, to view anti-homosexuality—or at least, homophobia—as one of the more serious forms of sexual deviation. The shift in public understanding around homosexuality gives us reason to hope for other shifts in the popular understanding of sexuality and sexual deviance.

Questions for Critical Thought

1. Can you think of any other types of sexual deviance that are being normalized? If so, what do you think are the processes behind the normalization of these sexual activities?
2. How has the double standard in regard to the expected behaviours of males and females structured research on the topic of sexual deviance?
3. Identify the reasons why sexual deviance is often limited to distinct parts of cities. What purpose might this serve?
4. Why might women choose to enter the sex trade? Is it always a choice?
5. Traditional heterosexual pornography is said to be gendered. How can homosexual pornography be just as gendered?
6. Between 20 and 40 per cent of the population is reportedly involved in some form of SM behaviour but doesn't define it as such. How would a theorist then explain the fact that it is such a stigmatized activity?

Recommended Readings

Butler, Judith. 1990. *Gender Trouble: Feminism and the Subversion of Identity*. New York: Routledge.

This classic study of gender and sexual identity is paramount for any understanding of queer theory. Butler examines traditional conceptions of identity and explains how they are produced and reproduced.

Cantú, Lionel. 2009. *The Sexuality of Migration: Border Crossings and Mexican Immigrant Men*. New York: New York University Press.

This innovative study explores experiences of Mexican men who have same sex with men and who have migrated to the United States. Until recently, immigration scholars have left out the experiences of gays and lesbians. Cantú situates his analysis within the history of Mexican immigration and offers a broad understanding of diverse migratory experiences ranging from recent gay asylum seekers to an assessment of gay tourism in Mexico, using methods that include archival research, interviews, and ethnographic research.

Laqueur, Thomas W. 2003. *Solitary Sex: A Cultural History of Masturbation*. New York: Zone Books.

This book details the changing nature of Western culture's obsession with masturbation, often thought to irreversibly harm its practitioners. Today, this belief—and the attendant anxiety—no longer persists. This makes masturbation both the "first truly democratic sexuality" and the "crack cocaine of sex": both addictive and readily accessible to all.

Laumann, Edward, et al. 2004. *The Sexual Organization of the City*. Chicago: University of Chicago Press.

Sex in the city occurs when opportunities and constraints lead the individual towards some sexual outlets and away from others. Sex markets—embedded in social networks, institutions, and social spaces—constrain the choices that people have to express their sexuality. The authors propose the existence of a "sex market," a spatial and cultural arena in which individuals search for sex partners.

Laws, D. Richard, and William T. O'Donohue, eds. 2008. *Sexual Deviance: Theory, Assessment, and Treatment*, 2nd edn. New York: Guilford Press.

This book provides authoritative perspectives on the full range of paraphilias. For each major clinical syndrome, a chapter on theory is followed by a chapter on assessment and treatment. Challenges in working with sex offenders are considered in depth, with a suitable appreciation for the influence of research, theory, culture, and politics in this socially charged area of public discourse.

Seidman, Steven. 2004. *Beyond the Closet: The Transformation of Gay and Lesbian Life*. New York: Routledge.

This study of gays and lesbians explores the experience of living "in the closet" and coming "out of the closet." The findings show differences in experiences from gays and lesbians of different generations, races, and classes. They also reveal changes in the "closet" as society has changed.

Recommended Websites

Heterosexual Deviance, Robert Keel On-line, University of Missouri–St Louis

www.umsl.edu/~keelr/200/hetsex.html

Professor Robert Keel runs this web page out of his personal website devoted to analyzing the ways in which gendered sexuality is a social construct. This site is particularly useful for students wishing to understand postmodern arguments against what many consider a rigid, gendered sexual script that makes many people "sexual deviants."

Prostitute Research and Education

www.prostitutionresearch.com/

Prostitute Research and Education is an NGO with the mandate to organize prostitutes and provide alternatives to the current forms of prostitution that exist in the United States. The website informs viewers as to laws, trafficking trends, and the latest research in prostitution.

The Sex Atlas, Erwin J. Haeberle, University of Berlin–Humboldt

www2.hu-berlin.de/sexology/ATLAS_EN/

This is a free, online English-language version of Erwin J. Haeberle's *Sex Atlas*. Originally published in 1981, the work remains a useful overview of many issues related to sex in society, including the way the human body is seen and the place of sex as a social convention in modern society.

Transgender Crossroads

www.tgcrossroads.org/

This is a portal website offers a myriad of information for transgendered people. It provides information on new books, civil liberties, laws, medical services, and some of the latest research concerning transgendered people.

The Society of Janus

soj.org/

This not-for-profit San Francisco-based agency aims to educate the public on "the art of safe, consensual and non-exploitative **BDSM**." Any understanding of **BDSM** as a practice or a lifestyle likely calls for a review of this advocacy group's website.

Magnus Hirschfeld Archive for Sexology

www2.hu-berlin.de/sexology/

Curated by Professor Edwin J. Haeberle of Berlin's Humboldt-Universtat, this is an extremely valuable resource focused on all manner of issues relating to sexuality. Truly international in scope, the website provides information on the political, cultural, and economic repercussions of sexuality and sexual deviance.

Recommended Movies

***Transamerica*, Dir. Duncan Tucker (2005)**

Bree (née Stanley), a pre-operative transsexual, learns about her 17-year-old biological son Toby days before her gender reassignment surgery. Bree's therapist requires she meet her son before undertaking her surgery, resulting in Bree and Toby going on a cross-country road trip. This film shows the difficulties transgendered people have sharing their identities with friends and family.

***The Laramie Project*, Dir. Moises Kaufman (2002)**

Based on one of the most widely known plays of the last 20 years, this film tells the real-life story of University of Wyoming student Matthew Shepard. In the fall of 1998, two thugs tied up and beat Shepard, who was openly gay, to death. The movie looks at both the event and its aftermath (including the trial), exploring how the residents of Laramie, Wyoming, perceived the incident.

***Capturing the Friedmans*, Dir. Andrew Jarecki (2003)**

One of the most controversial documentaries ever made, Jarecki's film provides a piercing look at the lives of the Friedman family of Great Neck, New York. Local police raided the Friedman home in November 1987 and arrested father Arnold and son Jesse on multiple counts of child molestation. This film uses home movies to examine the Friedmans' comprehension of, and response to, these events.

***Harold and Maude*, Dir. Hal Ashby (1971)**

This was one of Hollywood's attempts to represent the sexual counterculture of the late 1960s and early1970s. Harold, a death-obsessed teenager, falls in love with 79-year-old Maude, a woman with a decided *joie de vivre*. While Harold and Maude enjoy a strong emotional connection, the sexual component of their relationship disgusts all manner of onlookers and busybodies.

5 Substance Abuse

Learning Objectives

- To be able to define drug use and abuse
- To learn about the history of drug use and abuse
- To understand and analyze public reaction to substance abuse
- To learn the various sociological theories that explain drug abuse
- To understand the health effects of drug abuse
- To think of possible solutions to drug and alcohol abuse issues

Introduction

In this chapter, we will discuss various **consciousness-altering drugs** including alcohol, marijuana, cocaine, and heroin. These substances all change a person's mental state and can sometimes—depending on the drug and its use—lead to serious health risks for the user and for others. As we will see, there are close connections between drug use and important public safety issues that include crime and delinquency. That is why society has an interest in controlling the deviant use of a number of these **psychoactive substances**.

In Canada and elsewhere, the use of legal drugs such as alcohol, tobacco, and prescription medicine is much more common than the use of illegal drugs such as heroin and cocaine. Yet, our society focuses on *illegal* drug use as a problem while ignoring the harm done by *legal* drugs. This seeming irrationality reminds us that we socially construct all deviance—including our response to drug use. We choose to ignore certain problems and heighten the significance of others. Nowhere is this more obvious than in our view of drug abuse and drug addicts. In the media, people addicted to hard drugs are often portrayed as crazed, irrational, irresponsible, and unable to care for themselves. This is one way in which the media heighten attention to illegal drug use and heighten people's anxiety about this matter.

However, we cannot understand the persistence and vehemence of the drug debate unless we understand it as a form of "moral panic" about "addiction" at a particular point in human history. By **moral panic** we mean any popular controversy or dispute that provokes feelings and fears so intense they threaten the social order. Stanley Cohen, author of *Folk Devils and Moral Panics*, is credited with coining the term. According to Cohen (1972: 9), a moral panic occurs when a "condition, episode, person or group of persons emerges to become defined as a threat to societal values and interests."

Moral panics reveal and aggravate social tensions that are hard to resolve because, usually, the subject matter—sex, drugs, race, or another matter—is taboo. Once a moral panic begins, the media act as agents of moral indignation. At the very least, they excite concern merely by reporting the facts. Sometimes, they go well beyond this by purposely engaging in a moral crusade to mobilize public opinion. More often, the media are set in motion by **moral entrepreneurs**, who make public, increasingly loud claims about dangers to the social order. Typically, they target people who supposedly threaten the social order, whom Cohen has named "folk devils."

According to sociologists Erich Goode and Nachman Ben-Yehuda (1994), moral panics typically follow a pattern consisting of the following stages:

- ***Concern:*** Awareness grows that the behaviour of the group or category in question is likely to have a negative impact on society.
- ***Hostility:*** Hostility towards the group in question increases and a clearer division forms between "them" and "us," as the group comes to be viewed as "folk devils."
- ***Consensus:*** It becomes generally if not universally accepted that the group in question poses a real threat to society.
- ***Disproportionality:*** An action (or set of actions) is taken that is disproportionate to the threat actually posed by the accused group.
- ***Volatility:*** Public concern about the issue ebbs and flows rapidly and unpredictably, often with a sudden disappearance of public interest as media shift their focus to another topic.

Topics that have received this treatment in recent years include child pornography, Internet addiction, obesity, anorexia, and, of course, the "war on drugs."

As sociologists, we try to take a more measured, empirical approach to the topic of substance abuse; and doing so requires contextual, historical understanding. As Jacques Derrida (1992: 229) wrote, to define addiction (or abuse) we need "a history, a culture, conventions, evaluations, norms, [and] discourses . . . instituted on the basis of moral and political evaluations." As sociologists, we must beware of stereotyping drugs and the people who use them because at times the current prevailing ideas are ideological and political, not scientific. Often, there is no logic to our acceptance of some drug-using activities and our rejection of others.

The Social Role of Intoxication

The age-old relationship between drugs and deviant behaviour has two distinct but related aspects: one socio-cultural and the other biochemical. The biochemical effect of drugs is easily noted. Because of our body chemistry, drugs such as alcohol, cannabis, and opium have the power to alter our view of the world, relax us, lower our restraints, and (occasionally) cause us to see visions or have other unusual bodily experiences. Different drugs have different effects, but all commonly consumed drugs—including nicotine and caffeine—are psychoactive in one way or another.

At the same time, the social uses of and reactions to drugs vary historically and from one culture to another. In many cultures, drugs have had ceremonial value. The ways that people behave after consuming a drug depend in part on the society in which people have learned to use the drug and the effects they expect it to have. Consider the use of alcohol: as we can see by comparing drinking in different societies, the effects of alcohol are partly biochemical and partly social. Drunken behaviours dramatize or perform our understanding of biochemical states, but they also result from our expectations—how we expect (and hope) the drug will affect us. Because drunken behaviours are dramatizations of both biochemical states and their expected effects, drugs and alcohol are often used to ritualize unusual, even rule-breaking, behaviour.

The same drug may be used differently in different societies, often with different effects. The Mediterranean pattern of drinking, characterized by a continued intake of small amounts of alcohol, produces a sense of serene well-being and allows continued functioning throughout the day. The northern drinking pattern (referring to Northern Europe and groups of Anglo-Saxon descent) is characterized by an alternation between complete abstinence and occasional binge-drinking. This pattern is far more likely to result in aggressive, even violent, outbursts.

This latter drinking practice stems from a traditional stigmatization of alcohol for religious and health reasons. In Finland, for example, alcohol is isolated from everyday life. Thus, Finnish attitudes are very different from the ones prevalent in France, where alcohol is common and drinking is a routine part of daily life.

The Importance of Place

Situational factors are an important part of the drug-using experience. Different situations—locations, settings, and occasions—can encourage or discourage the use of drugs. They can also contribute to our sense that we are leaving the sober, routine world for a more unusual experience. That's why people are far more likely to consume alcohol (and drugs) in the company of others, at bars and restaurants or at parties, than alone at home. Much of this has to do with the facilitating role of other people.

Howard Becker (1953) asserts, contrary to still common ideas, that purely psychological theories about drug use, drug abuse, and drunken behaviour are inadequate. Marijuana use, for example—especially continued use—requires a sociological explanation, says Becker. In short, to smoke and appreciate marijuana, the drug must first be made available; then, knowledgeable people must teach the newcomer how to smoke the drug and how to detect and appreciate its physical effects. Without these situational, social influences, people will not become users of the drug. Thus, drug use must be viewed in a social and cultural context. And though we may not think so, because drinking is so common, this is as true of alcohol use as it is of marijuana.

Moreover, variations in the drinking environment—in a particular bar or restaurant—influence the amount people drink, how they act afterward, and even the likelihood they will drive while drunk. Barrooms are more or less likely to promote violence, depending on their situational characteristics. Noisier, smokier bars are more likely than average to produce excessive drinking and aggressive behaviour. Excessive heat or smoke, lack of bar staff, or servers who are drinking themselves also increase the risk of aggression in barrooms (Green and Plant, 2007).

Most violence in or near drinking places is associated with high levels of intoxication, and many patrons enjoy getting into a fight. For many, a fight after drinking is part of being a member of a macho male subculture. Group drinking (and fighting) for many men also symbolizes a rejection of middle-class values and constraints. This connection between drinking and violence—between group drinking, masculine identity, and the rejection of middle-class conventions—has a long tradition, stretching back to early working-class America, to frontier society and all-male work environments in North America, and to working-class pubs in early industrial Great Britain.

The ethic of masculinity has always been part of the "drinking and violence" problem, since men have always tended to act more aggressively masculine under the influence of alcohol. Part of this reflects the influence of the drinking place itself. The working-man's saloon has always offered men a same-sex space to indulge in "male" activities, where men could get drunk even as their authority was declining at home. Barroom attendance and all-male drinking became an expression of male independence early on.

However, people who drink in such places are likely to misjudge how much they have consumed and how drunk they are. Frequent, heavy drinkers are also likely to believe that heavy alcohol use is acceptable in their social reference groups, wherever they drink. They also overestimate the amount of alcohol that social and problem drinkers consume, and misjudge the criteria of problem drinking (e.g., frequency of intoxication). In short, heavy drinkers compare their own drinking to faulty estimates of drinking in reference groups so that their own drinking seems average or normal. In this way, as in others, the consumption of alcohol and substance abuse are profoundly social activities.

Factors Affecting Alcohol and Substance Abuse

Whether drinking becomes a problem, for an individual or for a society, depends on many circumstances. Alcohol—even drunkenness—is not a problem until it interacts with personal variables such as gender, class, and race to produce deviant, even dangerous, behaviour.

And, as we have said, situational factors also influence whether drinking and drunkenness pose a problem.

Under certain conditions, intoxication leads to violence, even homicide. In Canada—and even more in the US—interpersonal conflict often escalates into violence if the combatants are intoxicated and handguns are present. Various forms of personal pathology—including depression, mental illness, and homelessness—are associated with excessive alcohol use or childhood experiences involving alcohol. Alcohol and drugs sometimes cause these problems, sometimes they aggravate these problems, and sometimes they merely accompany them or show their presence.

The Importance of Demographics

The use of drugs, tobacco, and alcohol varies by age. Most people in our society are likely to first try these substances during their teen years, under the influence of their peers. By age 25, only a few people haven't tried tobacco and alcohol at least once.

The teen years are also a period in which people experiment with substance use that they will not continue later in life. During the teen years, substance abuse is more excessive, perhaps due to the influence of the peer group as opposed to parents. In young adulthood, substance abuse decreases slowly for many people, as they take on new social roles as parents and employees. For most teenagers, using or experimenting with drugs, though considered deviant, is usually "just a phase" of development. Some, however, find it difficult or impossible to escape this "phase," and consequently become failed or absent parents or largely unemployable.

Teen experimentation with alcohol and drugs, while offering a sense of "pseudo-adulthood," also socializes teenagers into deviant subcultures and roles. This increases the likelihood that they will continue to abuse substances and decreases their exposure to (and learning of) mainstream norms. However, most teens who experiment with alcohol and drugs pass through this stage without harming themselves or others. It is only when substance abuse continues into adulthood and interferes with job or family roles that it is seen as much more deviant.

As for the social construction of alcohol and drug problems, there are always cultural, historically specific reasons why—today—we consider substance use problems and deal with them in the ways we do.

The History of Drug and Alcohol Abuse and Public Reactions

Because drugs and alcohol have cultural meanings, popular thinking about who is permitted to use drugs and how they use them changes over time. Take the age limits on drinking. In modern youth culture, the use of alcohol for intoxication purposes is a key symbol of transition from childhood. Because alcohol consumption is formally restricted to adults, many people view gaining the legal right to consume alcohol as a "rite of passage" into adulthood.

However, public alcohol use was not always just an adult activity. In late-medieval England, when many boys did men's work, the same norms governed both men's and boys' access to alcohol, for example. New norms that limited boys' access to alcohol only came into effect when a shortage of jobs kept many boys from entering adulthood by achieving financial independence (Warner, 1998).

Two other developments in the early modern period coincided with reductions in juvenile access to alcohol. First, drinking gradually changed into an essentially recreational activity carried on outside the home in groups consisting mainly of males. Second, entrepreneurs introduced new and potentially more intoxicating beverages, first in the form of beer and later in the form of cheap spirits distilled from grain. So, as men did more of their drinking in public places and came to favour more powerful beverages, boys were increasingly excluded from the activity (ibid.).

Public drinking by women was not thought to endanger public virtue in England before the sixteenth and seventeenth centuries. But with the economic and social crises of the early modern period, women were pushed back into the home and obliged to do their drinking there (ibid.). By contrast, men continued to drink outside the home—and, often, mainly outside the home in the company of other men.

Changes in religious beliefs and practices have also influenced the use of drugs throughout history. Typically, drugs have been more widely and readily used by the followers of what we might call *expressive religions*. These expressive religions—for example, Roman Catholicism—use a variety of elaborate rituals and artifacts to celebrate religious observance. By contrast, *repressive religions*—for example, many Protestant denominations—tend to reject elaborate rituals and artifacts, calling instead for simplicity and modesty. Religious (and social) movements that set out to reform the world are usually repressive, since they rely on continuous, dedicated toil by their members. This requirement makes sobriety—as well as thrift, industry, planning, and efficiency—a central value of the religious subculture. No wonder, then, that the rise of Protestantism in Western Europe meant not only support for the spirit of capitalism, as Max Weber (1958 [1904]) tells us, but also support for the spirit of sobriety.

Time to Reflect: If the modern, capitalist age was driven by a religious value system (Protestantism) that called for sobriety, how do you account for the widespread use of intoxicating substances in today's modern world?

In the past hundred years, mass media have played an ever-increasing role in the construction of moral panic about drugs and alcohol, often boosting circulation or audience by raising fears about excessive drug use and its effects. Legislators and law enforcers have also benefited by promoting the idea that drugs pose a public problem that they are uniquely qualified to control. The RCMP's role here is clear in *Panic and Indifference: The Politics of Canada's Drug Laws* (Giffen et al.,1991). This study of the history of narcotics legislation shows that, though the original anti-opium legislation may have begun with hatred towards and fear of an almost exclusively male racial minority (i.e., the Chinese), it persisted and expanded because of self-aggrandizing efforts of bureaucratic lawmakers. It was in their occupational and professional interest to promote social concerns about narcotics that would justify more spending on the problem.

Within Canadian history, Judge Emily Murphy's *The Black Candle* (1922) illustrates the cultural meanings and popular attitudes towards drugs that prevailed during the 1920s and led to anti-drug legislation. In her book, Murphy describes drug use in Canada as a serious social concern, providing detailed information about the use of cocaine, opium, and what she termed a new *menace*—"marihuana." She strongly advocated for drug addiction to be recognized as a problem of law enforcement. Shortly after the publication of her book, legislation that specifically defined drug addiction as an issue of law enforcement was passed.

Reading Murphy's book today, we can see that her view of drug addiction was influenced by the racist attitudes of the period. In fact, Murphy admitted that her concern over drug addiction emerged because she was seeing a "disproportionate" number of Chinese people in her courtroom, and local detectives had given her a guided tour of opium dens in Vancouver's Chinatown. A year after the publication of her book, which first appeared as several *Maclean's* magazine articles, the exclusionary Chinese Immigration Act of 1923 was passed by Parliament.

Now, here's the paradox: ample research shows that alcohol causes people more harm than all the other drugs put together. So why, then, is alcohol still legal ? To answer this question we have to look at the temperance movement, which had been active and organized since the mid-nineteenth century in an effort to ban the sale of beer, wine, and spirits because of the social problems and harm caused by alcohol consumption, especially, in the view of these middle-class reformers, among the working classes. In Canada, prohibition became a local option in the late nineteenth century and numerous municipalities banned the sale of alcohol. Prince Edward Island, in 1901, became the first "dry" province, and other provinces followed during the World War I years. By 1930, the provincial prohibition laws had been repealed, except in PEI, which stayed dry until 1948. Some municipalities chose to remain dry, and a few across Canada remain so.

The prohibitionists, part of the first wave of the women's movement, failed in their central mission of preventing alcohol use. In fact, for a brief period they unwittingly succeeded in enriching black-market gangsters. Prohibition in the United States, which lasted nationally from 1920 to 1933, gave gangsters huge profits from an illegal traffic in bootlegged, often poisonous, alcohol.

Some Canadian distillery fortunes were made by supplying illegal alcohol across the US border, for even during the brief prohibition period in Canada, breweries, distilleries, and wineries were allowed to continue production for out-of-province export and for "industrial, scientific, mechanical, artistic, sacramental and medicinal uses" (Hallowell, 1988: 1765). Indeed, throughout the prohibition years, people who were ill could get a doctor's prescription for the purchase of alcohol at a drugstore. As Hallowell reports, during Christmas season when people sought holiday cheer, "long lineups" of "sick" people at doctors' offices suggested "veritable epidemics" of illness (ibid.).

Prohibition dramatized, in legislation, a status war between drinkers and abstainers in North American society. Between 1880 and 1920, the United States and Canada changed from rural, small-town societies to become urban societies with industry driving the economy. During that time, huge numbers of immigrants poured into the cities. In the US especially, they shifted economic and political control away from the native-born, white, Protestant, small-town middle class, which had run the country up through the nineteenth century. Symbolically, the effort to impose temperance through Prohibition in the US was a bid to turn the clock back to a time when society was uniform and dominated by middle-class Protestants.

In Canada, the French Catholic factor, especially in Quebec, had an ameliorating effect on rural–urban and class polarization, and Quebec had repealed its weak temperance legislation by 1919—thereby providing an early boon to the tourist industry in that province! The story of prohibition as it played out in North America suggests that societies seemingly plagued by deviance may actually suffer from too many rules.

The social factors that promoted laws against alcohol during the Prohibition era—notably, a status war between different parts of the population—are much the same as the factors promoting the modern "war on drugs." Today, for example, in the US the despised minority drug users are African-Americans. Ninety years ago, the despised minority drug (i.e., alcohol) users were immigrants. Yet, as sociologist Joseph Gusfield (1963) points out in his history of Prohibition, the effort to limit alcohol use was much more symbolic than practical. It was doomed to fail, and when it failed, it failed both symbolically and in practice. People continued to drink, and small-town Protestant teetotallers lost much of their political influence in the nation as a whole.

Congress repealed Prohibition partly because the legislators could see the harm it was doing. When regulated alcoholic beverages are unavailable, people will drink just about anything. In the 1920s and 1930s, many Americans died or went blind from drinking beverages that contained dangerous impurities or the wrong kind of alcohol (i.e., methanol instead of ethanol). This still occurs in some parts of the world, where poor and rural people cannot afford to buy licensed and regulated alcohol. In India in December 2011, for example, nearly 150 people were reported killed by a batch of methanol-based moonshine.

Today legal alcohol consumption per capita continues to rise in Canada and, as shown in Figure 5.1, the increase in British Columbia has been above the national average.

Nicotine Addiction

Cigarettes, too, contain a powerful drug, nicotine. Nicotine addiction, via cigarette smoking, first became widespread during the twentieth century. Tobacco use seems to have originated in South America, where the Native peoples used it for religious and medicinal purposes. Explorers returning from the Americas introduced tobacco to Europe, where it became fashionable in the seventeenth century but was, for a time, illegal and considered immoral.

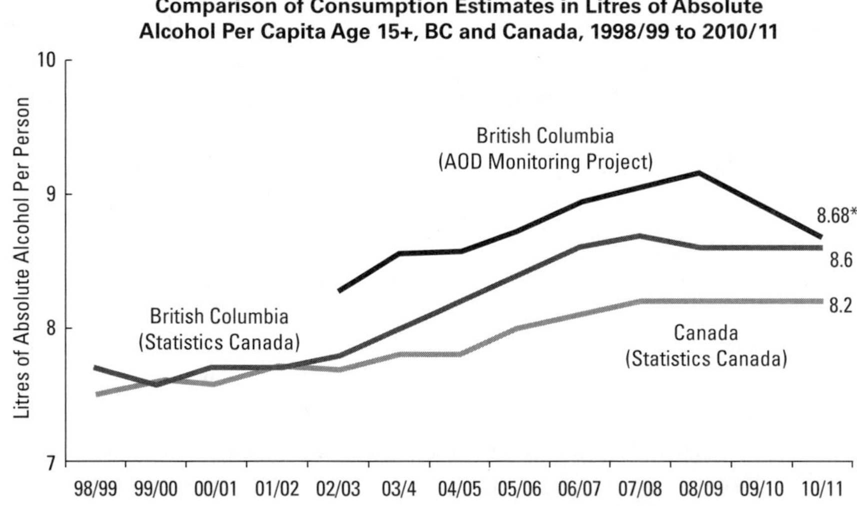

FIGURE 5.1 Growth in Alcohol Consumption, British Columbia and Canada, 1998–9 to 2010–11

Source: University of Victoria, Centre for Addictions Research of BC, at: <carbc.ca/AODMonitoring/ProjectComponents/AlcoholConsumption.aspx>.

During the world wars, governments promoted sending tobacco to those who were away fighting, as a symbol of patriotism and love. They encouraged and praised those at home for sending a carton of cigarettes overseas. However, after the war, new advances in medicine led to warnings about the harmful effects of tobacco, and attitudes towards tobacco use began to change. Accordingly, since the 1960s, men have greatly reduced their consumption of cigarettes. However, women and teenagers have increased their consumption over the same period. Today, women are almost as likely as men to smoke.

Prevalence rates for smoking remain especially high among young people, despite the proven health risks. Indeed, tobacco has long been the drug of choice for high school students. However, rates of smoking have declined drastically in recent years as taxation on cigarettes and, therefore, the cost of cigarettes have risen dramatically. According to a Health Canada survey published in 2010, the smoking rate among 16–19-year-olds dropped to 20 per cent in 2005 from 29 per cent in 2001. Teen smoking rates have fallen below that of the general population—which held steady around 21 per cent—for the first time in almost a decade (www.statcan.gc.ca/pub/82-625-x/2011001/article/11468-eng.htm).

One reason so many people smoke is because the harmful effects of tobacco are slow to develop. Unlike alcohol and other drugs, the harms associated with cigarettes are not as immediate. You can fail school because of cocaine addiction, or crash a car while drunk—these effects are immediately visible—but getting cancer from smoking, or even just suffering from receding gums, takes years. Most youth believe they will quit smoking before they ever begin to feel its negative effects, and many do so, but many others

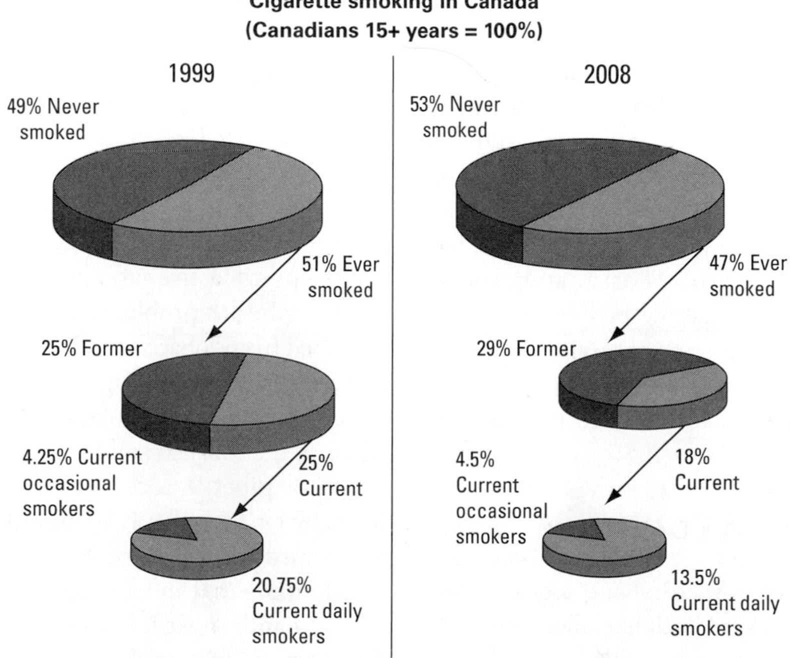

FIGURE 5.2 Reduction of Cigarette Smoking in Canada

Source: University of Ottawa, "Society, the Individual, and Medicine," at: <www.med.uottawa.ca/sim/data/Smoking_Rates_e.htm>.

cannot. So, for generations, cigarette smoking has remained a cultural habit, despite the changes to cigarette packaging in 2012 to include ever more graphic health warnings.

As a result, smoking continues to support a billion-dollar industry. For example, a recent report from Imperial Tobacco, Europe's second-biggest tobacco company and a major presence in the Canadian market, showed an operating profit of US$2.5 billion in the six months ending 31 March 2012. Sales volume in the UK continued to rise despite economizing among many smokers owing to the economic depression; however, profits fell in the Americas. Apparently, tobacco companies are now relying more on emerging markets to offset declining consumption and rising government taxes in Western Europe and North America. Imperial Tobacco CEO Alison Cooper said she was "pleased with the ongoing success of our key strategic brands," where the net revenue profit increase for the six-month period was 12 per cent (www.imperial-tobacco.com/files/financial/results/hy2012/index.asp?pageid=8).

If smoking were made illegal, legal tobacco profits would disappear entirely. On the other hand, as during Prohibition in US, smokers might use illegal means to get cigarettes and organized crime would move into marketing cigarettes. Fortunately, as the charts in Figure 5.2 show, people are increasingly avoiding smoking or giving it up after having started; as well, economic pressures and government taxes have reduced smoking somewhat.

Attitudes towards Drug Users

A large volume of medical and social research shows that the use of illicit narcotics—especially cannabis (marijuana and hashish)—is far less costly in physical and social terms than nicotine or alcohol. Yet the public continues to view illicit drugs—such as cocaine and heroin, but even including cannabis—as vastly more dangerous than these more common, legal substances.

On the whole, societal conceptions of drug addiction and drug addicts remain, as they were in previous eras, very negative. Though there is a growing understanding of drug addiction as a disease, many people continue to view drug addiction as immoral and wicked—a result of bad choices. There is, however, wider public support for treatment programs, thanks to the new medical discourse about drugs. As more people come to view drug addiction as a medical—and not a moral—problem, they are more willing to support treatment and harm reduction programs. This accounts for the increased engagement of public health researchers in all forms of alcohol and drug research, including the study of cigarette smokers.

The Activities and Characteristics of Substance Abusers

Tobacco

As we have said, tobacco is one of Canada's most popular legal drugs. Like alcohol, nicotine is a psychoactive substance that is to blame for many health problems. Nicotine is readily absorbed from tobacco smoke in the lungs and can enter the body through first-hand, second-hand, or third-hand smoke. It does not matter whether the tobacco smoke is from cigarettes, cigars, or pipes. A recent study of US households by Dr Jonathan P. Winickoff, a professor at Harvard Medical School, and his colleagues (2011) finds that most people are aware that second-hand smoke is harmful to children, but few are aware of the risks of carcinogens associated with third-hand smoke, i.e., the invisible residue left on furniture, clothing, and hair.

General risks associated with smoking cigarettes include a reduced sense of smell and taste, frequent colds, smoker's cough, gastric ulcers, chronic bronchitis, increase in heart rate and blood pressure, heart disease, stroke, and cancer. Research shows that cigarette smoking is Canada's largest cause of preventable disease and premature death. Male and female smokers lose an average of 13.2 and 14.5 years of life, respectively. This harm operates at every part of a smoker's life, starting in adolescence. Researchers argue that smoking is particularly dangerous for teens because their bodies are still developing and changing. The many chemicals in cigarette smoke can adversely affect this development.

Cigarettes, like alcohol and other drugs, have been implicated in major criminal activity—notably smuggling, to evade the payment of customs duties. In August 2008, two of Canada's "big three" tobacco companies, Imperial Tobacco and Rothmans Benson & Hedges, were ordered to pay more than $1 billion in criminal and civil penalties for arranging the wholesale shipment of cigarettes to the United States. These cigarettes were then smuggled back to Canada and sold at (illegal) bargain prices. Between 1989 and 1994, tax-free cigarettes were carried south by truck, most commonly through the Akwesasne First Nation reserve near Cornwall, Ontario, and the adjoining St Regis Mohawk reservation in upstate New York. From there, they were distributed to smugglers who brought them back to Canada to be resold at bargain prices on the street and in convenience stores. The goal, plainly, was to induce smokers to buy these brands and to maintain their share of the Canadian tobacco market.

Both companies admitted guilt, and at the end of the case Imperial Tobacco Canada Ltd agreed to pay a $200 million fine and Rothmans Benson & Hedges a $100 million fine. In total, the fines and settlement costs amounted to $1.15 billion—the largest ever levied in a Canadian court. This includes $815 million in civil damages to the federal, Ontario, and Quebec governments. However, some believe the tobacco companies actually received only lenient punishment. The penalties levied were far less than the billions of dollars lost to the federal and provincial governments through this smuggling; what's more, no charges were laid against company executives.

Alcohol

Alcohol researchers Naranjo and Bremner (1993) note that alcohol is used in most cultures, though people are well aware of physical, psychological, and social problems that may result from alcohol abuse. The chance and extent of harmful behaviour depend on several factors, including blood-alcohol concentration and the drinker's rate of alcohol metabolism. Harmful behaviours related to drunkenness include impaired driving, aggression, violence towards oneself and others, and various types of accidents.

A report submitted to Parliament's Standing Committee on Justice and Human Rights (Mann, 2008) concludes that:

> Drunk driving is one of the largest causes of alcohol-related death in Canada and other developed countries and, in Canada, is the largest criminal cause of death. Thus, it is very appropriate and commendable for Parliament to be considering ways to reduce those deaths. Juergen Rehm and colleagues, in their report on the costs of alcohol, tobacco, and other drugs, estimated the number of Canadians killed in alcohol-related collisions in 2002 to be 9,091, a number which for several reasons is acknowledged to be an underestimate.

The author of this report notes this is considerably more than the number of Canadians killed in combat in Afghanistan, about which there was great (and justifiable) public concern.

Similar statistics have been reported in the UK and Sweden. The risk of a fatal car accident increases dramatically with a driver's blood-alcohol level. The risks of falling, drowning, and fires also increase with degree of alcohol intoxication. At least one work-related accident in five may involve alcohol use. Finally, and not least, excessive alcohol consumption promotes aggressive behaviour and domestic violence, although we cannot readily tell whether this is a result of pharmacological effects or psychosocial effects, or a factor common to both.

Like some other drugs, alcohol is not intrinsically bad when used moderately and responsibly. People of all nationalities and cultures have used it for millennia. People drink alcohol to achieve its chemical effects: to relax, smooth social events, reduce tension, and slow down perceptual, cognitive, and motor functioning. The goal of drinking, then, is to escape from the stress, boredom, and frustration of everyday life and, often, to do so in the company of others, as part of a shared, sociable haze. Drinking becomes problematic only when it becomes excessive or addictive.

Binge drinking is an especially big problem on many college campuses; in fact, some Canadian and American universities are famous for being "party schools" with heavy drinking and drinking-related problems. Conceivably, some students attend these schools to take part in this drinking culture. Heavy drinking is characteristic of celebration by sports teams and their fans, for example. In the US, student drinking is even more of a concern than in Canada, since many undergraduates are under the national drinking age of 21. Various efforts have been proposed to combat problematic drinking on college campuses.

Deviant drinking takes either of two forms: heavy drinking in a moderate-drinking environment, or light drinking in a heavy-drinking environment. In each instance, one is led to wonder if the deviance is due to a faulty understanding of the local norms. Research into this problem on one college campus by Christopher Rice (2007) finds that you can reduce drinking among college students by correcting their misperceived drinking norms—that is, the amount they believe other people are drinking. People typically want to conform to the norms of their drinking reference group; however, different ethnic and racial groups seemingly have different drinking norms. Students are most willing to adjust their drinking when they are given information about the norms of their own group, rather than the overall average.

People consume a lot of alcohol each year, though per capita consumption patterns vary from one province to another (see, e.g., Statistics Canada, 2009). To some degree, provincial patterns reflect the age, sex, and ethnic ancestry of the population mix. Generally, provinces with more single young men and more Native people show the highest per capita rates of alcohol consumption.

In much the same way as alcohol can be used and abused, some believe that the excessive consumption of high-calorie foods can be seen as an addiction. Box 5.1 examines whether food should be regarded as an addictive substance, or if binge eating is incomparable to drug use.

Time to Reflect: What have you noticed about the types of people who consume alcohol most often on your college or university campus, and the occasions they do so? What is your school's policy on alcohol consumption?

Current Events

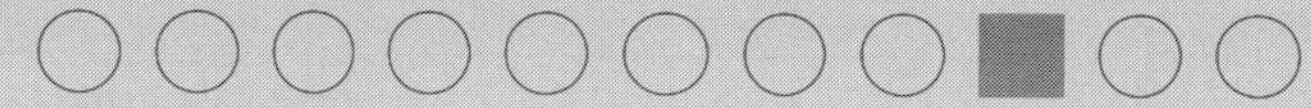

BOX 5.1

Binge Eating

A recent study suggests that excessive eating generates responses in the brain that resemble those seen in drug addicts. In this study, rats gorged themselves on high-calorie foods such as bacon and chocolate despite being aware that they would receive an electric shock for doing so (see www.cbc.ca/news/story/2010/03/29/junk-food-addiction-brain.html).

These results suggest that addicts consume substances—whether drugs or food—even when they are aware of the harm that will ensue. One of the co-authors of this study, Paul Johnson, a graduate student in molecular therapeutics at the Scripps Research Institute in Florida, suggested that overeating and obesity are typically linked with constant exposure and access to high-calorie foods. The other study author, Paul Kenny, a neurobiologist at the Scripps Research Institute, claims that overeating can develop into an obsessive, overwhelming habit very similar to that of drug use.

Terence Wilson of Rutgers University has come to a similar conclusion with regard to binge eating; the seemingly random, uncontrollable impulse to consume, he believes, is akin to the irrepressible need of drug addicts to use (Wilson, 2000: 91). Wilson proposes that treatment and counselling approaches currently used to help drug addicts should be applicable for people who overeat as well. Wilson reminds us that many obese binge eaters receive treatment from Overeaters Anonymous groups, which are structured according to the 12-step approach used by other addiction counselling programs such as Alcoholics Anonymous.

But Wilson also raises some valid points that suggest food cannot function as a drug—that is, it cannot be seen as an addictive substance in itself. Wilson points out that people who struggle with eating disorders (the definition of which includes binge eating) don't exhibit symptoms of dependence on, withdrawal from, or tolerance of certain foods, all of which are signs of addiction. If people can't use and abuse food as they do drugs, the treatment programs used to treat drug abuse will not sufficiently address the needs of obese overeaters (ibid., 88).

Evidently, more research must be conducted to confirm whether food may be classified as an addictive substance, or if binge eaters will benefit more from treatment options that are not geared towards addiction treatment.

Marijuana

Marijuana is the most widely used illicit drug in North America and likely the first illegal drug that teenagers will use, although many young people are first introduced to mood-altering substances through doctor-prescribed drugs, such as Ritalin, intended to modify unruly, hyperactive (and predominantly male) behaviour. As the data in Figure 5.3 show, most drug arrests and convictions in Canada are for marijuana. Indeed, in Canada, arrests for possession or sale of cannabis essentially drive the law enforcement program. However, as the same data indicate, after 1980, and especially between 1985 and 1995, more attention was given to other drugs, creating a larger gap between the total number of charges for drug offences and those for cannabis.

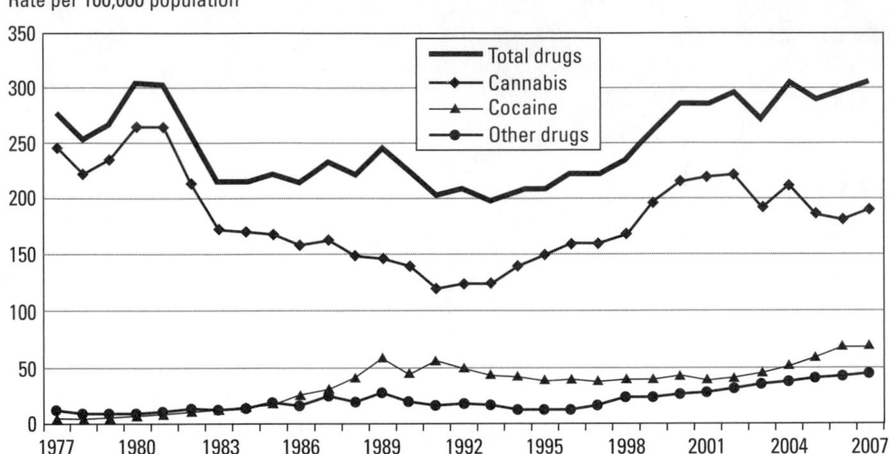

FIGURE 5.3 Police-Reported Drug Offence Rates, by Type of Drug, Canada, 1977–2007

Source: M. Dauvergne, "Trends in Police-Reported Drug Offences in Canada," *Juristat* (May 2009): Chart 2, at: <www.statcan.gc.ca/pub/85-002-x/2009002/article/10847-eng.htm#a5>.

The short-term effects of using marijuana include sleepiness, difficulty keeping track of time, reduced short-term memory, a reduced ability to do tasks needing concentration and co-ordination, increased heart rate, paranoia, hallucinations, and decreased social inhibitions. The long-term effects of smoking marijuana may include (for men) a decrease in testosterone levels, lower sperm counts, and difficulty having children; (for women) an increased risk of infertility; and (for both men and women) a heightened cancer risk (though this has been debated), decreased sexual pleasure, and psychological dependence requiring more of the drug to get the same effect.

Statistics Canada reports that in 2007, rates per 100,000 population for drug-related violations—mainly cannabis possession—were highest for individuals between the ages of 18 and 24, followed by 12–17-year-olds. The highest rates of drug offences were reported in British Columbia, Saskatchewan, and the Northwest Territories. In 2006–7, drug offences represented 7 per cent of all adult (criminal) and youth court cases. Figure 5.4 shows the relationship between cannabis use and the use of other illicit drugs in one province, Alberta, among those of ages 15 and over.

Many critics worry about marijuana's role as a potential **gateway drug**—that is, as a drug that leads to the use of "harder" drugs such as cocaine or heroin. However, for social and psychological reasons, people who are willing to try one type of drug may already be likely to try another drug. So, it is not the drug itself that causes further drug use. This process of **adverse selectivity** disappears when large numbers of people are using marijuana. Therefore, no particular "gateway" to other drug use is needed. Moreover, only a small fraction of all the people who use marijuana go on to using other, more addictive drugs.

Whether cannabis use is deviant largely depends on local and group norms and perceptions of risk. Despite speculation to the contrary, there is no real evidence to support the idea that abstainers are necessarily more poorly adjusted than users (or vice versa).

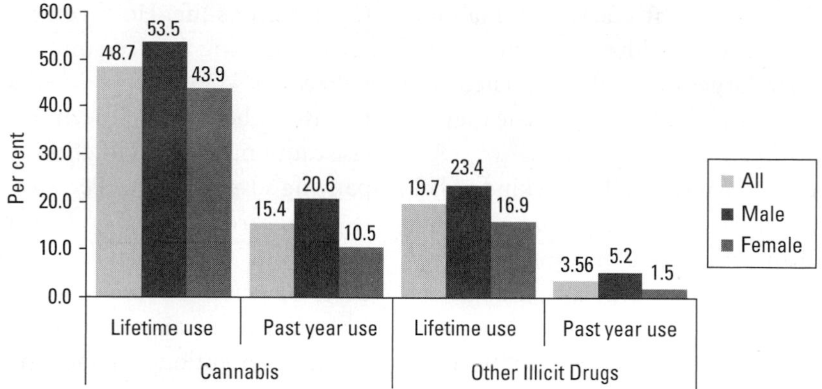

FIGURE 5.4 Lifetime and Past Year Cannabis and Other Drug Use among Albertans Aged 15 Years and Older, by Sex

Source: Alberta Alcohol and Drug Abuse Commission, *Canadian Addiction Survey 2004: Alberta Report* (Edmonton, 2006), at: <www.knowmo.ca/statistics/IllicitDrugs/Illicit_Drug_Use.aspx>.

However, a study by Tucker et al. (2006) suggests that abstainers do better according to various psychosocial measures. This longitudinal study compared Grade 12 marijuana abstainers, experimenters, and frequent users on psychosocial functioning during late adolescence and young adulthood. Those participating were recruited around ages 11–12 and assessed repeatedly until age 23. The results show that adolescent abstainers often fared better (and never fared worse) than marijuana users in school engagement, family and peer relations, mental health, and deviant behaviour.

Hallucinogens

No discussion of current drug use would be complete without a brief consideration of hallucinogens—psychoactive drugs that can change people's consciousness in ways that are often compared to dream states, trances, and meditation. Formally, they are defined as drugs that alter thought, perception, and mood, yet (as a rule) do not permanently impair intellect or memory, or lead to addiction.

Hallucinogens, though considered "modern" by many, are among the oldest drugs known to humanity; and they occur naturally in mushrooms, peyote and other cacti, and many other common plants. Cultures around the world have long used them for religious, medical, and recreational purposes. Historically, hallucinogens have been most commonly used for healing or in religious rituals. More recently, during the 1960s, hallucinogens—especially, so-called psychedelic drugs like **LSD**—played a major part in the counterculture, where they were associated with youth rebellion and a refusal to conform to adult behaviour norms.

Psychedelics are the most familiar type of hallucinogen. Some commentators, such as novelist Aldous Huxley, have argued that these drugs work by *disabling* the brain's ability to filter out certain perceptions, memories, and thoughts, suddenly making them available to the conscious mind. As a result, we can think of hallucinogens as *mind-expanding* or *consciousness-expanding*, for they increase the range of thought-experiences. Some drug "trips" can last as long as days, but most are much briefer. In recent years, illegal laboratories around the world have produced hundreds of new, largely unstudied psychedelics, and we are far from knowing how safe they are for human use.

Dissociative drugs are a second kind of hallucinogen. Unlike psychedelics, they kill pain, producing amnesia (loss of memory) and even stupor at higher doses. Typically, they detach people from the surrounding environment. People using them feel depersonalized, as though they are watching themselves from a great distance. Some users report out-of-body experiences (for example, flying through the sky) or a sense of robotic estrangement from their true selves. Probably the most common dissociative drug is nitrous oxide, commonly used by dentists to dull the pain of dental surgery.

Deliriants, a third kind of hallucinogen, induce a state characterized by confusion, loss of control, and sometimes even rage. Drug users feel effects that are like the experience of a high fever; presumably, their goal is to experience new, though not always pleasant, sensations. Natural suppliers of this group of drugs are the plants commonly known as deadly nightshade, angel's trumpet, jimson weed, and nutmeg.

Cocaine

Cocaine is an inhaled stimulant and has been used for centuries for religious, social, and medicinal purposes. It belongs to the class of drugs known as stimulants, which give the user a temporary illusion of limitless power and energy and leave the user feeling depressed, edgy, and craving more. The substance called *crack cocaine* is a chemically altered form of cocaine that users smoke.

For some, cocaine is highly addictive and may come to control every aspect of the regular user's life. However, many have succeeded in using the drug only as an occasional recreation. While users do seek a quick and intense high from cocaine, most of them exercise caution, fearing addiction and the accompanying adverse effects. Perceived risk of harm is, therefore, the major factor that affects level of use. Urban blacks were the first main users of crack cocaine in the United States. By contrast, cocaine use has been less widespread, contentious, or racially segregated in Canada. By estimate, less than 1 per cent of the Canadian population uses cocaine regularly. As with most other drugs, Canadian men are more likely than Canadian women to be users.

Drugs—even powder and crack cocaine—are used differently according to socio-economic background. In the Netherlands, for example, middle-class "party youth" occasionally use the drugs in clubs and discotheques for recreational purposes. Deprived "problem youth" from minority backgrounds add the drugs to already troubled multi-problem behaviour in their marginalized lifestyles. This implies that the problem to be solved is not drug use but social deprivation.

Heroin

Heroin is the most commonly injected drug in Canada for recreational use although, again, only a small fraction of the population reports using it. Heroin works fast, making it especially addictive. After an injection, heroin enters the brain through the bloodstream. Once in the brain, it changes to morphine and binds rapidly to opioid receptors. As a result, users typically report feeling a surge of pleasure, commonly called a *rush*. The intensity of this rush depends on how much of the drug is taken and how fast the drug enters the brain.

Tolerance to the drug develops with regular heroin use, meaning that the user must inject even more of the substance to achieve the same intensity or effect. In time, physical dependence and addiction increase until a user can no longer control desire and need. Withdrawal symptoms will occur if the user reduces or stops using the drug. Sudden withdrawal by a heavily dependent user in poor health can be fatal.

Mullen and Hammersley (2006) found that giving up heroin occurred after repeated tries and repeated treatments, often around major life changes. The men Mullen and Hammersley studied frequently relapsed, usually because of quitting without enough mental preparation. Others relapsed after returning to old places or situations; or because of the boredom of a life without heroin and an inability to cope with emotions previously suppressed by heroin use. Thus, many bounced back and forth between the deviant community of heroin injectors and the conventional neighbourhood. For drug use to end permanently, there had to be both a push away from the subculture and a pull towards the neighbourhood.

In closing, we should note that many prescription drugs have also made their way into the street drug market: they include Ritalin, the SSRIs, numerous painkillers such as OxyContin (now reformulated to reduce the possibility of its being crushed and transformed into an addictive street drug), and the various atypical (second-generation) anti-psychotics (e.g., Risperdol, Zyprexa) and typical (first-generation) anti-psychotics (e.g., Haldol). All are/have been sold on the street, by those for whom they are prescribed or by others who acquire them from prescription holders or by black market means. The illicit sale and use of these licit drugs, many of which are hugely harmful, are central to the issue of illicit drugs as a social problem.

Communities and Subcultures of Drug Users

Drug-using communities are interesting to sociologists for various reasons. As we have just seen, escaping from addiction to particular "hard" drugs like heroin will almost necessarily mean leaving the heroin-using community and forging a new life.

Members of drug communities often lead lives that are unusual, dangerous, and secretive, especially if they are committing criminal acts to get and use the drugs. They may also develop distinctive practices, customs, terminology, and safety and support systems. The more dangerous or difficult it is to get the drug, the more restrictive and mysterious the associated community. As a result, the communities of heroin or cocaine users are more unusual and distinctive than those of marijuana users, which, in turn, are more unusual and distinctive than those of alcohol or tobacco users.

In the process of getting and using drugs, community members will have needed to learn the skills to use the relevant paraphernalia. Hard-drug users need to know where to get the drugs, drug pipes, needles, and other equipment. They need to know how to smoke, swallow, or inject the drug to get a desired but non-lethal effect. Finally, they need to know how to appreciate and realize the effects of the drug.

As we mentioned earlier, research by Howard Becker (1953) provided valuable insight into how new marijuana smokers, through community membership, learn to sense and enjoy the effects of the drug (Box 5.2). Becker claimed that, without the right knowledge, the effects of marijuana might pass unnoticed or cause feelings of fear and discomfort. Becker believed that people have to learn to enjoy marijuana.

Classic Works

BOX 5.2

Howard Becker on *Outsiders*

In *Outsiders* (1963), Howard Becker set the groundwork for labelling theory as it is known today. He based his theories on his study as a participant-observer of marijuana users and jazz musicians. This analysis demonstrated that while members of these groups are labelled deviant because of their actions, their outsider status does not result from the intrinsic nature of their actions, but from how others respond to them. Deviance is thus created by larger social groups that reject and stigmatize smaller groups and label them as outsiders.

In his analysis, Becker dismisses a simultaneous model of deviance, in which background material (such as the role of broken families) is referred to but not situated in a causal sequence. In opposition to prevailing causal theories of addiction, Becker suggests that becoming deviant may well be a sequential *process*, but different factors are relevant at different stages in this progression towards becoming "outsiders." There is no single, typical pattern or sequence.

Becker suggests that this process requires deviants to learn socially supplied reasons for starting an activity, as well as a rationale for continuing it. Becoming a deviant is thus a process of progressively increasing commitment to a set of norms and institutions that endow the deviant action with meaning and value. Deviants are therefore also defined within their subgroup, rather than solely by the larger group that labels them; to be labelled "deviant" necessarily requires a commitment to an "outsider" group in addition to the rejection or labelling of this group by the larger society.

Outsiders emphasizes that the study of deviance must pay as much attention to the rule *enforcer* as it does to the rule *violator.* Instead of asking why they are deviant, the main question becomes: Why do we label such behaviour as deviant? This approach eliminates the assumption of wrongdoing present in models of dysfunction or mental illness. Becker (2005) underscores this in later writings, focusing on causal accusation: Who accuses who ? What do they accuse them of doing ? Under what circumstances are these accusations successful in the sense of being accepted by others (at least by some others)?

Drug users, like other deviants, often have a deviant lifestyle that may amount to a **deviant career**. Like any career, a drug-using career is made up of progressive stages of deeper involvement in the main (deviant) activity, the relevant community, and its subculture.

Where deviant communities and cultures exist, they lend support to individual desires to use drugs or commit other deviant acts. Psychological or individual explanations of drug use become less useful when a full-fledged community and subculture exist. Some urban sociologists have also noted that there is a particular geography to drug use and other deviant and criminal activities.

Certain parts of a city are more likely than others to contain places and people who can supply drugs, paraphernalia, and expert knowledge. Sociologist Donald Clairmont, in an unpublished manuscript (1973; also Clairmont and Magill, 1970) about the black slum in Halifax, Nova Scotia, named Africville, called these parts of a city **deviance service centres**, since various deviant needs and tastes can typically be satisfied in these areas (including drugs, prostitution, gambling, etc.). Such areas specialize in providing illegal goods and services, often developing in less prosperous parts of the city with limited economic opportunities and little police control. Africville was a particularly well-documented example 50 years ago: squatter housing combined with racial discrimination, poverty, and unemployment to encourage deviant and criminal opportunities.

Media Depictions of Substance Abuse

Substance abuse has long been a common subject in popular culture, encompassing the concerns of nearly every race, gender, and class. Around the turn of the century, readers all around the Atlantic world followed the cases of Sherlock Holmes who, like his modern counterpart Dr Gregory House of the television show *House M.D.*, was a drug addict (Holmes to opium, House to vicodin). Throughout the latter half of the twentieth century, the movie industry found it profitable to produce films with a focus on drug use and abuse, from the high-class, all-female "pill popping" featured in *Valley of the Dolls* (1967) to the low-class, all-male street drug use in *Trainspotting* (1996).

Over the last decade, movies and television have capably shown the class, gender, and race dynamics at play in issues relating to substance abuse. The films *Empire* (2002) and *Treed Murray* (2001) effectively speak to how society promotes the idea of "poor person drugs" (crack) and "rich person drugs" (cocaine), using racial and class stereotypes to vilify some drugs and not others. The HBO network, through shows such as *The Sopranos*, *Nurse Jackie*, and *The Wire*, has been exceptional in exploring these issues, looking at how drugs are consumed by the upper and middle classes and under classes, and at how different groups see their own place in drug culture.

While dramas treat drug use and abuse as a matter of some concern, marijuana use has remained an American comedy staple for four decades. The image of the lovable "pothead" came out of a 1960s counterculture that vehemently disagreed with the media's previous demonization of marijuana users in movies like *Reefer Madness* (1936). Beginning in Hollywood with the comedy duo Cheech Marin and Tommy Chong, marijuana culture has moved into popular television shows and movies, including *Half Baked* (1998), *That '70s Show* (1998–2006), and *Pineapple Express* (2008). This has made marijuana use, in many contexts, a value-free act of self-gratification.

Before popular culture considered marijuana use a laughing matter, many popular entertainers were already trading on the idea of the "lovable drunk." W.C. Fields, Red Skelton, Dean Martin, and Ed McMahon were among the most famous names in Hollywood between the 1930s and 1960s whose stage personas often cast them in the role of "lush," a humorous drunkard. With the growing understanding and acceptance of alcoholism's degenerative physical and social affects, however, the "lovable drunk" character gradually lost popular traction. More common today is the negative, troubled view of alcoholism seen in films like *Leaving Las Vegas* (1995).

Time to Reflect: How do you imagine public perceptions of drug use and drug users have changed over the past 20 years, and how would you account for these changes (if any)?

Theories about Drug and Alcohol Abuse

Functionalist Theories

Functionalist theories assert that drug and alcohol use are common because these substances fulfill an important social role—namely, they increase **social cohesion.** In this way, they contribute to the survival of the groups, communities, or societies to which drug users belong.

In some communities, the need for both cohesion and comfort are so great that drugs are bound to play an important role. This is especially true when traditional patterns and constraints break down. According to *social disorganization theory*, another functionalist approach, drug and alcohol abuse increases when institutions that have traditionally discouraged deviant behaviours, such as the family and the church, become less central in people's lives and therefore less effective in establishing and maintaining norms. Then, norms and values become unclear and people turn to deviant behaviour—in this case, to alcohol and drugs.

In short, people use and abuse drugs when traditional norms break down and the community is disrupted. Consider the Canadian Aboriginal population and its problem with addictive substances. With the arrival of European immigrants and the displacement of Aboriginal people from their traditional homelands and ways of living, alcohol abuse and suicide spread. These problems were compounded by racism, poverty, and residential schooling. Nothing seemed to stem this substance abuse problem because of a failure to address the issue of social disorganization: the loss of traditional controls and values. Interaction with white society had broken down traditional tribal societies, deprived the Aboriginal peoples of a sense of meaning, and destroyed the ability of family, community, and religion to control people's actions.

According to social disorganization theory, then, alcohol abuse resulted from all these factors. In addition, evidence suggests that Aboriginal peoples are less able than Europeans to metabolize alcohol effectively. Differences in alcohol tolerance are influenced by cultural factors that include diet, average body weight, and patterns of consumption. However, there is ample evidence suggesting that genetic factors are also at play. North Americans of European descent have a demonstrably higher alcohol tolerance and, therefore, less likelihood of developing alcoholism than First Nations people.

This is apparently the result of higher levels of alcohol dehydrogenase in their bodies, which is in turn an evolutionary result of many more centuries of exposure to drinking alcohol. This finding that alcoholism may have physiological roots has been strengthened in recent years by the discovery of a specific gene, CYP2EI, that regulates how fast people get drunk. People with the gene—an estimated 10–20 per cent of the population—are likely to get drunk after only a few drinks; and this low alcohol tolerance appears to protect them from becoming alcoholics themselves (see, e.g., Caetano and Clark, 1998; Fenna and Mix, 1971; Luczak et al., 2001; Mail et al., 2002; Yin et al., 1988).

There is no known cure for the genetic aspects of Aboriginal alcohol abuse. However, by reversing social disorganization and recovering a sense of community, Aboriginal people in some communities have been able to beat the alcohol problem, and some northern reserves have enacted local prohibition. That said, many Aboriginal communities remain in a state of desperate crisis, often because of other substance abuse. In some communities, for example, over 50 per cent of residents suffer from severe drug addiction from prescription painkillers, notably Percocet and OxyContin (recently reconfigured by the drug company to be less easily abused as a street drug providing an immediate and intense high). In fact, at Cat Lake in northwestern Ontario an estimated 70–80 per cent of adults in the community are addicted to the narcotics (www.cbc.ca/news/canada/thunder-bay/story/2012/04/15/thunder-bay-cat-lake-children-letter.html).

Another functional theory of drug abuse focuses on the gap between cultural goals and institutional means for satisfying those goals. According to Merton's (1957 [1938]) *theory of anomie*, excessive drinking results from a gap between culturally defined goals and socially approved means for reaching those goals. Society blames those who retreat to drugs and alcohol for their own weakness and failure. This protects society from blame and allows inequality to continue without change.

Symbolic Interactionist Theories

Issues of labelling and its effects are important to symbolic interactionists, as we have repeatedly seen. So, symbolic interactionists focus on the social meanings people associate with alcohol and drug use and the labels they attach to others who use drugs—labels like "stoner," "addict," or "alcoholic."

Symbolic interactionists are interested in seeing what kinds of people are labelled deviant, and why. Consider drinking as an example: most people drink alcohol at some time or another, and few are labelled "problem drinkers." Friendly social drinking is the code of the modern, advanced capitalist society. We associate drinking alcohol with relaxation and enjoyment—with "kicking back"—and within some groups and subcultures this approbation is extended to getting drunk. Yet, we also stigmatize and stereotype heavy drinkers in our society. We label some heavy drinkers "alcoholics" and hold various beliefs about them. Symbolic interactionists are interested in understanding the logic that underlies these labelling processes.

Symbolic interactionists, through a branch of study called **social constructionism**, are also interested in the processes by which we attach moralistic conceptions to social behaviours such as drinking. As mentioned earlier, sociologist Joseph Gusfield studied the **symbolic crusade** that led to Prohibition in the United States.

In the social construction and transformation of views on substance abuse, we often find a transition from ignoring the behaviour, to considering it immoral or irresponsible, and then to seeing it as a medical or psychological problem. This last stage is usually called the **medicalization of deviance**. In respect to the use of amphetamines ("speed"), Akihiko Sato (1996) notes six phases in the medicalization of deviance: *definition* (i.e., doctors labelling the abuse of speed as immoral); *prospecting* (i.e., doctors taking greater interest in the intoxication potential of speed); *claims-making* (i.e., doctors claiming the use of speed is a social problem that should be controlled); *legitimacy* (i.e., the government defining use of speed as a medical problem for purposes of regulation); *institutionalization* (i.e., lawmakers prohibiting the use of speed based largely on medical information); and *designation* (i.e., law-enforcers tightening the prohibition of speed use to keep speed users off the streets).

Like the social construction of a social problem, the medicalization of a social problem requires the collaboration of media, public figures, lawmakers, and medical experts.

Critical Theories

Some people benefit more from drug sales and drug laws than others. Alcohol and tobacco, for example, are produced and sold by the wealthy and powerful. Both of these industries are regulated and neither is considered illegal. They profit the stockholders of alcohol and tobacco companies while harming the heavy users, who are often poor.

The financial benefits to a few people result in widespread harm for the many. Consider the social costs of substance use and abuse in Canada. The best overall study of these costs is a report published in 2006, aptly titled *The Costs of Substance Abuse in Canada* and co-authored by Canada's leading addiction experts, led by Jürgen Rehm (Rehm et al., 2006). This study estimates that in Canada in 2002, the overall social cost of substance abuse was $39.8 billion; of this total, tobacco accounted for $17 billion or 42.7 per cent of the harm done, alcohol for another $14.6 billion (or 36.6 per cent), and illegal drugs for $8.2 billion (or 20.7 per cent).

The social cost of alcohol to Canada, $14.6 billion, included $7.1 billion for lost productivity due to illness and premature death, $3.3 billion for health care, and $3.1 billion for law enforcement. Other researchers have suggested that the costs of lost productivity resulting from alcohol use—due to missed days of work, arriving late for work, slowed work pace, mistakes, dismissal, and replacement—may be far higher: a total cost of $51 billion. Such estimation is always inexact but we cannot rule it out.

No wonder, then, that moral reformers in the nineteenth and twentieth centuries opposed alcohol use and tried to fight urban poverty by instilling traditional values—such as hard work, thrift, and family responsibility—in the poor population. The fight for sobriety and temperance became part of this effort to reform and control working-class men.

Similar efforts were made to control drug use by immigrant men. Consider two examples: opium in Canada and marijuana in the United States. The Chinese first brought opium to Canada, as well as a fondness for opium smoking, to ease the hardship of low wages in dangerous jobs and the difficulty of living in an almost exclusively male immigrant community. At first, the law offered no objections to either producing or possessing opium. Later, when people came to feel that Asian immigrants should be driven out of the country so that native-born labourers could take their jobs, the laws on opium changed.

Also, the laws against marijuana use in the US were biased against racial minorities and poor people—chiefly African- and Hispanic-Americans. In the 1960s, when these laws threatened to penalize college-aged children of the white middle class, police and courts scaled back their enforcement. However, they have continued to arrest and convict poorer whites and non-whites. As noted earlier, this conflict can best be viewed as a culture conflict, or status war, waged by whites against blacks, the native-born against immigrants, or middle-class people against poor people.

Feminist Approaches

Female alcoholics and drug abusers are less common than male alcoholics and drug abusers. They also are less visible because women traditionally and even today have been expected to occupy the private sphere—the home—whereas men to a greater extent have been socialized to live in and control the public sphere—paid employment, politics, the local watering place, the back alleys. Only so-called "bad" women conducted their lives in public to the extent that men did.

Gender differences abound in the realm of substance use. Where smoking is concerned, for example, women often have different reasons from men for smoking at all. Social factors play an important role in dictating who smokes, and it is more than the nicotine addiction alone that keeps women smoking. Social status—more than psychological or physiological makeup—influences who smokes and who quits. Also, women smoke under different circumstances than men; for example, they are more likely to smoke when they are under emotional pressure, whereas men smoke in more relaxed or neutral circumstances. Women are also much more likely than men to use cigarettes to cope with personal problems.

According to Health Canada (www.hc-sc.gc.ca/hc-ps/pubs/tobac-tabac/gsf-vsf/index-eng.php), women smoke for various reasons:

- to relax and take a break;
- to be sociable;
- to deal with stress and depression;
- to fight feelings of helplessness;
- to deal with anger and frustration;
- to avoid gaining weight;
- as a sign of control over their lives;
- because they are addicted.

Consequently, women most at risk usually fit one or more of the following categories:

- unemployed or with a low income or blue-collar job;
- less-educated;
- Aboriginal;
- francophone.

Lorraine Greaves's research on Canadian and Australian women leads to similar conclusions about the social role of tobacco:

- *Organizing social relationships.* Women report using smoking to equalize, bond, distance, defuse, or end relationships with others, including partners, children, and workmates.
- *Creating an image.* Women report using smoking to feel independent, different, stylish, accepted, and in a few cases, to stay thin.
- *Controlling emotions.* Women report using smoking to suppress or reduce negative emotions, anesthetize certain feelings, or, less frequently, to allow positive emotions to emerge.
- *Building a dependency.* On this theme, women report using smoking as a source of support, predictability, or controllability.
- *Finding an identity.* The women interviewed see their smoking as grounds for guilt, tension, contradiction, and a reason for self-castigation. As a result, the women reflect on their identity in terms of their smoking. (Greaves, 1996)

Alcohol is another drug that has had a gendered meaning in our history. For women, alcohol abuse has often been associated with male violence, especially domestic violence. Alcohol acts as a catalyst that ignites violence in already explosive domestic environments, with both male violence against female partners and female violence against males. Often, this violence translates into the physical, emotional, and sexual abuse of spouses and children.

Consequences of Drug and Alcohol Abuse

Social Consequences

Crime

Most drugs, when used excessively, result in unpredictable, deviant, and even criminal behaviour. Besides crimes associated with growing, processing, manufacturing, and trafficking illegal drugs, there are also crimes associated with drug use, committed by addicts to secure money to buy more drugs. Entire deviant subcultures and underground economies survive and thrive on the ability to traffic in illegal drugs. Crimes associated with securing money for drugs most often include theft, robbery, and prostitution. As tolerance to the drug increases and the addict requires larger and larger doses, the daily cost becomes more than most can afford and the associated crimes become more extreme or numerous.

Drunk driving is another common form of criminal deviance associated with alcohol abuse. Researchers estimate that drunk drivers are involved in more than one-third of the deaths caused by traffic accidents in North America. Drinking alcohol undermines a wide range of skills that are essential for carrying out these tasks. Besides, young people are both inexperienced drinkers and drivers, and thus they are especially dangerous drunk drivers.

Though the number of drug-related crimes fluctuates, such crimes remain common even if relatively minor. Desjardins and Hotton (2004) report, "after a period of decline throughout the 1980s and early 1990s, the rate of police-reported drug offences increased by 42 per cent between 1992 and 2002. In 2002, three in four drug-related incidents involved cannabis offences, most of which were for simple possession." Crimes and drug offence rates are closely related, as shown in Figure 5.5, below. Further, a recent Statistics Canada report notes that:

> In 2007, about one-quarter of drug-related incidents also involved at least one non-drug violation. This compares to 11 per cent of Criminal Code incidents in general. The offences most often associated with drug-related incidents tend to be relatively minor in nature. Administration of justice offences (such as failure to comply with an order or breach of probation) occurred in about one-third of all drug-related incidents as did property offences, usually possession of stolen goods. A weapon offence was involved in 14 per cent of drug-related incidents and 11 per cent were associated with a violent offence. (Dauvergne, 2009)

Poverty

Alcohol and drugs give the user a temporary escape from reality. As Merton tells us, drug and

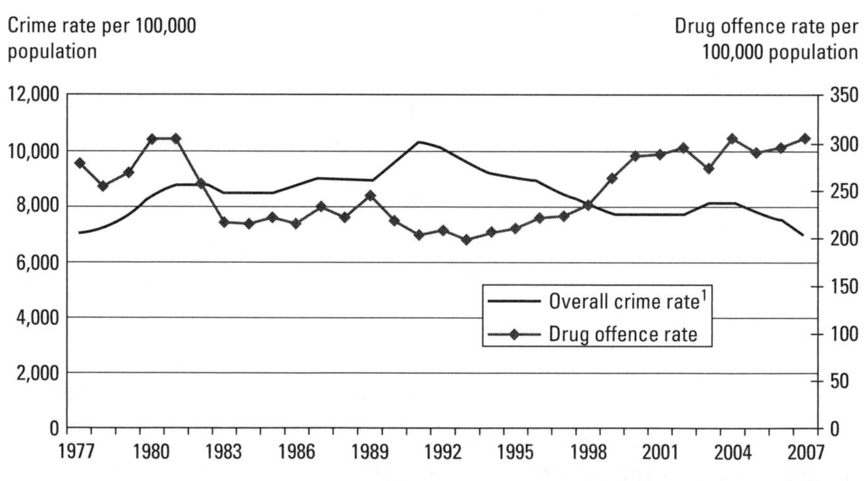

FIGURE 5.5 Police-Reported Crime and Drug Offence Rates, Canada, 1977–2007

[1]Excludes traffic offences, drug offences, and other federal statute offences.

Source: Mia Dauvergne, "Trends in Police-Reported Drug Offences in Canada," *Juristat* (May 2009): Chart 1, at: <www.statcan.gc.ca/pub/85-002-x/2009002/article/10847-eng.htm>.

alcohol use is a form of "retreatism"—an adaptation to anomie that poor people might find attractive. However, the connection between poverty and substance abuse is complex: sometimes substance abuse causes poverty, and at other times, poverty causes substance abuse.

In any event, substance abuse rarely improves the abuser's financial situation and often worsens it. Established drug habits are costly, and many addicts—unless they are gainfully employed—have to resort to prostitution, theft, and robbery to satisfy their habit. As well, addicts may undermine the economic well-being of the neighbourhood in which they live. High rates of addiction may increase social disorganization, homelessness, gang activity, and invasive drug trafficking and distribution systems.

> **Time to Reflect:** Given how much time and money people spend on healthy living and health care in our society, how do you explain the continued easy access to cigarettes and alcohol?

Health Consequences

Because drugs are psychoactive—they change people's consciousness—and they are at least potentially addictive, they are liable to harm people, especially those who are already unstable or socially vulnerable—those who are most attracted to addictive substances in the first place. We will discuss the risky teen behaviours associated with alcohol and drug use in Chapter 6.

Alcohol

Alcohol abuse today remains one of the major population health problems of our time because of its potentially harmful effects on people's health, welfare, and happiness.

Problems with health can begin when people consume more than two drinks per day, at which point alcohol may start to disrupt the normal body chemistry. Drinking too much alcohol, for too long a time, increases the risk of cancer of the liver, pancreas, mouth, tongue, pharynx, larynx, and esophagus. These risks are even greater for people who also smoke cigarettes.

Other effects of alcohol abuse may include gastritis (inflammation of the mucous membrane that lines the stomach), pancreatitis (inflammation of the pancreas), peptic ulcer (a raw area in the lining of the gastrointestinal tract), and an increase in blood-sugar level that causes diabetes. Diabetes, in turn, may lead to a variety of other medical problems and risks including heart disease, kidney disease, circulation problems, injuries from falls, and other accidents.

It is obvious that the health effects of excessive alcohol use described here translate into elevated health costs for the society as a whole, due to lost days of work and schooling, and disruption to family life—including an increased incidence of family violence.

Smoking

For decades, tobacco has been under heavy attack as a major contributor to many health difficulties. However, people rarely consider smoking to be one of our greatest drug problems. This failure to treat tobacco use as a drug problem is even more surprising when we compare it with social and legal concerns about marijuana use.

Cigarette smoke contains hundreds of substances. Carbon monoxide and tars, as well as nicotine, are the prime producers of the harmful effects. The carbon monoxide combines with hemoglobin in the blood, displacing oxygen and making the blood less able to deliver needed oxygen to tissues throughout the body. The tars contain carcinogens, or cancer-producing substances. Nicotine, besides being the drug that causes addiction, also raises LDL cholesterol (bad cholesterol) and lowers HDL cholesterol (good cholesterol) levels in the body, increasing the risk of atherosclerosis ("hardening" of the arteries) and cardiovascular disease.

Lifelong abstinence and avoidance of second- or third-hand smoke are the only proven ways to avoid health risks from tobacco use. Cessation—even after many years of smoking—reduces risk and harm for many tobacco-related conditions such as chronic breathing difficulties, cancer, and stroke.

Like excessive alcohol use, cigarette use translates into elevated health costs for the society, shortened working lives, and often the imposition of heavy care responsibilities on the family members of people with emphysema and other smoking-related diseases.

Drugs

The use of illegal drugs also carries societal costs. For example, the two major health effects of heroin abuse are infections and overdoses. Infections from heroin injection include cellulites, heart and vein infections, brain and lung abscesses, Hepatitis B, and HIV/AIDS. Other effects of heroin use include a decreased sexual desire, amenorrhea (absence of a menstrual period), and chronic constipation. These symptoms disappear when heroin use stops. However, both of these health issues create significant medical and hospital costs that are otherwise avoidable.

The health impacts of the abuse of so-called "recreational" drugs are largely hidden in our society. However, we can see them among the urban homeless populations, in the psychiatric wards of hospitals, and in countless homes across the country where young and not-so-young people remain cognitively impaired and socially unproductive or underproductive from the effects of LSD, ecstasy, mescaline, mushrooms containing psilocybin, the habitual overuse of marijuana, and a pharmacopoeia of other illicit drugs. Some others have taken their own lives.

That said, it is impossible to say whether these health impacts are a direct result of substance abuse or, rather, that substance abuse arose (with harmful consequences) in response to other problems: for example, poverty, homelessness, prolonged unemployment, mental illness, and so on.

Consequences of Illegal Drug Use

The greatest costs relating to substance abuse, it can be argued, flow from governmental attitudes towards the drug trade and drug use. Both the Canadian and American governments have undertaken a "war on drugs," and while American policies have proven much costlier, both nations have been greatly—and needlessly—burdened by these undertakings. Though illegal drug use is somewhat costly to the economy, as we have noted, these costs pale in comparison to the expenses burdening the justice system. In employing police, courts, and correctional services in the battle against illegal drug sales and use, the Canadian government spends approximately $2 billion each year on prosecuting drug-related crimes, according to the Canadian Centre on Substance Abuse (Rehm et al., 2006).

In the United States, the drug war began in the 1960s under President Lyndon Johnson and expanded dramatically through the 1980s, reaching unsustainable levels in the 1990s. A rise of "zero tolerance" laws meant to scare the public away from drug use has instead bloated American prisons at terrific public expense. The costs of mass imprisonment do not end with an offender's release, however. Those sent to prison on drug charges, like other prisoners, also come out less employable, less skilled, and less educated than the general population. For this reason and others, the "war on drugs" has created a new economic **underclass** of American citizens (Moore and Elkavich, 2008).

The passage by the Harper Conservative government of new crime legislation—Bill C-10—in March 2012 is likely to push Canada even further down the same path of spiralling costs for what many argue are few results, despite warnings from experts and practitioners from the US that this was the wrong path to take. The legislation, among other things, will impose harsher and **mandatory sentencing** for drug offences, and the Quebec government has stated that it will seek to ameliorate or skirt around costly changes mandated in the omnibus crime bill. In requiring new provincial prisons and additional administration, this new legislation could cost that province alone close to a billion dollars. Besides Quebec, other provinces—to no avail—have protested the tough-on-crime legislation (Blatchford, 2012).

While the debate over which drugs (if any) should or should not be legal is not easily solvable, the legalization of a widely used substance like marijuana could greatly alleviate the costs of the drug war. US economists Jeffrey Miron and Katherine Waldock estimate that the United States could save US$8.7 billion each year by simply not pursuing marijuana-related criminal charges. They also suggest that drug legalization could yield "sin tax" revenue of approximately US$46.7 billion, a profit that would more than cover the present costs of the drug war (Miron and Waldock, 2010).

Social Policy Implications

Much disagreement surrounds different strategies for "curing" substance abuse. Some believe that Alcoholics Anonymous (AA)—the original 12-step program—is the most successful of all addiction treatments, and it has been the model for many other programs. AA views the alcoholic as a member of a moral community. Thinking about alcoholism as a "disease" helps create a sense of kinship—of shared victimhood—among AA members.

AA founded its recovery program on a combination of religious and medical beliefs: first, that the addict needed to seek help from God and others to conquer his or her addiction; second, that addiction is a medically defined disease, not a personal failing. Today, most treatment centres use the 12-step approach. In recent years, however, other recovery movements have proposed alternative strategies. They have often challenged the religious basis of the AA program—as is the case with SOS (Secular Organizations for Sobriety)—and sometimes even disputed addiction as a disease.

Understanding drug and alcohol addicts as sick people, not immoral people, has promoted new ways of dealing with the problem legally as well as medically. For example, it has led to the introduction of Drug Treatment Courts, the first of which opened in Toronto in 1998. These courts sentence addicts to rehabilitation treatment rather than incarceration. In 2005, Justice Canada announced that "as part of its commitment under Canada's Drug Strategy to expand Drug Treatment Courts in Canada, the federal government is providing funding of more than $13.3 million over four years to help establish new courts in Edmonton, Regina, Winnipeg and Ottawa." Currently, about $3.5 million is allocated annually to support these courts and the previously established courts in Toronto and Vancouver (www.justice.gc.ca/eng/news-nouv/nr-cp/2005/doc_31552.html).

Drug education, in its widest sense, aims to change beliefs, expectations, norms, values, and behaviours in ways that reduce drug use and drug-related harm. Spending money on drug education programs in schools is one of the most effective ways a government can reduce drug use. Many schools and local communities have also developed strategies to prevent or reduce alcohol, drug, and tobacco use among youth. Often, they design such strategies to strengthen existing positive (anti-drug) peer interactions and social networks. As we will see in Chapter 6, the teen years are high-risk years, so school programs for adolescents put the most intensive effort into drug education where it is most urgently needed.

Likely, we will never be rid of recreational drugs, so it may be more prudent to adopt **harm reduction strategies** that regulate drug use. An important step in this direction has been taken at Insite, a legal supervised injection site in Vancouver. There, drug injectors are provided with clean needles to prevent the spread of deadly infectious diseases (such as hepatitis and HIV/AIDS) associated with needle-sharing. However, the federal government has been reluctant to support this initiative, claiming that the results of evaluation research are ambiguous—though they are not—and that such a harm reduction program promotes or excuses drug addiction. In April 2012 a four-year study conducted by University of Toronto and St Michael's Hospital researchers concluded that Toronto and Ottawa should have supervised drug injection sites similar to the Insite program in Vancouver, although it seems unlikely in the current political climate whether either city, the province of Ontario, or the federal government will act on this recommendation (see, e.g., www.cbc.ca/news/canada/ottawa/story/2012/04/11/ottawa-toronto-safe-injection-site-study-released.html).

Most arguments that support legalizing cannabis stress the practical benefits of legalization—for example, the opportunity to ensure quality control and to tax drug sales—and the harm done by failing to legalize these drugs. They note that, to a large degree, current laws do not work. Laws aimed at preventing drug use have no effect and drug use remains widespread. Criminal sanctions do not appear to affect drug use and efforts to control illegal drug use by law enforcement strategies regularly fail. Thus, a great deal of money spent on drug law enforcement is wasted.

What is amply evident is that people will continue searching for and using drugs that make them feel good and provide at least temporary escape from the difficulties of life. In fact, suppliers continue to find innovative ways to sell cannabis products while avoiding legal sanctions (see Box 5.3).

For the most part, recreational drugs are not a problem for society; crime resulting from drug dependence is the problem to be solved. The public concern about drugs is really a concern about crime—about the production, sale, purchase, and possession of illegal drugs, the commission of crimes to buy illegal drugs, the commission of crimes while under the influence of drugs, and the violent and corrupt behaviour of drug traffickers.

That said, the most popular recreational drugs—marijuana and hashish—are not physically addictive, but they can become psychologically addictive to a significant extent, and it is this addiction that must be avoided.

Decriminalization and Legalization

Many Canadians believe it is time to change the law regarding so-called "soft" drugs. However, it is important to distinguish between two alternative ways of dealing with recreational drugs such as marijuana: decriminalization and legalization.

Decriminalization means removing from the Criminal Code laws against marijuana possession and use—that is, eliminating all current penalties. **Legalization** means taking state control of the sale of these substances, as well as removing penalties for possession and

Current Events

BOX 5.3

"Spice": The Synthetic Pot Controversy

In 2009, advisers on drug policy advocated a ban on "Spice" products—smokable cannabis substitutes consisting of a synthetic blend of cannabinoids and spices. According to Professor David Nutt, at that time the chairman of the Advisory Council on the Misuse of Drugs in the UK, the products contain dangerous chemical compounds that can cause panic attacks, paranoia, withdrawal symptoms, psychosis, and even death. Since it is sold both on the street and online for relatively low prices, Spice is easily accessible, which exposes a large population to these new, largely unresearched, and dangerous compounds. This population includes people of all ages, since no age restrictions are currently in effect to prevent its sale to youth. It's also completely legal in many countries, and cannot be detected by typical drug screenings, since suppliers have been reconstructing new compounds to evade legal prosecution.

Because of this legal status, Spice is commonly referred to as a "legal high," and is typically advertised as a risk-free herbal alternative. Sometimes it is presented as potpourri or incense, but the labels on Spice products also frequently promote the substance as having similar effects to those of cannabis, while failing to admit that the natural herbal contents it contains have been supplemented by artificial compounds. And yet some of these compounds have more intense effects than THC (tetrahydrocannabinol), the main psychoactive substance in cannabis.

In the UK, Spice was identified as a Class B agent in December 2009; possession of such an agent is punishable by up to five years in prison and an uncapped fine. Following the approval of this ban, illegal compounds were still detected in Spice products, meaning that individuals purchasing this substance in the UK would be liable to fines and imprisonment. And yet suppliers continue to advertise these products as legal, harmless alternatives to cannabis. Thus, in addition to threatening people's health, Spice products have the potential to get their consumers into serious trouble with the law.

Consistent, more easily enforceable legislative action must be taken to protect people against the adverse effects of these drugs. Further research is also needed to confirm how extensive and damaging these effects may be. However, efforts to stop or even slow the trafficking of these products will continue to be hampered by the ability of suppliers to synthesize new, technically legal compounds that allow them to avoid becoming the targets of legal prosecution.

Interestingly, Professor Nutt was fired from his chairmanship of the Advisory Council barely two months after he had spoken out against Spice, following his criticism of the government's decision to upgrade the classification of cannabis to a Class B agent from the less restrictive and punitive Class C category.

Sources: Paul Dargan, Simon Hudson, John Ramsey, and David Wood, "The Impact of Changes in UK Classification of the Synthetic Cannabinoid Receptor Agonists in 'Spice'," *International Journal of Drug Policy* 22 (2011): 274–7; BBC News, at: <news.bbc.co.uk/2/hi/uk_news/8196953.stm>; BBC News, at: <news.bbc.co.uk/2/hi/8334774.stm>; Liana Fattore and Walter Fratta, "Beyond THC: The New Generation of Cannabinoid Designer Drugs," *Frontiers in Behavioural Neuroscience* 5, 60 (2011), at: <www.ncbi.nlm.nih.gov/pmc/articles/PMC3187647/>.

use. Legalization, which would allow the state to tax sales of the drug, would normally entail setting and enforcing quality standards, as the state does with other drugs and foods.

While legalization and decriminalization are both forms of harm reduction, legalization is better because it would erase a criminal drug trade and ensure safe drugs for consumers. Many look to the Netherlands as a source of evidence about the likely effects of decriminalization or legalization. Research there suggests that the modification of Dutch drug policy in 1976, to control the distribution, possession, and consumption of soft drugs (i.e., cannabis and derivatives), was intended only to reduce the progression to hard drug use. In the years since this de facto legalization of drug use, there has been no evidence that drug use increased in the Netherlands as a result of this policy.

However, in the past 30 years, the increased co-operation between European Union member states has made it increasingly difficult for individual countries like the Netherlands to pursue their own national policies on issues like drugs. The drug policy of the Netherlands, which aims squarely at harm reduction, has been under attack from various quarters in recent years. At the same time, many other European countries have been discussing drug policy reform, considering everything from the decriminalization or legalization of cannabis to the legal prescription of heroin. This debate has made the liberal Dutch approach a less isolated case than it once was.

Decriminalization of drug use currently has many supporters in Canada and elsewhere. There is little evidence suggesting that decriminalizing the use of soft drugs (e.g., those containing THC) results in dramatic increases in substance abuse, nor is there compelling evidence that it leads people to use heavily addictive drugs like heroin or cocaine. We know this because de facto relaxation of police efforts to control marijuana use in the last decade has not led to epidemics of marijuana use.

The use of non-prescription drugs remains illegal in Canada, but we can do little to monitor the quality of drugs available to users or the conditions under which people access and use these drugs. The illegality of drugs such as marijuana (except for those who are licensed to produce or use marijuana for medical purposes) leads users into indirect or direct contact with criminal elements that control the drug trade. Thus, although marijuana may not be a gateway drug per se, the subcultural social elements that profit from its illegal trade can be a gateway to more dangerous behaviours and to personal difficulties.

For example, recent research in Canada, the US, and Holland shows that when people buy "soft drugs" from friends they are less likely to progress to buying "hard drugs" than if they buy the "soft drugs" from professional drug dealers. Also, when drugs are illegal, users take fewer health precautions. For example, needles shared among heroin users spread HIV/AIDS. By driving the drug culture underground, the law works against public safety, good hygiene, and disease prevention.

Drug abuse is a serious problem for which there is no quick or easy solution. Though people disagree about drug legalization, Canada is evidently moving towards a harsher, more punitive regime with the omnibus crime bill that became law in 2012. This policy, uninformed by research evidence, will not likely have the desired consequences.

Conclusion

Drugs are common in our society and people hold many opinions about their use. However, drug use is not a social problem in itself. Drugs become a social problem when people abuse them and violate approved social practices, or when these drugs are used in ways (or to a degree) that cause bodily injury.

They also are a social problem when widely prescribed and popular pharmaceuticals do more harm than good, as arguably is the case with a wide range of psychoactive medications. In all of these instances, drug use becomes costly to society in terms of accidents and crime, family, lost work productivity, and health problems. We have noted that legally approved drugs like alcohol and nicotine can be even more addictive and harmful than legally disapproved drugs like marijuana. So, we cannot explain the prohibition of certain drugs on the basis of health concerns alone.

As we have seen, throughout history, people in power have made efforts to approve or disapprove, legalize or criminalize various kinds of drugs. These actions have rarely been a result of medical or scientific reasons alone. Usually, they have reflected prejudices against the drugs, the people who customarily use these drugs, or the pursuit of pleasure using drugs and alcohol.

The current laws protect the interests of large corporations that manufacture and sell alcoholic beverages, tobacco products, and prescription drugs. They oppose the interests of other drug producers (for example, marijuana growers). Yet, unwittingly, they protect a thriving black market that provides a fortune for organized criminals who wholesale illegal drugs and a living for the gang members and street retailers who keep the drugs flowing to eager buyers. Another set of laws would likely work better to reduce and prevent harm associated with drug and alcohol use.

This chapter has provided various explanations of drug abuse. Sociological explanations focus on the role of culture, social structure, and social interaction in producing drug use and abuse. From the standpoint of deviance research, drugs and alcohol show us the importance of understanding the cultural politics that determine our laws and enforcement practices.

Questions for Critical Thought

1. Evaluate the view that "since human beings are chemistry sets with an obvious desire to perform experiments on themselves, we spend far too much time and money trying to control a few of these experiments."
2. Discuss why some drugs are legal and others are illegal. In connection with this, explain what factors play a role in defining some drug use as a "drug problem."
3. Howard Becker explains that one must learn how to use marijuana. Is there any evidence that people also need to learn to use and enjoy other drugs—for example, alcohol, nicotine, ecstasy, or cocaine?
4. Do you support the decriminalization of marijuana? Use sociological theories you have learned in this chapter to support your views on the issue.
5. What is the evidence that harm reduction policies promote the use of injected drugs? What is the evidence that, on balance, they save and improve lives?
6. "Widespread drug use—of whatever kind—is symptomatic of a society in crisis." Evaluate this statement in respect to several different societies, communities, or groups for which you have information.

Recommended Readings

Frey, James. 2003. *A Million Little Pieces.* New York: Anchor Books.

This best-selling book—part memoir, part fiction—nicely illustrates the process by which a drug user can overcome circumstances to become a non-user. As an abuser of alcohol and drugs, Frey checks into a treatment facility and battles with AA's 12 steps. Controversy surrounded the book and its author when it was revealed that Frey had embellished his story, which had been published and advertised as a factual memoir. The supposedly non-fictional book is interesting as evidence of the entry of substance abuse into the popular consciousness, though its veracity is much in question.

McAllister, Patrick A. 2005. *Xhosa Beer Drinking Rituals: Power, Practice and Performance in the South African Rural Periphery.* Durham, NC: Carolina Academic Press.

Among the rural, Xhosa-speaking people of South Africa's Eastern Cape province, beer rituals became a crucial mechanism through which rural people developed and maintained social and economic relations while affording an alternative to the disillusionment and suffering of black urban areas.

McKnight, David. 2002. *From Hunting to Drinking: The Devastating Effects of Alcohol on an Australian Aboriginal Community.* London and New York: Routledge.

This book reveals the devastating effects of alcohol on Mornington Island, off the North Queensland coast of Australia. Drinking has become the main social activity on the island, and it now affects all community life. As the amount of alcohol consumed has risen, so have suicide and homicide rates.

Wilkins, John, and Shaun Hill. 2005. *Food in the Ancient World.* Oxford: Blackwell.

This book describes eating and drinking from early Egypt (4000 BCE) to the end of the Roman Empire (fifth century CE). Throughout these millennia, people in power viewed bars, taverns, hotels, and other public eating places with suspicion because of the political discussions and competitive drinking that often occurred.

Recommended Websites

Health Canada—Alcohol and Drug Prevention Publications

www.hc-sc.gc.ca/hl-vs/pubs/adp-apd/index-eng.php

This Health Canada site provides government reports on alcohol and drug abuse in Canadian society. While some of the reports are myopic in focus, most relate to a specific aspect of alcohol or drug abuse, such as the effect of substance abuse on youths, Aboriginals, or seniors.

MADD: Mothers Against Drunk Driving

www.madd.org/

Mothers Against Drunk Driving focuses its activism on education information for students. As one of the largest crime victim organizations in the world, MADD is able to generate quite a bit of attention towards research on alcohol use and abuse.

National Institute on Alcohol Abuse and Alcoholism

www.niaaa.nih.gov/

Run by the US Department of Health and Human Services, this website is dedicated to creating awareness regarding the social effects of alcohol abuse and alcoholism. Free publications, research links, news, and other resources for investigating the effects of alcoholism on society can be found here.

National Institute on Drug Abuse

www.drugabuse.gov/NIDAHome.html

The NIDA is an agency within the US Department of Health and Human Services. This site offers a broad array of links and online publications on substance abuse issues targeted for both the general public and medical professionals and academics.

World Health Organization: Substance Abuse

www.who.int/topics/substance_abuse/en/

The World Health Organization, a UN agency, is devoted to issues relating to global health and advocacy. This WHO site focused on substance abuse contains a large amount of data on international health issues and has a helpful listing of long-form publications and regional public health advocacy groups for further reference.

Recommended Movies

***Drugstore Cowboy*, Dir. Gus Van Sant (1989)**

This powerful film follows a group of prescription drug addicts who wander about the country, breaking into drugstores in search of a "fix." When one of them dies from an overdose, their leader calls on the group to get clean, even as his wife sets her mind to keep on using. The movie effectively shows the composition of a community based on drug use, as well as the ways in which people's decisions to use or not use drugs can alter their personal relationships.

***Leaving Las Vegas*, Dir. Mike Figgis (1995)**

Nicholas Cage won an Oscar for his role as the hopelessly alcoholic Hollywood screenwriter Ben, who leaves his old life behind and moves to Las Vegas. Once there, Ben meets Sera, a prostitute who agrees that she will not ask Ben to give up drinking. This film unflinchingly portrays the physical and mental disintegration alcoholics must cope with and the measures others must adopt to accommodate or enable alcoholic behaviours.

Grass, Dir. Ron Mann (1999)

Directed by one of Canada's great documentary filmmakers, this film recounts the history of marijuana culture in twentieth-century North America. Using a collage of educational films, exploitation pictures, and political and cultural history, Mann shows how attitudes towards marijuana changed drastically over the twentieth century. He also shows how political and popular views of the dangers and effects of marijuana often clash.

Trainspotting, Dir. Danny Boyle (1996)

Danny Boyle's interpretation of Irvine Welsh's gonzo novel explores the life of Mark Renton, a young heroin addict living in Edinburgh. Renton, sick of his life as it is, moves to London in pursuit of a normal life, only to have his addict friends Sick Boy, Begbie, and Spud show up. Boyle capably shows the effects of addiction by exploring how difficult it is for former addicts to leave behind both the physical and the cultural aspects of drug use.

PART III

Delinquency and Crime

6 Risky Behaviours and Delinquency

Learning Objectives

- To identify youthful risky behaviours and the influences motivating them
- To trace the history of juvenile delinquency and public reactions to it
- To examine delinquent subcultures
- To discuss delinquency in terms of the major sociological approaches
- To describe the communities and cultures that support juvenile delinquency
- To learn about the Youth Criminal Justice Act and its implications

Introduction

This chapter is about rule-breaking by Canada's youth and the efforts sociologists have made to understand this behaviour. It gives a brief survey of the research available on **delinquency** and crime among young people. Beyond that, it is about risky behaviour—behaviour that endangers the actor and other people.

Though most delinquency is risky, not all risky behaviour is delinquent. Formerly, traditional legal definitions of delinquency, in Canada and elsewhere, included behaviours that would not be considered criminal if committed by adults. This over-inclusiveness reflected good intentions: notably, a desire to protect youth against their own worst impulses. The law saw its role as providing moral guidance for youth who were getting into trouble or in danger of getting into trouble. In British common law and contemporary American family law, this is referred to by the Latin term *in loco parentis*, which means "in the place of a parent" or "instead of a parent."

Evidence of "anti-social" tendencies—for example, frequent truancy, underage smoking or use of alcohol, sexual activity, or an unwillingness to obey authority figures—was often considered grounds for invoking the law. Youth who were putting themselves or their futures at risk were thought to be in need of help from the juvenile authorities. Also, the law took "delinquency" to include a variety of behaviours that might serve as "gateways" to more serious criminal acts.

In the 1970s, delinquency came to be defined much more narrowly. The goal in narrowing "delinquency" was to protect the rights of juveniles from arbitrary—often discretionary and unregulated—exercises of authority. Another goal was to ensure that, while they were not treated like adult criminals, youth had the same legal rights as adults. As one indication of this, their records of delinquent activity were to be erased when they reached adulthood, so youthful mistakes would not permanently affect their adult lives.

In this chapter we explore various risky behaviours that include dangerous driving and unsafe sex. For adults, these behaviours are deviant—that is, they break rules and violate expectations. Some risky behaviour even breaks laws. However, the legal treatment of adult rule-breaking remains different—somewhat less restrictive—than the treatment of adolescent rule-breaking. A great many more adolescents drift into risky behaviour—including delinquency—than drift into crime as adults.

Many youth who read this book will have been, at some time or another, either victims or perpetrators of delinquent acts, or both. As sociologist David Matza (1964) wrote in his classic work *Delinquency and Drift*, many young people "drift" into delinquency armed with little more than **techniques of neutralization** and without a strong motivation to do harm. These so-called "techniques" provide varied excuses or justifications for rule-breaking and make the drift into delinquency easier morally, if not socially.

Matza believes that delinquents share the same values and attitudes as non-delinquents and need only the help of "neutralizing" excuses to break rules. The drift into delinquency is common, and so is the tendency for young delinquents to leave delinquency as they become young adults with adult responsibilities.

That said, the drift in and out of delinquency is not without consequences, even if the period of delinquency is brief. The time spent in delinquency is time spent at the expense of activities—whether educational, occupational, or social—that contribute to eventual adult success. Besides, social contacts made through delinquency are often at the expense of social contacts other young people make in the conforming world. Finally, skills that are useful in delinquent activity are often learned at the expense of skills useful in the conforming world.

A Snapshot of Risky Behaviour: The Case of Ontario

We begin this discussion with a brief overview of risky and delinquent behaviour by a sample of young people in Ontario. While youth in Ontario are not necessarily representative of all Canadian youth, they likely display the variety of youthful misbehaviours on display all over Canada. Equally important, the data describing Ontario youth come from an excellent survey of randomly selected young people—OSDUHS—the 2009 Ontario Student Drug Use and Health Survey (published in 2010), so we can trust these data implicitly.

The OSDUHS is the longest continuing school survey in Canada and second-longest in North America. It began with an agreement between several Toronto school boards and the Addiction Research Foundation (now, Centre for Addiction and Mental Health) to continually monitor the extent of drug use among their students. The first survey was conducted in 1968 and after several successful studies of Toronto students in Grades 7, 9, 11, and 13, it was extended to surveying all of Ontario. Since 1977, OSDUHS has surveyed thousands of students every two years; and with the passage of time, it has extended its attention to a variety of health issues besides addiction. The most recent (2009) study surveyed 9,112 Ontario students from 47 school boards, and (through statistical weighting) provides a valid picture of over one million Ontario students in Grades 7 to 12.

In the 2009 study, students were asked about 13 delinquent behaviours in which they might have engaged at least once during the past year. Among all students, the 13 behaviours ranked in the following manner, from most to least prevalent (CAMH, 2010: 12):

Fire setting	14 per cent
Theft of goods $50 or less	14 per cent
Vandalism	14 per cent
Assault	10 per cent
Ran away	10 per cent
Carried a weapon	7 per cent
Car theft/joyride	7 per cent
Sold cannabis	6 per cent
Theft of goods worth over $50	5 per cent
Break and enter	4 per cent
Gang fighting	3 per cent
Sold other drugs	2 per cent
Carried a handgun	1 per cent

Other findings include the following:

- Females are more likely than males to report running away from home. Males are more likely than females to report all of the other 12 behaviours.
- Defining "delinquent behaviour" as three or more of 11 behaviours surveyed repeatedly (excluding setting something on fire and carrying a handgun), 11 per cent of all students—an estimated 113,000 Ontario students—report "delinquent behaviour" as a general pattern.
- Males are significantly more likely than females to engage in such delinquent behaviour, by a 2:1 ratio (i.e., 14 per cent versus 7 per cent).
- Students in the higher grades (10 to 12)—at a rate of 14–15 per cent—are more likely than younger students to engage in delinquent behaviour.
- The research finds no significant variation in delinquent behaviour among the

different regions of Ontario. (For this reason, among others, we can feel confident generalizing these findings to other parts of Canada.)

The Developmental Course of Risk-Taking

As these data show, not all adolescents are delinquent or even dangerous risk-takers. In fact, some are militantly against such behaviour. However, some adolescents do take big risks and break the rules. Some even become "delinquents."

Typically, sociologists focus on the organization of urban gangs, delinquent subcultures, and limited opportunities for success in legitimate enterprises. These provide the ways we might begin to explain the risk-taking—even delinquent risk-taking—as a normal, understandable, and even rational behaviour. As a result, sociologists see most delinquency as a "normal"—that is, common and rational—social response to stresses and opportunities in the young person's environment. Sociologists concerned with preventing delinquency, therefore, direct our attention back to the social environment and ways it can be improved.

Young people, for their part, often see themselves as invincible, and these days—more than in the past—this is closer to being true. The Canadian life expectancy is nearly 81 years—higher for females and lower for males; and many youth are perfectly healthy, never having experienced a serious childhood illness. Also, a decade into the twenty-first century, the youth literacy rate is the highest ever. Most important, young people (far more than their parents) have learned to master the intricacies of instantaneous communication using every form of media, social media included.

Yet, this is not an easy time for young people. Unemployment rates are high among young people, especially those who have dropped out of school. Even among those youth still in school, many suffer from low self-esteem, stress, and depression. Many have been victimized by violence, neglect, or abuse at home; and ample evidence shows a direct link between these home experiences and undesired outcomes such as delinquency (also, school dropout, low self-esteem, and anti-social attitudes).

Some risky or delinquent acts are aimed at making money, although most are intended to gain or defend status, protect gang territory, or prove the youth's courage. Such behaviour occurs in all social classes, though the evidence of delinquency is clearest for poor youth in poor neighbourhoods. Children from low-income homes are most at risk of running into trouble with the law.

In general, we can say that people break the rules when they believe they have something to gain by doing so and they believe they have nothing to lose by doing so. So, young men—especially in gangs, tough schools, or dangerous neighbourhoods—may believe they have a great deal to gain by showing off their courage in reckless, rule-breaking ways. For example, they may expect to gain approval from their male peers and rise in the estimation of young women.

Equally important, young men—especially, those without significant restraints by family, school, or community—may feel like they have nothing to lose by acting this way. As we saw in Chapter 1, sociologist Travis Hirschi (1969) has developed a comprehensive theory to explain why individuals choose to conform to conventional norms and, by implication, why they break them. He assumes that everyone has the potential to become delinquent, and that social controls, not moral values, preserve law and order. Without controls, Hirschi argues, people are more likely to commit delinquent or criminal acts. According to this theory, delinquents defy moral codes because their attachment to mainstream society is weak. In turn, their attachment to society (and its laws) is weak because their attachment to family, school, and community is weak.

Four social bonds that routinely promote conformity are attachment, commitment, involvement, and belief; and all of these bonds are rooted in stable, healthy experiences of family, school, and community life. The first bond, **attachment**, refers to a person's interest in or attachment to others—especially parents, schools, and peers. The depth and quality of these attachments and the frequency of interaction (e.g., the time a child and parent spend together) are also important, leading to intimacy and identification. Hirschi states that a child's attachment to parents and school is more important than the bond formed with one's peers.

The second bond, **commitment**, refers to the time, energy, and effort spent in conventional lines of social activity, all of which tie an individual to the moral code of society. People who invest their effort building a good reputation and acquiring property are less likely to engage in criminal acts that endanger their social position.

The third bond, **involvement**, refers to a person's participation in activities that support the conventional interests of society, since such activities don't leave time to engage in delinquent or criminal acts. Such activities—which include going to school or work, engaging in an organized sport, or volunteering—insulate a juvenile from potential delinquency that may be a result of idleness. In general, any engagement with the law-abiding world increases conformity and reduces delinquency among young people.

Finally, **belief** in the laws of society—and in the people and institutions that enforce such laws—provides a fourth bond promoting conformity.

According to this theory, adolescents take risks and break rules if their bonds to conventional society are weak and they feel they have less to lose than other people. They lack the attachment, commitment, involvement, and belief that keep people law-abiding. They do not have a **stake in conformity**: a career, mortgage, or credit rating to endanger. As we will see, when young people do finally find mates or good career prospects, their risk-taking, delinquency, and chances of getting into trouble reduce enormously.

The Gendering of Delinquency and Crime

If this theory is correct, then young people socialized most strictly to embrace and practice these four "principles of conformity," as we might call them, will be least likely to break the rules. Through a combination of internal self-control and external (or imposed) control, they will be most likely to conform to the expectations of their parents, teachers, and others. Likely, this is a large part of the reason girls are better-behaved than boys, on average, as sociologist John Hagan has argued in his theory of power control (see Hagan et al., 1985; Hagan and McCarthy, 1997).

Hagan and his associates have attempted, with the **power-control theory**, to explain the observed interaction between class and gender in producing delinquency and crime rates. More specifically, they have tried to explain why working-class girls have lower rates of delinquency than their brothers, while middle-class girls have the same rates of delinquency as their brothers; and middle-class girls have higher rates of delinquency than working-class girls. Hagan's answer has to do with occupational and domestic inequalities.

In a two-parent (two-earner) middle-class family, the husband and wife have roughly equal work roles; this translates into roughly equal household power and shared child-rearing. This, in turn, translates into roughly equal treatment of sons and daughters. For a variety of reasons—not least, the absence of both parents from the home during the day—both sons and daughters are supervised loosely. Because of the middle-class value system, both sons and daughters are socialized to value success and mobility. In the capitalist economic system, this means they are taught to value risk-taking (within the framework of legally permitted behaviours). This lack of supervision and training in risk-taking increases the likelihood of delinquency by both sons and daughters equally.

By contrast, in a two-parent working-class family—with a stay-at-home or part-time working mother—the husband and wife have unequal work roles; this translates into an unequal household dominated by the husband and unequal treatment of sons and daughters. The father focuses on his instrumental responsibilities, granting sons greater freedom to prepare them for the traditional male role. The mother is left to closely supervise the children, especially the daughters, who are socialized into domesticity in preparation for a life like their mother's, focusing on domestic labour and consumption.

In this context, sons are encouraged to experiment and take risks. Daughters, on the other hand, are watched closely to prevent their participation in deviant or delinquent activities. This differential supervision of sons and daughters means a differential likelihood of delinquency.

As a result, working-class daughters are the least likely of all to engage in delinquent or criminal acts. Middle-class sons and daughters are more likely to engage in delinquent or criminal acts, and working-class sons may be equally likely to do so. Hagan argues that to understand crime rates we need to know about more than just class or poverty: we also need to understand the interaction between class experiences and gender experiences.

Bullying

When we discuss children and youth, a source of increased concern today is bullying—especially the use of violence or threatened violence against children at, or near, school. And, with the evolution of the Internet, much bullying has taken on the form of psychological rather than physical violence.

Bullying here is defined as the assertion of power through aggression. Bullies acquire power over their victims physically, emotionally, and socially. They can do this in many ways: by physical size and strength, by status within the peer group, by knowing the victim's weaknesses, or by recruiting support from other children to accomplish group bullying. Emotional and social bullying may perhaps be the most frequent and harmful forms. Bullying can be physical or verbal, direct (face-to-face) or indirect (through gossip or exclusion). With repeated bullying, the bully's dominance over the victim is established and the victim becomes increasingly distressed and fearful.

Bullying is a serious problem for those who engage in it, for its victims, and for the communities in which it takes place. It is not a normal part of growing up. It can make children feel frightened, sick, lonely, and unhappy. Unfortunately, childhood bullies are also more likely to develop anti-social behaviours (Farrington, 1993). Studies indicate that 30–40 per cent of children with aggression problems grow up to have problems with violence (Public Legal Education and Information Service of New Brunswick, 2009, at: www.legal-info-legale.nb.ca/en/abuse_and_bullying).

Time to Reflect: How is the emergence of cyberbullying on social media (e.g., Facebook) likely to change, and possibly worsen, children's experiences of growing up in our society?

Current Events

BOX 6.1

"Bully"

An updated version of a controversial video game called "Bully" was released in March 2008 by Rockstar Games, fuelling the debate between supporters and detractors that has been raging since the original was put out in 2006. The two games share a central plot, with 15-year-old Jimmy Hopkins trying to adjust to his new life at prep school by belittling his fellow students through a variety of means ranging from giving wedgies to using slingshots, itching powder, and baseball bats to inflict harm upon them. Points are awarded for humiliating classmates or causing them physical pain, as well as for targeting teachers for abuse.

Those who want to see the game banned claim that it models negative behaviour for teenagers, and encourages violent bullying of both students and teachers. Action taken against the original "Bully" includes the warnings of a school superintendent in Florida, who advised parents not to purchase the game for their children, as well as the refusal of two British venues to stock the game. A coalition of teachers from a variety of countries are advocating similar action be taken against "Bully: Scholarship Edition." The four million teachers that compose this coalition are trying to persuade vendors not to stock the game, claiming that it encourages youth to bully their colleagues and teachers, and thus seriously hampers the anti-bullying efforts and campaigns currently being made by many schools.

Further, some feel that Rockstar Games should be held responsible for violent acts committed by adolescents who have been exposed to or play games like "Bully." In 2006, Rockstar was sued by the relatives of three people who were murdered by an adolescent who had played the original "Bully." Prosecutors claimed that the offence wouldn't have occurred had it not been for the negative influence of the video game upon this teenager.

Others feel that banning or taking other forms of action against the game and its developers will have little effect. Assistant Professor Michael Hoechsmann, a McGill University expert on video game violence, suggests that banning the game won't miraculously create a safe, caring school environment; factors beyond "Bully" are encouraging bullying within schools as well. Hoechsmann also claims that there isn't sufficient evidence to prove that violent video games produce violent actions. Thus, while these two editions of "Bully" may have a negative influence on youth, attention must also be paid to other factors that could be encouraging bullying and violence in schools.

Sources: CTV.ca News, at: <www.cp24.com/servlet/an/local/CTVNews/20061023/bully_game_061023?hub=CP24Home500>; Jill Mahoney, "Teachers Demand Ban on Bullying Video Game," *Globe and Mail*, 4 Mar. 2008.

Canadian survey data (Bidwell, 1997) show that children become victimized for many different reasons; and there is no single type of victim. For some children, the following characteristics are present before bullying occurs; for others, they develop as a result of bullying.

- *Gender*. Boys and girls are equally likely to report being victimized.
- *Age*. Victimization decreases across grade levels: 26 per cent of children in Grades 1–3 report victimization compared to 15 per cent in Grades 4–6 and 12 per cent in Grades 7–8. Children in lower grades are more likely to be victims of older bullies, whereas children in higher grades are more likely to be victims of same-age bullies. Younger students experience more direct bullying, whereas older students experience more indirect bullying.
- *Temperament*. Victimized children have a tendency to be anxious and withdrawn. There is more evidence of this among preschool children than among school-aged children.
- *Physical appearance*. Research has not supported the popular stereotype that victims have unusual physical traits.
- *Self-esteem*. Victims often report low self-esteem, likely because of repeated exposure to victimization.
- *Depression*. Both boys and girls who are victimized report symptoms of depression such as sadness and apathy.
- *Anxiety*. Boys and girls who are victims of bullying report symptoms of anxiety such as tension, fears, and worries.

Bullying usually involves more than just the bully and the victim—85 per cent of bullying episodes occur in the context of a peer group. Although 83 per cent of students indicate that watching bullying makes them feel uncomfortable, observations indicate that peers assume many roles in the bullying episode: joining, cheering, watching passively, and, occasionally, intervening.

Some children hold a disadvantaged position within their social hierarchy and are thus more prone to disproportionate amounts of negative interactions with their peers. This problem has been recently aggravated by the widespread use of social media. The widespread availability of telecommunications gadgets among children has provided new media through which victimization can occur and cyberbullying has been recognized as a serious issue over the last few years. Bullying was experienced by adolescents through the Internet and via mobile phones at rates of 29 per cent and 24.6 per cent, respectively. This form of social network bullying is common among high school students, especially among girls (Buelga et al., 2006).

Instances of bullying that occur face-to-face are also largely unmonitored and underreported. However, cyberbullying may pose a greater threat to children's emotional well-being because it can happen virtually anywhere at any time. Cyberbullying can occur even while kids are in their homes and under parental supervision. Children can also send and receive numerous insults due to the instantaneous delivery of messages. Moreover, the Internet provides a new platform for sexual harassment. Compared to adults, female adolescents are at a much greater risk for unwanted sexual solicitation online (Baumgartner et al., 2010).

Adolescent Risk-Taking

Bullying is one place to begin a discussion of risky behaviour. Another is with alcohol and drug use, since substance abuse connects so well with other kinds of risky and delinquent activities. Problems related to adolescent drinking include interpersonal aggression, accidents and injuries, trouble with the police, and problems at school or work.

Drinking and Driving

Nowhere is the recklessness of youth more obvious than in motor vehicle accidents. Young men, of all drivers, have the highest risk of automobile accidents. As a result, automobile accidents—along with homicides and suicides—are the most common causes of death for young men.

The reasons are simple. Compared with older men, young men have less driving experience, more often drive at night, and are more likely to drive while drunk. Young drivers are more likely to take risks on the road and they are more often absorbed in talking or listening to music while driving. According to Mothers Against Drunk Driving (MADD), road crashes still remain the leading cause of death among teenagers and 45 per cent of these crashes are a direct result of impaired driving: 40 per cent of teenage drivers who are killed in road crashes have been drinking. As a result, young people—especially young men—have more automobile accidents and suffer more driving-related deaths than anyone else.

Alcohol and drugs are an indirect cause of many traffic accidents, deaths, and associated property damage. In a study of students in Grades 10–12, 13 per cent admitted to driving under the influence (DUI) of alcohol, and 31 per cent reported having driven in the last month with someone who was DUI. Males are also more likely than females to drink underage and ride with drunk drivers. Teen peers are more approving of males who drive after drinking than of females, it seems, and this approval may encourage males to repeat this behaviour. Boys often view dangerous driving as "cool," as feeling personally involved with their car, and they approve of other people's dangerous driving.

Much research has shown that dangerous driving by adolescents is correlated with other kinds of risky behaviour; and the riskiest driving is found among adolescents who binge drink—that is, consume more than five drinks in a sitting—and then drive. So, for example, Miller et al. (2007: 76) report that:

> Compared with students who drank alcohol but did not binge drink, binge drinkers were more likely to engage in health risk behaviors and to have poor school performance. Similar to our findings, other studies have shown that underage drinking is associated with other health risk behaviors, such as not wearing a helmet while cycling, engaging in sexual activity at an early age and with multiple partners, and using illicit drugs. It is important to realize that those students who engage in these other risk behaviors are more susceptible to adverse health outcomes, such as head injury from not wearing helmets, death resulting from lack of seatbelt use or fighting with weapons, or being infected with sexually transmitted diseases because of promiscuity and lack of protection.

Youth reporting the largest number of risky behaviours experience much higher injury rates—especially multiple injuries and severe injuries—than those reporting no high-risk behaviours. These results are consistent with the idea of a common factor underlying risky behaviour in traffic and criminal behaviour. Multiple-risk behaviours may play an important role in the social etiology of youth injury. Indeed, many factors—including driving ability, demographics, personality factors, masculine identity, the "culture of driving," and the immediate driving situation (e.g., are passengers male or female?)— contribute to the higher-than-average risk of motor-vehicle collisions that teenagers face in North America. Adolescent risk-taking, in cars and elsewhere, needs to be understood in this multi-factor context (Shope and Bingham, 2008).

Unsafe Sex as Risk Behaviour

As with smoking and drinking, unsafe sex is another health risk teenagers often run. Young people are less likely to take effective precautions before sex, resulting in unwanted pregnancy or the transmission of STDs. Inconsistent condom use is especially frequent between partners whose ages differ by two or more years. Some unsafe sex is a result of mating between younger, naive women and older, experienced, and possibly exploitive men.

Given the early age of first sexual intercourse, especially among urban, minority youth, the risk of sexually transmitted diseases is rapidly growing. Because of high-risk sex, these youths are putting themselves and others in danger of contracting venereal diseases. By some measures, this problem is improving.

A study of Canadian 15–19-year-olds (Rotermann, 2008) found that the proportion of teens who had had sexual intercourse at least once declined between 1996–7 and 2005. Also, the proportion who reported becoming sexually active before age 15 had decreased. However, many of those who *were* sexually active continued to take significant risks. For example, no significant change was reported in the likelihood of having multiple partners or, for males, using condoms. Forty per cent of males and 27 per cent of females in this age group reported having had multiple partners in the past year; and fully 20 per cent of boys and 30 per cent of girls reported not using a condom when they last had sex.

Like other risky behaviours, juvenile sexual behaviour thrives on unsupervised time. Many youth spend long periods without adult supervision and may have limited opportunities to take part in after-school activities (Cohen et al., 2002). More than half of sexually active youths report that they have had sex at home after school. As youths get older, parents are more willing to leave them on their own. Many parents have no choice, needing to work for pay outside the home. This gives the young people many opportunities for sexual activity at home. So, sexual activity and substance abuse increase with the amount of unsupervised time youths spend at home.

Unplanned sexual intercourse under the influence of alcohol or other drugs often increases the risk of inconsistent condom use. Men and women differ in their reasons for not using a condom. Women who fail to use condoms often say they feel there is little risk of pregnancy or of getting a sexually transmitted disease during sexual intercourse. Men who fail to use them are more likely to cite inconvenience or unavailability as their reason.

Typically, when condom use is discussed at all, women play a more active role in the negotiation and men play a more reactive role. Positive attitudes towards safe sex promote an open dialogue about condom use and condom use during intercourse. However, there is often no open dialogue, largely because the girl/woman is reluctant to risk her partner's anger by raising the issue.

Failure in School

Since most juveniles are required by law to be in school, delinquency can also have an effect on school performance. Failure in school is an important factor in predicting juvenile crime and future criminal behaviour. Adolescents who report doing poorly or very poorly in school are more than twice as likely to report getting drunk during the past year than those who report doing well.

Leaving school early reduces the chances that juveniles will develop the vocational and social skills we learn in school, such as learning to meet deadlines, to follow instructions, and to deal constructively with authority figures and peers. Research shows that, among Canadian 24-year-olds, the dropout rate, which was 16.6 per cent in 1990–1, had fallen to 8.5 per cent in 2009–10 (HRSDC, 2012). In turn, this means a large number of young Canadians are unqualified for well-paid jobs and, as a result, may resort to other, even illegal, means of earning money.

The Influence of Family and Peers

Parent–child relations are another a key influence on risky behaviour by adolescents. Where family relationships are tense and conflict-filled, adults have less control over teenagers' behaviour.

Family conflict disrupts parental control over children by reducing family attachment and parental supervision. The parents have less information over what their children are doing, and the children are less willing to comply with parental wishes. Adolescent drinking, for example, tends to increase when parental attachment and supervision decline. Authoritative parenting—which is loving and firm but fair—is the best parenting strategy, not only to prevent adolescent drug and alcohol abuse but, more generally, to raise happy, confident children.

Peers can also be important agents of socialization and are especially influential from late childhood through adolescence and early adulthood. The *peer group* is a group of interacting companions who usually share similar social characteristics (age, gender, social class, and religion, among others), interests, tastes, and values. Members of a peer group get to know one another well, in terms of interests, activities, and tastes, which become the foundation for close friendships (as well as strong enmities). The friendships of youth are especially intense because children and adolescents spend so much time together engaged in identical or similar activities.

Peers start to be an important reference group as soon as a child starts school, and they become more important through adolescence and early adulthood. The importance of peers as a reference group does not depend on school, however. For example, gangs also provide teenagers with emotional support and aid by providing a positive sense of self when schools or parents cannot. Street gangs are numerous, large, and significant precisely because they give their members opportunities to gain a positive self-image that no other social groups do.

Acceptance and status are key elements in the group dynamic. Adolescents are likely to behave in ways they believe other young people are behaving—to shape their behaviour, however risky, to the perceived norms of their own reference group. When a person's friends or associates engage in delinquency, that person feels pressure to go along with the group and imitate their behaviour. Most young people do not want to risk losing acceptance or status within their group by failing to go along with the group's thinking.

Time to Reflect: In your experience, what is the relative importance of parents and peers in shaping adolescents' behaviour patterns (including patterns of delinquency)? Explain how this works.

In the end, both family influences and peer influences (in the forms of approval, modelling, control, and support) affect risky behaviour among teens. Indeed, often, a tug of war results between family and peer influences. Consider the use of illegal drugs. If the peer group is using drugs, the youth will be inclined to at least try them, to show solidarity with the group. However, whatever the availability of illegal drugs, strong family ties are likely to discourage such drug use more than once.

In general, families characterized by strong adult–child relations and authoritative parenting practices make it less likely that family members will associate with potentially dangerous peers. This applies to drug use and other risky behaviours. Healthy family relationships also play a part in promoting the use of birth control and STD protection during adolescent intercourse. As a result, supportive families with strong parent–child relationships can increase a teenager's protection against STD infection.

Parents do this both by educating their children at home and by supporting the messages their children receive in the classroom. Also of huge importance are the school, the school system, and individual teachers. Some are poor or worse; some are excellent; and all are likely to have some influence on the child's behaviour (www.socialunion.gc.ca/ecd/2003/report2_e/c3e.html).

Researchers have disagreed about whether family structure or **family process** is the more important factor in determining adolescent risk behaviours. Some have stressed the importance of structure, noting, for example, that teens living with both biological parents are slower to begin risky sexual experimentation. Two parents at home are better than one, if they provide more supervision and control, as they are ideally able to do. On the other hand, parental conflict, abuse, or neglect tends to increase the risk of unwanted outcomes: pregnancy, delinquency, school failure, and risky drug-using behaviours, for example.

Some researchers (e.g., Deković et al., 2003) have shown the importance of family process variables as direct predictors of risky or anti-social behaviours by teenagers. These family process variables—especially the quantity and quality of parent–child interactions—are the best predictors of behaviour outcomes, and they mediate the effect of other family characteristics. As Deković et al. point out, the characteristics of parents and of family structure disappear when the effects of family interaction are taken into account. Said another way, if we want to predict anti-social youth behaviour, we should look at the interactions between spouses and between parents and children, not the number of parents or children, their genders, their classes, or their marital status.

We have mainly focused on family, school, and peer group, but other factors, such as television and advertising, also influence adolescent risk-taking. For example, television, movies, and music videos constantly promote the ideal of sexual activity as a main life-concern. They also play on youthful anxieties about attractiveness and popularity. So, for example, in efforts to recruit new smokers, cigarette advertisers play on women's anxiety about their appearance, especially their body-weight/shape concerns. Research shows that girls who smoke are more likely than average to be moderately overweight and especially sensitive to issues of body shape.

Defining and Measuring Delinquency

Not all risky behaviour is considered delinquency in the Canadian Criminal Code, though all delinquency is risky behaviour—if only because it brings the offender into jeopardy with the law.

Juvenile delinquency—a much studied topic in sociology—is connected with a wide variety of risky behaviours that include drinking, dangerous driving, and unprotected sex, as well as with school and family problems. What's more, these patterns of adolescent behaviour are relatively consistent throughout Canada and elsewhere in the industrial world. Here are a few generalizations that would hold true through most of the developed world:

- Delinquency is commonplace.
- Adults tend to be unaware of youth delinquency. As a result, much delinquency goes undiscovered, unrecorded, and unpunished.
- Boys tend to be more often delinquent than girls and, especially, more violent.
- Lack of parental supervision and frequent use of alcohol and drugs are reportedly associated with delinquency.
- High rates of delinquency translate into high rates of victimization, in two senses. First, areas with high delinquency rates are dangerous for everyone. Second, people who engage in delinquent acts are, reportedly, at a higher-than-average risk of victimization themselves.

The Activities of Juvenile Delinquents

Crime

Like the adult crime rate, which, according to Statistics Canada, "has been falling steadily for the past 20 years and is now at its lowest level since 1973" (www.statcan.gc.ca/daily-quotidien/110721/dq110721b-eng.htm), the rate of delinquency has been falling. This is particularly true of serious or violent offences, for both adults and juveniles (see Figure 6.1). Most of the youth crime is not classifiable as "severe" crime. Statistics Canada (Milligan, 2010) points out, "In 2008/2009, the types of cases processed in youth courts most often involved crimes against property (38 per cent) and crimes against the person (26 per cent). . . . As in past years, a small number of offences accounted for a large proportion of the youth court caseload in 2008/2009. Together, 10 offences represented

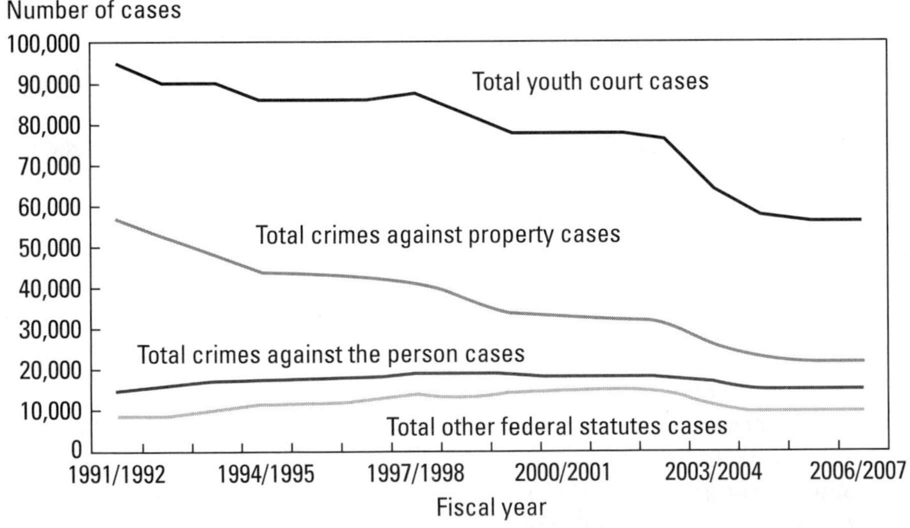

FIGURE 6.1 Declines in Youth Court Caseload, 1991–2 to 2006–7

Source: Adapted from Jennifer Thomas, "Youth Court Statistics, 2006/2007," *Juristat* 28, 4 (2008): Chart 1, at: <www.statcan.gc.ca/pub/85-002-x/2008004/article/10568-eng.htm>.

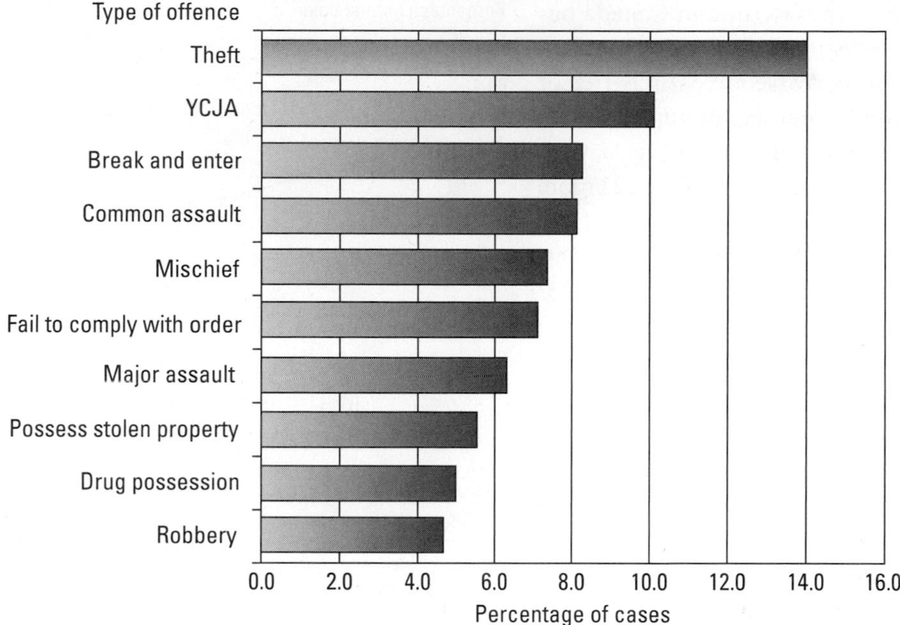

FIGURE 6.2 Youth Court: 10 Common Offences Accounting for over 75 Per Cent of Caseload, 2008–9

Source: Adapted from Shelly Milligan, "Youth Court Statistics, 2008/2009," *Juristat* (Summer 2010): Chart 2, at: <www.statcan.gc.ca/pub/85-002-x/2010002/article/11294-eng.htm>.

over three-quarters (76 per cent) of the total youth court caseload" (see Figure 6.2).

We know a great deal about the particulars of everyday delinquency in Canada. Highlights from a Statistics Canada report by Andrea Taylor-Butts (2010) show:

- Private residences were the most common site for youth crime (32 per cent), followed closely by commercial establishments (23 per cent), such as stores, office buildings, and gas stations, and outdoor public spaces (23 per cent), such as streets, parks, and parking lots.
- Violent youth crime (23 per cent) and youth drug violations (31 per cent) were more likely than other types of police-reported youth crime to occur on school property.
- Non-violent youth crime coming to the attention of police, especially property-related offences, took place in commercial establishments more often than other offence types.
- According to police-reported data, youth committed violent offences such as physical assault, sexual assault, and robbery with slightly greater frequency on weekdays than on weekends.
- Drug offences involving youth were more likely to occur on Friday followed by Thursday; and traffic violations were notably higher on weekends.
- Data indicate that after-school hours, between 3 p.m. and 6 p.m., were a peak time for violent (22 per cent) and non-violent (20 per cent) youth crime, while early afternoon (noon to 3 p.m.) was the most frequent time for youth drug offences (24 per cent) and nighttime (9 p.m. to midnight) for youth traffic violations (28 per cent).

The rate of youth crime in Canada has been decreasing since 1992. However, that is not to say we are entirely free of serious youth crime. For example, in 2009, 78 young Canadians aged 12 to 17 were accused of committing homicide, 23 more than in 2008. It was the second highest rate per 100,000 youth in over 30 years (www.statcan.gc.ca/daily-quotidien/101026/dq101026a-eng.htm). Some might use a statistic like that to generate a moral panic about youthful criminality or to justify the expansion of our prison system.

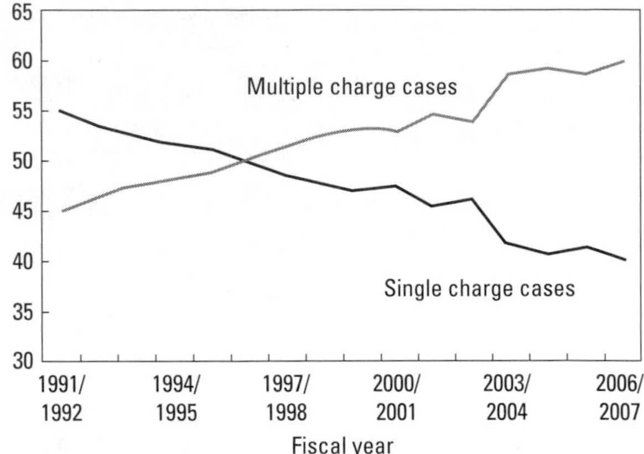

FIGURE 6.3 Multiple Charge Cases in Youth Courts, 1991–2 to 2006–7

Source: Adapted from Jennifer Thomas, "Youth Court Statistics, 2006/2007," *Juristat* 28, 4 (2008): Chart 3, at: <www.statcan.gc.ca/pub/85-002-x/2008004/article/10568-eng.htm>.

Statistics Canada reports that, "Despite a 4 per cent drop between 2009 and 2010, the youth violent CSI [Crime Severity Index] was 5 per cent higher than in 2000." However, it should be added that this statistic was lower in 2010 than in 2008. And like severe adult crime, severe youth crime has declined over the past decade or two. "The severity of youth crime has . . . declined over the past 10 years, including a 6 per cent drop in 2010" (Brennan and Dauvergne, 2011). What is most remarkable, perhaps, is the continued drop in youth court cases since the enactment of the Youth Criminal Justice Act in 2003–4. Yet, while the total number of cases is declining, the complexity of cases, consisting of multiple charges against the same youth, is increasing (Figure 6.3). We simply do not know if this indicates more case complexity or the greater eagerness of police to lay multiple charges in the hope of getting a conviction for one charge or another, often through plea-bargaining.

Motor Vehicle Theft

Far more common than violent crime among youth is property crime—for example, car theft. *Juristat* reports that, in 2007, youths aged 15–18 accounted for three in every 10 solved motor vehicle thefts, the highest vehicle theft rate of any age group (www.statcan.gc.ca/daily-quotidien/081215/dq081215c-eng.htm). And overall, motor vehicle theft rates are 10 per cent higher than a decade ago. In fact, Canada ranks fifth highest of 17 countries at risk of car theft, with 1.6 per cent of the Canadian population reporting being victimized by car theft in a given year. Most vehicles are stolen from parking lots, streets, and homes (garages, driveways).

For various reasons, these cases are rarely solved, whether the car is recovered or not. In general, the clearance rate for stolen vehicles is low: only 13 per cent of all vehicle theft incidents were "solved" by police—a rate of success comparable to that of other property crimes such as break-ins.

Impaired Driving and Other Traffic Offences

Another common offence among young adults, especially young men, is impaired driving. According to *Juristat*, the rate of persons accused of impaired driving offences in 2002 was highest among young adults between the ages of 19 and 24 and lowest for people 65 and over (Janhevich et al., 2003).

The good news is that, in the total population, impaired driving offences have been declining over the past 30 years; the 2010 rate was only 0.25 per cent, which is 0.46 per cent lower than the peak of 0.71 per cent in 1981 (www.statcan.gc.ca/pub/85-002-x/2011001/article/11523-eng.htm#a5). The reason is demographic—a change in the age composition of Canadian society. The aging of the Canadian population has meant a decline in the proportion of young people—those most likely to commit this offence (ibid.).

Coexisting Problems

Researchers who study delinquency and addiction know that people with a problem tend to have more than one problem at a time. The 2009 OSDUHS study mentioned earlier estimated the proportion of Ontario adolescents who suffer from (and display) the following four key problems: mental health problems (i.e., elevated psychological distress), alcohol abuse, drug abuse, and delinquent behaviour. They found that:

- A majority (53 per cent) of students surveyed report *none* of the four problems of interest. On the other hand, 2 per cent report all four problems, 6 per cent report three problems, and 11 per cent report two problems.
- The percentage reporting three *or* four problems is 8 per cent, representing about 89,000 Ontario students—a very large number of young people needing help.
- Older students (in Grade 12) are significantly more likely than younger students to experience all four problems, but there are no significant regional or male–female differences in the likelihood of experiencing three *or* four problems.

Communities and Subcultures of Delinquency

Though youth may sometimes feel isolated and all alone with their troubles, delinquency is social behaviour. We cannot understand individual delinquency unless we understand the social context—especially, the gang context—within which it usually is learned and practised.

We can trace the beginnings of the sociological understanding of gangs to classic works by Thrasher (1927), Whyte (1993 [1943]), and Cohen (1955). They all found that the gang offers members something they are missing: relief from the oppression of adult norms and excitement that socially accepted routines fail to provide. In doing so, the gang may also offer relief from feelings of loneliness and psychological distress (including depression and anxiety); in other words, it can provide the kind of support and security of a family a young person may need. To translate the OSDUHS findings into this context, the gang provides a large fraction of youth in mental distress with structured opportunities for gaining approval through such activities as delinquency, drug abuse, and alcohol abuse.

A group becomes a gang when it starts to form a clearer group consciousness, including a sense of rivals and enemies. Further, it attains the status of a gang when people in the neighbourhood want to break it up. Once the gang is threatened, its members come closer together and work to defend their membership. Thus, in Thrasher's conception, a gang is typically at odds with both society at large and the community within which the gang has formed.

By contrast, in his classic work, *Street Corner Society* (1993 [1943]), William Foote Whyte tells a slightly different story, in which the gang has an organic relationship with the community in which it forms. Whyte studied a slum district in Boston known as Cornerville. Occupied mainly by Italian immigrants, Cornerville was crowded with low-income, working-class people and had a high rate of juvenile delinquency.

Like Thrasher, Whyte says that gangs in Cornerville arise from the daily association of members over long periods of time. The stable composition of a gang, and a lack of social confidence that limits members' contact with outsiders, leads to high rates of social interaction within the gang. In turn, the in-group interaction produces a system of mutual obligations that is essential to group cohesion. The gang members—"corner boys"—have a code that obliges them to help each other when they can and to do each other no harm.

However, here Whyte parts company with Thrasher. Early sociologists believed that crime in poor US neighbourhoods resulted from social disorganization: the more disorganization, the more crime. After roughly 1940, however, with the publication of *Street Corner Society*, sociologists changed their views. They came to recognize that crime—especially organized crime in poor neighbourhoods—was *highly* organized. It was also intimately connected with the social, political, and economic life of the people in the community. Gang delinquency was an intrinsic part of city life—indeed, of national, corporate, and political life.

Albert Cohen provides a third influential theory of gangs in his book *Delinquent Boys* (1955). Cohen notes that gang members resist the pressures of home, school, and other agencies that attempt to regulate their activities, whether delinquent or not. He asserts that this resistance to authority is due to ineffective family supervision, the breakdown of parental authority, and hostility of children towards their parents. Given their community and family situation, delinquents of lower-class origin in particular create a counterculture to resist middle-class values. Thus, delinquency in Cohen's theory is about class struggle as well as the struggle against parents and related authority figures.

Thrasher, Whyte, and Cohen all point to a problematic relationship between delinquent gangs and the middle-class work ethic. Writers since then have acknowledged that youth gangs can have a wide variety of origins, activities, and purposes, but none have much to do with attaining traditional middle-class success values. Gordon (1995), for example, finds five distinct types of "young gangs": youth groups, youth movements, criminal groups, criminal business organizations, and street gangs.

Of particular interest to us are the last three of these categories. Criminal groups are groups of friends (mainly adults) who get together with the motive of committing a crime. Criminal business organizations are also groups of youth and adults who participate in criminal behaviours, and their sole motive is financial gain. Finally, street gangs are combined groups of youths and adults who form semi-organized groups for the purpose of profit. Unlike the others, the members of street gangs identify themselves through dress and by giving their gangs names.

Why do people join gangs and why do they leave them? Research on these questions used the files of 41 gang members held in British Columbia's provincial correctional centres; in addition, interviews were conducted with 25 of these inmates. The majority of these jailed gang members were 25 years of age or younger, male, and members of one of 11 gangs. Usually, the first contact with a gang occurred at a young age via a close relative or friend. All the respondents said that they had joined the gang gradually because of the rewards, material or psychological, that the gang offered. Speaking about joining the gang, members said things like "It made me feel proud"; "I felt more powerful, I had nothing else to do, and I had more friends if I joined"; and "It felt good, I felt protected" (Gordon, 1994). Others joined because of boredom and because the gang offered some excitement.

In time, young people leave the gangs to which they have belonged, and some gangs even disband. Some complain about low and unsatisfactory rewards, the high risk of arrest and imprisonment, and the new interrelations that develop and take precedence over criminal activity—for example, new relations with wives, girlfriends, and families (West, 1978).

In short, some young people join gangs to escape the negative aspects of their family lives; and they leave gangs when they have the prospect of establishing their own, independent family lives. But gangs are not the only social mechanism that enables this. Other disgruntled youth choose to live on the street.

Street Youth

For many youths, home is not a place of refuge but instead a source of abuse and a negatively charged emotional atmosphere. That is why some youth choose to run away from home. Others do not choose to leave but are instead throwaways; and many of these are gay, lesbian, and bisexual youths.

Leaving home to live on the street is hard and dangerous. A majority go for long periods without employment, and many have not been regularly employed since taking to the streets. For these young people, the three main methods of finding money for food and shelter are panhandling (75 per cent), social assistance, and crime. In terms of crime, many street youths rely either on prostitution or survival sex (a trade of sex for food, shelter, or drugs) (Gordon, 1994).

Life on the street is extremely dangerous, largely because of the other people who live there. Baron (1997), who studied 14 male street skinheads ages 15–22 in Edmonton, found that skinheads are drawn from homes characterized by extreme violence and oppression, experiences that left them likely to behave in violent ways. Their tendency to violence is intensified by school experiences, homelessness, and prevailing street norms that support aggressive behaviour.

However, there is no evidence that youth take to the street in order to become criminals. True, homeless or street youth show various forms of delinquency and crime. The classic work in this area is *Mean Streets: Youth, Crime, and Homelessness* by Canadian sociologists John Hagan and Bill McCarthy (Box 6.2). To research their book, Hagan and McCarthy collected survey and interview data from more than 800 homeless adolescents in Toronto and Vancouver. As well, they gathered data from 400 high school students to compare the backgrounds of youth who live at home with those who live on the street.

> **Time to Reflect:** Are "street youth" so unrepresentative of Canadian adolescents that we are unlikely to learn anything generally useful by studying them?

They found that, compared to youth in school, the majority of homeless youth come from dysfunctional families. These include

Classic Works

BOX 6.2

Mean Streets

The primary goal of John Hagan and Bill McCarthy's (1997) study was to examine how and why youths leave home for life on the street. Their research revealed that street kids' primary problems tend to begin with the life from which they fled; many progressed poorly in school and were involved with conflicts with school administration, which loosened their connections to their community. Many were also former residents of impoverished neighbourhoods, where they typically lived with their unemployed parents. The authors argue that as the pressure increases on these parents of lower socio-economic status, their parenting becomes less consistent and, often, more violent. All of these factors contribute to making youth feel as though life on the streets would be better than living at home.

But once they leave home, teenagers who lack social capital discover that they are incapable of meeting basic daily needs like food, shelter, and clothing. Many, therefore, engage in crime as a survival strategy, stealing food to satisfy their hunger and entering into professions such as prostitution to meet financial needs. Street youth thus develop a "criminal capital" to survive: they attain the "knowledge and technical skills that promote criminal activity, as well as beliefs or definitions that legitimize offending" (ibid., 138). This "capital" is acquired by becoming embedded within a network of other street kids who act as "a channel for the acquisition of information" (ibid.) and necessary skills.

Finally, Hagan and McCarthy note the different approaches taken by Toronto and Vancouver in dealing with homeless youth. BC's approach to dealing with homeless adolescents has been modified since Hagan and McCarthy's study was conducted. According to Housing Matters BC, an initiative designed to provide the homeless with affordable, safe housing, provincial funding for the Emergency Shelter Program has increased by 40 per cent. Homeless Outreach Teams have also been developed with the intent of helping homeless people gain access to necessities such as food, shelter, and clothing. The aim of both of these initiatives is to help homeless people transition from life on the streets to more stable, permanent living situations (www.bchousing.org/resources/About%20BC%20Housing/Housing_Matters_BC/Strategy_1.pdf; www.bchousing.org/Initiatives/Housing_Matters/Strategy).

At the time of this study, Toronto had adopted a social welfare approach through which organizations provide shelters like youth hostels. In opposition, Vancouver employed a crime control system where homeless adolescents are picked up by police and either jailed or returned to an abusive home environment. These latter strategies fail to "offer successful solutions to problems that cause youth to leave home in the first place" (Hagan and McCarthy, 1997: 108). Hagan and McCarthy assert that these differences result in the different youth crime rates in the two cities: crime rates are lower where adolescents receive social assistance to meet daily needs. Thus, underlying problems of family unemployment, inadequate education and training opportunities, and crime control responses to the effects of socio-economic marginalization increase the likelihood these youth will turn to crime.

Since *Mean Streets* was written, there have been continued cuts to social welfare spending, job losses in the unskilled and semi-skilled job markets, and ever-higher rates of male high school dropouts. More research is needed to understand how these cuts have affected homeless adolescents, and legislation that aims to solve the problems this population faces is necessary.

families experiencing severe economic strain that translated into dysfunctional parenting styles: into parental addiction, abuse, and neglect, for example. Indeed, a disproportionate number of street youth come from homes with family violence and sexual abuse. Once on the street, youths' lives are characterized by a daily search for food, shelter, income, and companionship. No wonder they turn to crime. If all the background variables are held constant, including prior involvement in crime, one factor consistently predicts their involvement in crime: a lack of the necessities of life (i.e., food, shelter, or source of income). Crime, for street youth, is a clear and practical response to need.

The influence of peers is another factor that increases their involvement in crime. Once they arrive on the street, youths become increasingly immersed in networks of other young people and adults for whom the street is "home," and many of these people are heavily involved in crime.

Employment is a turning point in the lives of street youth. In the same way that the street network encourages criminal behaviours, the work network promotes non-criminal behaviour. Employment comes to have an important dampening effect on the street youth's involvement in crime. Street youth who find stable, long-term employment become less involved in crime and generally spend less time hanging out on the street. A majority, with a stake in conformity, become ordinary, non-criminal citizens.

Runaway Youths

Reasons for fleeing the parental home are both psychological and social. Many street youths are "runaways," children who stray from their parental homes, rules, and expectations and, in these respects, violate the norms of society.

Various problems with interpersonal and family relationships, school, siblings, and parents shape adolescents' decisions to run away. Most street youths come from families that suffer serious emotional, mental, or substance abuse problems. Unlike street children in developing countries, these Canadian youth are rarely on the street for reasons of extreme family poverty, though family financial difficulties increase the likelihood of physical abuse, and abuse increases the likelihood of running away.

Homeless youth in Canada are most likely to come from broken families that are financially unstable or from reconstituted families (families comprising formerly married partners and their children) that are financially stable. Abuse aside, the children often come from "chaotic/aggressive families" and reveal a mixed pattern of youth aggression and parental skill deficit.

Sexual abuse is a common element in the stories of homeless youth. Here again, poverty is only a minor element. Both runaway males and females are likely to have been sexually abused. Among adolescent runaways interviewed in a Toronto shelter, one in three males and three in four females report having been sexually abused. Many male victims of sexual abuse report a fear of adult men. Another Toronto study also reports high rates of substance use and abuse, attempted suicide (30 per cent), loneliness, and depression among the street youth population (Adlaf et al., 1996).

Running away is usually a response to neglect, abandonment, and physical or sexual violence. Janus et al. (1995) estimate that 74 per cent of runaway males and 90 per cent of runaway females had been physically abused at least once. Most of these adolescents had been victims of chronic, extreme abuse experienced at a young age, often perpetrated by the biological parents and initiated before the first runaway episode.

Abused runaways are even more likely than those who were not abused to describe their parents in ways that suggest serious anti-social personality and drug problems. Parents are often the villains in these stories. Powers et al. (1990) report that, of New York runaways and homeless youth, 60 per cent had suffered physical abuse, 42 per cent emotional abuse, 48 per cent neglect, and 21 per cent sexual abuse.

Some runaways grow up to be homeless adults who display higher-than-average rates of criminal behaviour, substance abuse, mental illness, and other forms of deviant behaviour. A history of foster care, group home placement, and running away is especially common among homeless adults. The production of runaways and homeless children is the production of a new crop of adult rule-breakers and even criminals.

Media Depictions of Delinquency

Popular culture is, in many ways, intertwined with public conceptions of delinquency, as some cultural commentators claim that popular culture may itself be a cause of delinquency. Throughout the twentieth century, parents and civic leaders have expressed concern that positive media depictions of drug use, violence, gang culture, and other risky behaviours would tempt youths into delinquency. Debates on this issue escalated after the 1999 Columbine High School massacre in Littleton, Colorado.

Following two students' murder-suicide of 12 students and one teacher, some cultural commentators began pointing to the perpetrators' interest in the music of Marilyn Manson, KMFDM, and Rammstein and their interest in violent video games as causes of their behaviour. Researchers, however, began to provide convincing evidence that anti-depressant SSRIs were the triggering factor—one of the two Columbine shooters was on an increased dosage of an SSRI (the medical records for the other youth were sealed and remain so, though he likely also was on an SSRI, the side effects for which include suicide and homicide) (see, e.g., www.happinessonline.org/BeTemperate/pl.htm).

While popular cultural images of disaffection and deviancy may affect impressionable youths, there are no convincing empirical studies to show this is the case. In their own movies on this subject, Gus Van Sant (*Elephant*, 2003) and Michael Moore (*Bowling for Columbine*, 2002) came to no firm conclusions on the matter. Moore even went so far as to interview Marilyn Manson for his film; later, pointing out that *Bowling for Columbine* disproved the popular explanations, he called for an inquiry to examine the real cause of this and other tragedies—SSRIs (see psychiatricfraud.org/tag/michael-moore/).

Nonetheless, prominent American political figures such Connecticut Senator Joe Lieberman and former Florida Governor Bob Martinez have attempted to address delinquency in recent decades through crackdowns on "offensive" popular culture. The fact that, in 1989, Martinez was unable to ban the song "Me So Horny" by 2 Live Crew from radio play, and that Lieberman has been rebuffed in his attempts to staunch the growing violence in video games, suggests that ideas of culture directly causing delinquency hold little water with the public.

Rather than seeing juvenile delinquents as being made "bad" by culture, popular culture tends to portray delinquents as being born malevolent, as being spoiled by poor parenting, or as being misunderstood. The idea of delinquents as "born bad" is most common in horror movies like *The Bad Seed* (1956) and *The Omen* (1976), though it has little place outside of that genre. The idea of kids being turned delinquent is much more common, as one sees in sensationalized movies like *Kids* (1995) and *Thirteen* (2003), and more realistically in the characters found in *Rebel Without a Cause* (1955), *The Basketball Diaries* (1995), and the TV series *My So-Called Life* and the various incarnations of the *Degrassi* franchise. Even *West Side Story*, the hugely popular and award-winning Broadway musical (1957) and film (1961), explored the environmental factors related to delinquency and gang behaviour.

Beginning mid-century, television and film writers seemed more eager to see actions deemed "delinquent" as not being bad at all, but as rather as being legitimate expressions of self. Perhaps the culmination of this phenomenon was the development and popularity of Bart Simpson of *The Simpsons.* A self-professed "bad boy" who scribbles graffiti and engages in grifting, Bart is unapologetically himself and the show's writers, while generally sensitive to upholding positive moral values, choose not to "correct" Bart's behaviours (effectively refusing to reinforce puritanical moral standards). Rather, the show's writers formed Bart as an inevitable renegade, an adolescent whose behaviours distinguish him among the town's many well-meaning buffoons, bland do-gooders, and tolerated villains. Bart Simpson's popularity indicates that popular taste has room for both negative and positive depictions of delinquency.

Theories about Juvenile Delinquency

Functionalist Theories

Recall that functionalist theories of behaviour focus on the universality of the behaviour and explain the behaviour in terms of its supposed contribution to the social order.

Crime and delinquency are the result of social disorganization, according to functional theory, and result from defective attachment to the social order. Juvenile delinquency occurs because social bonds are weakened. Unsupervised households and neighbourhoods that lack cohesion, for example, are sources of social disorganization that produce personal disorganization and delinquency. Disorganized neighbourhoods lack the informal controls that help prevent delinquency, and they undermine the controlling functions of family, school, and peer group.

At the same time, many delinquent activities provide a new opportunity for cohesion—as in the formation of gangs, for example. As Whyte showed in *Street Corner Society*, gang delinquency may be tightly integrated with—and contribute to—the integration of political, economic, and adult criminal activity in a slum community. Additionally, juvenile delinquency and crime have their own functions for the youths, providing them with an "alternative world" that requires consensus and cohesion. Thus, delinquency may not always be functional for the adult world, but it is often functional for the adolescent world—in the sense of creating communal and subcultural boundaries around young people.

Symbolic Interactionist Theories

According to symbolic interactionists, people define themselves—including their identity, self-concept, values, and attitudes—through the process of social interaction. Labelling theory, for example, is concerned with the processes by which a deviant label is attached to specific people and their behaviour.

Labelling theorists recognize that an important result of the labelling process is its effect on the individual's identity and self-esteem. This process may have an especially forceful effect on young people. Some teenagers may respond to others' labels, at least in part, by accepting their judgement and engaging in behaviours that live up to, or down to, the given label.

A chilling example of this occurred in regard to the Columbine massacre—the two shooters were reportedly part of a group of school loners and gamers who called themselves the "Trench Coat Mafia," a label applied to them initially by a school jock. The term apparently originated from a fantasy scene in *The Basketball Diaries* in which the protagonist, dressed in a black trench coat, shoots students in his school.

Another result of labelling is that if a person's behaviour becomes known and labelled as deviant, opportunities for legitimate activity may diminish. Moreover, the possibility of associating with delinquent peers may increase as a result of the lack of respectable friends. By being labelled deviant and inadvertently associating with fellow delinquents, the individual increases his or her chances of deviant behaviour.

People behave the ways they think their reference group behaves. For that reason, changing people's behaviour often means changing what they know or believe about their reference group. For example, it may mean providing new or better information about how peers drink, drive, or have sex.

Critical Theories

Critical theorists reject the idea that any behaviour or arrangement benefits the entire society. For this reason, they assume that society will continually experience conflict between groups and continually change because of this conflict. Accordingly, critical theorists contend that juvenile delinquency is a result of class-based conflict between one or more groups.

Conflict can also result from a power struggle or arise between the legal system (judges, police officers, etc.) and minority groups who feel oppressed by it. It can even reflect a conflict between young people (and their value systems) and older people, many of whom are their parents. From this perspective, juvenile delinquency can be viewed as young people acting out against advantaged members of society.

In a society marked by poverty and class conflict, high rates of juvenile delinquency may indicate a deteriorating social fabric under conditions of rapid social change. Criminological theories suggest, however, that such conditions do not produce delinquency per se; instead, they force youth into pro-delinquent leisure activities—risky behaviours—with peers. Drinking, drug use, or automobile theft support delinquency and offer the infrastructure for it. The extent to which adolescents engage in pro-delinquent peer activities depends more on the cultural context that adolescents live in than on their personal experience in the family and in public.

Time to Reflect: Is it the position of sociology that poverty (or social inequality) leads to delinquency and that we can eliminate delinquency by eliminating poverty?

Critical theorists also recognize that the definition of what is criminal and what is delinquent reflects the desires, values, and interests of the most powerful groups and that these definitions not only change over time but conflict with the interests of less powerful groups—juveniles, in this case. Greater conflict and change in society mean that more rules are made and enforced. As a result, criminal and delinquent activity may increase from one time period to another simply because of an increase in the number of rules. What is best for middle-class members of society may not always be best for young members of the dispossessed **underclass**.

Feminist Approaches

As we have said, feminist theories focus on important differences between male and female behaviour and explain the differences in terms of differential opportunities and pressures in what have historically been male-dominated societies.

While recorded female crime has not increased much in certain areas—for example, homicides or serious assaults—it has increased in others, including delinquency and minor assaults. Two points of view contend about this increase in female criminality. One approach, represented by Adler (1975), argues that as women have become more involved in public life and the labour market, their opportunities for crime have increased and, therefore, so have their crimes. Critics respond that the increased criminality more likely indicates a reduced tolerance for female rule-breakers and a greater willingness to treat them the same as male rule-breakers.

The differential treatment of boys and girls by the juvenile justice system is well documented in the literature. Prior research has shown that police and courts often penalize girls for participating in behaviours that violate gender-role expectations and do not penalize boys the same way. Girls who exhibit behaviours typically found under the umbrella of "public peace" or status offences—including activities such as being sexually active, running away, staying out past curfew, staying out all night, being truant from school, or being disrespectful to parents—have traditionally been treated differently than boys.

Gangs have historically been recognized as androcentric (male dominated). Females in gangs were usually viewed as sexual objects or deviant tomboys who were no more than the affiliates of male gang members. Increasingly, however, female gang members are establishing themselves as equals to their male counterparts. Statistics Canada shows that between 1986 and 1990, there was a 29 per cent increase in the number of females charged by police (the numbers increased from 18,336 to 23,610). Despite this increase, in 2009, over 72 per cent of crimes were still committed by male delinquents (www.statcan.gc.ca/pub/85-002-x/2010002/article/11294-eng.htm).

The existence and development of female gangs are receiving more attention from experts. A recent study of female gang inmates (Scott and Ruddell, 2011) compared the characteristics of 337 Canadian adult female gang offenders with a matched sample of women offenders who were not gang members and concluded "that [the female gang members] were more likely to have been sentenced for violent offenses, had a greater number of prior youth and criminal convictions, and served prior terms of incarceration. Gang members were also assessed as having higher overall needs and risks, lower levels of motivation for change, and a higher risk of recidivism."

The current estimates of female gang membership, however, are hazy and unreliable. The best available expert opinion is that female gang members continue to be relatively few in number, especially in prisons (see, e.g., Mackenzie and Johnson, 2003).

Consequences of Juvenile Delinquency

All the delinquent and criminal youth behaviours we have discussed so far have important social and health consequences. Because they are risky behaviours, they often carry heavy costs.

Social and Health Consequences

Violence, though scarcely confined to youth, is one consequence of delinquency and risky behaviour more generally. Violent acts can have many types of health consequences, and repetitive violence can have major harmful effects on psychological well-being. Victims of intimate partner or dating violence, for example, have a greater risk of depression and self-directed violence. Further consequences are lowered self-esteem, anxiety, and alcohol and drug abuse.

Risky sex is a continuing problem because it causes unwanted pregnancies—with attendant problems of interrupted schooling, family conflict, and bad parenting—and spreads sexually transmitted diseases. Sex education in schools and programs like SHOP (School Health Opportunities and Progress), promoted by SIECUS (the Sexuality Information and Education Council of the United States), provide teenagers with important information about sex, sexual orientation, and substance use and abuse.

All three of these consequential problems—substance abuse, violence, and unsafe sex—are discussed at greater length in other chapters of this book. All of them, moreover, have significant effects on population health. For example, alcohol abuse increases the rates of traffic deaths; violence increases the rates of hospitalization, imprisonment, and family breakdown; and unsafe sex increases the spread of venereal disease and the risk of unwanted pregnancy.

Economic Consequences

Delinquency and crime have obvious economic consequences. Delinquents and criminals steal and destroy personal property, much of which is never recovered. Beyond that, crimes against persons, especially if violent, can result in lost days of work or school, and lost productivity for the society as a whole.

Nowhere are the economic consequences of crime more evident and more concentrated than in the communities of already poor people. Here, delinquency has the effect of undermining community cohesion and disrupting the education of those who are trying to escape to a better life. Aboriginal youths, for instance, have been of great interest to the Canadian government in the recent past, as the lifestyles found in the poorer communities in northern Canada and the subsequent feelings of limited opportunities and discrimination create particular problems for Aboriginal teens. Delinquency in these communities has been particularly harmful.

Another vulnerable type of community receiving more notice in recent years is the West Indian black community in Toronto and other large cities. Some have suggested dealing with delinquency and school dropout patterns, and attacking alienation particular to the black community, by chartering controversial "Afrocentric" schools. This idea grew out of concerns not just over the rates of delinquency in the community, but also about the ways in which delinquency might combine with social concerns like racism to create issues particular to the community. As we write, there are plans to extend Afrocentric education to the secondary school level, given the apparent popularity and success of an Afrocentric primary school.

There is general agreement among experts that education is a key factor in preventing delinquency. Clive Belfield and Henry Levin, for example, have argued that high school dropout rates are a key driver of delinquency rates. They found that, in one cohort of 12-year-old Californians, dropouts cost the state \$1.1 billion per year and, over their lifetimes, would account for \$10.5 billion in losses. They also investigated a cohort of 120,000 20-year-old high school dropouts, finding that group responsible for US$46.4 billion in losses to the state throughout their lives (Belfield and Levin, 2010). The simplest, most plausible solution to the financial burdens of delinquency, the study suggested, is to lower dropout rates. Nowhere would doing this have greater long-term economic and social consequences than in the communities of economically and racially disadvantaged people.

Social Policy Implications

Many communities have tended to ignore juvenile misbehaviour or punish it informally. A few have relied heavily on corporal punishment, as suggested by the traditional dictum, "Spare the rod and spoil the child." But no simple generalization is possible. As Table 6.1 shows, such traditional treatment of juveniles—at home, in school, and in the wider community—varies globally. Generally, there is a growing tendency to outlaw such casual violence towards children, whatever their misdeeds.

Today, economically developed societies aim a great deal of public effort at preventing and correcting risky behaviour, especially in the form of juvenile delinquency. However, the success of community programs in promoting good behaviour and reducing risky behaviour depends largely on parental actions. Families—especially parents—are intermediaries between their children, on the one hand, and community institutions, on the other.

Often, the quality of parent–child relations will influence whether teens are receptive to third-party messages about drinking, smoking, drug use, and safe sex. Though many children respect and listen to their parents concerning such third-party health messages, other children do not. Moreover, youths who reject parental authority are likely to reject professional health advocates as well—indeed, all figures of authority. Conversely, adolescents are more likely to participate in anti-smoking and alcohol prevention programs if they feel strongly attached to their parents and if their parents are non-smokers and, if they consume alcohol at all, responsible drinkers.

Strategies of arrest, probation, and incarceration do not seem to result in significantly

TABLE 6.1 Global Summary of Progress towards Prohibition of All Corporal Punishment of Children

	Prohibited in Home	Prohibited in Schools	Prohibited in Penal System		Prohibited in Alternative Care Settings
			As Sentence for Crime	As Disciplinary Measure	
Prohibited (no, of countries)	29	110	152	109	38
Not prohibited (no. of countries)	168	87	42	78	156
Legality unknown	–	–	3	10	3

Source: Adapted from Global Initiative to End All Corporal Punishment of Children, Dec. 2010, at: <www.endcorporalpunishment.org>.

improved juvenile behaviour; and the result is frequent recidivism. *Juristat* reports that in 1999–2000—when the most recent Canadian statistics were available—three-fifths of the nearly 57,000 convicted offenders between 18 and 25 years of age had at least one previous conviction, either in adult criminal court or youth court. Property offenders were especially likely to re-offend.

A majority of recidivists aged 18–25—64 per cent of males and 57 per cent of females—convicted in 1999–2000 had been convicted at least once for an offence committed before they turned 18. "Longer criminal histories tended to correspond with higher incarceration rates. Recidivists with multiple adult convictions had an incarceration rate nearly twice as high (41 per cent) as recidivists with a single adult conviction (22 per cent). Incarceration rates were higher for repeat offenders with an early age of first conviction" (Thomas et al., 2002), nearly twice as high for those first convicted at age 12 than for those first convicted at age 17.

Thus, punitive strategies do not seem to cure children of their delinquent tendencies. In fact, they may solidify these tendencies and lock people into criminal careers. We have argued in this chapter that juvenile delinquency is highly correlated with—and may be a subtype of—youth risk-taking behaviour. Current programs reduce risk not only by curbing risky sexual activity and substance use but also by "decreasing poverty; ensuring access to HIV testing, health care, general social skills training, and employment opportunities; and requiring community service for students" (Rotheram-Borus, 2000: S33).

Recreational programs help deal with the problem of youth supervision. They are a valuable addition to educational programs that provide useful information and keep youths off the streets, away from possible violence, substance abuse, and other risky behaviours. Such programs give youth an opportunity to socialize, use their energy in organized sports, and stay off the streets where they are more likely to get into trouble and engage in risky behaviours. Structured, safe, and enjoyable contexts provide youth with more than just encouragement to "say no" to risky behaviour; they provide something to which youth can "say yes."

Most experts believe that harsh punishments do not deter delinquent activities, so we should not bring juveniles into the harsh adult courts and prisons. Many members of the public believe that the punishments for delinquency are not harsh enough, especially when it comes to serious crimes such as murder. They would favour a symbolic, punitive exercise of the law, even if a more punitive law fails to reform juveniles or deter delinquency. For those youth who face the formal youth justice system, the new Youth Criminal Justice Act (YCJA), which came into force in 2003, includes sentencing principles that provide a clear, consistent, and coherent code for youth sentences. They are intended to reduce disparity and reflect a fundamentally fairer approach to sentencing.

The new legislation states that the purpose of sentencing is to hold a young person accountable for the offence committed by imposing meaningful consequences and promoting the rehabilitation and reintegration of the young person. The Act makes a new effort to ensure that similarly situated youth receive similar treatment for similar offences. Proportionality sets the framework or limits within which the needs of the young person committing the offence are to be addressed through the criminal justice system.

One of the new sentences available under the YCJA is the "custody and supervision order." This sentence is made up of two components: a period of custody and a period of supervision within the community, specifically, in the ratio of two-thirds custody to one-third supervision. This sentence is intended for a young person who is found guilty of a serious offence—that is, murder, attempted murder, manslaughter, or sexual assault—for which a non-custodial sentence would be inconsistent with the purpose and principles of youth sentencing. This sentence requires a plan for the intensive treatment and supervision of the offender, to assist the young person in the transition from custody to successful reintegration into the community.

Another option, the Intensive Support and Supervision Program, is a community-based program intended as an alternative to custody for young offenders who do not pose a threat to public safety and can be supervised within the community. To aid in the young offender's rehabilitation, this program provides closer monitoring and more support than conventional probation. Designed to address the particular needs and risks of particular youth, this sentence requires the young offender to attend non-residential programs at specified times and on conditions set by the court.

The YCJA recognizes that many young people are often brought into the formal justice system for minor offences that could be effectively dealt with in the community in less formal ways. While reserving the formal court process for more serious offences, the YCJA provides for a range of penalties and programs to deal with less serious crimes. Many provisions of this Act are intended to correct flaws in earlier delinquency legislation. Though the problem of juvenile crime has persisted through the years, the repertoire of interventions employed by juvenile justice officials has swung between punitive and rehabilitative policies and may continue to do so.

The omnibus crime bill of 2012, Bill C-10, has significant implications for young offenders. As reported by the CBC:

> Changes to the Youth Criminal Justice Act will impose tougher sentences for violent and repeat young offenders, make it easier to keep such offenders in custody prior to trial and expand the definition of what is considered a "violent offence" to include "creating a substantial likelihood of causing bodily harm" rather than just causing, attempting to cause or threatening to cause bodily harm. The new legislation will also require the Crown to consider adult sentences for offenders convicted of "serious violent offences" and require judges to consider lifting the publication ban on names of offenders convicted of "violent offences" even when they have been given youth sentences. Some of the concerns around these provisions raised by some of the professionals who work with young offenders include:
>
> - The publication of names of some young offenders will unjustly stigmatize them for life. Quebec has asked that provinces be allowed to opt out of this provision.
> - The changes shift the emphasis of the Act from rehabilitation to "protection of society," which critics say will put the focus on punishing young offenders rather than steering them away from a life of crime. Quebec, in particular, which prides itself on the success of the rehabilitative aspects of its youth justice system, has argued for stronger language prioritizing rehabilitation.
> - Stiffer, longer sentences will turn young offenders into hardened criminals and undermine any potential for rehabilitation.
> - As with other parts of the crime bill, critics say harsher sentencing rules

and increased emphasis on incarceration will disproportionately affect aboriginal and black Canadians, who are already over-represented in the criminal justice system. (www.cbc.ca/news/canada/story/2012/03/06/f-bill-c10-objections.html)

Future Trends

What can we expect in the future? The simplest answer may be less juvenile delinquency because the future will bring relatively fewer juveniles. Due to steadily declining rates of child-bearing since the mid-1960s, there are ever fewer young people in Canadian society.

The exceptions to this rule are found in high-fertility Aboriginal and immigrant communities. The result of continued low fertility, and a decline in young people, means a reduction in the numbers of young people at risk of delinquency, dangerous driving, substance abuse, and the other problems we have discussed in this chapter. As their numbers decline, society as a whole ages and fewer young people are at risk of breaking the rules.

Often, delinquency results from social disadvantage. So, for example, *Juristat* reports: "In 2004, the rate of youth crime on reserves was three times higher than the rate of youth crime throughout the rest of Canada .... Specifically, young offenders were accused of committing homicides on reserve at about 11 times the rate of young people so accused elsewhere in Canada, and were seven times more likely to be accused of break and enter and disturbing the peace" (Brzozowski et al., 2006).

Given the role that poverty and neighbourhood characteristics play in fostering juvenile delinquency and crime, it is likely that reducing poverty and the economic disparity between the affluent and poor members of our society would help reduce some forms of crime and delinquency among youths.

Families and schools are critically important domains in the prevention of youth substance abuse, for example. Because family life and school life are part of the problem, they must be part of the solution. In addition, the media, youth agencies, sports and arts groups, communities of faith, and municipal governments should augment efforts at the community level.

Conclusion

As we have seen, juvenile delinquency is a continuing concern in Canadian society, and people disagree about the best way to understand its prevalence. Competing approaches provide competing interpretations of delinquency and competing suggestions for control. We have taken the approach that delinquency is largely a result of several main factors, especially learned adolescent risk-taking, peer pressures to conform, and the lack of a stake in conformity.

In large part, these behaviours are rooted in cultural conceptions of masculinity that reward risk-taking and even delinquency. Though we claim (as a society) to value law and order, our media (including video games) provide a continuing celebration of male mayhem as the way to manhood, power, and popularity. As well, these behaviours are rooted in what some would describe as a continued decline of family and community life. Many children are short-changed by parental indifference, addiction, depression, negligence, or abuse; so it is little wonder they feel a lack of connection to "society" and its rules.

Learning risky behaviour, especially by boys, is something our culture has to remedy. Peer pressures to conform—especially to deviant gang norms—can be remedied only by offering youth competing activities that yield fulfillment and status. We can only hope that aging and maturation will, for most young people, bring a stake in conformity—as it has in the past for most juvenile delinquents. In the meantime, we need to reduce the risk and harm associated with delinquent adolescent behaviours. This we can do by improved public education, more sensitive parenting, and fairer, less stigmatizing strategies of control.

Questions for Critical Thought

1. The **culture of poverty** explanation holds that delinquents display traits such as a belief in fate, danger, luck, and risk-taking. Is this true of all delinquent acts? What is the major criticism of this theory?
2. The media portrayal of adolescent youth is overwhelmingly negative. In what ways (if any) is the media image of delinquent youth justifiable?
3. Some classic studies claim that gangs originate in youth playgroups. Explain how this is a functionalist approach.
4. According to Durkheim, where would one be more likely to find a higher crime rate: in a large city where people are unknown or in a small town where everyone knows each other?
5. What evidence could one use to prove delinquency is the result of parental influence? How could one prove that it was due to peer pressure?
6. The feminist approach mentions that males may be more deviant than females because of cultural ideas of masculinity. What aspects of masculinity lend itself to a deviant lifestyle?

Recommended Readings

Doob, Anthony, and Carla Cesaroni. 2004. *Responding to Youth Crime in Canada*. Toronto: University of Toronto Press.

This book dispels various myths—for example, that youth crime is on the increase, that females are becoming more violent, and that the gang problem in Canada is out of control. The authors argue that effective programs to deal with youth crime will most likely operate in preventive or diversionary institutions.

Laub, John H., and Robert Sampson. 2003. *Shared Beginnings, Divergent Lives: Delinquent Boys to Age 70*. Cambridge, Mass.: Harvard University Press.

Earlier longitudinal research on criminal activity has not followed delinquents much past the age of 30. This book, following 500 delinquent boys up to age 70, uses both qualitative and quantitative data to identify patterns of crime and profiles of criminal careers.

Thornberry, Terence P., et al. 2003. *Gangs and Delinquency in Developmental Perspective*. Cambridge, Mass.: Harvard University Press.

The findings of this book show that multiple developmental deficits lead youth to join gangs, but membership, in turn, leads to an increase in delinquency and violent behaviour, further disrupting normal adolescent development.

Warr, Mark. 2002. *Companions in Crime: The Social Aspects of Criminal Conduct*. Cambridge: Cambridge University Press.

This book reveals that most offenders are embedded in a network of friends and accomplices and subject to many forms of peer influence. It is this association with delinquent peers that causes delinquency. Delinquent peers are key in bringing about delinquency—the *main cause* of most criminal conduct.

Recommended Websites

Centre for Research on Youth at Risk

www.stthomasu.ca/research/youth/

Fredericton's St Thomas University curates this website, the entrée for the institution's research centre on issues relating to risky behaviours in youth. The site provides a variety of readings and links for Canadians looking to research juvenile delinquency issues, as well as a number of valuable data sets for a quantitative perspective.

Center on Juvenile & Criminal Justice

www.cjcj.org/links/index.php#rsd

The Center on Juvenile and Criminal Justice is also a private American service, though its website provides a more focused and academic investigation of the social issues surrounding juvenile crime. The website provides information and links on a great many issues, including government and non-government agencies, professional associations, and media sites.

Juvenile Delinquency (United Nations)

www.un.org/esa/socdev/unyin/documents/ch07.pdf

This is the seventh chapter of the United Nations' larger 2003 *World Youth Report*, compiled by the organization's Social Policy and Development Division. A dense but worthwhile read, the focus is on international and transnational juvenile delinquency issues.

RCMP

www.rcmp-grc.gc.ca/

In November 2002, the *Gazette*, an RCMP publication, published an issue on biker gangs, including biker history in Canada and what Canada is doing to stop biker gangs. This issue provides an excellent overview of biker activity in Canada.

Recommended Movies

***River's Edge*, Dir. Tim Hunter (1986)**

A teenager murders his girlfriend, whose body washes up on the edge of the river in their small, dismal hometown. All of the kids in town know who the murderer is, but nobody will turn him in, electing instead to forget through self-medication or by simply giving into their malaise. This film shows how delinquency is not simply the act of young people acting out, but it can also be passive, showing anger through alienation and disaffection as well.

***Mean Creek*, Dir. Jacob Aaron Estes (2004)**

Told in an inventive, cinéma-vérité style, this story takes place in a small town in Oregon, where a group of boys take a celebratory boat trip. Looking for revenge on one of their number (the town bully), the boys pull off a prank that takes an unexpected, and tragic, turn. This movie not only discusses issues relating to delinquency and risk-taking, but also provides valuable insights into the ways young people victimize each other.

***Dogtown and Z Boys*, Dir. Stacy Peralta (2001)**

This film revisits the troubled members of the celebrated mid-1970s Santa Monica skateboarding club the "Z-Boys." In their youth, the subjects were on the vanguard of skating culture, becoming counterculture icons and trendsetters. Directed by one of the club's members, Peralta uncovers the way fortune and celebrity combined with the negative socialization these kids received, showing how almost all of them died young or fell into severe drug addictions.

***Thirteen*, Dir. Catherine Hardwicke (2003)**

This sensationalistic movie follows Tracy, a Los Angeles teenager who morphs from being an excellent student and model daughter into a surly, sexualized delinquent. The popular Evie, who cleaves a bulwark between Tracy and her once-beloved mother, lures the protagonist into a life of sex, drugs, and risk-taking. While this borders on being a crass exploitation film (à la *Kids*), it is nonetheless a valuable reminder of why many adults fear and distrust adolescents.

7 Violent Crimes

Learning Objectives

- To understand the nature of violent crimes and public reaction to them
- To be familiar with the social characteristics of violent criminals
- To understand the characteristics of violent communities and subcultures
- To be familiar with theories about violent crime
- To understand the nature of various forms of family violence
- To understand the role of mass media in the portrayal of violent crimes
- To identify policies aimed at reducing violent crimes

Introduction

We study crime because it often has real consequences for people's safety, health, and general well-being. Victimization by criminals can cause people to lose trust in the existing social institutions and reduce their participation in community life. Because it is so important, we will discuss victimization again, in a separate chapter.

This chapter focuses on *violent* rule-breaking and especially on violent crimes. By "violence," we mean any act marked by great force, passion, or fierceness. Say "violent crime" and many Canadians will think of the serial murder of BC prostitutes by Robert Pickton, the gang violence in downtown Toronto on Boxing Day, 2005, that killed innocent shopper Jane Creba in its crossfire, the apparent gang-related killing at Toronto's Eaton Centre in June 2012 that injured several bystanders, or the Montreal massacre by Marc Lepine of 14 engineering students at École Polytechnique in 1989. The more historically minded readers might think of the abduction and murder of Quebec Labour Minister Pierre Laporte by members of the Front de libération du Québec (FLQ) during the October Crisis of 1970, or even of the notorious bank-robbing murderers, the Boyd Gang, who operated in Ontario in the late 1940s and early 1950s.

Others, however, will think of violent crimes committed closer to home: for example, the crime committed by an immigrant father, Mohammad Shafia, his son, and a second wife who murdered three daughters and a first wife for "dishonouring" their family by behaviour the murderers considered "godless" or immoral. Such honour killings are not rare throughout the world, even in Canada; and family violence is far more common than any other kind of violence, though less often the subject of newspaper reports. In this chapter we will talk about the less commonly discussed, though more common, forms of violence: **stalking**, domestic assault, and domestic homicide.

Currently, violent crime has been thrust into the limelight once again by a federal government that claims the average Canadian is afraid of violent crime, and this fear warrants longer, stiffer prison sentences in larger, more numerous prisons. One goal of this chapter is to evaluate this Conservative Party political agenda and the underlying notion that we are menaced by violent strangers who need to be put in jail and kept there.

We will see that, in fact, violence is unusual in Canadian social life and such violence as most people experience is close to home. Generally, Canadians get what they want by non-violent means: for example, through persuasion, bargaining, by offering benefits for co-operation, or by threatening to withhold benefits if co-operation is not forthcoming. Occasionally, we may need to make good on our threats to withhold benefits. However, for most people in most situations, even threats are unnecessary and unspoken. Usually, persuasion and bargaining are enough.

This tendency towards peaceful conflict resolution is not limited to Canada, however. In a recent book *The Better Angels of Our Nature* (2011), psychologist Stephen Pinker has argued that humanity as a whole has become ever less violent over the course of its history: that we are currently the least violent we have ever been, whether we look at warfare or violent crime, Canada or elsewhere.

For Pinker, violence represents an un-evolved mentality. For sociologists, violence represents a failure of social institutions—the breakdown of all other systems of interaction: persuasion, bargaining, and even threats. Violence, for sociologists, represents a failure to achieve agreement by peaceful means or, sometimes, even a failure to *consider* seeking agreement by peaceful means.

Violence is frightening, unusual, and therefore interesting (except to victims). For these reasons, it makes eye-catching news—though, as we will we see, the violent crimes featured in the media are not necessarily the ones we should be most concerned about.

Perhaps because of the media distortion, Canadians tend to believe that homicide is more common than it is. In reality, homicide is rare: in 1999, Canadian police services reported the lowest homicide rate since 1967, and between 1999 and 2009, rates remained relatively stable, as shown in Figure 7.1 (Beattie and Cotter, 2009). Yet, homicide continues to receive extensive media coverage both as news and as entertainment. The "life-threatening risk" that a homicide offender can pose always captures public interest—and fear.

That said, we must keep in mind that Canada is a diverse country, and the rates of violent crime differ markedly from one region to another. In particular, the West and the North have noticeably higher rates than are found in central and eastern Canada (Figure 7.2). This, as we will see, has something to do with demographics—the concentration of young, unattached men—and economics—the concentration of unemployed and poor people.

The same is true of other violent crimes: they have declined in recent decades. Today, the absolute numbers are high but the rates are lower than one or two decades ago. In 2010, police reported over 437,000 violent incidents, about 7,200 fewer than the previous year. Among the violent crimes with lower rates were attempted murder (–14 per cent), homicide (–10 per cent), robbery (–7 per cent), and serious assault (–5 per cent). In contrast, increases were reported among firearm offences (+11 per cent), criminal harassment (+5 per cent), all levels of sexual assault (+5 per cent), and abduction (+1 per cent). Almost every province showed a decrease in the severity of violent crime reported by police in 2010. The only exception

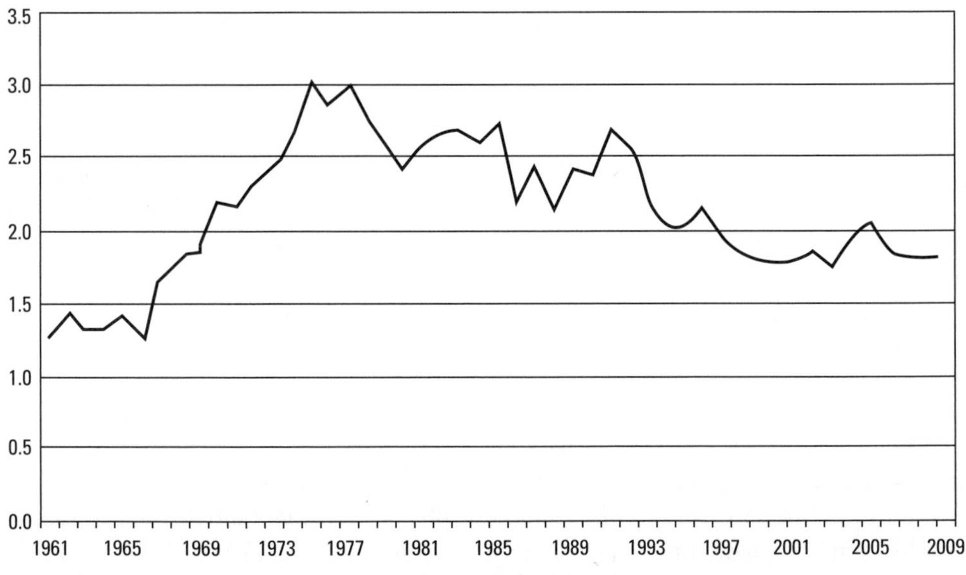

FIGURE 7.1 Rates of Homicide in Canada, 1961–2009

Source: Tina Hotton Mahony, "Homicide in Canada, 2010," *Juristat* (2011): Chart 1, at <www.statcan.gc.ca/pub/85-002-x/2011001/article/11561-eng.htm#a2>.

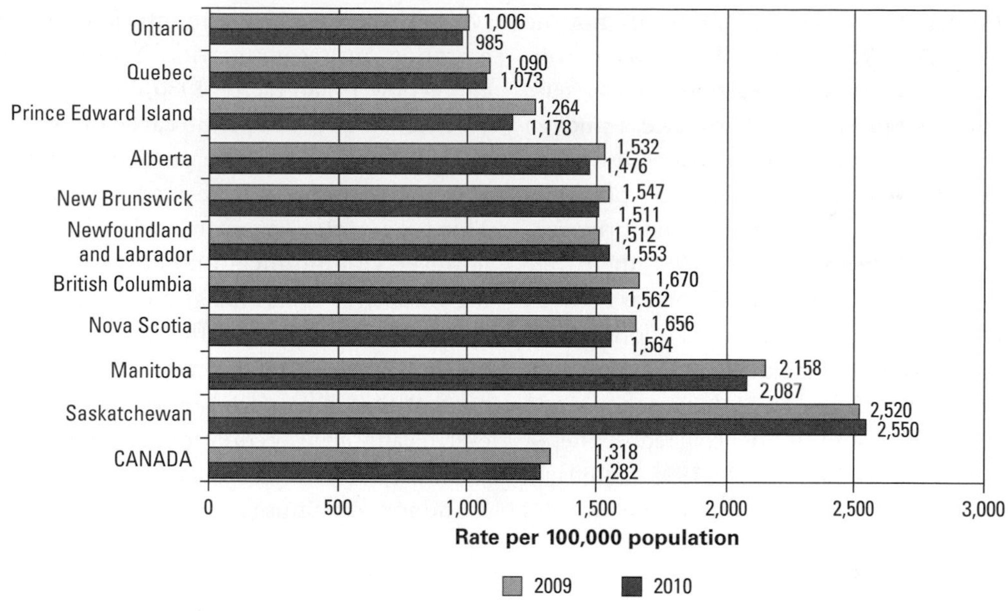

FIGURE 7.2 Violent Crime Rates for Canada and Provinces, 2009 and 2010

Source: Government of Alberta, Office of Statistics and Information, at: <https://osi.alberta.ca/osi-content/Pages/Factsheets/ViolentCrimeRatesforCanadaandProvinces.aspx>.

was Newfoundland and Labrador, where police reported a 13 per cent increase in violent crime, due primarily to a 37 per cent increase in robbery (Statistics Canada, 2011b).

Violent crimes are "high consensus" crimes, meaning that most people usually agree the crimes are dangerous and must be controlled or prevented. The concern over these crimes is both societal and personal. People want to protect themselves and their families against bodily harm, and most succeed in doing so. There are many forms of violence—public versus private, intended (planned) versus spontaneous, and so on. As a result, we need to consider various possible explanations. As we will see, sociological approaches to violence focus on social organization. These assume that violence occurs when the normal mechanisms of interaction—exchange, persuasion, altruism, or threats—fail to achieve the desired purposes.

For this reason we have consigned the discussion of organized crime to another chapter, on non-violent crime. Of course, organized crime sometimes uses violence—certainly, it uses the threat of violence—to achieve its desired goals. But violence is typically used as a last resort when other methods of persuasion fail.

Though we do not have reliable statistics over an extended period, it seems likely that Stephen Pinker is right: violent crime is indeed much less common today than it was a century ago. If violence occurs when stable, accepted, non-violent means of achieving the desired result are lacking, violence declines alongside the growth of **civility** that accompanies the development of nation-states (see, e.g., Elias, 1980). Nation-states bring about the "rule of law" by creating written codes, courts, prisons, and law officers with a monopoly on the legitimate use of violence: mainly, police officers and soldiers.

Of course, nation-states alone are not the whole answer. When the legitimate use of violence by authority figures is extreme, it may cause violence, not prevent it. For instance, a study in California showed that the increased use of the death penalty increases the incidence of unlawful violence. This is referred to as the "brutalization effect." Between 1957 and 1967, there were executions every two months, whereas between 1968 and 1991, there were no executions carried out. The homicide rate during the first period was twice as great as it was during the second period, when no executions occurred (Center of Juvenile and Criminal Justice, 1995). Similarly, studies in New York show that homicide rates typically increase in the month following an execution, once again showing the brutalization effect (Bowers and Pierce, 1980).

Often, fear is the prime cause of violence in human relations. One person expects the worst of another and pre-emptively attacks. This type of violence can often be avoided, however. Communication between competing groups (or individuals) can bring about a peaceful resolution when the conflict is caused by fear. Open communication can reduce a conflict that is based on needless fear; however, it cannot always prevent conflict based on other motives, for example, greed, or a desire for honour or status.

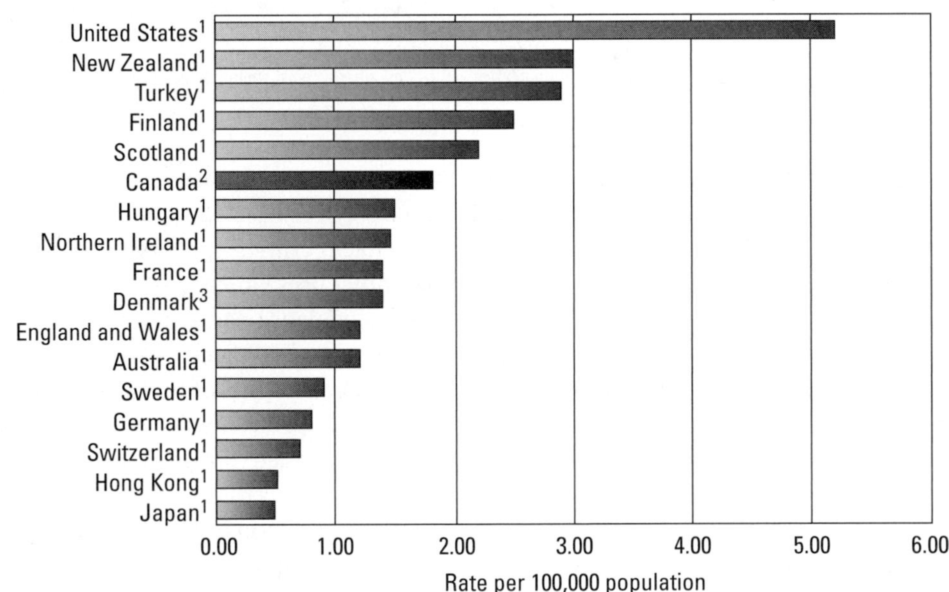

1. Figure reflects 2008 data.
2. Figure reflects 2009 data.
3. Figure reflects 2007 data.

FIGURE 7.3 Homicide Rates, Selected Countries

Source: Sara Beattie and Adam Cotter, "Homicide in Canada, 2009," *Juristat* (Fall 2010): Chart 1, at: <www.statcan.gc.ca/pub/85-002-x/2010003/article/11352-eng.htm>.

Often, **interpersonal violence**—including violent crime—is the outcome of a bargaining process between two people—the attacker and the victim—in which exchange, persuasion, appeals to altruism, and threats do not work. In other cases, the attacker and/or victim are not behaving rationally—that is, assessing their own best interests. It may occur when people have no legitimate means of redressing their grievances, as happens between gangs. People do not often behave rationally when the stakes are high, especially when they are unclear and diffuse.

Nowhere are conflicts less clear and more diffuse—hence, more irrational and violent—than in respect to issues of honour, pride, dignity, esteem, and "saving face." These issues are likely to arise in families, between friends and acquaintances, or in schools and workplaces. Often, these clashes occur in private places, where private violence is able to erupt without any public visibility or control. Thus, in Canada, incidents of physical assault and sexual assault are far more common types of violent crime than incidents of robbery, for example.

In connection with such irrational violence, let's not forget the role of gender in these events. Men are far more likely than women to act out violently, and there are social (as well as cultural, psychological, and probably genetic) reasons for this. Proving masculinity is often a factor in violent crimes by males against other males. It may sometimes also be a factor in attacks by males against females. However, violent acts that grow out of male efforts to show masculinity and physical courage, and to save face and seek honour, are not merely psychological responses to frustration. They are social and cultural and have a long history, as we will see. And, largely because societies differ in their socio-cultural history, they differ in their rates of homicide (see Figure 7.3).

The History of Violent Crime and Public Reactions

To seek respect (or honour) and take revenge for disrespect (or dishonour) are both old, established cultural practices in certain parts of the world, as is **feuding** to resolve a conflict. Though none of these is necessarily a crime, all remain important to our understanding of modern crimes of violence.

Feuding, Honour, and Human Rights

Feuds, **blood feuds**, or vendettas are ancient forms of inter-group violence intended to restore a group's honour by taking revenge on another group for having dishonoured it.

Perhaps owing to its connection with masculinity, feuding often has a sexual motive when groups are avenging the dishonour of a female group member. Though focused on women and sex, this behaviour is not to be confused with Western romantic or chivalric notions in which a prized woman is sought, wooed, idealized, cherished, and wed. In traditional societies with a strong sexual double standard, where women are viewed as property, if someone rapes or seduces an unmarried woman, her bride price is lowered because she is "damaged goods." Although women have been seen as property in both the historical chivalric notion and elsewhere, the reaction to the loss of a woman's "purity" has differed among societies. The goal then—depending on the society—may be to kill the seducer, kill the woman, or force the seducer (or someone else) to marry the woman, while taking revenge on the seducer's family.

In these traditional societies, women often have few personal rights; their feelings and experiences count for little. In some parts of the world, even today, women suffer violent abuse if they "dishonour" their spouse or their family by behaving too freely in any of many ways. The results are called **honour killings** and are practised in many Islamic societies. In Turkish society, for example, women are carriers and bearers of group identity. Women are physically abused when they violate the boundaries of their community's definition of acceptable femininity by dressing, speaking, or acting in non-traditional ways.

In Palestine, despite the criminalization of abuses inflicted on women, the murder of girls or women for allegedly committing "crimes of family honour" remains common (Shalhoub-Kevorkian, 2002; Hasan, 2002). A silent masculine conspiracy keeps sexist and gender-biased legal policies in place here. The entire matter of "honour" in such a society is a rationale for preserving male control over women. However, we could find examples of similar patriarchal attitudes and acts of violence in dozens of other traditional societies.

Such acts are less common in more modern, economically developed societies like Canada. Lindner (2002) notes a long-term historical shift from discourses of "honour" to discourses of "human rights" as the basis for codes of human behaviour. From this evolutionary perspective, there are clear differences between societies founded on "honour" as compared with societies founded on "human rights" with respect to their codes of behaviour and use of humiliation. Violence—both political and personal—is more common in the former type of society than in the latter. Both women and men suffer under the "honour" principle, though it is likely that women suffer more.

Since many men—even in Canada—still consider women property, this poses problems for law enforcement on how to deal with sexual assault by spouses. Canada is no stranger to the idea that a wife is the sexual property of her husband. Until it was amended in 1983, Canada's Criminal Code limited the offence of rape to favour the rights of men over women. The offence of rape needed proof that a man had sexual intercourse with a woman *other than his wife*, without the woman's consent. This offence was punishable by up to life imprisonment. However, it was thought impossible for a man to rape his own wife; she was his sexual property, obliged to provide sex on a particular occasion whether she consented to it or not.

Perhaps a more nuanced description would say that, in Canada and elsewhere, women historically negotiated their sexuality within marriage; before the existence of reliable birth control, they developed considerable self-control and had recognized negotiating power. Sexual relations were generally conducted under very much more restraint, with much greater attention to economic issues, much less "romanticizing" of relationships, more attention to practical matters because couples were raising more children, and with much more social support in communities and social institutions for those values. So, we cannot readily apply our own thinking to these people, who were acting at another time under different constraints.

In recent times we have come to understand that sexual behaviour, to be legal, requires consent. In 1983, Bill C-127 redefined the physical and sexual assault sections of the Canadian Criminal Code, abolishing the offence of rape and establishing three levels of assault. One level includes sexual touching or sexual intercourse without consent. The second includes (non-consenting incidents) involving a weapon or resulting in bodily harm. The third, aggravated assault/sexual assault, is the level in which the victim is wounded or disfigured (Duchesne, 1997).

Most important to our current discussion, Canadian law has also abolished the distinction between men and women—no longer supposing that only men can commit rape—and has ended spousal immunity. Sexual conduct between partners must now be fully consensual, whatever their marital status.

We have no way of knowing how well official statistics reflect the actual incidence of sexual assault. However, according to the most recent figures available (Statistics Canada, 2007), both police and victimization data show that rates of sexual victimization are five to six times higher among females than males, almost regardless of the type of sexual assault. The gap between female and male rates is slightly smaller for level 3 sexual assaults and "other sexual offences" than for level 1 and 2 sexual assaults, such as unwanted touching.

Being young, attending school, and participating frequently in evening activities all are factors that increase the risk of violent victimization, largely because of lifestyle factors we will discuss further in Chapter 10, on victimization. Accordingly, the rate of sexual assault for Canadians aged 15 to 24 was almost 18 times higher than the rate recorded for Canadians aged 55 years and older; and in 2007 over half (58 per cent) of sexual assault victims were under the age of 18, with children under 12 accounting for 25 per cent. The vast majority of these young victims were female (81 per cent).

Because young people are more likely to put themselves in "hot spots" where risks of assault are higher, the 2004 General Social Survey found that students had significantly higher-than-average rates of sexual assault, and people who participated in 30 or more evening activities per month had rates of sexual victimization that were 4.5 times higher than those who engaged in less than 10 evening activities in a month.

In sexual assault cases, males are usually the accused and females usually the victims. In fact, according to 2007 police-reported data, 97 per cent of the people accused of sexual offences were male. Rates of sexual offending were highest among people aged 12 to 17 (90 per 100,000 population), followed by 18- to 34-year-olds (55 per 100,000 population) and 35- to 44-year-olds (42 per 100,000 population).

Typically, the victims of sexual assault know their attackers well. Often the attackers are friends or acquaintances, and only in a minority of cases—somewhere between a third and a fifth of the cases—are they strangers. According to police reports, the accused attacker was a family member in nearly a third (31 per cent) of sexual offence incidents that came to the attention of law enforcement in 2007, with extended family members (10 per cent), the victim's parents (10 per cent), or some other immediate family member (7 per cent) identified most frequently as the accused. Not surprisingly, then, police-reported data from 2007 indicate that 68 per cent of aggravated sexual assaults occurred in or around someone's home (ibid.).

Defining Crimes of Violence

When we think about crime at all, we often first think about violent crime—about crimes like murder, attempted murder, manslaughter, assault, sexual assault, and robbery. Criminologists have given these types of offences the name *conventional crimes* precisely because they are the illegal behaviours that most people think of as crime (Koenig, 2000). They frighten people and make them feel unsafe. And because they fear it, some Canadians believe—largely without reason—that crime in general, and violent crime in particular, is on the rise. However, violent crime has stayed relatively steady at a level far lower than property crime. Consider the Canadian statistics on homicide and physical assault.

Homicide and Physical Assault

Homicide refers to the killing of one human being by another. Few would disagree that homicide is the most serious violent offence. It is also the *least* common criminal offence: there were only 554 Canadian homicides in 2010, one of the lowest totals since 1967.

Non-sexual assault, by contrast, is by far the *most* common violent crime. Both men and women are equally likely to be victims of non-sexual assault; however, men are more likely to be victims of assault in which a weapon is used.

As data from the economically developed societies have shown, the Canadian homicide rate, though higher than the world's lowest rate (that of Japan), is far lower than the world's highest rate (that of the United States). It is even lower than the recorded rates in countries we commonly regard as safe and progressive such as Finland and New Zealand. This low Canadian rate, compared to the US in particular, is largely due to the low rate of homicides involving firearms in Canada. Firearm use is relatively rare in Canada. If firearms, especially handguns, became more easily accessible in Canada, this homicide difference would likely change. However, other factors (such as range of social inequality) also explain the difference between Canada and the US.

It may be because of the influence of American media that some Canadians express concern about the danger posed by homicide, though the increased use of handguns by some urban gangs may also contribute. However, as noted earlier, the rates of homicide in Canada have declined since 1990, and they are currently below the 50-year average (though higher than the rates 50 years ago). Moreover, these rates have continued to decline in the past 10 years. More generally, all types of violent crime known to the police have dropped over this period, as shown in Figures 7.4 and 7.5.

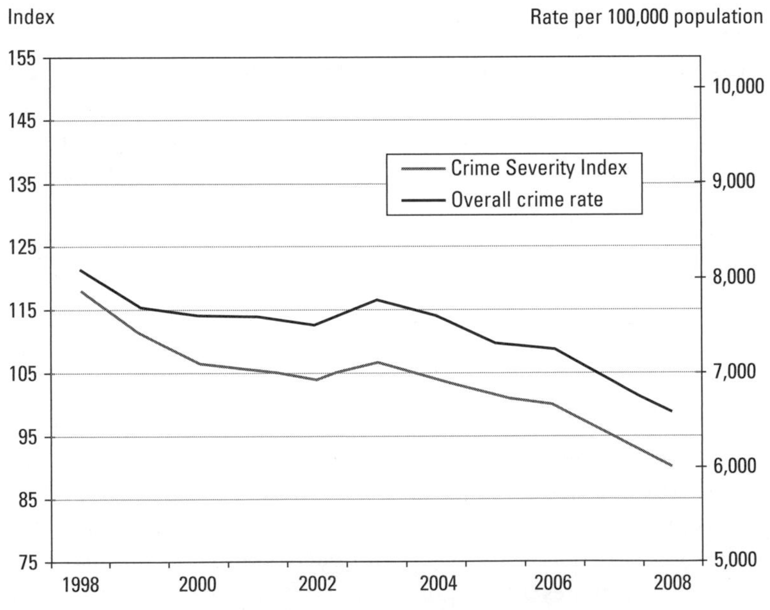

FIGURE 7.4 Police-Reported Crime Rate and Crime Severity Index, 1998–2008

Source: Marnie Wallace, "Police-Reported Crime Statistics in Canada, 2008," *Juristat* (July 2009): Chart 1.a, at: <www.statcan.gc.ca/pub/85-002-x/2009003/article/10902-eng.htm>.

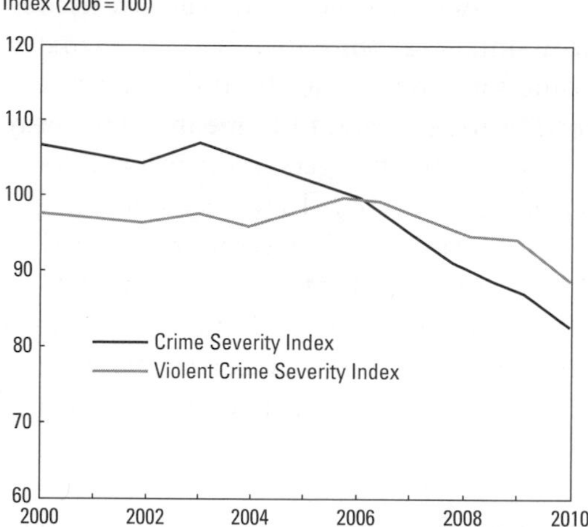

FIGURE 7.5 Police-Reported Crime Severity Indexes

Source: Statistics Canada, *The Daily*, 21 July 2011, at: <www.statcan.gc.ca/daily-quotidien/110721/dq110721b-eng.htm>.

Time to Reflect: What are the types of crime most often depicted in movies and on television? What are the types of crime most often perpetrated in Canadian society? How do you account for the difference between the reality and the depiction?

Sexual Assault

Like its non-sexual counterpart, sexual assault can be classified into three levels, according to whether a weapon was used and whether the victim was wounded, maimed, or disfigured. We can also distinguish between (1) "classic" rape, which involves forcing sexual intercourse on a stranger against his or her will; (2) acquaintance rape, which involves sexual assault involving someone the victim knows casually; (3) statutory rape, in which the victim is under the legal age of consent (typically 18); (4) marital rape, which involves a spouse; and (5) incest, which involves a member of the assaulter's immediate biological family.

As we have seen, women outnumber men as victims of sexual assault by a ratio of about 4:1. The disproportionate victimization of women has not changed much for as long as we have had reliable statistics on the matter. However, the interpretations put on sexual assault by the courts and by society at large have changed.

As Edwards (1981) has shown, legal definitions of sexual deviance are influenced by cultural and societal assumptions about gender and sex. Through the nineteenth century, most people seemed to hold the view that women were devoid of sexuality compared to men. Edwards suggests that this belief in "female sexual passivity" may have originated from the interpretation of biological differences in the sexes. The protruding nature of the male penis seemed to imply active sexuality in males, and the "inversion" of the female vagina implied that women were sexually passive. Edwards notes that both historically and cross-culturally, rape has been legally defined as an act that must occur between a male and a female and must involve penetrating the female's vagina by the male's penis.

This argument can be seen within the Canadian context. Before 1984, "rape" was still considered a criminal offence only when the offender was a male, the victim was a female and the act involved the forceful penetration of the female's vagina with the male's penis.

Today, we have a much better idea of the differences between male and female sexuality, and a much more complex idea of what constitutes sexual assault. Key to our current understanding is the idea of consent: in effect, *any* sexual activity is an assault unless both parties have consented.

Robbery

Robbery is another violent crime, but it is a crime against property: a form of theft that involves the use or threat of force. According to the most recent available Canadian statistics (2008), the nature and extent of robberies, as reported to police, has also changed during the past decade. Commercial robberies (e.g., bank and store robberies) have declined, while robberies occurring in residences and public transit facilities have increased.

Canadian police services reported about 32,000 incidents of robbery in 2008, accounting for 7 per cent of all violent crimes. Young men committed the vast majority of these robberies. In 2008, almost 90 per cent of those accused of robbery were male and nearly two-thirds were between the ages of 12 and 24. Money was the most common item reported stolen (37 per cent of all robberies), followed by personal accessories such as jewellery (18 per cent). Electronic devices such as cell phones, personal music devices, and computers, items that can be sold for a quick profit, were next at 15 per cent. Western Canada, particularly Manitoba, recorded the highest rates of police-reported robbery in the country—a pattern that is similar overall for violent crime rates.

Robberies tend to occur in public. In 2008, about half of all robberies were committed on the street or in another outdoor public location such as a parking lot or public transit facility. Another 39 per cent took place in a commercial establishment such as a convenience store or bank. The remaining 10 per cent were residential robberies. When we discuss victimization in Chapter 10, these statistics will make more sense in terms of "routine activity theory" and "location theory." In short, robberies occur where money is to be found and "guardians"—police and security forces—are absent.

In 2008, police also reported 2,700 home invasions—robberies that occurred in a private residence. The rate of home invasions rose 38 per cent between 1999 and 2005 and has been relatively stable since. Unlike other types of robbery, which tend to involve friends, acquaintances, schoolmates, or workmates, home invasions typically involve strangers. In 2008, 63 per cent of home invasions were committed by strangers, while just over one-quarter were committed by acquaintances.

Robberies are dangerous because they involve force and, often, weapons. Indeed, robberies committed with knives accounted for 29 per cent of all incidents. Firearms were involved in another 14 per cent of all robberies in 2008, down from 20 per cent a decade earlier. Between 1977 and 2002, the rate of robberies committed with a firearm declined steadily; since then, the rate has remained stable (Statistics Canada, 2010). The relative absence of firearms should reassure us that we are not moving rapidly in the direction of American criminality.

Stalking

Stalking—a type of relationship abuse that may evolve into violent physical, psychological, and sexual forms—has emerged as a relatively new form of violent crime in our society. This activity has gained much attention in recent decades because it is common and is associated with gendered abuse and violence.

Regrettably, Canadian statistics on stalking are hard to find and, often, the available ones are old, possibly outdated. That said, in all stalking cases for the year 1997, stalkers made overt threats to about 45 per cent of victims; spied on or followed about 75 per cent of them; vandalized the property of about 30 per cent; and threatened to kill or killed the pets of about 10 per cent. So, stalking is a frightening crime because the victim often has no idea what will happen next. This is very different from robbery, where the goal is (usually) a simple transfer of money from the victim to the criminal.

Stalking often follows a relationship breakup or rejection. In 1996, roughly 80 per cent of the 4,450 stalking victims in Canada were women, and 88 per cent of the people accused of stalking in these cases were men (Bunge and Levett, 1998). Most stalkers were former intimates: former boyfriends or husbands, in particular. Usually, the victims of stalking had to resort to help from the authorities and seek restraining orders to protect themselves.

The Social Characteristics of Violent Criminals

As we have already hinted, changing crime rates largely reflect the changing demographics of Canadian society. Consider this fact: according to Statistics Canada, in 2010 both the volume and severity of police-reported violent crime declined. The rate of violent crime fell 3 per cent from 2009, while the decline in the Crime Severity Index (CSI) was more notable, down 6 per cent. This marked the fourth consecutive decline in the CSI and the largest drop seen in more than a decade.

This fall in serious crime mirrors the decline of the proportion of men in the population aged 15–35. Birth rates "boomed" in Canada between 1947 and 1967, and the unusually large number of male babies soon became an unusually large number of young men. During the period 1965–1985, a short-lived explosion of criminal violence in Canada was the result of an increase in the number of young men. On average, violent criminals are younger than other people. Usually, people who are going to break the law start getting into trouble when they are young. The vast majority of young rule-breakers stop after their first or second brush with the police and courts.

In the last 30 years, however, as the Canadian population has aged and older people have come to outnumber younger ones, the rates of violent crime have fallen, then stabilized at a lower level than existed 20 or 30 years ago. Said another way, with the decline in fertility and the aging of the Canadian population, the rates of violent crime have dropped.

Of course, violence has not disappeared entirely. Leaving aside domestic violence, a small group we might call **violent predators** continue to commit serious crimes outside the home—among them robberies, assaults, and drug deals—often from childhood onward. These violent criminals are very dangerous, but also very rare.

Communities and Subcultures of Violence

We started this chapter by asserting that violence reflects the absence of order and the failure of other mechanisms for resolving disputes. Therefore, violence (in the form of duels, feuds, and otherwise) declines with the development of the rational–legal modern state and the rise of a fair judicial system.

To the extent that these systems are perceived to work by those they govern, violence should be reduced. However, we have also recognized that communities vary in the importance they attach to honour and respect, and in their willingness to use violence as a brave and masculine way of seeking respect. Thus, sociologists explain violence in terms of both social disorganization—an absence of regulatory mechanisms—and subcultural variations in the value placed on violence. Some societies hold values and beliefs that glorify aggression and violence, while others do not.

Sociologists have studied violent communities and subcultures to explain how values and belief systems contribute to violent criminal behaviour. In this respect, subculture theory is helpful in explaining why arguments between young males, for example, are the most common forerunner to homicide in our own society and elsewhere. Young men embrace identities and subcultures that encourage them to challenge each other in competitions for honour and respect.

This is most evident among inner-city youth who live according to a street code that justifies gaining respect from others through violence. In these inner-city subcultures, guns symbolize respect, power, identity, and manhood; they play a central role in starting, continuing, and intensifying youth violence. Violence becomes viewed as "suitable" behaviour for youth who are regularly exposed to violence, are gang members themselves, have family members or friends who are gang members, and have peer support for violence. In these subcultures, males who behave fearfully or seem unwilling to act violently are, ironically, likely to be threatened with violence.

In poor urban areas, as in peasant and tribal societies, all goods—including honour—are scarce. Honour is used to measure social worth, and in this subculture, people can gain it mainly through violence. That is because legitimate, peaceful channels are closed to them. People who live in more prosperous neighbourhoods can earn respect through their educational and career achievements, or through their possessions (clothes, cars, and so on). However, people who live in poorer areas, such as the inner city, may have to rely on strength, threats, or violent acts and tough anti-social acts to gain their peers' respect.

As viewed by the law-abiding middle-class society, inner-city neighbourhoods are chaotic, gang-dominated danger zones. As viewed by the local residents, the same neighbourhoods may seem dangerous but orderly. Gangs, after all, give minority youth an alternative opportunity to achieve social status, friendship, and upward mobility.

In every gang-dominated neighbourhood, engaging in violence is part of the lifestyle of the **subculture of violence** (Wolfgang and Ferracuti, 1967). Members of a violent community or gang internalize the norms of the subculture, which helps members justify their actions and reduce feelings of guilt. Members of the subculture who refuse to engage in violence are deemed cowardly and may be expelled from the group.

Wolfgang and Ferracuti (1967: 140) write, "a subculture implies there are value judgments or a social value system, which is apart from and a part of a larger central value system." A subculture of violence is a subculture in which violence plays a central role in "the lifestyle, the socialization process, [and] the interpersonal relationships of individuals living in similar conditions" (ibid.). Wolfgang and Ferracuti's subculture of violence theory can be summarized as follows: compared to other people, members of a violent subculture are particularly likely to respond to minor transgressions with lethal force because of a culturally defined need to protect their reputation and an aversion to legal forms of dispute resolution.

Family Violence

Just as violence within poor communities is historically common, so is violence within families. Violence among family members is as old as the family institution itself. However, the systematic study of family violence is a new branch of academic research, and also a new branch of law enforcement. It emerged only in the 1960s, launched by the publication of the first detailed case studies of seemingly inexplicable physical injuries that young children had suffered. Much of the difficulty in finding out the extent or prevalence of family violence is methodological.

Family violence is an umbrella term covering different kinds of violence, among different sets of family members. Besides the obvious forms of physical violence, we need to include sexual violence, such as child sexual abuse, incest, and marital rape, which are likely to include physical violence. As well, emotional abuse often accompanies these violent acts. For its victims, emotional abuse can be as painful and destructive of self-esteem and healthy emotional development as physical violence. Consider a few of the various forms of family violence that are common in our society.

Elder Abuse

Children and spouses are not the only victims of domestic violence; so are elderly parents. Research shows that elder abuse cases fall into three categories, determined by the type of mistreatment (physical, psychological, financial, or neglect), the relationship between victim and perpetrator, and the sex and race of the victims and abusers. In many cases, there is a complicated power or dependency relationship between the perpetrator and his or her victim.

Statistics Canada estimates that one elderly person in 10 is victimized by violent criminal abuse; but this risk of abuse, though large, is much lower than for younger people. Specifically, "The rate of violent victimization among seniors was almost four times *lower* [in 2007] than the rate for people aged 55 to 64, and almost 20 times lower than the rate for people aged 15 to 24." As with other kinds of assault, elder assault is usually committed by acquaintances or relatives (Statistics Canada, 2007b). Sometimes, adult children abuse their parents, who abused them in childhood.

Unlike child abuse, elder abuse receives little attention in our society, partly because it is a less common form of abuse and perhaps because we have less interest in the welfare of our elders than we do of our children. Also, many elders are hidden in the home, invisible to public institutions and law enforcers.

Child Abuse

Like elder abuse, child abuse comes in many forms; these range from sexual abuse to peer bullying, but their outcomes are similarly harmful. All forms of childhood abuse increase the likelihood of low self-esteem, anxiety, depression, and anti-social tendencies. Children are also put at risk of harmful outcomes by exposure to vicarious violence (e.g., witnessing violence between their parents).

Childhood abuse may later express itself in behavioural issues, addiction issues, or mental health issues such as post-traumatic stress syndrome (PTSD) (Becker et al., 2010; Lalor and McElvaney, 2010; Hughes et al., 2010; Luk et al., 2010). Abused children, in adulthood, are also more prone to future victimization and partner violence, compared to non-victims (Payne et al., 2010). Victimization even has an adverse effect on children's physiology, as it can affect the development of important brain functions that regulate child development (Coates, 2010).

According to Canadian police reports, close to 55,000 youth (aged 0 to 17 years) experienced physical and/or sexual assault in 2009. Of these, 30 percent were victimized by a member of their own family. Of these family cases, 81 per cent involved violence of the least severity (level 1 assault); aggravated assault and assaults with a weapon constituted 18 per cent of cases (Statistics Canada, 2011c).

However, we should not underestimate the importance of these "less severe" assaults. Even children who experience only minor physical harm are put at a heightened risk of significant long-term consequences. As noted, these long-term consequences include (but are not limited to) depression and low self-esteem. Victims of child abuse are also more likely than other children to engage in violent activities and have difficulty regulating their impulses.

Time to Reflect: Might child abuse by parents do more harm in Canadian society, where such abuse is less common, than it does in societies where abusive parenting is common and even considered "normal"?

Fortunately, we know a great deal about child abuse. In 2001, researchers Nico Trocmé and David Wolfe published a classic examination of child abuse—the first nationwide study of reported child maltreatment and the best Canadian study to date. Trocmé and Wolfe found that, in 1998, more than 135,000 cases of maltreatment were investigated by child welfare services, and 45 per cent of these cases were substantiated. Of the reported maltreatment cases, 31 per cent were cases of physical abuse, 10 per cent were cases of sexual abuse, 40 per cent were cases of neglect, and 19 per cent were emotional maltreatment or abuse.

This study, using Canadian data, verified and replicated the findings of earlier American studies noted above. It found, for example, that several main factors contribute to parental abuse of children, and of these, substance abuse is among the most important. Substance abuse occurs in a reported 40–80 per cent of families in which the children are victims of abuse. Children whose parents abuse alcohol and other drugs are three times more likely to be abused and more than four times more likely to be neglected than children from non-substance-abusing families. Parents' abuse of alcohol and other drugs can lead to a cycle of addiction, in which high rates of alcoholism and other incidents of substance abuse are reflected among children of addicts.

As in earlier studies, parent–child violence and exposure to inter-parental violence also are significant causes of adolescent behaviour problems. Witnessing violence between one's parents harms the emotional and behavioural development of children. As with responses to other family troubles, girls tend to internalize their emotions, experiencing higher levels of shame and guilt, while boys tend to act out.

Like other criminal violence, child abuse is gendered and so are its outcomes. So, for example, compared to non-victims, females who suffer abuse as children are more likely to suffer sexual victimization in adulthood and are more likely to indulge in high-risk sexual behaviours (Messman-Moore, 2010). Indeed, females who suffer abuse in childhood are vulnerable to adult re-victimization precisely *because of* their increased tendency to engage in risky sexual behaviour, such as having unprotected sex and sex with numerous sexual partners. For similar reasons, abused girls also put themselves at a greater risk for teen pregnancy (Lalor and McElvaney, 2010).

When young, children are less likely to understand the nature and severity of the abuse they suffer, so the effects of abuse—especially the effects of sexual abuse—may be slow to appear (Yancey and Hansen, 2010). But whether the child realizes it or not, abuse is a serious issue with important long-term consequences. Girls who suffer abuse as children are more likely than average to become victims of abuse in adulthood, and boys who suffer abuse as children are more likely than average to become abusers (Trocmé and Wolfe, 2001).

Not surprisingly, children who suffer from multiple types of abuse are likely to sustain the most harm. These children, whom Finkelhor et al.(2009) have labelled *poly-victimized*, display four main pathways to poly-victimization: "(1)

residing in a dangerous community, (2) living in a dangerous family (e.g. family violence), (3) having a chaotic, multi-problem family environment (e.g. unemployment), or (4) having emotional problems that increase risk behaviour, engender antagonism, and compromise the capacity to protect oneself."

Of these long-term predictive pathways, *emotional problems* are the most significant for younger children. These children with "emotional problems" have typically been victimized at an early age and tend to remain poly-victimized over the course of their lives. The researchers note that poly-victimization in childhood is likely to occur at major transition points in a child's life: for example, shortly before entry into elementary school and, again, before entry into high school. What is evident from research on child abuse is that the consequences of victimization may persist throughout a person's lifetime. Many abused children grow up to be depressed adults or abusing parents, passing on their dysfunction to mates, children, co-workers, neighbours, and others who know and rely on them.

However, these effects are not inevitable. Strong social support from adults—from relatives, neighbours, or teachers, for example—often helps to minimize the effects of victimization. Victimized children with high levels of social support are also less likely than other abused children to commit acts of delinquency in the future (Yancey and Hansen, 2010). Hence, the effects of chronic abuse—whether in the form of family abuse or schoolyard bullying, delinquent behaviour, or school failure—can be mitigated at the individual, family, or community levels.

Partner Violence

Partner violence is another type of domestic violence about which researchers know a great deal, and perhaps (in part) because of the greater public awareness and disapproval, the rates have declined in recent years.

In fact, *Juristat* (Beattie and Cotter, 2009) reports: "The rate of spousal homicide has generally been declining since the mid-1970s." Contributors to the decline in spousal homicide likely include changes in the structure of intimate relationships, increases in gender equality, better training for enforcement personnel, and improvements in the support provided for victims.

Intimate partner violence has been recognized as a serious problem since the early 1970s, largely because of the women's movement. Thanks largely to feminist research, we now understand that women are more likely to be abused by an intimate partner than by strangers, and they are likely to sustain significant injuries—emotional and psychological, as well as physical—from the abuse (Warner, 2010). Men who are abused by a partner are likely to get slapped, kicked, bitten, scratched, and/or punched, or experience verbal abuse. By contrast, women abused by a partner are more likely to experience serious violence, such as sexual assault, being choked, pushed, grabbed, shoved, and beaten (Statistics Canada, 2006a).

As noted, men are victimized by domestic violence, too, and they say so in anonymous victimization studies. However, they are less likely than women to report this victimization to legal authorities (Goldstein et al., 2008). Typically, they do not view female violence against them as a punishable offence (Dutton and Nicholls, 2005). They may also believe that legal authorities will be unsympathetic and that abusive women willing to perjure themselves will find a sympathetic judicial hearing.

Typically, the violence directed against men causes less physical harm than the violence directed against women, and cases of male abuse are not taken as seriously as those involving female victims (www.phac-aspc.gc.ca/ncfv-cnivf/publications/mlintima-eng.php). For instance, men often have worse legal outcomes than women in the criminal court trials of opposite-sex abuse (Edelson and Joa, 2010). Nevertheless, abused men may sometimes experience the same long-term harm as that experienced by female victims—outcomes that include increased anxiety, depression, and sexual problems (Coxell and King, 2010).

That said, women are far more likely than men to be harmed—and harmed seriously—by domestic violence. And despite the empowerment of women in recent decades, many are still disadvantaged, compared to their male partners, because of lower earning potential and heavier parental responsibilities. These factors make it harder for women, especially women with children, to escape an abusive marriage. And the longer the abuse goes on, the harder it is for an abused woman to escape. Prolonged abuse leads to constant fearfulness, learned helplessness (Seligman and Johnston, 1973), and ever-diminishing self-esteem—none of these being conducive to independent action (Goldstein et al., 2008; Luk et al., 2010).

Many of these victims develop battered woman syndrome (BWS), a subcategory of post-traumatic stress disorder (PTSD). Symptoms of BWS include the involuntary recall of abuse episodes, hyperarousal and hypervigilance, an irrational avoidance of places and things related to abuse, impaired social functioning, and body image distortion (Walker, 2006). BWS is sufficiently well recognized now that some courts have admitted it as evidence in defence of women accused of murdering or seriously harming an abusive partner.

However, homicide—a relatively rare occurrence—is just the tip of the iceberg where partner violence is concerned. In at least two-thirds of all cases, spousal homicide is preceded by a long history of abuse and assault. With possible homicide looming in the background, many battered spouses try to escape their domestic situation. In 2010, an estimated 45,150 women, many with children, were admitted to transition homes and emergency shelters across Canada because of domestic violence. Most of the children were under 10 years old. In many instances, women and children were turned away because the sanctuaries were full (Burczycka and Cotter, 2011).

As we said earlier in this chapter, violence reflects the breakdown of non-violent negotiation. This breakdown can happen under a variety of conditions, to be sure. It is particularly likely to happen where one or both parties are set on gaining and maintaining control over the other: on taking charge and keeping charge. Often, this mindset or inclination to control is associated with cultural notions of masculinity. Sometimes, it reflects psychological insecurity that goes back to childhood—for example, when a child learned to fear rejection by, or the loss of, a loved one through divorce or death.

Thus, we cannot minimize the importance of this mindset in studying domestic violence. Macmillan and Gartner (1999) have made a particularly valuable contribution to this in their analysis of data from Statistics Canada's *Canadian Violence against Women Survey* for the year 1993. They examine the effects of proprietary or "coercively controlling" attitudes on domestic violence, finding that, often, psychologically and physically abusive men fear the loss of their partner, whom they consider sexual and emotional property.

Men who practise a high level of coercive control—for example, insisting on always knowing where their partners are when they leave the household, what they are doing, and with whom they are doing it—are particularly abusive. Men who practise a high level of coercive control are more likely than other

Current Events

BOX 7.1

Family Violence in Canada: A Statistical Profile, 2009

Here are some up-to-date Canadian facts on domestic violence. Of the nearly 19 million Canadians who had a current or former spouse in 2009, 6.2 per cent or 1.2 million reported their partner or spouse had victimized her or him physically or sexually during the five years prior to the survey.

About 57 per cent of women who had experienced an incident of spousal violence in the five years prior to the survey reported that it had occurred on more than one occasion, as did 40 per cent of men. Rates of spousal violence were highest among certain segments of the population; in particular, among younger adults aged 25 to 34, those in common-law relationships, and those living in blended families.

Breaking up, threatening to break up, or having broken up are conditions that heighten the risk of violence dramatically. Spousal violence was four times more likely to occur between ex-spouses or partners than current spouses or partners. In 2009, 17 per cent of adults who had contact with an ex-spouse or partner in the previous five years reported their partner had physically or sexually assaulted them at least once. By contrast, among those with a current spouse or partner, only 4 per cent were physically or sexually assaulted during the five-year period prior to the survey.

In victimization surveys, women typically report more serious forms of spousal violence than men do. For example, in the 2009 study, 34 per cent of females who reported spousal violence on the survey said they had been sexually assaulted, beaten, choked, or threatened with a gun or a knife by their partner or ex-partner in the previous five years. This was three times the proportion for men, which was, however, 10 per cent.

There is some evidence that victims are less likely to report spousal violence to police than in the past. In 2009, 22 per cent of spousal violence victims said the police had learned of the incident, down from 28 per cent in 2004. Typically, the victims themselves brought incidents of spousal violence to the attention of police. About 23 per cent of female victims said they had reported the incident to police, compared with only 7 per cent of male victims.

As for the reasons for reporting, the vast majority of victims (89 per cent) said they reported the incidents to police to stop the violence and receive protection. Of those who reported the victimization to the police, over 6 in 10 were satisfied with the response they received.

Source: Abridged from Statistics Canada (2011a).

men to abuse their wives physically, sexually, and emotionally—often, in the most serious, systematic ways.

Because men are more likely than women to associate control with masculinity and, on average, are bigger and stronger than women, women generally run a much higher risk of murder by their spouse or ex-spouse than men: "Men who killed an ex-partner were most often motivated by jealousy (44 per cent), while arguments or quarrels (41 per cent) most often motivated women" (Fedorowycz, 2000). As well, "estranged husbands were twice as likely as current husbands to have multiple victims. When marital relationships were still intact at the time of spousal homicides, children were the most likely victims other than the spouse. In estranged marriages, the victim's new partner was the most frequent third-party victim" (ibid.).

A review of previous studies by the same researcher finds that violent husbands are likely to support a patriarchal ideology that holds positive attitudes towards marital violence and negative attitudes towards gender equality. However, patriarchal attitudes cannot be the whole story, because we see similar patterns of violence in same-sex couples, for example, among lesbians. Research has shown that partner violence may be just as prevalent in the gay and lesbian community as it is in the heterosexual community. Based on a review of the literature, Rohrbaugh (2006: 287) asserts that:

> Physical violence occurs in 11–12 per cent of same-gender couples, which suggests that domestic violence is an abuse of power that can happen in any type of intimate relationship, regardless of gender or sexual orientation. Although incidents of violence occur at the same rate in same-gender couples and cross-gender couples, the violence appears to be milder in same-gender couples. . . . Same-gender victims also suffer from the additional stress of severe isolation and the abuser's threats to expose the victim's sexual orientation in a hostile manner.

The empirical studies of this problem are still very few, and they are typically based on small, non-random samples. However, in general, many of the same factors associated with heterosexual domestic violence are found in cases of homosexual domestic violence. So, for example, a study of lesbian couples (McLennen et al., 2002) identified deficient communication and social skills, substance abuse, and the intergenerational transmission of violence as factors that predicted domestic violence in these couples. Two other predictive factors they identified are more likely to produce conflict in homosexual than in heterosexual couples: namely, internalized homophobia and status differential (within a gender-egalitarian relationship).

Media Depictions of Violent Crime

We cannot understand public perceptions and fears about crime without understanding media depictions of crime. Most people, after all, get most of their ideas about violent crime from the mass media, not from first-hand experience.

North American popular culture has an ambivalent view towards violence, alternating between an acceptance and approbation of violence as a means of solving problems or showing machismo, and denouncing violence as destructive and foolish. Television shows like *America's Most Wanted* and *Nancy Grace* have created sizable audiences out of public fears regarding violent crime, baldly painting violent criminals as moral degenerates and ever-present threats. Alternatively, a great number of action movies present violence (and even violent crime) as a glamorous and necessary act to uphold law and morality. Movies like *Network* (1976), *Mad City* (1997), and *15 Minutes* (2001) have, more helpfully, explored the ways in which the media play on viewers' sentiments by manipulating images of violence.

Violent crime certainly plays a prominent role in popular culture, often serving as a test of personal mettle and as a cause for sympathy with the victim. The non-fiction book *A Child Called "It"* (1995) tapped into public fears about child abuse, as the story of one boy's torture at the hands of his mother from ages 4–12 spent over two years on the best-seller list. Laurence Fishburne and Angela Bassett received Oscar nominations for their roles in *What's Love Got To Do With It?* (1993), a movie largely concerned with singer Tina Turner's brutal treatment at the hands of her then-husband, Ike Turner. More recently, dating singers Rihanna and Chris Brown made news when it came to light that Brown had severely beaten Rihanna, resulting in an international show of support for Rihanna and a still-present stigma for Brown.

As sympathetic as the public is to victims of violence in popular culture, however, there is at least as strong an appetite for depictions of violence that portray violence as delivering some "greater" goal. This slant is most potently portrayed in superhero and action movies, such as the *Batman* and *Death Wish* franchises, in which citizens take up violent vigilantism to great effect, and in the popular HBO series *Dexter*. Views of "acceptable" violence may go so far as to turn murder into something preposterous or humorous, as can be seen in gruesome movies like *Kill Bill I* and *Kill Bill II* (2003, 2004) and *Rambo* (2008), the latter film glorifying the hero's killing of 83 "bad guys." In these action films, people are treated as cannon fodder, their deaths made "acceptable" by rarely presenting the victims as individuals with lives and families of their own.

This acceptance of cartoonish violence in action films may bleed into how we discuss violence in other contexts. In recent years, Canadians concerned over expanding literatures on brain damage and permanent injury have very seriously discussed whether to try to minimize violence in hockey. While there are many public health concerns at play, movies like *Slapshot* (1977), *The Tooth Fairy* (2010), and *Goon* (2011), not to mention the popular CBC show *Hockey Night in Canada* (with the bellicose pro-fighting commentator Don Cherry), have tied hockey violence into popular conceptions of manhood. The glorification of hockey fighting—which is illegal in purely legal terms—has upheld violence in hockey and, it could be argued, in Canadian society.

Time to Reflect: Is there any way researchers could show decisively that prolonged exposure to media violence increases the risk of violent behaviour in everyday life?

Theories about Violent Crime

As usual in the field of deviance and crime, different sociological perspectives take different approaches to understanding violent crime. One sociological approach—the functionalist perspective—holds that violence is due to an organizational problem: the lack of peaceful strategies and mechanisms for resolving conflict. Another—the symbolic interactionist perspective—views violence as faulty interaction: a breakdown of the normal communication process. A third approach—the critical perspective—focuses on power imbalance.

Functionalist Theories

Recall that functionalist approaches to deviance converge on a few central tenets—namely, that crime is normal, universal, and unavoidable and that it is to be expected in any society. By implication, violent crime is also normal, universal, and in some sense "necessary." This approach leads to a theory about the relationship between violence and social (and personal) disorganization.

Gottfredson and Hirschi's (1990) *general theory of crime* usefully combines macro and micro perspectives in its emphasis on lack of self-control as a factor in criminal behaviour. Their theory, which applies to all criminal and deviant behaviours, stresses background factors that influence the tendency to commit crime. At the individual level, according to their theory, the origin of crime is low self-control, which stems from inadequate, ineffective, and inconsistent socialization by parents in early childhood. Crime, in this sense, is aimed at pleasure. A criminal's drive for pleasure is unconstrained by learned, internalized controls on behaviour.

According to this theory, people commit criminal acts because these acts provide easy satisfaction or they are exciting and pleasurable in themselves. People inclined to criminal acts, lacking self-control, are also likely to seek other easy pleasures that are not criminal. Most criminals lack diligence and persistence; they tend to act impulsively. These criminal acts need little if any learning; criminals do what they feel like doing. Their behaviour does not reflect a rational orientation, merely lack of self-control.

Not all people with low self-control commit crimes. However, low self-control increases the likelihood that someone will commit a crime. These chances are increased if the motivated offender has access to a suitable target—for example, money that lacks a "capable guardian." The absence of enough protection against crime, epitomized by social disorganization in the community, further intensifies the likelihood that a criminal will act out his or her impulses.

This theory adequately covers a great many situations—especially impulsive acts of violent behaviour. Crimes of violence are often referred to as **crimes of passion**, since they do not adhere to any rational course of action. However, this theory fails to explain the aggression and anger that some criminals show when committing their crimes, suggesting something beyond a mere absence of self-control. Also, it fails to explain crimes—even crimes of violence—that are premeditated, goal-seeking, or demand skills (e.g., the use of guns) that take time to learn.

Symbolic Interactionist Theories

Symbolic interactionism is typically less interested in the reasons people commit violent acts than in the results of these acts for the actor. As usual, the emphasis is on labels that are attached to violent criminals and the effects of such labelling. They also emphasize the interpretation—the attachment of meaning—to violent acts.

Rationalizations for violence are important and learned. Violent people interpret the situations in which they commit violent crimes as *requiring* violent actions. Athens (1997) states that an offender may use any of the four types of interpretation:

- The physically *defensive interpretation:* the offender believes the victim will attack or has already begun to attack.
- The *frustrative interpretation:* supposedly, the victim is resisting a specific course of action, or the offender is expected to co-operate with an unwanted action.
- The *malefic interpretation:* the offender believes that he or she is being belittled, sees the victim as evil, and thinks violence is the best way to deal with this.
- The *frustrative–malefic interpretation:* a direct mixture of the frustrative and malefic approaches, with the proviso that the victim is not only an adversary but loathsome as well.

Note that all these scenarios assume a set of beliefs about the situation, the enemy, and even the self. Athens (ibid.) distinguishes between a violent self-image, an incipiently violent self-image (those individuals seen as having a *willingness* to use violence instead of a *natural*

Classic Works

BOX 7.2

Elliott Leyton and the Rise of the Modern Multiple Murderer

Nothing is more violent than a serial killer, and in his book *Hunting Humans* (1986), Leyton outlines several controversial theories that he believes explain the behaviour of six American serial killers.

Contrary to the views of mental health professionals, Leyton asserts that multiple murderers are anything but "insane," helping to address the difficulties psychiatrists face assessing and rehabilitating serial killers. Correspondingly, Leyton feels that, mostly, these killers are "normal"—save for the absence of remorse and empathy towards their victims. He also asserts that their acts of murder were not episodes of blind or drunken rage, as is often the case with domestic and single murders. Rather, they were deliberate, purposeful, meticulously planned acts, since serial killers relish what they do (though pleasure is only part of the reason they kill).

The killings often have social motives. For example, Leyton describes the killings of the "Boston Strangler," Albert DeSalvo, as a protest against high society, and Mark Essex's killings as acts of war against racist, white-dominated society. He argues that multiple murders appear most often when new classes are emerging, and that multiple murderers typically come from declining and vulnerable lower-middle or upper-lower classes, making them obsessively class-conscious. Consequently, they try to find their sense of identity and fulfillment through their murderous acts, which usually involve victims specifically selected from the class directly above them.

Once caught, these killers often tried to justify their acts on some moral ground, lecture society, and even accuse the parents of the victims of contemptible behaviour. Multiple murderers thus seem to be motivated by what Leyton calls a *subpolitical campaign*; they kill out of social protest, rebellion, or revenge against a society that they feel has alienated and oppressed them, making them unable to feel content and satisfied with life. According to Leyton, then, multiple murderers are neither radicals nor revolutionaries, but they are by-products of the society in which they live; American society and culture are responsible for creating multiple murderers, and the killers point to key issues and stresses in society.

This book has led people to rethink the causes of serial murder. While the media often portray multiple killers as "monsters," Leyton tries to humanize them to explain their actions. Leyton's anthropological approach allowed him to incorporate a broader range of social factors than psychiatry usually covers, casting new light on the psyches of these killers.

disposition to use violence), and those with a non-violent image. To develop this typology, Athens interviewed violent offenders and asked them to assign a type of interpretation to themselves. Those who viewed themselves as non-violent interpreted the situations in which they committed the crime as physically defensive, whereas those who had a violent self-image interpreted their crimes in all four ways.

Critical Theories

Critical theories of crime and violence point to inequalities in society as the cause of deviant, including violent, behaviour. So, for example, nineteenth-century political theorist Georges Sorel (1994 [1908]: 9) declared that "proletarian acts of violence . . . are purely acts of war; they have the value of military demonstrations and serve to mark the separation of classes." Does this mean that critical theorists view all crimes as political acts? No, but the line dividing political from non-political acts of violence and other crime may be hard to draw.

Critical theorists believe crime—even violent crime—is unavoidable whenever groups have unequal levels of power and influence. One result is that as inequality increases in a society, crime will also increase. Declining wages cause increased rates of "quick cash" crimes, especially in societies that lack a social safety net of unemployment benefits, universal health insurance, and income security provisions. Violence often may be an unintended by-product of these acquisitive, hasty crimes.

As we noted earlier, people who are socially disadvantaged also are more likely to embrace violent subcultures of "honour" and "respect," leading to higher rates of crimes against persons. Deprived areas marked by poverty and inequality spawn social exclusion, alienation, and violence in pursuit of respect. Subcultures of violence emerge in poor neighbourhoods, not rich ones. That is because poverty and inequality are harmful to self-esteem; they are the results of the **hidden injuries of social class**, to use the words of historians Richard Sennett and Jonathan Cobb.

As a result, other things being equal, the homicide rates are highest in communities marked by low welfare-payment levels, a high percentage of female-headed families, and a high dropout rate from schools (Hannon, 1997).

Dahrendorf (1959) notes that violence, as a means of conducting conflict, diminishes through the regulation of conflict. There is less violence when conflict is more regulated, even if the motivators of conflict—for example, economic inequality or power imbalance—continue to exist. For conflict to be regulated, according to Dahrendorf, parties must recognize the conflict as an inevitable outgrowth of conflicting interests, be organized into groups, and agree to rules under which the conflict will take place. Such rules protect the survival of both parties, reduce potential injury to each party, introduce some predictability into the actions of each party, and protect third parties from undue harm.

This approach suggests that violence is a means of conducting conflict without ground rules and shared assumptions. Conditions of trust and common understanding are needed for people to conduct social life, even competitive or conflictual social life.

The critical perspective also notes that use of violence is not limited to the oppressed—people in privileged positions struggle to preserve their privileged status. They readily resort to criminal, even violent, acts if it will serve their purposes. For example, corporate crimes benefit the governing or upper class but harm the environment, place workers in danger (e.g., Westray Mine), and put the public at needless risk with dangerous products. This is a form of violence, since it endangers the lives and health of its victims. So, for example, some might consider the oversight in Walkerton, Ontario, which resulted in multiple deaths from polluted water, to be a crime of violence. It resulted from negligence by those most directly charged with overseeing the water supply and the removal of environmental protections by a government willing to risk lives to cut taxes and, thereby, gain more votes.

Feminist Approaches

Among various types of violent crime, feminists have focused on sexual assault for many reasons. First, it is a terrifying, dangerous, and humiliating experience that many women are subjected to and most women fear. Changing the laws related to rape, providing help and other services to women who have been raped, and finding ways to prevent rape are, therefore, important tasks facing society.

As we saw in an earlier section and will review in Chapter 10, sexual assault is a gender-based act of violence. Most of the time, the offenders are men and the victims are women. Therefore, though a small number of males—for example, men in prison—also experience sexual assault, this crime mostly victimizes women. An estimated one in three girls will be sexually assaulted in her lifetime, and one in seven boys will be sexually assaulted as well. According to the National Crime Victimization Survey (2005), 191,670 incidents of rape were reported to authorities in the US. According to Statistics Canada, there were over 22,000 cases of sexual assault reported to authorities in 2010. However, since only an estimated 30 per cent of cases are reported to authorities, the actual number of rapes is probably a lot larger (Brennan and Dauvergne, 2011).

A woman faces a greater risk of being sexually assaulted during her university career than at any other point in her life. This is because the greatest risk of victimization occurs between the ages of 16 and 24 in women, which coincidentally corresponds to the years they are at university. According to a (US) National College Women Sexual Violence Study, one in seven students receive unwanted sexual attention during their university years, and approximately 20–25 per cent of university women experience attempted or completed rape during their university careers. In actual numbers, the National Centre for Victims of Crime estimated that more than 100,000 university women are raped every year in Canada, and many more are raped in the US. Most often the rapist is a dating partner, classmate, or fellow student.

Sexual assault is a traumatic experience, and victims use varied psychological mechanisms to cope with the trauma. Many women try to minimize the experience or blame themselves to some extent. During the actual assault, many use disassociation, a process in which they psychologically distance themselves from the experience. When faced with a potential attack, some women choose not to resist physically because they feel their safety or life is at risk. This increases their sense of vulnerability and powerlessness.

In life as a whole, women are not necessarily more victimized than men, but they are less likely than men to perpetrate violence. In short, women continue to have far lower rates of violent criminality than men, in every category. Some argue that men's higher levels of testosterone predispose them towards disproportionate aggression and hostile actions. Others argue that socialization is to blame: that males are taught to use aggressive and violent behaviours, and conversely are *not* taught peaceful ways of controlling their aggressive and sexual urges. There is likely some truth to both assertions.

Time to Reflect: Is male violence an inevitable result of our cultural norms about "masculinity," and if so, what new norms of masculinity could we teach children that would eliminate some of this violence?

Consequences of Violent Crime

Social and Psychological Consequences

Much of the violence in our society begins or ends in families. For example, "According to the 1999 General Social Survey, children heard or saw one parent assaulting the other in an estimated 461,000 households, which represents 37 per cent of all households with spousal violence in the five-year period preceding the survey" (Dauvergne and Johnson, 2001). Adult victims were more likely to seek help from the police or from social services when children had witnessed the violence.

Data from the National Longitudinal Survey of Children and Youth show that children who are exposed to physical violence in the home are less likely to have positive or effective interactions with their parents. Parental rates of depression are higher and parenting quality is low. Children, under these circumstances, are more likely to display physical aggression, emotional disorders, hyperactivity, poor school performance, and delinquent acts against property.

Other effects of violent crime include the physical pain resulting from any injuries the victim suffers, lowered self-esteem resulting from victimization, and the emotional loss experienced by the family and friends of victims of homicide. Fear of crime is not only a problem for individuals; it is also a social concern: "If frightened citizens remain locked in their homes instead of enjoying public spaces, there is a loss of public and community life and a loss of 'social capital'—the family and neighbourhood channels that transmit positive social values from one generation to the next" (National Research Council, 1994).

Mental Health Consequences

The effects of violent crime on mental health are discussed in various places throughout this book, including the chapter on victimization below and the chapter on imprisonment (a situation where violence and fear of violence are rampant). In general, violence produces a general fear or anxiety that creates stress for everyone, especially the most disadvantaged and vulnerable in the population. And stress, as we know, tends to lower immune system resilience, increasing risks of illness and diminishing longevity.

The anxiety surrounding violence in a community also produces second-order effects that further heighten stress and risks of mental and physical illness. First, a climate of violence increases fear of crime by strangers, which leads people to isolate themselves in their homes. Second, a climate of violence increases distrust and the fear of neighbours and acquaintances, further isolating people from one another. This isolation, as well as the consequent loss of social cohesion, has harmful mental health effects, for example, increasing the risk of depression.

Third, a climate of violence diminishes people's confidence in public institutions such as the government and police, increasing their anxiety and often leading the state to intensify repressive efforts. This increase in repressive law enforcement may provide temporary relief from anxiety about criminal violence but sometimes leads to an increase in police violence, a new source of mental health problems. Finally, and by no means least important, a loss of confidence in public institutions (including the police) often supports the rise to importance of professional criminals. In dangerous, disadvantaged communities, these criminals often gain control over public life, bringing new sources of repression and danger, with consequent stresses and mental health issues.

In short, criminal violence—in all of these ways—tends to break down "civil society," that set of social and communal bonds that holds people together, providing comfort and support.

The people hardest hit are the victims themselves. Victims of violent crimes suffer more distress symptoms and stressful life events than non-victims and victims of non-violent crimes (Johnson, 1996). However, criminal victimization affects different people in different ways, even when the crime is identical. Resources such as social support, time, money, education, and the presence of other life stressors can affect one's resistance or vulnerability to stress. As for both physical and emotional trauma, the health effect of a crime also depends on the social context of violence. For example, lesbians, gays, and bisexuals who have been victimized by hate crimes report higher-than-average levels of depression, anxiety, anger, and symptoms of post-traumatic stress.

In general, victims of violent crime are reluctant to report their victimization to the police, especially victims of sexual assault, that is, women. Perhaps this is part of the reason that victims often suffer long and painful psychological effects of these victimization experiences. Victims of crimes are more likely than non-victims to suffer from PTSD, major depressive episodes, and various phobias. The reaction depends largely on the crime. Though victims are affected most, a high risk of homicide or assault in the community affects everyone.

Victims of sexual assault often suffer from rape trauma syndrome, a type of PTSD, as well as from other psychological reactions. For example, victims may feel terrified of the offender and fear for their lives. They may also feel humiliation, shame, and self-blame. If the attacker was an acquaintance, friend, or lover, the victim may have a hard time in future trusting other people and developing intimacy with them.

Males as well as females are harmed by sexual assault. Sexually abused boys, for example, report more high-risk sexual behaviour, including: the use of prostitutes; unprotected anal intercourse; a larger number of sexual partners; a lower rate of condom use; higher rates of sexually transmitted diseases; and higher rates of partner pregnancy. Typically, the sexual abuse has occurred through a violation of trust: sexually abused boys are more than four times as likely to have forced sexual contact with another person, most often another boy (often an older brother). And, as we have learned from news stories, many boys have been sexually abused by trusted adult authorities: by priests, teachers, scout leaders, and sports coaches, among others.

Physical Health Consequences

We can divide physical health outcomes of violent crimes into two groups: fatal outcomes and non-fatal outcomes. The fatal outcomes of crime are usually a result of an immediate injury inflicted on the victim. In 2009, for example, 610 people in Canada died as a result of homicides: "210 victims (36 per cent) killed by stabbing and 179 victims killed by a firearm (30 per cent). A further 20 per cent of victims were beaten, 7 per cent were strangled or suffocated and 7 per cent were killed by other methods such as vehicles, fire (smoke inhalation, burns), poisoning and shaken baby syndrome" (Beattie and Cotter, 2009).

There are long-term, lingering effects of non-fatal physical violence. Statistics show that rape victims are over four times more likely than non-victims to have considered suicide and 13 times more likely to have attempted it. Another study showed that women who report having suffered sexual abuse in childhood have a history of suicide attempts. Suicide attempts among sexually abused males are 14–15 times higher than among other males (Briere and Runtz, 1986; see also Bebbington et al., 2009).

Another potentially fatal outcome of violent sexual assault is HIV/AIDS. Victims of sexual assault who are penetrated orally, vaginally, or anally are at risk of contracting the virus that leads to AIDS and eventually death. It is impossible, however, to calculate how many victims have become HIV-infected due to sexual assault.

The non-fatal outcomes of violent crimes are many. As mentioned before, victimization harms people's health. Victims of crimes regularly report lower-than-average levels of well-being. Also, they report lower levels of perceived health, and younger victims report greater decrease in health than older victims. It is hard to pinpoint the precise long-term effects of violent crimes because of the diversity of injuries that occur. The physical effects of sexual assault are easier to discuss because of their common nature in many reported cases.

Economic Consequences

The fallout of violent crime results in a great many expenses, both on the individual and community levels. Violent deaths result in lost incomes and lost opportunities for the people who survive. Violent injuries incapacitate the victims, often leading to long-term disability, unemployment, or unemployability. The partners and close relatives of murder victims and victims of rape, disfigurement, and injury all suffer emotionally; often, this means lost days of work and diminished productivity at work. Violent crimes can also diminish family incomes through the death or disability of a spouse, by turning a two-income home into a one-income home, and by limiting marriage opportunities for a permanently injured or disfigured person.

However, the economic fallout of violent crime reaches far beyond the family, into society as a whole. The public costs of treating victims' physical and psychological injuries, and prosecuting and punishing the perpetrators of violent acts, are substantial. Medical costs are extremely burdensome for Canadian taxpayers, as the federal government estimated the 2004 costs of treating intentional injuries came out to $3.3 billion (Public Health Agency of Canada, 2004).

As for the public costs of punishment, violent crimes are more likely to warrant harsher-than-average punishments. A recent news report notes: "The cost of keeping a male inmate in prison rose from $88,067 per year in 2006 to $109,699 in 2009, according to the most recent data from [the 2011] *Corrections and Conditional Release Statistical Overview*" (*National Post*, 18 July 2011). These costs are even higher for women offenders: Canada's Correctional Investigator reported in 2010 that housing a female offender in a federal prison costs over $180,000 per year—a fact that makes the long-term detention of violent women especially burdensome (Office of the Correctional Investigator, 2010).

Widespread animosity towards violent criminals and the great cost of imprisoning them often increase public support for capital punishment because this is perceived as a cost-effective reaction to violence. However, the meticulous planning needed for capital trials and the lengthy post-conviction appeal processes mean that capital punishment is a far *more* expensive reaction to violent crime than long-term imprisonment. In California, for instance, the California Commission on the Fair Administration of Justice estimated that the death penalty system is 10 times as expensive to run as a justice system that has a maximum punishment of lifetime incarceration (CCFAJ, 2008). There are, it seems, no viable ways to punish violent offenders cheaply.

Social Policy Implications

The Criminal Justice System

As we noted at the beginning of this book, the Canadian criminal justice system is shaped like a funnel. Of the many crimes that are committed, few are reported to the police. Criminologists who study crime rates based on official government statistics refer to the unknown amount of unreported and unrecorded crime as the "dark figure" of crime. Of all the crimes reported to police, only a fraction result in arrests and charges. Moreover, only a fraction of the crimes resulting in charges end with convictions. Finally, only a fraction of the crimes that lead to conviction end with imprisonment. Thus, all the people in jail for violent offences represent only a tiny fraction of all offenders, and they are disproportionately young, poor, and socially isolated. However, there are huge law enforcement costs at every stage of the process.

The costs of our criminal justice system—of the police, courts, judges, prisons, and parole systems—are enormous; yet, many Canadians do not feel secure or well served by the system. They may not know precisely how few violent criminals are taken out of circulation for an extended period, but they sense that these numbers are small and that large numbers of violent people are walking the streets.

Part of the crime problem we face in Canada, as in most societies, is that many people feel dissatisfied with and distrustful of public institutions—politicians, police, judges, and lawyers. Though they dislike crime and criminals, they also dislike and distrust people in authority. This distrust may cause them to avoid reporting crimes or giving information to the police and courts. For example, in a recent shooting on a Toronto bus, a 10-year-old girl and her parent—innocent bystanders—were injured by gunfire. None of the 19 other passengers on the bus was willing to come forward with a description of the shooter.

In some countries, people may even use violence to take action (and from their perspective, justice) into their own hands to settle disputes. In these countries there is no professional police force, or the police and military have historically been used by the government to oppress dissidents. When the existing order is disrupted—as in Haiti or more recently in Iraq—there are no professional peacekeeping organizations to step in and enforce order and justice. The results are anarchy, crime, and sometimes a return to private revenge.

As we have seen, criminal behaviour is not fully rational. Yet, the criminal justice system is based on the principle of deterrence. This notion assumes that most crimes are rational acts in which the offender weighs the imagined benefits of committing the crime against the likelihood of being caught and the severity of the punishment. The "get tough on crime" approach often discussed in recent years in North America calls for maximizing punishment to increase deterrent effects and thereby lower crime rates.

We can see the problems that emerge with this perspective. A deterrence-based approach to criminal justice fails to acknowledge and address the individual, societal, economic, and political factors that encourage the existence of crime in the first place: unemployment, racial and gender inequality, poverty, the unequal distribution of resources and opportunities, and the criminalization of some activities and behaviours that might better be addressed in other ways.

Moreover, biases intrude into the criminal justice system, even in Canada, where Aboriginal and black minorities are over-represented in the prison population. Research has found discrimination against blacks in denied bail and in sentencing, especially for drug, sexual assault, and bail violations. The discrimination against Aboriginal and black people is strongest at the policing point (Roberts and Doob, 1997).

Conclusion

A widespread consensus in Canadian society, and most other societies, is that violent behaviours are wrong and should be harshly punished. Despite biases in reporting, criminologists know enough about crime to venture several inferences.

First, there is more fear about violent crime than the statistics warrant. The rates of homicide (also robbery, manslaughter, and attempted murder) have changed little over the past 40 years, and rates of assault have fallen since 1992. Homicides in Canada are rarer than in many other countries (Table 7.1).

Second, crimes of violence often result from fights between spouses or friends. This is especially true when women are the victims. Men are more likely than women to be attacked by mere acquaintances, or even strangers.

Third, crimes of violence, as we have seen, are more characteristic of certain kinds of people—in particular, young, poor men. To some degree, this demographic link is probably a result of the interaction of economic and social variables. Poor young men are more likely than other people to be out of school, unemployed, and without significant social responsibilities, for example.

To finish where we began, Canada is a safe place where violent crimes are rare—rarer, perhaps, than at any time in the country's history. Canadians are the beneficiaries of a stable government, reliable legal system, and a secure civil society. As a people, we are more oriented to human rights than to issues of honour—for example, we supply the poor with a social welfare net that aims to affirm their human rights and to reduce the felt need for crime (though this safety net, for many, is hardly adequate).

Yet many Canadians, including the federal government with its recent crime bill, are preoccupied with crime, even violent crime. That is rarely because they have been personally victimized by violent crime; likely, it is because they regularly view crime stories in the news or fictionalized crime dramas on television. The media, not personal experience, shape our fears about crime. However, statistics show that if we are young men, our fear of strangers and acquaintances may not be misplaced. If we are women (of any age), the statistics show that rather than fear these faceless strangers, we have more reason to fear our intimates—our dates, lovers, husbands, and past partners. Unlike the movies, where psychopathic strangers kill and maim innocent people, in real life the people we know pose the greatest danger.

TABLE 7.1 Homicides per 100,000 Population, Selected Countries

Country	Rate	Country	Rate
Honduras	82.1	Trinidad and Tobago	35.2
El Salvador	66.0	South Africa	33.8
Cote D'Ivoire	56.9	Colombia	33.4
Jamaica	52.1	Ethiopia	25.5
Venezuela	49.0	Kenya	20.1
Belize	41.7	Mexico	18.1
Guatemala	41.4	Russian Federation	11.2
US Virgin Islands	39.2	United States	5.0
Zambia	38.1	Canada	1.8
Uganda	36.3	Sweden	1.0
Malawi	36.0	Japan	0.5

Source: United Nations Office on Drugs and Crime, *2011 Global Study on Homicide* (Vienna: UNODC, 2011), at: <www.unodc.org/documents/southerncone/noticias/2011/10-outubro/Globa_study_on_homicide_2011_web.pdf>.

Questions for Critical Thought

1. What might account for the rising fear of crime? What social implications does this have for certain groups such as the elderly?
2. Assuming that gender is the most significant factor in the study of any crime, does the feminist approach provide the best lens of analysis? Argue for or against the use of the feminist perspective.
3. Hypothesize why crime rates are higher in remote regions such as Nunavut than in metropolitan regions.
4. Explain why families are hot spots of violence. Do families mirror what occurs on the streets?
5. Are strict gun regulations the answer to reducing crimes of violence? Choose a position and debate this issue.
6. Think about the ways in which violence is portrayed on television in crime/police dramas. How does this treatment compare with the picture of violence described in this chapter?

Recommended Readings

Collins, Randall. 2008. *Violence: A Micro-Sociological Theory.* Princeton, NJ: Princeton University Press.

Drawing on video footage, forensics, and ethnography, Collins argues that violence comes neither easily nor automatically. Only a few individuals are thought to be competent at violence, whether as genocidal atrocities against the weak or secret acts of terrorism and murder.

Jackson, Nicky Ali, ed. 2007. *Encyclopedia of Domestic Violence.* Milton Park, UK: Routledge.

This is the first-ever reference book written by leading international scholars in domestic violence research. The entries include topics such as battered women, child abuse, and dating violence and less discussed topics like ritual abuse, torture within families, domestic violence against women with disabilities, pseudo-family violence, and domestic violence within military families.

Palermo, George B., and Richard N. Kocsis. 2005. *Offender Profiling: An Introduction to the Socio-Psychological Analysis of Violent Crime.* Springfield, Ill.: Charles C. Thomas.

The authors point out that profiling occurs in all social interactions; all humans use superficial clues to predict the behaviour of others. A major premise of the book, and of most types of profiling, is that the criminal act committed is an expression of the offender's motivations, needs, and personality traits.

Perry, Barbara. 2001. *In the Name of Hate: Understanding Hate Crimes.* New York: Routledge.

Intolerance, bigotry, and negative attitudes and stereotypes about subordinate groups are prevalent among individual Americans; they create a rhetoric of hate, which begins at the "top." For most maligned groups—African-Americans, gays and lesbians, and recent immigrants—an environment of intolerance is shaped by negative political rhetoric.

Recommended Websites

Canadian Resource Centre for Victims of Crime

www.crcvc.ca/en/

This website advocates for individual victims and their families in order to assist them in obtaining needed services and resources and lobbies for victims' rights by presenting the interests and perspectives of victims of crime to government, at all levels.

Hate Crime in Canada: An Overview of Issues and Data Sources

dsp-psd.tpsgc.gc.ca/Collection-R/Statcan/85-551-XIE/0009985-551-XIE.pdf

Created by a subsidiary of Statistics Canada, this thorough review of the issues surrounding hate crime in Canada not only provides a literature review and an overview of legal policies regarding hate crimes, but also includes a lengthy bibliography for further research.

National Crime Prevention Strategy

www.publicsafety.gc.ca/prg/cp/ncps-en.asp

This government of Canada website discusses public safety and preparedness.

United Nations Data

data.un.org/Data.aspx?d=UNODC&f=tableCode%3A1

The United Nations keeps some of the most thorough global homicide data, and this website provides the most recent (though dated) information on the topic. The site also provides a sorting function to more effectively compare homicide rates for all UN member states.

Violence Prevention Alliance

www.who.int/violenceprevention/en/

A part of the World Health Organization's Global Campaign for Violence Prevention, this site offers a good introduction to international issues relating to violent crime. Valuable links are provided to a variety of international NGOs that focus on violence prevention and harm reduction.

Recommended Movies

***Boyz 'N The Hood*, Dir. John Singleton (1991)**

This film, which earned John Singleton the first Oscar nomination ever for an African-American director, is about three of the most common life paths open to impoverished black men in America—school, sports, and crime. When Ricky, a high school football star, is shot down by local hoods, gangbanger Doughboy and scholastically inclined Tre must decide how to respond. This daring political film shows how violent crime is not simply the result of personal pathology, but is often the result of cultures of violence, such as the one found in early 1990s south central Los Angeles.

***In The Bedroom*, Dir. Todd Field (2001)**

Young Frank Fowler is tragically shot and killed by his girlfriend's ex-husband, sending the lives of his parents, Matt and Ruth, into a downward emotional spiral. Frank's father throws himself into his work, shutting himself off from others, while Ruth feels disconnected from her life, passing her days in front of the television. This film splendidly articulates the difficulty victims of violence face in coping with their losses and the ways in which they grope for meaning and resolution.

***Monster*, Dir. Patty Jenkins (2003)**

Aileen Wuornos survived an abusive childhood, only to become a street prostitute and the girlfriend of fellow runaway and prostitute, Selby Wall. One night, Aileen shoots and kills a belligerent john and, finding she has a taste for killing the men who hire her, begins murdering her customers regardless of their behaviour. Part true crime and part vigilante story, this film reminds us that violence, and the roots of violence, are not limited by gender or sexual orientation.

***4 Little Girls*, Dir. Spike Lee (1997)**

Lee's moving foray into documentary filmmaking is a piercing investigation into the 1963 terror bombing of an African-American church in Birmingham, Alabama. The event, which saw the deaths of four girls, aged 11 to 14, received national press coverage, was memorialized in "Birmingham Sunday" by folksinger-activist Joan Baez, and played a major role in forwarding the civil rights struggle. The film takes a long, hard look at the event's perpetrators and the political and cultural fallout of their act, showing the ways in which people try to justify even the most abhorrent acts of violence.

8 Non-Violent Crimes

Learning Objectives

- To explain the development of non-violent crimes within a historical framework
- To understand how non-violent crime may be a normal reaction to social conditions
- To see how cultures and communities maintain non-violent crime practices.
- To describe the connection between crime and poverty within a sociological context
- To learn the effects that non-violent crime has on the perception of crime by citizens
- To examine various policies that can reduce non-violent crime

Introduction

The goal of most non-violent crimes—the topic of this chapter—is to get money or property, not to inflict harm. In such crimes, violence is rarely used and only if needed to bring about that goal. In this chapter, we focus on three types of non-violent crime: **organized crime**, business crime, and **street crime**. These include offences such as drug trafficking, prostitution, and bookmaking; white-collar offences such as embezzlement and fraud; and offences against property such as breaking and entering for the purpose of committing an indictable offence (e.g., theft), automobile theft, and shoplifting.

A great many "respectable" Canadians commit non-violent crimes every day, while others avoid doing so mainly because they fear being punished. Consider tax-cheating: according to a 2011 survey of Canadian adults commissioned by the Canada Revenue Agency (CRA), a sizable minority of Canadians—about 13 per cent—regularly cheat on their taxes, despite warnings from the CRA. For example, they pay cash under the table to get a cheaper price on services, and under-report their income. These law-breakers tend to think tax evasion is not a "big deal," use excuses for cheating, and think a lot of other people cheat on taxes, too. In terms of social background, this group tends to have relatively low education and income. As well, they are more likely than average to be self-employed men under 30 years of age. Compared to other Canadians, they are the least likely to see consequences attached to tax cheating, and among the least likely to fear getting caught. You probably wouldn't know this person was a criminal if you met him at a party or sat next to him on a bus.

Nearly half—an estimated 49 per cent of Canadian adults—pay exactly what they are expected (and required) to pay. That leaves nearly 40 percent of Canadians who are *potential* or occasional cheaters; they sometimes avoid paying taxes by making cash payments "under the table," for example. These occasional criminals fall into several categories, according to the CRA. "Rationalizers"(12 per cent of Canadians) tend to believe that taxation in Canada is unfair and try to rationalize or explain away their tax cheating. "Underground economists" (12 per cent) often pay cash to avoid tax if the opportunity arises, and are less likely than average to think tax cheating is risky. "Over-taxed opportunists" (15 per cent) feel they are over-taxed, look for opportunities to pay cash to avoid taxes, and believe that many others do so as well. They tend to think that Canadians in general are taxed too much.

However, these potential offenders are generally law-abiding and fear having to pay penalties, if found cheating. As well, according to survey results, they understand their civic responsibilities and know how revenues are spent. You probably wouldn't know *these* people were criminals if you met them at a party or sat next to them on a bus. Our point is that many types of non-violent crime are very common and, often, not easily noticeable.

Some readers may be surprised by the inclusion of organized crime in this chapter, for organized crime can be very noticeable and very violent—we know that from news reports of gang killings and (even more) from movie treatments of the Mafia. However, for the most part, organized crime relies on the quiet threat of violence—not its (noisy) perpetration. Indeed, it was one of the great, even legendary, accomplishments of Mafia chief Al Capone to have brought peaceful methods of governance to the main organized crime "families" in the 1930s. It is precisely this ability to "do business" without much violence, and without the public attention violence draws, that has made organized crime as profitable as it has been for the past 80 years.

Most people consider non-violent (property) offences wrong, but few wish to increase the severity of punishment, precisely because they are not *violent* crimes. People agree less about the social significance of non-violent crimes—for example, occasional tax evasion—than they do about violent crimes. So, though the non-violent crimes we discuss in this chapter are very different from one another, they have in common the important element of non-violence.

These crimes are also more frequent and repetitive than violent crimes. As we saw in Chapter 7, violent crimes often are committed against friends, acquaintances, or family members. Non-violent crimes are more often committed against strangers or, at least, against people not closely related to the criminal. Non-violent crimes even offer a way of life—an occupation or profession. As in other occupations, many of these criminal activities are learned through observation, apprenticeship, and imitation.

The crimes we discuss in this chapter are seemingly based on a rational calculation of costs and benefits—in fact, they are calculated, planned ways of making a living (or, like tax evasion, saving money). To summarize, where **acquisitive (non-violent) crime** is concerned, humans want to maximize their material well-being. However, humans also plan their actions and apply meanings to them. We cannot understand non-violent crime unless we understand these meanings and the ways criminals organize to achieve their goals.

Non-Violent Crime: Its Types and Variety

One of the persisting ironies of crime is that huge numbers of Canadians are victimized by it and many fear it. Yet, there is often little connection between the two: many who have been victimized are not fearful, and many who are fearful have never been victimized.

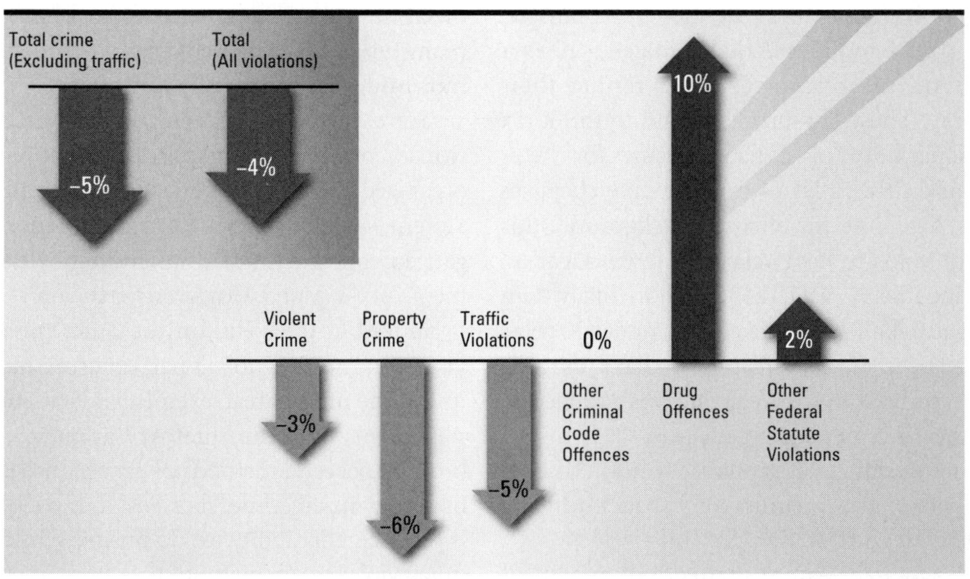

FIGURE 8.1 Crime Rates for Most Types of Crime Are Falling in Canada

Source: CBC News, at: <www.cbc.ca/news/interactives/crime-canada/>.

Further, the kinds of crimes people typically fear are those they are least likely to experience first-hand—especially crimes of violence. Most Canadians "experience" crimes of violence by viewing films and television dramas. Conversely, few television dramas are taken up with telling the stories of common, everyday, non-violent crimes—for example, stories of tax evasion, fraud, or theft.

In any given year, between 5 and 10 per cent of Canadian households directly experience theft, vandalism, or breaking and entering. Moreover, each of these types of victimization has increased slightly since 1993. It would be far-fetched to characterize this as an epidemic. However, it would be appropriate to note that a Canadian household is far more likely, in any given year, to experience one of these non-violent crimes than to experience a violent crime, a fatal accident, a severe illness (e.g., heart attack or cancer), or even a divorce. Note, finally, that all of these latter events are far more often considered major stressors in most people's lives. Crime victimization is also a stressor, but we often forget to count it in our calculations.

Organized Crime

One highly publicized form of crime is what we commonly call *organized crime*. Compared with juvenile delinquency, violent (domestic) crime, and amateur (street) crime, professional crime—for example, a career in automobile theft or embezzlement—is well organized. At the pinnacle of organized crime are transnational criminal organizations such as the Mafia.

Crimes committed by members of these criminal organizations are sometimes violent. This is especially true of "biker gangs," for example. However, most of the violence committed by these organized criminals is directed against other organized criminals. The most profitable business activities of such organizations are *non-violent*; they include prostitution, gambling, drugs, money laundering, and pornography.

There is organized crime in every country, and some of the organized crime in Canada has come about through immigration from various countries. In North America generally, organized crime has always been common among first- and second-generation immigrants and other deprived urban populations. Through the nineteenth and early twentieth centuries, a variety of immigrant groups—among them the Irish, the Germans, and the Jews—controlled crime in the large American cities before the Italians took over in the 1920s. Since then, organized crime in North America has continued to pass through other ethnic hands, seeing the emergence of black gangs, Puerto Rican gangs, Russian gangs, Chinese gangs, Vietnamese gangs, and, in Quebec, French-Canadian gangs.

Organized crime first became big business in the 1920s, when Al Capone negotiated peace among the competing US gangsters and Prohibition reduced the legal supply of alcohol. Criminal gangs, splitting up the available territory, could monopolize the illegal manufacture and delivery of alcohol for which the demand remained high. Gangsters quickly figured out that they could make a fortune by providing other illegal products and services such as drugs, gambling, and prostitution.

In the ensuing years, society changed and so did organized crime. In North America, large-scale crime became a more diversified, less visible business. Organized criminals also invested their profits in legitimate businesses such as real estate, trucking, and food, partly to "launder" the vast sums of money they earned through crime.

Today, organized crime is a topic of public concern all over the world. Increasingly,

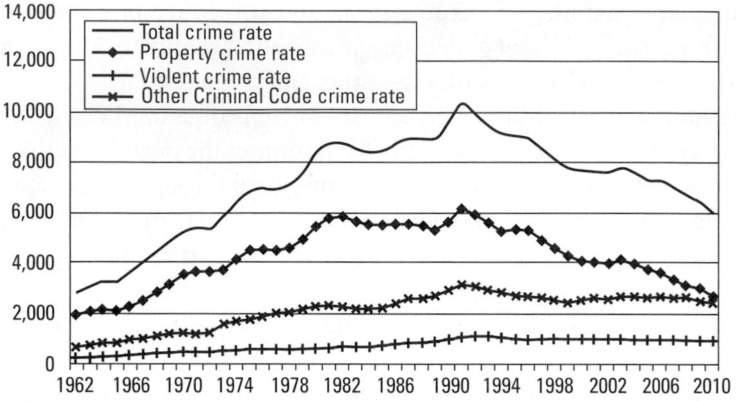

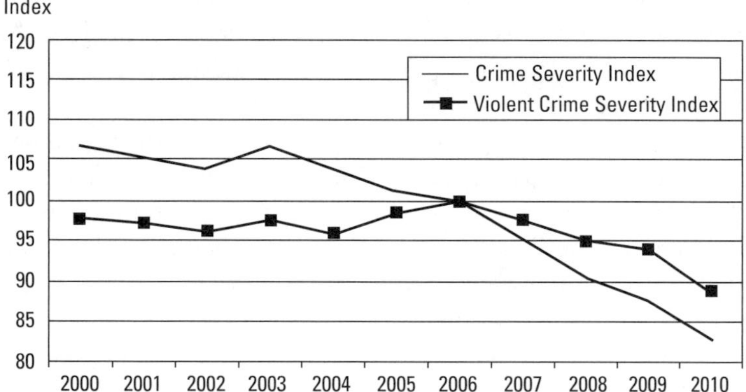

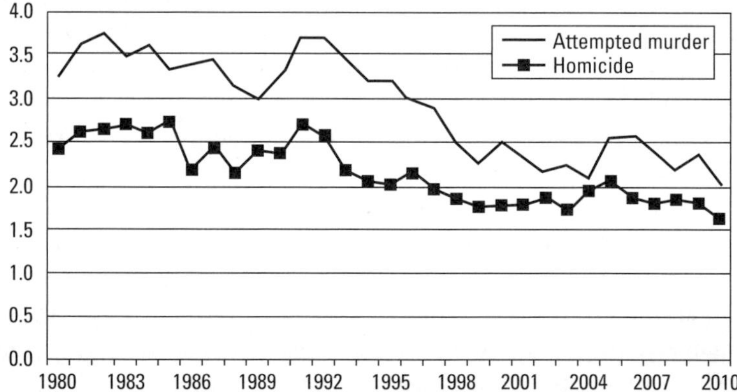

FIGURE 8.2 Decreases in Canadian Crime Rates: Police-Reported Crime Rates, Canada, 1962–2010; Police-Reported Crime Severity Index, Canada, 2000–2010; Attempted Murder and Homicide, Police-Reported Rates, Canada, 1980–2010

Source: S. Brennan and M. Dauvergne, "Police-Reported Crime Statistics in Canada, 2010," Charts 1, 2, and 6, *Juristat* (July 2011) at: < http://www.statcan.gc.ca/pub/85-002-x/2011001/article/11523-eng.htm>.

criminal organizations can cross national borders for illegal purposes, undermine democratic institutions through bribery and blackmail, threaten the stability of states in transition, and introduce new problems such as nuclear expansion, terrorism, and piracy.

Business Crime

Some crimes are committed neither by organized criminals nor by the urban poor; rather, they are committed by prosperous business people. There are, strictly speaking, two kinds of such business crime (or corporate or **suite crime**).

First, some business crimes are committed by corporations in their own corporate interest. Second, other business crimes—so-called **white-collar crimes**—are committed by business people or professionals in their own personal interest and often at the expense of the larger corporate body within which they work. Within large business organizations, hidden from view by bureaucratic rules and corporate liability, these individuals may commit criminal acts that cannot be easily observed, let alone prosecuted.

Sociologist Edwin Sutherland (1940, 1949) was the first to carry out systematic research on business crime, especially corporate crime (Box 8.1). Unlike amateur crime—for example, shoplifting—corporate crime victimizes millions of people; it robs businesses of billions of dollars each year, and it undermines the legitimacy of public institutions. Corporate crime has received ever more attention from investigators because the number and influence of business organizations have increased dramatically.

Fraud, such as insider trading (where people use private information in illegal ways) and falsifying account books (as Canadian/British executive Conrad Black is said to have done), provides the perfect example of self-interested business crime. Usually, frauds misrepresent a product or service. This misrepresentation allows the criminal to sell something of little or no value for a large amount of money and make a huge profit. Fraud relies on manipulating information, which means it often relies on what Goffman called "impression management." The high-tech industry, for example, is a perfect place for fraudulent activity; rapid growth, high stakes, and a huge potential for profits characterize this activity. In any "wildcat" environment, investigative procedures, internal controls, and good accounting practices are often lacking, and they are all essential weapons in the battle against corporate or personal fraud.

Nothing proved as perfect for fraudulent investment as the low-interest mortgage meltdown in the US in 2008. There, people without any secure means of payment, first, were induced to take home mortgages at impossibly low rates. These "toxic" mortgages, then, were rolled in with other notes and properties to create seductive investment opportunities that were, indeed, "too good to be true." When the mortgagees started to fail in large numbers, homes were repossessed, the housing market collapsed, and many banks, pension funds, and other investors lost a large fraction of their holdings.

Some financiers and corporate executives who were in the know pulled their investments before the system collapsed and walked away with millions of dollars in profits. Many other individuals and businesses went bankrupt. Many Americans, and to a lesser degree Canadians, are currently homeless and out of work because of this collapse; and the federal US government has had to use public funds—the revenues supplied by honest taxpayers—to secure the banking industry and the mortgage market.

Since Sutherland's groundbreaking work, business crime has evolved into a visible global problem. Governments around the world are putting more effort into fighting this form of crime that affects the economy, government, and public. Many business criminals rely on offshore banking and bank secrecy, as historically practised through Swiss bank accounts, to hide and launder billions of dollars stolen from people throughout the world. US treasury officials believe that 99.9 per cent of foreign criminal and terrorist money sent to the US is placed in secure accounts, making it safe from detection. Shell companies—also known as "mailbox" companies, international business corporations (IBCs), or personal investment companies (PICs) marketed by banks and accounting firms—launder money and hide profits from income taxes.

Some experts calculate that as much as half the world's capital flows are handled in these impossible-to-monitor offshore centres. For example, the International Monetary Fund (IMF) estimates that between $600 billion and $1.5 trillion of illicit money is laundered yearly through secret bank accounts. In crimes of this sort, the line is blurred between **corporate crime**, organized crime, and political crime (which we discuss in Chapter 9).

Time to Reflect: What do we learn from the (relative) failure to study and prosecute white-collar crime in North America? How might our theories of crime change if we studied it more?

Classic Works

BOX 8.1

Edwin H. Sutherland on *White-Collar Crime*

In *White-Collar Crime* (1949), Sutherland explores the widespread, yet neglected, crimes of corporations in the US. He shows that people of the upper socio-economic class also commit crimes, and argues that these crimes are relevant to any discussion of criminal behaviour. With this evidence of upper-class wrongdoing, Sutherland set out to create theories that would explain all criminal behaviour, white-collar and otherwise.

Sutherland examined court records of cases implicating large industrial and commercial corporations, finding that between 1900 and 1944, the 70 corporations he studied had committed 779 offences (not including 201 cases of patent or trademark violations), 158 of which were criminal offences. Sixty per cent brought at least four criminal convictions each. Sutherland notes that if these corporations had been individual people, they would have been termed *habitual criminals* in most states. In total, 980 adverse decisions (i.e., convictions) against the corporations were rendered, 583 by courts and 397 by administrative agencies. Of these, 60 per cent had been discovered within only 10 years of Sutherland's study (that is, between 1939 and 1949.)

The corporate offences Sutherland studied covered a wide range of activities, including restraint of trade; misleading advertising; financial fraud and violation of trust; violation of war regulations; the commission of unfair labour practices; and offences under other labour laws, especially with respect to wages and hours.

These corporate crimes were not unintended violations of technical rules—they were deliberate and consistent. The criminality of these corporations, like that of professional thieves, was persistent, and in that sense, many of the corporate offenders were recidivists—repeat offenders. Yet, the executives of these law-breaking corporations rarely lost any status among their business associates; rather, they were brazen about their law-breaking, often expressing contempt for law, government, and government personnel. In short, these white-collar crimes were deliberate, organized, and supported by a tolerant business subculture.

Sutherland ultimately suggests that such persistent, widespread crime by business people undermines the ideological justification for capitalism. No wonder Sutherland is remembered for coining the term *white-collar crime*, which we understand today as corporate crime committed by individuals of high socio-economic standing.

As these examples show, corporate and business crimes usually are carried out inside large organizations by people with more-than-average social status; however, most organizations want to keep these crimes secret to protect their public image. As a result, the public is slow to learn about these crimes, and (it would seem) few corporate criminals are prosecuted. This places unusual importance on the role of people within these organizations—so-called *whistle-blowers*—to step forward and reveal the details of these crimes to corporate auditors, the media, or law enforcement personnel. As the data in Table 8.1 show, whistle-blowing in the pharmaceutical industry (for example) can result in significant legal actions and the recovery (by the state) of huge sums of money.

As might be expected, whistle-blowing carries a great risk. As we see in Figure 8.3, the potential whistle-blower will typically make a careful assessment of this risk before reporting the criminal misdeed to others—even to superiors within the organizations. Often, organizations would prefer to ignore and hide such

TABLE 8.1 Whistle-Blower–Initiated US Federal Pharmaceutical Fraud Cases Settled between January 2001 and March 2009

Company and Year	Settlement (Millions of $)	Drug	Summary of Alleged Improper Conduct
TAP, 2001	875	Lupron	Inflated government reimbursement for prescription of its drug by reporting average wholesale price as significantly higher than the average sales price
Warner-Lambert, 2003	49	Lipitor and others	Violated best-price rules by offering rebates to private insurers*; gave kickbacks to private insurers for favouring drug on formularies
AstraZeneca, 2003	335	Zoladex	Inflated government reimbursement for prescription of its drug by reporting average wholesale price as significantly higher than the average sales price
Bayer, 2003	257	Cipro and Adalat CC	Sold relabelled drugs to private payers at discounted prices and then concealed this information to avoid obligation to pay such rebates to the government

TABLE 8.1 (continued)

Company and Year	Settlement (Millions of $)	Drug	Summary of Alleged Improper Conduct
Warner-Lambert, 2004	430	Neurontin	Aggressively marketed drug for off-label indications; gave kick-backs to high-prescribing physicians; made false statements about safety
Schering-Plough, 2004	346	Claritin	Offered underpriced and free goods and services to private sector that it did not offer to government programs
GlaxoSmithKline, 2005	150	Zofran and Kytril	Inflated government reimbursement for prescription of its drug by reporting average wholesale price as significantly higher than the average sales price
Serono, 2005	704	Serostim	Paid kickbacks to induce prescribing and falsified bioelectrical impedance analysis test results to make patients appear to be candidates for drug
King, 2005	124	Altace, Levoxyl, and others	Submitted inaccurate price data to the government, resulting in rebate amounts on its drug products that were lower than they should have been
InterMune, 2006	17	Actimmune	Conducted off-label marketing, including making false statements about drug efficacy to induce prescription writing and creating a "safety registry" to facilitate off-label sales
Bristol-Myers Squibb, 2007	515	Pravachol, Glucophage, and others	Conducted off-label marketing, including using misleading reprints and other sources, inducing prescription writing by offering rebates and gifts to off-label prescribing physicians, and holding continuing medical education meetings to induce writing of unapproved prescriptions
Cell Therapeutics, 2007	11	Trisenox	Conducted off-label marketing, including suppression of data about a dangerous side effect (acute promyelocytic leukemia differentiation syndrome) and manipulation of efficacy studies
Orphan Medical, 2007	20	Xyrem	Conducted off-label marketing, including organizing continuing medical education events with speakers describing unapproved uses of the drug and teaching physicians to falsify billing codes
Medics, 2007	10	Loprox	Conducted off-label marketing of an antifungal cream, approved for use in adults, for the treatment of diaper rash in children; misrepresented safety data
Merck, 2008	650	Vioxx and Pepcid	Failed to pay proper rebates to government programs and paid providers to induce prescriptions through payments for training, consultation, or research
Cephalon, 2008	425	Provigil, Gabitril, and Actiq	Conducted off-label marketing, including active help in securing government reimbursement for prescriptions for unapproved users
Eli Lilly, 2009	1400	Zyprexa and others	Conducted off-label marketing to children and to elderly patients in long-term care facilities; failed to provide information about drugs' side effects

*Best-price rules state that Medicaid must be granted the lowest price for drugs offered to any private purchaser.
Source: Aaron S. Kesselheim et al., "Whistle-Blowers' Experiences in Fraud Litigation against Pharmaceutical Companies," *New England Journal of Medicine* 362 (2010): Table 1, at: <www.nejm.org/doi/full/10.1056/NEJMsr0912039>.

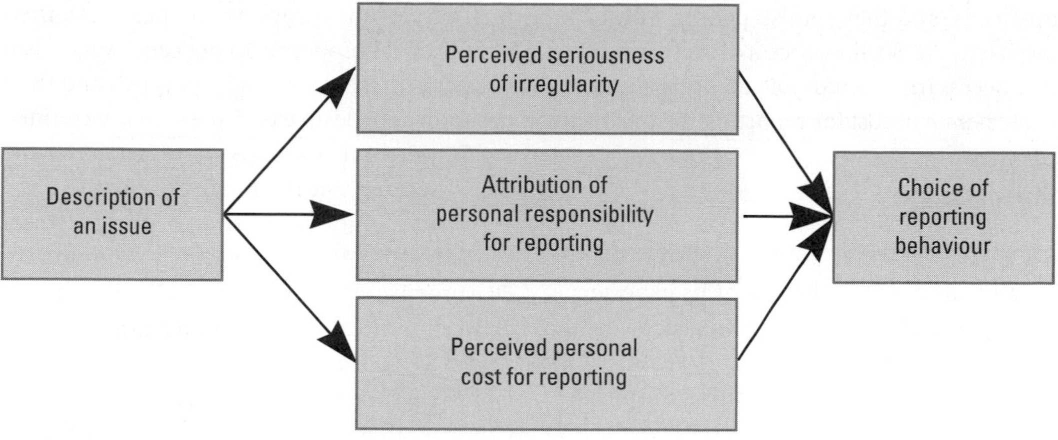

FIGURE 8.3 The Process of Risk Assessment

Note: The authors used an experimental study in which subjects were asked to judge the likelihood of reporting a questionable act and to assess the personal responsibility to report. Each subject completed six case studies. The subjects consisted of 145 managers and professional staff from public companies in Norway and the United States and from wholly owned US subsidiaries in France.

Source: Adapted from Joseph Schultz Jr et al., "An Investigation of the Reporting of Questionable Acts in an International Setting," *Journal of Accounting Research* 31 (1993): 75–103, at: <www.aim-hills.ph/projectpage/prs/research3_5.htm>.

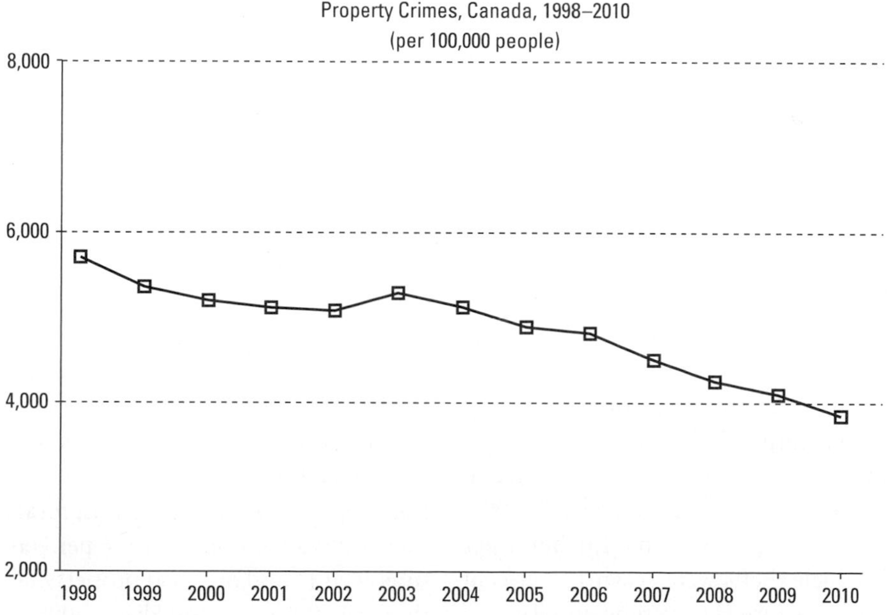

FIGURE 8.4 Declining Rates of Ordinary Property Crime

Source: Human Resources and Skills Development Canada, "Security—Crime Rates," in *Indicators of Well-being in Canada* (2012), at: <www4.hrsdc.gc.ca/.3ndic.1t.4r@-eng.jsp?preview=1&iid=57>.

misdeeds, and they punish people who bring them to light. So, the process of risk assessment will necessarily include calculations about the likely personal cost for reporting the misdeeds.

Street Crime

Far less spectacular are the everyday crimes we all hear about and some of us experience. Today, we call these *street crimes* because they often occur in public, in and around city streets. They include crimes like shoplifting, vandalism, break and enter, and car theft.

Street crimes are common because, of all crimes, they need the least skill, experience, technology, organization, or capital. Anyone can commit a street crime; as a result, amateurs commit the most. And because they occur in public places, street crimes are more likely to result in arrests than organized or business crimes. The result is that courts, jails, and prisons are filled with these amateur street criminals, most often people with little education, financial capital, or social capital. The opportunity to commit a street crime is, unlike business crime or even organized crime, readily available even to society's poorest people; but it is a far from secure means of making a living.

The Prevalence of Street Crime in Canada

Most street crimes, leaving aside simple assaults, are property crimes. According to *Juristat*, the rate of property crimes has been decreasing over the past two decades. Roughly 70 per cent of all Criminal Code offences (excluding traffic offences) reported to the police in 2009 were property crimes. Moreover, in 2009, the rate of break-ins dropped a further 4 per cent and vehicle thefts were down 15 per cent from the year before (Dauvergne and Turner, 2010). Statistics Canada notes: "The majority of criminal incidents reported to the GSS in 2009 were non-violent. More specifically, theft of personal property (34 per cent), theft of household property (13 per cent), vandalism (11 per cent), break-ins (7 per cent), and theft of motor vehicles/parts (5 per cent), accounted for 70 per cent of incidents recorded by the GSS." (Perrault and Brennan, op. cit.)

Official data show that ordinary street crime continues to be extremely common. In 2010, for example, there were 1.3 million property crime violations, including 536,151 thefts under $5,000 (not including motor vehicles) and 339,831 crimes of mischief (or vandalism). Compare these huge figures with those for the far more highly publicized acts of homicide, which numbered only 554 for all of Canada (www40.statcan.gc.ca/l01/cst01/legal50a-eng.htm).

Though it has lower rates of violent crime than the US, Canada has higher rates of property crime than the United States, for reasons that are not immediately apparent. The higher Canadian rate may reflect more confidence in the police and higher rates of reporting. Or it may reflect the larger number of gated communities, neighbourhood vigilante groups, and expensive home security systems in the US. Compared with 29 other countries taking part in the 2004 International Crime Victimization Survey (ICVS), Canada is near the average.

In fact, crime in Canada is representative of most industrial societies. The most common crimes reported are car vandalism and theft from a car. For almost all countries participating in the ICVS, the offences with the highest victimization rates were theft of personal property, theft from a car, and theft of a bicycle. In Canada, the highest victimization rate was for theft from a vehicle. Nearly 5 per cent of persons aged 16 and over had property taken from their vehicle (Sauvé and Hung, 2008). Statistics Canada notes: "Not all incidents of criminal victimization are reported to the police, of course. Across all participating countries [in the ICVS], slightly more than half the population (53 per cent) reported a victimization incident to the police. This rate is based on the reporting of five offence types comprised of theft from a car, theft of a bicycle, burglary, attempted burglary, and theft of personal property" (ibid.).

Although break-ins have continued to be common in Canada, the rate has steadily dropped since peaking in the early 1990s. For example, the 2009 rate was 42 per cent lower than a decade earlier. As well, motor vehicle thefts have dropped across the country. A *Juristat* report explains: "In 2009, police reported 108,000 motor vehicle thefts, an average of about 300 stolen vehicles each day. Since peaking in 1996, the rate of motor vehicle theft has been gradually declining. In 2009, the rate was 15 per cent lower than the year before and 40 per cent lower than a decade earlier" (Perreault and Brennan, 2010). The rates continued to drop in 2010, with a Canada-wide decrease in property crime of 6.4 per cent from 2009 (Figure 8.5). Only the three easternmost provinces saw slight increases, and, as with violent crime, these rates are higher in western Canada than in central and eastern Canada (compare Figure 8.5 and Figure 7.2).

The Demographic and Social Characteristics of Criminals

Racializing Crime, Criminalizing Poverty

Anyone who has looked at crime statistics knows that they are socially structured. The likelihood of committing a crime, being arrested, tried, and convicted varies between men and women, young people and old people, married people and single people, rich people

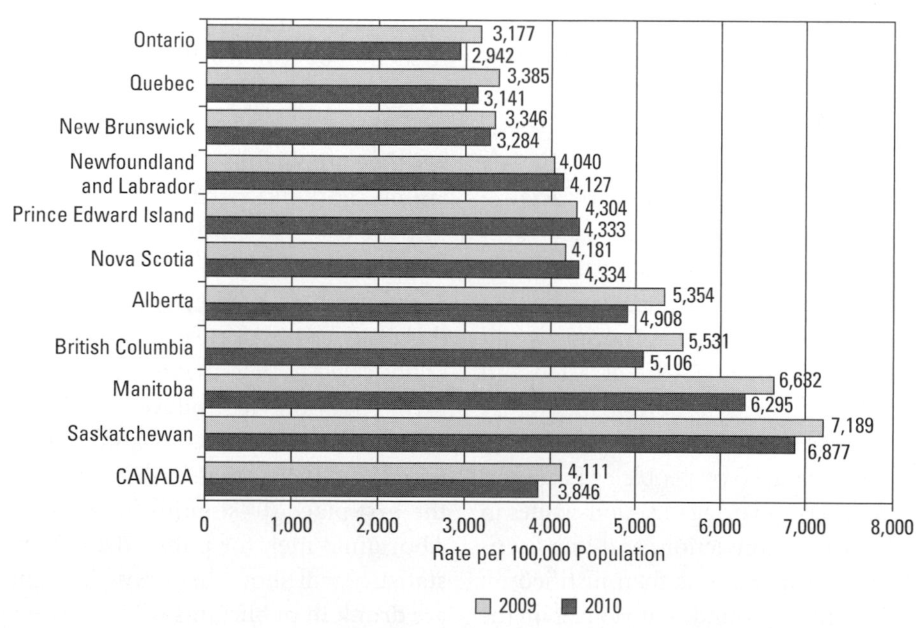

FIGURE 8.5 Property Crime Rates for Canada and Provinces, 2009 and 2010

Source: Government of Alberta, Office of Statistics and Information, at: <https://osi.alberta.ca/osi-content/Pages/Factsheets/PropertyCrimeRatesforCanadaandProvinces.aspx>.

and poor people, immigrants and natives, and people from different ethnic or racial backgrounds, for example. These sociological facts lead us to ask at least two questions: How can we explain these social variations, and what should our society do about them?

Consider the matter of race and class. In the nineteenth century, early social scientists and criminologists—influenced by prevailing views about biological determinism and eugenics—often explained crime in terms of weak or faulty genes. With the rise of modern social science in the twentieth century and vigorous campaigning against colonialism and racism, the crime–race link came to be understood in terms of class, poverty, socialization, and other social processes. Gradually, a more progressive view—that the racial composition of crime reflected patterns of racism and disadvantage in a society, not different patterns of immorality—came to dominate.

However, the earlier views were never completely erased. Even today, many people continue to hold racist beliefs that some groups are innately less moral and, in this sense, inherently more criminal than Canadians of a white, European background. As a result, there is a good possibility that we continue to racialize crime and criminalize race in Canada.

This "racialization" argument starts with the observation that a disproportionate number of visible minorities—especially Aboriginal and African-Canadian people—are arrested and jailed for crimes. That disproportion may reflect the tendency of the justice system, which continues to be dominated by people of European ancestry, to discriminate against non-whites in patterns of arrest, conviction, and imprisonment. The disproportion is then justified on seemingly scientific grounds—no longer on the theories of eugenics but on the grounds of social disadvantage: a culture of poverty, broken families, faulty socialization, and related notions.

The strongest support for this supposed racialization of crime comes from research on *racial profiling*. This is the tendency of police officers to over-select certain types of people for greater surveillance or inspection, on the grounds that they are statistically or demographically more likely than average to prove guilty of an infraction. Such racial profiling has been applied to people suspected of speeding or automobile theft; driving while under the influence of alcohol; drug possession; or, at international borders, suspected of terrorism.

Arguments surrounding this issue are far from resolved. In large part, there is still not enough evidence about the extent and motives behind such practices. The police (or border officials) are likely to say that racial profiling does not exist as such—or that it is merely a part of normal policing, which will invariably look for socio-demographic or behavioural signs that a crime is being committed. They may also say that this policing practice yields results that are in the public interest: a reduction of crimes and attempted crimes, for example.

Those subjected to such policing will likely say they are victims of harassment: that they are no more likely than anyone else to commit the crimes of which they are suspected and their civil liberties are being infringed. Moreover, they may (correctly) point out that this practice of selective policing—more generally, selective law-making and law enforcement—is bound to produce statistics for arrest and conviction that merely confirm the racially prejudiced beliefs that cause these practices in the first place. To simplify, if you only arrest Aboriginal men for public drunkenness, the statistics will show that only Aboriginal men are drunk in public; this will give rise to theories about the inherent flaws of Aboriginal men and the need to take special action against this group.

University of Toronto sociologists Scot Wortley and Julian Tanner (2006) have investigated racial profiling in the city of Toronto using results from their 2002 Youth Crime Victimization Survey. Doing so, they found that among their sample of 3,400 high school students, 50 per cent of black respondents revealed that the police had stopped them on two or more separate occasions within the last two years. In contrast, they found that only 17 per cent of white respondents and 11 per cent of Asian respondents reported being stopped by police within the same period of time.

A related process is the so-called *criminalization of poverty*. This is the process of selective law-making, law enforcement, and media coverage that highlights the link between crime and poverty and views the link as "natural"—upholding the idea that poor people are more criminally inclined than rich people. Like the tendency to racialize crime through selective surveillance, conviction, and imprisonment, the criminalization of poverty is likely to generate statistics that—in a seemingly dispassionate and scientific way—justify the practices and prejudices that generate those statistics.

Organized Crime

In recent decades, the scope and growth of organized crime have become globalized and spun out of control. Around the world we have seen a growing anxiety about the expansion of illegal markets, the increasing mobility of criminals across national borders, and the growing ability of criminals to infiltrate the legal economy and undermine political institutions.

The people who take part in organized crime are typically professional, or career, criminals. However, not all crimes—even professional crimes—are connected with what we call *organized crime*. Only some crimes need large-scale organization. For example, gambling and prostitution can bring huge profits but may not need much capital to organize. Other crimes, such as drug smuggling and trafficking, involve large overhead costs and need organization to fund and carry out. This leads to organized crime groups or syndicates—operations in which several criminal groups co-ordinate their crime. Criminals take over and invest in businesses that usually handle a high cash-transaction volume, mixing the illicit earnings with those of the legitimate business. Often, this is why criminals buy businesses—for example, restaurants, bars, nightclubs, hotels, currency exchange shops, vending machine companies, car washes, and other retail sales outlets—that yield huge gross receipts from cash sales.

Organized crime poses a serious threat to Canada's institutions, economy, and quality of life—even more so than common street crimes or attention-catching crimes of violence. For example, drug traders and other organized criminals have made money laundering the second largest global industry, with the circulation of "dirty" money estimated at $3 trillion worldwide. Organized crime groups are well known for their use of sophisticated technology to commit crimes such as currency and credit card counterfeiting and fraud, as well as fraudulent investment and telemarketing schemes.

Business Crime

Organized crime is viewed as the shady activity of shady people. Business crime is different: here, respected people of high social standing commit crimes during their normal workdays.

This "respectable" type of crime occurs at many different levels. Business crime may be committed by employees against companies (e.g., through embezzlement), by companies against employees (e.g., through violation of safety codes), by companies against customers (e.g., by price-fixing or fraudulent promises), or by companies against the public (e.g., by dumping toxic wastes into the air, land, or water). For business crimes by people in high-status occupations, we often use the term *white-collar crime*. As noted earlier, these crimes include insider trading; restraint of trade, such as monopoly; price-fixing; illegal rebates; infringement of patents, trademarks, and copyrights; and misrepresentation in advertisements.

The range of business crimes is very wide. Businesses may violate laws concerning food and drug quality and safety. Employers may violate laws regarding wages, hours, and public contracts. Politicians and government employees may violate laws (and gain personal profit) by supplying favours or confidential information to business firms. Accountants, lawyers, and others with financial responsibility may violate laws by embezzling money from trust funds.

The study of white-collar crime by sociologists, starting with Sutherland, introduced an important balance to an otherwise distorted picture of crime that highlights the study of common (street) crime committed by poor people. However, despite the better balance in representation, perpetrators of white-collar crime—who are better educated than average—are less often sentenced to prison and less often prosecuted by the criminal justice system. Instead, they may be disbarred from their profession or receive fines, which they can pay more easily than conventional criminals.

These penalties are far from proportionate to the harm done, since white-collar crime costs the Canadian economy a huge amount of money. One national organization estimates that insurance fraud alone costs policyholders $1.3 billion a year (Insurance Canada, 2003). No doubt, more recent estimates would be higher in the wake of the 2009 economic recession. Accordingly, Canada has devoted more attention to this crime problem in recent years. Ottawa has moved to crack down on corporate and securities crime by committing more resources to prosecuting white-collar offences and introducing tough penalties for illegal insider trading, with protection for whistle-blowers.

Street Crime

The public and media seem to pay closest attention to street crimes—often, penny-ante criminal acts by unsophisticated criminals—especially, criminal men. Most victims of street crime are men, and so are most of the perpetrators. As a result, any area with a high concentration of young men will likely have a high rate of street crime. A higher-than-average population density will also increase the rate of street crime because, by definition, these crimes occur in public places, usually where population density is greatest. For these reasons, street crimes are especially likely to occur in cities, in vacation spots during the peak season, on college campuses, and at public gatherings.

Some street crimes are a nuisance rather than a danger; what's more, they are clearly subcultural. Consider vandalism in the form of graffiti in public space. This is a non-violent crime, but it is also a type of communication among graffiti artists and between these artists and the public. It makes an implicit statement about who owns public space and how public space should be configured. And, evidently, people who create graffiti are often known to one another and share certain stylistic practices. In this sense, they make up a community and a culture of what others might consider "vandalism." Increasingly, courts are grappling with the legalities of policing public space around issues of graffiti (and other street "performances").

Graduating from amateur street crime to professional or career crime requires skills, like any other career. To enter a **criminal career** is to play multiple social roles, identify with crime, and make criminal activity a part of everyday life. Career criminals are not always connected with organized crime, although specialized criminals (such as safecrackers) may be. In comparison to amateur street criminals, professional criminals develop common attitudes towards themselves, their crimes, and the police, who are seen as the common enemy.

Many have remarked on the strange, almost symbiotic relationship between criminals and the police. Often, they come from similar social backgrounds and share similar social views. Over the course of time, they are likely to meet one another "professionally" and, sometimes, form relationships with one another. These conflicting relationships are the themes of popular police and crime dramas on television, which lead us to imagine that policing is exciting and heroic (see Ericson and Haggerty, 1997).

> **Time to Reflect:** How could you tell if a criminal is having a successful or unsuccessful "criminal career"? In what respects is it similar to other occupational careers people pursue?

Organized Criminals

Professional or career criminals belong to cultures and communities that are closely associated with organized crime. This illustrates how crime and deviance can give rise to "normal," well-organized subcultural activities.

Organized crime rings that currently exist in Canada include offshoots of the Chinese Triad, the Colombian Mafia, the Russian Mafia, and outlaw motorcycle gangs such the Hell's Angels, Outlaws, and Bandidos. Law enforcement agencies have connected these various groups to drug trafficking, prostitution, extortion, bribery, money laundering, assaults, and homicides.

Sociology, like journalism, has helped to disenchant our thinking by dispelling the idea that organized crime is an individualistic response to poverty. Early sociologists believed that crime resulted from poverty and that crime in poor neighbourhoods resulted from social disorganization: the more disorganized, the greater the incidence of crime. After 1940, however, with the publication of William Whyte's classic study, *Street Corner Society* (1993 [1943]), sociologists changed their views. They came to recognize that crime—especially crime in poor neighbourhoods—could be highly organized. It is also connected with the social, political, and economic life of the people in the community. Organized crime, we now know, is an intrinsic part of city, national, corporate, and political life.

We also know that modern organized crime acts at the intersection of legitimate and illegitimate business, family, and formal organization (see Ianni and Ruess-Ianni, 1983). Often, it has just as strong connections to white-collar crime as it does to vice crimes (such as drugs, pornography, and prostitution) that work through juvenile or amateur criminal associates. Organized crime often draws on the talents of professional and amateur, older and younger, criminals. This shows dramatically that crime is, indeed, a learned, organized, social activity with deep historical roots.

Organized crime, like other forms of secret organization, depends largely on friendship and kinship relations, which simplify the maintenance of order and conformity (see, e.g., Erickson, 1981; Simmel, 1906 [1902]). At the base of organized crime is the principle that sociologists have variously called **patronage** or **clientelism**. Originally, the word *client* meant "hearer" or "person who listens to advice." The client listened to the "patron," or boss. The relationship between patron and client is personal and endures for life, and this is as true in organized crime as it is elsewhere.

The organization of large-scale crime today is a particular mix of older and newer elements. Unlike bureaucracies, patron–client networks are based on unwritten and particularistic rules. The conditions that support and spread clientelism in modern cities are high unemployment, low wages, low education, and low levels of labour force participation (e.g., gendered work patterns). Where the state is largely organized by and for the most powerful members of society, organized crime constitutes—in some communities—an illegitimate state organized by and for the less powerful members of society.

For this reason, organized crime has survived in Sicily through all the political and economic changes that began in the late nineteenth century and accelerated after World War II. Key to its survival are ideas of trust and honour, and notions of crime and punishment, that can still be found among Sicilian peasants and Sardinian herdsmen. These ideas work well wherever people distrust the state, the police, and other major institutions and where material deprivation is common.

Organized crime flourishes in any community that meets four key conditions. First, organized crime is associated with conditions of scarcity and inequality. Second, it is associated with poverty and prejudice, keeping people from moving easily to another community to find work. Third, it provides protection wherever people lack equal legal or human rights or equal access to welfare, health care, and good-quality education. Finally, organized crime flourishes among people who lack human capital and cultural capital. All of these conditions can be found in certain parts of North America, Russia, and Sicily, as well as in Latin America and areas in Asia; in short, they can be found in almost every part of the world, which suggests we can expect to see a continuing survival and growth of organized crime.

In general, organized crime is most common and most extensive in societies characterized as "failed states," where the government does not enjoy the trust of its people and, partly for this reason, fails to govern. Some characteristics of failed states include demographic pressures, refugees, group grievances, human flight, economic decline, corruption, public lack of confidence in the state, poor public services, violations of human rights, and factionalized elites. Every failed state has a recent history of internal or external war, just as every failed community has a recent history of crime and violence.

No wonder, then, that piracy in recent years has flourished off the east coast of Africa, particularly Somalia, one of a number of such "failed states." Piracy has historically become established wherever a local government was unable to expel pirate coastal settlements or monitor the shoreline. Recent episodes have involved the seizure of ships, hostages, goods, and weapons. The most recent versions of piracy represent a dangerous combination of organized crime, international terrorism, and possibly civil warfare.

Current Events

BOX 8.2

The Ongoing Problem of Mafia-Enforced Extortions

Mafias manipulate vulnerable states by taking over and regulating both legal and illegal markets. A mafia, therefore, corrupts or takes on the role of the police force, ruthlessly abusing the coercive authority, which should be restricted to law enforcers of the state, for its own benefit. Corruption of other state institutions and representatives also allows mafias to gain and maintain power.

In the late 1990s, the citizens of Mumbai, India, experienced some of the worst manipulation and violence at the hands of organized crime elements. Over 100 people were left dead in 1998 as a result of "underworld" organized crime operations, extortions, and shootouts that were becoming increasingly less covert. When an economic recession reduced the mafia's profits from the film, property, and financing industries, it turned its focus towards ordinary citizens to make up for these financial losses. The police force failed to protect citizens from the mafia's extortion threats, as poorly salaried cops were easily bribed and the mafia's endless supply of sophisticated weaponry easily outstripped the poorly armed police. Mumbai's joint police commissioner and head of the crime branch, D. Sivanandan, urged citizens to refuse to "agree to pay up, or matters will only get worse." Yet citizens felt that co-operation with the mafia was the only way to avoid the threats, violence, and murders that were becoming increasingly prominent.

The problem persisted in Ercolano, just outside of Naples, until recently. There, the local Camorra demanded between 150 and 1,500 euros each month from businessmen, traders, entrepreneurs, and even priests. But in 2005, the overwhelming numbers of shops and businesses that had been forced to shut down due to their inability to pay extortion fees drove newly elected mayor, Nino Daniele, to retaliate. Through his active participation in anti-Camorra demonstrations, cancellation of municipal contracts with those companies thought to be associated with the Camorra, and passage of laws that enticed citizens to decline to pay extortion fees, Daniele has been a huge part of the solution to this ongoing problem in Ercolano. Radio Siani has also played a role in reducing the influence of the mafia by broadcasting messages that promote the law and denounce the mafia. As a result of these actions, roughly 250 Ercolano mafia members have been jailed, and 23 businessmen formerly abused by the mafia have come forward with accusations against 41 mobsters, who are currently having legal actions taken against them.

Corporate Crime

Corporate crimes against consumers are common, and the most common known perpetrators of corporate crime are small-scale businesses. Fewer major corporations are accused of corporate crime, though this may be because they are better able to resist further regulation due to their economic and societal power. Organizations engaged in corporate crime lie on the border between legal and illegal activity, making this kind of crime hard to enforce.

Very often, consumers are unaware of the corporate crime that has been perpetrated, because they lack the knowledge needed to assess the quality of a product they have purchased. Often, the harm has already been done by the time consumers recognize they have been victimized. Consider long-term health threats due to unmonitored chemical additives in food: it takes consumers a long time to associate their declining health with the product they have consumed. In most cases, consumers have been subjected to repeated victimization (each time they buy the product or they invest their money).

Corporate crimes involving food can have dramatic and sometimes fatal consequences for consumers. Consider food adulteration: food adulteration occurs whenever companies inject water into food or add other non-nutritious bulk substances to make it seem there is more. A recent and widely discussed form of this practice is the addition of so-called "pink slime" to hamburger meat. While such additives as pink slime may not be physically harmful to the consumer—at least, not immediately—they deceive the consumer about the value received for money and are economically wasteful. People are paying for products they think are nutritious that may be mostly made up of water, for example (or in the case of pink slime, made up of fat, bone, cartilage, and other meat waste).

Food fraud often occurs when companies import cheap foods from poor countries and then resell these under their own brand label. Consumers are misled into buying foods that may not have been prepared under the same safety or health precautions as would be required in Canada. Similarly, when inspection standards are lax, or inspectors have been bribed to okay faulty products, or when the machines used in processing are not properly cleaned, outbreaks of food poisoning can occur, sometimes leading to deaths.

Counterfeit goods are another source of consumer risk. For example, there have been reported cases of people getting burned by fake perfume. The cosmetics women (and men) smear on their skin often are toxic. Since such products are in direct contact with the body, the toxins from the cosmetics immediately are absorbed into the body or eaten. In some cases, certain cancers were proven to have been the long-term consequence of using a cosmetic.

And of course, many people have been victimized when purchasing "knock-off" versions of name-brand watches, purses, silk scarves, and other luxury products. On a much larger scale is the fraudulent sale of financial products: fake stocks or bonds that lack much if any real value. In recent years—especially since the worldwide financial crash of 2008—we have heard a number of highly publicized cases of people who entrusted their money to fraudulent investment corporations. The money, it turns out, was used for the personal gain either of the corporation or of high-powered people within the corporation. Companies like Enron and operators like Bernie Madoff come to mind in this instance. Often, their customers suffered tremendous financial losses.

Corporate offenders—for example, high-rolling stock traders—are able to manipulate their unsuspecting victims and avoid getting caught for many years, through the technique Erving Goffman (1963), in his classic work *Stigma*, called "impression management." This is the technique of controlling how other people see and react to them.

In most people, impression management is on automatic pilot, and we blend into a new role without too much thought of our behaviour. However, some people are able to exert tremendous self-control over their impression management and, like professional actors, they construct their personalities to appear pleasing to others. They work hard to fool their victims into believing that their created personality is who they are. The unwitting or naive victim is likely to accommodate to and trust the pleasing individual they encounter.

Offending fraudsters are further able to influence perceptions in social interaction by controlling and regulating information in three ways: ingratiation (show happiness to elicit goodwill), intimidation (getting others to obey), and supplication (getting others to be helpful). People who fall for such offenders are by no means unintelligent; they simply are unable to pick up on the deceit. Since such offenders have a large number of victims, it appears that the majority of people are unable to discover the deception. A well-known example of such an offender was Bernard Madoff, mentioned above, who got billions of dollars from thousands of investors. He did this by randomly rejecting some clients in order to make other clients feel special. His business built billions of dollars of profits through word-of-mouth promotion, without any actual product or investment being created.

Organizational Crimes against Employees

Another form of corporate crime occurs when the organization victimizes its own employees. This occurs when people higher up in management positions decide to endanger their workers by failing to keep safe working conditions, neglect to upgrade the equipment, and fail to train the employees.

Workplaces with higher-than-average risks of victimization include factories, oil rigs, and mines. A recent example is found in British Columbia sawmills, where explosions have taken lives and injured many because the time allowed for the necessary meticulous cleanup of combustible sawdust after a shift has been drastically cut.

In effect, the workers are sacrificed to the interests of the top managers and major shareholders. Large corporations are built on a hierarchical model. At the top is the corporation itself, with its own legal identity. The corporate directors do not see lower-level employees as essentially belonging to the corporation so much as being exchangeable units of labour. It is these lower-level employees who can be victimized by corporate crime (Pearce, 1993). Safety, health, and environmental violations often are outcomes of the directors' policies, while the worst violations are products of lower-level management decisions.

In principle, there are legal remedies and legal penalties in the event of injury or death in unsafe circumstances. In practice, the outcome often involves civil, not criminal, remedies. If the corporation is found to be at fault in the event of an injury or death, it is likely to pay a fine—at most. Yet, many corporations even avoid this degree of responsibility and punishment. They deny their responsibility for the situation, and portray the workplace accident as a tragic mishap rather than as a corporate crime.

Arendt (2003 [1971]) and Cohen (2001) describe four types of official denial that corporations use. These are: literal denial (i.e., nothing is happening or has happened), interpretive denial (i.e., what is happening or has happened is really something else), implicatory denial (i.e., what is happening or has happened is justified as self-defence or some other necessity), and passive denial (i.e., pay no attention to the situation at all). Interestingly, these defences nicely cover the rationalizations of *most* deviant behaviour. Most wrongdoers excuse their behaviour in these ways, as we noted earlier in a discussion of "techniques of neutralization" by delinquents. The difference is simply that major corporations can afford to hire the best lawyers to make these excuses on their behalf.

Media Depictions of Non-Violent Crime

Non-violent crime is often a source of irony or comedy in movies and television shows, perhaps because, in comparison to violent crime, white-collar and corporate crime is "invisible," meaning audiences may find it less threatening, or less interesting as dramatic fare. Also, people feel helpless against it so they vent their frustration by joking about it. Viewers seem more able to find humour in defrauding employers (*Office Space*, 1999), employees (*Fun With Dick and Jane*, 2005), or stockholders (*The Producers*, 1968) than they do in liquor store holdups or alleyway muggings for which police forces act on their behalf. Some long-running comedy shows satirize corporate executives who employ mercenary or illegal practices. Barney Stinson of CBS's *How I Met Your Mother* and Charles Montgomery Burns of Fox's *The Simpsons* are two such characters, though the former is portrayed as a lovable rogue, the latter as nearly sociopathic.

Like corporate crime, fraud (or "grifting") is a long-time comedy staple, which in the process provides information to alert and protect people about those sorts of behaviour. Throughout the twentieth century, popular books, movies, television shows, and comics have featured a variety of hustlers and con men. Classic films such as *Lady Eve* (1941), *Paper Moon* (1973), and *The Sting* (1973) showed audiences' and critics' general acceptance of comedy crooks. On radio and television, the lovable hustler has remained almost omnipresent. In the 1940s and 1950s, plot lines for Abbott and Costello movies and for TV shows *The Honeymooners* and *Amos 'n' Andy* frequently involved scams. That tradition carried on in the form of sitcom characters like Harry the Hat of *Cheers*, Blaine Sternin of *Frasier*, and Bender B. Rodriguez of *Futurama*.

Because nearly everybody pays taxes, tax fraud seems to be taken more seriously by both entertainers and audiences. Tax evasion is rarely used as a comedic premise, though a few films such as *The Mating Game* (1959) and *Harry's War* (1981) did attempt to mine the issue for laughs. More often, filmmakers portray tax fraud solemnly or judgementally. Director Brian De Palma depicted Al Capone's conviction on charges of tax evasion in *The Untouchables* (1987) as a triumph of good over evil. Alternatively, media outlets openly lamented the tax evasion convictions of singer Willie Nelson, rapper Ja Rule, and professional golfer Jim Thorpe, focusing on whether the convictions would negatively affect their careers.

Perhaps because it has only recently become a pressing issue, identity theft does not have a particularly long history in popular media. However, the sixteenth-century case of Martin Guerre is history's most famous and widely discussed example of identity theft. Several years after Guerre abandoned his wife in 1548, a new man showed up in the small French town of Artigat, appearing to be and fraudulently claiming to be the missing husband. The case was a sensation at the time and remains of historical interest today. The Guerre saga has resulted in two literary depictions by Alexander Dumas, the French film *Le Retour de Martin Guerre* (1982), the Hollywood production *Sommersby* (1993), and a litany of plays and musical renderings. Outside of movies that deal more broadly with computer hacking and fraud, however, the media have been slow to provide many works that focus solely on identity theft.

Theories about Non-Violent Crime

Functionalist Theories

The basic premise of functional theory is that the parts of society work together like parts of a living organism. As Merton said, crime may be one adaptation to the gap between the cultural (i.e., material) goals of society and the accepted means of achieving those goals.

Accordingly, this theory would predict the highest crime rates among the poorest members of society, since they are the least able to achieve our culture's goals by prescribed means and therefore have to resort to other (illegal) means. However, not everyone who is deprived of legitimate opportunities turns to a life of crime. Merton (1957 [1938]), in fact, identified four different ways in which people adapt to anomie: innovation, **ritualism**, **retreatism**, and rebellion. Crime, which Merton characterizes as "innovation," is only one of these four adaptations. Innovation, in turn, depends on the person's social environment, including his or her access to criminal culture and technology.

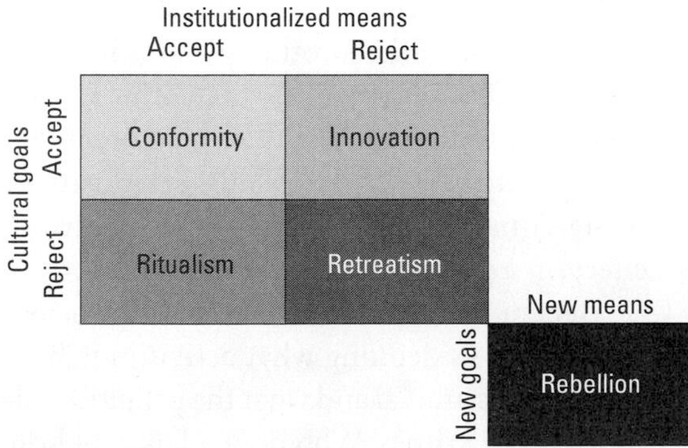

FIGURE 8.6 Robert K. Merton's Deviance Typology

Source: <en.wikipedia.org/wiki/File:Mertons_social_strain_theory.svg>.

According to Merton, all criminal innovations help preserve the workings of an unequal capitalist society by allowing poor people to imagine that they or their children will someday be rich. This is what makes strain theory a functionalist theory. Some theorists also believe that the incidence of non-violent crimes has increased in post-industrial societies because, despite major improvements in the quality of life, large numbers of people continue to experience *relative* deprivation, whereby the lives of others they see in their community and on television are more materially rich than their own. Thus, the theory of relative deprivation centres on how individuals subjectively perceive themselves as victims of disadvantage (Stiles et al., 2000).

> **Time to Reflect:** What are the theoretical advantages and disadvantages of thinking of crime as an "innovative" adaptation to anomie, as Merton does?

Regardless of the criminal's assumed motivation, functionalist theories also make clear the importance of social control. They assume that anyone is capable of delinquent or criminal behaviour and only control—self-control or external control—will prevent it.

Another functionalist theory relates poverty to social disorganization. As signs of social disorganization become more visible, poor communities degenerate into more crime. A vicious cycle of crime and disorganization is set in motion. This theory, commonly known as the **broken windows theory**, is best at explaining destructive property crime, especially vandalism. Along these lines, Wilson and

Keeling (1982) state: "If a window in a building is broken and left unrepaired, all the rest of the windows will soon be broken . . . one unrepaired window is a signal that no one cares and so breaking more windows will cost nothing." Similarly, if misconduct goes unaddressed, subsequent misconduct will follow.

Some believe that such tactics are successful in curbing more serious crime. However, others believe that they simply produce an "illusion of order" and while windows are being fixed, the window-breaker is getting away.

Symbolic Interactionist Theories

Symbolic interactionists focus on the ways people interpret behaviour and the ways their interpretations construct the social world.

Interactionist theories assume that crime, like other social activity, is learned through interaction with others and involves the development of a criminal self-concept. Deviance and crime are not direct products of the social structure but of face-to-face interactions and personal interpretations. Therefore, understanding criminal behaviour over the life course is only possible if we consider interactional—especially familial and neighbourhood—factors and their impact on early development. Adverse familial and neighbourhood contexts promote the socialization that results in antisocial behaviour.

This process involves at least two parts: differential association and labelling. First, some people learn specific skills and techniques in order to help them engage in criminal behaviour. For example, by becoming a member of an organized crime unit a person may learn how to obtain necessary weapons and how to influence key individuals. Second, some people learn to value criminality more highly than conventional behaviour. By associating with others who know how to commit crimes, people are more likely to learn to view these activities as more desirable than a conventional, law-abiding way of life. According to the differential association theory, then, learning to be criminal or delinquent involves socialization like that associated with learning any behaviour or value—for example, driving a car or practising Catholicism.

Another theory that has proved useful in explaining crime is *labelling theory*, which shifts attention away from the transgressor and towards the way that others react to the deviant. This theory suggests that whether others define or label a person as "deviant" is critical in the development of a pattern of deviant behaviour. Labelling perpetuates crime and delinquency because once people have been labelled they have fewer alternatives, and the deviant behaviour becomes a part of their social identity.

Critical Theories

According to critical theories, laws are used by the dominant social classes to control and punish those below them. Authority figures are simply using criminal law to maintain the status quo. This is suggested by a seeming bias against working-class people in policing, arrest, bail-setting, conviction, and punishment patterns. Because of the way the laws are enforced, some people are more likely than others to get caught and punished for their rule-breaking. Other factors (such as offence seriousness) being equal, race—like class—has a strong effect on a person's chance of incarceration.

Generally, the powerful members of society write the laws defining what activities will be considered criminal and what the penalties will be for those crimes. Who does what, and how the action is treated, clearly depends on how the action is interpreted. In turn, this depends on a person's status and authority in society.

However, the organization of criminal labelling is closely related to economic organization. On the one hand, capitalism—a system organized around the constant search for higher profits on invested capital—is pledged to protecting private property (i.e., private wealth). On the other hand, it is pledged to generating consumerism and strong desires for success and symbols of success. In short, the underlying cause of crime, for critical theorists, is inequality and the competition to attain culturally prized material goals.

Feminist Approaches

All feminist research is guided by the notion that personal life always has a political dimension—much like sociology's central idea of the connection between private troubles and public issues. Feminists have made important contributions to the study of deviance and crime by de-romanticizing the image of the criminal.

An important point needs to be made about the gendering of crimes discussed in this chapter. Organized crime, street crime, and white-collar or business crime have always been dominated by men. For example, organized crime "families" have tended to mirror the gender patterns observed in the traditional ethnic families from which they developed so that women have been excluded except as partners, associates, and helpers—never as bosses or key actors.

However, we are currently seeing an increase in the numbers of women being arrested, tried, convicted, and imprisoned for non-violent crimes. With the increase of women entering professional and managerial roles, the possibility of female business crime also has increased. This corresponds to a growth in women's opportunities to steal and embezzle as readily as men. Unfortunately, statistics on the extent of business crime are too incomplete to permit a clear indication of the degree to which this area of crime has become de-gendered.

Current Events

BOX 8.3

Faking Cancer for Personal Gain

Legal action has been taken against women who have been accused of faking cancer and acquiring large sums of money from supporters fraudulently. The first incident involved Ashley Kirilow, 23, who turned herself into the police in early August 2010 after she was accused of fundraising for the terminal cancer that she did not, in fact, have. The Burlington, Ontario, resident gathered supporters and donations after she posted various items on Facebook and MySpace, including pictures that implied she had lost her hair as a result of chemotherapy treatment. With the help of these supporters, Kirilow established a fundraiser that yielded thousands of dollars for her and for a charity she had (supposedly) founded to finance cancer research. Despite this charity never having been registered, volunteers claim that at least $20,000 was raised in its name, in addition to $9,000 generated by a benefit concert for Kirilow personally. Kirilow has admitted that she continued to marshal support for herself at these benefits by shaving her head and eyebrows, starving herself, and plucking her eyelashes in order to make herself look as though she was undergoing treatment. Mike Kirilow, Ashley's father, claims that Ashley told him she has never had cancer, adding to the evidence against her. Kirilow was charged with three counts of fraud under $5,000 as a result of fraud complaints filed with the police.

A woman from Timmins, Ontario, Jessica Ann Leeder, 21, also had fraud complaints filed against her, allegedly for pretending to have both stomach and lung cancer. By employing similar tactics to those used by Kirilow, Leeder collected thousands of dollars from supporters. Lianne Callegari, who was living with Leeder until 1 November, claimed she doubted the entire situation from the beginning. "But . . . it's kind of hard to call someone out on whether or not they have cancer," she said. It appears that Leeder tried to feign chemotherapy treatment much like Kirilow did; however, her claims to having lost her hair were questioned by Callegari, who asserts that Leeder hadn't lost her eyebrows. Further, Callegari claims that Leeder would "get her stories mixed up" when talking about the treatment she was undergoing. Like Kirilow, Leeder pleaded guilty to a charge of fraud over $5,000 on 8 November 2010. Each woman pleaded guilty within one week of the other.

Sources: Brendan Kennedy, "Second Person Accused of Faking Cancer, Raising Funds," *Toronto Star*, 8 Nov. 2010, at:<www.thestar.com/article/887401>; CBC News, "Woman Accused of Faking Cancer Appears in Court," 9 Aug. 2010; "Woman Faked Cancer to Raise Money," *Toronto Star*, 6 Aug. 2010; "Timmins Woman Accused of Faking Cancer to Get Money," *Timmins Times*; "Another Ontario Community Asks How Someone Could Fake Cancer," *Toronto Star*, 9 Nov. 2010.

Consequences of Non-Violent Crime

Making and enforcing laws is costly. So the first consequence of non-violent crime in Canada is the public cost associated with preventing crimes, apprehending and trying criminals, and imprisoning or otherwise punishing them.

According to Statistics Canada (Taylor-Butts, 2001), more than $1 billion was spent on the operation of courts in Canada in 2000–1, employing nearly 10,000 court staff and 2,000 judges. Legal aid expenditures increased by 2 percent in 2000–1 to $512 million. To give some idea of the costs involved more recently, consider a report from Ontario on the provincial costs of court operation: Spending in 2009–10 by Ontario's Court Services Division (Ministry of the Attorney General) was $403 million to operate 260 courthouses and pay 3,000 staff, down only slightly from two years earlier (www.auditor.on.ca/en/reports_en/en10/407en10.pdf). It is not hard to believe, then, that Canada-wide court costs today—both federal and provincial—are $1.4 billion, according to a recent report.

Another major cost of crime—especially non-violent crime—is correctional services (including imprisonment, parole, and probation services). A recent *Juristat* report noted that the $3.9 billion spent on adult correctional services in 2008–9 represented:

> a 7 per cent increase from the previous year when controlling for inflation. Operating expenditures increased for both the provincial and territorial system (+6 per cent), and the federal system (+8 per cent) . . . . [In the same year] the provinces and territories spent slightly over $1.4 billion to operate prisons, compared to about $299 million to supervise offenders in the community.

> It is usually more costly to house federal inmates than inmates in the provincial and territorial system. On average, in 2008/2009, institutional expenditures amounted to almost $323 per day per federal inmate, compared to about $162 per day per provincial or territorial inmate. The federal system, which houses and serves offenders sentenced to periods of custody of two years or more, requires higher levels of security as well as longer-term specialized programming. (Calverley, 2010)

Social Consequences

Organized Crime

The *Organized Crime Impact Study* (Porteous, 1998) was the first major attempt to examine key organized crime activities in Canada. According to this study, the illicit drug trade has the greatest impact on Canadian society, given its combined social, economic, and violence-generating effects. Governments and enforcement agencies are just beginning to assess the importance of this organized crime activity, which may cost Canadians over $1 billion per year.

Organized crime has increased in such volume and scope that it now threatens national and international security. Laundered funds provide financial support for drug dealers, arms dealers, terrorists, and other criminals to operate and expand their criminal empires. Criminals are able to manipulate banking systems in Canada and abroad in pursuit of their criminal activities. The police have trouble controlling transnational organized crime because of the ability of criminal organizations to conceal their activities beneath legal transactions, to act rapidly in exploiting new opportunities, and to reorganize themselves in response to law enforcement successes.

Few Canadians spend much time thinking about white-collar crimes such as fraud and embezzlement. However, these crimes carry significant costs for all of us. Increasing attention is being paid to the forms and costs of crime that make use of information technology. A few statistics on the extent of cyber-fraud are presented in Box 8.4. Millions of people are currently at risk of cyber-fraud and

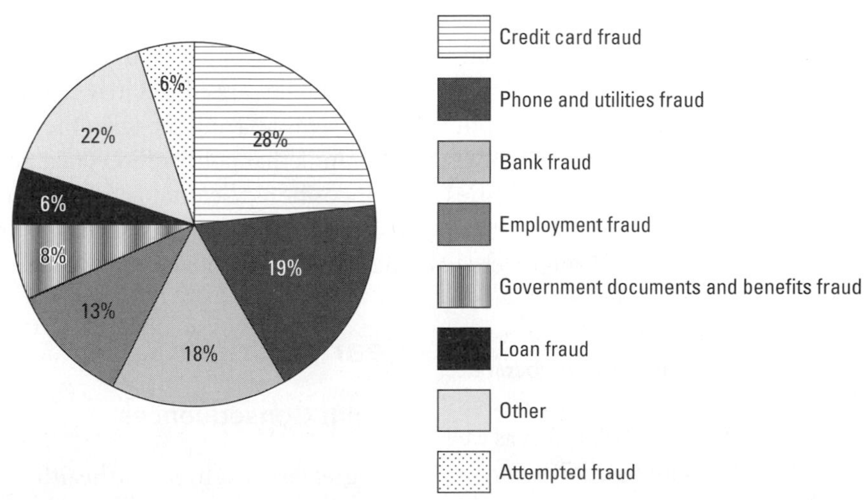

FIGURE 8.7 Types of Identity Theft

Source: <pottsestaxes.com/taxblog/?attachment_id=547>.

Current Events 

BOX 8.4

Facts on Fraud

- 29 per cent of Internet users have purchased goods from spam e-mails. The most commonly purchased items include sexual enhancement pills, software, adult material, and luxury items such as watches, jewellery, and clothing. *Botnets* are networks comprised of thousands of infected (or "zombie") personal computers, controlled remotely by criminals. They have enabled spammers to push down their costs through economies of scale.
- 9,977 Canadians reported that they had been victims of fraud in 2010. That means that 831 people were the victims of fraud each month or 27 people each day.
- 18,146 Canadians indicated that they had been the victims of identity fraud in 2010. These individuals lost $9,436,996 altogether.
- Canadians reported losses of $13 million to mass-marketing fraud in 2010.
- Organized crime is involved in close to 80 per cent of mass-marketing fraud.
- Total Canadian fraud losses, as estimated by the Commercial Crime Branch of the Royal Canadian Mounted Police (RCMP), are between $10 billion and $30 billion annually.
- 1,948 complaints were received in 2010 by the Canadian Anti-Fraud Centre regarding scam offers of foreign money; $2.6 million in total were reportedly lost.
- Only approximately 5 per cent of fraud victims report having been victimized.

Sources: <www.itfacts.biz/category/fraud>; CBC, "More Fraud Facts," 1 Apr.. 2011, at: <www.cbc.ca/marketplace/2011/wontgetfooledagain/facts.html>.

billions of dollars are being lost to a combination of fraud, hacking, and viruses.

Among the foremost are concerns about identity theft, which, as Figure 8.7 shows, comes in a variety of forms and venues. Fraudulent use of one's personal identity can result in huge indebtedness and ruined credit rating. New legislation and new strategies of detection and prevention are needed to deal with new criminal opportunities in cyberspace.

Besides the enormous financial costs of white-collar crime, there are social costs as well. Revelations of business and political corruption breed distrust and cynicism and undermine public confidence in the integrity of social institutions. People who think that all members of Parliament are crooks may refrain from voting or avoid paying the taxes they owe. People who think that police officers take advantage of their positions to commit crimes cease to respect the law. Thus, the costs of such crime go beyond the actual dollars involved in the crime itself.

Fear of Crime

Health Consequences

The greatest cost to public health results from the fear of crime. A recent study (Fitzgerald, 2008) using Canadian data demonstrates that while "the characteristics and perceptions of individuals are most important in explaining differences in fear among urban Canadians, a statistically significant portion of the variation in fear was attributable to the neighbourhood environment." This is because some aspects of the social and economic conditions of neighbourhoods directly affect people's behaviours and perceptions, regardless of their own personal characteristics or experiences. Second, people's perceptions of the level of crime and "social disorder" in the neighbourhood may explain variations in levels of fear.

Fear of crime is one of several factors in the social milieu that increases people's level of stress, regardless of their personal experiences. And, as a great deal of careful health research has shown, increases in stress over a long period result in reduced immunity, higher risks of infection, higher rates of depression, and a greater incidence of cardiovascular diseases.

Some people are at greater risk of victimization than others, as discussed in Chapter 10. Socio-demographic correlates of fear reflect the actual risk of victimization, or "vulnerability." Donnelly (1988) suggests that there are two kinds of vulnerability. "Physical vulnerability refers to a person's openness to attack and powerlessness to resist." On the other hand, "social vulnerability" refers to "the daily threat of victimization and an inability to cope with the economic and physical consequences of victimization."

Fearfulness has a loose relationship with actual risk. Researchers suggest three characteristics of lower-income neighbourhoods that may explain why residents are more fearful of crime. First, lower-income residents are more likely to see areas outside of their immediate block as foreign—outside their experience and control—and therefore fear those areas. A second factor is that lower-income communities have more diverse populations than higher-income neighbourhoods. Because of the diversity, residents are more likely to live among people whose lifestyles are different from their own. Third, less-educated and lower-income people are more vulnerable to the costs of victimization. They cannot afford to be deprived of what little they own or deal easily with the costs of injury (e.g., missing days of paid work).

Many, for example, fear the effects of crack houses, halfway houses, treatment facilities, or prostitution in their neighbourhood. They fear these facilities and services may bring the "wrong kind of people" into the neighbourhood, endanger their family, and lower housing values. On the other hand, bear in mind that many criminal activities are carried out in discreet ways, below the level of public consciousness and without any effect on their everyday lives.

Social integration (or organization) reduces these fears in three ways. First, integration reduces the proportion of strangers (as opposed to acquaintances) in the area; it increases familiarity. Familiarity, as we have seen throughout this book, always reduces fear and ignorance. Second, integration makes a larger number of networks with which people may associate themselves available; this association makes them feel safer. Finally, integration makes the everyday routines and lifestyles of others in the neighbourhood seem less strange—again, giving people the sense of security that comes with familiarity. Social organization means that people have ties to one another within the community. The longer people remain in the community, the stronger the local social bonds and the larger the membership in neighbourhood organizations.

In less integrated communities, most people learn about crimes through the mass media. By sensationalizing stories, the mass media create fears of crime that inflate actual risks. Reports of property crime fuel fears of violent crime, or vice versa. It is not the total number of crime stories that affects fear of crime but rather the proportion of crime stories in which the crimes are local, random, and sensational. If random and sensational crimes occur in a person's own locality, they induce fear. If they occur in other areas, people feel less fear and feel safe by comparison.

Time to Reflect: How would you account for the weak correlation between the amount of crime in a neighbourhood or community and the amount of fear people have about criminal victimization?

One result of fear about the risks of crime is that neighbourhoods do not want ex-convicts around. This can have a negative effect on programs that try to integrate people with criminal records into community life. As noted, a fear of crime can inhibit normal social interaction and alter everyday routines. In the end, this fear works against the rehabilitation and reintegration of convicted criminals and against public safety. It may also produce a fearful punitive atmosphere and calls for capital punishment, more policing, or fewer civil liberties.

Economic Consequences

With the rise of online banking and purchasing, as well as the proliferation of debit and credit cards, identity theft and mass-marketing scams have increased dramatically throughout the country. Reports of identity fraud (see Box 8.4) are only very low estimates, given that most identity theft goes unreported. One academic study, using survey data, estimated 6.5 per cent of Canadians (1.7 million) experience some form of identity fraud each year, requiring 20 million hours and $150 million to resolve fraud-related issues (Thomson, 2008).

Like identity theft, mass-marketing fraud is a growing concern in Canada. While people joke about the now-notorious e-mails from self-identified Nigerian princes asking for financial assistance, "advance-fee frauds" are actually a very serious problem. RCMP reports suggest mass-marketing fraud costs the Canadian public approximately $10 billion each year. Moreover, organized criminal bodies undertake nearly 80 per cent of this fraud, and those groups are more difficult to pursue than individuals. The international nature of mass-marketing fraud—issues related to extradition and varying international standards—also creates problems in addressing these issues.

Non-violent economic crime is not always the result of a malevolent outsider or group victimizing an innocent stranger, however. One of the most widely practised yet least discussed non-violent crimes in North America is tax evasion. The Canadian Revenue Agency secured only 323 criminal convictions on tax fraud charges between 2008 and 2009, imposing $29.2 million in fines. These convictions represent only a drop in the bucket of all tax evaders. In the United States, the Internal Revenue Service claims that 18–19 per cent of all income goes unreported, creating a "tax gap" in that country of nearly $500 billion (Feige and Cebula, 2011). General public ambivalence towards governments and taxation and an "everybody's doing it" attitude surely are at the core of the ubiquity of tax evasion.

Illegal sharing of movie and music files has become a very common form of non-violent crime. The motion picture and music industries have claimed that their recent financial problems are directly related to what industry representatives and the media call "piracy." The International Federation of the Phonographic Industry, a transnational body for the protection of record companies, reports that piracy has led directly to a 30 per cent decline in global music sales since 2004. Major American movie studios claimed to have lost $18.2 billion to piracy in 2005, a number the industry believes will only increase in time (LEK, 2005). Non-violent crime takes many forms and finds many victims, whether those victims are individuals, governments, or corporations.

Social Policy Implications

Given the role of poverty and economic inequality in fostering crime, it seems likely that reducing poverty and the gap between rich and poor would help reduce some forms of crime and delinquency.

If so, we need to create new jobs and to provide job training to people who lack satisfactory job skills. The jobs people receive must pay a living wage so that people can support their families. Further, there should be more investment in the institutions that prepare people for productive roles in society: at work, in families, and in schools. Failures in educational and family roles contribute to the inability of many young people to find and use legitimate job opportunities. Though difficult, it is easier to prevent crime by improving families and schools than by rehabilitating criminals with an ingrained criminal lifestyle.

Arresting people who commit crimes at least temporarily reduces the likelihood they will commit crimes again. While in custody, they cannot endanger the rest of society. Policing is important, and the police need resources and technology to do their job effectively. Increasingly, technology is playing an important role in the policing of crime. The growing international concern about electronic fraud and computer-related crime calls for more education and technological development in this area.

At the same time, technology has made a host of new crimes possible and has opened new avenues in which traditional crimes, such as fraud, can flourish. Electronic money laundering is one example. The illegal electronic transfer of funds challenges the legal system to develop new laws and adopt new strategies for coping with electronic crime.

Governments are working together to further the fight against **e-crime/cybercrime**. Its international scope and technological complexity have prompted several agencies to call for new resources and approaches to law enforcement. The RCMP and the Canadian Security Intelligence Service (CSIS) are among them. However, Canada's police forces and security agencies may lack the essential skills, technology, and personnel to meet the growing threat posed by computer-related crime.

Future Trends

Crime is not increasing in Canada; if anything, it is decreasing. This decrease is not because Canadians are becoming more virtuous, self-controlled, or prosperous but because Canadians are getting older. According to criminologist Peter Carrington (2001):

> all types of crime are forecast to decline, due to the continuing aging of the Canadian population. The overall recorded crime rate is expected to fall to 85 per cent of its 1999 level by 2026 and to 81 per cent by 2041. Recorded rates of

> crimes that are characteristic of teenagers and young adults, such as robbery and break and enter, should decrease slightly faster and farther; whereas crimes that are more characteristic of older adults . . . should be affected less by the aging of the population.

As we increasingly become an "information society," crime will raise the focus on the theft and abuse of information. However, police agencies will increasingly use new technology to detect crime and pursue the offenders.

The growing use of information technology (IT) has already had a marked effect on society and on crime. Information about ways to invade electronic systems—data, financial, or security systems, for example—is available more easily to more people. Besides providing great opportunities for crime involving technology, information communication technologies are providing better resources for law enforcers to fight crime.

Technology has made it possible to keep registries, reorganize law enforcement, and use high-tech gadgets that help keep unlawful acts under control. Technologies are revolutionizing police work, just as they are revolutionizing crime. In short, modern IT is fundamental to the commission—but also the detection, prevention, and control—of new forms of high-tech financial crime (McQuade, 2001). Again, it is hard to predict whether crime will increase—only that it will change and policing will change with it.

Globalization, too, is affecting technology, commerce, communication, and crime. Already, crimes on the Internet, drug dealing, and smuggling show the attraction of global crime and the difficulty this poses for national law enforcement. People who commit transnational crimes often live outside the jurisdiction of nations where the crime occurs; or other governments do not co-operate in apprehending them. This calls for integrating law enforcement agencies and introducing new technologies that strengthen the global interconnectedness of police and other law enforcement bodies.

Crime reaches further today than ever before. Once again, it is hard to tell whether globalization will increase crime or simply change the nature, scope, and scale of criminal operations. Thus, it seems likely that fraud, impersonation, and extortion will increase in the future; more crime will be committed outside national jurisdictions; and theft will increase—especially, theft focused on electronic services. Though demographic forces (chiefly, population aging) conspire to reduce crime, as Carrington has argued, technological forces work in the opposite direction, creating a wide range of new criminal opportunities. Law enforcement and the judicial systems alone will not be enough to combat new and more sophisticated forms of transnational crime.

As crime detection improves through advances in forensic science, criminals will find new ways of covering their tracks. Some may find high-tech ways of leaving false tracks leading away from a crime scene, while others resort to more drastic ways of destroying the crime scene altogether, through arson or explosives. Fraud—on the Internet and otherwise—will become the most common offence, being used for financial gain or to get information (e.g., identity theft).

The future of money, in its current physical (cash) form, will also have a major impact on crime. The criminal economy largely runs on the anonymity of cash—and the larger the denomination of banknotes, the easier criminal transactions become. With the increasing use of virtual cash in the form of credit cards and smart cards, some believe physical cash may eventually disappear, perhaps to be replaced by alternative anonymous forms of transactions. Others believe that "smarter" currency, such as the encoding of information on new plastic $100 and $50 bills, may replace our current money to minimize counterfeiting. Crime may have to concentrate on the electronic realm, where different, better detection methods will be necessary.

Corporate crime has serious economic, political, and even ideological effects, which is why the state has traditionally intervened in private business. However, in the past 15 years, responsibility and culpability for harmful practices have been redefined. As industries have been deregulated, risk management has taken the place of regulatory enforcement. Corporate crime has become normalized with the decline of the nation-state, an increase in failed and failing states, the growth of offshore banking centres, and the rise of global capitalism. This may continue.

Of all the changes that bear on the future of societies, and on the future of social problems, cyberspace, and the information that resides there, has had the greatest impact. One growing crime of the future is the theft of intellectual property. Today, the Internet shapes the relationship between consumers, producers, and knowledge, changing the way we view information and changing the relations of its production.

The result is the creation of worldwide virtual communities—communities of interest and shared viewpoints that are unhampered by distance or by traditional social barriers such as age, race, gender, and class. Not only does the Internet ease information sharing, commerce, and social support, it also allows people to create and try out new identities. People are able to stalk others on the Internet, to enjoy Internet sex or cybersexual affairs, and to spread false information about themselves and others. Also, the Internet enables people to sell fraudulent identities and products more easily than if they had to persuade customers face-to-face.

Conclusion

Within the bounds of the Criminal Code are many different kinds of crime. Widespread agreement in Canadian society—and in most other societies—is that violent crimes are wrong and should be harshly punished. In contrast, most agree that non-violent crimes are wrong but they do not wish to debate or increase the severity of punishments.

Despite biases in reporting, criminologists know enough about crime to permit several conclusions. As Statistics Canada has noted, "The police-reported crime rate, which measures the overall volume of crime, continued its long-term downward trend in 2010, declining 5 per cent from 2009. At the same time, the Crime Severity Index, which measures the severity of crime, fell 6 per cent . . . . The Crime Severity Index reached its lowest point (82.7) since 1998, the first year for which Index data are available" (www.statcan.gc.ca/daily-quotidien/110721/dq110721b-eng.htm). This does not mean society is moving towards an idyllic, crime-free state. Like the poor, crime will always be with us. Crimes committed for gain—for example, drug peddling, solicitation for prostitution, illegal gambling, and extortion—are often tied (however indirectly) to organized crime. On the other hand, a great deal of street crime is petty and amateur, not professional, much less organized.

Criminals, as we have seen, tend to be young, poor men, although the exact relationship between these demographic variables and criminal behaviour is complex and poorly understood. As we have suggested, the connection is probably a result of the interaction of economic, social, and cultural variables. As we will see in Chapter 12, preventing crime is probably easier than rehabilitating criminals, but doing so will require a re-conceptualization of our social order.

Finally, we have noted throughout this chapter that there is an important, and obvious, link between criminals and their victims. Most (though not all) crimes have victims; and most victimization (though not all) is a result of recognizably criminal behaviour. This raises interesting questions about the typical relationship between criminals and their victims; and it demands that we frame theories about victimization that are clearly connected to our theories about criminality. This we will do in Chapter 10. However, in the next chapter, we discuss a type of crime that is, in some respects, similar to corporate crime: crime committed by the powerful against the powerless.

Questions for Critical Thought

1. In what respects are non-violent crimes likely to be different from violent crimes in terms of causes and effects?
2. Brainstorm the different roles the mass media and the government can play in reducing the fear of crime among citizens.
3. To what extent does poverty play a role in producing crime? Discuss different methods that can be used to counter the effects poverty has on crime.
4. Critical theorists see capitalism as the root of the crime problem. Discuss how the levels of non-violent crime may be diminished within a capitalist society.
5. How would you rate the effectiveness of the penal system? Recommend changes that would make the system more effective.
6. Is it feasible to ask that top executives be held personally accountable for crimes that the corporation commits? Apart from financial ramification, is there any other way to hold corporations accountable for their crimes?

Recommended Readings

Haggerty, Kevin D., and Richard V. Ericson, eds. 2005. *The New Politics of Surveillance and Visibility*. Toronto: University of Toronto Press.

This collection of articles focuses on the theory of surveillance and visibility; the role of police and military surveillance; and the interplay of surveillance, electronic media, and consumer culture. The ideas of privacy, identity, and personhood are being redefined without democratic accountability.

Peterson, Ruth D., Lauren J. Krivo, and John Hagan. 2006. *The Many Colors of Crime: Inequalities of Race, Ethnicity, and Crime in America*. New York: New York University Press.

Race and ethnicity are central organizing principles in determining why, how, where, and by whom crimes are committed and enforced. They even condition the laws that make certain behaviours criminal and the responses to laws and crime that make some behaviours (and people) more likely to be defined as criminal.

Rapping, Elayne. 2003. *Law and Justice as Seen on TV*. New York: New York University Press.

Television plays to a popular fascination with law and justice, crime and punishment. As the author shows, this promotes a conservative (or fearful) attitude towards the "criminalization" of American life. Law-related television shapes the way Americans (and even Canadians) perceive justice, criminals, courts, and the law in general, promoting a distrust of those who work to rehabilitate and free criminals.

Simon, David R., and Frank E. Hagan. 1999. *White-Collar Deviance*. Boston: Allyn and Bacon.

This book discusses a new conceptualization of the terms *elite deviance*, *white-collar crime*, and *economic crime*. It includes both criminal and non-criminal deviance by individuals and organizations, as well as the conduct of the elite and non-elite.

Recommended Websites

Criminal Intelligence Service Canada

www.cisc.gc.ca/

This website contains comprehensive information regarding organized crime in Canada. The agency has released the *2010 Report on Organized Crime*, which highlights how organized crime affects our daily lives and what actions are being taken to reduce organized crime.

Facts about Organized Crime in Canada

http://www.cisc.gc.ca/annual_reports/annual_report_2007/document/annual_report_2007_e.pdf

This brief summary of the issues surrounding organized crime in Canada is from the archives of Public Safety Canada. Providing basic information on government policy regarding policing and prevention, this is a suitable introduction to the topic of Canadian organized crime.

National Crime Prevention Strategy

http://www.publicsafety.gc.ca/prg/cp/ncps-eng.aspx

This website has a comprehensive list of documents and research data available in its research and evaluation section. The purpose of the website is part of a greater government initiative to curb reactive responses to crime in favour of early intervention to prevent crime and victimization.

Corporate Crime Reporter

corporatecrimereporter.com/

The *Corporate Crime Reporter* is a quarter-century-old legal newspaper that discusses all manner of corporate crime and fraud. This publication is a very useful resource for studying corporate crime in America, as the website includes not only articles but also an extensive collection of interviews with legislators and jurists.

"Combating White Collar Crime in Canada: Serving Victim Needs and Market Integrity"

www.policecouncil.ca/reports/Kempa_Combating%20White%20Collar%20Crime%20in%20Canada_Kempa.pdf

This paper, written by Michael Kempa, a Professor of Criminology at the University of Ottawa, provides a recent (2009) interpretation of the state of white-collar and corporate crime in Canada. Researchers will find Kempa's three-page bibliography particularly helpful.

Recommended Movies

The Untouchables, **Dir. Brian De Palma (1987)**

Brian De Palma and screenwriter David Mamet based this critically acclaimed film on the 1960s television series of the same name. In Prohibition-era Chicago, federal agent Elliot Ness finds an underground economy dominated by crime boss Al Capone and a local police department unwilling to intervene in the alcohol black market. Despite the film's placement in the 1930s, its messages about underground economies and institutional corruption remain relatable.

Casino Jack, **Dir. George Hickenlooper (2010)**

Though a film of only middling quality, *Casino Jack* takes on the important issue of political ties to organized crime. Based on the experiences of Washington "super-lobbyist" Jack Abramoff, the film depicts Abramoff's teaming with businessman Michael Scanlon and their subsequent foray into shaping American governmental policy. The pair's ties to the Mob prove their ultimate undoing, however, recalling the role of organized crime in the careers of other twentieth-century politicians.

The Grifters, **Dir. Stephen Frears (1990)**

Frears followed up his wildly successful adaptation of *Dangerous Liaisons* (1988) with this punchy adaptation of Jim Thompson's 1963 classic pulp novel. The film trails the activities of a triumvirate of cons (two women, one man) who work in an uneasy alliance, fighting off evident sexual tension. Anjelica Huston received an Oscar nomination for her role in this excellent film noir, bringing enormous charm and nuance to her hustler character.

The Corporation, **Dir. Mark Achbar (2003)**

A critically acclaimed documentary look at the paradox of "business ethics," this film applies psychiatric and investigative techniques to examining a series of corporate case studies. Achbar eventually determines that corporations, which are becoming ever more powerful in modern society, regularly act immorally, leading to an amorality more generally among all of big business.

9 Political Crimes

Learning Objectives

- To understand the different forms of political deviance
- To examine corruption as a social problem
- To evaluate political crimes from a sociological perspective
- To learn the ways that political crimes affect social cohesion
- To understand some of the causes and outcomes of terrorism
- To understand the social, health, and psychological consequences of warfare

Introduction

This chapter is about rule-breaking by people with political goals or political power. Within this context, we also examine the creation of political crimes—the attachment of labels of deviance to people for their roles in political conflicts.

Many such political crimes take place during wars, and for this reason we will have occasion to discuss war repeatedly. At no point in recorded history has there been a complete absence of war. From this, it would be safe to assume that as long as people are around, war will be, too. Discussion, debate, protest, **rebellion**, and war are different ways of conducting political conflict, along a spectrum from peaceful to violent. War between nations is the largest-scale, most extreme version of political conflict. Civil wars and acts of **terrorism** are geographically limited versions of the same thing. So, by understanding war—its causes and effects—we can understand more about protest, rebellion, and other forms of deviant political conflict.

However, the problem of politicized labelling involves more than wars. Governments themselves commit "deviant," even criminal, acts. Most people would consider Hitler a war criminal, though he was the legal head of the German state when he committed his crimes against humanity. This problem came to the fore once again in a recent court case that tried Charles Taylor for crimes against humanity (Box 9.1).

As the example of Liberia's Charles Taylor suggests, the evaluation of political crime is difficult—mainly because it implies a comparative cross-national or historical focus. The unit of analysis is the state or society, and comparing societies inevitably raises complex methodological issues. First, there is the problem of deciding what kinds of "political crimes" to measure—that is, how many "actual events" need explaining. Second, there is the question of whether the society's legal authorities have recorded (let alone arrested, charged, or convicted people for) these political crimes. Typically, legal action against political criminals is least likely when the rule-breakers are highly placed in society. Third, it is difficult to find the victims of political crimes, or those who survived, and to get them to admit or report a crime against them. Thus, at each stage, errors are introduced into the data, making the comparison of societies difficult.

Corruption

The simplest form of political crime is **corruption**. Corruption includes a wide variety of activities, especially bribery, patronage, and fraud. *Bribery* is the payment of money or favours to an official for special consideration in the application of formal rules. *Patronage* is giving special consideration—including handing out contracts or jobs—to people based on friendship, kinship, or the expectation of favours in return. *Fraud* is any use of deception or false pretense for purposes of self-enrichment.

Political corruption is not supposed to happen in modern democratic societies, for several reasons. First, modern societies are bureaucratic, and bureaucracies are supposed to make honest, efficient use of resources. Usually, corruption is not efficient. In his classic analysis of **bureaucracy** as an ideal type, Max Weber distinguishes between bureaucratic and pre-bureaucratic forms of organization, such as patrimony or clientelism. Weber argues that bureaucracy arises historically as an organizational form precisely because patrimony and other forms are inefficient. Because of this inefficiency, pre-modern armies lose battles, businesses go bankrupt, and governments make wasteful or illegal decisions. Because

Current Events

BOX 9.1

Judging the Cost of Human Life

International judges sentenced former Liberian President Charles Taylor to 50 years in prison on 30 May 2012, saying he was responsible for "some of the most heinous and brutal crimes recorded in human history" by arming and supporting Sierra Leone rebels in return for "blood diamonds." The Special Court for Sierra Leone had convicted Taylor a month earlier on 11 charges of aiding and abetting the rebels who went on a brutal rampage during that country's decade-long war that ended in 2002 with more than 50,000 dead.

The 64-year-old warlord-turned-president is the first former head of state convicted by an international war crimes court since World War II, and judges said they had no precedent when deciding his sentence. Taylor will serve his sentence in a British jail. His lawyers, however, said they will appeal his convictions and that will likely keep him in a jail in The Hague, Netherlands, for months.

Prosecutor Brenda Hollis also said she was considering an appeal to extend the sentence. "It is important in our view that those responsible for criminal misconduct on a massive scale are not given a volume discount," Ms. Hollis said. "The sentence that was imposed today does not replace amputated limbs. It does not bring back those who were murdered," she said. "It does not heal the wounds of those who were victims of sexual violence and does not remove the permanent emotional and psychological and physical scars of those enslaved or recruited as child soldiers. . . . The purposely cruel and savage crimes committed included public executions and amputations of civilians, the display of decapitated heads at checkpoints, the killing and public disembowelment of a civilian whose intestines were then stretched across the road to make a check point, public rapes of women and girls, and people burned alive in their homes," Ms. Hollis wrote in a brief appealing for a 80-year sentence.

Prosecutors argued there was no reason for leniency, given the extreme nature of the crimes and Taylor's "greed" and misuse of his position of power.

Source: Adapted from Mike Corder, Associated Press, "Ex-Liberian President Charles Taylor Sentenced to 50 Years in Prison," *Globe and Mail*, 30 May 2012.

bureaucracy is a superior organizational form, owing to its greater efficiency, it supplants earlier forms. From this standpoint, corruption is a step backward organizationally.

Second, along similar lines, modern societies are founded (in principle) on scientific rationality, the rule of law, and democratic participation. These concepts distinguish modern societies from feudal and tribal-based societies. From this standpoint, corruption is a return to pre-modern practices. It favours a few interest groups or interested individuals—for example, financial contributors to the ruling political party or one's ethnic group (in the case of political leaders)—over everyone else.

Some might say that "particularism" in government decision-making is unavoidable and makes sense. At least people know whom they are favouring, and why. As well, people know that if they work for a particular party, they will be rewarded. Political systems that run on friendship—that is, on patronage and corruption—work consistently. As sociologist Robert Merton (1957 [1938]) showed in an early work on city politics, systems that run against patronage, on supposed universalistic principles, usually fail to meet their stated goals. They are far less predictable because they cannot reward and keep their supporters.

As the data in Figure 9.1 show, people in different societies have different degrees of tolerance for public corruption—specifically, bribery. Some accept the practice with resignation, while others resist it and seek to eliminate it. The World Values Survey, measuring the acceptance of public bribery on a scale from 1 to 10, shows considerable variation in the Western industrial nations, including Canada. The variation is even wider in non-Western, less-developed societies. Respondents were asked to judge whether accepting a bribe is "never justifiable" (rated 1), "always justifiable" (rated 10), or somewhere in between.

Russia is one of the most odious offenders, and the acceptance of corruption by the Russian people is having dire results on the success of post-Communist government. The prevalence of corruption there has reached a new phase of normalization. According to one poll conducted by Transparency International, two-thirds of the Russian people accept corruption as a normal part of economic and political life. Faced with these facts, the Russian president not only has avoided taking serious action against corruption but has even refused to discuss the subject. Yet, corruption hurts small businesses and foreign investors, siphons money to foreigners that is needed for growth inside the country, and destroys the legitimacy and structure of the state. The same is true in a country like Afghanistan, which has undergone extreme turmoil for the past generation and where, arguably, corruption is viewed as simply the cost of doing business with officialdom (see Figure 9.2).

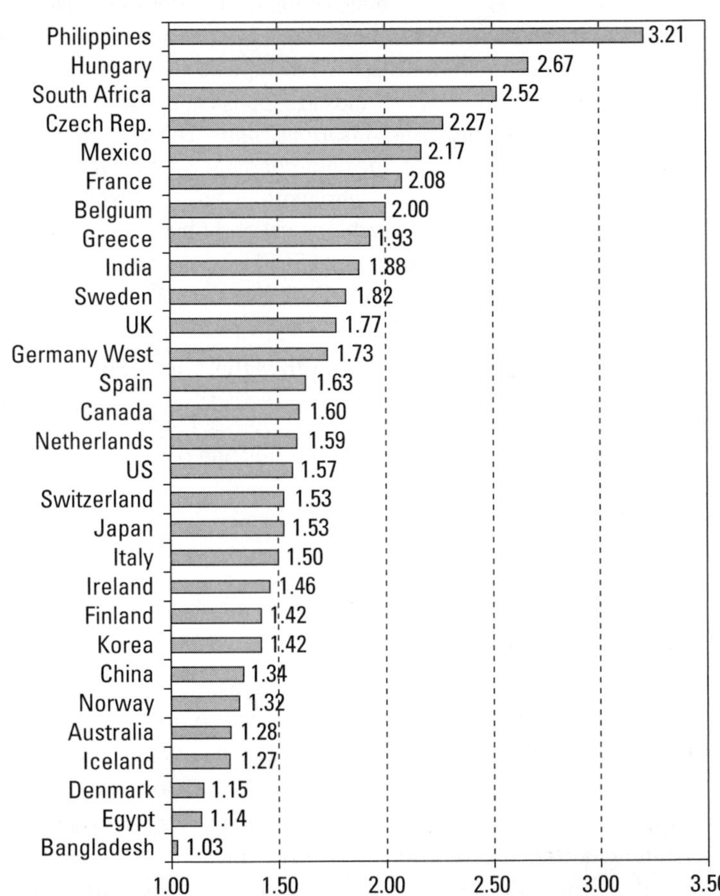

FIGURE 9.1 The Justifiability of Accepting a Bribe, Selected Countries

Note: Based on a scale of 1 to 10, where 1 = "never justifiable" and 10 = "always justifiable."
Source: Adapted from <micpohling.wordpress.com/2007/06/07/world-morale-someone-accepting-bribe/>.

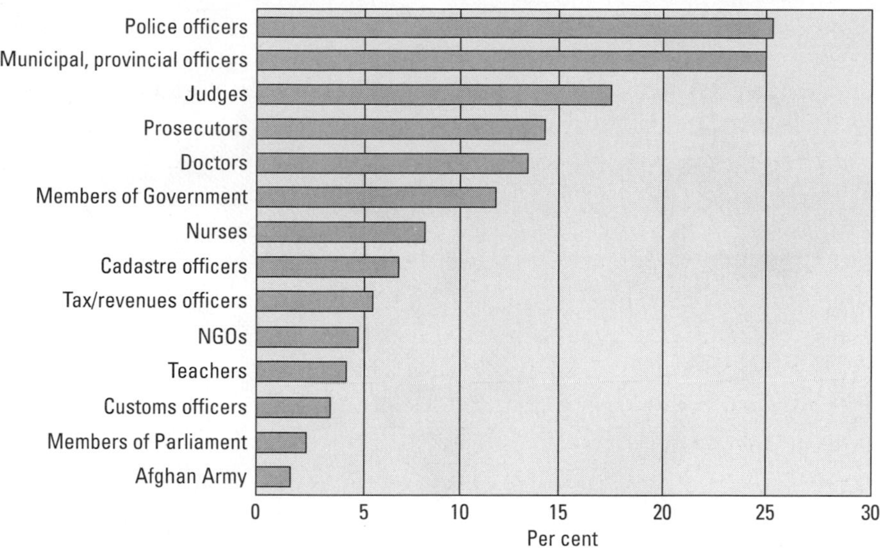

FIGURE 9.2 Percentage of Adult Population Who Paid at least One Bribe during the Last 12 Months, Afghanistan 2010, by Type of Public Official Requesting Bribe

Source: United Nations Office on Drugs and Crime, *Corruption in Afghanistan: Bribery as Reported by the Victims* (Jan. 2010), at: <www.unodc.org/documents/afghanistan/Anti-Corruption/Corruption_in_Afghanistan_Bribery_Reported_by_Victims_2010-Eng.pdf>, 25, Figure 9.

Political corruption is found worldwide and works at the highest levels of society, infiltrating global politics and economics. Only the extent of corruption varies from one society to another. Transparency International makes annual ratings of the business climate in different countries to assess the political honesty versus corruption. In the last few years, TI was able to put corruption on the worldwide policy agenda by calling attention to its widespread prevalence. Currently, Canada ranks sixth best on the scale of perceived corruption and ranks slightly below Denmark, New Zealand, Singapore, Finland, and Sweden—which are perceived as being less corrupt.

The least corruption is experienced by citizens living in countries with (1) high levels of economic development, (2) high levels of economic freedom, (3) long exposure to democracy, (4) a unitary (non-federal) structure, (5) Protestant traditions, and (6) a British legal culture. As the mapped data in Figure 9.3 show, political corruption—or at least perceived political corruption—is concentrated in the poorest societies of the southern hemisphere (i.e., in Africa and South America). As mentioned, corruption is high in Russia and the former Soviet republics. By contrast, political corruption is thought to be much less in North America, Australia, New Zealand, and Northern and Western Europe.

Treason

States and ruling classes use various methods to keep people from resisting or opposing the current ways of doing things. Considering the tendency for people to feel uncomfortable about violating the simplest social rules—for example, rules of table etiquette—imagine how hard it is to resist the demands of the state. Imagine, for example, marching in protest

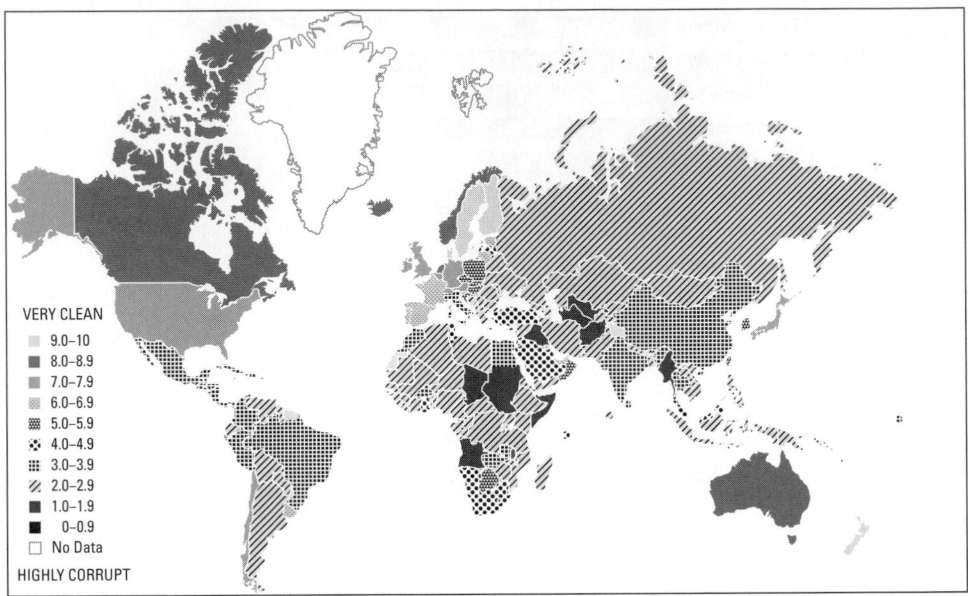

FIGURE 9.3 Corruption Perceptions Index: 2010 Results

Source: Transparency International, at: <www.transparency.org/policy_research/surveys_indices/cpi/2010/results>.

against a government policy or siding with an unpopular group of citizens. Some people do so, nonetheless, even under conditions of extreme danger, as has recently occurred in Egypt, Libya, Syria, and elsewhere in the Middle East and North Africa.

To protest the state's actions may seem impossible and useless. It may seem abnormal—crazy—to some, even to people we know and respect. In short, resisting institutions of power in our society demands unusual courage and a strong sense of *agency*—the ability to overcome internal and external obstacles and to act on our beliefs. However, the state usually fights back against those who protest. Sometimes they are even accused of, and charged with, treason—the state's strongest weapon against protest. *Treason* is a label given by the state to those acts that oppose its goals to the point of seeking to overthrow the government. In principle, criminalizing opposition to the state preserves social and political stability. Yet, when held in the wrong hands, the law against treason can be an instrument of despotism and terror—especially when states are unstable and rulers are willing to act despotically to secure their power.

> **Time to Reflect:** Why is political protest hampered, channelled, and sometimes even criminalized in democratic societies like Canada? Use the example of police treatment of protestors at the G20 conference in Toronto in 2010.

At the end of the political spectrum from corrupt politicians who use their power in

Current Events

BOX 9.2

The UK Expenses Scandal

The Great Expenses Scandal of 2009 in Great Britain included shocking and outrageous anecdotes, such as the use of taxpayers' money to fund the dredging of a moat around one MP's country estate, the building of a lavish house meant to accommodate another's ducks, and finally, the purchase of pornographic films by another. Other ridiculous expense claims made by MPs included non-existent mortgages, gardening, piano-tuning, pet food, pool maintenance, and bedding and upholstery. What made this abuse of parliamentary expenses all the more disturbing were the assertions put forward by MPs stating that they felt themselves to be perfectly justified in claiming these expenses.

The drama of 2009 has generated concern among Canadians that this sort of abuse could be committed in Canada, and certainly some abuses by Canadian cabinet ministers have come to light recently: the Defence Minister commandeering a military search-and-rescue helicopter to pick him up from his vacation retreat; the International Co-operation Minister switching her London hotel accommodations from a swanky five-star hotel to an even swankier hotel. However, several differences between the British and Canadian systems make gross abuses of office less unlikely than in the British case. First, the Canadian House of Commons deals far more strictly with expenses than Westminster. Second, Canadian MPs earn $157, 731 per year, while British MPs earn the considerably smaller salary of $100,000. The higher incomes received by Canadian MPs make them less likely than those in Britain to turn to their expense allowances in order to cover their personal costs. Third, British MPs bear the financial weight of housing costs that their Canadian counterparts do not. In order to cover these costs, British MPs are provided with a "second-home" allowance worth roughly $40,000 per year, since it is believed that each requires residences both in their home constituency and in London near Parliament. This allowance is thus meant to assist British politicians in paying for their living accommodations, and permits them to claim expenses on second homes. The 2009 scandal essentially arose because of the vague rules governing this allowance; the MPs felt it within their rights to claim the outrageous expenses discussed earlier.

Not surprisingly, this scandal has also stirred up a great deal of fervour among British citizens, and has generated considerable support for reform. Many feel that the British Parliament should be remodelled based on North American systems, with fixed-term parliaments, a fully elected upper chamber, and a written constitution in the manner of the US. However, others believe that the problem lies with the people committing these offences, rather than with the system that allows them to do so.

Sources: *Vancouver Sun*/Canada.com, at: <www.canada.com/story_print.html?id=de977e31-2572-4043-91f3-ee701215b340&sponsor=>; Alex Massie, "Expense Account; London's Reform Plan: Copy Congress," *The American Conservative*, 8 Aug. 2009.

self-interested ways, there are powerless people who run the greatest personal risks to live according to moral principles. Consider draft dodgers. Sociologist John Hagan (2002) analyzed the lives of Americans who, like himself, resisted the Vietnam War draft by "dodging" and "deserting" military service. Some viewed these expatriates as traitors, and, had they returned to the US, they would have been imprisoned. In the late 1970s, they finally were granted amnesty. However, in the largest political exodus from the US since the American Revolution, during the 1960s and early 1970s more than 50,000 young Americans migrated to Canada. Once in Canada, these selective service and military "criminals"—these "traitors"—were assimilated as new Canadians, becoming unexpected symbols of Canadian sovereignty.

It was no small thing for the Canadian state to go against American wishes on this matter, yet Canada had the courage to do so. Many of these new Canadians remained in Canada and contributed to their adopted country in important ways; some felt an ambivalent citizenship and even today are less likely than average to participate politically by voting in Canadian federal elections; some returned to the US.

Riots and Collective Protests

Riots are another type of protest against authority. Riots can be a form of political protest that suggests grassroots dissatisfaction with the government, and sometimes riots related to sporting events break out, as happened in Vancouver in 2011 after the Canucks lost in the Stanley Cup final, and more than a half-century earlier, the famous Richard Riot occurred in Montreal after Canadiens' star Maurice Richard was suspended for the season and the playoffs following an altercation with an on-ice official. Of course, soccer riots have been an all-too-common occurrence in Africa, Asia, and Europe for many years, at times resulting in many deaths. Emotional, violent, and localized collective behaviours, *riots* have outcomes that are unplanned and unpredictable because they are undirected.

In Canada, riots have been a relatively uncommon form of political expression, compared with Europe and Latin America. Exceptions to this rule include the Winnipeg General Strike of 1919 and the G20 riots in Toronto in 2010. This relative tranquility has something to do with the control exercised by police in Canada: riots need aggressive protestors and police that are even more aggressive. Research shows a tendency towards softer, more tolerant policing of protest in Western democracies. From this standpoint, police behaviour at the 1997 Asia-Pacific Economic Co-operation (APEC) summit in Vancouver (where Canada hosted rulers of less democratic regimes in a ritual celebration of economic globalization) was an exception to this rule. There, in the face of protests about undemocratic regimes elsewhere, especially against the Sukarno regime in Indonesia, the Canadian government and police used harsh tactics popularly believed to be more characteristic of those other regimes.

Riots have been far more common in the United States, particularly in connection with youth protest, black–white relations, and racial discrimination. During the 1960s, urban rioting in the United States was an enormous concern because it resulted in the destruction of much private and public property, looting, and civil disorder. Research on rioting then concluded that rioting both expresses social tensions and reflects weak or inadequate external control.

Usually, such rioting is set off by an incident involving the police in a minority neighbourhood, where some actual or believed violation of accepted police practice has taken place. Social control starts to break down and some people see the opportunity for looting. If, at this point, order is not restored, the riot moves into a third stage that includes arson, gunfire, and harsh countermeasures by the police and militia. In short, the violence intensifies on both sides.

Though North American protest movements today are less violent and smaller in scope than in the 1960s, demonstrations continue in various locations around the world, and protesting has become an accepted way of expressing dissatisfaction with social affairs. In 2005, and again in 2007, riots based on race and class erupted in the northern suburbs of Paris, where many Arabs, blacks, and other ethnic minorities live in poor housing, largely isolated from the rest of society. They continue to experience high rates of unemployment, feel ignored and disenfranchised, and view the police as indifferent if not active enemies.

Much debate in sociology centres on the degree of social structuring in riots. Generally, researchers conclude that some kinds of people are more likely than others to participate, and often the participants are linked to one another by **social ties** as well as by shared motives. A large fraction of the community is likely to get involved—especially young men. Often, people cannot say exactly why they are rioting, or they express their motives in overly general terms of dissatisfaction. The mass media may also play a role in the riots, spreading the rationalizations and symbols of identification that rioters come to use.

Torture

There has been increasing concern in recent years about the use of torture by both governments and their opponents—as both a means of punishment and a means of threat or persuasion. Increasingly, therefore, we are coming to view torture as an important political crime.

The word *torture* comes from the Latin word meaning "to twist" or "to wring"—as in twisting someone's arm behind their back until they comply with your wishes. The goal of torture is to inflict severe physical (or mental) pain. Sometimes this is done as a goal in itself, to punish for a past misdeed. Sometimes it is done to drag information out of the tortured person.

Torture has been outlawed by the Geneva Conventions on warfare and widely criticized by organizations such as Amnesty International. Yet, many developed countries still use torture in warfare to extort information or to punish misdeeds. Here, once again, the United States has played a leading role. The torture used by American troops against prisoners at Abu Ghraib prison in Iraq and at Guantanamo in Cuba has been widely publicized now, thanks to photographs supplied by some of the torturers themselves and to information supplied by people who survived or escaped from these places. What's more, it has become clear that torture is not only a casual, brutal activity practised by overzealous guards. It is part of a standard interrogation and imprisonment policy devised by the CIA and the US Department of Defense.

However, the United States is not alone in its use of torture. Other advanced, supposedly liberal societies have used torture, especially against political prisoners. A prime example is the alleged use of torture by British forces against the insurgents in Northern Ireland in the second half of the twentieth century. As in Iraq, Afghanistan, Syria, and other societies where torture has been used, the torture of Irish rebels—or *terrorists*, as they were called—was justified through the argument that national security demanded the sternest measures—the reason provided being that any steps can and should be taken to extort information from terrorists if it will save the lives of British, American, or other more highly valued soldiers and civilians.

This rationale, that savage and extreme means are justified if the goal—safety—is just, also was used to justify dropping atomic bombs on Hiroshima and Nagasaki in 1945. More recently, Canadian police wielding

Tasers have used it to justify the ostensibly unintentional killings of civilians. Where torture and death are not the immediate goal of such actions, they are viewed as merely regrettable by-products of the need to keep order. Most incidents of torture today—for example, subjecting prisoners to "waterboarding" to simulate drowning—are intended and preventable.

Does torture work? Some think it does. However, the quality of information gained in this way is questionable. People will confess to almost anything if they are tortured. Often they will even provide false information; information gained from torture is always suspect and uncertain at best. In the long term, torture does not work. It erodes the tradition of rule of law and undermines civil liberties that are thought to distinguish our society from those we fight against. It tarnishes the reputation of the torturer and his or her society and inflames hatred against the hypocritical society that perpetrates this practice. So, in the end, the torturer pays a price for seeking information and compliance through causing pain (Sansani, 2004).

Sexual torture has been used against women as a technique of warfare and intimidation and is widely used in Africa today (for example, during warfare in the Congo, Somalia, and Sudan). However, the use of sexual torture is not limited to women. Using research collected by the Sexual Assault Investigation Team at the International Criminal Tribunal for the Former Yugoslavia (UCTY) in the mid-1990s, Carlson (2006) has found evidence of male sexual assaults during war—especially the infliction of blunt trauma to the male genitals. This largely invisible offence is widespread in several contexts around the world as a form of sexual torture against political prisoners and as a way of attacking prisoners sexually, emotionally, and politically.

Though torture likely was known to primitive and archaic societies, the use of state torture as a matter of policy became widespread as societies shifted from agrarian to industrial and advanced capitalist societies (Cohen and Corrado, 2005). Today, advanced liberal, capitalist states are more likely to employ state torture against the citizens of other countries and to engage private "security" (i.e., torture) organizations or surrogate countries (e.g., Syria) in which to carry out these forbidden activities.

The History of Protest, War, and Rebellion and Public Reactions

Most people consider *war* to be an armed conflict between two countries or two groups within a country. However, we can expand this definition to include undeclared battles, civil conflicts, guerrilla wars, covert operations, and even terrorism. In some countries, war even includes the use of military and police forces against the citizenry. Sociologists Francesca Cancian and James W. Gibson (1990) suggest that some countries can be said to possess a "war system," in which key social institutions—economies, governments, and even cultural practices—promote warfare as a normal and comprehensive aspect of their lives.

The most interesting thing to note about warfare is that, though the absolute numbers of dead have grown over the past five centuries or so—culminating in massive bloodshed during the twentieth century—the percentage of people killed in wars has diminished. In fact, a higher proportion of people were killed in pre-industrial warfare, before states as we know them today existed, than are killed in present-day wars. This is illustrated in Figure 9.4, which shows estimates of the proportion of adult males killed in different kinds of societies: tribal, pre-industrial, and state societies.

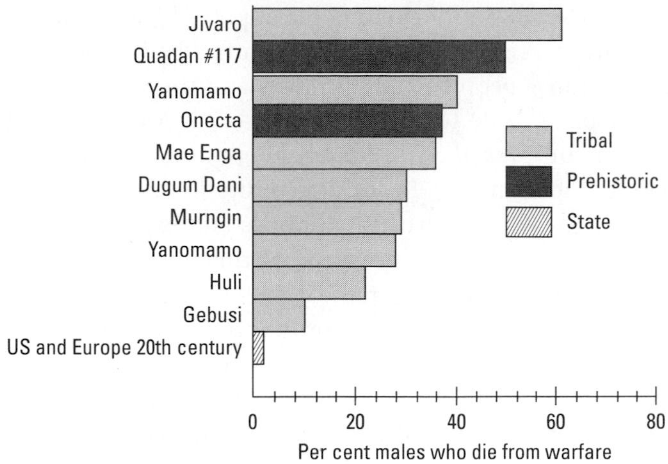

FIGURE 9.4 Male Deaths in Warfare

Source: Lawrence H. Keeley, *War Before Civilization: The Myth of the Peaceful Savage* (Oxford: Oxford University Press, 1996), accessed at: <en.wikipedia.org/wiki/War_Before_Civilization>.

The causes of war are many and complex, and seldom is a conflict fought for a single reason. One of the most common causes of war is a dispute over natural resources, such as land and oil. Another cause is a difference of ideological beliefs. World War II was in many ways a global conflict between democracy and fascism. The Cold War between the United States and Russia, roughly 1945–89, was a global conflict between capitalism and communism. Today, some even assert that conflict in the Middle East is a "clash of civilizations" between Christian West and Islamic East. Such conflicts are less likely to be resolved through negotiation or signing a peace treaty, since they are fought over fundamental beliefs that have not been harmonized.

Like nation-states pursuing their national goals through violence, terrorists are often motivated by ideological beliefs to commit acts of violence against those perceived to be the enemy, including civilians. Followers of the Muslim fundamentalist leader Sheik Omar Abdel Rahman, who considers the US oppressive and immoral, perpetrated the 1993 bombing of the World Trade Center in New York City, for example. Similarly, followers of Osama bin Laden carried out the destruction of the World Trade Center in 2001. It was only in 2011, a full 10 years later, that Osama bin Laden was killed by American troops in Pakistan.

As short a time as two centuries ago, most wars were small in absolute terms, fought on a local scale between neighbouring groups. With advances in military technology, war now can be waged between parties who are thousands of miles apart, such that the killers and the victims may never even see one another face to face. No wonder, then, that the twentieth century has been called the bloodiest 100 years in human history.

Wars have changed in other ways. Between 1500 and 1950, most wars were fought in Europe. Since then, most of the world's wars have been fought in economically developing (low-income) nations, even when European or North American states have been involved. Currently, dozens of military conflicts are active in the world, many of which are intra-national. As well, with terrorists increasingly targeting civilian populations rather than military stations, war zones have shifted from secluded outposts and isolated bases to crowded urban centres.

Violent Political Protest

As societies industrialize and (usually) become democratic, movements of political protest typically become less violent. Political protest continues in many forms, however, varying in duration, reasons for initiation, scope of activities, degree of engagement in collective violence, motivations of the participants, and means for mobilization for action. Some protests become violent, but in countries like Canada, violent political protests are uncommon. In that respect, the violence of the Front de libération du Québec (FLQ)—most widely remembered in connection with the October Crisis of 1970—was uncharacteristic.

The FLQ was a national terrorist group that wanted to see Quebec separate from Canada and set itself up as an independent nation. The group's actions first became violent during the 1960s, when they began bombing national symbols such as mailboxes and monuments in Quebec. Throughout the decade, as the frustration of radical Québécois nationalists grew, the bombings became more violent and sophisticated. In October 1970, members of the FLQ kidnapped visiting British trade official James Cross and provincial Labour Minister Pierre Laporte.

Those responsible for the kidnapping threatened to murder both Cross and Laporte unless their demands were met by the federal government—then under the leadership of Prime Minister Pierre Trudeau. These demands included a public broadcasting of an FLQ communiqué expressing their political belief that English-Canadian culture and American imperialism were overtaking Quebec culture. Trudeau and the federal government responded by imposing the War Measures Act, which allowed for the indefinite suspension of civil liberties. Laporte's body was eventually found in the trunk of a car, and shortly thereafter, the crisis was resolved when Cross was safely released in exchange for his kidnappers' safe exile to Cuba. Those involved in the killing of Laporte were tried and convicted for their crimes.

Ultimately, political protest has social and economic roots, reflecting a bad fit between people's cultural goals and the means available to achieve them—what Merton called *rebellion* in his typology of adaptations to anomie. In addition, protest typically accompanies frustrated hopes and expectations—indeed, expectations that may have been rising more rapidly than the means to satisfy them. However, protest is not merely a result of psychological excitement or ideological conviction; it has a practical side as well. Protest also requires resources and organization: cash, weapons, information technology, and co-operation from influential individuals, for example. Though some movements of protest are spontaneous, brief, and disorganized, most are planned and rooted in both formal and informal networks of social contact. The most developed form of social protest is exemplified by a revolution.

Revolution

Zimmermann (1983: 298) defined revolution as "the successful overthrow of the prevailing elite by a new elite who, after having taken over power, fundamentally change the social structure and therewith also the structure of authority."

Though revolutions are events of immense political and moral contradiction, and sometimes occasions for celebrating the heroic and the idealistic, they rarely achieve their original goals. Whatever their goals and high ideals, revolutions invariably substitute one form of restrictive power for another. They rarely replace despotism with a secure democracy, and often they replace one form of despotism with another. Even if they do not achieve their intended goals at home, revolutions affect other countries and the world as a whole. This was true of the French Revolution, the Russian Revolution, the Chinese Revolution, the Cuban Revolution, and many other smaller-scale revolutions.

Revolutions grow out of failed governments. Revolutionary crises in France, Russia, and China, for example, developed when the old aristocratic regimes failed to meet emerging social and economic challenges (Skocpol, 1979). According to Skocpol, pre-revolutionary France, Russia, and China were "fully established imperial states." Since these states were not fully bureaucratic or parliamentary, however, they could not offer representatives of the dominant class an opportunity to take part in political decision-making. As a result, the landed aristocracy developed a "self-conscious collective organization." It was in a position to "obstruct monarchical undertakings that ran counter to their economic interests" (ibid.). Their obstructions had the unintended consequence of destroying the military and administrative integrity of the imperial state. In effect, the landed aristocracy undermined its own traditional position in the society.

This finding was supported by earlier research on revolutions by Moore (1966), who showed that the outcome of a revolution depends largely on which social classes attack the ruler. When the attackers are mainly peasants, as in China, Vietnam, and Cuba, the result is a Communist regime that introduces land reform and social equality. When the revolutionaries are independent farmers, artisans, and other "middle-class people," the result is likely to be parliamentary democracy, as in England, France, and the United States. However, when the attackers are primarily military—supported by a coalition of the landed aristocracy, Church, and large business interests—the result is fascism, as in Germany, Italy, and Spain.

Rebellion

Rebellion, in common terms, is armed opposition by a portion of the citizenry to an established government or other authority. The difference between a *rebellion* and a *revolution* lies in the outcome. If the rebellion succeeds in overthrowing the government and making significant social and political changes, then it is considered a revolution. If, as with the so-called Rebellions of 1837 in Upper and Lower Canada, the government is not overthrown, or few changes result, then the act is considered a rebellion. Everyone who engages in rebellion against a government is liable to the criminal penalties of treason established by that government. If a rebellion becomes widespread, involving a considerable proportion of the country, and the rebels receive the recognition of foreign nations, the government in charge treats captured rebels as criminals. If the rebellion succeeds, and the rebels form a new government, the rebels are no longer criminals: they are heroes and rulers.

In 1837, Canada experienced a series of insurrections against the colonial rule of Great Britain, known as the Rebellions of 1837. These rebellions were driven by frustration over the oligarchic and politically irresponsible governments Britain had installed. Patronage and corruption were rife; the ruling families used wealth and power at their own convenience. The brief episodes of fighting in Upper Canada (present-day Ontario) and Lower Canada (present-day Quebec) were part of a single crisis where responsible government was at issue. By the time the crisis ended in 1838, hundreds had been killed and thousands more were refugees. Following Lord Durham's investigative report to the English Parliament, the road was cleared for responsible government in Canada and, eventually, independence.

Both revolutions and rebellions are acts of deviance and crimes against government. To repeat, whether history views the rebels as heroes or villains depends on whether they win. Winners typically rewrite the history books to show themselves as heroes conforming to a higher standard of moral conduct; losers are vilified, with a few exceptions. Louis Riel, a nineteenth-century Métis rebel in western Canada, continues to be celebrated by Native people and francophones but ignored by most Canadians. William Lyon Mackenzie, leader of the unsuccessful 1837 rebellion in Upper Canada, is mostly forgotten.

More common than rebellions and revolutions are **populist movements**, which have always been common in Canada. By "populist" we mean movements aimed at moving power back to individual voters, rather than their representatives, elites, or backroom brokers. In this regard, the "referendum" as a means of political decision-making is an example of populist politics.

Some grassroots movements have resulted in the formation of new political parties in western Canada, notably, the Social Credit Party and the Co-operative Commonwealth Federation (CCF, which later became the New Democratic Party or NDP), and led to the Winnipeg General Strike in 1919. The early part of the twentieth century was a time of significant change within Canada while the country struggled to respond to a massive influx of immigrants, expansion in western Canada, the impact of urbanization, two world wars, a major drought, and economic depression. A variety of new populist initiatives emerged out of these national economic tragedies, especially in the West where waves of immigrants created a more varied population mix than in any other part of the country.

Political populism in twentieth-century Canada comprised several important elements: a view of society expressing traditional Christian values associated with personal industriousness, thrift, and family attachment; criticism of industrial or big business capitalism as harmful to the interests of independent, small-scale commodity producers; and criticism of the political corruption resulting from control of political parties and institutions by large-scale finance, industrial, and manufacturing capitalists.

Populist movements in Canada have most often succeeded when led by people like Tommy Douglas (CCF) and William Aberhart (Social Credit), who could articulate regional grievances and exploit new techniques of communication such as radio and television. Populist sentiment in Canada continues among some members of the Conservative Party, especially the western wing of conservatism formerly associated with the Social Credit Party.

Increasingly, movements of protest around the industrial world are driven by non-class-based issues including environmentalism, civil rights, anti-racism, and feminism (Inglehart, 1985). They tend to recruit middle-class, highly educated young people—in Canada and elsewhere—who de-emphasize traditional working-class interests in wages and job security and may not be connected to any mainstream political party.

This departure from past practice suggests considerable uncertainty and instability in political protests of the future. Walzer (1965), in writing about the English revolution of 1640, referred to a similar phenomenon as a "revolution of the saints." Such protest is driven by ideologies, not interests, and free-forming social groups, not social classes. This kind of protest sometimes recruits highly educated people with many ideas about building a better society. Alternatively, as with the Paris riots, it recruits less educated, underemployed people, also with many ideas about building a better society.

> **Time to Reflect:** If you and your collaborators were planning to organize a political protest movement, what three steps would you propose taking first?

Communities and Subcultures of Protest, War, and Rebellion

Like other types of deviant behaviour, protest activity is socially structured. Typically, protestors—like other deviants—form communities and subcultures to provide one another with support. Rioters do not qualify as a subgroup, since their actions are short-lived, but it is certainly true of bandits, revolutionaries, guerrillas, and terrorist bands. We will consider each of these briefly.

Bandit Communities

Historian Eric Hobsbawm (1959) defines banditry as a "primitive" form of organized social protest—primitive in the sense of being small-scale, with few resources, and occurring in pre-industrial (agricultural) societies, without any long-term political agenda. Banditry, from this standpoint, is a pre-class, pre-ideological formation.

In pre-industrial societies, the poor often protected the bandit, regarded him as their hero, and turned him into a "mythological" figure (ibid.). The most famous bandit protestor in our Anglo-dominant tradition is Robin Hood, who inhabited Sherwood Forest in England. Like other bandits, Robin Hood received support and protection from the common people. In return, he tried to live up to his role as protector. As a social rebel, Robin Hood stole from the rich and gave to the poor, and he did not kill except in self-defence or to avenge wrongs.

Many criminals adopt a bandit pose in order to succeed. An example is Pablo Escobar, leader of one of Colombia's most notorious drug cartels until he was gunned down a Colombian police task force in December 1993. Although many Colombians disapproved of his involvement with drugs, from the 1970s to the early 1990s Escobar enjoyed protection by living among the poorest Colombians outside of Medellin. The poor helped Escobar successfully evade the government for an extended period. Despite the large rewards offered and news of Escobar's use of violence, torture, and assassination to secure his goals, he retained the support of the poor by enriching them with a small fraction of his drug-based wealth. For example, he had built homes for more than 200 poor families in a section named Barrio Pablo Escobar. Escobar once even told his brother that he felt like a modern version of Robin Hood. After his death, thousands of young, poor mourners gathered around Escobar's coffin while the rest of Colombia celebrated.

As Hobsbawm notes, banditry is a pre-political phenomenon in the sense that it does not lead to a stable political structure nor does it contest power within stable political institutions (such as Parliament). Banditry is not about political parties and platforms. Once the bandit dies, his rebellion is over, unless followers maintain the effort.

Revolutionary Communities

In modern times, **political protest movements** are more likely to orient themselves to forming parties and contesting power through institutionalized channels. However, in their early stages, political protest movements often are small, unstable, and cliquish.

Canadian sociologist Roger O'Toole (1977) wrote an important study of the subculture of a small revolutionary group, or sect, in Canada, the League for Socialist Action (LSA), a revolutionary organization in the 1960s that claimed leadership of the Canadian working class and the Canadian revolution it anticipated. It accepted the basic Trotskyite view of the need for **world revolution**. Group members viewed reformist social democrats and trade-union bureaucrats as enemies propping up a capitalist social system that Trotsky had diagnosed 30 years earlier as being in its death agony.

The LSA promoted and strengthened these views by recruiting members and maintaining group cohesion. Besides its regular public forums, the LSA held meetings, showed films, and had social gatherings. The LSA youth also held gatherings, talks, parties, and poetry readings. The LSA members engaged in a very full social life.

The group leadership invited members to work as a moral and intellectual elite operating in semi-secrecy. Recruitment was the bestowal of a high honour, and the individual decision to join was seen as a voluntary act of total commitment for life to the LSA cause and organization. The LSA membership increased dramatically in the 1960s from the combination of Canadian youth radicalization and French-Canadian nationalism in Quebec and the lowering of barriers to membership. Moreover, the leadership involved its members in group activities to ensure that they remained "uncontaminated" by capitalist propaganda.

The LSA had what Breton (1964), in the context of ethnic communities, has called **institutional completeness**. Stable revolutionary communities or cell communities satisfy human needs for interaction and support. Second, they tend to produce new roles, rules, and cultural values. Third, through the establishment of a wide range of services and activities, they make it possible to live without having much, if any, contact with the "outside world." At the end of the decade, LSA members contributed to the Waffle movement in the NDP until its expulsion from the party in 1972. The LSA decided to remain in the NDP, while some of its members left to become allied with other Communist groups.

Guerrilla Communities

Guerrillas are soldiers in an irregular or undeclared war—usually a civil war. They, too, form communities for mutual support. Guerrillas and terrorist groups share some perspectives, such as surprise tactics; both have the tendency to discredit the government through successful attacks. Often, terrorists have kept their numbers small to preserve secrecy or have alienated large numbers of the public through indiscriminately violent means—for example, the bombing of subways in Madrid, which claimed nearly 200 civilian lives in 2004. Terrorist groups can work with fewer members and a smaller skill set than guerrilla forces.

Guerrilla groups try to maintain control and influence in the community. They have to work more openly than terrorists do and use more focused methods of violence. They also use propaganda tactics and persuasion to hold control; only if that does not work do they use threats and terrorism. According to Mao Zedong, the leader of the Communist revolution in China, there are five components to a successful guerrilla movement: mass support, party organization, military organization, favourable terrain, and economic strength.

The Khmer Rouge is a case in point. The Cambodian Khmer Rouge's main goal was to bring about an egalitarian communist society and a glorification of peasant life. They attempted their goal by mass deportations from the cities, enforced labour in the fields, and mass murders in "the killing fields."

Sometimes, guerrillas are merely isolated soldiers fighting a rearguard, often losing, action against the enemy.

Terrorist Communities

Terrorists are often motivated by a political or social cause, such as the promotion of an ideology, a struggle for the control of religious expression, or the desire to overthrow what is perceived to be an oppressive government or authoritative body. Terrorism is best viewed as a "poor man's war," a war that is evidently fought by new rules. Most generally, *terrorism* can be defined as any act employing the unpredictable use of force by an individual or group intended to undermine the legitimate authority of a government or state plus increase terror or fear among the general population.

The roots of terrorism can be found in the religious, ethnic, nationalist, political, economic, and social differences that prevent people from living together in peace. A rational cost-benefit analysis—not reckless impulse—leads them to this conclusion, often in view of various frustrating or limiting social, political, economic, and personal conditions. Terrorists primarily are men with a higher-than-average education from middle- to upper-class backgrounds, with specific skills and strong political motivation. Increasingly, terrorist organizations in the developing world recruit younger members. Often the only role models these young people have to identify with are terrorists and guerrillas.

Experts generally view terrorism as a different form of soldiering, with the usual motives: to protect home and country. Jeffrey Simon (2001: 338) writes that "what limited data we have on individual terrorists suggests that the outstanding common characteristic is normality." As in the formation of social movements, the formation of terrorist groups relies on social networks to recruit members. Because terrorist activities are generally organized and carried out in secret, social networks are important as a source of social control over the recruits, in order to ensure their trustworthiness.

On this matter, we learn a lot from the work by Professor Bonnie Erickson (1981) on "secret societies." Secret societies hold a particular importance for religion and politics, precisely because of their potential for hidden, long-term political crime. Simmel (1906 [1902]) defines a *secret society* as a social unit characterized by reciprocal relations that are governed by secrecy. Members of the society are concerned with protecting their most important ideas, sentiments, and information. They do so by controlling the flow of public information.

Political, religious, and other secret societies, such as the staunchly Protestant Freemasons and Opus Dei within the Catholic Church, often include rituals to promote bonding and build on elaborate hierarchies of authority. These structures help to preserve group cohesion, a consciousness of boundaries and belonging, and a greater group willingness to yield obediently to the leader's authority. Conditions in the larger society influence the development of these subgroups. For example, secret societies are most likely to form under conditions of political oppression and totalitarian regimentation. They are also likely to develop where groups such as the Irish Republican Army (IRA) or Al-Qaeda form to carry out secret political goals. Whenever the participants are at risk of death for their political views and activities, as is often the case for terrorists, secret societies form to carry out these political goals.

However, not all terrorism is opposed to the state in power. *State-sponsored terrorism* is the state-sanctioned use of terrorist groups to facilitate foreign policy objectives. In the eyes of the current US government, there are four countries on the list of states that sponsor terrorism: Cuba, Iran, Sudan, and Syria (US Department of State, 2011). Of the four countries, three are Middle Eastern/North African with mainly Muslim populations. Other governments might compile other lists. In the eyes of some, the United States might be viewed as a state that sponsors terrorism to destabilize foreign governments and undermine progressive political movements.

As Frantz Fanon made clear in his classic work, *The Wretched of the Earth*, under conditions of colonial oppression and struggle, nothing less than the identity and selfhood of the colonized person is at stake (Box 9.3). Under such extreme conditions, we should not be surprised to see oppressed people taking extreme actions.

Media Depictions of Political Crime

Political crime remains a common source for drama in popular entertainment. Genocide, corruption, and resistance are universal, powerful themes, and the art based on these themes tends to hold sway with broad audiences. Protest music has long been an important popular response to political crime and it remains a vibrant art form today. The peak of protest music was likely the mid-twentieth century, when labour and civil rights advocates like Woody Guthrie, Bob Dylan, Joan Baez, Paul Robeson, Malvina Reynolds, and Pete Seeger produced new material and refashioned spirituals to denounce societal inequities, racial segregation in the southern United States, and the Vietnam War, which they believed contradicted principles laid out by the country's Constitution. The results of these labours, songs such as "Blowin' in the Wind" (1963), "A Change Is Gonna Come" (1963), and "Strange Fruit" (1939), are remembered today.

Authors, like musicians, have produced a great many popular works on political crime, particularly in the second half of the twentieth century. The Holocaust led to an extraordinary body of literature, leading to a deluge of popular plays, movies, and television shows. Works like Elie Wiesel's *Night* (1955), Edward Wallant's *The Pawnbroker* (1961), Anne Frank's *The Diary of a Young Girl* (1947), and Art Spiegelman's *Maus* (1986) developed enormous followings and entrenched the Holocaust as a source of literary inspiration. Discussions of political crime extend even into comic books that feature characters who exist outside the law as a response to systemic corruption, like Batman or the Punisher. In 2007, Marvel Comics ran a storyline that saw the iconic Captain America assassinated for his political beliefs. Political crime certainly has a broad literary reach.

Hollywood has capitalized more than any industry on political crimes, turning out a procession of films about genocide and corruption. These films have been especially prevalent since 1949, the year *All the King's Men*, which focused on the career of a corrupt southern governor, won the Oscar for best picture. Since then, films such as *Hotel Rwanda* (2004), *Nixon* (1995), *All the President's Men* (1976), and *Fahrenheit 9/11* (2004) have earned critical praise and large audiences. Even many of Hollywood's most beloved comedies, including *Bananas* (1971), *Duck Soup* (1933), and *Dr. Strangelove* (1964), have lampooned the sad realities of totalitarianism, revolution in the developing world, and executive abuses of power. Given the traumatic events of the mid-century Holocaust, World War II, and Cold War, filmmaker interest in political crime is understandable.

Popular television shows have been more hesitant to explore political crime and, when doing so, have taken a softer tone. In 1969, after the stars of *Smothers Brothers Comedy*

Classic Works

BOX 9.3

The Wretched of the Earth by Frantz Fanon

Frantz Fanon, a theorist and activist in the Algerian national liberation movement, wrote *The Wretched of the Earth* in 1961. This fierce condemnation of colonialism is titled for the oppressed peasants living in the European colonies of Africa, Latin America, and Asia. This title comes from the first line of the first stanza of *The Internationale*, the anthem of the international Communist movement, which had been translated and reinvented in many versions, and is an expression of that movement's goals. In English, a version of the anthem reads roughly as follows:

Arise, wretched of the earth
Arise, convicts of hunger
Reason thunders in its volcano
This is the eruption of the end
Of the past let us wipe the slate clean
Masses, slaves, arise, arise
The world is about to change its foundation
We are nothing, let us be all
This is the final struggle
Let us gather together, and tomorrow
The International
Will be the human race.

The book is a call to violence, but it is also an analysis of the mental pathologies caused by suffering under colonial rule. By internalizing the views of the colonizers, the colonized perpetuate their own economic and political oppression through a lack of self-respect and continued sense of worthlessness. Fanon believed that to overcome this system in which black is associated with evil and white with good, a new way of thinking was needed. This new rationality would include self-respect and a sense of identity among the oppressed. In addition, armed violence, or revolution, would be necessary: "This utopian desire, to be absolutely free of the past, requires total revolution, absolute violence" (Fanon, 1965 [1961]: 37). Such extreme violence would purify, destroying not only the category of white, but that of black, too, since they define each other by their mutual opposition. Violence also reinforces the new way of thinking Fanon aimed to promote since it proves the oppressed, too, are able to act, allowing the colonized people to see for themselves that they are capable of gaining and exercising power. In contrast, peaceful solutions would fail to provide the self-respect necessary to "cure" the natives and convince them of their own power and sovereignty. Only through independence and violence can the oppressed take charge of their lives and lessen their reliance on the colonizer. And since colonialism is inherently violent, only sustainable through violence against the colonized, violence against the colonizer is the only solution. It alone can cure and unify the colonized, and it is the only language that can be shared with colonialism.

Hour criticized American foreign policy in Asia and the handling of the Vietnam War, CBS replaced the show with the politically unadventurous *Hee Haw.* The modern show to most enthusiastically engage the subject of political crime was *Arrested Development.* The Fox sitcom, which ran during the height of the Iraq War, showed pictures of US Defense Secretary Donald Rumsfeld shaking hands with Saddam Hussein, saw one of its principal characters accused of "light treason," and had three other characters targeted by the government for assassination. *Arrested Development,* which was singularly adventurous, was cancelled after three seasons.

Theories about Protest, War, and Rebellion

Functionalist Theories

The consistency with which large numbers of people systematically try to kill one another suggests that war must have a social *function,* and that it may even be viewed as a social institution. Paradoxically, conflict increases social cohesion and group identity by creating a common cause for which people can fight. During a war, internal squabbles between political parties, ethnic communities, and special interest groups are put aside temporarily as the entire nation bands together to defeat a common enemy. Only when this larger antagonist is no longer a threat to national well-being do the intra-national conflicts resume.

A second function of war is the economic mobilization that comes with war-making efforts. For example, Canadian participation in World War II led to increased employment and production, helping to end the economic downturn of the Great Depression. Even after the war, Canadians rode the economic momentum through several more decades, experiencing prosperity and growth in all aspects of society. After the war, the gross national product doubled, industry developed exponentially, and consumer spending rose with the baby-boom generation. This was made possible because the Allies won the war. European countries took time to recover from the war. The German and Japanese economies suffered significant setbacks in the years immediately after the conflict.

Wars also lead to scientific and technological innovations that remain beneficial and functional for society in peacetime. For example, the Internet was an invention of the US Pentagon—an emergency communications network against the possibility of a nuclear war. Spinoffs of World War II include jet engines and nuclear power.

A close connection develops between a society's inclination to make war, its military institutions, and its strategic culture. *Strategic culture* is the collective belief or rationale about the use of force in international politics that has been based on the experiences of that group. A state's military behaviour is based on its shared historical experiences in war, so each state will have its own unique strategic culture. As a result, some populations will be more willing to see the nation use violence. This inclination may affect policy-making and a country's "response and conduct in the international sphere" (Rummel, 1994).

Symbolic Interactionist Theories

This paradigm sees society as a product of continuous, face-to-face interactions among individuals in different social settings. For example, symbolic interactionists examine the ways in which governments and media influence popular attitudes towards war and conflict.

The media, through cartoons and action shows, instill aggression and a habit of resolving conflicts with physical force as early as childhood, mostly in boys. GI Joe, "cowboys and Indians," and green, plastic army men—among other childhood toys and games—implicitly teach young people that war is a noble and heroic adventure, that the "good guys" always win, and that national patriotism is crucial to victory.

In times of war, people use a specific language to talk about and legitimize the combat and minimize the emotional impact of massive deaths that will ensue. Soldiers on both sides are not "murder victims"; they are "casualties." And these casualties are celebrated: during Canada's engagement in Afghanistan, for example, the bodies of dead military personnel were transported first to the air base at Trenton in eastern Ontario and then from Trenton along the Trans-Canada Highway (Highway 401) to Toronto. This 170-kilometre stretch of highway was formally renamed the "Highway of Heroes" and citizens would gather on overpasses along the route to cheer the fallen heroes.

The now unavoidable killing of innocent civilians is referred to impersonally as "collateral damage." Nuclear missiles are not weapons of mass destruction; they are "peacekeepers." The stereotyping of enemies—focusing on ethnic, racial, and cultural differences—is a common way of dehumanizing the enemy, making him an easier victim and war more "justifiable." The stereotyping may reflect current anxieties—for example, fears about Islamic extremism in the Middle East—but like all stereotypes, they are exaggerated. Even the term *terrorist* denotes a particular point of view—lack of sympathy—about the person in question. Bear in mind that one person's "terrorist" is another person's "freedom fighter."

The concept of war itself may be given a positive spin in popular culture, as when the term is used in initiatives like the "war on drugs," the "war on poverty," the "war on cancer," and even the "war on terrorism." In recruitment materials, the military stresses honour, courage, and sacrifice for the greater good as defining characteristics of the ideal soldier. Their well-groomed uniforms and combat decorations are designed to command respect and admiration from the public. The government often stresses the importance of military preparedness as vital to national prosperity. In reality, the military tends to recruit young, undereducated men and women from economically depressed areas and subjects them to unrelenting discipline.

Critical Theories

Protest, revolution, and terror occur where change can no longer be attained through discussion. Accordingly, groups or governments that try to prevent the expression of disagreement and conflict will often intensify those measures and produce more violent forms of politicking, including protest, rebellion, and even civil war.

Critical theory also emphasizes how war (and other conflict) benefits some groups—most notably ruling classes, corporations, politicians, and the military—but not others. The government in power tends to benefit from war, since war against a common enemy has a unifying and patriotic impact on the citizenry, and victory, should it come, wins admiration and gratitude and therefore improves the chances of re-election. At a macro level, even the foreign aid intended to help Third World countries ultimately benefits First World nations. According to this perspective, wars are fought by nations seeking to increase their level of power and influence on the global level or seeking to perpetuate the subordination of lesser nations.

Wars are particularly beneficial for the military establishment. Historically, military forces and their resulting communities were authoritarian, hierarchically stratified, and traditional in their values. Like other bureaucracies, military establishments fight to increase their power and resource base. At the same time, military forces derive their effectiveness from the fact that they are total institutions. They must re-socialize recruits and turn them into killing machines. Military bureaucracies are well organized to achieve this kind of socialization.

Time to Reflect: What effects do continual or frequent warfare have on war-making societies? Are these effects mainly positive, negative, or both?

In a society with a highly developed "war system," such as the United States, military people often become involved in a variety of semi-public, semi-political activities that are not traditionally the responsibility or expertise of the military. The military establishment is relatively unimportant in Canadian society, but in some societies the military is a means of upward social mobility in the same way as a career in law, religion, business, or academe may be in another society. As a result, underemployed military people—military men without wars to fight or other means of distinguishing themselves—are a potent threat to the social order. They may be counted on to foment rebellion and conflict. In this sense, they become a self-interested political class. The military elite have posed a continuing problem in Pakistan and Myanmar, for example, and in many South American nations.

Civil wars, revolutions, and protests are even closer to the conflict perspective, since they cast light on the internal contradictions in a particular society. For Marx and Engels (1988 [1848]), the earliest critical theorists, history is driven by class conflict and the replacement or overthrow of one ruling class by another. Marxist approaches to revolution emphasize the importance of the struggle between social classes and the contradiction within the mode of production between the force and the relations of production. Contemporary Marxists who treat class conflict as the essential feature of Marxist analysis are likely to see revolution as the uncertain outcome of a complex combination of forces, mainly class consciousness, historical circumstance, political organization, and the repression of the working class.

Feminist Approaches

With few exceptions historically, men—not women—have fought wars. Men are also more often the leaders of a nation and, therefore, are more likely to be in the position to declare wars against one another.

This socialization of masculinity and militarism begins in childhood. Stereotypically, boys wage make-believe wars with GI Joe figurines, while girls play with dolls and act out domestic routines like baking and child-rearing. When women have participated in military campaigns, they have usually filled stereotypical "female" roles as nurses and clerical workers. Ostensibly, "Barbie" is a military surgeon or nurse and not a front-line soldier.

As the twentieth century progressed and feminist groups gained political and social influence, more varied opportunities became available for women in the military. As warfare has become more technological and less reliant on individual, face-to-face armed combat, women have been able to enlist in any military position available to men. Currently, women are able to serve in most ranks and divisions of the Canadian military.

A gender issue related to war is the fate of civilians of a war-torn region. During World War II, the Japanese military forced up to 200,000 young women into prostitution as "comfort women" for military personnel; many eventually died from sexually transmitted diseases and torture. During the more recent conflicts in Bosnia, Rwanda, Congo, and almost certainly in other hostile regions as well, women were raped, beaten, and killed by roving bands of soldiers. Despite prohibitions outlined in the Geneva Conventions, rape, assault, and enforced prostitution of women continue to occur in armed conflicts today.

International feminist activists and women's organizations have played an important role in recent prosecutions of war crimes committed against women, especially rape and sexual enslavement (Cooper, 2002). Feminists successfully pressured the UN to designate crimes against women as prosecutable human rights abuses and to include female prosecutors and judges in tribunals. So, for example, the Hague war crimes tribunal convicted three men for their role in the mass rape of Muslim women during the conflict in Bosnia.

Particularly worrying is the problem of **gendercide** as a human rights violation. Gendercide against women typically involves rape, which has come to be recognized as a war crime. Against men, such crimes generally involve the selective separation of young civilian men "of military age" (i.e., 18–45) from old men, children, and women of all ages for punishment, torture, and execution.

Collective rape has garnered much worldwide attention in recent years, but systematic documentation and empirical research are still lacking. It is defined as a pattern of sexual violence perpetrated on civilians by agents of a state or political group and measured through two indicators of occurrence or nonoccurrence in various countries and years. Green (2007) collected data from three news sources—*World News Digest Facts on File*, the *New York Times*, and *Reuters Business Briefs*—and recorded information of the timing, location, perpetrators, and victims. In total, 37 episodes of collective rape were identified. Episodes were more prevalent in Africa and Asia and in the 1990s compared with the 1980s. The perpetrators were most often agents of a government (such as the military), but political civil groups were also implicated.

However, sexual violence—including sexual torture—is not limited to women. Oosterhoff et al. (2004) note that public awareness of the widespread use of sexual torture as a weapon of war increased after the war in the former Yugoslavia in the early 1990s. Sexual torture has serious mental, physical, and health outcomes, for men as well as for women. In Croatia, many men were sexually tortured. Based on interviews in 2000 with 16 health professionals and data from the medical records of three centres providing care to refugees and victims of torture, the study found evidence of rape and other forced sexual acts, full or partial castration, genital beatings, and electroshock. Yet, few men admit being sexually tortured or seek help, and professionals may fail to recognize cases. Few perpetrators have been prosecuted, mainly because of a lack of political will.

Finally, there is some evidence of women's role in another aspect of politics: namely, as sources of honesty and clean government. As the data below suggest, governments with a higher proportion of women legislators, such as those found in Scandinavia and Western Europe—tend to be less corrupt. It is not clear, however, whether an increase in women's influence brings about political "housecleaning" or whether societies with higher (i.e., more progressive) moral standards are readier than others to elect a large number of women legislators.

Consequences of Protest, War, and Rebellion

Social Consequences

Wars come at enormous economic costs. Currently, the US is spending $1 billion per day on military efforts. The vast expenditures devoted to developing and maintaining the world's military forces take away from each nation's resources for other social programs. The (estimated) trillion dollars spent annually by the world's leaders on national defence could just as easily be spent instead on reforesting the planet, increasing energy efficiency, protecting croplands from soil erosion, feeding and educating the world's poor, and developing environmentally friendly, renewable sources of energy (Renner, 1993a; 1993b).

Beyond the dollars spent directly on the world's war-fighting machines, trillions more are wasted every year on repairing the physical damage to buildings and infrastructure (roads, bridges, public transit, hospitals, and waterways) and on trying to remediate the environmental destruction caused by war and terrorism. Property damage incurred during World War II, for example, is estimated to be in the neighbourhood of $260 billion. The damage caused by the terrorist bombings of the World Trade Center in New York City and the Alfred P. Murrah Federal Building in Oklahoma City each cost the United States government and private companies $500 million to repair.

Wars can also destroy the cultural heritage of a nation or region. For example, during the civil war in Afghanistan, the Taliban destroyed a Kabul museum that was one of the richest and most famous in the world, and two huge, culturally significant Buddhist figures. In addition to the tremendous economic toll that war and conflict have on society, another consequence is purely human. For many people, morale is shattered by the effects of hostile combat. Although countries or groups that win a war may enjoy a general improvement in spirits, many people will experience the war as gruelling and perpetually haunting.

For instance, after the Vietnam War, veterans returned to the United States disillusioned, unable to understand their purpose in the conflict and the lack of sympathy from fellow Americans. Of course, war also affects civilians—even those who are sheltered from the physical horrors of combat. For those who are not so sheltered, and who survive, such as those in Iraq during the initial American "shock and awe" aerial bombardment in 2003, the emotional, psychological scars can be long-lasting and result in mental illness.

Revolution

Use of the term *revolution* seems appropriate when it refers to changes that have major and often unanticipated consequences. Most revolutions cause dramatic changes in the way people live, for better and for worse. Revolutions reveal internal cleavages between those who support and those who oppose the new order. There will always be people who oppose political change: not all people are revolutionaries and not everyone disagrees with the existing government. This cleavage can cause further conflict in the society.

After some revolutions, the general population suffers from a new government's lack of attention to domestic problems. Almost every revolution is followed by a period of famine, poverty, deprivation, class conflict, and even greater unrest among the general public. As American political activist Florence Kennedy once said, "Oppressed people are frequently oppressive when first liberated. . . . Somebody's foot on their neck or their foot on somebody's neck" (Peter, 1977).

Political Violence

Political actions often involve a degree of violence. This is truer for rebellions and revolutions than for conventional political protest in the contemporary era. However, throughout the twentieth century we saw a level of violence—both inside and outside warfare—that was unparalleled in earlier times.

Political violence differs from other kinds of violence in that representatives of one political or national group inflict it to perpetuate or change the relative political status of another political or national group or to prevent that group from achieving the changes its members desire. Rationalizations commonly are devised to justify the extent of violence, its effects, or its lack of fairness. Rationalizations may even make the slaughtering of soldiers an acceptable cost of war but the slaughtering of civilians—what R.J. Rummel has termed **democide** (Figure 9.5)—a criminal horror; these distinctions are socially and politically constructed, if not morally meaningful.

The process of rationalization begins by distinguishing "us" from "them." A group defined as outsiders or strangers is easily vilified and attacked—is easily viewed as a means to an end or as fully expendable. The most horrific aspect of this process is *genocide*, the systematic and planned execution of an entire national, ethnic, racial, or political group. The most infamous case of attempted genocide was the Holocaust during World War II. In all, six million Jews were killed, many in concentration camps like Auschwitz, where an estimated one million died. The Romani people (gypsies), homosexuals, the mentally disabled, and others were also systematically murdered at this time because of their race and because of perceived physical and mental weaknesses.

Issues involving war crimes fall into at least four categories: assigning responsibility for criminal acts; trying and punishing the criminals; bringing about national reconciliation; and ensuring that a nation remembers its criminal past and learns from it. The International Criminal Court, which opened on 1 July 2002 upon the ratification of the Treaty of Rome, is a permanent tribunal for the prosecution of war crimes and crimes against humanity.

However, the calls for international war crime tribunals are sporadic, due to tensions between selfishness and idealism within liberal states. Moreover, the war crimes tribunals are physically unable to process hundreds of thousands of trials. Nonetheless, these tribunals are at least better than acts of vengeance by the aggrieved parties. Right actions following wrongdoing, such as changing institutions, reparations, or apologies, may help bring about healing and peace.

This is fine in theory. In practice, it may be very difficult to help people restart and reorganize their lives after their community has been ravaged by genocide. Babic (2002) studied the return of war migrants to their homes in the former Yugoslavia, with an emphasis on the problem of social interaction between different ethnic, immigrant, and native groups in Brodsko-Posavska County. He focused on 180 war migrants, including returnee Croats, Serbs, and refugees/immigrants. He found that the coexistence of the antagonistic Croats and Serbs remains a problem in the state of Croatia. The returnees are burdened with memories of the recent conflicts, human and material losses, and issues of forgiveness and compromise. Ironically, all three groups contend that, *before* the war, they valued peaceful coexistence. Today, the groups differ in their perception of who is responsible for the war.

National self-examination has been a continuing problem after wars and war crimes, but nations approach their history in different ways. The Federal Republic of Germany (West Germany), for example, was slow to acknowledge its role in the Holocaust. While

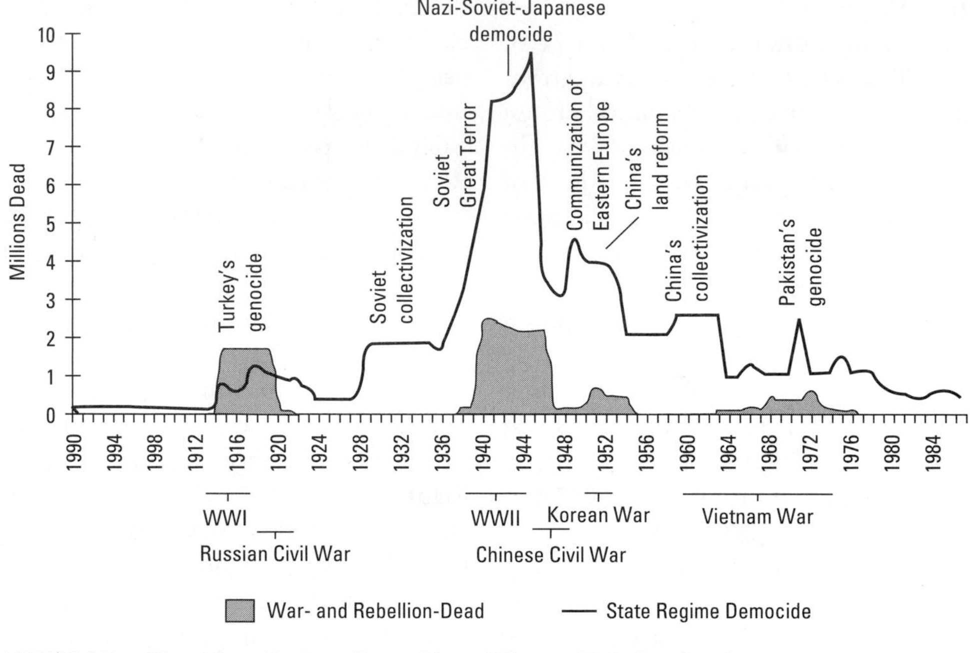

FIGURE 9.5 Plot of State Regimes Democide and War- and Rebellion-Dead

Source: R.J. Rummel, *Power Kills: Democracy as a Method of Nonviolence* (New Brunswick, NJ: Transaction, 1997), at: <www.hawaii.edu/powerkills/SOD.FIG23.2.GIF>.

the interpretation remained basically the same throughout the existence of East Germany (the German Democratic Republic, 1949–90), the main focus of West Germany changed several times. At first, textbooks to a certain extent maintained Nazi positions (in accordance with conservative nationalist policy) on many questions of national interest, engagement, and expansion. Gradually, authors changed their underlying theories about National Socialism. The theory of "totalitarianism"—that is, of Communism and National Socialism as hostile twin brothers—was officially promoted in West Germany, where Nazism was not seriously discussed in the continuity of German history and society until the 1980s.

For all victims and analysts of political violence, at least in the West, the Holocaust remains the benchmark against which all other crimes against humanity are judged. The Holocaust likely sped up the development of a "war crimes" concept, culminating in the International Criminal Court in The Hague.

Environmental Consequences

War not only results in loss of human life, but also causes extensive environmental damage—intentional and unintentional. For example, during the Gulf War, Saddam Hussein ordered the release of an estimated 11 million barrels of oil into the Arabian Gulf, causing irreparable damage to local marine life. The wanton pollution created by the Iraqi army was expected to affect crop yields in countries as far away as India.

Military operations also harm the environment in peacetime. According to Calhoun (1996: 60), the United States military is the largest producer of hazardous materials in the country, and "decades of improper and unsafe handling, storage, and disposal of hazardous materials while building and maintaining the world's most powerful fighting force have severely polluted America's air, water, and soil."

Landmines remain a serious cause of death and injury long after wars have ended. The Ottawa Treaty—formally, the Convention on the Prohibition of the Use, Stockpiling, Production and Transfer of Anti-Personnel Mines and on their Destruction—came into force on 1 March 1999. Signers of the treaty agree to destroy their existing stocks within four years of signing and that they will not use, develop, manufacture, or trade in anti-personnel landmines. To date, the treaty has been signed by 155 countries and ratified by 153. Another 40 have yet to sign on, including the United States, which has claimed that mines are still necessary along the border between North and South Korea. There is continued progress in the discovery and destruction of landmines in signatory nations, but we have no complete account of the numbers of landmines remaining. By some estimates, they exceed 100 million, and they pose a special danger because they move with flooding, erosion, and other land movements (Landmine & Cluster Munition Monitor, at: www.the-monitor.org/index.php/LM/The-Issues/FAQs).

Health Consequences

Terrorism and War

War invariably results in the most immediate and final health consequence—death. Military conflicts in the twentieth century have resulted in the deaths of over 100 million soldiers and civilians—more than the total number of casualties in all previous wars in human history combined (Porter, 1994). Other approximations vary according to whether deaths stemming from war-related famine and disease are included.

Renner (1993b) calculated that 75 per cent of all military deaths since the reign of Julius Caesar occurred in the twentieth century. In part, this is due to the large population today: 90 per cent of all the people who ever lived were alive in the twentieth century. However, one cannot deny the century's unique technological and organizational capabilities for war-making. The rapid rise in humanity's capacity for killing is clear from a comparison of the world wars. World War I claimed the lives of eight million soldiers and one million civilians. The two atomic bombs dropped on Hiroshima and Nagasaki in World War II killed 250,000 Japanese civilians. In all, 17 million combatants and 35 million civilians were killed during World War II.

Improved technology alone is not to blame for the high death toll. People, not machines, make war. After all, in the civil war in Rwanda a decade ago, over 800,000 people died within a three-month period. Most were killed by machetes—broad swords—not guns. However, advanced military technology increases the likelihood that a high death toll will result, and thus, we are far beyond what machetes could possibly accomplish. Currently, the nuclear weapons in major military arsenals are over 4,000 times as powerful as the atomic bombs dropped on Japan. Friedman and Friedman (1996) estimate that a nuclear war today would kill 160 million instantly. Exposure to war also increases the risk of health problems and lowers life expectancy.

Time to Reflect: Is limiting the scale of warfare an attainable goal? Is it a worthwhile goal, or should we aim at eliminating warfare altogether?

Just as death is an unavoidable consequence of war, so too are physical and psychological injuries. In general, the number of military personnel and civilians who are injured or maimed during a war exceeds the number of deaths. Part of common military strategy is to maim rather than kill the enemy, since it requires more resources to care for the wounded than to discard their bodies. Cambodia has been called the *land of the one-legged man*, referring to more than 30,000 individuals—mostly rural citizen farmers—who have had limbs amputated as a result of accidentally detonating concealed anti-personnel mines.

Surviving a war physically unscathed does not guarantee complete well-being. Many veterans of war suffer the much slower torture of psychological disorders. Much of the mental health literature on the effects of war has focused on PTSD, which had previously been studied under names like *shell shock*, *concentration camp syndrome*, *survivor syndrome*, and *war neurosis* (Summerfield, 2000). Although initially considered by military officers as an expression of cowardice, PTSD is now recognized as a legitimate form of psychological distress produced by a traumatic experience, whether criminal victimization, sexual assault, or military combat. Soldiers returned from Afghanistan and Iraq often have difficulty fitting back into civilian society, and can become involved in family violence, homicides, and hostage takings, and, statistically, as a consequence of trauma, they have suffered greater losses at home than in theatres of war. In the US, "Veterans kill themselves at a rate of one every 80 minutes. More than 6,500 veteran suicides are logged every year—more than the total number of soldiers killed in Afghanistan and Iraq combined since those wars began" (Kristof, 2012).

Due to its unexpected, severe, and occasionally random nature, and because its targets are most often unsuspecting civilians who are sheltered from large-scale violence, terrorism is particularly likely to cause psychological trauma. The Oklahoma City bombing by domestic terrorist Timothy McVeigh was a shocking experience for all Americans, particularly for survivors of the blast and for the families and friends of survivors and victims. Risk factors for the development of psychological dysfunction include a pre-war history of mental instability, as well as the effects of war on family, social, and economic statuses.

Even worse is political violence inflicted by governmental authorities. "When the police force of a governing political authority shoots randomly into a group of demonstrating opponents to warn dissidents and strike fear into potential demonstrators, that is political violence or terrorism" (Held, 1997). The rationale behind governmental violence is to show future activists that political protest will not be tolerated.

In Canada today, such incidents are rare, and officials are expected to maintain the safety of any political protests. Freedom of speech and expression allows people to demonstrate in front of a provincial legislature or the Parliament buildings as long as they do so in an organized and peaceful fashion.

Economic Consequences

It is very difficult to gauge the cost of political crimes given the far-reaching collateral consequences of those crimes. Genocide is a particularly significant political crime, though its costs are almost impossible to measure. According to the United Nations Outreach Program on the Rwandan Genocide, causes of genocide are mostly systemic and require wide-scale investment in public works as both a redress for past slaughters and prevention of future ones. The war and decimation left Rwanda in need of legal and medical establishments, orphanages, schools, and an economy. The international community should, the UN claims, make a heavy investment in Rwanda to ensure the country's youth will be capable of future nation-building, escaping further cycles of poverty (UN, 2012).

The needs of Rwandans are not unique, insofar as all populations subject to genocide require financial assistance to recreate and revive their decimated cultures. In addition to spending billions of dollars in helping victims of genocide, the international community would be wise to invest in stopping genocides before they happen. The US government, through the United States Holocaust Memorial Museum, engages in research aimed at understanding the causes of genocide, having developed a number of prevention initiatives in high-risk countries. This institution put aside $200 million for grants and loans that, it is hoped, will aid in the development of local and national economies. Perhaps by lessening systemic financial ills, agencies can staunch genocidal threats.

Genocide is not the only political crime that is both expensive and difficult to address. Terrorism is remarkably costly, with the expenses going well beyond tracking and prosecuting terror suspects. Terrorism's political implications often make governments feel compelled to respond to acts of terror in extreme, perhaps unnecessary, ways. In response to the attacks on the World Trade Center on 11 September 2001, the Port Authority of New York and New Jersey elected to build a replacement "Freedom Tower" that will cost an estimated $3.3 billion. Few would fault the city for wanting to make such a powerful statement, but the tower's construction is not necessarily financially prudent.

Perhaps the most widely condemned—and certainly the most controversial—responses to terrorism in history were the post-9/11 American attacks on Afghanistan (in 2001) and Iraq (in 2003). Aside from the moral implications of the invasions, Operations Enduring Freedom and Iraqi Freedom have shown how enormously expensive it is to address terrorism militarily. According to the Congressional Research Service, the American government approved $1.283 trillion for military operations in Iraq and Afghanistan between October 2001 and March 2011 (Belasco, 2011). The astronomical costs of the American government's ongoing response to the attacks on the World Trade Center show the incredible potential collateral costs of terrorism.

The Dominant Ideology as Normative System

Very few citizens resist the dictates of their government in a forceful way. Instead, most people conform to their country's rules and social expectations, for many good reasons.

Consider the role of the **dominant ideology**: in Marxian theory, it is the set of common values and beliefs shared by most people in a given society, framing how the majority think about a range of topics. The dominant ideology is also understood to reflect, or serve, the interests of the dominant class in that society—the bourgeoisie. This theory is summarized in the slogan "The dominant ideology is the ideology of the dominant class." Dominant ideologies support the status quo or existing power structure. We call them *dominant* to point out their role in controlling people. Whether an ideology is dominant can be learned only through empirical research. We consider an ideology dominant if the most powerful or socially dominant groups in society sponsor it and if it also supports the interests of these groups.

The popular belief in "winners" and "losers"—in people getting what they deserve and deserving what they get and in social action being a game with a scoreboard—is an ideology that is dominant in this sense. In turn, the dominant ideology is an important part of popular culture and entertainment. In American culture, for example, high value is placed on war and heroism. This ideology makes it easy for American politicians to mobilize public sentiment behind activities like the Iraq War and, before that, the long-standing Cold War.

Italian Marxist Antonio Gramsci defined ideology as a view of the world that is implicit in all works of consciousness: in art, law, economic activity, and all aspects of individual life. Rather than supporting the use of propaganda and brainwashing, Gramsci favoured the concept of *hegemony*, or moral/spiritual supremacy, which encourages a class to translate its own world view into dominance. He urged Soviet Marxists to adopt a non-Bolshevik strategy based on persuasion, culture, and mass participation.

Dominant ideologies influence political life indirectly as well as directly, by shaping *public opinion*. Since the bourgeoisie own the media, they can select which ideas are represented there, and, in broad terms, they select just those ideas that serve their interests. As well, they impute certainty or "facticity" to opinions that are often in flux (in matters of science, policy, and so forth), creating something out of nothing.

Political and other public opinion polls contribute to this illusion-making (or what Marx called *false consciousness*), but journalists play a far larger role when they report propaganda under the guise of news. *Propaganda* is any idea or doctrine that is spread for the purpose of influencing people's opinions and actions. In this sense, Sunday school lessons, advertising, and election campaigns all are or can be vehicles of propaganda. In fact, propaganda is any information that represents itself as pure, unquestionable truth.

Our "institutions of information"—the mass media; schools and universities; even, in some instances, religious institutions—continue to spread the belief that people are free to make of their lives whatever they want to. Right paths and wrong paths, so we are led to believe, are freely chosen. Hard work and merit are rewarded. Sloth and crime are punished. Under these beliefs, government and other collective bodies, such as trade unions, actively interfere with people's right to choose. These kinds of ideas, trumpeted by leaders of business through the mass media they control, are appealing enough to survive year after year.

Social Policy Implications

What are we to do about political crimes—including corruption, torture, terrorism, war crimes, and other mass murder of civilian populations? The first thing is to encourage and support an independent press. Many have remarked on the decline of independent political reporting under recent administrations, especially in the US. In many countries, there has *never* been a tradition of independent reporting, and journalism has become one of the most dangerous professions to pursue—many journalists are murdered each year. In North America, declining revenues have made newspapers more reluctant than ever to challenge the powerful or to risk public disapproval. Yet, without courageous reporting, the public is never going to learn what their government is actually doing.

Along similar lines, social scientists have a role to play—as public intellectuals—in revealing and explaining the political crimes in our midst. So far, too many social scientists have been content to write research studies that will be read by only a handful of other scholars. If we are to understand and improve our society, we need to expect more of our scholars and researchers.

Truth and reconciliation commissions can bring past abuses into the open, as has been the case, for example, in South Africa. It remains to be seen whether Canada's Truth and Reconciliation Commission on residential schools will have a positive impact, or any impact at all beyond segments of the Aboriginal community. As we have seen in a variety of countries, ignoring these abuses—corruption, patronage, the harmful and violent "othering" of segments of society, and other crimes—won't work. People simply lose confidence in the political process; at the very least, they disengage from political parties, ignore public affairs, and refuse to vote. Only rarely do people mobilize in political movements to overthrow the government or even to demand reforms. On the other hand, threatening to punish the wrongdoers—the corrupt or criminal politicians—is unlikely to work. This strategy polarizes people and leads them to hide information.

Finally, and just as important, a society needs to learn from the revelations of wrongdoing, taking steps to regulate government more effectively to prevent future misdeeds. Of course, this assumes citizens' willingness to study their own society—to learn about its problems and possible solutions—and to participate in the correction of a malfunctioning government. Some will say this is too much to expect of the average person. Yet, the underlying premise of democracy is precisely that it is a government *by the people.* In a country like Canada, public engagement and participation should be the rule, not the exception. Otherwise, we will continue to get the governments we deserve.

Conclusion

Criminalizing protest is one method that states use to keep the ruling class in power and to control the extent of protest. Alternately, criminalizing excessive violence in warfare is one method that states use to reduce the number of civilian casualties. In neither case does criminalization work well to limit violence once warring passions are inflamed.

In this chapter we have discussed protests, rebellions, revolutions, and wars, and the crimes associated with them. In countries such as Canada and the United States, political conflict is seen in two forms: through institutionalized participation, which involves public polls and voting; and political protest, which involves demonstrations and rallies about numerous issues on the political agenda.

Canadians are fortunate in having witnessed relatively little overt political violence since the Winnipeg General Strike nearly a century ago and the On-to-Ottawa trek of unemployed workers in 1935. Many would argue that this is because Canada is a democratic country, and in democratic countries political participation is typically non-violent. By contrast, many countries in the world still are not democratic, violent political participation is ongoing, and political crimes are common.

Questions for Critical Thought

1. Define the notion of "political crime" and discuss any political crime that has been perpetrated by government.
2. Merton speaks of *anomie* as a gap between cultural goals and the ability to achieve them. How would he have characterized war deserters from the United States to Canada?
3. Historically, military societies were authoritarian, hierarchically stratified, and traditional in their values. Explain why democracies such as the United States have been engaged in wars.

4. Think about the ways that the media help to manufacture consent for war. What role, if any, has the media played in recent conflict?
5. How do sociologists account for the fact that many terrorists are middle- to upper-class men with a higher-than-average education?
6. No century has seen as much violence carried out in the name of governments as the twentieth century. In a democratizing world, with organizations like the United Nations, how can we make sense of this?

Recommended Readings

Chomsky, Noam. 2003. *Hegemony or Survival: America's Quest for Global Dominance.* New York: Metropolitan Books.

Noam Chomsky's book is the first in a series that examines America's imperial tendencies. Chomsky, a renowned linguist and peace activist, explores how America has tried to preserve its supremacy through the use of its military.

Dallaire, Romeo. 2004. *Shake Hands with the Devil: The Failure of Humanity in Rwanda.* New York: Carroll and Graf.

This is a first-hand account of the genocide in Rwanda by the Canadian soldier who led the under-supported and failed UN Assistance Mission for Rwanda (UNAMIR) in the mid-1990s. Dallaire describes the horrible events he witnessed that the international community tried to ignore.

Lorey, David E., and William H. Beezley, eds. 2002. *Genocide, Collective Violence, and Popular Memory: The Politics of Remembrance in the Twentieth Century.* Wilmington, Del.: Scholarly Resources Books.

This book discusses various incidents of collective violence, ranging from decades-long genocide to short-lived massacres. The goal is to highlight the importance of "social memory" in healing the wounds caused by state-sponsored political violence.

Scheper-Hughes, Nancy, and Philippe I. Bourgois, eds. 2004. *Violence in War and Peace: An Anthology.* Malden, Mass.: Blackwell.

This book argues that violence occurs along a continuum, ranging from individual action and responsibility to communal and state sponsorship. The authors believe that violence begets violence and that the most violent acts often involve conduct that is socially permitted—even encouraged—rather than condemned as deviant.

Recommended Websites

Transparency International

www.transparency.org/

Transparency International is an NGO committed to providing information about global corruption. This website provides links to research on corruption in business and government, as well as information on how to reduce corruption.

United Nations Office on Drugs and Crime

www.unodc.org/unodc/index.html?ref=menutop

The UNODC provides extensive information, news, and data on all aspects of crime, from domestic abuse to terrorism, with links to the various categories of criminal activity and UN action. Of particular relevance here is the link to the 2003 UN Convention against Corruption.

Web Genocide Documentation Centre

www.ess.uwe.ac.uk/genocide.htm

Run by Professor Stuart Stein of Bristol's University of the West of England, this is a valuable, though visually unattractive, compendium of reference materials on issues relating to genocide. This well-organized site caters to students looking for a brief overview of important genocide-related topics.

World Bank

www.worldbank.org/wbi/governance/

The World Bank's governance and anti-corruption division provides information and research about global corruption. The main goal of this initiative is to alleviate poverty by eliminating corrupt practices and promoting good governance.

Your No Counts!

www.unodc.org/yournocounts/

Run by the United Nations, the *Your No Counts!* campaign is an international effort dedicated to fighting government corruption throughout the world. Working in conjunction with the United Nations Development Programme and the UN's Office on Drugs and Crime, the program provides many valuable links to anti-corruption sites.

Recommended Movies

***Pan's Labyrinth*, Dir. Guillermo del Toro (2006)**

Mexican director del Toro's work is alternately charming and terrifying, weaving elements of magical realism into a story about totalitarianism, fascism, and guerrilla resistance. Set in the aftermath of the Spanish Civil War, a shy young girl, Ofelia, feels alienated from her stepfather, a high-ranking commander in General Franco's army. Ofelia routinely escapes to a magical world that borders on reality while war rages on around her.

***Missing*, Dir. Costa-Gavras (1982)**

Costa-Gavras (Constantinos Gavras), who also directed the classic political thriller *Z*, helms this pointed attack on American complicity in the military coups common to South America at the time. Charles Horman, a left-wing American activist, goes missing in the unnamed country (thinly veiled Chile). Both the country's ruling junta and local American representatives ignore Horman's wife and father, who come looking for his body. This powerful, award-winning film's critique of American policy in Central and South America raised the ire of the American government at the time of its release.

***Born on the Fourth of July*, Dir. Oliver Stone (1989)**

Iconoclastic director Stone's follow-up to *Platoon* (1986), this film gave Stone his second Oscar win for best director. Based on the memoirs of Vietnam War veteran Ron Kovic, the movie follows the principal character's path from deeply patriotic soldier to disabled ex-marine and, finally, to anti-war activist. Though focused on a particular war, Stone speaks more broadly to the unjustness of war itself and the place of free speech at times of war.

***The Sorrow and the Pity*, Dir. Marcel Ophüls (1969)**

One of the most famous documentaries ever made, this is an epic treatise on French memories and realities of the Nazi occupation of Vichy France. While the French often discuss their resistance movement, Ophüls explores the more common realities of collaboration. The director interviews French citizens who remember the occupation, getting their thoughts about wartime anti-Semitic films and pro-Vichy propaganda.

10 Victims of Crime and Victims of Conscience

Learning Objectives

- To learn how people can be victimized in different ways
- To understand the leading theories about criminal victimization
- To see the special importance of location (place) for victimization
- To recognize that vulnerable populations are at highest risk
- To focus on the dangers facing homeless people, sex workers, and Aboriginals
- To question the role of religion as a source of victimization

Introduction

This chapter is about victimization—the targeting of an individual or group for subjection to crime, unfair treatment, or another wrong. As noted in earlier chapters, people think about deviance in various ways, and this book has reflected much of that variety. In fact, we might even name the types of deviance according to their victims: these names might include "victims of crime," "victims of non-crime," "victims of conscience," "crimes without victims," and "ordinary rule-benders." Let us briefly consider each of these in turn, and then consider two of them at length.

Discussing "victims of crime" takes us to the heart of debates about the purpose of social control. This kind of victimization reminds us of the reason we have laws, police, courts, and prisons. Criminal victimization is harmful: we can identify the harm done and the people harmed. At the opposite pole are **crimes without victims**, crimes for which people are punished for behaving in ways that do not (obviously) harm anyone. One example is punishment for the use of recreational drugs such as marijuana. Public support for the punishment of such "crimes" is often weak. However, politicians avoid removing these laws for fear of offending small but vocal minorities in the electorate. Instead, they allow the police to leave these laws unenforced or selectively enforced.

Viewed from another angle, the opposite of "victims of crime" are "victims of non-crime," people who suffer because the government has failed to regulate dangerous activities. We have already discussed some of this in Chapter 8; however, it is useful to review the issue of corporate or white-collar crime. Consider the non-regulation of financial activities that resulted in the meltdown of the world's economy in 2008; the continued, unregulated pollution of the environment by large industrial or farming concerns; and the non-enforcement of many consumer safety or workplace safety laws.

Much of the first half of this book discussed a fourth face of deviance—what we might call "ordinary rule-benders." This term includes people with deviant appearances (for example, freaks and geeks) or unusual sexual preferences, and people who are otherwise non-conformists (whether we consider them rebels, kooks, weirdos, whiners, or disturbed). These people do things a little differently from other people without, at least obviously, hurting anyone. So, they are not criminals and they do not have apparent victims, but we treat them as deviant nonetheless.

Finally, there are people we might call "victims of conscience." These people bend the rules or even break them because their principles will not let them conform to society's dominant beliefs. They can be important when they challenge the "received wisdom of society"—whether religious, political, or moral. In their own time, other people may consider them cranks or troublemakers and, therefore, ridicule them, throw them in jail, or even put them to death. Consider the fates of Socrates, Jesus, and Galileo—each persecuted for their beliefs by the religious and political leaders of their time. Or consider the more recent examples of Gandhi and Nelson Mandela.

Such "victims of conscience" appear in various social forms: as heretics, whistle-blowers, conscientious objectors, war resisters, or merely bohemians and members of the counterculture. Eventually, people may remember many of them as heroes and heralds of a new society. Yet, in their own time, a fearful power structure and an ignorant populace may victimize them. Later in this chapter, we will discuss the particular role of organized religion in suppressing deviant new thinking and victims of conscience. First, however, we will discuss "victims of crime"—a central concern in the criminological approach to deviant behaviour—and the relation of these victims to "the normality of crime."

Classic Works

BOX 10.1

Émile Durkheim and "The Normality of Crime"

Crime is present . . . in all societies of all types. . . . .the acts thus characterized are not the same everywhere; but, everywhere and always, there have been men who have behaved in such a way as to draw upon themselves penal repression. What is normal, simply, is the existence of criminality. . . . [This] is not to say merely that it is an inevitable, although regrettable phenomenon due to the incorrigible wickedness of men; it is to affirm that it is . . .an integral part of all healthy societies. . . .

Crime is normal because a society exempt from it is utterly impossible. Crime . . . consists of an act that offends certain very strong collective sentiments. In a society in which criminal acts are no longer committed, the sentiments they offend would have to be found without exception in all individual consciousness, and they must be found to exist with the same degree as sentiments contrary to them. Assuming that this condition could actually be realized, crime would not thereby disappear; it would only change its form. . . .

Imagine a society of saints. . . . Crimes . . . will there be unknown, but faults which appear venial to the layman will create there the same scandal that the ordinary offense does in ordinary consciousness. If, then, this society has the power to judge and punish, it will define these acts as criminal and will treat them as such.

What confers [a criminal] character upon [people] is not the intrinsic quality of a given act but that definition which the collective conscience lends them. If the collective conscience is stronger, if it has enough authority practically to suppress these divergences [from the collective type] . . . it will designate them as criminal.

Crime is, then, necessary; it is bound up with the fundamental conditions of all social life and by that very fact it is useful. . . . From this point of view . . . the criminal no longer seems a totally unsociable being, a sort of parasitic element . . . introduced into the midst of society. On the contrary, he plays a definite role in social life. Crime, for its part, must no longer be conceived as an evil that cannot be too much suppressed. There is no occasion for self-congratulation when the crime rate drops noticeably below the average level, for we may be certain that this apparent progress is associated with some social disorder. . . . If crime is not pathological at all, the object of punishment cannot be to cure it, and its true function must be sought elsewhere.

Source: Abridged from Émile Durkheim, "The Normality of Crime," in Durkheim (1938 [1895]).

Theories about Victims and Victimization

In this section of the book, comprising the last three chapters, we dispense with the discussion of competing paradigms—of functional theory, critical theory, and symbolic interactionism, in particular—and carve up the literature differently. This is because, in the scholarly research on victimization, social control, and punishment, the contributions are not easily or usefully distinguished as belonging to one or another of these three paradigms. Instead, in this chapter and the next two, we will organize the theoretical discussions as they appear in the scholarly literature.

Four main theories are commonly used to explain why some groups of people are more likely to be victims of crime than others, and they do not fall neatly into one or another of the major paradigms. These are **routine activity theory**, lifestyle theory, deviant place theory, and victim precipitation theory.

Routine Activity Theory

Routine activity theory states that crime depends mainly on opportunities, and opportunities are created by activity patterns. Thus, victimization is a predictable result of how and where people spend their time. Mustaine and Tewksbury (2000) argue that criminal acts are also promoted by situations that involve alcohol and drug use, for example, or unsupervised interactions with violent people. As a result, individual lifestyle and social affiliations largely shape our risks of victimization (Jennings et al., 2010). This influence is especially obvious in gangs: gang membership is strongly correlated with victimization, even after controlling for demographic variables such as education, poverty, and unemployment (Taylor et al., 2007).

Routine activity theory predicts that victimization results from the convergence of likely offenders and suitable targets with an absence of capable guardians. Therefore, the growth of victimization will reflect changes in the character of our routine activities—criminal and otherwise—and the increased opportunities for victimization in modern urban life. Automobiles, vacations, college enrolment, female labour force participation, and new consumer goods all improve our lives. However, they also provide new occasions for criminal behaviour by creating new routine activities and increasing our exposure to dangerous situations.

Changes in opportunity structures (e.g., new technology) can also increase the convergence of motivated offenders and suitable targets in the absence of capable guardianship. In this respect, think of cyberspace as providing a new set of criminal opportunities. The Internet has changed consumer practices and expanded opportunities for cyber-fraudsters to target online consumers, and has increased people's exposure to motivated offenders. In Florida, for example, researchers have found that socio-demographic characteristics such as age, sex, and education shape routine patterns of online activity (e.g., time spent online and online purchasing patterns). These, in turn, shape the likelihood of being targeted for fraud online, thus explaining the effect of socio-demographic characteristics on victimization (Pratt et al., 2010).

As noted, capable guardianship is an important element of routine activity theory, though it is often neglected. Reynald (2010) interviewed residential guardians—informal agents of social control in a specific locality who may include neighbourhood watch groups and self-appointed vigilantes, among others—to examine the factors that made them "capable" of disrupting opportunities for crime. Three key aspects of capable guardianship were identified: a willingness to supervise, an ability to detect potential offenders, and a willingness to intervene when necessary.

Routine activity theory can be applied to both domestic and non-domestic, less intimate types of victimization. Consider victimization by robbery. Using official police records, interviews, and participant observation in Tianzhi city, China, Xu (2009) examined the victimization of motorcycle taxi drivers. His research showed that migrant motorcycle taxi drivers, who came to the city illegally and are unregistered there, are robbed more often than are resident motorcycle taxi drivers. In general, their nighttime work patterns increase the chances of their being robbed, both by increasing their exposure to likely offenders and by reducing the presence of capable guardians. In addition, like other illegal or marginalized workers—for example, sex workers in Canada—migrant workers suffer the added risk because of a lack of protection.

Hot Spots, Targets, and Guardians

Hot spots, a key concept in routine activity theory, are locations where the risks of crime are especially high; they include downtown entertainment districts and tourist attractions. In many cities, hot spots also include dancehalls, bars, and nightclubs. On average, young people are at much higher risk of being victims of violent crime than older people are because young people are more likely to visit public hot spots.

However, not all hot spots are public places. They can be private places, too. For example, throughout Canada, family homes are "hot spots" of victimization. In family homes, likely offenders are often close to familiar, likely victims; and often, the so-called guardians are themselves the perpetrators of violence.

Workplaces are also hot spots of victimization. A Statistics Canada report (Léséleuc, 2007) using police-reported and self-reported data from 24,000 households, found that nearly one-fifth of all incidents of violent victimization, including physical assault, sexual assault, and robbery, occurred in the victim's workplace. Seven out of 10 incidents of workplace violence were physical assaults, and men and women were equally likely to report having experienced workplace violence. However, incidents involving male victims were about 50 per cent more likely to result in injuries.

Violence in the workplace was found to be especially common in certain employment sectors. For example, one-third of all violent workplace incidents involved a victim who worked in social assistance or health-care services, such as hospitals, nursing, or residential care institutions. Victimization rates were also high among people working in accommodation (that is, hotel) or food services, retail or wholesale trade, or educational services. Violent incidents that occurred in the workplace were twice as likely to be reported to the police as those occurring outside of the workplace.

As well, schools can also be hot spots for victimization. In Canadian research on bullying, Pepler, Jiang, Craig, and Connolly (2008) found 60 per cent of girls and 48 per cent of boys in Grade 1 said they had been bullied in the previous two months. Bullying typically declines with age. Yet, even in Grade 9, 45 per cent of boys and 32 per cent of girls reported having been bullied in the previous two months. And even among students in Grade 12, 15 per cent of boys and 10 per cent of girls reported they had been bullied over the same period.

Current Events

BOX 10.2

"Bullycides"

Two sets of parents have recently placed the blame for their children's suicides on the bullying and cyber-bullying they endured. Seventeen-year-old Courtney Brown reportedly committed suicide after having been bullied for months both at school and on Facebook, according to her parents. The mother of 15-year-old Jenna Bowers-Bryanton similarly reported that her daughter took her own life because she had been harassed at school and through a social networking site. The parents of these girls publicly appealed for increased and intensified action to be taken against bullying, adding to the chorus of negative sentiments that have recently surfaced with regard to this increasingly prevalent issue.

In response to these so-called "bullycides" and the pleas for action they have generated, a group titled Nova Scotia Parents Against Bullying began campaigning for a new law, which they hope to have titled "Jenna's Law," that would make counselling mandatory for youth who are identified as bullies. Those who support the implementation of this law feel that most bullies have been victims of bullying themselves, and that these adolescents therefore require professional help to address the emotional issues that seem to be causing (or at least contributing to) their tormenting of others.

In addition, the Nova Scotia government has founded a task force to investigate youth cyber-bullying, with the aim of strengthening provincial and school policies intended to prevent, manage, and intervene on bullying. Education Minister Ramona Jennex announced that teachers, police, parents, and mental health professionals would be invited to participate in the task force, which will provide the province with a recommended action plan, based on the information gathered in a series of meetings and focus groups with students across the province and input gathered from the public via an online survey.

Sources: "Nova Scotia Announces Task Force to Examine Prevalence of Cyberbullying," *Globe and Mail*, 6 Apr. 2011; CBC News, "Bullied Teen's Death Sparks Campaign," 28 Mar. 2011; Jennifer Taplin, "Parents, Teachers, Police and Mental-Health Professionals to Take Part in Task Force," *Metro Halifax*, 7 Apr. 2011.

These authors also conclude from available international data that Canada compares poorly with many other countries in respect to bullying. They report, "Canada ranked a dismal 27th out of 35 countries on 13-year-old students' reports of bullying and victimization, respectively. . . . Across all categories of bullying or victimization, Canada consistently ranks at or below the middle of the international group. Moreover, . . . our position on the international stage across all age and gender categories has slipped compared to other countries" (prevnet.ca/BullyingFacts/BullyingStatistics/tabid/122/Default.aspx).

Prisons, not surprisingly, are especially dangerous places for violent victimization. In fact, inmates of many "total institutions," including mental hospitals and nursing homes, risk victimization every day. Common offences against prisoners include assault, robbery, threats of violence, theft from cells, and verbal abuse. Prisoners are at particular risk of physical assault by other inmates, as well as theft of personal property.

Another key concept in routine activity theory is *suitable targets*. Suitable targets are people who are regularly exposed to crime or for other reasons have heightened vulnerability. Location aside, some people are simply more likely than others to be victimized. The risk of violent victimization is higher among certain demographic groups than others. For example, young Canadians (aged 15 to 24 years), people who are single, people who live in an urban area, and people who have a household income under $15,000 all are more likely to be crime victims (Gannon and Mihorean, 2005).

Risks of victimization are even higher for Aboriginal people—especially young Aboriginal people—than they are for young people in general. Self-reported violent victimization is generally highest among Canada's disadvantaged. People with higher-than-average risks of being victims of violent crimes self-identify as homosexual, self-identify as Aboriginal, or have some form of activity limitation or physical handicap, for example. Figure 10.1 shows the victimization rates for selected disadvantaged and marginalized groups in Canada.

People who are powerless or appear powerless are at higher-than-average risk of crime and violence. Three characteristics that put people at risk of victimization are the victim's target vulnerability (e.g., physical weakness or psychological distress), target gratifiability (e.g., female gender for the crime of sexual assault), and target antagonism (e.g., ethnic or group identities that may spark hostility or resentment).

As we have noted several times, women risk certain kinds of victimization more than men do. In this sense, they are especially suitable targets. For example, women are more likely than men to be killed by a spouse, former spouse, intimate partner, or date. Men, by contrast, are more likely to be killed by a stranger or acquaintance. Most acts of violence against women are carried out in private places, such as the home, although some public places also can pose risks. Women run higher-than-usual risks in certain situations, such as when using public transport, living near a park, or drinking alcohol. Women are much more likely to be victims than men are, especially if they eat out often and spend time socializing.

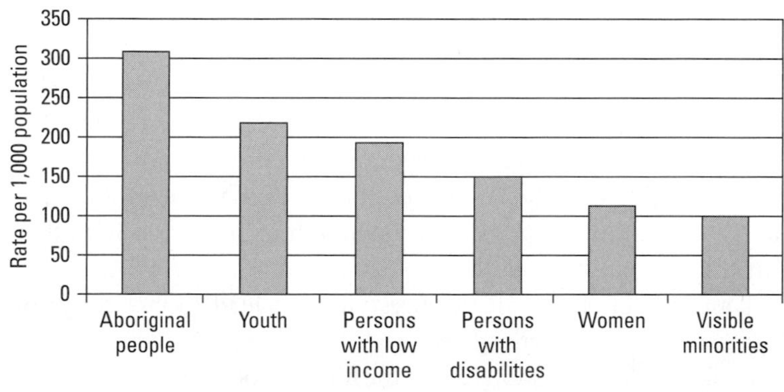

FIGURE 10.1 Victims of Violent Crime, Selected Disadvantaged Groups, Canada

Note: "Violent crime" includes sexual assault, assault, and robbery.
Source: Department of Justice Canada, *JustResearch* no. 13 (2005): 59, at: <www.justice.gc.ca/eng/pi/rs/rep-rap/jr/jr13/jr13.pdf>.

Public places increase the risk of rape for women; and women workers, women students, and younger women generally are at a much greater risk of rape than women who are less mobile. However, homes remain the hottest hot spots for women. Situational context—the where and when of a sexually violent crime—is an even better predictor of rape attempts than victim or offender characteristics. In Chapter 7, we considered recent data on violence in the home. Clearly, women and children run a higher risk of victimization than men.

The elderly are also at a higher risk of victimization. Elderly people, though running less risk than youth, are more at risk than middle-aged people, especially for crimes of robbery, intimidation, vandalism, and forgery or fraud swindles. Robbery is the most serious violent offence committed against elderly victims, and men and women are equally likely to experience it. Such robberies often take place outside the home during routine activities.

At the other end of the age spectrum, juveniles aged 12–17 are more likely than adults to be victims of violent crimes. Compared with adult victims, juvenile victims are more likely to know their victimizer and to be involved in perpetrating violence themselves. Among other suitable targets, immigrants and ethnic minorities are also at higher risk of victimization, especially with crimes against persons. We often refer to these as hate crimes when they are motivated by a person's race, ethnicity, religion, or other distinguishing characteristic. Statistics Canada (www.statcan.gc.ca/daily-quotidien/110607/dq110607a-eng.htm) reported on hate crimes for 2009:

- In 2009, Canadian police services reported 1,473 hate crimes, an increase of 42 per cent from the previous year.
- Overall, mischief was the most common type of hate crime, accounting for more than half (54 per cent) of all incidents. Incidents motivated by sexual orientation were more often violent, at about three-quarters (74 per cent) of all such incidents.
- Race or ethnicity was the most common motivation for police-reported hate crime (54 per cent) in 2009, followed by religion (29 per cent) and sexual orientation (13 per cent).
- For both victims and persons accused of hate crime, the rate peaked among those aged 12 to 17 and generally decreased with increasing age.

Interestingly, in regard to crimes against persons, targets (i.e., victims) and victimizers often have similar characteristics because they share similar routine activities and meet one another regularly. No wonder, then, that intra-racial violence is more common than inter-racial offences: victims and offenders often live in the same neighbourhood; and, often, both victims and offenders belong to groups that experience social exclusion (Blumstein, 2010). People tend to spend time in the company of other people who are like themselves, so they are likely to victimize or be victimized by people like themselves. This also applies to people in the same age group, though (as we have seen) it does not apply to people of the same gender.

Lifestyle Theory

Lifestyle theory, as mentioned earlier, builds on the idea that victimization depends on a person's lifestyle. People with high-risk lifestyles are more likely to be victimized than people with low-risk lifestyles. Men who regularly go to bars, for example, are much more likely to be victimized than men who spend their evenings at home, watching television with their pet dog.

Risky lifestyles can lead to victimization anywhere. So, for example, Nofziger (2009) showed that the lifestyles of juveniles can lead to violent victimization at school. Analyzing data from the US National Survey of Adolescents, Nofziger found that both indirect victimization (e.g., witnessing violence) and direct victimization (e.g., sexual or physical assault) are common at schools. Juveniles who lead a deviant lifestyle, i.e., often engaging in delinquent activities, significantly increase their odds of both direct and indirect victimization. Even within the (relatively) controlled school setting, juveniles who lead deviant lifestyles are at a high risk of victimization. Consider, therefore, how much more dangerous life can be outside of schools.

Among frequent drug users, for example, violent victimization is not uncommon. Criminals also often risk victimization because of their association with other criminals. And when they interact with other criminals, they cannot always rely on legal authorities for protection. Moreover, they sometimes become the targets of retaliatory behaviour.

Deviant Place Theory

Deviant place theory states that people who live in dangerous social areas are at greater risk of victimization. In these high-risk places, people fall victim to crime because of the sheer volume of crime in their neighbourhood, which increases their risk of encountering criminals. Typically, poverty, unemployment, disorganization, and a large number of young males characterize high-risk areas.

Thus, deviant place theory—related to social disorganization theory—refers to the risks associated with living in "bad areas of town." It links high victimization rates to the presence of poverty and unemployment, common in such urban areas. The best way to avoid victimization, according to this theory, is to move to a "better" neighbourhood.

Many studies have shown that population turnover increases the crime rate and residential stability decreases it. In short, crime flourishes in communities where the population turns over rapidly because an unstable population cannot unite to address local crime issues. Note that these findings about the effects of social disorganization apply mainly to cities. Homicides occur less often in rural areas; also, the characteristics of rural homicides vary from those committed in urban settings (Cronin, 2009).

Applying Theories to the Homeless

The above three theories—routine activity theory, lifestyle theory, and deviant place theory—all are helpful in explaining the victimization of homeless people. Not surprisingly, homeless people are victimized far more often than other people are, and this can be largely explained by their location, their lifestyle, and their routine activities.

As lifestyle theory would argue, living on the streets increases their risk of victimization by exposing homeless people to criminals and crime. As well, the homeless often take part in risky activities necessary for survival, such as begging, selling drugs, or selling sexual favours. This lifestyle also puts homeless people at a high risk of being victimized. Since homeless women are more likely to resort to selling sex for money than homeless men, their chances of being sexually assaulted are much higher than those of homeless men or women who do not live on the street.

Homeless men occasionally resort to criminal activities such as robbery and dealing drugs, and, as criminals, are more likely than average to be assaulted (Whitbeck et al., 2001). The perpetrators of crimes against homeless people are typically other homeless people. Random violence also occurs, because many homeless people are on edge with hunger, drugs, alcohol, or mental illness. Some homeless people use violence to protect themselves or their property from harm by other homeless people (Garland et al., 2010). Occasionally, homeless people are the victims of non-economic crimes, such as hate crimes committed by teenage thrill-seekers (ibid.).

Many of the homeless also carry a personal history of victimization into their current lives. Roughly one-third of homeless women report having experienced childhood physical or sexual abuse, which studies have linked to subsequent homelessness (Hudson et al., 2010). Victimized children are more likely than other children to run away from home during adolescence; occasionally, this lands them on the street. The results of childhood abuse are long-lasting. Homeless women who experienced rape in childhood are almost four times as likely to experience sexual assault in adulthood as those who were not so abused as children (ibid.).

All of the mental health issues that homeless people disproportionately experience, compared to the general population, contribute to a higher risk of victimization. This is true regardless of race or age or other demographic features.

Deviant place theory also helps us understand why homeless people are criminally victimized more often than members of the general population. Homeless people tend to live in urban areas where jobs and supports are more plentiful. However, they are usually concentrated in less well-off parts of the city. Therefore, homeless shelters are also located in poorer parts of the central city; but this is also where crime risks are higher (Snow and Mulchahy, 2001).

Finally, routine activity theory helps us understand the vulnerability of homeless people to victimization. First, homeless people are available and suitable targets: they carry their property around with them and lack the protections of a locked home. They bed down in unsafe spaces—alleys, empty lots, abandoned buildings, and other areas that residents overlook. Second, homeless people also lack capable guardians such as relatives, friends, and people in authority; this leaves them especially vulnerable to violent attack. Many homeless people have friendly relations with other homeless people. However, these street friends can rarely serve as proper guardians, since they are vulnerable themselves, financially and otherwise.

Finally, homeless people are continually exposed to potential offenders such as addicts, ruffians, and street criminals. In fact, homeless people themselves fit into this category of potential offenders, which helps to explain why homeless people usually victimize other homeless people. Homeless women who sell sexual favours for money run added risks. Though they are likely to associate with clients who are not homeless, homeless women may be sexually assaulted by members of the general population or by homeless individuals (Garland et al., 2010).

Victim Precipitation Theory

Victim precipitation theory proposes that people create their own risks of being victimized—through verbal provocation, body language, or wearing certain types of clothes, for example. People may do this either passively or actively. Active precipitation involves attacking first or acting provocatively. Passive precipitation involves a victim unknowingly motivating the offender (for example, by being part of a group that threatens another group).

This theory builds on the obvious fact that some people are repeated victims of crime while other people rarely or never suffer victimization. This alone makes us wonder if the repeat victims are doing something they should avoid. The notion that some people are prone to victimization reminds us that there is a similar literature on accident proneness. One of the earliest pieces of research on accident victimization (Rawson, 1944) put forward the idea that some people were, for psychological reasons, more prone to having accidents than others.

In the decades that followed, psychologists did many studies to find and identify the personality configuration that led to this proposed accident proneness. They were never able to do so, because it doesn't exist (Rodgers and Blanchard, 1993). Today, researchers recognize that a variety of factors cause people to have multiple accidents. Some of these are physiological factors, for example, problems with balance that cause people to fall or black out. Others are situational factors that cause people to be in places (e.g., neighbourhoods) or with people likely to cause an accident—for example, being with a dangerous driver. Additionally, much of the research on workplace injury has identified management, technology, and other working conditions that lead to multiple accident risks.

Cultural values also play a part. In Chapter 6 we noted that some groups in the population—young men, in particular—tend to behave in ways that increase the likelihood of dangerous, harmful outcomes for themselves and others. However, we argued that this was due to subcultural notions of manhood, not personality characteristics rooted in the genes or childhood socialization. Young men pay higher automobile insurance premiums than older men or women of any age because they drive recklessly to appear masculine.

With victimization as with accidents, our culture tends to "blame the victim"—hold the victim responsible for bad things that happen to him or her (and give others credit for good things that happen). In our culture, we tend to seek individualistic explanations of life experiences rather than structural explanations, and elements of this attitude can be seen in all of the theories discussed above.

Of course, all the theories examined so far are compatible with regular, repeated victimization. People who are suitable targets (e.g., for reasons of disability or age) are likely to remain suitable targets. People who lead dangerous lives because of their occupation (e.g., prison guard, nightclub bouncer, or paid escort) will be in danger so long as they practise this occupation. And people who live in dangerous neighbourhoods, usually because of poverty, will continue to live in such neighbourhoods until they became wealthier.

Victim precipitation theory is controversial, however, because of its seeming tendency to single out women for their own victimization. In particular, the theory seems to blame women for physical and sexual attacks they suffer at the hands of men—whether as dates, wives, or prostitutes. This theory seems to argue that women bring about their own victimization by dressing provocatively or leaving their typical roles. By this reasoning, women are to blame if they are raped—an outrageous allegation for most women and an idea that reflects outdated, prejudiced views of both men and women. Though most women would consider this a biased approach to victimization, some researchers continue to advance this theory. For example, Franklin (2010) used survey data collected from a sample of college sorority and non-sorority women to study rape victimization among sorority members at US colleges.

On the one hand, Franklin finds that rape experiences are common for both sorority women and non-sorority women. These common experiences include sexual assault, verbal coercion resulting in sexual intercourse, and threats of force or force resulting in attempted or completed rape. On the other hand, Franklin finds that sorority women are more likely to engage in what she considers vulnerability-enhancing behaviours—behaviours correlated with various forms of sexual assault.

Sorority women, according to Franklin, are more likely to drink too much, and her data show that women who get drunk more often are more likely than other women to engage in risky behaviours, reducing their ability to assess and respond to danger cues and increasing their risk of victimization. As well, compared to non-sorority women, sorority members are more willing to put themselves in close quarters with fraternity men, and women who spend more time close to fraternity men are more likely to experience victimization, especially sexual assault.

Yet, in another study, Moor (2009) claims to find no empirical support for victim precipitation theory. Moor measures women's exposure to several forms of sexual violence (including sexual assault and physical and verbal sexual harassment) using data from a sample of Israeli college students. She finds a high prevalence of all forms of sexual violence among the students sampled, similar to the prevalence documented in other Western societies. However, she identifies no sign of a typical victim profile.

According to Moor, victims of sexual violence are not distinguishable from other women in characteristics often linked to the precipitation of sexual violence: for example, revealing style of dress, lack of self-confidence, and stereotypical attitudes towards women's roles. No single variable distinguishes between women who experience sexual violence and those who do not.

Although Canadians like to think of their country as a safe place—the peaceable kingdom—Canada stood just above the average among 30 Western countries in the 2004–5 International Crime Victimization Survey. Seventeen per cent of Canadians 16 and over reported that in the previous year they had been victims of crime, which for the purposes of the survey included a total of 10 property crimes and crimes against the person (Figure 10.2).

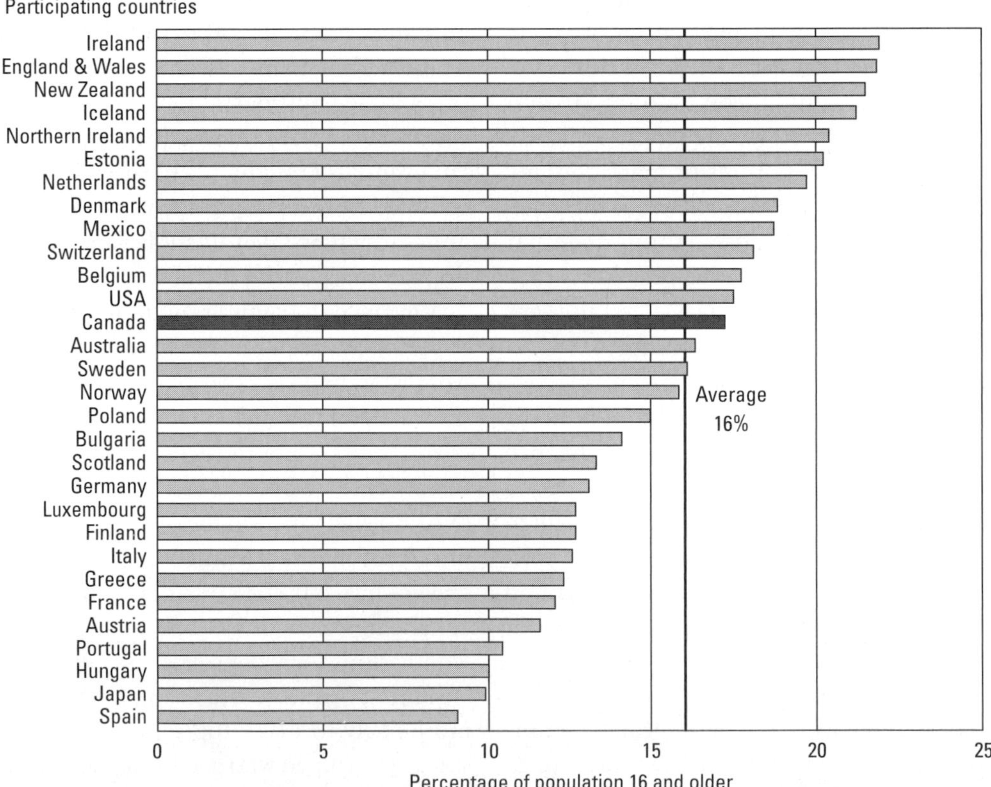

FIGURE 10.2 Rates of Victimization, Selected Countries

Source: Julie Sauvé and Kwing Hung, "An International Perspective on Criminal Victimization," *Juristat* (Dec. 2008): Chart 1, at: <www.statcan.gc.ca/pub/85-002-x/2008010/article/10745-eng.htm>.

Victimization and the Case of Sex Workers

For years, the police were aware that women from Vancouver's Downtown Eastside were disappearing, but they did little about it. They may have felt that since these women were involved in the sex trade, their disappearance was not only not surprising, but "expected." That may be one reason serial murderer Robert Pickton chose all of his victims from the sex trade in Vancouver. As victims, they were available, vulnerable, and largely ignored (if not actively despised).

In Canada, prostitution is legal. However, street soliciting and brothels have been illegal, and therefore "job" communication has to be kept hidden from the police. Sex workers in Canada are at an extremely high risk of being criminally victimized, especially by physical and sexual assault. Like homeless women, sex workers run a continuing risk of violence throughout their lives (Surrat et al., 2004).

Women sex workers who walk the city streets in search of trade are at an especially high risk of assault, rape, murder, and other types of physical violence. The male perpetrators of these crimes are varied; muggers, drug dealers, police, potential customers, and sometimes even people who pass by. As deviant place theorists would note, sex workers spend a great deal of time on the streets in areas known for high rates of crime, increasing their risk of victimization.

However, other issues contribute to their victimization as well, including gender inequality and discrimination against women (Weitzer, 2000). Class and racial discrimination are also prevalent. Most street sex workers are impoverished minority women who lack the education and skills to compete for other work opportunities. Aboriginal women offer a prime example of this, and their disrupted cultural background contributes to their vulnerability. In addition, many of these women are impoverished or homeless, further increasing their risks of victimization.

The lifestyle of sex workers also increases their risk of victimization. As lifestyle theory would point out, the prevalence of drug and alcohol use among sex trade workers both increases their attractiveness as targets and inhibits their ability to make proper risk assessments on the job. Sex workers often begin their evening work sober; but after their first client, they become drunk or high before returning to the streets for other clients (Surrat et al., 2004). This not only puts sex trade workers at increased risk for contracting sexually transmitted diseases, but also for physical and sexual violence.

Routine activity theory helps us recognize other factors that play a significant role. Street prostitutes are available targets since they roam the streets in search of customers. Second, sex workers most often ply their trade in private places, without guardians around to protect them from danger. While working the streets, sex workers expose themselves to homeless people, people on drugs, and people looking for trouble. However, even in a bedroom, there is a risk of victimization by a client under the influence of drugs or alcohol, or for whom sadism is part of the pleasure.

The Victimization of Aboriginal People

In Canada, as in the United States and elsewhere, Aboriginal people are over-represented as victims of violence, including intimate partner violence (Brownridge, 2008). As with sex workers, all the victimization theories we have examined—routine activity theory, lifestyle theory, location theory, and victim precipitation theory—contribute to an overall explanation of Aboriginal vulnerability.

Current Events

BOX 10.3

The Decriminalization of Prostitution

In June 2011, the Ontario Court of Appeal heard two starkly opposing views in the case regarding the decriminalization of prostitution in Canada. (The Court handed down its landmark decision in March 2012, as discussed in Chapter 4.) First, the federal government asserted that it is not responsible for defending people who "choose" to participate in behaviours that may be hazardous. In addition, those countries that have taken this approach have seen both the demand for and supply of prostitution rise, since decriminalization undeniably establishes an environment that excuses or even encourages the actions of sex traffickers, suggesting to them that they are free to go about their "business."

In contrast, those who support the move towards decriminalization suggest that prostitutes need to be able to protect themselves from the risks inherent to the sex industry. Prostitutes are unable, for example, to speak to potential clients for long enough to evaluate how dangerous they may be. Further, sex workers are unable to effectively defend themselves, since the laws prevent them from hiring bodyguards.

However, the real issue may lie not with the laws surrounding the sex trade but with the existence of the industry itself. Decriminalization or legalization, according to Melissa Farley of Prostitution Research and Education, will do nothing to protect or help sex trade workers. In fact, she argues against the conceptualization of prostitution as legitimate "work" or as a "job" since the majority of prostitutes did not consensually or willingly enter into the business, but were forced to participate due to a lack of alternatives for survival (Farley, 2004).

Further, prostitution is an inherently discriminatory industry, putting (primarily) females at risk of sexual violence. The sex trade is inextricably tied up in gender inequality; certain attitudes allow the industry to function, including the belief in the superiority of men over women and the right of men to use women as sexual objects. Because the industry operates based on these unjust, discriminatory views, decriminalization or legalization merely perpetuates social and gender inequality and sexual exploitation.

Thus, Farley and others suggest that the unjust, abusive, and oppressive sex trade industry should no longer be normalized or diminished as a necessary (albeit unfortunate) part of society. Rather than merely altering the laws that keep women in the sex trade, women should have access to alternative means of survival. To accomplish this, the social inequality and discrimination that underpin prostitution must be abolished.

Sources: Norma Ramos, "We Must Punish Prostitution's Buyers," *Globe and Mail*, 28 June 2011; "Prostitution Case at Ontario Court of Appeal Sees Judges Grill Federal Lawyers on Sex Trade Dangers," *The Huffington Post*, 13 June 2011.

According to Perreault (2011), Aboriginal people are twice as likely as non-Aboriginal people to become victims of violence such as assault, sexual assault, or robbery. They are also significantly more likely to be victims of homicide. Between 1997 and 2000, the average homicide rate for Aboriginal people was 8.8 per 100,000 population—almost seven times higher than the rate for non-Aboriginal people (1.3 per 100,000 population).

The General Social Survey (GSS) conducted by Statistics Canada in 2004 found that Aboriginal people were over twice as likely as non-Aboriginal people to experience some form of violent victimization such as an assault, sexual assault, or robbery. No other minorities, immigrants, or native-born were at the same risk of victimization; the rates of victimization were even lower among immigrants than non-immigrants (68 versus 116 per 1,000 population (Gannon and Mihorean, 2005). For violent victimization, the Aboriginal rate was 206 incidents per 1,000 population as opposed to 81 per 1,000 in the non-Aboriginal population (Chartrand and McKay, 2006).

Here, in summary, are some recent facts about Aboriginal victimization in Canada:

> In 2009, 37 per cent of Aboriginal people self-reported being the victim of a crime compared to 26 per cent of the non-Aboriginal population.
>
> Aboriginal people reported sexual assault incidents at a rate of 70 incidents per 1,000 people, compared to 23 per 1,000 non-Aboriginal people.
>
> Those aged 15 to 24 years were the victims in nearly half (47 per cent) of non-spousal violent incidents reported by Aboriginal people, whereas they represented 22 per cent of the Aboriginal population aged 15 and over.
>
> Aboriginal women were almost three times more likely than non-Aboriginal women to report that they had been a victim of spousal violence in the past five years.
>
> Aboriginal victims of spousal violence were also more likely to report that they have feared for their life or that they had been injured as a result of the violence.
>
> Violent crimes involving an Aboriginal victim (67 per cent) were more likely than incidents with a non-Aboriginal victim (52 per cent) to be related to the alcohol or illegal drug use of the perpetrator. (Perreault, 2011)

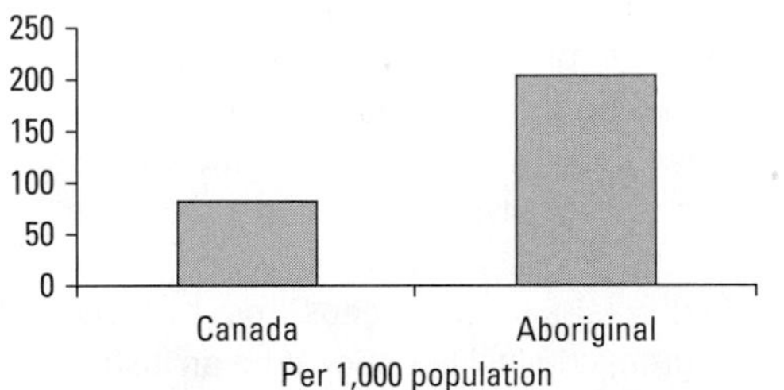

FIGURE 10.3 Violent Victimization Rates: Aboriginal and Non-Aboriginal Populations

Source: Chartrand and McKay (2006: 20, Chart 2).

Location theory is helpful in understanding Aboriginal victimization. Aboriginal people are much more likely to be victims of homicide than non-Aboriginal people are. In large part, these high rates of victimization reflect the dangerous places many Aboriginal people live. According to the 2004 General Social Survey, residents of the northern territories were three times more likely than provincial residents to experience violent victimization, such as sexual assault, robbery, or physical assault.

However, other factors also influence the high rates of victimization among Aboriginal Canadians. Consider their often impoverished lifestyles. The unemployment rate among Aboriginal people was nearly double that of the non-Aboriginal population in 2007 (10.6 per cent compared to 5.9 per cent). As well, a larger proportion of Aboriginal people live in poor, overcrowded housing than do non-Aboriginal people in Canada (11 per cent versus 3 per cent) and in homes in need of major repairs (23 per cent versus 7 per cent). Bad living conditions increase household stress and, in this way, increase the risk of violence.

Finally, the Aboriginal population is younger on average than the rest of the Canadian population, with a median age of 27 compared to the Canadian median age of 40. Almost half (48 per cent) of the Aboriginal population in Canada is under the age of 25. All of these factors—poverty, unemployment, crowding, and youth—are associated with crime and victimization in the general population, as well as among Aboriginal people. However, they are more common among the Aboriginal population, especially in Canada's North.

Classic Works

BOX 10.4

Edwin M. Schur's *Crimes without Victims*

Based on the labelling theory popularized by Howard Becker and Edwin Lemert, Edwin M. Schur, in *Crimes without Victims: Deviant Behavior and Public Policy* (1965), argued for the decriminalization of "victimless crimes."

"Crimes without victims" are consensual acts by adults that break the rules prescribed in law—for example, selling or sharing marijuana. In these acts, no third party is involved or evidently harmed. Therefore, no third party has a reason to complain to the police or present evidence against these rule-breakers. Usually, these acts are also hidden from public view, so police are not likely to witness them without having advance notice. Schur also argues that "criminal laws do not always effectively curb the behavior they proscribe," and therefore these "laws . . . are highly ineffective from the standpoint of sheer deterrence" (Schur, 1965: 6). Yet, such laws may also be influential in that they show the weakness or incapability to deter unwanted behaviour, and thus bring the law into disrepute for seeking to deter behaviour that is popularly accepted.

Schur suggests that attempting to inhibit such behaviour through criminal law "seems particularly likely to create secondary deviance and to set the stage for police corruption and demoralization" (ibid.). For example, the efforts to catch and punish homosexuals, when homosexual acts were still illegal, increased homosexuals' vulnerability to blackmail and other forms of police corruption. Secondarily, the laws alienated homosexuals from society, humiliating and demoralizing them.

The criminalization of homosexual behaviour was defended until quite recently. Many believed that a failure to do so would lead to sexual experimentation, moral drift, and social decay—including the disappearance of the family. Some who continue to fear or dislike homosexuality would say, even today, the legalization of homosexual marriage has completed this process of weakening the modern family and, with it, modern society. Similarly, some may still believe homosexuals are mentally ill and need psychiatric treatment, though such views have been removed from the DSM—the "Bible" of the psychiatric profession.

The notion of "victimless crimes" forces us to consider what a society needs from its laws, courts, and police. It forces us to ask how, and to what degree, criminal law should be an instrument of social policy. While the idea of "crimes without victims" has been essential in the legalization of homosexual acts and abortion in Canada, it continues to play a role, 50 years after Schur's influential book appeared, in discussions related to marijuana and other drug use.

Victims of Conscience

Consider now a different victimization: victimization of conscience. By this, we mean the victimization some people suffer because they feel morally obliged to break society's rules, which they consider wrong or immoral, then suffer punishment for acting according to their conscience. It is important for us to remember that deviance is not always bad. In fact, deviance is often good and necessary—like a forest fire that clears the way for new trees. This may be one reason deviance is universal: found in all places at all times. It can have positive effects on society.

One of the founders of sociology, Émile Durkheim, made this very point in a classic statement about the normality of crime (and deviance) in *Rules of the Sociological Method* (see Box 10.1). Now consider also the dilemma posed by crimes without victims. These crimes may or may not benefit society; but it seems likely that their punishment will harm society, for reasons outlined in Box 10.4.

Time to Reflect: Can you think of people who are harmed or who suffer from "crimes without victims"? Is this still the case when certain behaviours and activities are decriminalized?

As we saw in the excerpt from Durkheim (Box 10.1), crime can be viewed as a normal and even necessary part of life. There is no society without crime. Precisely what makes up a crime in any given society, however, varies over time and place. For example, adultery may be a punishable crime in one place and moment in history, but not in another. Only a few crimes, such as murder, are considered crimes in all societies, although even here societies differ in what they consider murder—that is, culpable killing.

This leads Durkheim to wonder why crime is found everywhere, and what value (if any) crime may have for the survival of societies. He concludes that crime has an "indirect utility," that is, all societies need to be able to change, and precisely this openness to change leaves room for deviance and crime.

As well, crime also has a direct value or utility. Like the forest fire that results in change and renewal within an ecosystem, a crime challenges and destroys some aspect of the prevailing order. In this sense, it clears the way for change. Sometimes, it even installs the change. In hindsight, we may come to view the crime as a type of progress. Every successful revolution, when it first occurs, is considered a crime, at least by the people in power. Yet, with the installation of new leaders, the revolution is no longer a crime but a heroic act, honoured, and celebrated. Besides, even when a "criminal" is not celebrated in his or her own time, honours may come later. This was true, for example, of the Greek philosopher Socrates, put to death for inciting immoral thoughts among his young students. Today, we view Socrates as a hero, not a criminal.

In the cases of Socrates and other famous "criminals" like Jesus, Galileo, or, more recently, Mahatma Gandhi, Nelson Mandela, and Martin Luther King—the rule-breakers are punished for violating conventional beliefs and going against prevailing authority. Their courage costs them years in prison, if not their lives. Their independence sets an example for others and opens the door to new thinking and new behaviour by others. They may be deviants and criminals, but they are conscientious ones; and they are victimized by society for their trouble.

Thus, many crimes—especially victimless crimes, including so-called crimes against morality or "public order"—are potentially useful to society. To repeat a theme in this book, most psychologists treat crime (deviance more generally) as something pathological; and they look for psychological causes or faulty values in the mind of the criminal. By contrast, Durkheim viewed crime as a product of society, not individuals. Crime is normal and can have positive social functions, though it may not always do so. Crime is also normal in that no society is so repressive that everyone conforms all the time. Thus, deviance and crime are always possible, by the mere fact that rules exist and people have choice about when and whether to obey them.

However, as we have also seen, crime has indirect benefits for society, in that it elicits punishment and control, and these societal responses are also important for social survival. By eliciting punishments and arousing collective sentiments against the rule-breaker, crime clarifies society's support for the rule that has been broken. Thus, crime has the unexpected effect of strengthening moral consensus in the society: it creates and strengthens social cohesion. As Durkheim (1938 [1895]) says elsewhere in the same essay, "Crime brings together upright consciences and concentrates them." Punishment in this sense becomes an occasion for the celebration of social consensus or solidarity.

How, then, should we compare the social benefits of crime (which is generally considered bad) with religion (which is generally considered good)? Each contributes to social cohesion, but each does so in a different way; and the two are usually opposed to each other.

Religion as a Source of Control and Deviance

Religion is largely concerned with enforcing social control on behalf of a shared, and supernaturally sanctioned, moral code. Yet for Durkheim, everything in social life needs moderation and balance. As Durkheim makes clear in his classic work *Suicide* and elsewhere, there can be too little social control and too much social control. In each instance, the effects on individuals and on society are harmful.

Not surprisingly, then, religion can be a force for good and for bad. When religious control is relatively weak (as, for example, in Protestantism compared to Roman Catholicism, by Durkheim's reckoning), one result is an increase in suicide. However, religious or other types of control can be harmful if they are excessive. Then, they create repression, which can have harmful psychological and social effects on civilized society.

Beyond that, religions may set repressive, unattainable moral and behavioural standards. They also target particular types of people for surveillance, control, and punishment. Religions, for example, tend to be designed for and by men, to serve male interests. No wonder, then, that women have been especially targeted for religious repression and persecution.

Leaving aside the segregation and unequal treatment of women in Orthodox Judaism and Islam, consider the mistreatment of women in the history of Christianity. During the period referred to as "the Burning Times," roughly the fifteenth to seventeenth centuries, large numbers of women were accused of witchcraft and condemned by the Church, often for no other reason than that they were women. Witches were accused of harmful magic and consorting with the Devil.

The theology of the times made the witch craze possible. Women were seen as the carriers of evil: susceptible to the advances of the Devil from whom they derived their powers through a pact; sexually insatiable; the greatest danger to Christian society. The most famous witch-hunters' manual, *Malleus Maleficarum*, prepared by two Dominican priests, was published in 1486 and went through six editions before 1500, at least 15 editions by 1520, and another 16 by 1669. It was translated from the Latin into German, French, Italian, and English, was extensively quoted in later manuals, and soon spread into civil law.

It may be by chance that more women were accused: in many areas, the "witch" became a convenient scapegoat, and all the ills affecting a district could be blamed on her or him. People who did not fit in—for example, those who uttered curses or who were seen as bad neighbours—were more likely to be targeted by an untutored peasantry as witches and as the source of local problems. Further, the witch craze was conducted by civil authorities as well as by the churches, so it is unjust to blame the churches alone for this craze. During this period, culminating in the sixteenth and seventeenth centuries, civil as well as ecclesiastical courts condemned both women and men. However, women were far more often condemned than men were.

By the end of the period, a woman's place was to be as an adjunct to her husband, if she had one. Seen in a broader context, the process of accusation, trial, torture, and execution of thousands of "witches" proved to be one method by which men were able to restrict women's lives to a greater extent than was the case before or since.

Two anthropologists, Child and Whiting (1953), analyzed the characteristics of societies in which a belief in witches and witchcraft is especially marked. In their survey of over 50 cultures around the world, they find that belief in witchcraft is most common in societies that impose severe behavioural and moral training on young children to control their aggressive impulses. Wherever the child training is most severe, there the culture is most likely to believe in witchcraft and punish witches. This fact suggests, as Freud would suggest, that suppressed aggression seeks indirect outlets, and witchcraft provides such outlets.

Of course, belief in witchcraft is not the only outlet for suppressed aggression: other outlets include warfare, patriotism, racism, and superstition. In fact, Adorno et al. (1950) found all of these tendencies were correlated in the people possessing what they call "authoritarian personalities." Thus, religion—if too controlling—can stifle creativity and freedom; it can also produce pathologies of violence, aggression, and distorted thinking. Said another way, it can create "victims of conscience" who appear to be witches, traitors, or other dangerous deviates.

Today, many religions are not controlling and punitive, and for many people religion is irrelevant and exercises no control over their lives. Responding to this widespread lack of interest, religious denominations have tried harder than in the past to embrace a wider, more welcoming view of differences. This has been the response of religion to "secularism." Ironically, secularism has also brought about the development of religious fundamentalism in many parts of the world (see Berger and Zijderveld, 2009).

Our present-day society is often called a "secular society," and by that we mean that people today are less religiously inclined than they were a century or two ago. People are less inclined to attend churches or think about the supernatural. People today often speak of our society as being, among other things, a technological or scientific or, as Weber called it, a "rational-legal" society. This refers to a society in which people are "disenchanted" or demystified about the natural world, and disinclined to explain natural phenomena by invoking supernatural causes.

Still, religion is a distinctive approach to life and it trains people to think in particular ways about morality, deviance, and control. We get the clearest idea about the difference between secular and religious approaches to these topics if we contrast religion with science. People discussed this difference a great deal throughout the nineteenth and twentieth centuries. Indeed, there was virtual warfare between science and religion around topics like Darwin's theory of evolution. Darwin's thinking posed a significant challenge to a literal interpretation of the Old Testament. Today, this debate has largely died down, though not disappeared. Still, a large gap remains between science and religion, and specifically between the ways that science and religion carry out their inquiries.

Science is a cultural and social orientation towards the search for knowledge. It is morally neutral—the goal of science is to advance knowledge, not to proclaim a particular morality. This fact is reflected in the way scientists do their empirical research, obeying the "norms of science" identified by Robert Merton (1973 [1942]) as "CUDO": communalism, universalism, disinterest, and organized skepticism. Moreover, science advances by independent disinterested research, a public review of findings, and the application of universal criteria of judgement. Most important of all, science demands organized skepticism. All scientific claims are critically evaluated and all conclusions are considered "tentative," awaiting disproof.

By contrast, religious scholarship is rarely disinterested. It is often organized and funded by religious organizations or by colleges with religious affiliations. For this reason, it is unlikely that, say, a Catholic scholar will conclude the Vatican is all wrong about papal infallibility or that the Gospels are a hoax. Scholars and other religious commentators who step too far outside the accepted institutional boundaries risk ridicule, exclusion, expulsion, excommunication, or even, in Islam, a fatwa (death sentence).

Religious debates are rarely public; often, they are carried out "internally," so the Church can continue to present a united front to the outside world. A final key point is that religions do not encourage or even necessarily approve organized skepticism. Churches and religions are built on faith. They do not regard their values, beliefs, and holy documents as current "best guesses" about the supernatural. Therefore, they are usually unwilling to change their values and beliefs. True, religions vary in their flexibility and adaptability under pressure. However, taken as a whole, a religion can never be as flexible and adaptable as a science, because science demands no commitment whatever to traditional beliefs. Indeed, science rejects such commitments. That said, when science is applied to create technology and, therefore, profit for some people, its "purity" and neutrality can be quickly compromised: the oil and gas industry, space exploration, and the development of new pharmaceuticals are three prime examples.

Throughout the nineteenth and twentieth centuries, "nationalism" provided many people with a sense of meaning and purpose. In some especially patriotic countries like the US, nationalism and patriotism continue to be very powerful, much more so than in Canada, for example. They have often been linked to religious belief and combined secular, nationalist, and other ideological elements in vast public rituals. In such powerfully patriotic societies, we also find efforts at thought control around secular, political matters (e.g., opposition to communism or Islam).

Think of major American sporting events such as the Super Bowl. These rival or even surpass religious events as occasions for ritual celebration. Indeed, one can view the Super Bowl as nothing less than a full-fledged civic religious festival, bringing together powerful elements of sports, politics, and myth. A recent

Super Bowl halftime show even included militaristic and nationalistic aspects in its allusions to the post-9/11 "war on terror." The goal of this display was to justify the American war in Iraq by representing it in terms of "American" values and the virtues of democratic citizenship, all in the context of sports coverage.

Thus, nationalism or, more broadly "civil religion" has the same effect as denominational religion in its efforts to control people's thoughts and behaviours. However, in most societies, churches and religious beliefs tend to be longer-lived and more controlling than secular institutions and beliefs.

Churches tend to be "greedy" institutions, demanding people's loyalty in thought and action. For centuries, prejudice and discrimination were freely expressed against religious minorities throughout Europe, culminating in the Holocaust—the biggest religion- and race-based pogrom in human history. We do not have to dig very far back in history to come across instances of abuse and violence against religious minorities, let alone reasons for continuing suspicion and distrust. Often, minority groups have been stigmatized, discriminated against, excluded, and even punished for their failure to hold the correct views.

At the extremes, religious groups have promoted genocide (think of the Spanish Inquisition against Jews and Islamic Moors, for example) and suppressed particular groups (whether women, religious minorities, or others with "unacceptable" qualities). Many believe that Catholicism and Islam continue to support anti-democratic regimes in much of the world today. By contrast, other religions—Hinduism, Buddhism, and Confucianism—play little role in politics (although it is worth noting that Confucianism was a basis for Japanese fascism during World War II).

In multi-ethnic and multi-religious states such as the US, Britain, and Canada, the separation of politics from religion has been good for politics and it has been good for religion, because religious groups have been protected by multicultural tolerance. The problem we face in Canada and other multicultural nations is whether to give priority to religious tolerance over concerns about the rights of, say, women within religious groups.

Religions today chiefly help people develop and achieve fulfillment by exploring their spiritual needs, and some believe this goal is incompatible with partisan political involvement. Giving religions an overt political role can pose a great challenge to safeguarding citizenship rights for women and other minority groups. This is because many religious codes define civil, political, and social rights and duties in ways that systematically encourage different treatment of women and men, girls and boys (as well as heterosexuals and homosexuals; and members of other religions). In addition, while we want to protect religious freedom, we do not want to give religious groups the right to discriminate in this way. The trick is to find a way of protecting both equal citizenship and religious accommodation.

Throughout the twentieth century, sociologists predicted that religion would decline in importance, often basing their work on the ideas of Émile Durkheim, who made the assumption that religion and religious expression would change as society changed. Indeed, "mainstream" Judeo-Christianity did shift to a more humanist orientation, connected to so-called "**secularization**." Many scholars have studied secularization in Western societies, noting a steadily dwindling influence of religion in public life.

Today, many people are more likely to give their allegiance to their community or society than to their church. The process some have called "societalization" refers to how people increasingly connect to an abstract "society," not to a community in which every person knows everyone else. In North America and Europe, most people look to society—a large, shapeless entity made up of organizations run on bureaucratic principles—to provide for their needs. People regularly find and work at jobs, read and watch the news, attend school, and vote in elections. All of these activities put them into contact with a society that regulates their activities, often through the state.

In Canadian society, no single religious organization dominates, so none could possibly control the state, even if it tried. Most Canadians follow a form of Christianity (though not all of these are churchgoers), but those who are church members belong to many different churches or denominations. Many others adhere to other religions, including Islam, Buddhism, and Judaism, or to Aboriginal spirituality. Some groups even draw on the teachings of several religions and philosophies: Unitarians, for example, formally admit contributions and teachings from many religions and religious leaders, specifically naming Christianity, Judaism, humanism, and earth-based religions.

Sociologists today are actively re-examining the relations between religion and citizenship, or what we might call "the search for civility" within a religious context. Of course, some religions remain more repressive than others, and this is reflected in their political tolerance or lack thereof. Ever since sociologist Sam Stouffer began to measure political tolerance more than half a century ago, US studies have shown that church attendance and denominational affiliation significantly influence whether individuals willingly extend civil liberties to fringe groups.

Today, some people believe that religion and politics can, and should, be separate. We should not view religion as an inevitable impediment to civility—to living well together—and we need to learn how to harness the religious impulses that, visibly, remain strong in modern societies. However, we should recognize that, historically, religions have tended to control people, stigmatize deviants, punish nonbelievers, and exclude "heretics." The modern world, characterized by scientific and rational-legal thinking, has little room for institutions that produce victims of conscience.

Media Depictions of Victimization

The very idea of "**victimization**" is so powerful and widespread that the reputations of movie and television stars are occasionally done or undone by whether someone is seen as having been victimized.

For example, the long-running tabloid headlines regarding Jennifer Aniston's "betrayal" by her former husband, Brad Pitt, and Angelina Jolie play on the idea of Aniston's victimhood, much to Aniston's financial benefit, since it has kept her in the public eye. While having a "victim identity" can certainly help a celebrity curry public favour, claims of victimization can also damage a popular star's career. In 2011, *Twilight* star Kristen Stewart, angry about the paparazzi's intrusions into her life, compared unsanctioned photos to rape. This caused a remarkable outpouring of anger and Stewart quickly apologized for casting herself in the same light as a victim of rape.

Victimization is a common storyline in popular movies, television, and literature, as writers look to exploit the emotions of the audience by playing on the common fear of unjust punishment and corrupted innocence. Bullying is one of the more common manifestations of these themes, remaining a popular form of victimization in popular culture. In recent years, movies like *Drillbit Taylor* (2008), *Mean Creek* (2004), and *The Education of Charlie Banks* (2007) have reflected this concern about the issue of child and adolescent bullying. Television shows like *Hung* and *The Office*, as well as movies including *Joe Somebody* (2001), have been more open in discussing bullying as an adult issue, too.

These denunciations of bullying usually involve denouncing violence in a tempered, thoughtful way. Many popular culture outlets, however, are much more focused on the harsh retribution of those who victimize others, as the success of shows like *To Catch a Predator* and *Law & Order: SVU* suggest. One can see these values in the HBO show *Dexter*, as the titular character (and hero) is a murderer of murderers. An even more extreme example can be seen in the 2010 release of *I Spit on Your Grave*, a remake of a film Roger Ebert called "a vile bag of garbage." The movie follows a rape victim as she exacts clear, torturous murder against her rapists.

As the very existence of *I Spit on Your Grave* as a widely released film shows, many writers have tapped into a widespread desire to revel in the victimization of victimizers. Nowhere is this more evident than in the three popular crime novels by Stieg Larsson and the three Swedish movies based on them—so popular they are being remade by Hollywood, the first of which, *The Girl with the Dragon Tattoo* (2011), was widely acclaimed.

While one might argue that the public's eagerness to enjoy victimizers' comeuppance is itself a collective, public denunciation of violent deviance, the opposite seems the case. In fact, we have seen a growing trend in popular culture to fetishize many forms of violent victimization. The last decade has seen the remarkable ascendancy of a film genre known colloquially as "torture pornography," with movies like *Hostel* (2005) and *Saw* (2004) that focus on mutilation and murder, usually with little plot or character development. Today's torture films tend to have little narrative thrust, the "stories" revolving largely around the grisly persecution and victimization of innocent people and, in turn, the grisly response of the victim.

Economic Consequences of Human Trafficking

By **human trafficking** we mean the sale and transport of and profit from human beings who are forced to work for others, a practice generally considered the modern equivalent of slavery.

Activities like human trafficking and sex slavery, forced labour, and involuntary servitude have the most fundamental global economic effects of any form of victimization. These practices enrich a few brokers at a disastrous expense to the vulnerable populations (often children or teenagers) who are the victims. Those trafficked usually come from dire circumstances, perhaps shattered home lives, extreme poverty, or cultures of violent civil unrest (Zhang and Pineda, 2008). Unfortunately, there is a seemingly limitless supply of exploitable people, a fact that has allowed human trafficking to become the third largest transnational criminal activity in the world, after weapons dealing and the drug trade (Mullaly, 2008).

It is difficult to guess how many people human trafficking victimizes, given how widespread the practice is. The United States has estimated in its *Trafficking in Persons Report* there are 12.3 million people globally who are enslaved in forced or bonded labour or sexual servitude at any given time (US Department of State, 2010). This may be a conservative estimate, however, as British sociologist Kevin Bales and his colleagues believe that the number may be more than twice as large, estimating as many as 27 million people (Bales et al., 2009).

Whatever the estimates, clearly an enormous number of people are caught up as victims of human trafficking.

The widespread existence of human trafficking speaks to its profitability. As early North and South American colonists learned from their enslavement of imported black slaves, forced labour has the potential to be extremely profitable, whether in harvesting sugar cane or working in a sweatshop. One estimate of the yearly profits from global slave labour suggests these victimized populations produce US$31.6 billion in revenue. Given the huge amount of money to be made, any effective attack on the trade networks must, according to the International Labour Organization (ILO), include a confiscation of the financial assets of human traffickers (Belser, 2005).

While discussions of forced prostitution, child soldiers, camel jockeys, and indentured servitude may suggest to some that human trafficking is relegated to the developing world, this is untrue. The ILO estimates that nearly half of all profits from human trafficking—US$15 billion—come from industrialized nations. Further, the Federal Bureau of Investigation believes that human trafficking is a $9.5 billion business within the United States alone (Siskin and Wyler, 2010). Given the media focus on enslaved sex workers in Asia and child soldiers in Africa, it may seem surprising to hear that North America accounts so largely for global human trafficking. However, as with many other topics we have discussed, estimation procedures vary and so do the resulting estimates.

Social Policy Implications of Victimization

An analysis of the impacts of victimization in Canada (Aucoin and Beauchamp, 2007), based on survey data collected in 2004, indicates that no easy recipe exists for dealing with this problem. First, the analysis—using the most recent available Canadian data—shows that victims incur a wide variety of physical, emotional, and financial costs as a result of their victimization. Many of these costs are hard to measure in dollar terms, a type of measurement often required for social policy-making. Equally problematic, people's fears about being victimized often bear little relation to their personal experiences or to the experiences of anyone in their community. It's true that experience with victimization affects people's perceptions of personal safety and opinions of police effectiveness. However, many other factors also affect these perceptions just as much, including media coverage and political posturing.

For example, some victims react more fearfully than others. Variables that shape the reaction to criminal victimization include age, a prior history of victimization, general perceptions of crime, the severity of crime experienced, and the relationship between victim and offender.

Moreover, victim responses are not easily convertible into dollars; and because different kinds of victims react differently to the same crime, measuring the cost to society is extremely difficult, making the policy response difficult. The problem starts with defining what to measure. Then, there is the question of whom to measure. For example, we know that others are often affected indirectly, including the family and close friends of the victim. Also in question is the length of the measurement period: the effects of some types of victimization linger longer than is the case for other types.

In these terms, the easiest types of assessment involve property crimes—theft, embezzlement, or vandalism, for example. As a consequence, the policy implications here are easiest to assess. The effects of property crimes like these are shortest-lived and affect the fewest people, outside the victim him- or herself. These types of victimization are remedied by insurance compensation and prevented by strict regulation, good policing, and sensible security precautions.

The hardest types of assessment involve crimes against the person, especially crimes of violence like assault, robbery, or kidnapping. Many of these happen in homes, schools, or workplaces, among kin, friends, or acquaintances. The effects of these crimes are longest-lived and affect the widest range of people besides the immediate victim. The most striking example, in the Canadian context, is the victimization caused to Aboriginal people by the residential schools: the immediate victims were children removed from their families, robbed of their culture and language, and in many cases physically or sexually abused; but the families, too, were victimized, as were the communities (see Frideres, 2011: 57–79).

In addition, the social disruption in this instance—the victimization—has carried on to later generations because those individuals, families, and communities that were initially victimized were unable to pass down the essential values and beliefs that are the glue of any society. Victimization in such an instance becomes a form of post-traumatic stress disorder on a societal level.

Because crimes of violence often involve victimization by intimates in private spaces, they are hard to police and hard to prevent. The social policy implications, therefore, are more likely to involve public education, strategies to encourage the reporting of violent incidents, and counselling for the victims and their family members. Sometimes, more than counselling is needed, and may include lengthy and costly medical, nursing, or other therapeutic interventions. Caregivers may also be needed for extended periods. Policy-makers need to ensure that the costs of these interventions are adequately covered; otherwise, the victim of a crime endures additional (financial) victimization during the recovery period.

Conclusion

We have seen in this chapter that some people are victims of crime; for this, they deserve our protection and support. Other people are victims of conscience; they, too, deserve our protection and support, or at least tolerance. The hallmark of a modern, secular society is a willingness to grant different opinions and points of view, so long as these do not injure others. In large part, most Canadians have come to embrace this outlook, and Canada, as a result, is a relatively tolerant, peaceful, safe, and secure country.

Thus, as Durkheim has suggested, we can be victimized by too little social order (as crime-ridden communities show) or by too much social order (as the Spanish Inquisition showed). In neither instance is the problem that human beings are naturally bad: it is that some forms of social organization are better than others for preventing victimization.

It is no wonder, then, that a debate—in a new form—continues between religion and science, and it has implications for crime as well as for deviance. This is a debate over control and punishment, about whether to tolerate deviance we cannot control or try to eliminate it through harsher, if usually ineffective, means. Briefly, the debate is about harm reduction versus standing on principle. A person from a more traditional, conservative, or religious background would argue that we should make every effort, through laws and punishments, to show our disapproval of crime and other rule-breaking. In other words, the argument goes, wrong is wrong and should be punished, and we must stand on principle to see that it is. We should do this even if these laws and punishments fail to achieve the desired result or deter further crime. Indeed, our response to failure should be to ramp up the law-making, threatened punishment, and spending on police enforcement. This view is reflected in the omnibus crime bill recently passed by the federal Conservative government.

On the other hand, if proposed harm-reduction strategies, such as the decriminalization and legalization of some offences, were to work as expected, they would reduce the danger to society—reduce victimization—and reduce recidivism among the violators. These strategies will not appear as morally principled as strict rules and harsh punishments, but they can be more effective. Science and rationality are, typically, concerned with outcomes—they are (indeed) pathways to desired outcomes. Religion, though supposedly a pathway to desired outcomes (for example, to moral living and Heaven after death), may be a dead end, at least where social planning is concerned.

Therefore, the debates between science and religion are not yet over. The job of sociologists who study deviance, crime, and control is to understand our society's needs and goals, and to think clearly about how these might be satisfied. In this book, we have made a start in that direction.

Questions for Critical Thought

1. "There is no rule-breaking without a victim." Analyze this statement and explain why you agree or disagree.
2. Why are private places even riskier than public places for most types of victimization? What are the implications of this for social policy?
3. Find at least one aspect of homeless victimization not explained by the current theories about criminal victimization; and discuss the kind of research needed to study this aspect.
4. Would the Aboriginal population suffer less victimization if it were socially and economically integrated with the rest of the Canadian population? If yes, what is standing in the way of such integration?
5. "Systems of religious oppression are socially useful because they create the condition for their own overthrow." Analyze this statement, saying what you think it means, whether you agree, and why (or why not).
6. How well do theories about victims of crime apply to victims of conscience? Try using one example (e.g., Jesus or Galileo) to see the benefits of doing so.

Recommended Readings

Child, Irvin L., and John W.M. Whiting. 1953. *Child Training and Personality*. New Haven: Yale University Press.

This much-debated book uses data from the anthropological Human Relations Area Files to test Freudian theories about the relationship between child-rearing practices, especially weaning, and adult behaviour. Interestingly, it finds strong relationships between severe child-rearing experiences and adult beliefs in witchcraft.

Erikson, Kai. 2004. *Wayward Puritans: A Study in the Sociology of Deviance*, rev.edn. Boston: Allyn and Bacon.

This book clarifies the role of moral boundaries in human societies, how boundary crises may arise, and the effects of these boundary crises on crime-finding and punishment. In this way, Erikson helps to illustrate Durkheim's functional theory of crime and provides a non-psychological understanding of punitiveness.

Freud, Sigmund. 1989 [1927]. *Religion: The Future of an Illusion.* New York: W.W. Norton.

Freud declares that "Religion is comparable to a childhood neurosis." This view, which reveals a great deal about Freud's understanding of morality and convention, also provides an insight into his views of punishment for unconventional thoughts and behaviour. It also helps us understand why crime is normal and why civilization brings social evolution but also discontent.

Schur, Edwin M. 1965. *Crimes without Victims: Deviant Behavior and Public Policy.* New York: Spectrum Books.

As discussed earlier, this classic work seeks to clarify the social role of laws that criminalize behaviour offensive to some people's morality but harmful to none of the participants.

Recommended Websites

Criminal Victimization in Canada (2009)

www.statcan.gc.ca/pub/85-002-x/2010002/article/11340-eng.htm

This recent Statistics Canada survey provides up-to-date information on reported victimization in Canada. The study is helpful not only in understanding the ubiquity of violent and non-violent forms of victimization, but in showing how arrest rates and conviction rates vary by region.

Public Safety Canada

www.publicsafety.gc.ca

This is the website of the federal government's Public Safety Office, which oversees all federal-level matters relating to crime, crime prevention, corrections, and imprisonment. The Public Safety Office also is involved in crafting public policy to address these issues.

Policy Centre for Victim Issues

www.justice.gc.ca/eng/pi/pcvi-cpcv/index.html

Run out of the federal Department of Justice, this site has many links to criminal justice publications, news agencies, legislative bodies, and victims' services. The Policy Centre for Victim Issues is very helpful in understanding how the government attempts to address the needs of victims.

World Society of Victimology

www.worldsocietyofvictimology.org/

This body, which aims to develop the academic study of victimology, is a not-for-profit NGO with a consultative status with the Economic and Social Council of the United Nations. The World Society's website provides links to resources in this burgeoning field of study and also provides a list of print publications and non-affiliated research bodies in the field.

Joint Center on Violence and Victim Studies

www.washburn.edu/ao/jcvvs/index.html

This American inter-university collective brings together three victimization studies programs, located at Washburn University, California State University-Fresno, and the University of New Haven, in the hopes of further developing the field of victimology. While the site provides a broad listing of resources for studying victimization issues, it is also a useful resource for students considering advanced study in the field.

Recommended Movies

***Philadelphia*, Dir. Jonathan Demme (1993)**

In the first Hollywood film to openly discuss AIDS and to seriously equate homophobia with other forms of discrimination, Tom Hanks plays Andrew Beckett, a talented gay lawyer at a conservative law firm. Upon discovering that Andrew has AIDS, the firm fires him, leading Andrew to hire the homophobic black lawyer Joe Miller to represent him in a wrongful termination case. Joe comes to realize that the discrimination Andrew faces is very much akin to the racism he himself has faced, and Demme suggests that to condone or ignore one form of discrimination is to implicitly accept the idea of bigotry itself.

***The Accused*, Dir. Jonathan Kaplan (1988)**

Jodie Foster won an Oscar for portraying Sarah Tobias, an uneducated woman of few means and a substantial joie de vivre who is gang-raped at a local bar. Despite the horrible nature of the crime, Sarah's rapists receive plea bargains from the district attorney, as defence lawyers threaten to suggest that Sarah was "asking" to be raped, given her sexual indiscretions and party-hard lifestyle. Kaplan vividly underscores the ways in which poor women can be repeatedly victimized by the justice system, excoriating the hypocrisy of a court that would accept a suggestion that women are responsible for their own rape.

A Soldier's Story, Dir. Norman Jewison (1984)

This movie, based on the Pulitzer Prize-winning production *A Soldier's Play*, ably shows how violence can build upon itself, leading victimizers to become victims themselves. Taking place in the 1940s at Louisiana's Fort Neal, a group of black soldiers are gathered under the abusive Sergeant Waters. When Sergeant Waters is found dead, Captain Davenport investigates the matter, finding that any of the men—not to mention local white supremacist groups—could be responsible.

Inglourious Basterds, Dir. Quentin Tarantino (2009)

Directed by one of modern cinema's most popular auteurs, this film represents the continued sense of grievance victimized groups feel, even after many decades. During World War II, an American band of Nazi killers search Vichy, France, for prey, earning the nickname "The Basterds" from the Third Reich. In crafting this fantasy, Tarantino taps into the residual anger of those groups still affected by Nazi brutality, a sentiment that all victimized groups may understand.

PART IV

What Comes Next?

11 Social Control

Learning Objectives

- To consider common types of informal social control in use
- To examine the characteristics of each type of social control
- To study the particular value of informal control in small settings
- To see the unintended outcomes of informal sanctions
- To judge the effectiveness of social, material, and psychological controls
- To understand why corporal punishment may backfire

Introduction

In this chapter, we discuss several of the most important and perplexing issues around deviance and crime—those associated with the notion of "social control." These concerns go to the root of the topic of deviance and crime and indeed go to the root of sociology's interest in the basis of social order. By *social control*, sometimes called *informal control*, we mean the regulation of people's behaviour by other people in ordinary social settings. This occurs without any of the trappings of formal rule enforcement: without police officers, courts, jails, and so on.

But how do ordinary people regulate other people's behaviour without all the formal trappings of official law enforcers? Why, how, and when do these informal strategies work, and when don't they work? And, by implication, under what circumstances must we consider informal controls failures and resort to formal means of social control?

To understand this kind of informal or ordinary social control, let's start with **social norms**. Social norms are the collection of informal, often unspoken, rules, guides, and standards of behaviour that prevail in a society or an organization. The authority or origin of many of these rules may be vague and diffuse. However, the community's readiness to punish norm violation can be swift and harsh. People follow these informal rules and obligations largely because failing to do so may result in feelings of guilt or shame, gossip, ostracism, and even violence. The authority of these rules rests in "the group," since all group members rely on relations of reciprocity and trust between individuals in the "community" (O'Donnell, 2007). Even mild criticism—a disparaging glance or expression of disapproval, for example—may be enough to worry the rule-breaker, as such signals often serve as a prelude to ostracism or more severe penalties.

So, people have good reasons for keeping the rules and avoiding group sanctions, however mild. Sometimes even their lives may depend, in practical ways, on preserving good relationships with others. However, that is not the whole story. As social animals, people also crave the good opinion of others, their company, and their approval or good opinion. Because they base their opinions of themselves largely on how they believe other people view them, they are likely to feel punished—bruised even—when other people disapprove.

Well-socialized people can feel guilt or shame even without the enforcement of social norms by others. This, George Mead would say, is rooted in learned views of the "generalized other" in childhood. Paradoxically, informal social control can be extremely effective, even though it is inexpensive to administer and often almost impossible to see. It seamlessly punishes the rule-breaker and silently rewards the conformist with esteem, trust, and, most important, co-operation.

Informal social control, then, is like a wonder drug: almost free, almost painless, almost invisible, and something that almost always works. In this chapter, we will seek a clearer understanding of how social controls bring about order and conformity—most of the time. We will also ask about its hidden costs and harms.

Some believe that control and conformity are explainable in individual terms: everyone obeys the rules because everyone (individually) gains from doing so and loses by not doing so. Others believe altruistic rewards and punishments—*strong reciprocity*—also play an important role in promoting co-operation. Consciously or unconsciously, groups preserve themselves by rewarding conformity and punishing deviance. Some believe that is how the human race has survived and evolved. For example, Wiessner (2005) uses data from conversations among the Ju/'hoansi (!Kung) Bushmen to argue that self-interest may not be good enough to explain the reasons people bear the costs of conformity and norm enforcement. By default, strong reciprocity and altruism must be at work. Somehow, we are hard-wired to do what social survival requires us to do, according to evolutionary psychologists.

That said, the wellspring of altruism is always hard to locate, especially in large, complex, individualistic societies (like our own) as opposed to small tribal societies. Some say that altruism is built into the human psyche, but that is impossible to prove. Certainly, all religions call for altruism and obedience, yet our society is increasingly secular. All families and communities require some measure of self-sacrifice, but great (not small) altruism is so rare that the few true altruists are widely viewed as saints. So, again by default, it is easiest to explain conformity as a reaction to social control and a self-interested obedience to social rules. It is easier to demonstrate that people "behave themselves" and stick to the straight and narrow because of informal controls and reciprocal exchanges than it is to show they do so because of altruism and a need for self-sacrifice.

"Social control" is a uniquely sociological (and anthropological) idea to be distinguished from, say, political control, military control, police control, or even legal control. Social control identifies mainstream society and its social relationships as sources of control in our lives. The concept of social control centres on "civil society" as an important location in human lives—a portion of society that is just as important as the state and economy, for example, yet less well studied.

And just as the state and the economy make demands on us—the one demanding our taxes and the other our time—so does civil society, demanding our conformity. This conformity—like taxes and wage labour—comes with a cost, in the form of repression. Sigmund Freud suggested there are direct connections between social control and repression. Through repression, according to Freud, social control opens the door to shame, guilt, and fear we all associate with failing to live up to society's rules. These, as Freud proposed, are the fundamentals of neurosis. Civilization, as Freud argued, invariably demands social order, which it mainly achieves through repression. As a result, civilization is naturally, inevitably repressive.

This, in turn, implies civilization—social life—is necessarily neurosis-producing and the cause of much of the unhappiness, depression, anxiety, addiction, and other forms of deviance discussed in this book. Of course, we haven't all become hermits and recluses, mental cases or alcoholics, as this theory might suggest. Freud would say that is because most of us learn to sublimate our urges: to channel and translate them into socially acceptable behaviours, like work and study. For many people, Freudian theory is an untestable theory with too many escape clauses; for others, it remains endlessly suggestive and a shortcut to understanding our public enthusiasm for an endless number of new obsessions that include gaming, gambling, shopping, Internet pornography, and other diversions that are pathological when taken to extremes (Box 11.1).

Some people overwork to sublimate their so-called libidinal energy or sexual impulses; some write symphonies or plays, while others climb mountains or collect antique cars. People "innovate" not only for the reasons that Merton noted in his classic essay on anomie—namely, to achieve their socially desired goal by illegitimate means—but also in response to blocked opportunities and blocked impulses.

They innovate because social life demands innovation psychologically, as well as socially and economically.

So, in discussing social control we realize we need to discuss whether social control is good or bad, a source of security or a source of repression. If social control is harmfully repressive, we need to find out if it can function more creatively.

How Groups Protect Themselves

People do not merely think and interpret other people's actions or respond to constraints and opportunities presented to them. They also take purposeful action to further their own interests and protect the groups to which they belong. Sociological theories—associated with research on small groups and social systems (see Homans, 1974)—provide us with a starting point to understanding group influences and especially the ways that groups protect themselves against deviant activities and identities.

People use many informal tactics to control one another, but these fall mainly into two categories: rewarding desirable behaviour and withholding rewards for undesirable behaviour. Rewards between spouses, for example, include respect, love, sex, friendship, emotional support, and sometimes money. This is not to say that all people are socialized to be manipulative, or to conduct their relationships in exploitive ways. It *is* to say that people are rarely saints and most people, most of the time, engage in exchange with one another. In long-term, stable relationships, our social exchanges are so ingrained and reciprocal that they are virtually invisible as such. However, when exchanges break down, so do relationships. Then people stop dating, break up, get divorced, or stop phoning.

At ground level, among real people in real situations, shared, interlinked, mutually rewarding histories of life together are the effective sources of control. We toe the line so we will get more of the "good stuff" and avoid the "bad stuff."

Time to Reflect: Thinking back over enduring relationships you have (or have had) with certain people, which techniques of informal control have worked best and which ones have backfired? Or are all of your relationships based on such control mechanisms?

Managing Social Rewards

We all like to think of our personal, intimate relationships as being somehow unique and unlikely to yield to formal or abstract analysis and generalization. Yet, sociologists tend to view families as having certain important similarities. Moreover, they also have certain important similarities to other groups and organizations. This means that we can use what we know about families to better understand small organizations—for example, workplaces, teams, bands, or gangs—and we can also use what we know about small organizations to better understand families.

Sociologist Marvin Olsen (1978) argues that all social organizations—families, classrooms, workplaces, and so on—use social control to maintain their boundaries, regulate member activities, perform key functions, and perpetuate order. If we take this seriously, we can view societies in a new way: as a social organization. From this standpoint, key features of a family include a role structure (parent, child, student), a division of labour (chores, income), often, a power structure (head of household, decision-making processes), the accumulation and use of collective resources (furniture, bank accounts), and an organizational culture and normative structure (holidays, daily rituals).

Second, Olsen asserts that informal social control is accomplished mainly through two processes: social sanctioning (i.e., by administering rewards and punishments) and social management (i.e., by shaping the social settings in which people act). Social sanctioning is easy to understand and needs little elaboration: simply, people typically behave in ways that will win them rewards and evade punishments. This means that people—friends, family members, teachers, bosses, and even strangers—who can supply rewards and

Classic Works

BOX 11.1

Sigmund Freud's Civilization and Its Discontents

In *Civilization and Its Discontents*, Freud seeks to explain why humanity seems discontent with and bitter towards civilization. He suggests that repressed sexuality results in a surplus of libidinal energy that, in a civilized society, must be turned inward; however, doing so leads to a sense of guilt and discontent.

Freud bases his theory on three assumptions, the first being that the goal of human life is to seek happiness. This can be achieved through direct, momentary pleasure and by avoiding pain. Civilization, Freud argues, was created to ensure the latter, even at the expense of the former—for example, by controlling and channelling sexual drives. Thus the cost of civilization (and the safety it brings) is a drop in our sexual pleasure.

Second, Freud sees humans in a constant battle between two fundamental instincts: Eros, the instinct directed to life and love, and Thanatos, the instinct directed to death and aggression. While Eros seeks to bind all humans together in society, Thanatos seeks the opposite. However, Eros is also restricted by society in that building and upholding civilization demands limits on sexuality. This control channels surplus libidinal energy into socially acceptable creativity, such as art and music. Further, Eros channels sexuality into marriage and monogamous romance. However, this may be an inadequate use of sexual energy. Consequently, men and women always have a surplus of libidinal energy available for non-sexual activities such as artistic and cultural pursuits.

Third, Freud sees aggression, violence, and even warfare as inevitable. Given its negative nature, Thanatos invariably gives rise to aggressive thoughts and impulses. To deal with this buildup of aggression, the individual's superego directs it at the ego, causing people to feel guilty about their aggressive (and sexual) thoughts, even if they do not act on them. By constantly attacking the individual for these "wicked" thoughts, the superego acts as a guardian of civilization. However, the combined effect of repression and guilt can, when taken to an extreme, lead to neurosis.

Often, the controls imposed by society, especially the moral ones, prove too limiting and thus lead to deviance or neurosis. Every advance in civilization—accompanied by more order, organization, and repression—increases guilt and discontent. So, ironically, social "advances" lead to more neurosis or deviance. Civilization fails to make us happy, yet seems to be necessary; and even this imperfect necessity is in constant danger of collapse, through wars and violence.

punishments during an interaction will be able to exercise social control.

Social management is a slightly more complicated notion, since it refers to a way of achieving control. A clever manager does not manipulate her workers by obvious threats or rewards. It is too costly to keep providing rewards to gain compliance, and it is risky to keep threatening punishment. Often, the latter strategy backfires; organizationally, nothing is worse for a manager than to threaten punishment and then fail to deliver on it or fail to deliver a punishment that is strong enough to control the wayward worker. It is far better to organize the social environment so that other people (e.g., co-workers) do the rewarding and punishing and so that internal controls (shame, guilt, fear) do most of the work. In short, then, social management refers to the creation of opportunities and constraints that influence or change the actions of group members.

Consider exercising control over a problem gambler in the family setting. Often, rewards (affection, attention, sex) are not sufficient, and naked threats simply drive the gambler out of the house, fuelling his or her desire to be somewhere else (e.g., the casino). One way around this is to increase couple intimacy through a wider range of shared activities and shared friends. This can be used to manage problem gambling in two ways. First, a problem gambler's activities become more highly visible, constantly under surveillance by the spouse or partner. This visibility can have the effect of controlling or limiting rule-breaking behaviour. Second, the gambler's time, money, and energy are being steered into couple-based activities. If handled properly, a spouse can use this kind of social management to change and redirect the gambler's behaviour.

Olsen further states that organizations use bureaucratization to rationalize and control their functioning and help them reach their goals. Of course, the typical family does not "bureaucratize." However, families, like bureaucracies, sometimes have pressing goals, and these force them to search for ways to achieve their goals more efficiently. For example, a need to streamline may arise when a family member develops a gambling problem. How can, and how should, a family reorganize itself to achieve the most effective and efficient response to this development? Often, families can be amazingly creative in these situations, given their usually limited resources.

Olsen also notes that social control means setting up procedures for organizational survival:

- training or socializing members;
- sharing common goals;
- establishing a division of labour;
- developing a consistent set of norms and rules;
- co-ordinating organizational activities;
- creating procedures for resolving conflicts;
- transmitting procedures for changing the organization.

This list, though incomplete, hints at the wide range of activities a social unit typically undertakes to survive as a group, an organization, or a society. These strategies, and others, are used interpersonally to bring about compliance with rules and expectations.

Strategies of Social Control

In the sections that follow, we look briefly at a number of different tactics, methods, and strategies that groups use to enforce informal social control. All of these are familiar, yet—as is so often the case in sociology—we see them differently when we view them in new situations or compare them with unlikely groupings.

Threat

Consider "threat": we have all been threatened at one time or another. Stated simply, a threat is a warning of imminent danger or harm. It may also be an enemy's promise to carry out unwanted actions—the delivery of punishment or withholding of rewards—if we fail to comply with his stated wishes.

Threats—both stated and unstated—play an important part in informal social control. Often, unstated or implied threats work even better than stated or explicit threats; we are more frightened of something that is only vaguely evident than something that is clear. For example, we would be more frightened by a boss's threat to "cut our pay" than by his more specific threat to "cut our pay by $10 an hour." However, as stated earlier, threats are generally a weak form of control. If the threatened punishment, when delivered, proves less significant than expected, it will be considered a failure. This failure will rob the one who threatens of the ability to control either implied or explicit threats in the future.

Yet, the uncertainty, weakness, and volatility of the threat process also make threats potentially dangerous. The conflict is likely to escalate quickly and unpredictably—and even get out of hand—if one failed threat has to be followed by another even bigger threat. This is one reason that heated arguments—even between intimates—can quickly turn violent. It is also why some people who prefer to use threat as a means of control—such as the police and gang members—carry guns, which they are prepared to use. Guns are the final threat and are usually more persuasive than other threats.

In recent years, the discussion of "threat" in sociology has focused on macro-social events that threaten entire communities, groups, races, or nations and the circumstances under which this "sense of threat" is perpetuated. Often discussed are the ways the US has used threat—backed up by guns—to ostensibly protect itself and control others. So, for example, many writers have focused on the sense of threat created by 9/11. They note that, through the Bush administration, the US government used this sense of threat to control public opinion and public behaviour, even to the point of denying citizens their constitutionally protected civil liberties.

There is no denying that a sense of threat about terrorism has permeated the West since 9/11, and it has influenced the way Americans view all world events—for example, the way they view piracy. The National Security Strategy of the United States (NSSUS) equates piracy to terrorism, shifting the focus away from piracy as theft towards the threat of terrorism at sea, or "floating bombs." Since 9/11, it has been increasingly difficult to ensure distinctions are made between terrorists (who use violence for political ends) and pirates (who use violence for profiteering ends) (Engels, 2007).

The preoccupation with national security has also affected people's thinking about international refugees. Even outside the US, in Canada and Australia, controversy exists about the status of refugees and the national responsibility for taking refugees. Watson (2007) studied three notable refugee "crises" in each state to examine political responses. In Australia, the three crises are the 1979 Indo-Chinese boat people exodus, the 1992 boat arrivals, and the 2001 Tampa affair. In Canada, he examined the 1979 Indo-Chinese boat people exodus, the 1986–7 boat landings, and the 1999 boat arrivals. He found that, whenever refugees could be characterized as security threats, the leaders of receiving societies were likely to adopt policies designed to "protect" the state rather than the refugees.

The sense or experience of threat is likely to generate a process sociologists have called **othering**—a tendency to view some people as outsiders and some outsiders as people unlike, or perhaps even less than, oneself. Since the Madrid and London public transportation system bombings of 2004 and 2005, which killed 191 and 52, respectively, there has been an increased concern about security throughout Western Europe. Often, this fear has resulted in "bordering practices" against the "other"—that is, to practices and public policies that focus on differences between us/"other," inside/outside, and insider/outsider distinctions—and denial of the right to "otherness." Paradoxically, one might argue that this preoccupation with security will continue so long as there is a preoccupation with "otherness" (Akinwumi, 2007). The tendency to "otherness" will maintain a sense of threat long after the conditions that cause it have disappeared.

Environmental threats have also produced fearfulness and manipulated people's sentiments. These threats to society can have various origins—dangerous waste disposal, industrial pollution, and chemical spills, for example. However, people respond differently to threats. First, some people are simply more predisposed—psychologically and demographically—to feel threatened by any specific risk. So, for example, Crowson et al. (2006) found that right-wing authoritarianism and social conservatism were significant predictors of support for restricted human rights during the US-led "war on terror" and for US military involvement in Iraq.

Second, people's views of risk and threat are mediated by the views and opinions of others with whom they are in social contact. This reflects the two-step flow of mass communication hypothesized by Katz and Lazarsfeld (1955) in their key studies of public opinion over 50 years ago. People usually like to discuss the information they take in, especially if that information is confusing or troubling. As a result, their own sense of threat will reflect the views of people around them and, also, the availability of people with whom to discuss their own views.

A diffuse sense of threat, whether real or constructed to promote state purposes, can have real, unforeseen, and hard-to-contain effects. This would argue against readily using threat as a technique of social control. Yet, of course, threat is used every day for just that purpose.

Persuasion

Persuasion is another common method of control. This process of advising is aimed at convincing the listener to take a specific course of action—for example, to obey the stated rules rather than break them. By its nature, persuasion is friendly or neutral, not threatening or negative in its tone. It gains its effect by the apparent wisdom and objectivity of the argument. Therefore, the effectiveness of persuasion will depend on the seeming credibility of the speaker (the persuader) and the evidence he or she uses to support the argument.

Usually, social psychologists think of persuasion micro-sociologically, as an interpersonal process equivalent to coaxing. However, macro-sociologically, persuasion can be related to what social constructionists call *claims-making.* These are the processes by which groups create and promote claims they hope will be granted credibility or legitimacy by the mass public. It is by this method they hope to persuade the public to behave in certain ways—for example, to support an initiative to fund certain activities and ban others.

A sociologist who has written extensively about the power of persuasion in "claims-making" is Joel Best (1995, 2003). Best is interested in the "rhetoric" that claims makers use when they try to depict criminal or deviant acts as significant social problems meriting societal concern. The media, according to Best, become claims makers when they try to transform incidents of random crime into instances or examples of "larger problems." Best has investigated the role the media has played in a number of moral panics, including the satanic scare, the anti-cult movement, the apparent "missing children" epidemic, and the Halloween scare (when the media covered reports of sharp objects allegedly found in Halloween candy).

We are all being persuaded all the time, often by mass media messages. Some of these messages are clear and plain in their aims, while others are far more devious. In Chapter 2, we examined the effects of mass media portrayals in shaping social norms about appearance—in effect, persuading many (young women in particular) to lose weight, undergo cosmetic surgery, or buy beauty-enhancing clothes and adornments. However, increasingly, the media are used for purposes of political propaganda and "social marketing"—that is, to bring about changes in people's beliefs and behaviours unrelated to consumerism.

Sometimes these processes are used for good purposes. Das et al. (2008) assessed the effectiveness of different fundraising messages. Earlier research had shown the importance of "message framing." The most effective fundraising messages should combine abstract, statistical information with a *negative* message frame and anecdotal evidence with a *positive* message frame. (For example, in the first case, "An estimated 62 per cent of all teenagers who eat tuna fish sandwiches for lunch will die horribly of brain cancer." In the second case, "Little Johnny Smith came home from school yesterday to get the best surprise he could ever imagine: dad had packed the car for a family trip to Disneyland.") In addition, donations are reportedly higher in response to messages that address charity goal issues: for example, "Your gift will go directly towards buying new wheelchairs for children with disabilities in Rwanda."

Unfortunately, persuasive communication strategies can be used for both good and bad purposes. On the one hand, anti-smoking labels on cigarette packages have been effective in inducing smokers to quit and preventing non-smokers from starting to smoke. On the other hand, cigarette companies wage their own battle for the hearts and lungs of smokers, using the best persuasive techniques they can imagine. Norman (2007), looking at the battle between science and the tobacco industry, found that smoking policies from 1964 to 2005 reduced the influence of the cigarette industry over the public mind. In this period, anti-smoking interpretations of scientific evidence were widely accepted, extended, and deepened. Policy convergence—the implementation of public views in public anti-smoking policy—occurred much later, after 1990. What this shows is that it may be easier, and more important, to persuade the public than (try) to persuade legislators.

We will see later that it is hard to persuade the public of everything through advertising: efforts to sell atheism through an advertising campaign have proved more hostility-provoking than efforts to sell gambling, drinking, escort services, and pornography, for example (see Box 11.2).

Shame

Shame is a painful sense of disgrace or embarrassment arising from the memory, or exposure, of dishonourable and offensive acts. Shame is a strongly felt emotion that is, therefore, often deeply etched in a person's memory; shame conditions the person to behave and not behave in particular ways that become habitual and may be socially limiting. Shame also has important social causes and effects. It is rooted in social norms whose violation causes a sense of disgrace; and, in some communities, it may translate into a loss of face, social ostracism, and ridicule—all social consequences.

Shame and shaming are powerful, unseen factors that influence people's social behaviour. Often shame, or fear of shame, keeps people from taking socially or personally useful actions. Rutten (2006), for example, argues that shame—viewed as a feeling of social inadequacy and (the anticipation of) public humiliation—may hold back worker activism. This sense of shame, which inhibits personal confrontations between workers and employers, may often be embedded in a personalized (i.e., patron–client) relationship with the boss. So, shame may serve as an obstacle to face-to-face confrontation and claims-making and may present a barrier to political protest. This is one reason why Marx insisted that the first step in class mobilization was the development of class awareness and an understanding that class membership must transcend other loyalties.

Many victims of sexual attack or abuse feel shamed and are often unwilling to speak out about the abuse or even report the crime to the proper authorities. For example, Latino cultural concerns around shaming experiences associated with sexual abuse include attributions of blame for the abuse, feelings of fatalism, issues about virginity, sexual taboos, fears of a shameful future, and, for boy victims, concerns about machismo and fears of homosexuality (Fontes, 2007). Here, as with the example of workplace shame described above, the victim needs to transcend a traditional, personal way of viewing his or her experience. To see oneself as the member of a victimized group or category may seem impersonal and cold, but it is also oddly freeing from feelings of shame or guilt.

Time to Reflect: In some societies, shame is often used as a means of informal social control. In what kinds of societies (or communities) would shame work best? Explain your thinking.

For similar reasons, shame often controls the behaviour of abused women. Researchers in Holland interviewed women in two shelter homes for battered women. Many of these women had failed to disclose intimate partner abuse to their family doctors. Their main reasons were shame and fear of retaliation (Wester et al., 2007). The women mainly wanted a solution to their physical problems and were undecided about accepting help to tackle their abuse problems. Those who did enter discussion with their doctor were often pleasantly surprised. Although the family doctor did not play an important role in solving their abuse problems, an open and empathic attitude was helpful and encouraging to these women.

The tendency to feel shame apparently varies across cultures and between genders. Silfver (2007) studied cultural and gender differences in guilt and shame in samples of Finnish and Peruvian adolescents. As expected, the Peruvians were more collectivistic and traditional than the Finns, and this made the Peruvians more prone to guilt and shame. However, this cultural difference also magnified the gender difference.

Gender differences in values were smaller for the Peruvians than for the Finns: both male and female Peruvians were equally inclined to feel guilt and shame. By contrast, among the Finns—generally less likely to feel shame than the Peruvians—males were much less likely than females to feel shame. The results support the view that psychological gender differences are greater in modern, individualistic societies (e.g., Finland) than in traditional, collectivist societies (e.g., Peru). Stated another way, though social differences between men and women tend to shrink in industrial societies, psychological differences expand, owing to a slower change in women's norms and socialization than men's.

Guilt

Guilt is the remorse a person may feel for breaking a rule or committing a shameful act. Like shame, to which it is related, guilt plays an important part in controlling people socially, from the inside out. As Freud (1961 [1929]) wrote in *Civilization and Its Discontents*, "The different religions have never overlooked the part played by the sense of guilt in civilization. What is more, they come forward with a claim . . . to save mankind from this sense of guilt, which they call sin." This is a reminder that all the mechanisms of control we have discussed so far—including threat, persuasion, shame, and guilt—are forms of *social control*, a result of social learning and social manipulation by our parents, schools, political leaders, and churches.

Shame and guilt are emotions that often (in fact, ideally) result when people break, or consider breaking, social rules. The servants of conscience or superego, they "monitor" our thoughts and control our actions. However, shame and guilt have different effects on personal development, engaging different emotions and producing different behaviours. Shame often results in social withdrawal, anger, and aggression, while guilt incites prosocial behaviour. Shame is associated with deviations from ideals that significant others hold for us; guilt is associated with deviations from moral standards we hold for ourselves. Viewing the situation from outside, we can see that focusing on the action committed causes guilt, whereas focusing on the self who committed the action causes shame—though most people are unaware of these processes taking place. By any standard, guilt results from an independent, internal assessment of one's own behaviour, according to one's own standards (Fromson, 2006).

The capacity for having a sense of guilt is largely rooted in childhood socialization because our personal standards of behaviour are rooted there. We would expect better-behaved children to have higher levels of guilt or, at least, to have parents with higher levels of guilt. To test this, Cornell and Frick (2007) studied children between the ages of three and five and their mothers. As rated by their preschool teachers, compared to uninhibited children, better-behaved or more controlled children had higher-than-average levels of guilt and empathy, regardless of the parenting they had received. Less inhibited (worse behaved) children were characterized by either inconsistent parental discipline and lower-than-average levels of guilt; or by authoritarian parenting and higher-than-average levels of guilt.

Does imprisonment lead to feelings of guilt about misbehaviour? Does it, in this way, get people to go straight? Hosser et al. (2005) repeatedly interviewed over 400 young male offenders from six different detention centres. The researchers found that feelings of guilt predict lower rates of recidivism; however, these effects are not statistically significant. They did, however, find one seeming exception to this rule: feelings of guilt following a violent delinquent act reduce the likelihood of further delinquency. So, at least in this case, guilt has some proven capacity to control behaviour.

In sociology, much of the discussion of guilt is about collective guilt—guilt shared by a group or social category over wrongs committed in the past against other groups or social categories. So, some men feel collective guilt about past (or continuing) discrimination against women. Miron et al. (2006), who studied men's experience, found that collective guilt is an emotion that emerges when members of a dominant group—for example, men—sense their relationship with a disadvantaged group—for example, women—is illegitimate, that is, not morally defensible.

Along similar lines, Feather and Boeckmann (2007) examined Australian men's views of workplace gender discrimination, feelings of collective responsibility and guilt for discrimination, and judgements of affirmative action. Statistical analyses showed, as in the previous study, that men's reports of collective guilt predicted attitudes towards women's entitlement. That is, men who believed women were unfairly disadvantaged were most likely to support affirmative action for women. That said, men were more likely than women to believe women bear some responsibility for their own disadvantage.

In general, feelings of guilt about inequality (or disadvantage) are least in societies that most strongly embrace the legitimacy of social inequality. Acceptance of inequality in North American—especially US—society is widespread. The tendency of all groups—poor included—is to accept the social status quo. Generally, white Americans (both men and women) feel guilty about their social advantage only if they believe they are receiving an *unfair* advantage and their own group is responsible for the disadvantage suffered by another group (e.g., by African-Americans) (Mallett and Swim, 2007).

Since guilt is an uncomfortable emotion, most people try to avoid feeling it. When faced with potentially guilt-inducing occasions, they usually try to neutralize their feelings of guilt or deny them. In 1957, Sykes and Matza introduced **neutralization theory** as a way of understanding how people could overcome their feelings of guilt so they could break the social rules. The dominant belief at the time was that offenders commit crimes because they embrace a subcultural rule set that opposes the conventional rules of society and values law-breaking. Sykes and Matza rejected this view, arguing instead that despite their rule-breaking, delinquents preserve a strong bond to conventional society and want to see themselves as "good."

To bridge this gap between a felt need to break the law and another felt need to be morally worthy, criminals use neutralization techniques to relieve expected guilt. This line of argument applies to many adult street criminals as well as to the juvenile delinquents Sykes and Matza studied. It also applies to mothers who smoke and men who enjoy the benefits of gender inequality.

For those with a functioning conscience, ignorance and denial are useful ways of avoiding guilt. For example, if you knew something bad was about to happen and you didn't try to prevent it, you might feel guilty. So one strategy is to ignore the problem: don't read the newspapers, don't discuss the problem, don't join social movements, and so on. Using ethnographic and interview data from a rural Norwegian community, Norgaard (2006) describes how people avoided thinking about climate change because doing so would make them feel insecure, helpless, and guilty, and in this way would threaten their sense of identity. Consequently, members of this community held information at a distance as part of emotion management—a way of socially organizing denial. In this community, the process of denial was carried out by using a cultural stock of social accounts to achieve a "selective interpretation" of reality.

In fact, sociologists have often remarked that most people want to remain unaware of social problems and the work (by police officers, social workers, and others) that goes into controlling these problems and keeping them out of sight. Since out of sight is out of mind, selective ignorance is a useful way to avoid feelings of guilt that could not be otherwise easily denied or neutralized.

Gossip

Gossip is the practice of idle talk or rumour. Under some social circumstances, gossip is a powerful source of social control, since it spreads information that can mobilize shame, guilt, or ridicule against others by undermining their reputation.

Gossip is sociologically interesting because, though it originates in particular individuals and spreads through identifiable social networks, it can mobilize (or simulate) the force of public opinion. Indeed, the more anonymous the sources of the gossip, the more it will seem objective and unbiased—though the gossip may have originated with a single self-interested, trouble-making individual. That said, gossip is well known to combine a mixture of truth, exaggeration, and falsehood. It is socially effective because, most of the time, people cannot easily separate the truth from the exaggeration and falsehood.

Gossip works best in social networks and communities (including schools and workplaces) that are small and concentrated. It usually requires the object of gossip to be well known to those who are gossiping (people do not typically gossip about strangers). Therefore, people are most likely to gossip about their kin, neighbours, friends, or workmates. (Of course, when they do so over the Internet, many others are likely to hear about it!) It is in these smaller settings that gossip, or fear of gossip, is most likely to control behaviour. Under certain conditions, gossip can even result in vigilantism and murder.

Gossip is a form of persuasion that works through repetition and through the suggestion—almost the insistence—that there is a group consensus or norm about something. Another form of control through persuasion that works in similar ways is advertising. After a century of learning how to advertise everything from shirt collars to hemorrhoid cream, mouthwash to fantasy casino experiences, people have even turned their advertising intelligence to selling religion or, as in Box 11.2, anti-religion. Here as elsewhere, the goal is to persuade through logic, innuendo, and moral uplift. But though people are willing to be sold hemorrhoid creams and fantasy casino experiences, they resist the selling of atheism as though this were a singularly noxious product.

Like advertising, gossip is about promoting particular values and behaviours, using simple images and storylines. Those who gossip in effect negotiate their own and others' identities, using gossipy storytelling. It is important to note that gossip is a kind of debate or negotiation about the best way to interpret and evaluate other people's behaviour. In the process, both the moral stature of the "gossip" and the person gossiped about come into consideration.

In a gossip session, a social "misdeed" may be viewed as a serious matter and receive criticism or, conversely, be treated playfully and celebrated. Whether the gossip group chooses to approve or disapprove of the questionable behaviour can rarely be predicted. The setting of boundaries and application of sanctions are constantly being negotiated. Thus, "othering"—placing people outside the boundary of acceptability—is an emergent process, as are the creative conversational strategies that achieve it (Jaworski and Coupland, 2005).

When the subject of gossip is not present, the process—the character assassination—will

Current Events 

BOX 11.2

Advertising, Faith, and Atheism

The message, "There's probably no God. Now stop worrying and enjoy your life," appeared on the sides of buses across London, England, in late 2008. This campaign, which aims to promote the views and opinions of non-religious individuals, was initially conceptualized in opposition to the religious ads featured on public transportation vehicles; these messages incorporated the web address of one group that assured all non-Christians they would spend "all eternity in torment in hell."

Of course, many religious groups and individuals were infuriated by the atheist campaign. *Christian Voice*, among others, suggested the ad failed to adhere to the advertising code. In its appeal to the Advertising Standards Authority, this group argued that the claims made in the campaign were not grounded in truth, and that they could not be validated. Complaints were also reportedly filed with the ASA claiming that the ads were insulting and degrading to people of faith.

In addition to the turmoil the atheist campaign inspired among religious groups in London, substantial commotion was generated when humanist, atheistic groups in other countries, including Canada, proposed that the ads be displayed on their own public transport. The ads spread from the British Humanist Association, which funded the original London-based campaign, to the Freethought Association of Canada, which has assisted in the establishment of the ads in Toronto, Calgary, and London, Ontario. However, the acceptance of the campaign in some Canadian cities did not go entirely smoothly. Halifax rejected the ads, and at first the Ottawa Transit Committee refused to display them on its buses. Eventually, the Humanist Association of Ottawa won its case against OC Transpo, and the ads were featured on Ottawa buses, bringing atheist advertising to yet another Canadian city.

Sources: *Ottawa Citizen*/Canada Online, at: <www2.canada.com/components/print.aspx?id=dcad334f-f28e-4f6c-9c09-2a8458cd73f3&sponsor=>; Mark Sweney, "ASA Clears Atheist Bus Campaign Ads," *The Guardian*, Jan. 2009; Ariane Sherine, "All Aboard the Atheist Bus Campaign," *The Guardian*, Oct. 2008; "How the Atheist Bus Campaign Started," Humanist Association of Ottawa.

likely proceed unimpeded. When the subject of gossip is present, then he or she is turned into a "non-person" within the group who is "physically present but interactionally absent." Often, jokes are used to signal that the morality-laden gossip messages are intended in good fun; no such levity is needed when gossip occurs behind people's backs. Indeed, if the subject of gossip is present and participating in the discussion, then the process may become conflictual, with the person talked about directly challenging the others and their interpretation. In short, the course of the conversation, and outcome of gossip, will depend in some part on the identity of group members and their participation in the process (Handelman, 1973).

The connection between gossip and social integration is two-sided. Gossiping about members of a "rival" group can reinforce the values and standards of the in-group. However, Elias and Scotson (1965) stress that gossip does not always have an integrating function. What's more, the relationship between gossip and integration may be reciprocal. Often, it is the level of group integration that determines the extent to which its members gossip, not vice versa. Typically, the more connected group members feel to each other, the more they will gossip.

Gossip can be viewed as a form of conversation in which group norms about a supposed misdeed evolve. Assessments worked out during gossip sessions shape how members of a peer group make sense of their experience and take stances towards a particular target (the person gossiped about). So, for example, Goodwin (2007) describes a gossip session among 11-year-old American girls who were excluded from a softball game by the team's captain and his girlfriend. The girls voiced their views—and worked out an agreement—about the way members of their age group should treat one another. Of course, some girls participated more than others. And using words as well as body language, participants declared their right to offer views on the matter. In these ways, people devise and express notions of culture and morality.

As everyone knows, gossip can hurt or improve a person's reputation. What varies from one society to another is the content of the gossip and the way qualities are evaluated. For example, the Tsimane women of Bolivia gossip about the attractiveness of group members. They also gossip about one another's maternal and housekeeping abilities, trustworthiness, social intelligence, wealth, and status; these are all factors that influence a woman's overall attractiveness rating. Unlike some other groups, reports of promiscuity have no significant effect on a woman's status for attractiveness (Rucas et al., 2006).

Conventionally, gossip has been closely associated with women, and some researchers have wondered why. One answer is that gossip is a form of indirect aggression, and women are more likely to use indirect aggression than men, who more typically use direct aggression. This is a result of the way they were socialized as children. Boys are taught to throw punches; girls are taught to throw offensive innuendoes.

In many social settings, boys are taught, permitted, or encouraged to use direct physical or verbal aggression, and girls are taught to use less direct forms of aggression that prominently feature gossip. Almost all studies of adults have found this same sex difference in the use of physical aggression. Hess and Hagen (2006) exposed young adult women and men to the same aggression-evoking stimulus. As conventional wisdom would predict, they found that women had a stronger need than men to express aggression indirectly, even after controlling for their differing social norms and needs for approval.

Women's gossip even has a place in the rituals of some tribal groups. According to Innes (2006), Muskogee women are linguistically active in ceremonial public spheres, though in different ways from men. One of the rituals women perform in these contexts is "gossip," which some Muskogee men describe as a dangerous activity. Here, the women use gossip in ritual ways—as in a celebrity roast or Mardi Gras revel—to criticize and embarrass the people who normally are in charge—in this case, the menfolk. This gossip gives women power and to some degree equalizes the power imbalance between men and women. Seemingly, tribe members agree that women's gossip is a powerful activity whose use is generally positive for Muskogees.

Gossip can keep people from breaking the rules, and this may be socially and even personally beneficial. However, fear of gossip can also harm people by limiting their willingness to act in ways that could help them. For example, people may be reluctant to seek help with psychiatric problems out of a fear of gossip.

This fear of gossip also plays a role in keeping some women from undertaking professional activities with men outside the office. Morgan and Martin (2006) studied the ways out-of-office settings affect women's sales careers. They found that in "heterosocial" settings, where both sexes are normally present—for example, in hotels or restaurants—traditional interaction rules apply. Women and men eating or talking together tend to be viewed as heterosexually linked pairs, even if their relationship is professional. As a result, women and men who work together outside the office risk becoming targets of gossip. Such problems are less common in "homosocial" settings, where men typically predominate, such as golf courses and strip clubs, as women tend to be excluded or are only present in small numbers.

The biggest problem with gossip—as with advertising—is that it spreads information that may be exaggerated or even false, and cannot be easily verified. Will we be better able to assess the veracity or credibility of gossip in the future? Probably not. In fact, it may prove more difficult. Kibby (2005) notes that e-mail communication, for example, fosters an environment where messages have an inherent "truth value," and senders are less restrained in the types of messages they send.

This is especially the case in regard to cyberbullying, also discussed in Chapter 6, which in some instances has led to target suicides (Box 10.2). When combined with convenience and ease of communication, and an ability to contact huge numbers of people simultaneously, e-mail becomes a rapid and effective mechanism for gossip, rumour, and urban legends. Thus, electronic media have simplified the distribution of gossip on an unprecedented scale, which means that they may become an even more important source of social control than ever. The conviction in March 2012 of ex-Rutgers University student Dharun Ravi for using a webcam to spy on his roommate, Tyler Clementi, during a gay encounter and then inviting others to view an encounter on webcam might send a clear message to social media users that what you do or say may be held against you in court.

Or it may not: Ravi received a 30-day jail sentence, a fine, and community service. Clementi, days after his roommate spied on him in September 2010, jumped to his death from the George Washington Bridge connecting New Jersey and New York City.

Exclusion/Ostracism

Exclusion—also known as ostracism or shunning—is the removal or expulsion of people from a social group or the refusal to allow them to join that group. It may also accompany other forms of social control—for example, shame, ridicule, or gossip. Or it may work on its own, silently controlling behaviour by cutting people off from access to contacts, relationships, and resources they need. Many people suffer ostracism without even knowing—or knowing why—they have been "voted out."

The most dramatic version of ostracism is imprisonment, meted out by the formal criminal justice system. Essentially, when a prison sentence is handed down, the convicted offender is expelled and removed from society—sometimes temporarily, sometimes indefinitely, and sometimes for life. Removal from the social group implies a loss of the rights associated with group membership—in the US, for example, the right to vote. While many US states reinstate an offender's right to vote once the person is released from prison, others do not. Today, 35 US states restrict voting privileges of offenders while they are on parole; 30 states restrict voting rights of offenders who are on probation; and in both Kentucky and Virginia, disenfranchisement is permanent for former felons.

All of us can expect to be excluded or ignored at one time or another—or to ignore and exclude someone else. In this sense ostracism is a common social process that permeates our society. Zadro et al. (2004) examined ostracism to determine the characteristics of ostracizers and their victims. They found that, psychologically, ostracizers show a low need for affiliation and an insecure attachment style. In other words, they don't have much need for other people and don't tend to bond strongly. On the other hand, people targeted for ostracism are especially vulnerable, with a preoccupied attachment style. This means they are anxious and emotionally expressive, often experiencing high levels of worry and impulsiveness. They react to ostracism in especially visible ways, which may account (in part) for why people target them.

Ostracism appears to both upset the victim and satisfy the ostracizer. It has the effect of making the victim feel bad and the perpetrator feel good or sometimes guilty—depending on the victim's reaction. To show this, Poulsen (2006) studied four-person groups in which three were given the role of perpetrator and told to exclude the fourth, an unsuspecting target. The research found, unremarkably, that targets expressed more negative feelings and perpetrators reported more guilt. Targets also viewed specific perpetrators more negatively than other perpetrators; equally, perpetrators came to view their targets less favourably than they viewed themselves or other perpetrators. This shows that ostracism, though intended to control behaviour, may have the unintended effect of isolating the target, increasing hostility between the target and community members, and—in that way—increasing the chance of further deviance.

Time to Reflect: Under what conditions is it not possible to ostracize people to control their behaviour? Under what conditions does ostracism work better than other methods of control?

In another experiment (Zadro, 2005), participants acted out a five-minute train ride in which two participants ignored or argued with a target sitting between them. Targets who were ignored—ostracized—later reported even lower satisfaction levels than the targets of argument. By contrast, the participants who ostracized the target person reported higher satisfaction levels than those who argued with the target. In other words, ostracism can be satisfying if you are the perpetrator, though not if you are the victim. For victims, it is even more punitive—more unsatisfying—than being the target of argument and criticism.

The effectiveness of ostracism as a means of social control is largely due to its symbolic and emotional effect. As a result, people suffer when they are ostracized, even if they suffer no material deprivation. Van Beest and Williams (2006) asked: If being included meant losing money and being ostracized meant keeping money, would individuals still be upset by ostracism? Even when being ostracized meant keeping more money than other players, victims found that ostracism was painful. In a second study involving Cyberball, victims felt worse when given no positive attention—that is, when ignored or ostracized—than when they received punitive attention.

This experience of pain through ostracism may also explain why, historically, **ghettos** have produced anger and identity distortion. In important respects, the ghetto can validly be compared to other institutions also dedicated to the forced confinement of dispossessed and dishonoured groups, such as refugee camps and prisons (Wacquant, 2004). Ghettos and ghettoization can represent concrete, extreme versions of collective ostracism. They achieve ostracism through the operation of four elements—stigma, boundaries, confinement, and institutional encapsulation—that together help the perpetrator accomplish economic exploitation as well as social ostracism.

As a result, the ghetto is a special form of collective violence—a total institution in urban space. This involuntary segregation makes ghettoization quite different from voluntary ethnic self-segregation—more similar to the historical Jewish ghettos of European cities than to the self-selected neighbourhoods—the Chinatowns, Little Italies—that most people are familiar with today, where people of common ethnicity reside in an urban enclave for reasons of social support and networking.

Ostracism, though historically effective as a means of social control, has lost some of its effectiveness in a fragmented and mobile world. Though people still have a deep fear of exclusion and exile, social ostracism in the modern world is likely to be temporary and insignificant (Pelusi, 2007). For most of human history, group membership was necessary for survival. Then, as social and geographic mobility increased, people became members of an ever-growing circle of families. Today, that circle is made up of large numbers of anonymous individuals creating easily permeable subgroups. These groups may be less emotionally meaningful than social groups in the past, but they are also less exclusionary. And since people's social ties are weaker, exclusion is also less significant to them.

For those who are (or have been) members of relatively insular, homogeneous groups and cultures, however, exclusion can have a huge impact because personal identity, and even survival, is so closely linked to group identity. Thus, the practice of shunning in some religious sects and banishment, as traditionally practised in some tribal societies, can be devastating. Similarly, excommunication of someone from the Catholic Church who is deeply devout will have a greater and more deleterious effect than the excommunication of someone for whom institutionalized Catholicism is not so central to personal life and identity.

Corporal Punishment

Unlike other types of control we have discussed, corporal punishment—especially, the corporal punishment of children—covers a wide range of penalties that scourge the body as much as the mind or spirit. Corporal punishment is an especially interesting type of social control because it is commonly used in mild forms, especially in families. As practised in families, it may accompany other forms of social control we have discussed—shame, exclusion, and so on.

Corporal punishment, as we are discussing it here, is physical punishment or assault that, under section 43 of Canada's Criminal Code, is *exempt from prosecution*: "Every schoolteacher, parent, or person standing in the place of a parent is justified in using force by way of correction toward the pupil or child, as the case may be, who is under his care, if the force does not exceed what is reasonable under the circumstances." Although section 43 is a legal defence for assault, the courts have never been able to define what force—in degree or nature—is "reasonable under the circumstances." Canadian courts have excused various bodily and emotional injuries—for example, bleeding, bruising, chipped teeth, long-term pain, psychological trauma, and the sexual humiliation of young girls—under section 43. Punishment, which most of us would view as cruel and unusual for adults, is often excused when applied to children.

The idea behind corporal punishment is that physical pain will make a person stop misbehaving. As well, the threat or fear of such punishment will deter others from similar rule-breaking. Corporal punishment has as its chief virtue ease of delivery. Any adult can easily whack a small child. What's more, the human body is richly supplied with nerve receptors that provide gateways for pain. At one time or another, many different techniques have been used to punish, threaten, or control people.

Most legal systems throughout the world have banned corporal punishment. Even "protectors"—fathers, husbands, schools, and asylums, for example—are no longer allowed free rein in using corporal punishment to correct the behaviour of their traditional wards—children, wives, students, and lunatics. Yet, out of public view, some parents continue to spank or whip their children. Some husbands also continue to beat their wives, although this is almost universally forbidden by the law. Also, some institutions continue to abuse the people who are forced to live within their walls. This, too, is outside the law but hard to regulate.

Research shows that, as with capital punishment, corporal punishment is least acceptable in the most developed and progressive societies—New Zealand, Canada, Scandinavia, and north-western Europe, for example. It remains acceptable only in less developed societies and parts of the United States (Figure 11.1 and Table 11.1).

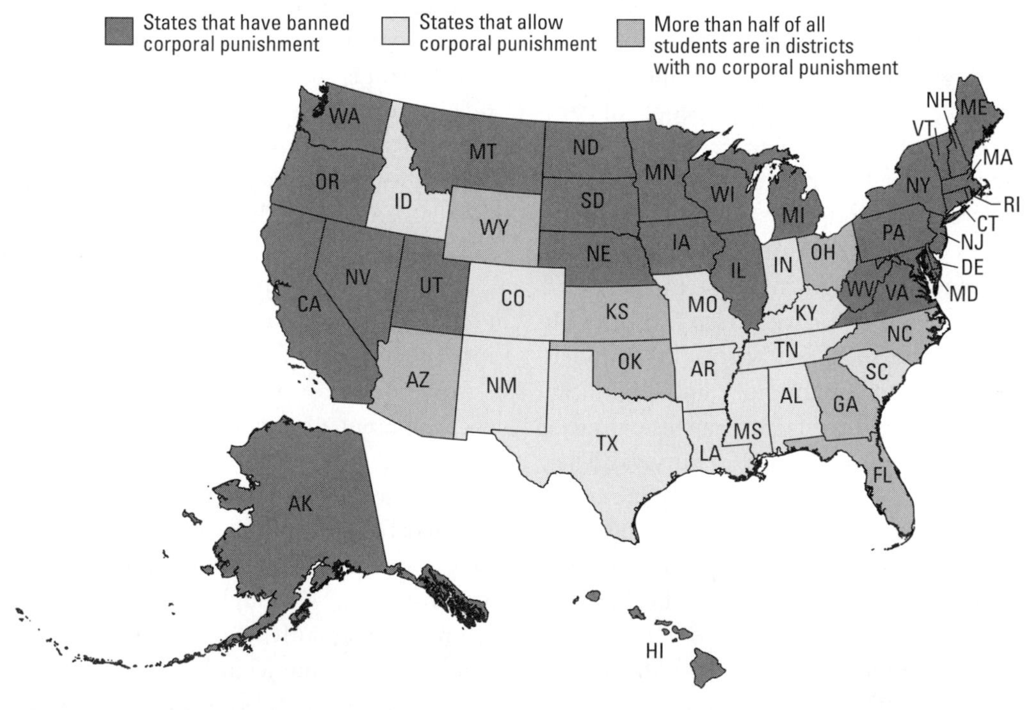

FIGURE 11.1 States with Corporal Punishment—USA

Source: US Department of Education, "Civil Rights Data Collection," 2006, at: <www.stophitting.com/index.php?page=statesbanning>.

TABLE 11.1 Legality of Corporal Punishment Worldwide, 2011

Country	Prohibited in the Home	Prohibited in All Schools	Prohibited in Penal System, All Uses
Australia	No	No	No
Austria	Yes	Yes	Yes
Belgium	No	Yes	Yes
Canada	No	Yes	Yes
Czech Republic	No	No	Yes
Denmark	Yes	Yes	Yes
Finland	Yes	Yes	Yes
France	No	Yes	Yes
Germany	Yes	Yes	Yes
Greece	Yes	Yes	Yes
Hungary	Yes	Yes	Yes
Iceland	Yes	Yes	Yes
Ireland	No	Yes	Yes
Italy	No	Yes	Yes
Japan	No	Yes	Yes
Luxembourg	No	Yes	Yes
Mexico	No	No	No
Netherlands	Yes	Yes	Yes
New Zealand	Yes	Yes	Yes
Norway	Yes	Yes	Yes
Poland	No	Yes	Yes
Portugal	Yes	Yes	Yes
Slovakia	No	Yes	Yes
Spain	Yes	Yes	Yes
Sweden	Yes	Yes	Yes
Switzerland	No	Yes	Yes
Turkey	No	Yes	Yes
United Kingdom	No	Yes	Yes
United States	No	No	No

Source: Adapted from Global Initiative to End All Corporal Punishment of Children, 2011, at: <www.endcorporalpunishment.org/pages/pdfs/reports/GlobalReport2011.pdf>.

Also, as with capital punishment, the research literature on corporal punishment consistently shows that this mode of control is largely ineffective. In fact, it is often counter-effective. Often, corporal punishment teaches people to act violently toward others, breeds hostility toward the punisher, and increases the likelihood the punished person will secretly break the rules. In these ways, corporal punishment backfires, just like ostracism, shaming, and threatening. These methods of control all drive a wedge between the perpetrator and the victim, creating hatred and a need for revenge.

People who are controlled by corporal punishments—especially by severe punishments—are unlikely to accept the punishment as just, compared with people who are reasoned with. They are unlikely to internalize the moral norms on which the punishment is premised. True, they may recognize the superior force of the punisher, comply with his or her wishes, and pretend to have internalized the norms; however, they will look for opportunities to violate the norms with impunity.

So, if our goal is to teach people—especially children—the difference between right and wrong, corporal punishment is one of the least effective ways to do so. All corporal punishment does is prove the (temporary) superiority of force over reason. It teaches the child to look for an opportunity to pass the punishment along to someone smaller or weaker.

In the past, corporal punishment was as common in schools as it was in homes. Consider Ireland: although people argued against it there in the 1950s, corporal punishment remained an accepted practice into the early 1980s. Rules governing the proper use of corporal punishment in schools were regularly violated. Yet, there was little effort to challenge the authority of teachers or penalize them for excessive punishment. People also took for granted the right of parents to punish their children as they saw fit. They believed parents had not only the right but also the responsibility to discipline their children. When an abuse came to light, courts were more likely to send the victimized child to an industrial school than punish the abusive parents.

School managers throughout this period enjoyed the same rights as parents to discipline the children in their care, and the Department of Education avoided interfering. After 30 years of continued pressure, corporal punishment was finally banned in Ireland in 1982 (Maguire and Cinneide, 2005).

The Canadian Teachers' Federation (CTF) opposes the use of corporal punishment in public schools yet "supports the retention of section 43 of the Criminal Code of Canada." In a 1993 discussion paper, the CTF expressed concern that repealing section 43 would criminalize child care. Using force to break up a fight between students, for example, could lead to assault charges, and without section 43 there would be no defence.

Today, corporal punishment persists in family homes, mainly in the form of spanking. Canadian data show that many children and youth are spanked at one time or another, but some experience much worse. A significant degree of the violence that does occur within the family arises as excessive "correction" or physical discipline. Indeed, as noted, section 43 of the Criminal Code lets families use "reasonable" force to correct children.

As the gatekeepers to the courts, the police have to decide what this means and they vary significantly in the ways they respond to corporal punishment of varying kinds and degrees. Some variation is inevitable given the normal exercise of police discretion. However, a lack of clarity in the law adds to the confusion and undermines the efforts to reduce violence in children's lives (Landau, 2005).

Much research has been done, in Canada and elsewhere, on the factors that incline parents to use corporal punishment on their children and the effects of this punishment on children's well-being. We still do not know whether the psychological harm caused by corporal punishment is universal or depends on the child's view or interpretation of the punishment and the specific cultural context. Most evidence shows that physical punishment by parents has a consistently negative effect on children's behaviour. For example, it increases the likelihood of delinquency and reduces the quality of school performance (Millar, 2007).

Yet, many Canadian parents continue to approve of—and use—corporal punishment, especially if they experienced corporal punishment themselves in childhood. In reproducing the parenting practices they experienced in childhood, parents often pass these practices on to their children. According to a survey of adults in Quebec, most respondents approved of spanking, even though they recognized that corporal punishment may do harm (Gagnė et al., 2007). For two-thirds of these respondents, spanking was a common childhood experience. Older respondents who were spanked in childhood, and believe that spanking never or seldom results in physical injuries, are most for spanking. On the other hand, respondents who reported more severe physical violence or psychological abuse in childhood were less in favour of spanking.

In this intergenerational transmission of physical (or corporal) punishment, women often reproduce the behaviour of their own punitive mothers and men the behaviour of their own punitive fathers. Marital dissatisfaction increases the intensity of corporal punishment by fathers, though it has no similar effect on mothers, perhaps reminding us that men tend to act out their aggressive feelings directly, whereas women do not (Lunkenheimer et al., 2006).

Childhood experiences are not the only factors that influence parents' use of corporal punishment. Current difficulties—domestic violence, feeling the need for or receiving mental health services, unemployment, health issues, lack of social support, and prior child welfare involvement—have even more influence on parenting practices, including corporal punishment. In short, corporal punishment is more often used on children by parents who are poor, stressed, and abused (Barrett, 2007). This would seem to contradict any views that corporal punishment is something parents administer to their children wisely, humanely, and with clinical detachment.

Other research supports the view that, among families living at or near the poverty level, parental distress is a significant predictor of child maltreatment. What's more, the less social support a parent has, the more serious the child maltreatment is likely to be. As one might imagine, a parent's childhood history of maltreatment is the second highest predictor. Other important influences on child maltreatment are the parent's educational attainment and his or her belief in the value of corporal punishment.

Child maltreatment can have serious long-term outcomes—for example, increasing the risk of depression in both childhood and adulthood. Children exposed to physical, sexual, sibling, or peer abuse often suffer severe depression; children exposed to corporal punishment, domestic violence, or other family abuse at home also experience significant problems at school (Charles, 2007).

Other research shows that corporal punishment is associated with increased odds of major depression, alcohol addiction, and "acting out" in adulthood, even after adjusting for socio-demographic variables and parental bonding. Adults who experienced physical punishment as children—but no other abuse—are at higher risk of adult psychopathology than adults who had experienced no physical punishment or abuse. From this, researchers infer that corporal punishment creates childhood distress that can lead to adult psychopathology (Afifi et al., 2006). Worse things can be done to children—especially emotional and sexual abuse—but we must do away with the idea that corporal punishment, by itself, is inconsequential.

Of course, people interpret their experiences and respond to their interpretations; they do not respond mechanically to their social environment. So, the chance a child will become depressed or aggressive (i.e., act out) is mediated by interpretations of the parent giving the punishment. In turn, this interpretation depends on the parent's usual parenting style. Research shows that mothers who *approve* of corporal punishment use it routinely whether they feel distressed or not, while mothers who *disapprove* of corporal punishment use it only when they feel distressed. Second, and probably related to this finding, spanking is more likely to produce depressive symptoms in children of mothers who *disapprove* of corporal punishment than in children of mothers who *approve* of corporal punishment (McLloyd and Smith, 2002).

These findings can be interpreted in several ways that all point in the same direction. Spanking has a harmful effect on children only when—or because—(1) it is provided by a stressed parent in an anxious environment; (2) it reflects the parent's fleeting need to lash out at the child, despite contrary views about spanking; or (3) it reflects a parenting style that is hostile, inconsistent, or unpredictable.

Harmful spanking is by no means rare. In a study of a sample of college students, Turner and Muller (2004) found that, as reported in national studies, roughly 40 per cent of the sample had experienced some corporal punishment when they were 13 years old. Those who had suffered corporal punishment were more likely than average to report depressive symptoms, independent of any history of abuse and/or other forms of punishment. Similar to McLloyd and Smith's study (2002), parental anger while delivering corporal punishment was the strongest predictor of depression among these students. Spanking by an angry parent, then, does the worst damage to children. Reportedly, spanking has fewer adverse effects if the child has high self-esteem.

One justifiable concern about corporal punishment is that it will promote other forms of aggressive or dangerous behaviour. An example is school bullying, and research has found that children subjected to corporal punishment at home are more likely to bully other children at school. School bullying is a major social problem in most countries. Often, school administrators and teachers are held responsible for bullying at school, though the real causes lie elsewhere—usually at the bully's home. Thus, despite rigorous efforts to prevent this problem, bullying continues to afflict most schools. To solve the problem of bullying, we need to address children's lives at home, not school. Figure 11.2 illustrates the cycle or typical sequence of bullying activities.

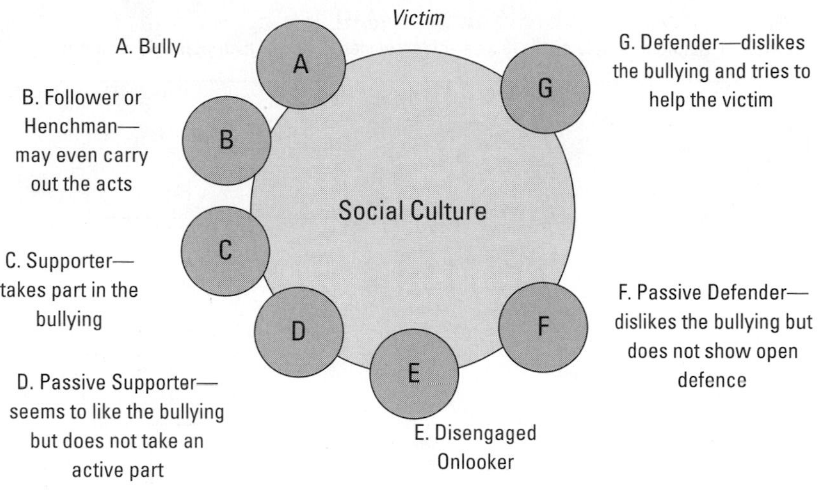
Victim
A. Bully
A
B. Follower or Henchman—may even carry out the acts
B
Social Culture
C. Supporter—takes part in the bullying
C
D. Passive Supporter—seems to like the bullying but does not take an active part
D
E. Disengaged Onlooker
E
F. Passive Defender—dislikes the bullying but does not show open defence
F
G. Defender—dislikes the bullying and tries to help the victim
G

FIGURE 11.2 The Cycle of Bullying

Source: <bullyingintodaysworld.blogspot.com/2011/09/bullying-statistics.html>.

Even though bullying at school is associated with abuse that children suffer first in their homes, bullying and victimization at school often become social scripts with their own history and logic.

Cross-cultural research by Dussich and Maekoya (2007) surveyed university students in Japan, South Africa, and the United States. In all three countries, they found significant connections between physical harm in childhood and three types of bullying experience: being a bully, being bullied, and being both a bully and bullied. They found the manner in which physically abused children cope with their early victimization at home has a bearing on their tendency to bully others or suffer victimization at school. Bullying is not as common in Canada or the US as it is elsewhere. The rates of bullying are much higher—over twice as high—in parts of Central Europe, the former USSR, and the Baltic nations.

No simple pattern emerges from these statistics, but one suspects there are social and cultural variations behind these differences. Interestingly, a correlation appears to exist between the high rates of bullying in these European countries and high rates of suicide (see Table 3.3).

Recent research on cyberbullying in the US illustrates its extent and forms. Figure 11.3 indicates the extent and types of such bullying in one American school district, and additional research points to an extensive prevalence of this practice (see, e.g., www.cyberbullying.us/research.php). Much of this will be familiar to readers of this book who have recently left the years of prime bullying risk.

Corporal punishment experienced in childhood may not only increase the likelihood of bullying; it may also influence dating violence in adolescence. In a sample drawn from 36 universities in 19 nations, 56 per cent of all students reported experiencing corporal punishment at home and 30 per cent reported assaulting a dating partner; 7 per cent even reported having injured one. Most important, students who had been physically punished at home were more likely than average to assault and injure a dating partner (Douglas and Straus, 2005).

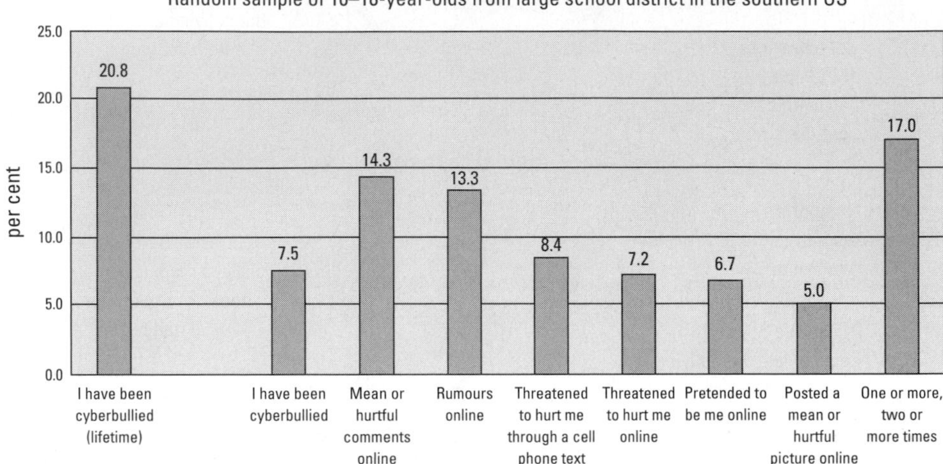

FIGURE 11.3 Cyberbullying Victimization

Source: Cyberbullying Research Center, at: <www.cyberbullying.us/research.php>.

The use of corporal punishment is apparently declining. Throughout Europe, countries have been banning the practice. For example, in 2000, the German government passed a law banning corporal punishment in families, and people have complied with this ban. Recent surveys reveal a significant decrease in the prevalence of corporal punishment and a high acceptance of the legal prohibition. General awareness of the legal limits on parental use of corporal punishment increased significantly after the law was passed. Thus, outlawing corporal punishment has had an impact on family violence against children in Germany (Bussmann, 2004).

Similarly, over the past 70 years, Sweden has imposed a series of legal reforms aimed at wiping out the corporal punishment of children in homes, schools, and institutions. The most recent of these reforms took place in 1979 when Sweden became the first nation to directly abolish corporal punishment. The goals of this ban were to affirm children's rights to personal security and to tell the public that physical punishment is neither acceptable nor defensible. The legislation has worked. Available evidence confirms that acts of violence against children have declined dramatically in Sweden in recent decades. Today, corporal punishment is rare, serious assaults on children are uncommon, and child abuse deaths are rare (Durrant and Janson, 2005).

In Canada and elsewhere, corporal punishment is increasingly viewed as unacceptable. Perhaps this will mean a greater use of other damaging means of social control on children, such as threat, shame, guilt, or ostracism. Hopefully, it will mean a greater use of persuasion and other positive means of influencing behaviour through advice, example, and kind supervision.

Time to Reflect: In most modern countries, most people oppose the use of corporal punishment, except under special circumstances. What circumstances do you think would justify corporal punishment?

Media Depictions of Informal Control

Perhaps because informal social control is often intended to be subtle or subliminal, it seems less present in popular movies, television, and books than formal mechanisms do. Through the influence of cultural and media theorists such as Marshall McLuhan, Daniel Boorstin, and Noam Chomsky, however, the public has developed some appetite for this topic. The popularity of the Comedy Central program *The Daily Show* starring Jon Stewart, for instance, is largely attributable to the public's desire for humorous meta-commentary on the ways the media present images and ideologies to the public.

Modern public conceptions of informal control, in large part, are attributable to two of the most popular and acclaimed books of the twentieth century, Aldous Huxley's *Brave New World* (1932) and George Orwell's *Nineteen Eighty-Four* (1948). Both books, written as dystopian visions of a totalitarian future, focus on governmental intrusions into private life and express concern over how power elites coerce or encourage specific modes of public thinking. Huxley depicts a future in which recreational sex and drug use are means of preoccupying public attentions from other issues. Orwell famously envisioned governments using public festivals, patriotism, and lotteries to produce an illusion of prosperity, augmented by direct surveillance (formal control).

Huxley, Orwell, and *The Daily Show*'s Stewart all speak to how media outlets use images and language to coerce informal control. They largely avoid the issues of religion, heritage, and tradition, however. Discussing religion as social control has always been touchy in North America. In 1927 Sinclair Lewis, who would later be awarded the Nobel Prize for literature, published his novel *Elmer Gantry*, about the political and personal ambitions of a cynical, self-serving Protestant minister. The book resulted in a political firestorm, earning the author death threats, a ban in Boston, and the mantle of "Satan's Cohort" from the Reverend Billy Sunday. Over the last few decades, in movies such as *Life of Brian* (1979), *Saved!* (2004), and *Jesus Camp* (2006), North Americans have more openly exposed themselves to popular entertainment that overtly discusses the social controls commonly found in the religious practice.

Immigration and culture have also provided fodder for discussions on social control. Many recent films openly discuss these issues. One is *Bend It Like Beckham* (2002), which speaks to the difficulty of a first-generation Londoner in getting permission from her traditional Punjabi Sikh father to play organized soccer. Indeed, this intergenerational conflict over child behaviour—how to dress, who to date, what activities to participate in—is a popular theme in movies and books about immigrants and their children. We could easily think of a dozen, and they all—more or less effectively—capture the dramatic shift in family dynamics that sociologists have written about for over 90 years, since the publication of Thomas and Znaniecki's classic work, *The Polish Peasant in Europe and America* (1918–20).

Consequences of Social Control

Economic Consequences

Informal control can be expensive to practice, as it requires strong, forceful, yet sometimes invisible control. For this reason, religious leaders with grand ambitions about spreading the word often feel an economic pinch.

The Church of Jesus Christ of Latter-day Saints (the Mormon church) provided a well-publicized example of the role of major money interests in church affairs in 2008. That year, the LDS engaged in vigorous fundraising on behalf of Proposition 8, a California ballot measure aimed at illegalizing same-sex marriage. The church ultimately collected millions of dollars and waged a public campaign on behalf of the church's values. Given the proposition's slim passage, the church's ability to raise money may have given the movement just enough strength to convince a wavering electorate.

While religious activism requires money, and not simply ideas, to affect change, even the LDS seems stingy compared to the secular advertising industry. For decades, North American businesses have poured billions of dollars into print, radio, and television advertising, launching widely reviled practices such as the now-illegal practice of subliminal advertising and the still-legal practice of product placement in movies and on television. Advertisements constantly strive to guide public taste, leading companies to spend ever more on promoting their products. The rise of the Internet has increased advertising revenues to dizzying heights, as Harvard Business School professors John Deighton and John Quelch estimate online advertising is now a $300 billion industry (Hamilton Consultants, with Deighton and Quelch, 2009).

In some ways, big-money religious proselytizing and advertising are similar, as the desires of each are clear from the outset. The LDS wants the public to believe in Mormon doctrine, whereas McDonald's wants the public to believe in the McGriddle. For this reason, the trend of media concentration in North America is troublesome, whereby ultra-rich media empires consolidating disparate outlets through mergers, binding corporate interests without transparently expressing what those interests are.

Canadian media are particularly prone to media concentration, as a small number of major financial powers in the country dominate the airwaves. In 2000, the BCE Corporation created a $4 billion alliance with Thompson Corp. and renamed itself Bell Media. It now owns CTV and its 33 affiliates, TSN, Discovery Channel, the Comedy Network, and 27 other specialty channels. It also controls 33 radio stations, and, until late 2010, controlled the *Globe and Mail*. With enormous financial clout, companies like Bell Media are able to deeply, yet indirectly, affect public opinion through control of media messaging, a fact that carries enormous political and social implications.

Conclusion

Informal social control has always existed and has always evolved to meet new challenges. The study of history reveals that deviance, crime, and social control are found in every society. They merely change their features over time.

Of course, these variations over time and place are not random. They are socially patterned, and the task of sociology is to discover those patterns. One attempt to do this has been especially creative. Sociologist Norbert

Elias, in his two-volume study *The Civilizing Process*, shows us the connection between the development of state control and self-control, as seen in the development of civility and good manners.

Elias points out that we cannot reasonably separate informal control from formal control. The two change together. There is a complex relationship between crime, control, the rise of states, and socio-economic development. In general, the rise of states lays the groundwork for more security and more conformity. Socio-economic development increases the opportunities for deviance and crime and also increases the opportunities for control.

More tolerance today for variant behaviours is evident in our day, owing largely to state approval and to a pluralistic society. Likely more crime also is committed in the world today because there is more around to steal and, with more material inequality in the world, a higher motivation to steal it. Further, it is more difficult to monitor people in large cities than in small towns or rural communities.

At the same time, with socio-economic development comes a revolution in social control. We see a series of counterbalancing forces in the modern state. Within each country, an increase in national wealth increases economic inequality; but in most industrial nations this process is counterbalanced by a tax system that redistributes the wealth, thus reducing inequality—in Marxist terms, just enough to prevent an uprising of the underclasses. (Globally, however, there has been much less redistribution of wealth between rich and poor countries to counterbalance economic inequality.)

Within each country, an increase in national wealth goes together with the development of state institutions. However, there are both positive and negative sides to the growth of modern nation-states. On the negative side, these nation-states enjoy an unparalleled capacity for coercion and surveillance. The rise of state bureaucracies made death camps possible—more generally, the "iron cage of modernity," as Weber called it. The rise of scientific testing and measurement—within state bureaucracies and outside state bureaucracies (e.g., in education and business)—made oppression by norms of "normalcy" possible, as Foucault contends.

On the positive side, the development of a strong central state has promoted the rule of law and the spread of civil rights. (In this respect, China is perhaps the most glaring counter-example.) Even the rise of civility—good manners—as Norbert Elias showed, has relied on the rise of nation-states. Our responsibilities as citizens have been listed in laws and regulations but so have our rights as citizens, including the right to freedom from discrimination.

As a result, today in modern industrial societies we are limited, and at the same time protected, by more written laws, regulations, and rules than ever before. In the face of this growth of legislation, it is difficult—maybe impossible—to say if people are more controlled or less controlled than they were in the past, because they are controlled less by brute force than by socialization. As noted, most modern states do not allow corporal punishment, and the number of modern states that do will likely decrease. People are still free to practise the art of control by threat, shame, guilt, and ostracism—and, of course, persuasion; however, some of these forms of social control are less useful in large, mobile societies.

Amid the proliferation of so-called *formal* controls by the state and its institutions, the *informal* controls continue to work, but sometimes they operate more weakly than in the past. People express less concern today about honour, shame, saving face, preserving reputation, and being gossiped about, for example. Some people even want to be gossiped about, and they use Facebook and Twitter, for example, to ensure the largest possible number know about their latest nefarious doings.

The strongest surviving concerns about honour, shame, and so on are found in small, relatively closed communities—in cliques, classrooms, villages, offices, families, and old-age homes—where they are likely to do the most damage and where state protections are most difficult to enforce. The "politics of reputation" continues to exercise a mighty control in these circumstances, far from the important activities of great figures and powerful institutions.

So, as we move forward in the twenty-first century, we are hard-pressed to answer the most interesting questions, theoretically and practically: What is the ideal relationship between civil society and the state, between informal social control and formal social control? Is social control, on balance, liberating or repressive, stifling or creative? Conversely, is deviance in a society more a sign of health or a sign of pathology, a sign of weakness or of strength? We argued in Chapter 10 that some people are victimized by their conscience—by a moral sense that they have to break the formal rules to be true to themselves. These are unquestionably strong people—sometimes, morally strong people in a morally weak society. As Durkheim showed us, might is not always right.

Finally, a debate continues to rage in deviance and criminological literature on the origins of criminal behaviour, on the one hand, and the best ways to control it, on the other. Clearly, these two topics are related. What we do know is (1) multiple causes contribute to criminal behaviour, and they interact with one another in complicated ways; and (2) we have had little success in rehabilitating criminals, so (many believe) it may make more sense to try to prevent crime than try to cure it.

Yet, this observation leads to further disagreements. If we are to prevent crime (and other associated forms of undesirable behaviour, like drug abuse or interpersonal violence), where in the life cycle do we have to intervene, and what can we do? Does the problem start in families, through neglect, abuse, faulty parenting, and uninformed socialization; in primary schools, through academic failure and damaged self-esteem; in peer relations, by learning unproductive or delinquent life skills; or does it start even earlier, outside the family, in the realm of poverty, economic inequality, racism, unemployment, and job-related stresses? Are we importing some of our society's problems from other countries where poverty and violence are even more severe? Can we do anything more through informal socialization or must we leave criminal deviance to the correctional system?

One thing we do know is that problems will arise in societies where people are continuously uncertain about whether norms will or will not be obeyed and defended. This uncertainty invites intolerance, deviance, and victimization. But we also know that people, to obey voluntarily, must be convinced that the formal rules are fair and just. Informal control shows that people, left to their own devices, can often create and enforce order together. Sometimes the state's intervention is an improvement and sometimes it isn't. In the next chapter, we discuss formal punishment and the problems attending that particular intervention.

Questions for Critical Thought

1. How does a group or community decide what rules to make and enforce and how to enforce them?
2. What are the most and least effective ways of persuading people to go with a plan of action? Under what conditions is persuasion likely to work better than threat?
3. How are shame and guilt likely to backfire, leading to behaviour that is the opposite of what is being demanded?
4. List some examples of situations you have seen when ridicule did not work as a means of social control. Explain the likely reasons it failed to control behaviour.
5. Would you agree that spanking is a form of child abuse and should be punished? If so, what kind of punishment would be appropriate?
6. Imagine and describe a society, or group, in which corporal punishment would not likely have harmful effects on the child.

Recommended Readings

Butler, Judith. 2004. *Precarious Life: The Powers of Mourning and Violence.* London and New York: Verso.

To examine how norms are established based on the inclusion of some groups and exclusion of other groups from what is considered "humanity," Butler explores the indefinite detention of prisoners at Guantanamo Bay, censorship of public debate, the nation-building politics of mourning, and the media's demonization of the Middle East.

Condry, Rachel. 2007. *Families Shamed: The Consequences of Crime for Relatives of Serious Offenders.* Cullompton, UK: Willan.

The book focuses on how the relatives of criminals make sense of their experiences, individually and collectively; how they describe the difficulties they face; whether they are blamed and shamed by others; and, above all, how they cope with supporting someone yet not excusing his or her actions.

Feagin, Joe R., and Vera Hernan. 2001. *Liberation Sociology.* Boulder, Colo.: Westview.

The text concerns itself with raising consciousness and defines liberation sociology as an activist rather than an academic sociology. The authors, who criticize the false notion of "objectivity" and warn against misleading data, are cheered by the large-scale influx of women and people of colour into the field of sociology.

Young, Jock. 2007. *The Vertigo of Late Modernity.* Los Angeles: Sage.

This book deals with the impact of major social issues on the modern world and the ways that societies and individuals respond, including issues of identity and questions of the normal and the "other," deviance and disorder, social exclusion and the underclass, work and welfare, punitive cultures, immigration, and terrorism.

Recommended Websites

Corporal Punishment

www.apa.org/releases/spanking.html

A comprehensive overview, from the American Psychological Association, of the effectiveness of spanking as a means of punishment and control.

Fairness & Accuracy In Reporting

www.fair.org/index.php

This is the most accessible and valuable website currently devoted to exploring corporate media inaccuracies and fallacies. The site features a vast archive of stories relating to faux-news and disinformation, as well as a regular podcast, blog, and a collection of reports and studies.

Rumour and Gossip

www.apa.org/science/psa/apr05gossip.html

Provided and maintained by the American Psychological Association, this website provides useful information and references on two of the most important means by which people maintain informal social control.

Shame and Psychotherapy

www.columbiapsych.com/shame_miller.html

This study argues that although shame has a central role in people's lives, it has been little studied and is little understood. As the author points out, shame is related to a family of painful emotions including humiliation, embarrassment, feelings of low self-esteem, belittlement, and stigmatization.

Sociological Images

thesocietypages.org/socimages/

"Sociological Images" is an extremely entertaining blog devoted to critiquing gendered and racialist media messages. This frequently updated site provides a litany of amusing examples of preposterous, misogynistic, and racist advertisements, as well as proposed teaching aides.

Recommended Movies

***Idiocracy*, Dir. Mike Judge (2006)**

Private Joe Bower, the US Army's most average soldier, is mistakenly frozen for five centuries, only to wake up and find that the devolution of human intelligence over the last 500 years made him the smartest man in the world. Given Judge's history as the creator of *King of the Hill*, *Office Space*, and *Beavis & Butthead*, *Idiocracy*'s flip, absurd tone is hardly surprising. As silly as the film is, however, it does speak ably to the risks posed by corporate sloganeering and society's general "dumbing down."

***Network*, Dir. Sidney Lumet (1976)**

Network anchor Howard Beale learns he is about to lose his job to a much younger man, causing Beale such grief that he announces on national television that he will commit suicide during his final episode. Beale does not kill himself, but he rails against the state of the world and of television, subsequently becoming the most popular media figure in America. Arguably the greatest film made about television, and one of the finest American films of any type, Lumet's satire seems truer today than ever before. Two comedy-dramas—*The Truman Show* (dir. Peter Weir, 1998) and *Pleasantville* (dir. Gary Ross, 1998)—are outstanding dystopian depictions of the pervasive influence of television on modern society.

***Mean Girls*, Dir. Mark S. Waters (2004)**

Cady Heron, an American who had previously been living in Africa, moves to suburban Illinois and finds herself subsumed by a group of popular girls known as "the Plastics." Tina Fey wrote this hit comedy, a pithy film that cleverly interrogates the formulation and dynamics of female cliques in high school. While the film would be even more cutting had it vigorously explored the class and race dimensions of popularity, this remains a very clever film about social divisions and belonging.

***Trembling Before G-d*, Dir. Sandi Dubowski (2001)**

This movie uncovers the tumultuous lives of gay and lesbian Hasidic and Orthodox Jews. David has been going to therapy for 10 years in an attempt to "cure" his homosexuality, while Michelle was disowned by her Orthodox family after filing for divorce from an ill-conceived marriage. Covering cases in New York, Florida, California, Israel, and Britain, Dubowski looks at how observant Jews attempt to maintain both their religious faith and their sexual identity.

12 Formal Punishment

Learning Objectives

- To understand the purposes of punishment
- To examine the different types of commonly used punishments
- To study the history and effectiveness of capital punishment and imprisonment
- To learn about the development of fines and penalties as punishment
- To identify problems associated with programs of rehabilitation, probation, and parole
- To consider the value of restorative justice as an alternative

Introduction

Thinking about punishment has changed gradually over time, and so have punishments. Once, most punishments were quick and harsh, but today they are more likely to be slow and supposedly remedial. Today, most people in developed societies assess punishments in terms of their effectiveness, not their moral intention. However, this is not universally true. For instance, victims of crime and supporters of the victim's rights movement continue to demand the right to express their moral outrage against crime. They believe this will recognize the harm caused by criminal behaviour and ensure that due punishment is meted out. Many members of the public also support the need for harsher punishments to show society's outrage when atrocious crimes are committed. Most citizens today also ask questions about punishment: Which punishments will work best to prevent crime? Which will reduce the likelihood of recidivism? Which will make society safer and healthier in the long-run?

So far, no final, decisive answers to these questions have been found. As a result, societies continue to vary widely in their uses of different types of punishment. Our goal in this chapter is to survey various forms of punishment from a sociological perspective. We will try to understand why these punishments are employed and ask whether they achieve their socially intended goals. Finally, we will try to make sense of this subject within the sociological approaches we have used throughout this book.

Definition of Punishment

What, precisely, do we mean by *punishment*? For purposes of this book, we will use a definition of punishment suggested by philosopher Anthony Flew (1954), who proposes that a punishment must have the following features:

- it must be unpleasant;
- it must result from, or follow, an offence;
- punishment must be imposed after a formal process of fact-gathering, detection, arrest, and trial;
- the person punished must be the offender;
- the punishment must occur in this world, not the afterlife; and
- to distinguish it from revenge or remorse, punishment must be exacted by a person in authority—not by the victim or the offender him- or herself.

This definition of punishment fits with the specific goals of punishment that are listed below, which form the basis for decision-making by people obliged to put general principles into practice—especially judges, lawyers, and legislators. It is also congruent with philosophical thought and philosophers' interest in the role of law in society.

Goals of Punishment

Legal philosophers have debated the purposes of punishment for centuries; these purposes fall into five main categories:

- taking retribution for criminal behaviour;
- deterring the criminal and others from committing crimes in the future;
- rehabilitating criminals so that they do not commit further crimes;
- restoring the victim and the community;
- incapacitating the criminal so that he or she cannot commit further crimes.

Retribution

One of the oldest goals of punishment is **retribution**: literally, "payback" for harm done, or "an eye for an eye." According to philosopher Immanuel Kant, morality demands that penal laws be based exclusively on the principle of retribution. Kant (1887 [1797]) argues punishments are only moral and just if they fit the crime—that is, if they are proportionate to the crime. So, for example, the execution of murderers would be just, but the execution of petty thieves would not.

The idea of retribution continues to have significant public appeal, especially when applied to punishment for serious crimes, such as child abuse or murder. It does not have quite the same public resonance, however, when applied to punishments for less serious offences, such as trespassing or creating a public nuisance. In addition, retributive punishments do not address two of the key concerns that many people today have about crime: prevention (deterrence) and harm reduction.

Prevention or Deterrence

The second, commonly accepted, purpose of punishment is **deterrence**: dissuading people from committing crimes by showing that if they do, they will be caught and painfully punished. Punishments based on deterrence may be "specific" (i.e., aimed at deterring the particular criminal being punished from committing new crimes), "general" (i.e., aimed at deterring others from committing such crimes), or both.

Cesare Beccaria (1738–94) had an enormous influence on the development of criminology as a discipline. He was one of the first philosophers and politicians to put forward the view that criminal punishment should not be aimed at retribution but instead at the prevention, or deterrence, of crime. Beccaria (1764) argued that deterring people from committing crimes was more socially useful than exacting retribution from criminals after the fact. He believed that people would act rationally to avoid the unpleasantness of punishment. This meant that, to be effective, punishments must not only be unpleasant; they must also be certain, publicly observable, and swift.

Beccaria did not believe in the death penalty as a just or effective deterrent to crime. However, deterrence arguments have been widely used to justify harsh criminal regimes, including those that rely heavily on the execution of criminals. The idea of deterrence continues to have much popular appeal, particularly at times when crime is perceived to be on the rise and the public is convinced that something must be done to stop it.

Rehabilitation

The third purpose of punishment is **rehabilitation**: helping convicted criminals become law-abiding members of society. If our goal is to make society safe in the long term, and we cannot accept the idea of execution or life imprisonment, we may decide that rehabilitation is the best way to ensure our collective safety.

This is an old idea, dating back many centuries. Appalled by the prison conditions of the day, prison reformers in late eighteenth-century England began to lobby for the humane treatment of prisoners. Many of the prison reformers were Quakers, who strongly believed all human beings could reform by "coming to God" through solitary reflection and repentance. Hence, the new "penitentiaries" built in nineteenth-century England (and elsewhere) became correctional and rehabilitative facilities and not merely holding places for convicts. Quaker mental hospital reform is the only bright light in the horrendous history of mental hospitals.

Early rehabilitation efforts were aimed at changing the character or "disciplining the soul" of the prisoner through exposure to religion and severe personal treatments. These included continuous solitary confinement and silence, harsh personal discipline, and rigorous work schedules. By contrast, rehabilitation efforts today focus on the provision of supports and supervision to ensure that prisoners refrain from crime when they "reintegrate" into law-abiding society. They sometimes also supply education or vocational training, help finding housing, supervised probation and parole, alternative measures for young offenders, and programs that provide offenders treatment for mental illness and substance abuse.

Restoration

The fourth purpose of punishment is to repair the harm done by the commission of a crime and to "restore" the victim, the offender, and the community to a healthy state.

Restorative justice focuses on ways of ensuring that offenders take responsibility for the harm they have caused and that victims of crime have a "voice" in determining the punishment. Where possible, restorative justice also seeks to ensure that the offender makes restitution to the victim and repairs any harm done to the community. The ultimate goal is to help all community members maintain their confidence in public safety and the justice system.

Restorative justice may be carried out in a number of different ways but usually it requires direct communication between the offender and the victim (and, in many cases, with community members as well). Once the parties understand why the offence took place and the harm it has caused, ideally, they can then reach an agreement on how the offender can "right the wrong." In short, offenders are expected to take responsibility for their actions and make amends.

The effectiveness of restorative justice in preventing crime has not yet been thoroughly assessed, and the future of restorative justice is not yet clear. Nevertheless, the popularity of this approach to justice is strong in Aboriginal communities and growing elsewhere in Canadian society.

Incapacitation

A final purpose of punishment is to incapacitate people who not only have inflicted harm but are believed to be a continuing danger to society. Banishment and execution have accomplished this goal in the past; today, most modern societies rely on imprisonment. We will have a great deal to say about imprisonment in the course of this chapter.

Time to Reflect: Of the various reasons for punishment mentioned above, which do you find the most compelling (or persuasive) and which least compelling?

Punishment in Canada

Before we look more closely at different types of punishment, it is useful to have some understanding of how formal punishment works in Canadian society.

The Legal Framework

The Canadian Charter of Rights and Freedoms guarantees all people accused of an offence a fair trial. It also states that no one convicted of an offence can be subjected to punishment that is "cruel and unusual." For this reason, Canada has abolished capital punishment and all forms of corporal punishment within the penal system.

Today, there are three main kinds of punishment in Canada: imprisonment, **community supervision** (e.g., probation and parole), and fines. Section 718 of the Criminal Code sets out the principles that judges must follow when sentencing criminal offenders:

> 718. The fundamental purpose of sentencing is to contribute, along with crime prevention initiatives, to respect for the law and the maintenance of a just, peaceful, and safe society by imposing just sanctions that have one or more of the following objectives:
>
> (a) to denounce unlawful conduct;
> (b) to deter the offender and other people from committing offences;
> (c) to separate offenders from society, where necessary;
> (d) to assist in rehabilitating offenders;
> (e) to provide reparations for harm done to victims or to the community; and
> (f) to promote a sense of responsibility in offenders and acknowledgment of the harm done to victims and to the community.

The Criminal Code also states that all sentences must be proportionate to the gravity of the offence and the degree of responsibility of the offender; and that alternatives to imprisonment must always be considered, particularly for Aboriginal offenders. In addition, the Youth Criminal Justice Act sets out a host of special rules—emphasizing rehabilitation and alternatives to imprisonment—for sentencing young offenders. (We have already discussed the case of younger offenders in Chapter 6.)

Crime and Punishment

Canadian conviction and punishment rates have been falling since 1995, in parallel with the falling crime rate (www.statcan.gc.ca/pub/85-002-x/2010002/article/11292-eng.htm).

The vast majority of recent convictions do not involve the type of serious, violent crime (e.g., rape and murder) that we hear so much about in the media. All types of homicides and all types of sexual offences, taken together, generally account for under 2 per cent (<5,200) of criminal cases (www.statcan.gc.ca/pub/85-002-x/2010002/article/11293/tbl/tbl1-eng.htm). The most common offences are theft under $5,000, common assault, mischief, break and enter, motor vehicle theft, and failure to comply with a court or probation order (Dauvergne and Turner, 2010).

Generally, the people sentenced in these cases are not the devious criminal masterminds we see in movies. Instead, they are poor, undereducated, single, unemployed, and (unless they have been convicted of impaired driving) under 35. They are disproportionately male and Aboriginal and likely to have substance abuse or mental health problems. The relatively few women who are sentenced are most often convicted of a property crime, and the vast majority (about 80 per cent) have a history of sexual or physical abuse, substance abuse, or mental health problems.

Most recently, of all offenders, 7 in 10 were sent to a prison or jail and 3 in 10 were in community supervision. On any given

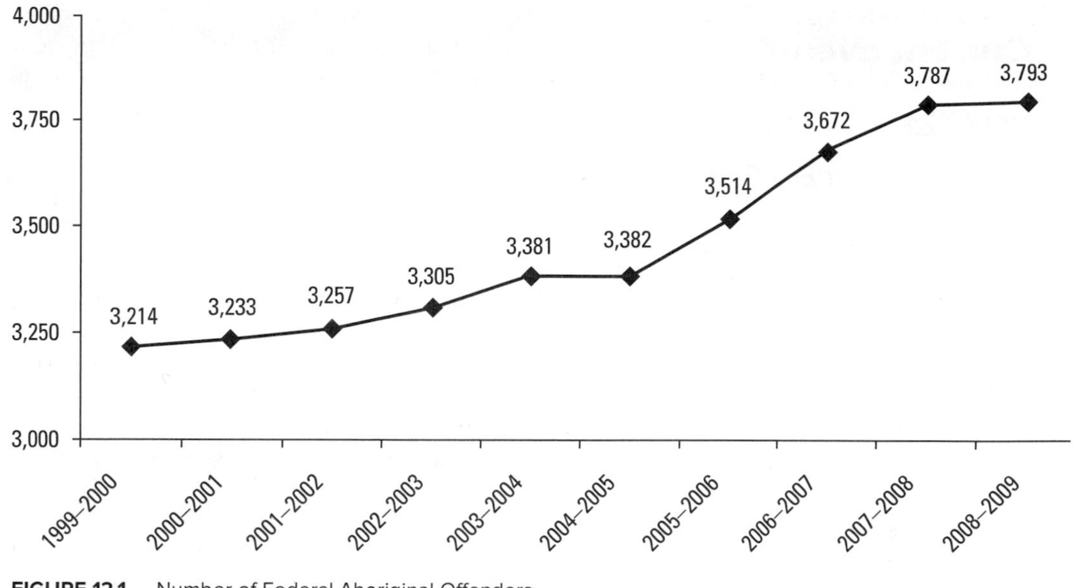

FIGURE 12.1 Number of Federal Aboriginal Offenders

Source: Office of the Correctional Investigator, "Presentation to the Canadian Human Rights Commission," Apr. 2010, at: <www.oci-bec.gc.ca/comm/presentations/presentations20100407-eng.aspx>.

day in 2008–9, there were 120,000 Canadian adults under a community supervision order (usually probation) and another 37,000 in jails and prisons serving their sentences. Only about 8,000 of these people were sent to a federal prison to serve their time, a disproportionate fraction of whom were Aboriginal (Figure 12.1). Federal prisons house only those offenders who receive a sentence of two years or more, and most criminal sentences are considerably shorter than that (Calverley, 2010).

Is Canada a punitive country? That depends on which other countries we compare it to. As we will see, there is a significant division between richer and poorer nations in the type and severity of punishments used. Like Canada, most modern, wealthy industrial nations have abolished the death penalty and have imprisonment rates in the same general range as Canada's. It is probably fair to say that Canada is "in the middle" on the punitive scale, compared to the countries to which it is most similar, although the present federal government has pushed the country in a more punitive direction with its recently passed omnibus crime bill (Box 12.1).

The one notable exception to this is the United States, which takes a far more punitive attitude to crime than Canada—or any other modern, industrialized country—in the sense that the US arrests, convicts, imprisons, and executes far more people per capita than the rest.

The Types and Characteristics of Punishment

Capital Punishment in International Perspective

Capital punishment is the state-sanctioned killing of a convicted person, according to the rule of law. Capital punishment was, likely, the earliest form of punishment. Many punishments listed in the Code of Hammurabi—the first known legal code, proclaimed by the Babylonian ruler in 1760 BC—are capital punishments.

Current Events

BOX 12.1

The Pitfalls of Bill C-10

Bill C-10, or the "Safe Streets and Communities Act," which was passed into law in March 2012, is the federal Conservatives' blueprint for getting tough on crime. Among other changes, the new crime bill creates new criminal offences, instigates longer and more mandatory minimum sentences, and establishes harsher sentencing for youth.

Yet the extent to which crime actually needs to be fought with this new, harsher legislation remains questionable. In the last decade, the crime rate in Canada has dropped 17 per cent—in 2010, the crime rate sat at its lowest since 1973. However, costs associated with the penitentiary system increased by 87 per cent from 2005–6 to 2011—increased expenditure that is in direct opposition to the low and declining crime rate.

This rise in spending will be exacerbated by Bill C-10, as more mandatory and longer sentences will result in more inmates, and will consequently generate a need for more jails. One solution, which has been adopted in BC, is to contract out the building of prisons to private owners. Yet this "solution" seems to create a range of new problems, as American experience has shown.

First, public prisons boast superior inmate health care and security, as well as lower recidivism rates, making them more effective in general than privately owned jails. Second, because the owners of private penitentiaries have a financial interest in keeping their prisons well populated, they will support legislation and policies that aim to increase the number of people who are incarcerated and the length of time they spend in jail. Thus, privately funded prisons also create the moral and ethical issue of unjust punishment. A conflict of interest is built into the system.

What's more, Bill C-10 may actually make the recidivism rate rise, and thereby intensify the very problem of crime that it's trying to solve. By implementing mandatory incarceration for minor, non-violent crimes, the crime bill ensures that the perpetrators of less serious offences will be exposed to more dangerous criminals, and consequently will have the opportunity to learn about and participate in more serious criminal activities. Prolonged minimum sentences are also problematic, since people are more likely to re-offend when they spend longer amounts of time in jail.

A more effective use of taxpayers' money might have been to address factors that have been recognized to have an impact on crime, such as high rates of child poverty and mental illness. Nonetheless, appearing to get tough on crime sells well with a sizable portion of North American voters.

Sources: Daphne Bramham, "Tough on Crime and Good for Profits," *Vancouver Sun*, 22 July 2011, at: <www2.canada.com/vancouversun/columnists/story.html?id=810d483f-3afo-4faf-873e-b17022c4ed50>; Brennan and Dauvergne (2011); Canadian Civil Liberties Association, "Bill C-10, the Omnibus Crime Bill: Unwise, Unjust, Unconstitutional," at: <ccla.org/omnibus-crime-bill-c-10/>; Trinda L. Ernst, "10 Reasons to Oppose Bill C-10," *Toronto Star*, 14 Nov. 2011, at:<www.thestar.com/opinion/editorialopinion/article/1086785--10-reasons-to-oppose-bill-c-10>.

Traditionally, capital punishment came in various forms. For example, Zoroastrian penal law in ancient Persia (present-day Iran) distinguished different types of crimes and sins according to the severity of each crime. Capital crimes, offending the basic norms of Zoroastrian ethics and ritual or threatening the political interests of the state, were offences deemed worthy of death. Types of capital punishment then in use included crucifixion, stoning, beheading by the sword, and burning.

Today, the range of capital crimes (and the range of capital punishments) is much smaller than in the past. Leaving the US aside, most industrial societies have either banished the death penalty or stopped applying it. Conversely, many less developed societies still use the death penalty (Figure 12.2).

There are several possible reasons for the early importance of capital punishment and its later decline. One obvious explanation is that many other punishments, such as probation, parole, or even imprisonment, are slow and costly to taxpayers. In short, those punishments presume the existence of a mature, relatively prosperous state—something that did not exist in most places for most of human history. By contrast, capital punishment needs nothing but an executioner.

Interestingly, countries that practise capital punishment (see Figure 12.3) are also countries that commonly practise corporal punishment and torture. They tend to be societies with an authoritarian or dictatorial government or without a strong rule of law and without protected civil liberties. They may also be theocratic; that is, countries where the justice system is based on religious law (e.g., sharia law in Islamic countries).

In his classic work, *The Division of Labor in Society* (1964 [1893]), Émile Durkheim explained that, in communities with a high degree of social similarity or homogeneity, one could find what he called **repressive justice**. Repressive justice is a preference for law enforcement that is rigid, harsh, and cruel. In a repressive society, people hold black-and-white views about morality and justice. Punishment merely

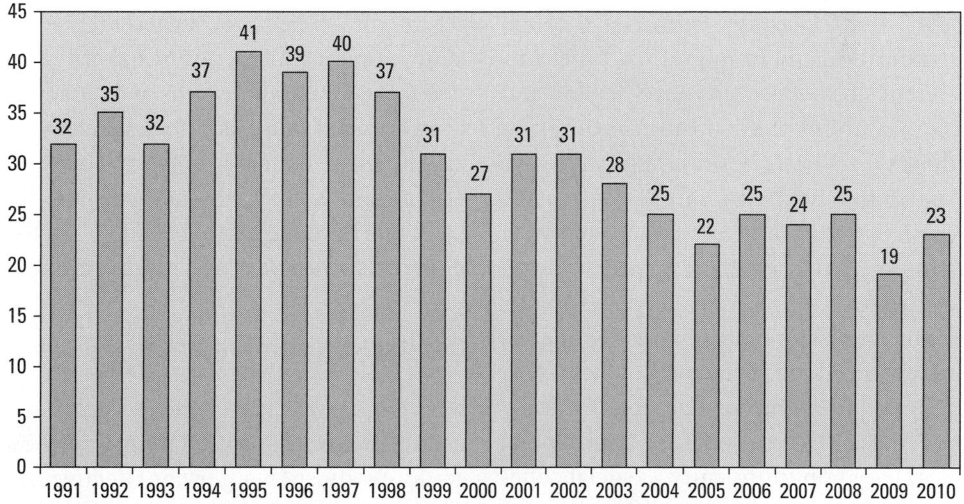

FIGURE 12.2 Number of Countries Carrying Out Executions, 1991–2010

Source: Amnesty International, *Death Sentences and Executions 2010* (London: Amnesty International, 2011), at: <www.amnesty.org/en/library/asset/ACT50/001/2011/en/ea1b6b25-a62a-4074-927d-ba51e88df2e9/act500012011en.pdf>.

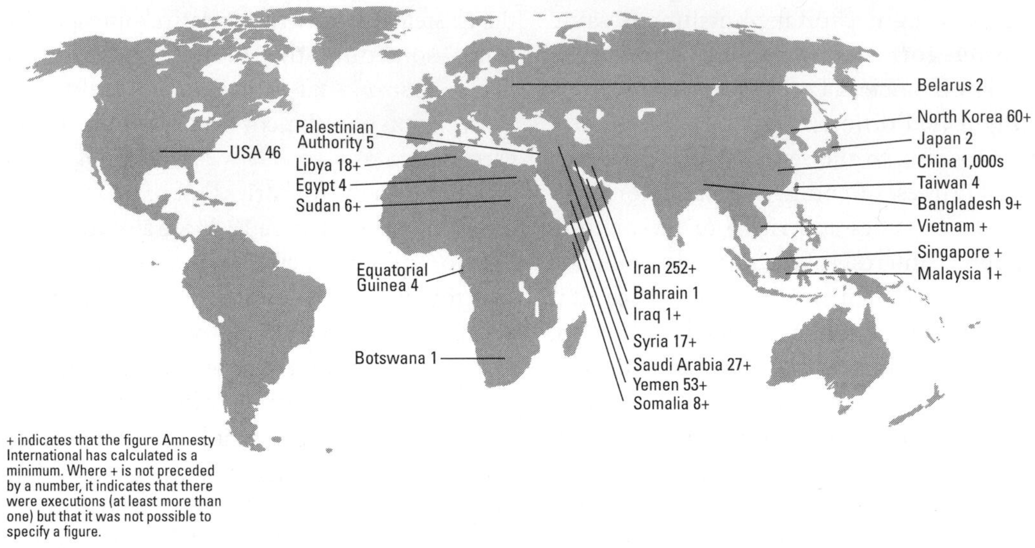

FIGURE 12.3 Number of Executions Worldwide, 2010

Source: Amnesty International, *Death Sentences and Executions 2010* (London: Amnesty International, 2011), at: <www.amnesty.org/en/library/asset/ACT50/001/2011/en/ea1b6b25-a62a-4074-927d-ba51e88df2e9/act500012011en.pdf>.

affirms the moral boundaries of people who lack any moral doubt about right and wrong. These are the communities where support for capital punishment is most likely to be found.

With the widespread decline of social similarity over the last two centuries, through industrialization and immigration, for example, societies have become more flexible and less certain about their moral boundaries. In industrial societies, repressive justice gave way to what Durkheim called **restitutive justice**. This outlook is less concerned with punishment than with making amends and curing the social ills that caused the crime. We might even say restitutive justice is concerned with reducing harm, not inflicting pain. As societies industrialize, they typically become more diverse, change from social cohesion based on uniformity to social cohesion based on interdependent difference, and come to rely on restitutive rather than repressive justice.

Does capital punishment deter crimes that are planned and executed in cold blood? Seemingly not. There is no evidence that capital punishment deters people from committing crimes since, usually, they don't think they will get caught. As Beccaria suggested, it is the certainty of punishment, not the severity of a *possible* punishment that seems to dissuade people from crime. If our goal is to deter crime—even violent crime—there is no strong evidence the distant and unlikely threat of capital punishment will have the needed effect. Therefore, we must seek other ways of deterring crime.

Capital Punishment in the US

Who on earth is in favour of putting other people to death? It is hard to imagine how one could justify such a gory, ineffective punishment, or why one would even try to do so. Yet, the facts are there: some countries do indeed put criminals to death for "capital" crimes.

Among the top 10 nations of the world ranked in terms of number of prisoners on death row, the US (at #2) is the *only* economically developed, "modern" nation to still use the death penalty. The other nine nations, in descending order, are all less economically developed: Pakistan (at #1), Thailand, Kenya, Bangladesh, Burundi, Uganda, Tanzania, Nigeria, and Sudan (*The Economist*, 2009). The US, therefore, is in odd company. That the US, as a democracy, ranks so high in death-row inmates can be partly understood in terms of its justice system and appeals process; China, for example, which executes more prisoners than the rest of world combined, does not appear on this list, nor do such countries as Iran, North Korea, and Yemen. In these countries the opportunity for appeal is limited and capital punishment can be swift.

The statistics for the US are somewhat misleading, since decisions to use, or not to use, the death penalty are made at the state level, not the national level. Capital punishment was briefly banned across the country by the United States Supreme Court (1972–5); but since 1976, states have been free to use the death penalty—if they wish. Across the country, there were 1,260 executions between 1976 and 2011. The 50 states vary widely in their support for (or opposition to) capital punishment. Some states, in this sense, are more like Pakistan (that is, in favour of capital punishment) while others are more like Norway or Holland (that is, outlawing capital punishment).

Figure 12.4 shows the state-by-state use of capital punishment in the US and the wide regional variations in its use. There are currently 15 jurisdictions that do not have a law

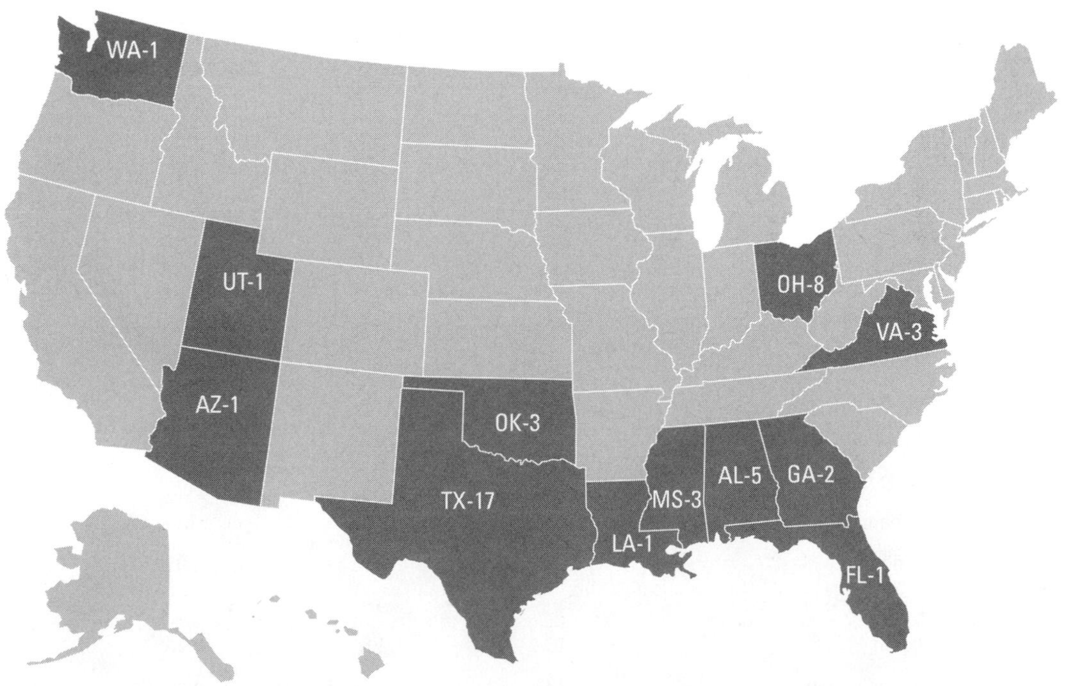

FIGURE 12.4 US Executions in 2010

Source: Death Penalty Information Centre, *The Death Penalty in 2010: Year End Report* (Washington, Dec. 2010), 6, at: <www.deathpenaltyinfo.org/documents/2010YearEnd-Final.pdf>.

authorizing the use of capital punishment and a number that have had no (or few) executions since 1976. In fact, close to half of all American states make no, or almost no, use of the death penalty. This includes most of the high-population states in the Northeast and Midwest: for example, Illinois recently suspended all capital punishments.

The main users of capital punishment are in the American South, which accounted for 1,034 of the 1,260 executions carried out in the US since 1976. Texas alone accounted for 471 of these. Why? How do we account for these regional variations in support for capital punishment?

Support for the Death Penalty

Pollsters have been tracking support for the death penalty in the United States for many decades, and though support remains strong, with 62 per cent in 2010 favouring capital punishment for those convicted of murder, this represents a drop from 78 per cent support in 1996.

Race, religion, and political affiliation all influence support for the death penalty, as does geographic region. Table 12.1 shows that whites support the death penalty much more strongly than African-Americans, Hispanics, and other minorities. There is also a strong relationship between support for the death penalty and political affiliation. Whereas 50 per cent of Democrats support the death penalty, 78 per cent of Republicans do. This is explained by the fact that people with different political views—Democrats versus Republicans—also tend to have different social and cultural characteristics.

TABLE 12.1 American Views on the Death Penalty

	Favour (%)	Oppose (%)	Don't Know (%)
Total	62	30	9
Republican	78	16	7
Democrat	50	42	7
Independent	62	30	8
Protestant	65	26	9
White evangelical	74	19	7
White mainline	71	21	8
Black Protestant	37	49	14
Catholic	60	32	8
White Catholic	68	26	6
Hispanic Catholic	43	45	13
Unaffiliated	61	32	6
Top influence on views			
Religion	45	55	n.a.
Other influence	73	27	n.a.

Note: Percentages may not add to 100 per cent due to rounding.
Source: Adapted from Pew Forum on Religion & Public Life, "Public Opinion on the Death Penalty," 23 Sept. 2011, at: <www.pewforum.org/Death-Penalty/Public-Opinion-on-the-Death-Penalty.aspx>.

The influence of religious affiliation is one determining factor. Table 12.1 shows there is strong support for capital punishment among members of all religious groups, in particular white evangelicals, and somewhat less support from those without a church affiliation. Another recent survey (Pew Center on the States, 2008) found that race appears to be an even stronger predictor of support for capital punishment than religion, a finding reflected in Table 12.1.

The Role of Race

One clear fact about capital punishment in the US is that African-Americans are disproportionately affected by it. Though they make up only about 12.5 per cent of the American population, African-Americans account for 35 per cent of the people executed since 1976 (www.deathpenaltyinfo.org/race-death-row-inmates-executed-1976). For that reason, it is impossible to understand capital punishment in the US without understanding its history of race relations.

Indeed, some argue that capital punishment in the US today is merely a continuation of the historic oppression of African-Americans since the end of slavery. Up to the time of the American Civil War, the laws surrounding slavery had given white citizens unofficial power to use violence in upholding the social order—after all, people were merely disciplining and managing their human property. With the end of slavery after the Civil War, violence to preserve the social order continued, especially in the South. Some believe capital punishment is the new form of violence against black (formerly enslaved) people.

As this theory would predict, capital punishment is more common in regions of the US where slaves were most numerous—also, where lynching was common in the late nineteenth and early twentieth centuries. To *lynch* is to punish through mob law by hanging. The term is most closely associated with practices in the southern United States during the period of Reconstruction that followed the American Civil War. Lynchings were most common there between roughly 1880 and 1930, mainly carried out by members or friends of the Ku Klux Klan, a racist organization pledged to torment and expel African-Americans, Jews, Catholics, and other foreigners who threatened the traditional, small-town, Protestant, white, southern way of life.

David Garland argues that public lynchings served as a form of "collective ritual" for those taking part in them. Doubtless because of this historic connection between slavery, lynching, and capital punishment, researchers find higher-than-average support for capital punishment among people who hold racist views or live in former slaveholding communities. For example, using historical data, Vandiver et al. (2006) found a strong geographical relationship between nineteenth-century slavery and twentieth-century executions. Since 1976, 90.6 per cent of executions occurred in states that had supported slavery before the Civil War, whether or not they were in the Confederacy or inside the traditional boundaries of the South.

Alternatives to the Death Penalty

But once a society does away with capital punishment for serious crimes, what alternatives remain?

Efforts to remove capital punishment run up against criticisms of alternative punishments. As one might expect, there are arguments against life imprisonment, just as there are arguments against capital punishment. Villaume (2005) asserts that a life in prison without parole is a "semantically disguised sentence of death." One of the greatest problems experienced by prisoners serving life sentences is boredom. Some might say the alternative to execution is boring a prisoner to death, which is to trivialize the problem. That aside, research shows imprisonment also carries significant dangers to safety, physical health, and mental health well beyond boredom.

Note, however, that capital punishment and imprisonment are not actually alternatives. In a sample of 100 nations, Ruddell (2005) found that nations that continue to use the death penalty also have higher-than-average rates of imprisonment. Nowhere is this more obvious than in the US. Not only is the US one of the few industrialized countries to retain the death penalty; it also imprisons more of its citizens (per capita) than any other country in the world. By this standard, the US is the most repressive modern nation in the world, despite its constitutional commitment to life, liberty, and the pursuit of happiness.

Canada's imprisonment rate has varied between 105 and 120 prisoners per 100,000 of the population over the last few years (Statistics Canada, 2009b). Imprisonment rates far lower than ours prevail in Japan, Switzerland, and the Scandinavian countries (Finland, Sweden, Denmark, and Norway). On the other hand, imprisonment rates are far higher in the US, Russia (and members of the former Soviet Union), China, Singapore, and some rapidly developing nations such as South Africa and Brazil. This variation tells us we need to look for sociological reasons to explain why some nations punish their citizens more commonly and more harshly than others.

Time to Reflect: What do you imagine are the major pros and cons of imprisoning large numbers of wrongdoers?

Imprisonment

Imprisonment is one of the world's most common types of punishment. It is both universal and ancient in its use. In general, prisons are intended to separate wrongdoers from law-abiding citizens and, in doing so, to protect the bad from the good. Prisons are also intended to punish wrongdoers, inspire rehabilitation, and assist in the reintegration of convicts into society. In this sense, prisons are supposed to be a site of not only punishment but also re-socialization or re-education.

Like policies on capital punishment, policies on imprisonment are often guided by ideology and political considerations. These are reflected in the wide and well-documented international variation in imprisonment rates (Figure 12.5).

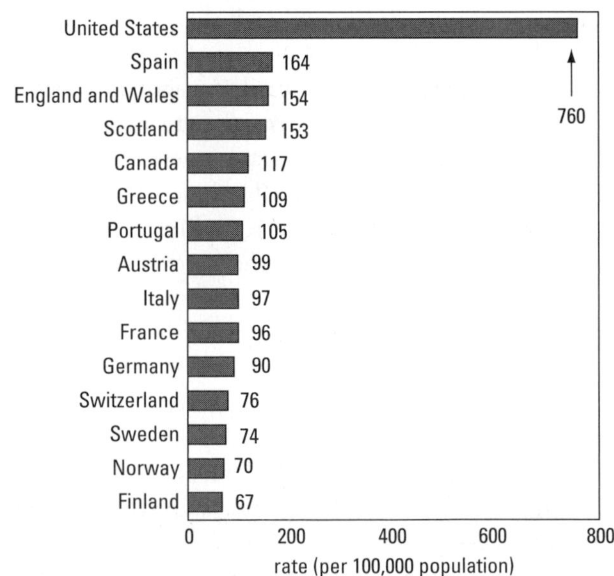

FIGURE 12.5 Incarceration Rates, Selected Western Countries

Source: Adapted from Statistics Canada, "Adult and Youth Correctional Services: Key Indicators," *The Daily*, 8 Dec. 2009, at: <www.statcan.gc.ca/daily-quotidien/091208/dq091208a-eng.htm>.

Researchers began to study prisons and prisoners systematically in the early twentieth century. Sociologist Donald Clemmer (1940) developed his **prisonization** theory out of such research. He noted that, by their nature, prisons degrade people, pressure them, and take away their rights. In this way, they make people less competent, rather than more so. They debilitate people, rather than rehabilitate them. The reason is that, in prisons, degrading treatment is organizationally unavoidable. Without it, prison officials cannot easily control such a large community of (usually) young men. Yet, this treatment, which keeps peace in the prison, also has unintended and undesirable effects. It alienates prisoners and unites them against the prison administration. A prison subculture, growing out of everyday prison life, reflects and hardens this alienation.

Michel Foucault (1975), however, doubts these outcomes are either unintended or unexpected. On the contrary, he writes, the purpose of prison is to punish people through discipline, rather than through corporal punishment or torture, for example. It is not to rehabilitate them, for rehabilitation may be impossible. It is to control them and, in controlling them, to mould them into disciplined, obedient people. This can only be achieved by breaking their resistance and their will.

Recidivism

The flip side of harsh control is that prisoners learn the prison subculture, especially its anti-administration values and codes of conduct. As well, through contact with more experienced inmates, prisoners gain new criminal skills, often learning to behave in even more undesirable and violent ways. They end up with an identity that is more deviant than they had brought into the prison.

Sociologist Erving Goffman (1961) wrote that all residential facilities that try to shape inmate behaviour—including prisons, mental hospitals, concentration camps, military barracks, monasteries, convents, and even boarding schools—are "total institutions." They degrade people, strip away old identities, impose uniformity of dress and behaviour, limit personal freedom, and, through social isolation and stigma, create new identities. And, as Goffman observed, this process always stamps an inmate with the institution's character and makes him or her *less* prepared for the outside world.

To varying degrees, this may be true of all institutions today. For example, large workplaces often have strict guidelines regarding behaviour (towards co-workers, clients, and oneself), a dress code, limitations of personal freedom (although most are implemented to maintain broader societal norms), and some may even "brainwash" individuals through their corporate training programs to propagate the success of their corporation. So, the phenomenon of prisonization is, perhaps, only the most extreme version of a common experience in modern society. We all are controlled by routines, surveillance, and artificially imposed controls on normative behaviour.

Prisonization, as Clemmer calls it, produces well-socialized prisoners: people who fit into the inmate society but who function poorly outside of it. As their release from prison approaches, inmates often feel great stress. After release, they often commit even more crimes—in some cases, even more violent crimes—and many end up back in prison. This process leading to re-imprisonment is called **recidivism** or the **revolving door**.

Although the extent of recidivism is difficult to measure, a number of Canadian studies have consistently found large numbers of offenders returning to the criminal justice system—and smaller numbers of offenders returning many times.

- One study found that 60 per cent of the offenders between the ages of 18 and 25 who were convicted in criminal court in 1999–2000 had at least one prior conviction. Of this group of recidivists, 72 per cent had multiple convictions (Thomas et al., 2002).
- Another study that looked at a group of offenders released from federal custody found that 43 per cent were reconvicted within two years. The reconviction rates were much higher for Aboriginal offenders than for non-Aboriginal offenders (Bonta et al., 2003).
- A third study, looking only at Saskatchewan data, tracked released offenders over a four-year period, between 1999 and 2004. The researchers found that rates of further arrest and re-conviction were highest for Aboriginals and for those who first entered the system at a young age. As well, recidivism was higher among those who had served a prison sentence than among those who had been sentenced to a fine or probation (Johnson, 2005).

Mass Imprisonment in the US

Though Canada and the US are similar in many respects, they are very different in the ways they punish rule-breakers. The US imprisonment rate has exploded over the last 35 years and is now more than five times higher than it was in 1970. What strikes all observers is the weak relationship between this increase in imprisonment rates and the growth in serious or violent crime. As in Canada, US crime rates have been *declining* since the mid-1990s. However, the growth in US imprisonment continues unabated. In 2009, the US had about 1.6 million Americans in prison on any given day. As noted earlier, Americans now imprison more of their citizens (per capita) than any other nation on earth.

Garland has considered the broad social and economic shifts that led some Western democracies—and especially the US—to adopt more punitive attitudes to crime in the late twentieth century (Box 12.2). Though researchers continue to debate the longer-term, social structural forces involved, the policy path to mass imprisonment in the US is well documented. During the 1970s, when violent crime was increasing, Americans began turning towards penal policies that favoured a more punitive, "tough on crime" approach. These policies were developed and passed by state legislatures throughout the 1980s and 1990s and went by various names: *zero tolerance* policies, *three strikes* laws, *mandatory minimum* sentences, *truth in sentencing*, *no frills* prisons, and *boot camps* for juvenile offenders.

Some part of this movement to harsher punishment was focused on winning the "**war on drugs**," the theory being that drug use was one of the main reasons for the perceived rising tide of violent crime. Another significant influence was the growth of the victims' rights movement, which was successful in persuading legislators that the criminal justice system was too lenient and tilted in favour of criminals.

Harsher punishments, in most states, were accompanied by civil measures intended to penalize offenders after release from prison, as well as expressing society's continuing disapproval of criminal conduct. Many states passed laws that placed lifetime bans on the rights of convicted felons to vote or to receive welfare benefits, food stamps, public housing, federal health care, or higher education benefits. American penal policies moved towards longer, non-discretionary terms of imprisonment in institutions offering no rehabilitation or "re-entry" programs. The discretionary sentencing authority of

BOX 12.2

David Garland's *Punishment and Modern Society*

In *Punishment and Modern Society*, David Garland (1990) suggests the study of punishment should be a central object of social theory, worthy of careful attention from mainstream sociology. He argues that punishment is an institution central to all social organization. Garland (1990: 4) writes that "modern penal institutions are currently experiencing a crisis of self definition," evident in the "rising crime rates, recidivism, and prison unrest," which "seriously undermines faith in the rehabilitative ideal and in penal institutions generally."

According to Garland, the systematic study of punishment has become a specialty sub-field wracked with conflict and lacking in consensus. This dissention among scholars is especially important given that penal institutions "are destined to a degree of futility in their capacity to control crime." With the major societal and economic changes of the late twentieth century, the new politics of crime control have become ever less effective, though more expressive and instrumental.

Garland believes that only the "mainstream process of socialization," not the penal system, will be "able to promote proper conduct on a consistent and regular basis." That is, punishment is not the solution to crime. Garland also addresses the need for an alternative theoretical approach to scholarship in this field, suggesting that punishment should be developed and analyzed like other social institutions, for example, like education. The problem is the lack of a "detailed appreciation of the nature of punishment, of its character as a social institution, and of its role in social life" (ibid., 9).

In particular, the penological approach taken by criminologists and the criminal justice system serves only to address "the efficacy of various mechanisms of crime and control." Garland proposes a pluralistic method to attain "a fuller understanding of the social determinants and social consequences of punishment." He uses Durkheim's theory to suggest that punishment can increase social solidarity. Television and other forms of media that portray criminals and their punishments create an audience for public punishment: a crowd of onlookers sitting at home watching TV.

Yet the reaffirmation of social rules and the solidarity created in public displays of punishment are still an important aspect of the institution. We don't attend public hangings, but we watch the dramatized struggle of good and evil on crime shows every night of the year.

judges in many instances was taken away. Significantly, Canada's new omnibus crime bill moves this country in the direction of the failed US policies.

Criminal Proceedings in Canada

As noted earlier, punishment comes at the end of a long deliberative process—a process that is slow, complex, and costly. Here are some statistics that sketch out the complexity of this process:

- *Criminal cases are numerous.* Adult criminal courts in Canada completed over 390,000 cases in 2008–9, involving more than one million charges.

- *Criminal cases are slow.* The amount of time it takes to dispose of a case in adult criminal courts declined recently from 128 days in 2004–5 to 124 days in 2008–9.
- *Cases involving trials are the slowest.* Cases involving a trial had twice the median elapsed time (255 days) of those cases where there was no trial (113 days).
- *Most cases end in convictions.* In 2008–9, the accused person was found guilty in two-thirds of cases, and only 3 per cent of cases resulted in an acquittal. Most of the remaining cases were either stayed, withdrawn, dismissed, or discharged.
- *Convictions result in one of three main outcomes.* A term of probation was the most frequently imposed sanction (45 per cent of guilty cases); a term of imprisonment was imposed in 34 per cent of cases; and a fine was given in 30 per cent of cases (www.statcan.gc.ca/pub/85-002-x/2010002/article/11293/hl-fs-eng.htm).

The processes are similar in one other respect: many of the people convicted of crimes are sentenced pursuant to a plea bargain struck between the prosecutor and the defence attorney. The bargain may require an acknowledgement of guilt on a lesser charge in return for a reduced sentence—a shorter imprisonment, probation instead of imprisonment—or, for relatively minor offences, payment of a "fine" in the form of a donation to a related local NGO or agency such as Crime Stoppers in return for having the charge dropped. Research on plea bargaining has often questioned whether the process is just or if, instead, it discriminates against poor people or racial minorities. Some would argue that many of the people in jail are people who, because of inadequate legal representation, agreed to imprisonment when, with a thicker wallet, they might have won an acquittal.

Legal aid, which varies across jurisdictions and from one case to another, is supposedly available to all people—including low-income people—charged with criminal offences. However, in practice, unless the case is serious, complex, and likely will result in significant jail time, the individual who cannot afford to hire a lawyer must often make do with duty counsel—lawyers who provide free advice on a rotating basis during court days. This puts a great many first offenders and young offenders into a position of great legal vulnerability.

The Canadian legal process is a lot like the US legal process, since both have their roots in the English common-law tradition. However, there are important differences, reflecting different histories and different constitutional provisions. That is why the US still has capital punishment and much higher rates of imprisonment than Canada.

Moreover, unlike the US rate, Canada's imprisonment rate has not changed much since 1960 (Doob and Webster, 2006). This stability contrasts with the rapidly increasing imprisonment rates in the United States and in England and Wales. Canadians have largely escaped several of the wider forces or "risk factors" at the root of higher imprisonment in other countries. These include—but are not restricted to—a history of racial segregation as in the United States and an attack on social redistribution by conservative governments in both the US and the UK. The fragmenting of Canadian politics, owing to regionalism and multiculturalism and a weak central government, also has kept Canada from adopting the same punitive policies as the United States and England and Wales. Whether this trend will continue with a federal Conservative majority and the recent omnibus crime bill remains to be seen.

Other recent changes could lead to a different, more punitive response. For example, economic globalization has increased Canada's integration into the US social and cultural orbit and may promote harsher policies and fewer social supports for the populations that typically supply the largest numbers of imprisoned criminals. High rates of immigration to Canada from impoverished nations may also increase crime rates and calls for harsher penalties (ibid.).

As we have repeatedly seen, comparisons between various countries show that prison rates do not always vary in direct proportion to crime rates. Prison rates do, however, reflect prevailing politics, ideology, and public opinion. As a result, Canadian prison rates are a reflection of Canadian culture. Low, stable imprisonment rates in Canada result from traditions of multiculturalism and minority empowerment, as well as Canadians' desire to distance the country from the punitive excesses of their American neighbour (Brodeur, 2007).

Imprisonment Rates of Racial Minorities in Canada

Canadian jurisdictions do not regularly keep or publish criminal justice statistics about the representation of all racial groups in Canadian jails and prisons. However, available studies show that some groups are more likely to be imprisoned than others.

In particular, the 1995 Commission on Systemic Racism in the Ontario Criminal Justice System found that, along with Aboriginal people, Canadian blacks were over-represented in Ontario jails. Similarly, the National Parole Board reported that in 2007–8, blacks made up 7.3 per cent of prisoners in federal prisons but only 2.5 per cent of the Canadian population as a whole. Significant public debate continues about whether this reflects racist attitudes in the Canadian justice system or broader social, cultural, and economic factors that increase the likelihood that members of these groups will commit crimes.

The dramatic over-representation of Aboriginal people in Canada's jails and prisons has received scholarly attention for quite some time. In 2007–8, Aboriginal people represented about 3.1 per cent of the adult Canadian population but accounted for 18 per cent of all admissions to jails and prisons (www.statcan.gc.ca/pub/85-002-x/2009003/article/10903-eng.htm). This over-representation is particularly acute in some of the western provinces. For example, in Saskatchewan, Aboriginal people comprise close to 80 per cent of the prison population but only 10 per cent of the adult population. The contrast between Aboriginal and non-Aboriginal imprisonment rates is even more striking among female inmates. Aboriginal women account for 87 per cent of all women imprisoned in Saskatchewan.

These Aboriginal offenders are also younger, less educated, less likely to be employed at the time of their admission to prison, and more likely to reoffend than non-Aboriginal offenders. Over 90 per cent of all Aboriginal offenders in Saskatchewan were also found to have a substance abuse problem. At the same time, Aboriginal people are also more likely to be victims of crime, particularly violent crime, than non-Aboriginal people. On-reserve crime rates are three times higher than crime rates in the rest of Canada, and on-reserve violent crime rates are eight times higher (Brzozowski et al., 2006).

Community Supervision

People have long known that imprisonment is a limited way of preventing crime. Community supervision (with probation and parole) is another approach, aimed at avoiding the negative aspects of imprisonment and integrating offenders back into the society they have offended.

Current Challenges for Community Supervision

The success of community supervision can be measured in a number of different ways. Criminologists generally agree that probation is less harmful to offenders, and less expensive to the public, than imprisonment. But does it keep the public safe? And does it help in the rehabilitation of offenders and their reintegration into society?

There are at least three significant challenges currently facing parole and probation officers, who are mandated with achieving solutions to these challenges.

First, there appears to be a conflict between the "policing" role of community supervision (i.e., making sure the offender obeys all conditions and is not a risk to society, etc.) and the "rehabilitation" role (i.e., assisting the offender in reintegrating into society). Due to the lack of resources, the enforcement role is often the only role a probation or parole officer can fully play. Some probation officers believe criminals are becoming more violent and harder to control. As a result, probation work often produces frustration, disappointment, and anger. For many probation officers, their supervisory roles conflict with their advocacy roles (Gregory, 2007).

Second, many offenders lack the private supports needed to help them reintegrate into society: often, they lack strong and supportive families and live in (or return to) disadvantaged communities with high crime rates. Though parole and probation officers play an important role in helping the released convict reintegrate into society, the prisoner's family also has an important role to play. Brooker (2006) found family members were not only sources of support during imprisonment but also provided emotional and instrumental support for inmates after they were released. Many respondents viewed family members as valuable helpers in gaining employment and finding a place to live after their release from prison.

Third, many offenders have complex needs that call for a wide variety of services not readily available in all communities (e.g., substance abuse programs, mental health services, counselling, anger management, time management, employment and housing assistance, etc.). In particular, the de-institutionalization of psychiatric patients, which began in the 1960s, has resulted in a well-documented, ever-increasing mentally ill population in the nation's prisons and jails. A related pressure comes from the large number of offenders suffering from drug and alcohol addiction. The traditional criminal justice system is ill-equipped to deal with these sorts of problems, and collaboration with social service and health agencies requires a large investment of time and training.

Many jurisdictions are now looking at ways of controlling the spiralling costs of imprisonment. It is clear that the key sources of cost have less to do with rising crime rates than with recycling prisoners from prison to probation and parole to home and back again. Most probation and parole programs simply are not succeeding in the task of reintegrating offenders back into society. Recent research has also confirmed that most of the prison population comes from a relatively few disadvantaged communities—communities that are outside the mainstream of social, political, and economic life (Allen and Stern, 2007).

Probation

Probation is a correctional method under which a convicted offender is given a suspended sentence or conditional discharge and is released on conditions prescribed in a probation order. Courts may also direct offenders to comply with a probation order in addition to a fine or after serving a sentence of imprisonment.

Probation began as a humanitarian effort to allow first-time and minor offenders a second chance. In this respect, it was like the gentler and more flexible treatment of juveniles discussed in Chapter 6. Early probationers were expected to obey the law and behave in a morally acceptable fashion. Officers sought to provide moral leadership to help shape probationers' attitudes and behaviours in relation to family, religion, employment, and free time. By doing so, early probationers were given the chance to prove themselves and possibly even lessen their sentence.

During the 1920s through the 1950s, major developments in psychology led probation officers to shift their emphasis from moral leadership to therapeutic counselling. The officer became more of a clinical social worker whose goal was to help the offender solve psychological and social problems. In turn, the offender was expected to become actively involved in the treatment. Rehabilitation became the primary goal of probation, and this gave the officer wide discretion in defining and treating the offender's problems. In the 1960s, however, major social changes challenged earlier assumptions about corrections. Increasingly, rather than counselling offenders, probation officers stressed reintegrating offenders, providing them with concrete social services such as help with employment, housing, finances, and education.

In the late 1970s, probation changed yet again as the goals of rehabilitation and reintegration gave way to "risk management." This approach, still dominant today, seeks to minimize the risk that an offender will commit a new offence. This role stresses neither therapy nor advocacy; instead, it reflects a reduction of services for the benefit of the probationer and focuses instead on "community protection."

While under probation, the probationer must satisfy the conditions set by the probation order. These conditions may include regularly meeting with the probation officer, keeping a job, obeying a curfew, living where directed, abstaining from unlawful behaviour, performing community service, attending anger management and/or other courses, participating in a 12-step program such as Alcoholics Anonymous, following the probation officer's orders, and not fleeing the jurisdiction. Probation may be revoked if the probationer breaches any of the stated conditions. If a breach does occur, the offender will be arrested and have to return to court—in which case, the court (in its discretion) may revoke probation and order the offender to serve time in jail or prison.

If an offender commits another offence while on probation, he or she will be arrested and brought back before the court. Then, it is highly likely probation will be revoked and the offender ordered to serve time in jail or prison.

In 2008–9, Canadian courts issued about 117,000 probation orders. In addition, they made 11,514 orders for "conditional sentences," which operate much like probation orders but are available only for less serious offences. (For the purposes of our discussion, conditional sentences are treated the same as probation orders.) In 2008–9, therefore, about 128,500 offenders were ordered into the supervision of provincial probation services.

Breaches of Probation Orders

We do not have much information about the frequency of probation breaches in Canada. One study of probation outcomes in Canada (2003–5) found that 25.5 per cent of probation orders were breached in Saskatchewan, and 36.8 per cent were breached in Alberta. This suggests that there is some significant variation from one province to the next.

The same study found that Aboriginal offenders had significantly higher rates of breach than non-Aboriginal offenders. There was also a big difference based on the age of the offender: younger people were much more likely to breach a probation order than older people. The breach rate ranged from 8.3 per cent (for non-Aboriginal offenders over the age of 45 in Saskatchewan) to 57 per cent (for Aboriginal offenders under 25 in Alberta). As suggested earlier, a breach of probation occurs whenever an offender fails to meet one of the conditions in his or her probation order. For example, missing a regular meeting with a probation officer will trigger a breach.

The most recent available Canadian study has concluded that probation works better than custody for reducing the risks of recidivism. In a comparison of two groups of adult offenders, one in custody and the other under supervision in the community:

> Adult offenders who spent their sentence under supervision in the community were far less likely to become re-involved with correctional authorities within 12 months of their release than those who were in a correctional institution. . . . In four provinces, 11 per cent of people who were on community supervision became re-involved with correctional authorities within 12 months of their release in 2003/2004. Among those in custody only, 30 per cent were re-involved, a proportion that was more than double the proportion of those on community supervision (11 per cent). (Statistics Canada, 2006b)

Regrettably, it was impossible in this study to control statistically for prior criminal history. However, the study did take into account a history of breaching conditions of supervision, which was a significant influence on the likelihood of further offences:

> There are mandatory conditions of community supervision imposed in the case of probation and conditional sentences. However, judges may also impose additional optional conditions such as the requirement to attend counselling and/or treatment, abstain from drugs and/or alcohol, or perform community service. A breach occurs when an offender violates a condition of supervision. This study showed that the proportion of adults who returned to the correctional system within 12 months of their release from community supervision was twice as high for those with a history of breaching conditions as for those with no history of breaching. (ibid.)

Parole and Statutory Release

Parole and statutory release are means of overseeing offenders who have been imprisoned in federal penitentiaries but have been released to serve part of their sentence in the community.

Parole in Canada began at the end of the nineteenth century with the Ticket of Leave Act. This Act authorized the Governor General in Council (the federal cabinet) to grant to any convict sentenced to imprisonment in a federal penitentiary a licence to be at large in Canada during a specified portion of his or her term of imprisonment, under specified conditions. The Governor General in Council could also revoke or alter this licence by an order in writing.

The ticket of leave reflected an already growing concern that imprisonment could harm rather than help people, especially young offenders and first-time offenders. As well, parole could be used to lessen disparities in prison sentences. Finally, it was a cost-saving measure since it was (and still is) cheaper to release some inmates early rather than keep them in prison. Released from prison on parole, the convict could return to supporting himself and his family—the most desirable outcome.

Here are some statistics to provide a sense of the magnitude of the parole operation in Canada. In 2009–10, 13,531 offenders were imprisoned under federal custody and another 8,709 were in "conditional release." The Parole Board of Canada explains that "Conditional Release includes those federal offenders conditionally released on day parole, full parole and statutory release and those on long-term supervision orders including those paroled for deportation and temporary detainees whether detained in a penitentiary or a provincial jail." Of those offenders who had applied for day parole or full parole, 66 per cent of applicants had received federal day parole and 41 per cent of applicants had received federal full parole.

Of these, a majority had successfully met the conditions for completing their parole: specifically, 87.4 per cent had successfully completed day parole (Figure 12.6) and 76.5 per cent had successfully completed full parole. In addition, 24,139 pardons were granted in 2009–10—fully 98 per cent of all applicants received pardons. The National Parole Board notes that "Since 1970, more than 400,000 Canadians have received pardons. 96 per cent of these are still in force, indicating that the vast majority of pardon recipients remain crime-free in the community" (pbc-clcc.gc.ca/infocntr/factsh/parole_stats-eng.shtml).

Incomplete though this discussion may be, these statistics lay to rest three myths or concerns that some Canadians may have about the parole system. First, getting a parole is not a "sure thing" and the Parole Board turns down many applicants after careful consideration. Second, getting out on parole is not likely to result in further violations or significant danger to the community; a majority of offenders meet their parole conditions, as required.

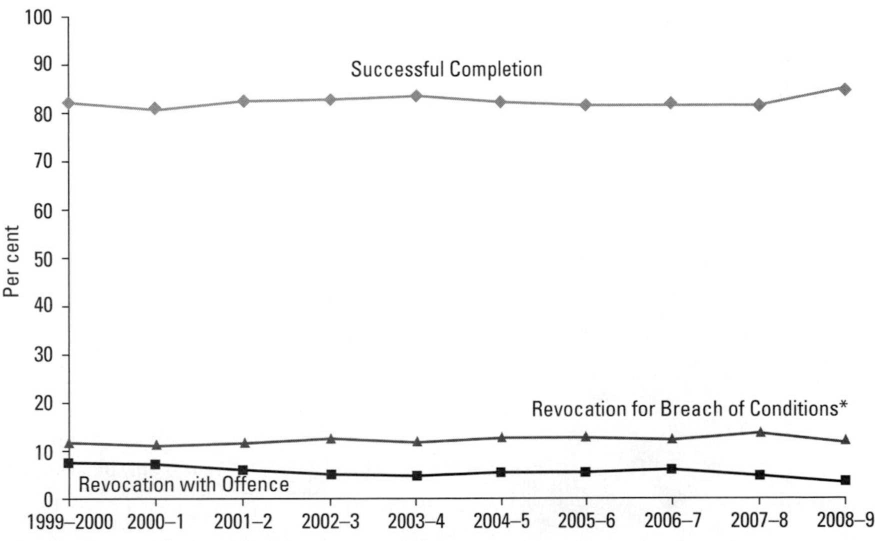

FIGURE 12.6 Day Parole Outcomes

Source: Public Safety Canada, *Corrections and Conditional Release Statistical Overview, 2008* (Ottawa, 2008), 91, at: <www.publicsafety.gc.ca/res/cor/rep/_fl/2008-04-ccrso-eng.pdf>.

Third, the high rate of pardons indicates a concern with avoiding the permanent stigmatization of offenders, since such stigmatization often contributes to recidivism.

Time to Reflect: If you were a parole officer, charged with overseeing dozens of convicts released from prison, how could you tell if the parolees were making good progress in their efforts to integrate into society?

To some extent, parole and statutory release in Canada today still reflect these concerns and principles. Both are governed by the Corrections and Conditional Release Act (CCRA). Under the CCRA, prisoners must apply for parole to the National Parole Board. The Board has authority to make decisions about the parole of individual prisoners, subject to the rules about eligibility set out in the Act. The CCRA states that the protection of society is to be the chief consideration in the corrections process. The Parole Board may only grant parole if it is satisfied that parole will help the offender reintegrate into society as a law-abiding citizen and that the offender will not present an undue risk to society.

The CCRA also provides for the "statutory release" of most inmates after they have served one-third of their sentence. Prisoners do not have to apply for this: it is automatic if a prisoner meets the requirements set out in the CCRA. (Offenders serving life sentences are not eligible.) However, the Parole Board can set conditions for statutory release and revoke the release for failing to meet those conditions. In addition, the Correctional Service of Canada may recommend that an offender be denied statutory release if it believes the offender is likely to commit any offence causing death or serious harm, a sexual offence involving a child, or a serious drug offence. Figure 12.7 provides a snapshot of the percentage breakdown of Canada's total offender population and their status as of April 2009.

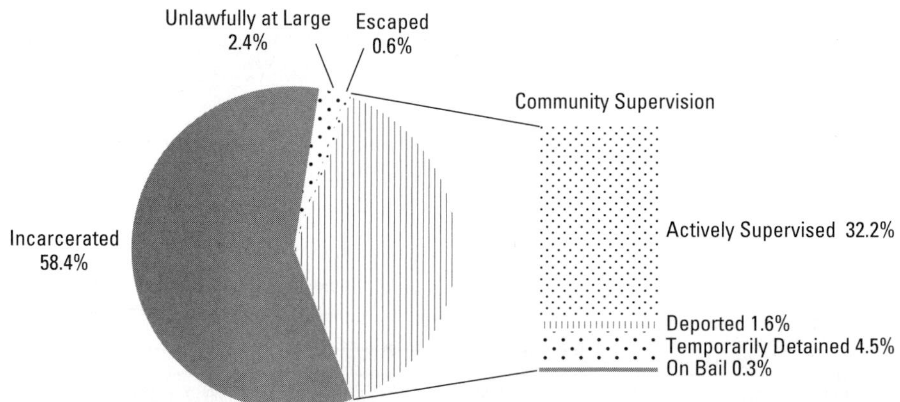

FIGURE 12.7 Total Offender Population as of 12 April 2009

Source: Public Safety Canada, *Corrections and Conditional Release Statistical Overview, 2008* (Ottawa, 2008), 37, at: <www.publicsafety.gc.ca/res/cor/rep/_fl/2008-04-ccrso-eng.pdf>.

Breaches of Parole and Statutory Release

The Canadian media give a lot of attention to parole violations; yet concerns about crimes, especially violent crimes, committed by prisoners on parole are somewhat exaggerated. The National Parole Board reports that between 1975 and 2006, 320,000 prisoners were released from prison on parole or statutory release. Of these, only 409 (or 0.013 per cent) committed a homicide while on parole or statutory release (National Parole Board, 2007a, 2007b). In 2007, about 0.6 per cent of those on parole and about 2.2 per cent of those on statutory release committed any violent offence. A vast majority of supervised offenders complete their parole or statutory release period successfully, although parolees are more successful than offenders on statutory release. When parole and statutory release *are* revoked, they are most likely to be revoked for a breach of conditions, rather than for the commission of an offence.

Fines and Penalties

Fines and other financial penalties have long been used to punish people who break less serious regulatory rules, traffic rules, crimes against public order, or crimes against property. These are crimes that must be discouraged but do not call for imprisonment. They are also crimes people are likely to disagree on in terms of their seriousness and the weight of punishment they deserve. In Canada, fines are used primarily as penalties for traffic offences, drug possession, disturbing the peace, and various regulatory offences (e.g., failing to pay appropriate tax under the Income Tax Act).

Fines and financial penalties are premised on the notion that people, seeking pleasure and fleeing pain, will be deterred from repeating a behaviour that costs them money. However, assigning cash fines and penalties to influence behaviour raises certain key questions. First, for what kinds of crimes and misdemeanours should these penalties be used? Second, how should the penalties be set—that is, how high is too high and how low is too low? Third, will the potential offender come to think of such penalties as a licence to commit the crime? Fourth, what should be done if the offender cannot afford to pay the fine? After all, the true "cost" of a mandatory fine of a certain amount is far greater for someone with little or no income than it is for someone who has more financial resources.

Fines and other **diversionary penalties** seem to work well enough for various delinquencies. For example, Kelly et al. (2003) evaluated an individualized treatment program for adolescent shoplifters. In this research, juveniles charged with shoplifting were randomly assigned to treatment and control groups. Their treatments combined fines, community service, monetary restitution, written essays, anti-shoplifting videos, apology letters, and individual or family counselling. Of the treatment group 88 per cent completed their assigned treatment. Compared to the (untreated) control group, the treatment group displayed significantly less recidivism over a two-year follow-up period. In short, this multi-method punishment seemed to work well.

Fines and financial penalties work only if they detect crimes in a timely fashion and punish them to a degree the offender cannot ignore. As we saw in Chapter 8, corporate crime is widespread but much of it goes undetected and undeterred. When detected and prosecuted, corporate crime rarely results in large penalties. Do these penalties work as intended? One of the difficulties in answering this question has to do with the difficulty in punishing corporate offenders. Since they are inanimate, corporations cannot feel pain in the same way as human beings. And there are inevitably difficult questions about who, in a large corporation, should be held responsible for committing the offence and whether the corporation as a whole should pay for it.

The long-term effects of prosecution may not all be negative. Cloninger and Waller (2000) studied 132 cases of corporate fraud involving 71 major firms. The evidence suggests that executives often engage in illegal activity in hopes of increasing share price. That is, they expect to make money for stockholders and presumably they do, more often than not. In that case, paying a fine is merely the cost of doing (prosperous) business.

So, at best the effectiveness of fines and financial penalties for corporate crime as a punishment is mixed. On the other hand, fines and financial penalties cost relatively little to impose and they bring money into the general revenues of the state, for use in the public interest. In these respects they are far different from imprisonment and probation, punishments that are slow and expensive.

Restorative Justice

As Durkheim would have expected, today researchers everywhere are considering the value and applicability of what he called *restitutive justice* (compared with *repressive justice*) and what others are now calling *restorative justice.* The underlying idea is that lawbreakers should be forced to make restoration or pay compensation to the person, people, or community harmed by their behaviour. This compensation may involve an expression of remorse (e.g., an apology), repayment for lost or damaged property, and hours of community service. It may also involve public discussion or mediation of any remaining conflict.

Restorative justice emphasizes repairing the harm caused by criminal behaviour. Practices and programs reflecting restorative purposes respond to crime by identifying and taking steps to repair harm, involving all stakeholders, and transforming the traditional relationship between communities and their governments in responding to crime.

Some of the programs and outcomes typically identified with restorative justice include:

- victim–offender mediation;
- conferencing;
- Aboriginal sentencing circles;
- victim assistance;
- ex-offender assistance;
- restitution;
- community service.

Three principles form the basis for restorative justice: work to restore the well-being of those who have been injured; give those most directly involved and affected by crime an opportunity to participate in the response if they wish; and preserve a just and peaceful public order. Accordingly, most restorative programs are characterized by four key practices:

- bring victims, offenders, and community members together to discuss the crime and its aftermath;
- oblige offenders to take steps to repair the harm they have caused;
- reintegrate both victims and offenders into the community;
- include everyone with a stake in the crime to participate in its resolution.

Note here that restorative justice—as defined above—does not meet the first of Anthony Flew's criteria for punishment: that it should be *unpleasant.* Clearly, people who support restorative justice believe that the goals of justice can be achieved without significant or lasting unpleasantness for the offender.

In a sense, restorative justice begins with what South Africa enacted through its lengthy truth and reconciliation process: admissions of guilt and regret and efforts to accept the wrongdoer back into the community. The need for truth, reconciliation, and repayment arises out of four paradoxes of criminal justice reform: good goals do not matter and may, in fact, be a hindrance (e.g., expressions of outrage may not improve society); major changes come about when disparate coalitions merge to make them possible; the structure of incentives matters more than the content of feelings or thoughts (e.g., people behave well when we reward good behaviour); and whatever we do in our lives will, if we are lucky, become the foundation that others who follow us will find in need of change (Clear, 2004).

Though we can see links with the restitutive justice Durkheim discussed a century ago, some have identified restorative justice as a new model of criminal justice, replacing the adversarial approach's insistence on assigning blame and imposing punishment. Restorative justice stresses healing the victim's injuries and remedying his or her losses. Restorative justice moves the focus of criminal justice away from the lawbreaker to the harm done to the victim and community.

Some critics are concerned that restorative justice programs may have the negative effect of "widening the net" of social control. They believe that restorative justice programs will encourage law enforcement officials to seek conviction and sentencing of individuals who would otherwise not have been processed through the criminal justice system if the only sentencing options available were more severe forms of punishment. Whether that concern is warranted remains to be seen.

Victim–Offender Reconciliation

The first step in restorative justice is the admission of harm done and an apology to victims. However, cultures will vary in their views on this matter. Takahashi (2005) asked American and Japanese university students their views about suitable punishment for minor property crimes. Findings show that US students tend to believe retribution is the primary goal of punishment, while Japanese students believe that rehabilitative treatment is equally important. Also, nearly half of Japanese respondents believe apology is an important part of punishment for a property crime, compared with only 18 per cent of their US counterparts. Thus, to judge from these results, restorative justice would be far easier to implement in Japan than in the US.

Victims' experiences in the justice system may help or hinder their healing. Restorative justice aims to heal the suffering caused by victimization. However, some victim advocates have expressed concern that restorative justice may *increase* victims' suffering. For example, participation in a mediation program that brings together the criminal and his or her victim may be more painful for the victim. Only under some circumstances will participation in such a program help victims recover. Far more research is needed before we have final answers to these questions (Wemmers and Cyr, 2005). Until then, victims will continue to use their personal discretion when deciding if they wish to see the offender again.

Community–Offender Reconciliation

Although some restorative justice programs focus mainly on reconciling the victim and offender, many also have a community element, recognizing that crime not only damages individual victims but the community as a whole. Similarly, full reconciliation requires that the offender be reintegrated into the community. A good example is the case of Reena Virk in BC: she was murdered by schoolmates in 1997, and one of her killers received community reconciliation in 2006.

In Canada and the US, peacemaking circles combine community and restorative justice principles and have received international attention in recent years (Coates et al., 2003). These are tribunal meetings between everyone affected by the crime, which allow individuals to communicate their thoughts and feelings to one another. Peacemaking circles are already used in many Aboriginal communities in North America. In South St Paul, Minnesota, for example, peacemaking circles have long been used in schools and communities. Research finds they are effective in holding local offenders accountable for the harm they caused, assisting crime victims, and fostering a greater sense of connection among all those affected.

Media Depictions of Formal Punishment

In past decades, there were many media depictions of capital punishment, though rather fewer depictions of probation, parole, and restorative justice. Most of all, the media have lavished great attention on life in what Goffman called "total institutions" like prisons, military barracks, and mental hospitals.

Popular culture today tends to treat the death penalty in a simplistic fashion. Very few movies that deal with crime and punishment in North America depict the death penalty today (perhaps because it is a contentious legal and philosophical issue). Those films that do look at the practice rarely delve deeply into its meaning. Exceptions are *Dead Man Walking* (1995), a realistic and moving look at a death-row killer and a nun's attempt to understand him and to bring him some semblance of inner peace before his execution. *The Green Mile* (1999) is a fantasy that depicts the looming death sentence of a gentle, magical giant who beneficently cares for a pet mouse and cures the ills of people he encounters. *I Want to Live!* (1958) is the story of a woman who has been framed for a murder and whose reputation as a petty thief and a woman of loose morals have led to her being on death row hoping for a stay of execution.

These films portray prison life and execution both as personal tragedies and as means of institutional control perpetrated upon people who are not understood as human beings, may be innocent of the crimes for which they were convicted, and who might have done great good if they were allowed to live.

When movies and television depict prisons and mental hospitals, they rarely show how, exactly, these institutions exert their control. There are only a small number of famous depictions of mental asylums that show institutional processes, namely *One Flew Over the Cuckoo's Nest* (1975) and *Girl, Interrupted* (1999). Both films explore how hospital administrators use physical restraints, drugs, medical treatments, or psychological intimidation to force patients into compliance. Films that explore the mechanisms of asylums are rare, though, as are films that look at the military's use of formal control.

Though Hollywood has produced many war films, few movies look at the process of "programming" soldiers. Notable exceptions are *Full Metal Jacket* (1987) and *Body Snatchers* (1995), which speak to this issue fleetingly. *Good Morning, Vietnam* (1987), which satirizes America's involvement in the Vietnam War, highlights the unquestioning, inhumane, and unintelligent perspectives of some officers, who fulfill their roles like office personnel, rather than as men who recognize the lives of the people under their control—including the enemy—are valued human beings.

Imprisonment may be the mode of formal control to receive the most attention in the mass media. The "prison film" developed into its own genre over the twentieth century, setting out clear, distinct conventions. Most prison films feature stock scenes that even casual moviegoers may recognize. For instance, these films often feature a cafeteria fight scene, prisoners playing sports, a psychopathic guard, and a wise, older prisoner. Though these tropes do not always contradict the realities of prison life, they offer viewers little in the way of legitimate insight into the structural mechanisms at work in total institutions.

The proliferation of prison movie tropes does not, in itself, indicate that movies always portray prison life ineptly. To the contrary, movies such as *The Shawshank Redemption* (1994) and *Cool Hand Luke* (1967) have accurately preserved much of the mood of prison life. These works depict the toil, danger, and corruption inherent in large, isolated institutions. *Shawshank Redemption* accurately portrays the hazards of prison life and the desperate plight of those who try to survive "on the outside" after having served long sentences.

Popular media's willingness to repeatedly note the harshness of prison life, especially in sensationalist television shows like *Oz* or *Prison Break*, emphasize the decency of many prisoners and the corruption of institutional punishment. This perspective is commendable, given the political rhetoric over the last three decades about luxurious, non-punitive "prison spas" and "Club Feds."

Consequences of Imprisonment

Employment Rates and Income

Prison is bad for people in a great many ways, not least because it wrenches them out of normal, everyday life and renders them less competent to re-enter it. Consider the problems of finding and keeping a job.

Employment is important for an ex-convict, both as a source of income and as a key to his or her successful reintegration into society. In fact, employment issues may have even contributed to the situation that led to imprisonment. That said, research suggests that imprisonment may harm the convict's abilities to gain employment after release. A longitudinal study of employment experiences after release from prison in three American states (Illinois, Ohio, and Texas) found the following:

- Eight months after prison, 65 per cent of respondents had been employed at some point but only 45 per cent were currently employed.
- Most respondents relied on family and friends for income after release, more so than legal employment.
- Respondents who held a job while in prison and those who participated in job-training programs while incarcerated had better employment outcomes after release.
- Once in the community, 48 per cent of respondents wanted but were unable to participate in programs to improve their work skills, most commonly because they were unaware of program availability.
- Most respondents who found work did so by speaking with friends and family; however, the most successful strategy for long-term employment was returning to a previous employer.
- Respondents who were employed and earning higher wages after release were less likely to return to prison the first year out. (Visher et al., 2008: 1)

Admittedly, it is difficult to isolate the effect of a prison record on ex-convicts' employment histories, given that many of them were previously employed in insecure secondary jobs. Indeed, this past history itself complicates the problem of integrating young, inner-city men back into the labour market after imprisonment. Yet, one cannot doubt that imprisonment worsens a former inmate's chances of getting a good job.

Inequality

Through its effect on employment and otherwise, the expansion of the prison system in the US had a dramatic general effect on social inequality, given the extreme disparities in imprisonment for African-American men born since the 1960s.

Engagement in the prison system disrupts the life course, produces enduring disadvantages, and fosters a class of social outsiders that undermines citizenship. Just when economic opportunities for unskilled young men were already collapsing in American inner cities, more punitive policies undermined the goal of rehabilitation. So, in recent years, high rates of imprisonment among cohorts of young African-American men with little schooling have effectively eroded the citizenship of young African-American men, weakening their integration into American society. Though less thoroughly documented, the same has happened to young Aboriginal men in Canada, to a lesser extent perhaps owing to lower overall imprisonment rates in Canada.

Families and Children

The outcomes of imprisonment go well beyond their effects on work, income, and social class. "Collateral consequences" of mass imprisonment affect social and family life as well. In Canada and elsewhere, the vast majority of people in prison are men. Women are a distinct minority in prisons. This is, in part, because judges and juries are reluctant to imprison women, especially if they are mothers or mothers-to-be. In turn, this reflects a concern with the effects of imprisonment on family relationships, marital relationships, parental relationships, and children. (Of course, it should also be noted that most serious offences are committed by men, and this affects the imprisonment rates as well.)

Being sentenced to prison is a disruptive force that often results in job loss and family breakup. Most prisoners have little or no income before entering prison and therefore are unable to pay child and family support while in prison, often leaving families dependent on welfare.

In view of the shortage of basic social services in the United States today, for some, a life in prison may seem preferable and easier to adapt to than a chaotic and stressful life at home. Impoverished women—lacking mental health services, substance abuse treatment, domestic violence intervention, and other social welfare support for themselves and their partners—sometimes even engage the criminal justice system for help and protection in their relationships with marginalized men. In this way, women with imprisoned partners undergo "secondary prisonization"—that is, reliance on the correctional facility as the most powerful public institution available to help them.

Increasingly, due to the continuing "war on drugs," women are being imprisoned, too, and as a result, even more families are suffering the collateral damage of imprisonment. An estimated 63 per cent of imprisoned women have one or more minor children, and most report having lived with their children before imprisonment. Children of imprisoned parents are a relatively invisible population in the research on the collateral effects of imprisonment, yet they suffer long-term effects. For example, Huebner and Gustafson (2007) found that, in adulthood, the children of imprisoned mothers are more likely than average to be convicted of a crime or sentenced to probation.

Health Consequences

Not surprisingly, imprisonment is associated with new health risks. For example, the number of mentally ill prisoners in US prisons is nearly five times the number of those in mental hospitals. Howard Sapers, Canada's Correctional Investigator, in his 2010 report to Parliament, estimated that one in four new admissions to the federal corrections systems is mentally ill. He notes: "It is a sobering and cautionary experience to walk through any of Canada's federal penitentiaries or provincial jails today. . . . federal penitentiaries are fast becoming our nation's largest psychiatric facilities and repositories for the mentally ill. As a society, we are criminalizing, incarcerating and warehousing the mentally disordered in large and alarming numbers" (Office of the Correctional Investigator, 2010). Of course, the conditions in prison also increase the risks of developing mental illness. In addition, large numbers of inmates contract communicable diseases while in prison, most commonly hepatitis C and HIV. Eventually, most of these inmates are released into the community, spreading disease in the general population.

Research by Schnittker and John (2007), using high-quality data from the National Longitudinal Survey of Youth in the US, has identified some of the direct and indirect effects of imprisonment. The findings show that imprisonment has powerful effects on health that only show up after release. The number of occasions a person has been imprisoned does not seem to matter. Indeed, the evidence for a causal effect is much weaker among persistent recidivists and those serving exceptionally long sentences.

Any imprisonment, for however long, has negative effects, and typically the first contact is the most important, a finding that suggests the stigma associated with imprisonment is a crucial factor in ill health. In part, the health effect of imprisonment after release is due to the negative effects on employment, earnings, and marital stability, and all of these have long-lasting, secondary effects; but these are not the main causes. Mainly, the health effect is due to residual effects of stigmatization and stress on the immune system, leading to a heightened risk of multiple illnesses.

Ironically, for many disadvantaged people, being in prison is not the unhealthiest thing that can happen to them. Recent research by Curtis (2011) finds that fathers who have previously been incarcerated at some time are markedly more likely than other men to rely on medications for physical or mental health problems—implying the long-term ill health consequences discussed by Schnittker and John. By contrast, recently incarcerated repeat offenders have relatively less likelihood of being in poor health, compared to those who have never been to prison. Curtis (ibid., 341) suggests that, other things being equal, the relatively good health of recidivists "may be related to prison health care and the overall disadvantaged circumstances of these fathers."

Economic Consequences

Almost all means of formal control—imprisonment, institutionalization, or hospitalization—are enormously expensive to undertake. Costs include the initial cost of purchasing land, along with building, staff, and operation costs, all of which are heavy financial burdens. The rise of mass imprisonment in the United States and, to a lesser extent, in Canada and Great Britain resulted in public crises over prison and juvenile detention centre funding. Politicians who debate this issue generally take one of two positions: the government should maintain high levels of imprisonment, offsetting the costs through privatization and cuts to other areas; or the government should simply lessen prison populations. The former view is the more politically popular, while the latter is more practical.

Despite the austerity of Canadian inmates' living conditions, imprisonment remains extremely expensive. Corrections Canada reports spending $110,223 on each male held in maximum security each year, a number that leaps to $150,867 for women. The costs drop dramatically, to around $70,000, for medium- and low-security inmates, and to $52,000 per year for provincial inmates. While much less, these are still substantial costs and represent a comfortable income for an entire family at the lower levels. This leads one to wonder if that kind of investment in poorer families might result in far less need for jails and prisons.

What's more, these costs have been exacerbated by a recent rash of federal prison construction, estimated at $517 million in 2011. This trend has upped public costs of imprisonment from $1.6 billion in 2006 to a projected $2.98 billion in 2011, according to Corrections Canada. A recent news report in the *National Post* reveals that:

> Figures on the cost of Canada's federal corrections system appear in the annual Reports on Plans and Priorities of the Correctional Service of Canada. By 2013–14, the cost of the federal penitentiary system will have almost doubled to $3.147 billion, according to budget projections. Recent government reports on the cost of Canada's jails show costs rising on all fronts. . . . The cost of staffing Canada's federal prisons has . . . increased significantly, with 5,745 more staff hired at Corrections Canada since the Conservatives took power. Staffing numbers have risen from 14,663 in 2005–06 to 20,408 full-time equivalents in 2011–12, according to Reports on Plans and Priorities. (Davis, 2011)

As was noted in the section on violent crime, some members of the public mistakenly believe that use of the death penalty could mitigate the costs of housing egregious offenders, such as murderers and pedophiles. This is a faulty presumption, as capital punishment is a monumentally costly and time-consuming practice. Because of the punishment's severity, the possibility of executing a wrongfully convicted person, and existing legal protections from cruel and unusual punishment, American states take on major court costs in pursuing the death penalty.

Social Policy Implications

Total state spending in the US on corrections was $12 billion in 1987. In 2007, it was over $74 billion, and these costs will continue to grow (bjs.ojp.usdoj.gov/index.cfm?ty=tp&tid=5). While the costs in Canada are much more modest, there can be no doubt that large-scale imprisonment poses a huge fiscal burden for government budgets, reducing the ability to spend on other pressing needs, such as education and health care.

Whichever country we look at, we find that some forms of punishment can help to defray the costs of punishment, and these typically are more commonly used in the socially progressive countries of Scandinavia and northwestern Europe. Universally, lengthy imprisonment is the most costly form of punishment—and it is the least cost-effective if our goal is to reduce recidivism and increase social re-integration. For these reasons, the increase of mandatory prison sentences and building of "super-prisons" are the most irrational, ineffective strategy imaginable—a testament to an irrational ideology, not research. By contrast, probation, parole, and community service are cheaper and more effective approaches—though, of course, none of these is cheap and none is perfectly effective.

The other social policy implication to notice is that remedial measures, such as imprisonment, parole, probation, and reintegration, are far inferior—in the long run—to preventive strategies. Better support for families and schools would produce Canadians who are less likely to commit serious crimes and, therefore, less likely to need costly, lengthy punishment in adulthood. The resistance to greater investment in this preventive approach is partly ideological—a preference for punishment over kindness to persons who commit crimes, perhaps—and partly a result of the uncertainty of preventive measures. If someone commits a crime, we know we haven't prevented it. If someone doesn't commit a crime, we don't know if and how a crime may have been prevented.

Conclusion

In this chapter we have seen that people hold various conflicting ideas about the purposes of punishment and the permissible range of punishments. Capital punishment is one of the oldest forms of punishment, and while used less often today than in past centuries, it remains in use even in some developed societies, such as the US.

Imprisonment has become a central means of criminal punishment, though we are well aware that it fails to achieve most of its stated goals. Increasingly, researchers are looking into the conditions that exist within prisons to find out whether those who are imprisoned are also being punished by sheer neglect. In some countries there has been an explosion in the inclination to imprison people for reasons that have nothing to do with increases in the rate of violent crime. More often than not, the people most at risk of imprisonment are the same people at risk of capital punishment: poor, young men from minority group backgrounds. Thus, we come to realize that imprisonment is not a kinder alternative to the death penalty, nor does it select in favour of people from privileged backgrounds. Rather, except for corporate crime and the rare crimes of passion, the privileged in society are not driven to commit crimes in the same manner as those of less privilege.

As people seek more effective, enlightened alternatives to execution and imprisonment, some have come to embrace the notion of restitutive or restorative justice. Others have re-embraced the rehabilitative ideal. In doing so, they have considered the additional services and supports families and communities will need if they are to reduce recidivism and help offenders reintegrate into society. We do not know yet whether these approaches will yield better results, but early findings suggest that they may be better for victims, communities, and offenders than the alternatives we have discussed in this chapter.

Questions for Critical Thought

1. What do states and societies that use capital punishment as a means of controlling their population have in common?
2. What are the pros and cons of alternatives to capital punishment (e.g., life in prison without the chance of parole)? Consider other alternatives, too.

3. "Imprisonment often does more harm to people left on the outside than it does to the people who have been imprisoned." Discuss the merits of this statement.
4. Should victims be allowed to influence decision-making in criminal courts or parole deliberations? Why or why not?
5. "Female criminals are likely to pose the biggest correction problems of the future." Do you agree? Discuss and explain your answer.
6. Would it be cheaper to prevent crime than to correct it through punishment? And would preventive strategies be more effective than correctional strategies? If you answered "yes," why do you think we still punish lawbreakers?

Recommended Readings

Gottschalk, Marie. 2006. *The Prison and the Gallows: The Politics of Mass Incarceration in America.* New York: Cambridge University Press.

This book argues that feminists, the victims' rights movement, prisoner rights advocates, and death penalty opponents all contributed to the push for mass incarceration by promoting policies attractive to conservatives. Gottschalk urges us to favour (instead) citizenship, rights, and the protection of children and families.

Western, Bruce. 2006. *Punishment and Inequality in America.* New York: Russell Sage Foundation.

This book explains some of the reasons behind the explosion in imprisonment rates over the past 30 years. It focuses attention on the economic and social consequences of mass incarceration, especially with regard to the poor economic prospects of former inmates, the effect this has had on their family lives, and how it has perpetuated the cycle of crime.

Whitman, James Q. 2003. *Harsh Justice: Criminal Punishment and the Widening Divide between America and Europe.* Oxford: Oxford University Press.

The author argues that America's susceptibility to degradation and harsher punishment practices is precisely linked to America's historic lack of an aristocracy. He argues both Tocqueville and Durkheim failed to understand the link between traditions of social hierarchy and the dynamic of degradation in punishment.

Zimring, Franklin E. 2003. *The Contradictions of American Capital Punishment.* Oxford: Oxford University Press.

Zimring asks: Why is the US the only developed Western nation to currently have the death penalty, and what is it about US history and culture that supports an affinity for this ultimate use of government power? He suggests that the reason for the predominantly southern character of the American death penalty is cultural. The death penalty culture of the contemporary South, he argues, comes from the same culture of vigilante justice that once led to lynchings.

Recommended Websites

Amnesty International

www.amnesty.org/

Amnesty International is the most important international organization devoted to international human rights, including the rights of prisoners and death-row inmates. The site features a variety of links to other organizations, helpful news stories, and national Amnesty branches.

Death Penalty Information Center

www.deathpenalty.org/

Dedicated to ending the death penalty in US states—especially California—this website provides important resources about capital punishment and progress reports about various projects that include increasing the visibility of opposition to the death penalty, energizing and mobilizing clergy and faith communities, and giving voice to men and women who were wrongfully convicted.

Elizabeth Fry Society/John Howard Society

www.elizabethfry.ca/caefs_e.htm; www.johnhoward.ca/

These two prison reform and prisoner advocacy organizations work on behalf of women (Elizabeth Fry) and men (John Howard) who have become entangled in the criminal justice system. Named after English reformers and advocates of the nineteenth and eighteenth centuries, respectively, these NGOs offer a wealth of information at their websites, from research reports and fact sheets to press releases and annual reports.

National Parole Board

www.npb-cnlc.gc.ca/

This website explains the mission, goals, and legislation underlying the work of Canada's National Parole Board and provides a capsule history of its development.

Public Safety Canada

www.publicsafety.gc.ca/

Public Safety Canada provides information about emergency management, corrections policy, national security, crime prevention, and law enforcement policy. This agency is responsible for developing legislation and policies governing corrections, implementing innovative approaches to community justice, and providing research expertise and resources to the corrections community.

Sentencing Project

www.sentencingproject.org/template/index.cfm

This engrossing American website covers all manner of sentencing issues relating to age, race, gender, and class. The site provides helpful geographical breakdowns of sentencing practices, using maps and graphs to show the effects of sentencing on neighbourhoods and voting patterns.

Recommended Movies

***Cool Hand Luke*, Dir. Stuart Rosenberg (1967)**

Luke Jackson, played by Paul Newman, is sent to a Florida prison camp after damaging some parking meters and runs afoul of violent prison mates, stupid and cruel overseers, and a system that allows atrocities to happen. The film, which tells a brutal story in realistic fashion, is notable for its fine acting: Newman was nominated for an Academy Award and George Kennedy won as best supporting actor for his role as "top dog" among the convicts.

***Dead Man Walking*, Dir. Tim Robbins (1995)**

Susan Sarandon won an Oscar for her portrayal of Sister Helen Prejean in this stirring film. Living in rural Louisiana where she serves the poor, Prejean receives a letter from convicted murderer Matthew Poncelet, who faces execution for a pair of murder-rapes. The nun tries to understand how somebody becomes as deranged as Poncelet, while serving as the man's counsellor, adviser, and confidante and ministering to the families of his victims.

***The Shawshank Redemption*, Dir. Frank Darabont (1994)**

One of the finest movies about imprisonment in the past 20 years, this film tells the story of a prison friendship between two men, Andy Dufresne (played by Tim Robbins)—a young banker imprisoned for murdering his unfaithful wife and her lover—and his close friend Red (played by Morgan Freeman). Red—a prison insider and entrepreneur—teaches Andy the prison ropes, and in the process they transform each other's lives.

***Scared Straight!*, Dir. Arnold Shapiro (1978)**

This movie, which won an Oscar for best documentary and has maintained a consistent popularity for over 30 years, relays the experiences of 17 juvenile delinquents sent to a New Jersey prison and left to spend a day being lectured by dangerous criminals behind bars. This look at prison life gave the kids, and gives the viewer, a fascinating understanding of the brutality of life "in the can."

Glossary

Acquisitive (non-violent) crime: Crime undertaken for the purpose of acquiring or gaining property (including money) through theft, robbery, fraud, extortion, or otherwise.

Adverse selectivity: A process whereby certain types of people are selected or gravitate into certain types of relationships, giving the false impression the relationship causes an undesired outcome. For example, post-cohabiting marriages are more likely to dissolve than ones not preceded by cohabitation, likely because of adverse selection (i.e., cohabitation attracts people more willing to dissolve an unsatisfactory relationship).

Anomie theory: Derived from the works of Émile Durkheim and Robert Merton, an explanatory theory related to the breakdown, confusion, or conflicts that disturb societal norms that describes how a lack of consensus and certainty about society's values and goals leads to a loss of effectiveness in regulating society's collective life and the lives of its members.

Appearance norms: Rules or expectations we hold about the ways people are supposed to look. Approximating these norms is important for social acceptance. Though different subcultures often hold slightly different norms, the mass media promote widely held ideal appearance norms.

Asylums: Erving Goffman's 1961 work based on fieldwork in a US mental hospital that traces the moral career of a mental patient and provides a general account of the workings of total institutions.

Attachment: The greater commitment to social conformity on the part of youth whose parents are authoritative and promote obedience to social rules, as shown by researchers who study delinquency. This shifts attention to the conditions that promote attachment in childhood and adolescence, and away from broader environmental factors.

Authoritarian personality: A type of personality, first described in 1950 by Theodore Adorno, characterized by rigidity and a desire for conformity and submission to authority. Authoritarians believe in a system in which some individuals control, while others are controlled, leading to a condition of dominance and submission in society.

Belief: A bond promoting conformity to the laws of society, whereby the individual accepts and believes in the people and institutions that enforce such laws.

Blood feud: A cycle of retaliatory violence based on what are often generations-old conflicts. Blood feuds begin with killing or dishonouring someone and end with the victim's family seeking vengeance by killing or otherwise punishing the culprit or the culprit's relatives.

Broken windows theory: Theory stating that the best way to protect law and order in a community is to strictly enforce all rules of public behaviour, even the most trivial ones (e.g., vandals breaking windows). In other words, an orderly, well-kept apartment building or neighbourhood will attract significantly less delinquency, crime, or disorderly behaviour than a building or area in poor repair.

Bureaucracy: A hierarchically organized body of administrative officials (such as in government or a large company) with clearly defined procedures and tasks to accomplish, distinct spheres of authority determined by formal rules and regulations, and the routine channelling of information through these positions.

Civility: Behaviours that are culturally defined as polite and refined, i.e., the ideal relationships among people in a community that encourage behaviours that are the foundations for easy and safe social interaction.

Clientelism: A form of hierarchical organization based on personal relationships between superiors and subordinates (patrons and clients), most often found in traditional (economically undeveloped) regions. Under this system, powerful, rich patrons promise protection and other benefits to poor, powerless clients in exchange for votes, labour, and other forms of loyalty.

Collective rape: Sexual violence perpetrated on civilians by agents of a state or political group.

Commitment: The time, energy, and effort spent in conventional lines of social activity, all of which tie an individual to the moral code of society.

Community supervision: A range of programs, including probation, parole, and "statutory release" (i.e., the legally mandated release of prisoners after they have served a certain proportion of their sentences), aimed at supervising convicted offenders in the community, rather than in jail or prison. These programs are generally aimed at avoiding the negative impacts of prolonged incarceration and assisting prisoners in making the transition from prison to community.

Consciousness-altering drugs: Substances used to temporarily change one's mental state. Common drugs such as alcohol and marijuana can be used for this purpose, though LSD, peyote, mescaline, and other natural and artificial drugs are also common.

Contagion: The spread of an opinion, belief, or behaviour, usually through contacts between members of the same social network. It may also spread as a result of a mass media message—a song, book, or movie, for example.

Corporate crime: Crime committed on behalf of a corporation that victimizes consumers, competing businesses, or governments. It can lead to major social, financial, or physical harm, though often no criminal law has been violated.

Corruption: The violation by public officials of standards of public conduct in the pursuit of unsanctioned personal gain. In some societies, these unsanctioned acts are widely accepted as normal, especially as they pertain to legal or administrative rules.

Crimes of passion: Usually violent crimes committed impulsively against a spouse or loved one because of sudden, strong feelings such as rage or jealousy. This form of crime is the polar opposite of premeditated (planned, intended, and non-impulsive) crimes.

Crimes without victims: Crimes for which people are punished for behaving in ways that do not (obviously) harm anyone. One example is punishment for the use of recreational drugs such as marijuana.

Criminal career: The series or sequence of delinquent and criminal acts committed over a person's lifespan, ranging from childhood through adulthood. Sociologists believe that criminal careers are like other occupational or educational careers, with clear stages, progressions from stage to stage, and (often) rituals of passage.

Critical or conflict theories: Theories, such as Marxism, feminism, and post-colonialism, that are critical of society as it is currently constructed and that base their analysis on the view that conflict and change are inherent to social relations and that the disadvantaged are in conflict with the powerful. These theories stress that conflicting interests within society—e.g., rich/poor, capitalist/working class, male/female, ethnic or racial majority/minorities—are the normal condition of society, not an abnormal or dysfunctional state.

Cultural capital: Derived from the work of Pierre Bourdieu (1984 [1979]), knowledge of the proper ways to use symbols, ideas, tastes, and preferences associated with a particular society or social class. People who acquire more cultural capital—often through higher education—tend to have better access to elite social circles, better jobs, higher incomes, and even higher-status mates.

Culture of poverty: The idea that poverty is perpetuated through a sense of fatalism that leads the underclass to inherit poverty, a concept developed by anthropologist Oscar Lewis from his study of rural migrants to Latin American cities, especially Mexico City. This culture of poverty is comprised of fragments of rural and urban culture, mixed with pessimism and self-destructiveness.

Decriminalization: The abolition of criminal penalties for particular acts, such as the possession and use of drugs or certain activities related to prostitution.

Definition of the situation: A central concept for symbolic interactionists, coined by William Isaac Thomas and Florian Znaniecki, that describes the subjective meaning an individual gives to a situation, since the subjective aspects are what influence behaviour in the situation. Individuals construct meanings for situations on the basis of their personal experiences, needs, and wishes while drawing on the customs and beliefs of their social group.

Degradation ceremonies: Ceremonies used to shame and undermine the identities of people in total institutions so they might be refashioned according to proper societal or institutional standards. These ceremonies include stripping the individual of personal belongings and enforcing uniform, often severe, appearance norms.

Deinstitutionalization: The process of releasing patients from long-stay mental institutions into smaller, less isolated community-based homes or institutions. Goffman's 1961 study of total institutions provided encouragement to people who wanted to see deinstitutionalization take place, for whatever reason.

Delinquency: Any misdeed or neglect of duty by young people. Today in Canada, we use the term *young offenders* to distinguish those who break the written laws and who will be subject to punishment according to rules specially devised for people not yet deemed adults.

Democide: The large-scale murder of citizens by the government in power, by a variety of means, including assassination, starvation, imprisonment, and warfare by the state against its own people.

Deterrence: A legal and criminological concept that reflects the view that punishment should prevent crime by imposing significant costs on those who commit crimes. Deterrence may be directed at the specific offender who committed the crime (*specific deterrence*), the society at large (*general deterrence*), or both.

Deviance service centres: Parts of a city most likely to provide opportunities for deviant activities such as drug purchasing, prostitution, or gambling. Most deviant service centres can accommodate many different deviant desires.

Deviant career: A career begun by an individual who creates a deviant self-identity and identifies with a deviant subculture. Often, the societal reaction to deviant acts leads people to consider themselves deviant.

Differential association theory: Theory arguing that crime is learned through contact with people who define criminal acts in favourable ways. Just as people learn to be law-abiding, so do they learn to be criminal. Given this central importance of learned values and skills, differential association theory rejects explanations of crime that focus on individual psychopathology.

Differential illegitimate opportunity: Closely related to *strain theory*, a concept contending that individuals commit crimes when their chances of being caught are low. The criminal subculture forms in areas with an established organization of adult crime that provides the opportunity for young people to learn the "tricks of the trade."

Discrediting or discreditable features: Visible, or potentially visible, stigmatizing attributes that require people to take actions to hide these features so they are not stigmatized or excluded. In effect, this allows them to "pass" as normal. Once someone is "discredited," that person's behaviour changes to that of someone acknowledging his or her place as a social outsider.

Diversionary penalties: Fines or community service orders that offer alternatives to incarceration as a way of punishing relatively minor or regulatory offences.

Dominant ideology: Marxist concept associated with the idea that in class-stratified societies, the ruling class controls both material production and the production of ideas and ideologies. Through this dominance, meaning systems of the working class are shaped to support the status quo, undermining efforts by the subordinate class to defend its own interests.

E-crime/cybercrime: Criminal offences, such as fraud and other crimes involving the manipulation of information, committed on the Internet, typically making use of advanced technology.

Family dysfunction: The condition of a family in constant conflict or suffering from misbehaviour or abuse by individual members, especially when other members accommodate (i.e., hide or normalize) such actions. Children who grow up in dysfunctional families, which may include a parent suffering from substance abuse or addiction, may grow up believing that such a family state is normal.

Family process: Practices—particularly parenting practices—that reflect the cohesion and flexibility of the family and predict risky activities by young people. They include things such as maternal monitoring and parent–child communication.

Fetishism: The obsessive interest with an object, particularly as a sexual preoccupation, such as articles of clothing. Fetish objects are usually body parts not commonly considered erogenous, such as feet.

Feuding: Long-running fights between two or more groups—often kin groups—beginning when one group feels it has been insulted or wronged, leading to retaliation and guilt-by-association. Feelings of anger, fear, and resentment cause a cycle of vengeance, making it difficult for the feud to end peacefully.

Functionalism: One of sociology's oldest strains of thought, which argues that any society establishes practices that will help it survive "in equilibrium." Robert Merton distinguished between *manifest functions*, which have intended consequences, and *latent functions*, which have just as important unintended consequences, of which society members are often unaware.

Gateway drug: The idea that a less dangerous or addictive drug may cause users to experiment with more dangerous drugs. For example, some argue marijuana commonly leads to the use of "harder" drugs, such as cocaine or heroin.

Gendercide: The systematic killing of members of a specific sex, usually women. Though the term is technically sex-neutral, it is used almost exclusively in feminist writing to refer to female victims of male violence.

General theory of crime: Theory that children must develop self-control by early adulthood or they will not develop it at all, and therefore crimes in adulthood are a result of faulty childhood socialization.

Ghettos: Inner-urban areas characterized by the spatial concentration of disadvantage. Historically, the term has been associated with particular ethnic groups—for example, urbanized Jewish populations in Europe and inner-city black populations in the United States.

Harm reduction strategies: Public health strategies to minimize the damage caused by potentially dangerous lifestyle choices. This approach assumes that many risky behaviours, such as smoking, casual sex, prostitution, and recreational drug use, cannot be totally eliminated, so a more realistic goal is to take steps to minimize their potential harm.

Hate crimes: Crimes committed out of racial, religious, or sexual prejudice, targeting minority groups. Such crimes, often violating anti-discrimination laws, are usually against groups such as Jews, blacks, and gays.

Hidden injuries of social class: Effects of social inequality, such as feelings of humiliation and subordination among poor people that may lead to the maintenance of social inequality. People who feel worthless may support the status quo because they have been made to believe they are to blame for their own condition.

Homophobia: A pathological fear of or aversion to homosexuality, coined by George Weinberg in *Society and the Healthy Homosexual* (1972).

Homosociality: All-male social worlds, more generally understood as same-sex relationships that are not romantic or sexual in nature.

Honour killings: Killings, particularly of women, carried out because the victims are believed to have committed dishonourable acts that bring shame to the family or the wider community. Thus, women may be killed, usually by their own fathers or brothers, for refusing an arranged marriage, having suffered a sexual assault, seeking a divorce, or committing adultery or fornication.

Hot spots: Areas in a city where the risks of crime are especially high, usually because the area draws many vulnerable victims and policing is relatively light.

Human trafficking: The sale and transport of and profit from human beings who are forced to work for others, a practice generally considered the modern equivalent of slavery.

Institutional completeness: The degree to which an ethnic or racial community can perform all the necessary services required by its members. This completeness provides community members with a parallel, alternate set of institutions and makes unnecessary dealings with members of the larger society.

Interpersonal violence: The abusive exertion of force, including emotional and verbal abuse, often causing injury to person or property.

Intimate partner violence: Physical abuse or violence, including homicide, perpetrated against a spouse, ex-spouse, boyfriend, or girlfriend, usually preceded or accompanied by a history of verbal and/or sexual abuse.

Involvement: A person's participation in activities, such as school and work, that support the conventional interests of society because such activities don't leave time to engage in delinquent or criminal acts.

Labelling theory: Theory that analyzes the social processes involved in the attribution of characteristics to acts, individuals, or groups, so that the greater problems associated with deviance are *secondary deviations*—a result of social labelling.

Legalization: The control and regulation by the state of formerly illegal activities, such as prostitution or the traffic in marijuana, thereby removing penalties for participation in those activities and providing revenues to the state through taxation.

Leisure class: Those wealthy people whose lack of real productivity and conspicuous consumption, characterized by prodigal wastefulness, distinguishes them from poorer people, a term introduced by Thorstein Veblen (1979 [1899]).

Male gaze: Feminist concept holding that males impose an unwanted gaze on females, reflecting an unequal power relationship. To conform to the demands of this gaze, women will often try to meet the ideals of female beauty, though few second-wave feminists believe such conformity will permit women to enjoy the gaze.

Mandatory sentencing: A legal regime under which a judge must impose a specified sentence on a convicted offender that thus prohibits judges from looking at the circumstances of individual cases and exercising sentencing discretion. In the US, mandatory sentencing laws have been widely adopted (particularly in relation to drug offences) and have contributed to the increase in American imprisonment rates.

Medicalization of deviance: The extension of the authority of medical professionals into areas where lay people once dominated, resulting in the medical profession gaining greater social control over certain deviant acts once considered crimes or moral lapses and treating these as medical illnesses.

Mental illness: Changes in thinking, mood, or behaviour (or some combination of these) associated with significant distress and hindered functioning.

Moral entrepreneurs: Active promoters of "morality," such as politicians, police, religious leaders, and media members, who use their resources as rule-makers, campaigners, and enforcers to create an awareness of issues and to shape public policy, in other words, those who define deviance and morality and create the rules and apply them once they come into existence.

Moral panic: A process—usually led by moral entrepreneurs and the mass media—that arouses social concern and, often, overreaction to certain deviant behaviours, which may be fairly trivial in nature or frequency. Moral panics have occurred over a wide range of social problems, including football hooliganism, child abuse, Satanism, AIDS, and many adolescent subcultural activities.

Neutralization theory: Gresham Sykes and David Matza's theory of delinquency in which the delinquent uses *techniques of neutralization* to deny the legitimacy of the dominant order. Neutralization techniques include denying the victim, condemning the condemners, denying injury or responsibility, and appealing to higher loyalties.

Organized crime: Crime in which large groups of people, hierarchically organized, engage in ongoing criminal activities, including extortion, drugs, prostitution, human trafficking, gambling, money laundering, theft, and the provision of illegal goods and services.

Othering: The process of imagining someone as alien to, or different from, one's own group, typically involving the attribution of negative characteristics to another person and excluding that person from membership in one's own group.

Paraphilias: Sexual behaviours considered deviant because in the form of persistent, intense obsessions—including fantasies of, or urges towards, pain, humiliation, non-consensual sex, or sex with children—they may interfere with a capacity for sexual activities with consenting adult partners.

Patriarchy: Meaning "rule of the father," any social system in which males rule their households and society in general. In a patriarchy, men achieve and maintain social, cultural, and economic dominance, passing this privilege down from one generation of men to the next.

Patronage: A system for exchanging favours or aid among individuals or organizations, closely related to *clientelism*. In some societies, patronage describes the corrupt use of state resources for group, family, ethnic, or race-based interests in exchange for electoral support.

Political corruption: Illegal acts by political officeholders who violate the rules associated with their official duties for illegitimate personal gain. This does not include the misuse of government power for purposes of political repression (e.g., illegal wiretapping of political enemies).

Political protest movements: Social movements organized to protest a particular political event or situation in hopes of swaying public opinion heard and, ultimately, influencing government policy. Government policy, economic circumstances, and social structures can limit political protest, which may lead to further protests.

Populist movements: Social and political movements that seek change and purport to represent the common person, or "little man," though populist policies are often difficult to enact in entrenched party systems.

Post-traumatic stress disorder (PTSD): The lingering effects, ranging from loss of self-esteem and fearfulness to panic attacks and severe emotional disturbance, caused by a traumatic experience, whether a vehicle accident, a physical assault or rape, or warfare.

Power-control theory: A combination of class and control theories on deviance that seeks to explain the effects of familial control on gender differences in crime. Because girls are more closely controlled than boys—especially in patriarchal households—there are gender differences in delinquency, with boys much more likely to commit deviant acts.

Prisonization: A term used by David Clemmer to describe the degradation of prisoners, their socialization into prison life, and their subsequent inability to function effectively outside the prison environment.

Psychoactive substances: Chemical substances that act on the central nervous system to alter brain function, creating new perceptions, moods, and behaviours. Psychoactive drugs may be used recreationally, for ritual/spiritual purposes, therapeutically, or as a means of augmenting the mind; see also *consciousness-altering drugs*.

Queer theory: A social theory asserting that conventional theory has been dominated by an entrenched male–female gender binary divide, creating deeply held and uninspected assumptions about personal sexuality. Queer theory has promoted a great deal of work on topics such as fetishes, drag, cybersexuality, sado-masochism, and the "radical sexual fringe."

Rebellion: An event that, usually through the use of violence, seeks to overturn the established social and political order. A successful rebellion, at the state level, is normally called a revolution.

Recidivism: Repeated criminal offences by previously convicted criminals. High rates of recidivism indicate the failure of the justice system to rehabilitate or deter lawbreakers. On an individual level, recidivism may indicate engagement in a criminal career.

Rehabilitation: The legal and criminological view that punishment should be aimed at reforming criminals and helping them become law-abiding, productive members of society.

Repressive justice: A term used by Durkheim to describe a system of rigid and harsh law enforcement found in "primitive" or relatively homogeneous societies with a high degree of social similarity and rigid views about morality. Repressive justice is primarily concerned with exacting revenge against those who cause harm to others by committing crimes.

Restitutive justice: A term used by Durkheim to describe a system of law enforcement in modern, culturally diverse societies. Restitutive justice is more concerned with making amends for criminal conduct, and curing the social ills that cause crime, than with exacting revenge for criminal behaviour.

Restorative justice: A set of approaches to criminal punishment aimed at ensuring that the criminal takes responsibility for his or her actions and that the victim, the criminal, and the community are all restored to a healthy state.

Retreatism: One of Robert Merton's five modes of adaptation to *anomie*, characterized by rejection of the means and goals of conformity; see also *ritualism*.

Retribution: A legal and criminological view that punishment should be aimed at ensuring that criminals pay for their crimes according to the degree of harm they have inflicted on others.

Revolving door: Metaphor for *recidivism* that portrays the criminal justice system as unable to prevent criminals from becoming repeat offenders—hence, in one door; out the other.

Ritualism: In Robert Merton's *anomie theory*, the acceptance of societal means and rejection of its goals, in other words, a mechanical conformity to law and order without any commitment. In this respect, it is similar to his "bureaucratic personality."

Romantic love: A traditional notion used to describe the relationship between two people who feel an intimate—often sexual—attachment, and thus a deep emotional connection.

Routine activity theory: An explanation of crime in terms of routine—that is, repetitive and unexceptional criminal opportunities result from well-established patterns of behaviour by the victim.

Secondary deviance: An important stage within the theory of deviant identity formation whereby the deviant, having passed through the amorphous primary deviance stage when the first deviant acts are committed, has internalized deviant activity into the self-concept to form a more permanent deviant identity. Secondary deviance gives rise to deviant careers and subcultures.

Secularization: The tendency of a culture, in modern society, to de-emphasize religious beliefs, practices, and institutions. Often, this decline in religious commitment is measured by attendance at religious ceremonies, commitment to orthodox beliefs, and engagement in religious activities.

Sexual fetishism: An obsession with materials and objects not conventionally viewed as erotic. The nature of sexual fetishism is widely debated as some consider it a sexual disorder, while others see it as enhancing a "normal" relationship.

Sexual gaze: The feminist concept that men eroticize and objectify women while denying or ignoring women's non-sexual selves. In this way, the female is transformed into a mere object of desire; see also *male gaze*.

Sexual property: The notion that someone can be monopolized for sexual use by another person, thus the subordination, especially sexual, of (primarily) women by men in a society where women are objects of exchange and possession.

Social bond theory: Theory proposing that strong bonds to family, school, and peers are important in preventing delinquency—as are a commitment to conventional lines of action, involvement in conventional activities, and a belief in a "common value." When social bonds are weak, youth drift together into delinquent groups and activities.

Social capital: The connectedness of people, so that social connections—like money—are a type of capital or resource and can be useful in "buying" social relations, including employment opportunities and support when ill or in emotional or economic difficulty. Social capital is also characteristic of communities, with some communities having more connectedness, and therefore greater well-being, than others.

Social cohesion: The close integration of people into groups or communities to which they belong, achieved through social bonds, shared interests and values, and other forces that keep people connected over time.

Social constructionism: A general term stressing that society and humans actively create social life together—including perceptions of, and reactions to, social objects and interactions. So, for example, any society's reaction to a drug is socially constructed in that it is specific to a particular society and a particular moment in history.

Social disorganization theory: Theory attributing the frequency and manner of deviance to the breakdown, or absence, of communal institutions that encourage conformity and co-operation. Often, this disorganization is seen in the decline of traditional institutions such as families, schools, churches, and local communities.

Social exclusion: The rejection of certain groups of people owing to their behaviour, physical appearance, or background. One's opportunities in life are strongly affected by social exclusion, and any person deviating from the societal norms, whether this deviance can be altered or not, may become subject to social exclusion, which can be either coarse or subtle in its form.

Social norms: Informal rules, guides, and standards that establish what is considered culturally desirable and appropriate in a particular society. Norms are distinguished from laws in that they are informal and not enforced through the power of the state.

Social ties: That which links people together socially. Paradoxically, weak social ties—for example, between acquaintances—have their own strength as they are the bedrock of important social networks through which valuable information flows. Networks of strong ties—for example, between close friends and blood relations—tend to be much smaller and, for this reason, sometimes less useful.

Stake in conformity: The idea that a person with strong social bonds is less likely to commit crimes because he or she has an investment in future successes through obedience to social rules. Conversely, young people drift into delinquent activity when they lack a stake in conformity, resulting in a greater likelihood of associating with delinquents and a greater opportunity to commit delinquent acts.

Stalking: The obsessive pattern of following, observing, or contacting a person of interest. A stalker may follow a victim to and from that person's home or work and may even look up their personal information in an attempt to monitor or contact the victim.

Status offences: Acts that are only considered offences when committed by juveniles but not when committed by adults (e.g., running away from home). This means that the nature of the offender, as well as the offence, defines law enforcement.

Stigma: Any devaluing physical or social feature that disqualifies an actor from full social acceptance since the characteristic is often taken to denote a moral failure of some kind—for example, obesity denoting sloth. The effects of a stigma are different depending on whether the discreditable feature is visible (obvious) or invisible (i.e., only potentially stigmatizing).

Strain theory: The theoretical approach that sees social structures as possibly pushing people to commit crimes for "structural" reasons; closely related to Robert Merton's *anomie theory*. These structural causes affect how an individual perceives his or her socially defined needs and influence the possibility an individual will turn to crime to satisfy these needs.

Street crime: Any criminal offence carried out in public places—for example, pickpocketing, drug dealing, prostitution, vandalism, even graffiti. Though street crime is often public, it can also occur in private, against private property.

Subculture of violence: The idea that high rates of violence arise in communities where violence is an acceptable form of behaviour. People in certain subcultures resort easily to violence when angered or frustrated. This is a result of social encouragements to violence, a lack of support for other forms of conflict resolution, and frustrated opportunities for success.

Suite crime: Crime committed by a business corporation or by individuals who are closely identified with a business corporation; also called *white-collar crime*. Typically, suite criminals are white-collar professionals, compared with street criminals who are more often from lower socio-economic origins.

Symbolic crusade: A systematic effort by moral entrepreneurs to call attention to a supposed moral problem while elevating their own status by characterizing other groups as threatening or deviant. Symbolic crusades are often status wars as much as they are efforts to achieve practical or material advantage.

Symbolic interactionism: A social scientific approach concerned with the meanings we use to decode everyday life, using observation and/or participant observation in fieldwork and intimate familiarity to understand the underlying forms of social interaction. These meanings do not "reside in the object" but must be seen as coming out of social processes, with human actors actively interpreting and constructing their realities.

Techniques of neutralization: Methods of self-justification or rationalization used by delinquents to temporarily neutralize their value system, allowing them to excuse their behaviour and commit acts that (presumably) they wouldn't normally allow themselves to commit.

Terrorism: Politically motivated action that combines psychological and physical violence against an enemy. Individuals, small groups, and large groups can all carry out terrorist acts, the goal being to have the enemy capitulate and meet their demands.

Total institutions: A term used by Erving Goffman to describe certain types of social institutions (such as mental hospitals, prisons, and military camps) that bureaucratically process large numbers of people. These institutions use similar techniques to strip away residents' existing identities and "remake" them according to the needs, values, and norms of the institution.

Underclass: A group outside mainstream society, below the main class and social status hierarchies. Groups comprising the underclass often include people in short-term or low-paid work, migrant workers, single parents, and the elderly. The term implies derogation and social criticism, and probably derives from Karl Marx's notion of the "lumpenproletariat."

Victimization: The singling out of an individual or group for subjection to crime, unfair treatment, or other wrong.

Violent predators: Those who commit combinations of dangerous, violent acts, usually over long criminal histories that often begin with juvenile delinquency. These offenders pose unique problems for the justice system since they refuse to give up violence, regardless of any treatment or punishment.

Voyeurism: Generally, the activities of those with a sexual interest in watching others engage in private behaviours such as undressing, engaging in sexual intercourse, or urinating.

"War on drugs": An anti-drug campaign undertaken in the United States to reduce the sale and use of illegal drugs. It has been ongoing since the 1980s and has relied extensively on strict sentencing and harsh penalties for drug-related offences.

Werther effect: "Suicide contagion" that follows the suicide of a well-known person as reported in the media or within a community, after Goethe's *The Sorrows of Young Werther* (1774), about a lovesick young man who takes his own life, which precipitated an epidemic of suicides in Europe at that time. The Werther effect has occurred in some Canadian Aboriginal communities in recent years.

White-collar crime: The illegal acts and misdeeds of middle-class members of the business world; see also *suite crime*.

World revolution: A Marxist concept that the overthrow of capitalism will require the involvement of and take place in all countries, although such revolution will not necessarily happen all at one time.

Youth movements: The mobilization of young people for certain social, political, or cultural goals. Historically, youth movements have played an important political role in different parts of the world, thanks in part to a smaller *stake in conformity*.

References

ABC News. 2004. "Poll: American Sex Survey," 21 Oct. At: <abcnews.go.com/Primetime/PollVault/story?id=1569218page=1>.

———, Yola M. Zdanowicz, and Reginald G. Smart. 1996. "Alcohol and Other Drug Use among Street-involved Youth in Toronto," *Addiction Research* 4, 1: 11–24.

Adorno, Theodor W., et al. 1950. *The Authoritarian Personality*. New York: Harper & Brothers.

Afifi, Tracie O., et al. 2006. "Physical Punishment, Childhood Abuse, and Psychiatric Disorders," *Child Abuse & Neglect* 30, 10: 1093–1103.

Agnew, Robert. 2001. "Building on the Foundation of General Strain Theory: Specifying the Types of Strain Most Likely to Lead to Crime and Delinquency," *Journal of Research in Crime and Delinquency* 38, 4: 319–61.

Akers, Ronald L. 1985. *Deviant Behavior: A Social Learning Approach*, 3rd edn. Belmont, Calif.: Wadsworth.

Akinwumi, Akinbola E. 2007. "Within/Without the Locus of Otherness: Europe, Societal (In)Security and the New Topicalities of Fear," *International Journal of Baudrillard Studies* 4, 1 (Jan.).

Allen, R., and V. Stern, eds. 2007. *Justice Reinvestment: A New Approach to Crime and Justice*. London, Ont.: International Centre for Prison Studies, King's College.

American Psychiatric Association (APA). 2004. *Diagnostic and Statistical Manual of Mental Disorders*, 4th edn.

Anderson, David C. 1994. "Crime Funnel: Arithmetic of the Criminal Justice System," *New York Times*, 12 June.

Arendt, Hannah. 1963. *Eichmann in Jerusalem: A Report on the Banality of Evil*. New York: Viking.

———. 2003 [1971]. "Thinking and Moral Considerations," in. J. Kohn, ed., *Responsibility and Judgment*. New York: Schocken Books.

Athens, Lonnie. 1997. *Violent Criminal Acts and Actors*. Urbana: University of Illinois Press.

Atkins, D.C., D.H. Baucom, and N.S. Jacobson. 2001. "Understanding Infidelity: Correlates in a National Random Sample," *Journal of Family Psychology* 15, 4: 735–49.

AuCoin, K., and D. Beauchamp. 2007. "Impacts and Consequences of Victimization, GSS 2004," *Juristat* 27, 1.

Babic, Dragutin. 2002. "Forgiveness and Reconciliation as a Prerequisite for Coexistence: A Process Which Has Already Begun or a Utopian Challenge? [The Case of Brodsko-Posavska County]," *Revija za Sociologiju* 33, 3 and 4: 197–211.

Bales, Kevin, Zoe Trodd, and Alex Kent Williamson. 2009. *Modern Slavery: The Secret World of 27 Million People*. London: Oneworld Publications.

Baron, Stephen W. 1997. "Canadian Male Street Skinheads: Street Gang or Street Terrorists?" *Canadian Review of Sociology and Anthropology* 34, 2: 125–54.

Barrett, Betty J. 2007. "The Impact of Childhood Sexual Abuse on Adulthood Parenting: Untangling the Effects of Childhood Adversities, Intimate Partner Violence, and Other Adulthood Risk Factors," *Dissertation Abstracts International. A, The Humanities and Social Sciences* 67, 9: 3589.

Baumgartner, Susanne E., Patti M. Valkenburg, and Jochen Peter. 2010. "Unwanted Online Sexual Solicitation and Risky Sexual Online Behavior across the Lifespan," *Journal of Applied Developmental Psychology* 31: 439–47.

Beattie, Sara, and Adam Cotter. 2009. "Homicide in Canada, 2009," *Juristat* 30, 3.

Bebbington, Paul E., Claudia Cooper, Sarah Minot, Traolach S. Brugha, Rachel Jenkins, Howard Meltzer, and Michael Dennis. 2009. "Suicide Attempts, Gender, and Sexual Abuse: Data From the 2000 British Psychiatric Morbidity Survey," *American Journal of Psychiatry* 166: 1135–40.

Beccaria, Cesare. 1764. *Of Crimes and Punishments*. English translation at: <www.constitution.org/cb/crim_pun.htm>.

Becker, Howard. 1953. "Becoming a Marijuana User," *American Journal of Sociology* 59: 235–42.

———. 1963. *Outsiders: Studies in the Sociology of Deviance*. New York: Free Press.

———. 2005. "An Introduction to the Danish and Brazilian Editions of *Outsiders*." At: <home.earthlink.net/~hsbecker/articles/danishintro.html>.

Becker, K.D., J. Stuewig, and L.A. McCloskey. 2010. "Traumatic Stress Symptoms of Women Exposed to Different Forms of Childhood Victimization and Intimate Partner Violence," *Journal of Interpersonal Violence* 25, 9: 1699–1715.

Belasco, Amy. 2011. "The Cost of Iraq, Afghanistan, and Other Global War on Terror Operations Since 9/11," Congressional Research Service, 29 Mar.

Belfield, C.R., and H.M. Levin. 2010. "Investments in K–12 Education: What Works?" in Arthur J. Reynolds et al., *Childhood Programs and Practices in the First Decade of Life: A Human Capital Integration*. New York: Cambridge University Press.

Belser, Patrick. 2005. *Forced Labour and Human Trafficking: Estimating the Profits*. Geneva: International Labour Office, Mar.

Bentham, Jeremy. 1995 [1787–91]. *The Panopticon Writings*, ed. Miran Bozovic. London: Verso.

Bérard, Guy. 1993. *Hearing Equals Behavior*. New Canaan, Conn.: Keats.

Berger, Peter, and Anton Zijderveld. 2009. *In Praise of Doubt*. New York: HarperCollins.

Besserer, S., et al. 2001. "A Profile of Criminal Victimization: Results of the 1999 General Social Survey," Catalogue no. 85–553–XIE. Ottawa: Statistics Canada.

Best, Joel. 1995. "Constructionism in Context," in Best, *Images of Issues*. Hawthorne, NY: Aldine de Gruyter, 337–54.

———. 2003. "Social Problems," in Larry T. Reynolds and Nancy J. Herman-Kinney, eds. *The Handbook of Symbolic Interactionism*. Walnut Creek, Calif.: Altamira, 981–96.

Bidwell, N. 1997. *The Nature and Prevalence of Bullying in Elementary Schools*. Regina: Saskatchewan School Trustees Association, Research Report 97–06.

Blatchford, Andy. 2012. "Quebec Refuses to Implement Harper's Crime Bill," *Globe and Mail*, 13 Mar. At: <www.theglobeandmail.com/news/politics/quebec-refuses-to-implement-harpers-crime-bill/article2367776/>.

Blumer, Herbert. 1937. *A Substantive Introduction to the Social Sciences*. New York: Prentice-Hall.

———. 1971. "Social Problems as Collective Behavior," *Social Problems* 18: 298–306.

Blumstein A. 2010. "Economic Conditions and Minority Violence," *Criminology and Public Policy* 9, 4: 659–63.

Blumstein, P, and P. Schwartz. 1983. *American Couples*. New York: Morrow.

Bonta, J., M. Dauvergne, and T. Ruggae. 2003. *The Reconviction Rate of Federal Offenders*. Ottawa: Solicitor General of Canada.

Boritch, Helen, ed. 1997. "Prostitution," in *Fallen Women: Female Crime and Criminal Justice in Canada*. Toronto: Nelson.

Bourdieu, Pierre. 1984 [1979]. *Distinction: A Social Critique of the Judgment of Taste*, trans. Richard Nice. Cambridge, Mass.: Harvard University Press.

Bowers, William, and Glenn Pierce. 1980. "Deterrence or Brutalization: What Is the Effect of Executions?" *Crime and Delinquency* 26: 453.

Brennan, Shannon, and Mia Dauvergne. 2011. "Police-Reported Crime Statistics in Canada, 2010." At: <www.statcan.gc.ca/pub/85-002-x/2011001/article/11523-eng.htm>.

Breton, Raymond. 1964. "Institutional Completeness of Ethnic Communities and the Personal Relations of Immigrants," *American Journal of Sociology* 70, 2: 193–205.

Briere, J., and M. Runtz. 1986. "Suicidal Thoughts and Behaviours in Former Sexual Abuse Victims," *Canadian Journal of Behavioural Science* 18: 413–23.

Brodeur, Jean-Paul. 2007. "Comparative Penology in Perspective," *Crime and Justice* 36: 49–91.

Bronstein, Phyllis, et al. 1996. "Family and Parenting Behaviors Predicting Middle School Adjustment: A Longitudinal Study," *Family Relations* 45: 415–26.

Brooker, Dale J. 2006. "Exploring the Expectations and Attitudes of Recently Released Inmates from the Texas Prison System: A Focus of Familial Support in the Reentry Process," *Dissertation Abstracts International. A, The Humanities and Social Sciences* 66, 9: 3469-A.

Brownridge, D.A. 2008. "Understanding the Elevated Risk of Partner Violence against Aboriginal Women: A Comparison of Two Nationally Representative Surveys of Canada," *Journal of Family Violence* 23: 353–67.

Brzozowski, Jodi-Anne, Andrea Taylor-Butts, and Sara Johnson. 2006. "Victimization and Offending among the Aboriginal Population in Canada," *Juristat* 26, 3. At: <www.statcan.gc.ca/pub/85-002-x/85-002-x2006003-eng.pdf>.

Buelga, S., M. Ravenna, G. Musitu, and M.S. Lila. 2006. "Epidemiology and Psychosocial Risk Factors Associated with Adolescent Drug Consumption," in S. Jackson and L. Goossens, eds, *Handbook of Adolescent Development*. London: Psychology Press, 337–69.

Bunge, V.P., and A. Levett. 1998. *Family Violence in Canada: A Statistical Profile*. Ottawa: Statistics Canada; Ministry of Industry.

Bureau of Justice Statistics. 2004. *Sourcebook of Criminal Justice Statistics*. Washington: US Bureau of Justice Statistics Clearinghouse.

Burczycka, Marta, and Adam Cotter. 2011. "Shelters for Abused Women in Canada, 2010," *Juristat* (June). At: <www.statcan.gc.ca/pub/85-002-x/2011001/article/11495-eng.pdf>.

Burgess, Ernest W. 1967 [1925]. "The Growth of the City: An Introduction to a Research Project," in Robert E. Park, Ernest W. Burgess, and Roderick D. McKenzie, eds, *The City*. Chicago: University of Chicago Press, 47–62.

Bussmann, Kai-D. 2004. "Evaluating the Subtle Impact of a Ban on Corporal Punishment of Children in Germany," *Child Abuse Review* 13, 5: 292–311.

Caetano, R., and C.L. Clark. 1998. "Trends in Alcohol-Related Problems among Whites, Blacks, and Hispanics: 1984–1995," *Alcoholism: Clinical and Experimental Research* no. 22: 534–8.

California Commission on the Fair Administration of Justice (CCFAJ). 2008. *Final Report*. Santa Clara, Calif.: CCFAJ. At: <www.ccfaj.org/documents/CCFAJFinalReport.pdf>.

Calverley, Donna. 2010. "Adult Correctional Services in Canada, 2008/2009," *Juristat* (Fall). At: <www.statcan.gc.ca/pub/85-002-x/2010003/article/11353-eng.htm>.

Canadian Broadcasting Corporation (CBC). 2008. "Post-Traumatic Stress Disorder May Affect up to 70,000 New Yorkers: Sept. 11 Study," 11 Sept. At: <www.cbc.ca/health/story/2008/09/11/sept11-health-effects.html>.

Canadian Institute for Health Information (CIHI). 2008. *A Framework for Health Outcomes Analysis: Diabetes and Depression Case Studies*. Ottawa: CIHI.

Canadian Women's Health Network. 2002. *Child and Youth Trafficking and Prostitution in Canada*, by Kathleen O'Grady. At: <www.cwhn.ca/resources/sex_trade/index.html>.

Cancian, F.M., and J.W. Gibson. 1990. *Making War, Making Peace: The Social Foundations of Violent Conflict*. Belmont, Calif.: Wadsworth.

Carlson, Eric Stener. 2006. "The Hidden Prevalence of Male Sexual Assault during War: Observations on Blunt Trauma to the Male Genitals," *British Journal of Criminology* 46, 1: 16–25.

Carlyle, Thomas. 1846. *Sartor Resartus*. New York: Wiley & Putnam.

Carrington, Peter J. 2001. "Population Aging and Crime in Canada, 2000," *Canadian Journal of Criminology* 43, 3: 331–56.

Center of Juvenile and Criminal Justice. 1995. "How Have Homicide Rates Been Affected by California's Death Penalty?" (Apr.): 2–3.

Centre for Addiction and Mental Health (CAMH). 2010. *The 2009 OSDUHS Drug Use Report*. Toronto: CAMH.

Cernkovich, Stephen A., and Peggy C. Giordano. 1987. "Family Relations and Delinquency," *Criminology* 25, 2: 295–322.

Charles, Herman. 2007. "Childhood Victimization: Toward a More Comprehensive Perspective Based on a Secondary Analysis of Data from the National Youth Victimization Prevention Study," *Dissertation Abstracts International. A, The Humanities and Social Sciences* 67, 10: 3726.

Chartrand, Larry, and Celeste McKay. 2006. *A Review of Research on Criminal Victimization and First Nations, Métis and Inuit Peoples 1990 to 2001*. Ottawa: Department of Justice Canada, Jan. At: <www.justice.gc.ca/eng/pi/rs/rep-rap/2006/rr06_vic1/rr06_vic1.pdf>.

Child, Irvin L., and John W.M. Whiting. 1953. *Child Training and Personality*. New Haven: Yale University Press.

Choi, K.H., J.A. Catania, and M.M. Dolcini. 1994. "Extramarital Sex and HIV Risk Behavior among U.S. Adults: Results from the National AIDS Behavioral Survey," *American Journal of Public Health* 84, 12: 2003–7.

Clairmont, D.H. 1973. "The Development of a Deviance Service Centre," unpublished manuscript, Dalhousie University.

——— and D. Magill. 1970. *Nova Scotia Blacks: An Historical and Structural Overview*. Halifax: Dalhousie University.

——— and ———. 1971. *Africville Relocation Report*. Halifax: Dalhousie University.

Clear, Todd R. 2004. "Thoughts about Action and Ideology in Criminal Justice Reform," *Contemporary Justice Review* 7, 1: 69–73.

Clemmer, D. 1940. *The Prison Community*. Boston: Christopher Publishing.

Cloninger, Dale O., and Edward R. Waller. 2000. "Corporate Fraud, Systematic Risk, and Shareholder Enrichment," *Journal of Socio-economics* 29, 2: 189–201.

Cloward, Richard, and Lloyd Ohlin. 1960. *Delinquency and Opportunity*. New York: Free Press.

Coates, D. 2010. "Impact of Childhood Abuse: Biophysical Pathways through which Adult Mental Health Is Compromised," *Australian Social Work* 63, 4: 391–403.

Coates, Robert B., Mark Umbreit, and Betty Vos. 2003. "Restorative Justice Circles: An Exploratory Study," *Contemporary Justice Review* 6, 3: 265–78.

Cohen, Albert K. 1955. *Delinquent Boys: The Culture of the Gang*. Glencoe, Ill.: Free Press.

Cohen, D.A., et al. 2002. "When and Where Do Youths Have Sex? The Potential Role of Adult Supervision," *Pediatrics* 110, 6: 66.

Cohen, Irwin M., and Raymond R. Corrado. 2005. "State Torture in the Contemporary World," *International Journal of Comparative Sociology* 46, 1 and 2: 103–31.

Cohen, Stanley. 1972. *Folk Devils and Moral Panics: The Creation of the Mods and Rockers*. London: MacGibbon & Kee.

———. 2001. *States of Denial: Knowing about Atrocities and Suffering*. Cambridge: Polity Press.

Connolly, P.H. 2006. "Psychological Functioning of Bondage/Domination/Sado-Masochism (BDSM) Practitioners," *Journal of Psychology and Human Sexuality* 18, 1: 79–120.

Cooley, Charles. 1902. *Human Nature and the Social Order*. New York: Charles Scribner's Sons.

Cooper, Sandi E. 2002. "Peace as a Human Right: The Invasion of Women into the World of High International Politics," *Journal of Women's History* 14, 2: 9–25.

Cornell, A.H., and P.J. Frick. 2007. "The Contribution of Parenting Styles and Behavioral Inhibition to the Development of Conscience in Preschool Children," *Journal of Clinical Child and Adolescent Psychology* 36: 305–18.

Coxell, A.W., and M.B. King. 2010. "Adult Male Rape and Sexual Assault: Prevalence, Re-victimization and Tonic Immobility Response," *Sexual and Relationship Therapy* 25, 4: 372–9.

Cronin, George. 2009. "Structural Determinants of Homicide in Rural Pennsylvania," *Dissertation Abstracts International, A: The Humanities and Social Sciences* 69, 08.

Crowson, Michael H., Teresa K. Debacker, and Stephen J. Thoma. 2006. "The Role of Authoritarianism, Perceived Threat, and Need for Closure or Structure in Predicting Post-9/11 Attitudes and Beliefs," *Journal of Social Psychology* 146, 6: 733–50.

Curtis, M.A. 2011. "The Effect of Incarceration on Urban Fathers' Health," *American Journal of Men's Health* 5, 4: 341–50.

Dahrendorf, Ralf. 1959. *Class and Class Conflict in Industrial Society*. Stanford, Calif.: Stanford University Press.

Dalla, R. 2002. "Night Moves: A Qualitative Investigation of Street-Level Sex Work," *Psychology of Women Quarterly* 26: 63–73.

Das, Enny, Peter Kerkhof, and Joyce Kuiper. 2008. "Improving the Effectiveness of Fundraising Messages: The Impact of Charity Goal Attainment, Message Framing, and Evidence on Persuasion," *Journal of Applied Communication Research* 36, 2: 161–75.

Dauvergne, Mia. 2009. "Trends in Police-Reported Drug Offences in Canada," *Juristat* (May). At: <www.statcan.gc.ca/pub/85-002-x/2009002/article/10847-eng.htm>.

——— and Holly Johnson. 2001. "Children Witnessing Family Violence," *Juristat* 21, 6, Catalogue no. 85–002–XIE. At: <www.statcan.gc.ca/pub/85-002-x/85-002-x2001006-eng.pdf>.

——— and John Turner. 2010. "Police-Reported Crime Statistics in Canada, 2009," *Juristat* 30, 2 (Summer). At: <www.statcan.gc.ca/pub/85-002-x/2010002/article/11292-eng.pdf>.

Davis, J.A., and T. Smith. 1991. *General Social Surveys, 1972–1991*. Storrs: University of Connecticut, Roper Center for Public Opinion Research.

Davis, Jeff. 2011. "Prison Costs Soar 86% in Past Five Years: Report," *National Post*, 18 July. At: <news.nationalpost.com/2011/07/18/prison-costs-soar-86-in-past-five-years/>.

Davis, Kingsley. 1937. "The Sociology of Prostitution," *American Sociological Review* 2: 746–55.

Dekovi , M., J.M. Janssens, and N.M. Van As. 2003. "Family Predictors of Antisocial Behavior in Adolescence," *Family Process* 42, 2: 223–35.

D'Emilio, John. 1983. *Sexual Politics, Sexual Communities*. Chicago: University of Chicago Press.

Derrida, Jacques. 1992. "The Rhetoric of Drugs," in Derrida, *Points . . . Interviews, 1974–1994*, ed. Elizabeth Weber, trans. Michael Israel. Stanford, Calif.: Stanford University Press.

Desjardins, Norm, and Tina Hotton. 2004. "Trends in Drug Offences and the Role of Alcohol and Drugs in Crime," *Juristat* 24, 1.

Donnelly, P.G. 1988. "Individual and Neighborhood Influences on Fear of Crime," *Sociological Focus* 22, 1: 69–85.

Doob, Anthony N., and Cheryl Marie Webster. 2003. "Sentence Severity and Crime: Accepting the Null Hypothesis," *Crime and Justice* 30: 143–95.

——— and ———. 2006. "Countering Punitiveness: Understanding Stability in Canada's Imprisonment Rate," *Law & Society Review* 40, 2: 325–67.

Douglas, E.M., and M.A. Straus. 2005. "Assault and Injury of Dating Partners by Male and Female University Students Worldwide," *Child Maltreatment* 10, 2: 124–35.

Duchesne, Doreen. 1997. "Street Prostitution in Canada," *Juristat* 17, 2, Catalogue no. 85–002–XPE. At: <dsp-psd.tpsgc.gc.ca/Collection-R/Statcan/85-002-XIE/0029785-002-XIE.pdf>.

Durex. 2005. *Give and Receive: 2005 Global Sex Survey*. At: <www.durex.com/gss>.

Durkheim, Emile. 1938 [1895]. *The Rules of Sociological Method*. Chicago: University of Chicago Press.

———. 1951 [1897]. *Suicide: A Study in Sociology*, trans. J.A. Spaulding and G. Simpson. New York: Free Press.

———. 1964 [1893]. *The Division of Labor in Society*. New York: Free Press.

Durrant, Joan E., and Staffan Janson. 2005. "Legal Reform, Corporal Punishment and Child Abuse: The Case of Sweden," *International Review of Victimology* 12, 2: 139–58.

Dussich, John P.J., and Chie Maekoya. 2007. "Physical Child Harm and Bullying-Related Behaviors: A Comparative Study in Japan, South Africa, and the United States," *International Journal of Offender Therapy and Comparative Criminology* 51, 5: 495–509.

Dutton, D.G., and T.L. Nicholls. 2005. "The Gender Paradigm in Domestic Violence Research and Theory: Part 1—The Conflict of Theory and Data," *Aggression and Violent Behavior* 10: 680–714.

Eaton, William W., et al. 1994. "Panic and Panic Disorder in the United States", *American Journal of Psychiatry* 151, 3: 413–20.

Economist, The. 2009. *Pocket World in Figures*. London: *The Economist*.

Edelson, M.G., and D. Joa. 2010. "Differences in Legal Outcomes for Male and Female Children Who Have Been Sexually Abused," *Sex Abuse* 22, 4: 427–42.

Edwards, Susan. 1981. *Female Sexuality and the Law*. Oxford: Martin Robertson.

Elias, Norbert. 1980. *The Civilizing Process: The History of Manners*, vol. 1. New York: Pantheon.

——— and John L. Scotson. 1965. *The Established and the Outsiders: A Sociological Enquiry into Community Problems*. London: Sage.

Engels, Jeremy. 2007. "Floating Bombs Encircling Our Shores: Post-9/11 Rhetorics of Piracy and Terrorism," *Cultural Studies: Critical Methodologies* 7, 3: 326–49.

Erickson, Bonnie H. 1981. "Secret Societies and Social Structure," *Social Forces* 60, 1: 188–210.

Ericson, Richard V., and Kevin D. Haggerty. 1997. *Policing the Risk Society*. New York: Oxford University Press.

Fanon, Frantz. 1965 [1961]. *The Wretched of the Earth*. New York: Grove Press.

Faris, Robert E., and H. Warren Dunham. 1939. *Mental Disorders in Urban Areas: An Ecological Study of Schizophrenia and Other Psychoses*. Chicago: University of Chicago Press.

Farley, Melissa. 2004. "Prostitution Is Sexual Violence," *Psychiatric Times* (special issue, Oct.): 7–10.

——— and Howard Barkan. 1998. "Prostitution, Violence against Women, and Post-traumatic Stress Disorder," *Women & Health* 27, 3: 37–49.

Farrington, D.P. 1993. "Understanding and Preventing Bullying," in M. Tonny and N. Morris, eds, *Crime and Justice*, vol. 17. Chicago: University of Chicago Press, 381–458.

Feather, N.T., and Robert J. Boeckmann. 2007. "Beliefs about Gender Discrimination in the Workplace in the Context of Affirmative Action: Effects of Gender and Ambivalent Attitudes in an Australian Sample," *Sex Roles: A Journal of Research* 57, 1 and 2: 31–42.

Fedorowycz, Orest. 1999. "Homicide in Canada—1998," *Juristat* 19, 10, Catalogue no. 85–002–XIE. At: <dsp-psd.tpsgc.gc.ca/Collection-R/Statcan/85-002-XIE/0109985-002-XIE.pdf>.

———. 2000. "Homicide in Canada—2000," *Juristat* 21, 9, Catalogue no. 85–002–XIE. At: <dsp-psd.tpsgc.gc.ca/Collection-R/Statcan/85-002-XIE/0090185-002-XIE.pdf>.

Feige, Edgar L., and Richard Cebula. 2011. "America's Underground Economy: Measuring the Size, Growth and Determinants of Income Tax Evasion in the U.S.," unpublished report.

Fenna, D.L., and O. Mix. 1971. "Ethanol Metabolism in Various Racial Groups," *Canadian Medical Association Journal* 105: 472–5.

Finkelhor, D., R. Ormrod, H. Turner, and M. Holt. 2009. "Pathways to Poly-victimization," *Child Maltreatment* 14: 316–29.

Fischer, Benedikt, et al. 2002. "The Socio-legal Dynamics and Implications of 'Diversion': The Case Study of the Toronto 'John School' Diversion Programme for Prostitution Offenders," *Criminal Justice* 2, 4: 385–410.

Fitzgerald, John. 2008. "Fear of Crime and the Neighbourhood Context in Canadian Cities," Catalogue no. 85–561–M. Ottawa: Statistics Canada.

Flew, Anthony. 1954. "The Justification of Punishment," *Philosophy* 29, 111 (Oct.): 291–307.

Fontes, Lisa Aronson. 2007. "Sin Verguenza: Addressing Shame with Latino Victims of Child Sexual Abuse and Their Families," *Journal of Child Sexual Abuse* 16, 1: 61–83.

Foucault, Michel. 1967. *Madness and Civilization: A History of Insanity in the Age of Reason*, trans. Richard Howard. New York: Random House.

———. 1975. *Discipline and Punish: The Birth of the Prison*, trans. Alan Sheridan. New York: Pantheon Books.

———. 1980. *Power/Knowledge: Selected Interviews and Other Writings, 1972–1977*, ed. Colin Gordon. London: Harvester.

———. 2005 [1961]. *Madness and Unreason: History of Madness in the Classical Age*. London: Taylor & Francis.

Franklin, Cortney Ann. 2010. "Sorority Affiliation and Rape-Supportive Environments: The Institutionalization of Sexual Assault Victimization through Vulnerability-Enhancing Attitudes and Behaviors," *Dissertation Abstracts International, A: The Humanities and Social Sciences* 70, 09.

Freud, Sigmund. 1961 [1929]. *Civilization and Its Discontents*. New York: W.W. Norton.

Frideres, James S. 2011. *First Nations in the Twenty-First Century*. Toronto: Oxford University Press.

Friedman, George, and Meredith Friedman. 1996. *The Future of War: Power, Technology, and American World Dominance in the 21st Century*. New York: St Martin's Press.

Fromson, Paul M. 2006. "Evoking Shame and Guilt: A Comparison of Two Theories," *Psychological Reports* 98, 1: 99–105.

Gagne, Marie-Helene, et al. 2007. "Predictors of Adult Attitudes toward Corporal Punishment of Children," *Journal of Interpersonal Violence* 22, 10: 1285–1304.

Gagnon, John H., and William Simon, eds. 1967. *Sexual Deviance*. New York: Harper & Row.

Gannon, Maire, and Karen Mihorean. 2005. "Criminal Victimization in Canada, 2004," *Juristat* 25, 7. At: <www.statcan.gc.ca/pub/85-002-x/85-002-x2005007-eng.pdf>.

Garland, David. 1990. *Punishment and Modern Society: A Study in Social Theory*. Oxford: Oxford University Press.

Garland, T.S., T. Richards, and M. Cooney. 2010. "Victims Hidden in Plain Sight: The Reality of Victimization among the Homeless," *Criminal Justice Studies* 23, 4: 285–301.

Giffen, James, Shirley Endicott, and Sylvia Lambert. 1991. *Panic and Indifference: The Politics of Canada's Drug Laws—A Study in the Sociology of Law*. Ottawa: Canadian Centre on Substance Abuse.

Glenn, N.D., and N. Weaver. 1979. "Attitudes toward Premarital, Extramarital, and Homosexual Relations in the U.S. in the 1970s," *Journal of Sex Research* 15: 108–19.

Goffman, Erving. 1959. *The Presentation of Self in Everyday Life*. Garden City, NY: Doubleday Anchor.

———. 1961. *Asylums: Essays on the Social Situation of Mental Patients and Other Inmates*. Garden City, NY: Doubleday Anchor.

———. 1963. *Stigma: Notes on the Management of Spoiled Identity*. Englewood Cliffs, NJ: Prentice-Hall.

Goldstein, S.E., D. Chesir-Teram, and A. McFaul. 2008. "Profiles and Correlates of Relational Aggression in Young Adults' Romantic Relationships," *Journal of Youth and Adolescence* 37: 251–65.

Goode, Erich, and Nachman Ben-Yehuda. 1994. *Moral Panics: The Social Construction of Deviance*. Cambridge, Mass.: Blackwell.

Goodwin, Marjorie Harness. 2007. "Participation and Embodied Action in Preadolescent Girls' Assessment Activity," *Research on Language and Social Interaction* 40, 4: 353–75.

Gordon, Robert. 1994. "Incarcerated Gang Members in British Columbia: A Preliminary Study," Research and Statistics Directorate, Department of Justice, Ottawa.

———. 1995. "Street Gangs in Vancouver," in J. Creechan and R. Silverman, eds, *Canadian Delinquency*. Toronto: Prentice-Hall.

Gottfredson, Michael R., and Travis Hirschi. 1990. *A General Theory of Crime*. Stanford, Calif.: Stanford University Press.

Gracia-Arnaiz, M. 2010. "Fat Bodies and Thin Bodies: Cultural, Biomedical and Market Discourses on Obesity," *Appetite* 55, 2 Oct.): 219–25.

Greaves, Lorraine. 1996. *Smoke Screen: Women's Smoking and Social Control.* Halifax: Fernwood.

Greeley, A.M., R.T. Michael, and T. Smith. 1990. "Americans and Their Sexual Partners," *Society* (July–Aug.): 36–42.

Green, Jennifer Lynn. 2007. "Collective Rape: A Cross-National Study of the Incidence and Perpetrators of Mass Political Sexual Violence, 1980–2003," *Dissertation Abstracts International. A, The Humanities and Social Sciences* 67, 7: 2772.

Green, Joanna, and Martin Plant. 2007. "Bad Bars: A Review of Risk Factors," *Journal of Substance Use* 12, 3: 157–89.

Greenberg, B.S., J.D. Brown, and N.L. Buerkel-Rothfuss, eds. 1993. *Media, Sex and the Adolescent.* Creskill, NJ: Hampton.

Gregory, Paul David. 2007. "Refocusing on Adult Probation: Theory versus Practice," *Dissertation Abstracts International. A, The Humanities and Social Sciences* 67, 11: 4343.

Guidroz, Kathleen. 2001. "Gender, Labor, and Sexuality in Escort and Telephone Sex Work," *Dissertation Abstracts International. A, The Humanities and Social Sciences*, 62, 6: 2252-A.

Gusfield, Joseph. 1963. *Symbolic Crusade: Status Politics and the American Temperance Movement.* Urbana: University of Illinois Press.

Hagan, John. 2002. "Class and Crime in War-time: Lessons of the American Vietnam War Resistance in Canada," *Law and Social Change* 37, 2: 137–62.

———, A.R. Gillis, and John Simpson. 1985. "The Class Structure of Gender and Delinquency: Toward a Power-Control Theory of Common Delinquent Behavior," *American Journal of Sociology* 90, 6: 1151–78.

——— and Bill McCarthy, in collaboration with Patricia Parker and Jo-Ann Climenhage. 1997. *Mean Streets: Youth Crime and Homelessness.* New York: Cambridge University Press.

———, Bill McCarthy, and Holly Foster. 2002. "A Gendered Theory of Delinquency and Despair in the Life Course," *Acta Sociologica* 45, 1: 37–46.

Hallowell, Gerald. 1988. "Prohibition," in James H. Marsh, ed., *The Canadian Encyclopedia*, vol. 3. Edmonton: Hurtig, 1765.

Hamilton Consultants, Inc., with John Deighton and John Quelch. 2009. *Economic Value of the Advertising-Supported Internet Ecosystem.* Cambridge, Mass. At: <www.iab.net/media/profile/Economic-Value-Report.pdf>.

Handelman, Don. 1973. "Gossip in Encounters: The Transmission of Information in a Bounded Social Setting," *Man* 8, 2: 210–27.

Hankivsky, Olena, with S. de Leeuw, J. Lee, B. Vissandjée, and N. Khanlou, eds. 2011. *Health Inequities in Canada: Intersectional Frameworks and Practices.* Vancouver: University of British Columbia Press.

Hannon, Lance. 1997. "AFDC and Homicide," *Journal of Sociology and Social Welfare* 24, 4: 125–36.

Harvey, J.H. 1995. *Odyssey of the Heart: The Search for Closeness, Intimacy, and Love.* New York: W.H. Freeman.

Hasan, Manar. 2002. "The Politics of Honor: Patriarchy, the State and the Murder of Women in the Name of Family Honor," *Journal of Israeli History* 21, 1 and 2 (Part 2): 1–37.

Health Canada. 2001. *Special Report on Youth, Piercing, Tattooing and Hepatitis C.* Toronto: Youth Culture Inc.

———. 2003. "Canada's Drug Strategy." At: <www.hc-sc.gc.ca/index-eng.php>.

Heisler, M., et al. 2004. "The Health Effects of Restricting Prescription Medication Use Because of Cost," *Medical Care* 42, 7: 626–34.

Held, Virginia. 1997. "The Media and Political Violence," *Journal of Ethics* 1, 2: 187–202.

Hess, Nicole H., and Edward H. Hagen. 2006. "Sex Differences in Indirect Aggression: Psychological Evidence from Young Adults," *Evolution and Human Behavior* 27, 3: 231–45.

Hirschi, Travis. 1969. *Causes of Delinquency.* Berkeley: University of California Press.

Hobsbawm, Eric J. 1959. *Primitive Rebels: Studies in Archaic Forms of Social Movement in the 19th and 20th Centuries.* New York: W.W. Norton.

Hoffman, Martin L. 1979. "Development of Moral Thought, Feeling, and Behavior," *American Psychologist* 34, 10: 958–66.

Homans, George C. 1974. *Social Behavior: Its Elementary Forms*, 2nd edn. New York: Harcourt Brace Jovanovich.

Horkheimer, Max. 1999 [1937]. "Traditional and Critical Theory," in Horkheimer, *Critical Theory: Selected Essays*, ed. M. O'Connell. New York: Continuum Press, 188–243.

Horwitz, Allan. 2007. "Response to Schwartz, Mirowsky, and Wheaton," *Health* 11, 3: 321–26.

Hosser, Daniela, Michael Windzio, and Werner Greve. 2005. "Shame, Guilt, and Delinquency: A Study of Repeated Offending with Adolescent Prisoners," *Zeitschrift fur Sozial Psychologie* 36, 4: 227–38.

Huddy, Leonie, Stanley Feldman, and Christopher Weber. 2007. "The Political Consequences of Perceived Threat and Felt Insecurity", *Annals, American Academy of Political and Social Science* 614, 1: 131–53.

Hudson, A.L., K. Wright, D. Bhattacharya, and K. Sinha. 2010. "Correlates of Adult Assault among Homeless Women," *Journal of Health Care for the Poor and Underserved* 21, 4: 1250–62.

Huebner, Beth M., and Regan Gustafson. 2007. "The Effect of Maternal Incarceration on Adult Offspring Involvement in the Criminal Justice System," *Journal of Criminal Justice*, 35, 3: 283–96.

Hughes, T., S.E. McCabe, S.C. Wilsnack, B.T. West, and C.J. Boyd. 2010. "Victimization and Substance Use Disorders in a National Sample of Heterosexual and Sexual Minority Women and Men," *Addiction* 105: 2130–40.

Human Resources and Skills Development Canada (HRSDC). 2012. "Indicators of Well-Being in Canada." At: <www4.hrsdc.gc.ca/.3ndic.1t.4r@-eng.jsp?iid=32>.

Hunt, M. 1974. *Sexual Behavior in the 1970s*. Chicago: Playboy Press.

Hurd Clarke, Laura, and Meredith Griffin. 2007. "The Body Natural and the Body Unnatural: Beauty Work and Aging," *Journal of Aging Studies* 21, 3: 187–201.

Ianni, Francis, and Elizabeth Ruess-Ianni. 1983. *A Family Business: Kinship and Social Control in Organized Crime*. Cambridge, Mass.: MIT Press.

Inciardi, James A., and Hilary L. Surratt. 2001. "Cross-Cultural Approaches to Harm . . . on the Brazil Experience," *Substance Use and Misuse* 36: 201–12.

Innes, Pamela. 2006. "The Interplay of Genres, Gender, and Language Ideology among the Muskogee," *Language in Society* 35, 2: 231–59.

Ishida, K., P. Stupp, M. Melian, F. Serbanescu, and M. Goodwin. 2010. "Exploring the Associations between Intimate Partner Violence and Women's Mental Health: Evidence from a Population-based Study in Paraguay," *Social Science and Medicine* 71: 1653–61.

Jacobson, Bobbie. 1986. *Beating the Ladykillers*. London: Pluto.

Janhevich, D., M. Gannon, and N. Morisset. 2003. "La conduite avec facultés affaiblies et autres délits de la route," *Juristat* 23, 9.

Janus, Mark David, et al. 1995. "Physical Abuse in Canadian Runaway Adolescents," *Child Abuse and Neglect* 19, 4: 433–47.

Jaworski, Adam, and Justine Coupland. 2005. "Othering in Gossip: 'You Go Out You Have a Laugh and You Can Pull Yeah Okay but Like . . . ,'" *Language in Society* 34, 5: 667–94.

Jennings, W.G., G.E. Higgins, R. Tewksbury, A.R. Gover, and A.R. Piquero. 2010. "A Longitudinal Assessment of Victim–Offender Overlap," *Journal of Interpersonal Violence* 25, 12: 2147–74.

Johnson, Holly. 1996. "Violent Crime in Canada," *Juristat* 16, 6.

Johnson, Sara. 2005. "Returning to Correctional Services after Release: A Profile of Aboriginal and Non-Aboriginal Adults Involved in Saskatchewan Corrections from 1999/2000 to 2003/4," *Juristat* 25, 2, Catalogue no. 85–002–XIE.

Kangasvuo, Jenny. 2007. "Insatiable Sluts and Almost Gay Guys: Bisexuality in Porn Magazines," in Susanna Paasonen, Kaarina, Nikunen, and Laura Saarenmaa, eds, *Pornification: Sex and Sexuality in Media Culture*. New York: Oxford University Press.

Kant, Immanuel. 1887 [1797]. *The Philosophy of Law: An Exposition of the Fundamental Principles of Jurisprudence as the Science of Right*, trans. W. Hastie. Edinburgh: Clark.

Karp, David. 1996. *Speaking of Sadness: Depression, Disconnection, and the Meanings of Illness*. London: Oxford University Press.

Katz, E., and P.F. Lazarsfeld. 1955. *Personal Influence: The Part Played by People in the Flow of Mass Communications*. Glencoe, Ill.: Free Press.

Keeley, Lawrence H. 1996. *War before Civilization: The Myth of the Peaceful Savage*. Oxford: Oxford University Press.

Kelly, Thomas M., Daniel B. Kennedy, and Robert J. Homant. 2003. "Evaluation of an Individualized Treatment Program for Adolescent Shoplifters," *Adolescence* 38, 152: 725–33.

Kibby, Marjorie D. 2005. "Email Forwardables: Folklore in the Age of the Internet," *New Media & Society* 7, 6: 770–90.

Kinsey Institute. Data from Alfred Kinsey's Studies. At: <www.kinseyinstitute.org/research/ak-data.html>.

Kinsey, A.C., W.B. Pomeroy, and C.E. Martin. 1948. *Sexual Behavior in the Human Male*. Philadelphia: Saunders.

Kite, Lindsay. 2011a. "The Lies We Buy: Defining Health at Women's Expense," Nov. At: <www.beautyredefined.net/wp-content/uploads/2011/03/Kite-Lindsay-NCA-Paper-Defining-Health-at-Womens-Expense.pdf>.

______. 2011b. "Redefining Health Part 1: Measuring the Obesity Crisis," *Beauty Redefined*. At: <www.beautyredefined.net/redefining-health-part-1>.

Knight, W. Andy, and Tom Keating. 2010. *Global Politics: Emerging Networks, Trends, and Challenges*. Toronto: Oxford University Press.

Koch, Jerome, Alden Roberts, Myrna Armstrong, and Donna Owen. 2007. "Frequencies and Relations of Body Piercing and Sexual Experience in College Students," *Psychological Reports* 101: 159–62.

Koenig, Daniel J. 2000. "Conventional Crime," in Rick Linden, ed., *Criminology: A Canadian Perspective*, 4th edn. Toronto: Harcourt Brace, 396–428.

Kristof, Nicholas D. 2012. "A Veteran's Death, the Nation's Shame," *New York Times*, 15 Apr. At: <www.nytimes.com/2012/04/15/opinion/sunday/kristof-a-veterans-death-the-nations-shame.html?pagewanted=all>.

Lai, Y., and M. Hynie. 2010. "Community Engagement and Well-being of Immigrants: The Role of Knowledge," *Canadian Issues* (summer): 93–7.

Lalor, K., and R. McElvaney. 2010. "Child Sexual Abuse, Links to Later Sexual Exploitation/High-Risk Sexual Behavior, and Prevention/Treatment Programs," *Trauma, Violence, and Abuse* 11, 4: 159–77.

Landau, Tammy C. 2005. "Policing the Punishment: Charging Practices under Canada's Corporal Punishment Laws," *International Review of Victimology* 12, 2: 121–38.

Larcher, Lorenz, Ingo Plötzeneder, Stefan Riml, and Peter Kompatscher. 2011. "Management of Complications Following Aesthetic Procedures Can Lead to Significant Additional Cost," *Journal of Plastic Reconstructive Aesthetic Surgery* 64, 8: 1096–9.

Laumann, Edward O., J.H. Gagnon, R.T. Michael, and S. Michaels. 1994. *The Social Organization of Sexuality: Sexual Practices in the United States*. Chicago: University of Chicago Press.

LEK. 2005. *The Cost of Movie Piracy: A Report Prepared by LEK for the Motion Picture Association of America*. At: <www.archive.org/stream/MpaaPiracyReort/LeksummarympaRevised_djvu.txt>.

Lemert, Edwin. 1951. *Social Pathology: A Systematic Approach to the Theory of Sociopathic Behavior*. New York: McGraw-Hill.

Lenius, S. 2001. "Bisexuals and BDSM: Bisexual People in a Pansexual Community," *Journal of Bisexuality* 1, 4: 69–78.

Lerner, Debra, and Rachel Mosher Henke. 2008. "What Does Research Tell Us about Depression, Job Performance, and Work Productivity?" *Journal of Occupational & Environmental Medicine* 50, 4: 401–10.

Léséleuc, Sylvain de. 2007. *Criminal Victimization in the Workplace, 2004*. Ottawa: Centre for Justice Statistics, Statistics Canada.

Leyton, Elliott. 1986. *Hunting Humans: The Rise of the Modern Multiple Murderer*. Toronto: McClelland & Stewart.

Lim, K.-L., P. Jacobs, A. Ohinmaa, D. Schopflocher, and C.S. Dewa. 2008. "A New Population-based Measure of the Burden of Mental Illness in Canada," *Chronic Diseases in Canada* 28, 3: 92–8.

Lindner, Evelin Gerda. 2002. "Gendercide and Humiliation in Honor and Human Rights Societies," *Journal of Genocide Research* 4, 1: 137–55.

Lombroso, Cesar, with Gina Lombroso-Ferrero. 1972 [1911]. *Criminal Man, According to the Classification of Cesare Lombroso*. New York: Putnam.

Lowman, J. 1998. "Prostitution Law Reform in Canada," in Institute of Comparative Law in Japan, ed., *Toward Comparative Law in the 21st Century*. Tokyo: Chuo University Press.

Lubell, Keri M. 2001. "Gender, Social Isolation, and Psychopathology: Making Sense of Male–Female Differences in Suicide Mortality," *Dissertation Abstracts International. A, The Humanities and Social Sciences* 62, 2: 799-A.

Luczak, S.E., et al. 2001. "Binge Drinking in Chinese, Korean, and White College Students: Genetic and Ethnic Group Differences," *Psychology of Addictive Behavior* no 15: 306–9.

Luk, J.W., J. Wang, and B.G. Simons-Morton. 2010. "Bullying Victimization and Substance Use among U.S. Adolescents: Mediation by Depression," *Prevention Science* 11, 3: 355–9.

Lunkenheimer, Erika S., et al. 2006. "The Intergenerational Transmission of Physical Punishment: Differing Mechanisms in Mothers' and Fathers' Endorsement?" *Journal of Family Violence* 21, 8: 509–19.

McClennen, J.C., A.B. Summers, and J.G. Daley. 2002. "Lesbian Partner Abuse Scale," *Research on Social Work Practice* 12, 2: 277–92.

Mackenzie, Andrew, and Sara L. Johnson. 2003. *A Profile of Women Gang Members in Canada, 2003*. Ottawa: Research Branch, Correctional Service of Canada, No. R–138, Apr.

McLloyd, V.C., and J. Smith. 2002. "Physical Discipline and Behaviour Problems in African-American, European-American, and Hispanic Children: Emotional Support as a Moderator," *Journal of Marriage and Family* 64: 40–53.

Macmillan, Ross, and Rosemary Gartner. 1999. "When She Brings Home the Bacon: Labor-Force Participation and the Risk of Spousal Violence against Women," *Journal of Marriage and the Family* 61, 4: 947–58.

McQuade, Samuel C. 2001. "Cops versus Crooks: Technological Competition and Complexity in the Co-evolution of Information Technologies and Money Laundering," *Dissertation Abstracts International. A, The Humanities and Social Sciences* 62, 4: 1589-A.

Maguire, Moira J., and Seamus O Cinneide. 2005. "'A Good Beating Never Hurt Anyone': The Punishment and Abuse of Children in Twentieth Century Ireland," *Journal of Social History* 38, 3: 635–52.

Maher, L. 1997. *Sexed Work: Gender, Race, and Resistance in a Brooklyn Drug Market*. Oxford: Clarendon Press.

Mail, Patricia D., et al. 2002. *Alcohol Use among American Indians and Alaska Natives: Multiple Perspectives on a Complex Problem*. Bethesda, Md: National Institute on Alcohol Abuse and Alcoholism, Research Monograph No. 37.

Mallett, Robyn K., and Janet K. Swim. 2007. "The Influence of Inequality, Responsibility and Justifiability on Reports of Group-based Guilt for Ingroup Privilege," *Group Processes & Intergroup Relations* 10, 1: 57–69.

Man, Guida. 2001. "From Hong Kong to Canada: Immigration and the Changing Family Lives of Middle-Class Women from Hong Kong," in Bonnie J. Fox, ed., *Family Patterns, Gender Relations*, 2nd edn, Toronto: Oxford University Press, 420–38.

Mandel, Howie. 2009. *Here's the Deal: Don't Touch Me*. New York: Bantam.

Mann, Robert. 2008. "Reducing Alcohol-Related Deaths on Canada's Roads," presentation to the Standing Committee on Justice and Human Rights, Parliament Hill, Ottawa, 12 Feb.

Marcuse, Herbert. 1955. *Eros and Civilization: A Philosophical Inquiry into Freud*. Boston: Beacon Press.

Marx, Karl, and Friedrich Engels. 1988 [1848]. *Manifesto of the Communist Party/The Communist Manifesto*, ed. Frederic L. Bender. New York: W.W. Norton.

Matza, David. 1964. *Delinquency and Drift*. New York: John Wiley & Sons.

Meldrim, Harmon. 2005. *The Impact of Marital Infidelity on the Offended Spouse: How Christian Women and Men Cope*. Charleston, SC: BookSurge Publishing.

Merton, Robert K. 1957 [1938]. "Social Structure and Anomie," in Merton, *Social Theory and Social Structure*, 2nd edn. New York: Free Press.

______. 1973 [1942]. "The Normative Structure of Science," in Merton, *The Sociology of Science: Theoretical and Empirical Investigations*. Chicago: University of Chicago Press.

Messman-Moore, T.L., K.L. Walsh, and D. DiLillo. 2010. "Emotional Dysregulation and Risky Sexual Behavior in Revictimization," *Child Abuse and Neglect* 34: 967–76.

Millar, Paul. 2007. "The Effect of Family Law on Canadian Children," *Dissertation Abstracts International. A, The Humanities and Social Sciences* 67, 11: 4340.

Milligan, S. 2010. "Youth Court Statistics, 2008/2009," *Juristat* (Summer). At: <www.statcan.gc.ca/pub/85-002-x/2010002/article/11294-eng.htm>.

Mills, C. Wright. 1959. *The Sociological Imagination*. New York: Oxford University Press.

Miron, Anca M., Nyla R. Branscombe, and Michael T. Schmitt. 2006. "Collective Guilt as Distress over Illegitimate Intergroup Inequality," *Group Processes & Intergroup Relations* 9, 2: 163–80.

Miron, Jeffrey A., and Katherine Waldock. 2010. *The Budgetary Impact of Ending Drug Prohibition*. White Paper no. 30. Washington: Cato Institute.

Mood Disorder Society of Canada. 2009. "Quick Facts: Mental Illness and Addictions in Canada." At: <www.mooddisorderscanada.ca/documents/Media%20Room/Quick%20Facts%203rd%20Edition%20Referenced%20Plain%20Text.pdf>.

Moor, A. 2009. "Prevalence of Exposure to Sexual Violence among Women in Israel: Preliminary Assessment," *Social Issues in Israel*, no. 7 (Winter): 46–65.

Moore, Barrington. 1966. *Social Origins of Dictatorship and Democracy: Lord and Peasant in the Making of the Modern World*. Boston: Beacon Press.

Moore, L.D., and A. Elkavich, 2008. "Who's Using and Who's Doing Time: Incarceration, the War on Drugs, and Public Health," *American Journal of Public Health* 98, 9 (suppl.): S176–80.

Morgan, Laurie A., and Karin A. Martin. 2006. "Taking Women Professionals Out of the Office: The Case of Women in Sales," *Gender & Society* 20, 1: 108–28.

Moser, Charles, and J.J. Madeson. 1996. *Bound to Be Free: The SM Experience*. New York: Continuum.

Mullaly, Siobhan. 2008. "Human Trafficking and Human Rights: Roots Causes and Consequences," Keynote Address, Human Trafficking: Law and Policy Responses, Garden Court Chambers, London, 1 Mar.

Mullen, Kenneth, and Richard Hammersley. 2006. "Attempted Cessation of Heroin Use among Men Approaching Middle Life," *Drugs: Education, Prevention and Policy* 13, 1: 77–92.

Murphy, Emily. 1922. *The Black Candle*. Toronto: Thomas Allen.

Murray, Stephen O. 1996. *American Gay*. Chicago: University of Chicago Press.

Mustaine, Elizabeth Erhardt, and Richard Tewksbury. 2000. "Comparing the Lifestyles of Victims, Offenders, and Victim–Offenders: A Routine Activity Theory Assessment of Similarities and Differences for Criminal Incident Participants," *Sociological Focus* 33, 3: 339–62.

Naranjo, C.A., and K.E. Bremner. 1993. "Behavioural Correlates of Alcohol Intoxication," *Addiction* 88, 1: 25–35.

National Parole Board. 2007a. *Performance Monitoring Report 2006/7*. Ottawa: National Parole Board.

———. 2007b. "Fact Sheet: Parole Statistics." Ottawa: National Parole Board.

National Research Council. 1994. *Understanding and Preventing Violence: Social Influences*, vol. 3, eds Albert J. Reiss and Jeffrey A. Roth, Panel on the Understanding and Control of Violent Behavior. Washington: National Academies Press.

Nofziger, Stacey. 2009. "Deviant Lifestyles and Violent Victimization at School," *Journal of Interpersonal Violence* 24, 9: 1494–1517.

Norgaard, Kari Marie. 2006. "'We Don't Really Want to Know': Environmental Justice and Socially Organized Denial of Global Warming in Norway," *Organization & Environment* 19, 3: 347–70.

Norman, Ruth Trexler. 2007. "Contest for the Meanings of Science in the Debate over Framing Cigarettes," *Dissertation Abstracts International. A, The Humanities and Social Sciences* 67, 12: 4686.

Nye, F. Ivan, with Howard M. Bahr et al. 1958. *Family Relationships and Delinquent Behavior*. New York: John Wiley & Sons.

O'Donnell, Patrick S. 2007. "Social Norms and Law: An Introduction," *Theory and Science* 9, 2.

Office of the Correctional Investigator. 2010. *Annual Report of the Office of the Correctional Investigator 2009–2010*. At: <www.oci-bec.gc.ca/rpt/annrpt/annrpt20092010-eng.aspx>.

Olsen, Marvin. 1978. *The Process of Social Organization: Power in Social Systems*. New York: Holt, Rinehart & Winston.

Oosterhoff, Pauline, Prisca Zwanikken, and Evert Ketting. 2004. "Sexual Torture of Men in Croatia and Other Conflict Situations: An Open Secret," *Reproductive Health Matters* 12, 23: 68–77.

Ost, Suzanne. 2002. "Children at Risk: Legal and Societal Perceptions of the Potential Threat That the Possession of Child Pornography Poses to Society," *Journal of Law and Society* 29, 3: 436–60.

O'Toole, Roger. 1977. *The Precipitous Path: Studies in Political Sects*. Toronto: Peter Martin.

Overstreet, S., and S. Braun. 2000. "Exposure to Community Violence and Post-Traumatic Stress Symptoms: Mediating Factors," *American Journal of Orthopsychiatry* 70: 231–7.

Park, Robert E. 1937. "Cultural Conflict and the Marginal Man," introduction to Everett V. Stonequist, *The Marginal Man: A Study in Personality and Culture Conflict*. New York: Charles Scribner's Sons.

Parsons, Talcott. 1951. *The Social System*. New York: Free Press.

Paulicelli, Eugenia. 2002. "Fashion, the Politics of Style and National Identity in Pre-Fascist and Fascist Italy," *Gender and History* 14, 3: 537–59.

Payne, B.K., G.E. Higgins, and B. Blackwell. 2010. "Exploring the Link between Self-Control and Partner Violence: Bad Parenting or General Criminals," *Journal of Criminal Justice* 38: 1015–21.

Pelusi, Nando. 2007. "Clinging to Your Crew: Today Social Ostracism Is Likely Temporary—and Far from the End of Your World," *Psychology Today* (May–June): 34–6.

Pepler, D., D. Jiang, W. Craig, and J. Connolly. 2008a. "Developmental Trajectories of Bullying and Associated Factors," *Child Development* 79 (Mar.): 325–38.

———, ———, ———, and ———. 2008b. "The Development of Bullying," *International Journal of Adolescent Mental Health* 20 (Apr.): 113–19.

Perreault, Samuel. 2011. "Violent Victimization of Aboriginal People in the Canadian Provinces,

2009," *Juristat*, 11 Mar. At: <www.statcan.gc.ca/pub/85-002-x/2011001/article/11415-eng.pdf>.

______ and Shannon Brennan. 2010. "Criminal Victimization in Canada, 2009," *Juristat* 30, 2. At: <www.statcan.gc.ca/pub/85-002-x/2010002/article/11340-eng.htm>.

Peter, Laurence J. 1977. *Peter's Quotations: Ideas for Our Time*. New York: Quill/William Morrow.

Pew Center on the States. 2008. "One in 100: Behind Bars in America 2008." At: <www.pewcenteronthestates.org/>.

Piaget, Jean. 1932. *The Moral Judgment of the Child*. New York: Harcourt, Bracc.

______. 1954 [1937]. *La construction du réel chez l'enfant/The Construction of Reality in the Child*. New York: Basic Books.

Pope, Whitney, and Nick Danigelis. 1981. "Sociology's One Law," *Social Forces* 60: 496–514.

Porteous, Sam. 1998. *Organized Crime Impact Study: Highlights*. Ottawa: Solicitor General of Canada.

Porter, Bruce D. 1994. *War and the Rise of the State: The Military Foundations of Modern Politics*. New York: Free Press.

Poulsen, Joan Rose. 2006. "Coping with Social Ostracism: How Differences in Coping Strategies and Aspects of the Situation Influence Outcomes for Targets of Ostracism," Ph.D. dissertation, Michigan State University.

Powers, Jane Levine, John Eckenrode, and Barbara Jaklitsch. 1990. "Maltreatment among Runaway and Homeless Youth," *Child Abuse and Neglect* 14, 1: 87–98.

Pratt, Travis C., Kristy Holtfreter, and Michael D. Reisig. 2010. "Routine Online Activity and Internet Fraud Targeting: Extending the Generality of Routine Activity Theory," *Journal of Research in Crime and Delinquency* 47, 3: 267–96.

Prus, Robert, and Scott Grills. 2003. *The Deviant Mystique: Involvements, Realities, and Regulation*. Westport, Conn.: Praeger Press.

Public Health Agency of Canada. 2002. *A Report on Mental Illnesses in Canada*. At: <www.phac-aspc.gc.ca/publicat/miic-mmac/>. (12 Apr.2005)

______. 2004. "The Economic Burden of Injury in Canada." At: <www.phac-aspc.gc.ca/injury-bles/ebuic-febnc/index-eng.php>.

Quinney, Richard. 1974. *The Social Reality of Crime*. Boston: Little, Brown.

Radziszewska, Barbara, et al. 1996. "Parenting Style and Adolescent Depressive Symptoms, Smoking, and Academic Achievement: Ethnic, Gender, and SES Differences," *Journal of Behavioral Medicine* 19, 3: 289–305.

Rawson, Arnold J. 1944. "Accident Proneness," *Psychosomatic Medicine* 6, 1: 88–94.

Rehm, Jürgen, et al. 2006. *The Costs of Substance Abuse in Canada 2002*. Ottawa: Canadian Centre on Substance Abuse.

Reiss, Albert J. 1951. "Delinquency as the Failure of Personal and Social Controls," *American Sociological Review* 16: 196–207.

Renner, Michael. 1993a. "Environmental Dimensions of Disarmament and Conversion," in Kevin J. Cassidy and Gregory A. Bischak, eds, *Real Security: Converting the Defense Economy and Building Peace*. Albany: State University of New York Press, 88–132.

______. 1993b. "Preparing for Peace," in L. Starke, ed., *State of the World 1993*. New York: W.W. Norton, 139–57.

Reynald, Danielle M. 2010. "Guardians on Guardianship: Factors Affecting the Willingness to Supervise, the Ability to Detect Potential Offenders, and the Willingness to Intervene," *Journal of Research in Crime and Delinquency* 47, 3: 358–90.

Rhodes, G. 2006. "The Evolutionary Psychology of Facial Beauty," *Annual Review of Psychology* 57: 199–226.

Rice, Christopher. 2007. "Retest Reliability of Self-Reported Daily Drinking: Form 90," *Journal of Studies on Alcohol and Drugs* 68: 615–18.

Richters, Juliet; Richard O. de Visser, Chris E. Rissel, Andrew E. Grulich, and Anthony M.A. Smith. 2008. "Demographic and Psychosocial Features of Participants in Bondage and Discipline, 'Sadomasochism' or Dominance and Submission (BDSM): Data from a National Survey," *Journal of Sexual Medicine* 5, 7: 1660–8.

Roberts, Julian V., and Anthony N. Doob. 1997. "Race, Ethnicity, and Criminal Justice in Canada," in Michael Tonry, ed., *Ethnicity, Crime, and Immigration: Comparative and Cross-national Perspectives*. Chicago: University of Chicago Press, 469–522.

Rodgers, Mark D., and Robert E. Blanchard. 1993. *Accident Proneness: A Research Review*. Oklahoma City: Civil Aeromedical Institute, Federal Aviation Administration, US Department of Transportation.

Rohrbaugh, Joanna Bunker. 2006. "Domestic Violence in Same-Gender Relationships," *Family Court Review* 44, 2: 287–99.

Rotermann, Michelle. 2008. "Trends in Teen Sexual Behaviour and Condom Use," *Health Reports*

19, 3: 1–5. At: <www.statcan.gc.ca/pub/82-003-x/2008003/article/10664-eng.pdf>.

Rotheram-Borus, M.J. 2000. "Expanding the Range of Interventions to Reduce HIV among Adolescents", *AIDS* 1 (Supp.) (14 June): S33–40.

Rucas, Stacey L., et al. 2006. "Female Intrasexual Competition and Reputational Effects on Attractiveness among the Tsimane of Bolivia," *Evolution and Human Behavior* 27, 1: 40–52.

Ruddell, Rick. 2005. "Social Disruption, State Priorities, and Minority Threat: A Cross-National Study of Imprisonment," *Punishment & Society*, 7, 1: 7–28.

Rummel, R.J. 1994. *Death by Government*. New Brunswick, NJ: Transaction.

———. 1997. *Power Kills: Democracy as a Method of Nonviolence*. New Brunswick, NJ: Transaction.

Rutten, Rosanne. 2006. "Shame and Worker Activism: Emotional Dynamics in Face-to-Face Encounters", *Qualitative Sociology* 29, 3: 353–72.

Sampson, Robert J., and John H. Laub. 2002. "Life-Course Desisters? Trajectories of Crime among Delinquent Boys Followed to Age 70," *Criminology* 41, 3: 555–92.

Sansani, Inbal. 2004. "Responses by Health Care Providers in Ireland to the Experiences of Women Refugees Who Have Survived Gender- and Ethnic-based Torture," *Women's Studies International Forum* 27, 4: 351–67.

Sato, Akihiko. 1996. "On the Creation of Philopon-Crime in Japan from the Perspective of the Medicalization of Deviance," *Soshioroji* 40, 3: 57–76.

Sauvé, Julie, and Kwing Hung. 2008. "An International Perspective on Criminal Victimisation," *Juristat* 28, 10. At: <www.statcan.gc.ca/pub/85-002-x/2008010/article/10745-eng.pdf>.

Schnittker, Jason, and Andrea John. 2007. "Enduring Stigma: The Long-Term Effects of Incarceration on Health," *Journal of Health and Social Behavior* 48: 115–30.

Schroeder, Jonathan E. 1998. "Consuming Representation: A Visual Approach to Consumer Research," in Barbara B. Stern, ed., *Representing Consumers: Voices, Views and Visions*. New York: Routledge, 193–230.

Schur, Edwin M. 1965. *Crimes without Victims: Deviant Behavior and Public Policy*. New York: Spectrum Books.

Scott, Terri-Lynne, and Rick Ruddell. 2011. "Canadian Female Gang Inmates: Risks, Needs, and the Potential for Prison Rehabilitation," *Journal of Offender Rehabilitation* 50, 6: 305–26.

Sedlak, Andrea J., and Diane D. Broadhurst. 1996. *Executive Summary of the Third National Incidence Study of Child Abuse and Neglect*. Washington: US Department of Health and Human Services, Administration for Children and Families, Administration on Children, Youth and Families, National Center on Child Abuse and Neglect.

Sellin, Thorsten. 1938. *Culture Conflict and Crime*. Jersey City, NJ: Social Science Research Council.

Shaffer, David 1988. "The Epidemiology of Teen Suicide: An Examination of Risk Factors," *Journal of Clinical Psychiatry* 49 (supp.): 36–41.

Shalhoub-Kevorkian, Nadera. 2002. "Femicide and the Palestinian Criminal Justice System: Seeds of Change in the Context of State Building?" *Law and Society Review* 36, 3: 577–605.

Shaw, Clifford R., et al. 1929. *Delinquency Areas*. Chicago: University of Chicago Press.

——— and Henry D. McKay. 1942. *Juvenile Delinquency in Urban Areas*. Chicago: University of Chicago Press.

Sheldon, William. 1940. *The Varieties of Human Physique: An Introduction to Constitutional Psychology*. New York: Harper.

Shope, Jean, and Raymond Bingham. 2008. "Teen Driving: Motor Vehicle Crashes and Factors That Contribute," *American Journal of Preventive Medicine* 35, 3S: S261–71.

Shrank, William H., Niteesh K. Choudhry, Joshua N. Liberman, and Troyen A. Brennan. 2011. "The Use of Generic Drugs in Prevention of Chronic Disease Is Far More Cost-Effective Than Thought, and May Save Money," *Health Affairs* 30, 7: 1351–7.

Silfver, Mia. 2007. "Gender Differences in Value Priorities, Guilt, and Shame among Finnish and Peruvian Adolescents," *Sex Roles: A Journal of Research* 56, 9–10: 601–9.

Simmel, Georg. 1906 [1902]. "The Sociology of Secrecy and of Secret Societies," *American Journal of Sociology* 11, 4: 441–98.

Simon, Jeffrey D. 2001. *Terrorist Trap: America's Experience with Terrorism*, 2nd edn. Bloomington: Indiana University Press.

Simons, Leslie Gordon, and Rand D. Conger. 2007. "Linking Mother–Father Differences in Parenting to a Typology of Family Parenting Styles and Adolescent Outcomes," *Journal of Family Issues* 28, 2: 212–41.

Skocpol, Theda. 1979. *States and Social Revolutions: A Comparative Analysis of France, Russia, and China*. Cambridge: Cambridge University Press.

Smith, Tom W. 1998. *American Sexual Behavior: Trends, Socio-demographic Differences, and Risk Behavior*. Chicago: NORC Report.

Snow, D.A., and M. Mulchahy. 2001. "Space, Politics, and Survival Strategies of the Homeless," *American Behavioural Scientist* 45, 1: 149–69.

Sorel, Georges. 1994 [1908]. *The Violent Muse: Violence and the Artistic Imagination in Europe*, eds Jana Howlett and Rod Mengham. Manchester: Manchester University Press.

Spitzer, Brenda L., Katherine A. Henderson, and Marilyn T. Zivian. 1999. "Gender Differences in Population versus Media Body Sizes: A Comparison over Four Decades," *Sex Roles* 40, 7 and 8: 545–65.

Sprecher, Susan, Pamela C. Regan, and Kathleen McKinney. 1998. "Beliefs about the Outcomes of Extramarital Sexual Relationships as a Function of the Gender of the 'Cheating Spouse'," *Sex Roles* 38, 3 and 4: 301.

Sprott, Jane B., Anthony N. Doob, and Jennifer M. Jenkins. 2001. "Problem Behaviour and Delinquency in Children and Youth", *Juristat* 21, 4, Catalogue no. 85–002–XPE. At: <www.statcan.gc.ca/pub/85-002-x/85-002-x2001004-eng.pdf>.

Statistics Canada. 2006a. *Measuring Violence against Women: Statistical Trends*. Ottawa: Statistics Canada Catalogue no. 85–570.

______. 2006b. "Outcomes of Probation and Conditional Sentence Supervision," *The Daily*, 15 Dec. At: <www.statcan.gc.ca/daily-quotidien/061215/dq061215b-eng.htm>.

______. 2007a. "The Nature of Sexual Offences." At: <www.statcan.gc.ca/pub/85f0033m/2008019/findings-resultats/nature-eng.htm>.

______. 2007b. "Seniors as Victims of Crime," *The Daily*, 6 Mar. At: <www.statcan.gc.ca/daily-quotidien/070306/dq070306b-eng.htm>.

______. 2007c. *Measuring Violence against Women: Statistical Trends 2006*. Ottawa: Statistics Canada Catalogue no. 85–570–XIE.

______. 2009a. "Control and Sale of Alcoholic Beverages", *The Daily*, 20 Apr. At: <www.statcan.gc.ca/daily-quotidien/090420/t090420b1-eng.htm>.

______. 2009b. "Adult and Youth Correctional Services: Key Indicators," *The Daily*, 8 Dec. At: <www.statcan.gc.ca/daily-quotidien/091208/dq091208a-eng.htm>.

______. 2010. "Police-Reported Robbery Statistics," *The Daily*, 25 Mar. At: <www.statcan.gc.ca/daily-quotidien/100325/dq100325b-eng.htm>.

______. 2011a. "Family Violence in Canada: A Statistical Profile," *The Daily*, 27 Jan. At: <www.statcan.gc.ca/daily-quotidien/110127/dq110127a-eng.htm>.

______. 2011b. "Police-Reported Crime Statistics," *The Daily*, 21 July. At: <www.statcan.gc.ca/daily-quotidien/110721/dq110721b-eng.htm>.

______. 2011c. *Family Violence in Canada: A Statistical Profile*. At: <www.statcan.gc.ca/pub/85-224-x/85-224-x2010000-eng.pdf>.

Steinberg, Laurence, et al. 1994. "Over-Time Changes in Adjustment and Competence among Adolescents from Authoritative, Authoritarian, Indulgent, and Neglectful Families," *Child Development* 65, 3: 754–70.

Stiles, Beverly L., Xiaoru Liu, and Howard B. Kaplan. 2000. "Relative Deprivation and Deviant Adaptations: The Mediating Effects of Negative Self-Feelings," *Journal of Research in Crime and Delinquency* 37, 1: 64–90.

Summerfield, Derek. 2000. "War and Mental Health: A Brief Overview," *British Medical Journal* 321: 232–5.

Surrat, H.L., J.A. Inciardi, S.P. Kurtz, and M.C. Kiley. 2004. "Sex Work and Drug Use in a Subculture of Violence," *Crime and Delinquency* 50, 1: 43–59.

Sutherland, Edwin H. 1927. "Is There Undue Crime among Immigrants?" *National Conference of Social Work*: 572–9.

______. 1939. *Principles of Criminology*, 3rd edn. Philadelphia: J.B. Lippincott.

______. 1940. "White Collar Criminality," *American Sociological Review* 5: 1.

______. 1949. *White-Collar Crime*. New York: Dryden Press.

Swami, Viren, Rebecca Miller, Adrian Furnham, Lars Penke, and Martin J. Tovée. 2008. "The Influence of Men's Sexual Strategies on Perceptions of Women's Bodily Attractiveness, Health and Fertility," *Personality and Individual Differences* 44, 1: 98–107.

Sykes, Gresham M., and David Matza. 1957. "Techniques of Neutralization: A Theory of Delinquency," *American Sociological Review* 22, 6: 664–70.

Takahashi, Yoshiko. 2005. "Toward a Balancing Approach: The Use of Apology in Japanese Society," *International Review of Victimology* 12, 1: 23–45.

Tallman, Laurna. 2010. *Listening for the Light: A New Perspective on Integration Disorder in Dyslexic Syndrome, Schizophrenia, Bipolarity, Chronic Fatigue Syndrome, and Substance Abuse*. Marmora, Ont.: Northern Light Books.

———. 2011. *Hemispheric Integration and the Ears: A Scientific and Inclusive Paradigm of Human Behaviour including the Mild and Severe Forms of Mental Illness*. Marmora, Ont.: Northern Light Books.

Tarde, Gabriel. 1903. *The Laws of Imitation*, trans. E.C. Parsons with an Introduction by F. Giddings. New York: Henry, Holt & Co..

Taylor, T.J., D. Peterson, F.A. Esbensen, and A. Freng. 2007. "Gang Membership as a Risk Factor for Adolescent Violent Victimization," *Journal of Research in Crime and Delinquency* 44, 4: 351–80.

Taylor-Butts, Andrea. 2001. "Justice Spending in Canada, 2000–2001," *Juristat*. At: <www.statcan.gc.ca/preview-apercu/85-002-x/8108328-eng.pdf>.

———. 2010. "Where and When Youth Commit Police-Reported Crime," *Juristat* 30, 2. At: <www.statcan.gc.ca/pub/85-002-x/2010002/article/11241-eng.pdf>.

Teets, J.M. 1997. "The Incidence and Experience of Rape among Chemically Dependent Women," *Journal of Psychoactive Drugs* 29, 4: 331–6.

Tepperman, Lorne, and Jana Weerasinghe. 1994. "Suicide and Happiness: Seven Tests of the Connection," *Social Indicators Research* 32: 199–233.

Thio, Alex. 1998. *Deviant Behavior*, 5th edn. New York: Addison-Wesley Longman.

Thomas, Domenic. 2003. "Fashion Matters: *La Sape* and Vestimentary Codes in Transnational Contexts and Urban Diasporas," *French Issue* 118, 4: 947–73.

Thomas, Mikhail, Howard Hurley, and Craig Grimes. 2002. "Pilot Analysis of Recidivism among Convicted Youth and Young Adults, 1999/00," *Juristat* 22, 9. At: <publications.gc.ca/collections/Collection-R/Statcan/85-002-XIE/0090285-002-XIE.pdf>.

Thompson, A.P. 1984. "Emotional and Sexual Components of Extramarital Relations," *Journal of Marriage and the Family* 46: 35–42.

Thomson, Julia. 2008. "1.7 Million Canadians Are Victims of Identity Fraud," *McMaster Daily News*, 17 Nov. At: <dailynews.mcmaster.ca/story.cfm?id=5800>.

Thrasher, Frederick. 1927. *The Gang*. Chicago: University of Chicago Press.

Toby, Jackson. 1957. "Social Disorganization and Stake in Conformity: Complementary Factors in the Predatory Behavior of Hoodlums," *Journal of Criminal Law, Criminology and Police Science* 48: 12–17.

Tomatis, Alfred A. 1996. *The Ear and Language*. Norval, Ont.: Moulin.

———. 2005. *The Ear and the Voice*, trans. Roberta Prada. Lanham, Md: Scarecrow Press.

Trocmé, Nico, and David Wolfe. 2001. "Canadian Incidence Study of Reported Child Abuse and Neglect," in *Family Violence in Canada: A Statistical Profile*. Ottawa: Canadian Centre for Justice Statistics. At: <www.statcan.gc.ca/pub/85-224-x/85-224-x2001000-eng.pdf>.

Tucker, J.S., et al. 2006. "Are Drug Experimenters Better Adjusted Than Abstainers and Users? A Longitudinal Study of Adolescent Marijuana Use," *Journal of Adolescent Health* 39, 4: 488–94.

Turk, Austin. 1969. *Criminality and Legal Order*. Chicago: Rand McNally.

Turner, H., and P. Muller. 2004. "Long-term Effects of Child Corporal Punishment on Depressive Symptoms in Young Adults: Potential Moderators and Mediators," *Journal of Family Issues* 24: 1–23.

United Nations (UN). 2012. Outreach Programme on the Rwanda Genocide and the United Nations. At: <www.un.org/en/preventgenocide/rwanda/>.

Unnever, James D., and Francis T. Cullen. 2007a. "Reassessing the Racial Divide in Support for Capital Punishment: The Continuing Significance of Race," *Journal of Research in Crime and Delinquency* 44, 1: 124–58.

——— and ———. 2007b. "The Racial Divide in Support for the Death Penalty: Does White Racism Matter?" *Social Forces* 85, 3: 1281–1301.

US Department of State. 2010. *Trafficking in Persons Report*. Washington.

US Department of State. 2011. "State Sponsors of Terrorism." At: <www.state.gov/j/ct/c14151.htm>.

van Beest, I., and K.D. Williams. 2006. "When Inclusion Costs and Ostracism Pays, Ostracism Still Hurts," *Journal of Personality and Social Psychology* 91: 218–28.

Vandiver, Margaret, David Giacopassi, and William Lofquist. 2006. "Slavery's Enduring Legacy: Executions in Modern America," *Journal of Ethnicity in Criminal Justice* 4, 4: 19–36.

Veblen, Thorstein. 1979 [1899]. *Theory of the Leisure Class*. Harmondsworth, UK: Penguin.

Vergun, Pamela Bea, Sanford M. Dornbusch, and Laurence Steinberg. 1996. "'Come All of You Turn to and Help One Another': Authoritative Parenting, Community Orientation, and Deviance among High School Students," presentation to American Sociological Association meeting.

Villaume, Alfred C. 2005. "'Life without Parole' and 'Virtual Life Sentences': Death Sentences by Any Other Name," *Contemporary Justice Review* 8, 3: 265–77.

Visher, Christy, Sara Debus, and Jennifer Yahner. 2008. "Employment after Prison: A Longitudinal Study of Releases in Three States," Research Brief, Oct. Washington: Urban Institute, Justice Policy Centre. At: <www.urban.org/UploadedPDF/411778_employment_after_prison.pdf>.

Wacquant, Loic. 2004. "What Is a Ghetto? Building a Sociological Concept," *Revista de Sociologia e Politica* 23 (Nov.): 155–64.

Walker, L.E. 2006. "Battered Woman Syndrome," *Annals, New York Academy of Sciences* 1087: 142–57.

Walzer, Michael J. 1965. *The Revolution of the Saints: A Study in the Origins of Radical Politics*. Cambridge, Mass.: Harvard University Press.

Warner, Jessica. 1997. "The Sanctuary of Sobriety: The Emergence of Temperance as a Feminine Virtue in Tudor and Stuart England," *Addiction* 92: 97–111.

———. 1998. "Historical Perspectives on the Shifting Boundaries around Youth and Alcohol: The Example of Preindustrial England, 1350–1750," *Addiction* 93: 641–57.

Warner, T.D. 2010. "Violent Acts and Injurious Consequences: An Examination of Competing Hypotheses about Intimate Partner Violence Using Agency-based Data," *Journal of Family Violence* 25: 183–93.

Watson, Scott D. 2007. "The Securitisation of Humanitarian Migration (Canada, Australia)," *Dissertation Abstracts International. A, The Humanities and Social Sciences* 67, 12: 4696.

Weber, Max. 1958 [1904]. *The Protestant Ethic and the Spirit of Capitalism*. New York: Charles Scribner's Sons.

Webster, Cheryl Marie, and Anthony N. Doob. 2007. "Punitive Trends and Stable Imprisonment Rates in Canada," *Crime and Justice* 36: 297–369.

Weis, D.L., and M. Slosnerick. 1981. "Attitudes toward Sexual and Nonsexual Extramarital Involvements among a Sample of College Students," *Journal of Marriage and the Family* 43: 349–58.

Weiss, M.D. 2006. "Mainstreaming Kink: The Politics of BDSM Representation in U.S. Popular Media," *Journal of Homosexuality* 50, 2 and 3: 103–32.

Weitzer, R., ed. 2000. *Sex for Sale: Prostitution, Pornography, and the Sex Industry*. New York: Routledge.

Wemmers, Jo-Anne, and Katie Cyr. 2005. "Can Mediation Be Therapeutic for Crime Victims? An Evaluation of Victims' Experiences in Mediation with Young Offenders," *Canadian Journal of Criminology and Criminal Justice* 47, 3: 527–44.

Werner, Cynthia. 2009. "Bride Abduction in Post-Soviet Central Asia: Marking a Shift toward Patriarchy through Local Discourses of Shame and Tradition," *Journal of the Royal Anthropological Institute* (new series) 15: 314–31.

West, W. Gordon. 1978. "Serious Theft as an Occupation," paper presented at Society for the Study of Social Problems meeting.

Whitaker, Robert. 2010a [2002]. *Mad in America: Bad Science, Bad Medicine, and the Enduring Mistreatment of the Mentally Ill*. New York: Basic Books.

———. 2010b. *Anatomy of an Epidemic: Magic Bullets, Psychiatric Drugs, and the Astonishing Rise of Mental Illness in America*. New York: Crown.

Whitbeck, L.S., D.R. Hoyt, K.A. Yoder, A.M. Cauce, and M. Paradise. 2001. "Deviant Behaviour and Victimization among Homeless and Runaway Adolescents," *Journal of Interpersonal Violence* 16, 11: 1175–1204.

Whitty, M.T. 2005. "The 'Realness' of Cyber-cheating: Men and Women's Representations of Unfaithful Internet Relationships," *Social Science Computer Review*: 23: 57–67.

Whyte, William Foote. 1993 [1943]. *Street Corner Society: The Social Structure of an Italian Slum*, 4th edn. Chicago: University of Chicago Press.

Wiederman, M.W. 1997. "Extramarital Sex: Prevalence and Correlates in a National Survey," *Journal of Sex Research* 34, 2: 167–75.

Wiessner, Polly. 2005. "Norm Enforcement among the Ju/'hoansi Bushmen: A Case of Strong Reciprocity?" *Human Nature* 16, 2: 115–45.

Wilson, G. Terence. 2000. "Eating Disorders and Addiction," *Drugs and Society* 15, 1 and 2: 87–102.

Wilson, J.Q., and G.L. Keeling. 1982. "Broken Windows," *Atlantic Monthly* 249, 3: 29–38.

Winickoff, J.P., S.E. Tanski, R.C McMillen, K.M. Ross, E.A. Lipstein, B.J. Hipple, J. Friebely, and J.D. Klein. 2011. "Acceptability of Testing Children for Tobacco-Smoke Exposure: A National Parent Survey," *Pediatrics* 127, 4: 628–34.

Wolfgang, Marvin and F. Ferracuti. 1967. *The Subculture of Violence: Towards an Integrated Theory in Criminology*. London: Tavistock.

World Health Organization (WHO). 2001. "The World Health Report 2001: Mental Disorders Affect One in Four People", press release, *WHO/42*, 28 Sept. At: <www.who.int/inf-pr-2001/en/pr2001-42.html>. (30 Apr. 2005)

———. 2004. "World Suicide Prevention Day—10 September 2004." At: <www.who.int/mediacentre/news/releases/2004/pr61/en/>.

Wortley, Scot, and Julian Tanner. 2006. "Immigration, Social Disadvantage and Urban Youth Gangs: Results of a Toronto-Area Survey," *Canadian Journal of Urban Research* 15, 2: 1–20.

Wyler, Liana Sun, and Alison Siskin. 2010. *Trafficking in Persons: U.S. Policy and Issues for Congress*. Washington: Congressional Research Service. At: <fpc.state.gov/documents/organization/139278.pdf>.

Xu, Jianhua. 2009. "The Robbery of Motorcycle Taxi Drivers (Dake Zai) in China: A Lifestyle/Routine Activity Perspective and Beyond," *British Journal of Criminology* 49, 4: 491–512.

Yancey, C.T., and D.J. Hansen. 2010. "Relationship of Personal, Familial, and Abuse-Specific Factors with Outcome Following Childhood Sexual Abuse," *Aggression and Violent Behavior* 15: 410–21.

Yin, S.J., T.C. Cheng, and C.P. Chang. 1988. "Human Stomach Alcohol and Aldehyde Dehydrogenases (ALDH): A Genetic Model proposed for ALDH III Isozymes," *Biochemical Genetics* no. 26: 343–60.

Zadro, Lisa, K.D. Williams, and R. Richardson. 2004. "How Low Can You Go? Ostracism by a Computer Lowers Belonging, Control, Self-Esteem, and Meaningful Existence," *Journal of Experimental Social Psychology* 40: 560–7.

———, ———, and ———. 2005. "Riding the 'O' Train: Comparing the Effects of Ostracism and Verbal Dispute on Targets and Sources," *Group Processes and Interpersonal Relations* 8: 125–143.

Zhang, Sheldon X., and Samuel L. Pineda. 2008. "Corruption as a Causal Factor in Human Trafficking," in Dina Siegel and Hans Nelen, eds, *Organized Crime: Culture, Markets, and Policies*. New York: Springer, 41–56.

Zimmermann, E. 1983. *Political Violence, Crises and Revolutions: Theories and Research*. Cambridge, Mass.: Schenkman.

Index

11 September 2001, 297, 340

Aberhart, William, 282
Aboriginal people: breach of probation and, 385–86; homicide rate, 316–17; imprisonment and, 371, 383, 394; juvenile delinquency and, 194, 198; living conditions, 317; median age, 318; mental illness and, 88; obesity and, 52; offenders, *371*; residential schools, 298, 327; sexual assault and, 317; substance abuse and, 154–55; suicide rates, 83; unemployment rates, 317; victimization of, 309, 315–18
Aboriginal women: as sex workers, 315; spousal violence and, 317
Abu Ghraib prison, 277
accidents, automobile, 178; victimization, 312–13
A Child Called "It," 220–21
acquisitive (non-violent) crime, 236, 401; *see also* non-violent crime
addiction: Derrida on, 137; public perception of, 136, 144; *see also* alcohol abuse; drug abuse; substance abuse
adolescents. *See* youth
Adorno, Theodor W., et al., 20, 117, 118, 321
adverse selectivity, 148, 401
advertising, 360; fashion and, 44; as persuasion, 346
Advisory Council on the Misuse of Drugs, 163
Afghanistan: corruption in, 272, *273*; post-9/11 attacks on, 297
African-Americans: capital punishment in US and, 377; imprisonment and, 394
Africville, 152–53
age: alcohol and, 139; bullying and, 177; sexual assault and, 209
agency, 274
aging: women and, 35
Agnew, Robert, 8
Akers, Ronald L., 15
Akwesasne First Nation, 145
Alberta Children's Service, 109
alcohol: age limits on, 139; effects of, 137; patterns of use, 137; personal pathology and, 139; rates of consumption, *142*, 146; situation factors in use of, 138, 139; violence and, 138
alcohol abuse, 145–46, 165; anomie and, 155; crime and, 157–58; critical theories and, 155–57; demographics of, 139; factors affecting, 138–39; feminist approaches to, 156–57; functionalism and, 154–55; genetic factors and, 154; health consequences of, 159–60; history and public reactions, 139–44; media depictions of, 153; poverty and, 158–59; risks of, 146; social consequences of, 157–59; social costs of, 156; social policy implications of, 161–64; symbolic interactionism and, 155; women and, 157
Alcoholics Anonymous (AA), 161
Al-Qaeda, 285
altruism, 335, 336
Amnesty International, 277, 399
anomie theory, 8, 401; Durkheim on, 6; Merton on, 8, 38, 54–55, 155, 255, 280, 336; ways of adapting to, 8, 38, 255, 280
anorexia nervosa, 48, 49, 60–61
anorexics, holy, 48
anti-depressants, 75, 84–85
anti-homosexuality, 127, 130; as form of sexual deviance, 117–18
anxiety disorders: bullying and, 177; co-morbidity and, 78
appearance: actual versus ideal, 36–37, 37–38; bullying and, 177; class and, 41; clothing and, 41–42; deviant subcultures and, 55; eating issues and, 49–54; fashion industry and, 42–44; fashion models and, 47–48; gender and, 40; identity and, 39–40; measuring, 36; media and, 38, 63; norms, 35–39, 401; punk, 46–47; social meaning of, 39–42; social norms and, 342; women and, 35–36, 49, 58–59
appearance deviation, 63–64; anomie and, 55; consequences of, 35, 59–61; critical theories and, 58–59; economic consequences of, 62–63; features of, 35; in films, 38–39; functionalism and, 54–55; health consequences of, 60–61; intentional and unintentional, 35; multiculturalism and, 62; social consequences of, 60; social policy implications of, 61–62; symbolic interactionism and, 55–58
Arendt, Hannah, 15, 253
Arrested Development (television program), 288
Asia-Pacific Economic Co-operation (APEC) summit, police behaviour at, 276
asylums, 69
Asylums (Goffman), 39, 83, 87, 401
atheist campaign, on London buses, 347
Athens, Lonnie, 222–23
attachment, 10, 174, 401; family and, 11
attention deficit hyperactivity disorder (ADHD), 71
authoritarian personality, 117, 118, 321, 401

Babic, Dragutin, 293
Bales, Kevin, et al., 325
bandit communities, 283
Baron, Stephen W., 187
bars: drinking and, 138
battered woman syndrome (BWS), 218
BDSM (bondage and discipline, dominance and submission, and sadism and masochism), 112–13, 119, 130
beauty: industry, 62–63; measuring, *37*; *see also* appearance
Beccaria, Cesare, 368, 374
Becker, Howard, 16, 138, 151; *Outsiders*, 152
Bedlam (Hospital of St Mary of Bethlehem), 69
Belfield, Clive and Henry Levin, 194–95
belief, 10, 174, 401
Bell Media, 360
Bend It Like Beckham (film), 359
Benjamin, Walter, 20
Bentham, Jeremy, 26
Bérard, Guy, 75, 77
Best, Joel, 341–42
Better Angels of Our Nature, The (Pinker), 203
Bill C-10 ("Safe Streets and Communities Act"), 161, 230, 372; changes to YCJA in, 197–98
Bill C-127, 208
binge eating, 53, 146, 147
bin Laden, Osama, 279
bipolar disorder, 74
bisexuality, 105, 119
Black, Conrad, 239
Black Candle, The (Murphy), 140–41
Bleuler, Paul, 77
Blumer, Herbert, 13, 16
body characteristics: measuring, 37, *37*; typical, *50*
Body Mass Index (BMI), 50; attractiveness and, 53
body piercing, 44, 61, 63
Boritch, Helen, 123–24
Bouchard-Taylor commission, 62
Bourdieu, Pierre: *Distinction: A Critique and Judgement of Taste*, 40; on habitus, 40–41
Bowers-Bryanton, Jenna, 308
Bowling for Columbine (film), 190
Boyd Gang, 203
boys: as "free to deviate," 10; victims of sexual assault, 227; *see also* men, young
Brave New World (Huxley), 359
break-ins, 245
Breton, Raymond, 284
bribery, 270, 272, *272*
British Columbia: homeless adolescents in, 188
broken windows theory, 255–56, 401
brutalization effect, 206
Bryant, Kobe, 115
bulimia nervosa, 50
"Bully" (video game), 176
bullying, 175–77, 307–8, 356–57; cycle of, *357*; definition of, 175; suicide and, 308
bureaucracy, 401; Weber on, 270–71
bureaucratization: social control and, 339
Burke, Brian, 115
business crime, 239–44, 247–48; against employees, 253; four types of official denial of, 253; as global problem, 240; range of, 248; *see also* corporate crime

California Commission on the Fair Administration of Justice, 228
Cambodia: war injuries in, 296
Canada Revenue Agency, 235, 262
Canada's Drug Strategy, 161
Canadian Centre on Substance Abuse, 31, 160
Canadian Community Health Survey, Cycle 2.1, 105
Canadian Institute for Health Information (CIHI), 75, 77
Canadian Mental Health Association (CMHA), 92, 98
Canadian Security Intelligence Service (CSIS), 263
Canadian Teachers' Federation (CTF), 354
Canadian Violence against Women Survey (Statistics Canada), 218
cancer, faking, 257–58
Cancian, Francesca and James W. Gibson, 278
cannabis, 144; lifetime and past year use by Albertans, *149*; *see also* marijuana
capable guardianship, 306–7
capital: criminal, 188; cultural, 42, 402; social, 42, 85, 226, 407
capital crimes, 373, 374
capitalism, 8, 20, 257
capital punishment, 28, 370, 397; decline in, 373; international perspective, 371–74; race and, 377; in US, 374–78
Capone, Al, 235, 237, 254
careers, 4; deviant, 152, 403; criminal, 10, 249, 402
Carlson, Eric Stener, 278
Carlyle, Thomas, 43; *Sartor Resartus*, 39, 40
Carpenter, Karen, 48, 84
Carrington, Peter, 263–64
Cat Lake, Ont., 155
Causes of Delinquency (Hirschi), 10
Centre for Addiction and Mental Health (CAMH), 93, 98, 172

cheating. *See* marital infidelity
Chicago School, 6–7, 10, 15, 16, 86
child abuse, 215–17; gender and, 216; poly-victimization, 216–17; runaway youth and, 189–90; substance abuse and, 216
Child, Irvin L. and John W.M. Whiting, 321; *Child Training and Personality*, 328–29
children: development of self, 14; effects of maltreatment, 355–56; guilt and, 344; obese, 51, 52; in prostitution, 107; trafficking of, 130
Children Now, 39
Chinese immigrants: opium smoking and, 156
Chinese Immigration Act (1923), 141
Christianity, 324; women in, 320
Christian Voice, 347
churches, 323
Church of Jesus Christ of Latter-day Saints (Mormon Church), 360
cigarettes: smuggling, 145; *see also* smoking
cities: Chicago School on, 6–7; creative, 116; secrecy in, 7
civility, 205, 401
civilization: Freud on, 338
Civilization and Its Discontents (Freud), 338, 344
Civilizing Process, The (Elias), 360–61
civil society: social control and, 336
claims-making, 155, 341–42
Clairmont, Donald, 152–53
clash of civilizations, 279
class, 20; conflict, 192, 290; crime and, 256–57; fashion and, 42–44; habitus and, 41
Clementi, Tyler, 349
Clemmer, Donald, 379
clientelism, 250, 401
Cloninger, Dale O. and Edward R. Waller, 390
clothing, 41–42; identity and, 39–40; pockets, 40; punk, 46–47; revealing and hiding bodies, 40; uniforms and dress codes, 41; *see also* appearance
Cloward, Richard and Lloyd Ohlin, 9
Code of Hammurabi, 371
Cohen, Albert K., 185; *Delinquent Boys*, 186
Cohen, Stanley, 253; *Folk Devils and Moral Panics*, 136; on moral panics, 19
Cold War, 279, 298
Columbine High School massacre, 85, 190, 192
comic books, 286
Commission on Systemic Racism in the Ontario Criminal Justice System, 383
commitment, 10, 174, 402
communities, 4; deviant, 15
community supervision, 370, 371, 383–84, 402
conditional release, 387
condom use, 179
conflict analysis, 20
conformity, 3, 8, 335, 336; Merton on, 38; social bonds that promote, 174; stake in, 9–10, 174, 408
Congressional Research Service, 297
Conservative Party, 282
conspicuous consumption, 60
conspicuous waste, 60
constitutional psychology, 49
consumerism, 257; appearance and, 58; fashion and, 44
contagion, 402; suicide, 79
conviction rates, 370–71, 382; *see also* imprisonment rates
Cooley, George, 13, 16
Cool Hand Luke (film), 393, 400
Cooper, Alison, 144
Co-operative Commonwealth Federation (CCF), 282
coprophilia, 129
Cornell, A.H. and P.J. Frick, 344
Cornerville, 186
corporal punishment, 351–58, 361, 370; acceptability of, 352; banning of, *195*, 352, 358; bullying and, 356–57; dating violence and, 357; effects of, 355; in family homes, 354; history of, 354; ineffectiveness of, 354; police discretion in laying charges, 355; US states with, *352*; worldwide legality of, *353*; youth and, 195
corporate crime, 28, 224, 240–41, 251–53, 402; consumers and, 251–52; future of, 265; involving food, 252; penalties for, 389–90
Correctional Service of Canada, 388, 396
correctional services: costs of non-violent crime, 258–59
Corrections and Conditional Release Act (CCRA), 388
corruption, 270–73, 402; global perceptions index, 273, *274*; worldwide, 272–73
Costs of Substance Abuse in Canada, The (Rehm et al.), 156
counterfeiting 252, 265
"covering," 57
Creba, Jane, 203
crime, 3, 12–13; actual versus apparent, 22; benefits for society, 320; conventional, 209; drug and alcohol abuse and, 157–58, 162; Durkheim on, 319, 320; gender and, 25–26; general theory of, 12, 222, 404; globalization of, 264; as innovation, 255; juvenile delinquency and, 182–84; low self-control and, 222; against morality or public order, 319–20; normality of, 305; of passion, 222, 402; prostitution and, 108;

Quinney's six propositions of, 23; social disorganization theory, 186; street youth and, 189; value of, 319; without victims, 402
crime rates, 18, 237, 372; declining, 182, *236*, *238*, 263, 265, 380; police-reported, *210*
Crime Severity Index (CSI), 213; declining in Canada, *238*, 265; police-reported, *210*, *211*
Crimes without Victims (Schur), 318
Criminal Code of Canada, 244; corporal punishment in, 351–52; delinquency in, 181; rape in, 208; rates of incidents, *19*; section 43, 354; section 718, 370
criminal justice system, 228–29; biases in, 229; costs of, 229; deterrence approach to, 229
criminal proceedings: in Canada, 381–83
criminals: corporate, 252–53; non-violent, 245–54; organized, 249–51; risk of victimization, 311; violent, 213
criminology, xi, 368; critical, 20, 22–27
critical (conflict) theories, 4, 19–28, 29, 402; appearance issues and, 58–59; critical criminology, 22–27; drug and alcohol abuse and, 155–57; juvenile delinquency and, 192–93; mental illness and, 87–90; non-violent crime and, 256–57; political crimes and, 289–91; rational choice theories, 27–28; sexual deviance and, 122–27; social policy implications of, 28–29; theory of culture conflict, 21–22; violent crime and, 223–25; *see also* feminist approaches; postmodern approaches
Croatia, 293
Cross, James, 280
Crowson, Michael H. et al., 341
"CUDO" (communalism, universalism, disinterest, and organized skepticism), 322
"Cultural Conflict and the Marginal Man" (Park), 8
culture conflict, theory of, 21–22
cultures, 4
Curtis, M.A., 395
Cyberball, 350
cyberbullying, 177, 349, 357, *358*
cyber-cheating, 104
cyber-fraud, 259–60
cyberspace: crime in, 265; *see also* e-crime/cybercrime

Dahrendorf, Ralf, 22–23, 224
Daily Show, The (television show), 359
Daniele, Nico, 251
Darwin, Charles, 322
Das, Enny, et al., 342
Davis, Kingsley, 120; "The Sociology of Prostitution," 107–08
Dead Man Walking (film), 392, 400
death penalty: alternatives to, 377–78; costs of, 396; in films, 392; in US, 375, 376; *see also* capital punishment
decriminalization, 402; of marijuana, 162, 164
degradation ceremonies, 39, 41, 403
Deighton, John and John Quelch, 360
deinstitutionalization, 14, 83, 84, 87, 95–96, 384, 403
Deković, M., et al., 181
delinquency (juvenile), 10, 171–72, 198–99, 403; activities, 182–85; adolescent risk-taking and, 173–74, 177–80; class and, 174–75, 186, 192–93; coexisting problems, 185; communities and subcultures of, 185–90; crime and, 182–84; critical theories and, 192–93; definitions of, 171; drift into, 171; economic consequences of, 194–95; families and parental control, 11–12; feminist approaches to, 193; functionalism and, 191; future trends in, 198; gender and, 10, 172, 174–75, 193; influence of family and peers, 180–82; measuring, 181–82; media depictions of, 190–91; parent-child relations, 195; punishments for, 196; punitive strategies, 195–96; social and health consequences of, 194; social policy implications of, 195–98; symbolic interactionism and, 191–92; unsupervised time and, 179; weak attachment to society and, 174
Delinquency and Drift (Matza), 171
delinquent behaviour: definition of, 172; Ontario youth, 172–73
Delinquent Boys (Cohen), 186
D'Emilio, John, 114
democide, 293, *294*, 403
democracy, 299
demonstrations, 276–77; *see also* protests
depression, 74, 75; bullying and, 177; causes of, 75; rates of, 76; suicide and, 79
Derrida, Jacques: on addiction, 137
DeSalvo, Albert ("Boston Strangler"), 223
Desjardins, Norm and Tina Hotton, 158
deterrence, 28, 368, 374, 403
deviance, 3; gender and, 25–26; medicalization of, 155, 405; necessity of, 319; rates of, 18; secondary, 16, 57, 407; socialization and, 14–15
deviant place theory, 311; homeless people and, 312
deviant service centres, 7, 153, 403
Diagnostic and Statistical Manual of Mental Disorders (DSM), 89, 90, 112
dieting, 49, 63
differential association theory, 15, 403; eating disorders and, 55; non-violent crime and, 256; punk culture and, 55
differential illegitimate opportunity, 9, 403

dignity, 3
disability: causes of, *73*; sexuality and, 126–27
discipline, techniques of, 12
Discipline and Punish (Foucault), 26
discredited/discreditable features, 56, 403
dispositions, xiii; *see also* punishment
Distinction: A Social Critique of the Judgement of Taste (Bourdieu), 40
Division of Labor in Society, The (Durkheim), 373
divorce: gender and, 24
Dix, Dorothea, 69
domestic assault, 203
dominant ideology, 297–98, 403
Donnelly, P.G., 261
double standard, sexual, 102–3, 108, 109, 130, 207
Douglas, Tommy, 282
draft dodgers, 275–76
drinking: adolescent, 180; binge, 146, 178; college students and, 146; and driving, 145–46, 158, 178–79, 184–85; problem, 138; social, 155; *see also* alcohol abuse
drug abuse: attitudes towards, 136, 144; communities and subcultures of, 151–53; crime and, 157–58; critical theories and, 155–57; feminist approaches to, 156–57; functionalism and, 154–55; harm reduction strategies, 162; health consequences of, 159–60; poverty and, 158–59; risk of victimization, 311; social consequences of, 157–59; social policy implications of, 161–64; as social problem, 164–65; symbolic interactionism and, 155
drugs: adolescents and, 181, 183; biochemical effects of, 137; cocaine, 144, 150; consciousness-altering, 136, 402; consequences of illegal, 160–61; crack, 150; deliriants, 150; dissociative, 150; gateway, 148, 404; hallucinogens, 149–50; hashish, 144, 162; heroin, 144, 150–51; legislation and, 140–41, 161; marijuana, 16, 138, 140, 147–49, 151, 153, 156, 162–64; for mental illness, 85–86; prescription, 147, 151, 165; psychedelic, 149; psychoactive, 75, 136, 406; rave culture and, 47; recreational, 160, 162; religious beliefs and practices, 140; situation factors in use of, 137–38; "soft" and "hard," 164; stimulants, 150
Drug Treatment Courts, 161
Dudley, Jared, 115
Durham, Lord, 281
Durkheim, Émile, 5, 323, 327, 362; on anomie, 6; on crime, 319, 320; *The Division of Labor in Society*, 373; egoism and, 9; on normality of crime, 5; "The Normality of Crime", 305; on restitutive justice, 374, 390, 391; *Rules of the Sociological Method*, 319; on social change, 5; *Suicide*, 5–6, 80; on suicide, 5–6, 9, 78–79, 80, 86, 320
Dussich, John P.J. and Chie Maekoya, 357
dysthymia, 74, 75

East Germany, 294
eating disorders, 49–54, 63, 73; anorexia nervosa, 48, 49, 60–61; binge eating and, 53, 146, 147; bulimia nervosa, 50; differential association theory and, 55; fashion models and, 48; health consequences of, 60–61; symbolic interactionism and, 57–58
Eaton Centre (Toronto), gang-related shooting at, 203
École Polytechnique, 203
e-crime/cybercrime, 263, 403
education: drug, 161–62; mental illness and, 93–94; prevention of delinquency, 194–95; sex, 103, 194
Edwards, Susan, 211
egoism, 9
elder abuse, 215
elderly people: risk of victimization, 310
Elephant (film), 190
Elephant Man, The (film), 38
Elias, Norbert: *The Civilizing Process*, 360–61
Ellis, Henry Havelock: *Psychopathia Sexualis*, 104
Elmer Gantry (Lewis), 359
employment: Aboriginal people and 317; imprisonment and, 393–94; mental illness and, 92, 93; street youth and, 189
Enlightenment, 26
Enron, 252
environmental threat, 341
erectile dysfunction, 127
Erickson, Bonnie, 285
Escobar, Pablo, 283
escort services, 107; *see also* prostitution
Essex, Mark, 223
evolution, theory of, 322
exclusion, 349–51
excommunication, 351
ex-convicts: employment and, 393; fear of, 262
executions: countries carrying out, *373*; in US, *375*; worldwide, *374*; *see also* capital punishment
exhibitionism, 112
experiences, gendering of, 25

"fallen woman," 123–24
false consciousness, 298
families, 5; "broken," 10; delinquency and structure of, 174–75; juvenile delinquency and, 198; parental

control in, 11–12; patriarchal, 10; prevention and treatment of mental illness, 94–95; rituals, 11; rule enforcement, 11; runaway youths and, 189; sense of attachment and, 11; sex trade and, 107; social bonds of, 10; suicide and, 83
family dysfunction, 83, 403
family process, 181, 403–4
family structure: adolescent risk-taking and, 181
family violence, 214–20, 225–26; child abuse, 215–17; elder abuse, 215; partner violence, 217–20; statistical profile in Canada, 219
Fanon, Frantz: *The Wretched of the Earth*, 286, 287
Faris, Robert and H. Warren Dunham, 70–71
Farley, Melissa, 316
Farley, Melissa and Howard Barkan, 128
fashion: class and, 42–44; industry, 63; models, 47–48; *see also* appearance
fear, of crime: 226, 237, 260–63; economic consequences of, 262–63; health consequences of, 260–62
fear: of reporting crime, 229; violence and, 206; of violent crime, 230
Feather, N.T. and Robert J. Boeckmann, 345
Federal Bureau of Investigation, 326
Federal Republic of Germany (West Germany), 293–94
feminist approaches, 24–26, 29; to appearance, 58–59; to drug and alcohol abuse, 156–57; to juvenile delinquency, 193; to non-violent crime, 257; to political crimes, 290–91; to sexual deviance, 123–25; to violent crimes, 224–25
fetishism, 102, 112, 130, 404; sexual, 112, 407; transvestic, 112
feuding, 207, 404
feuds, blood, 207, 401
films: business crime in, 254; crime in, 237; death penalty in, 392; homosexuality in, 118; identity theft in, 254; illegal file-sharing, 262–63; imprisonment in, 392–93; institutions in, 392; juvenile delinquency in, 190–91; mental illness in, 84; organized crime in, 254; overweight people in, 38; political crimes in, 286; prison, 392–93; protest and, 286; social control in, 359; substance abuse in, 153; torture, 325; victimization in, 324–25; violence in, 221; violent crime in, 220, 221
fines and penalties, 370, 389–90
Finland: alcohol use in, 137; guilt and shame in, 343–44
firearms: used in robberies, 212; use in Canada, 210
Fitz Mary, Simon, 69
Flew, Anthony, 367, 390
Florida, Richard, 116
folk devils, 136
Folk Devils and Moral Panics (Cohen), 136
food: corporate crime involving, 252
Foucault, Michel, 26–27, 29, 90, 125–26, 128, 361; *Discipline and Punish*, 26; *The History of Sexuality*, 126; *Madness and Unreason*, 88–90; on mental illness, 88–89; on pleasure, 126; on prisons and imprisonment, 26; on punishment, 379; on surveillance, 59, 84; techniques of control, 27
France: alcohol use in, 137; wearing of Islamic headscarf in schools in, 62
Frankfurt School, 20
Franklin, Cortney Ann, 313
fraud, 239, 264, 270; cases initiated by whistle-blowers, 241–42; facts on, 260; mass-marketing, 262
French Revolution, 43
Freud, Sigmund, 89, 104, 112, 321; on civilization, 338; *Civilization and Its Discontents*, 338, 344; *The Future of an Illusion*, 329; social control and repression, 336
Friedman, George and Meredith Friedman, 295
Front de libération du Québec (FLQ), 203, 280
frotteurism, 112, 128
functionalism, 4, 5–13, 29, 404; appearance issues and, 54–55; drug and alcohol abuse and, 154–55; early theories, 5–9; juvenile delinquency and, 191; mental illness and, 86; non-violent crime and, 255–56; political crime and, 288; sexual deviance and, 119–20; social control theories, 9; social policy implications of, 28; violent crime and, 221–22

G20 riots, 276
Gagnon, John H. and William Simon, 106, 120
game play, 14
gangs, 191, 214; biker, 237; conflict or violent, 9; criminal, 9, 237; criminal business organizations, 186; criminal groups, 186; gender and, 193; reasons people join and leave, 186–87; street gangs, 186; victimization and, 306; youth, 180, 185–87
Garland, David, 377, 380; *Punishment and Modern Society*, 381
gay and lesbian movement, 116, 121
gender, 25–26; appearance norms and, 40; bullying and, 177; delinquency and, 10, 172, 193; divorce and, 24; gangs and, 193; inequality, 24; mood disorders and, 75; romantic love and, 102–3; sexual assault and, 209, 211; sexual deviance and, 123; smoking and, 156–57; suicide and, 79; victimization and, 25; violence and, 207, 208
gendercide, 291, 404
General Social Survey, 209, 225, 317
Geneva Conventions, 277, 291
genocide, 293, 296–97
Gentry, Alvin, 115

Germany: corporal punishment in, *358*
Gerretsen, John, 129
ghettos, 351, 404
Giffen, James, et al.: *Panic and Indifference*, 140
Girl, Interrupted (film), 100, 392
girls: aversion to risk, 10; child abuse and, 216
Girl with the Dragon Tattoo, The (film), 325
globalization: crime and, 264
"God Save the Queen" (Sex Pistols), 46
Goffman, Erving, 239; *Asylums*, 39, 83, 87, 401; *The Presentation of Self in Everyday Life*, 56; on stigma, 56, 57; *Stigma*, 57, 252–53; on total institutions, 83, 95, 379, 392
Goode, Erich and Nachman Ben-Yehuda, 136
Good Morning, Vietnam (film), 392
Goodwin, Marjorie Harness, 348
Gordon, Robert, 186, 187
gossip, 346–49
Gottfredson, Michael R. and Travis Hirschi, 12–13, 222
Gracia-Arnaiz, Mabel, 63
graffiti, 248–49
Gramsci, Antonio, 298
Great Expenses Scandal (Great Britain), 275
Greaves, Lorraine, 157
Green, Jennifer Lynn, 291
Greenberg, B.S. et al., 39
Green Mile, The (film), 392
groups, 351; dominant versus subordinate, 23; social control and, 335; ways to protect themselves, 337
Guantanamo, 277
guerilla communities, 284–85
Guerre, Martin, 254
guilt, 344–46; collective, 344–45; gender and cultural differences in, 343–44; *see also* shame
guns, 340; *see also* firearms
Gusfield, Joseph, 142, 155

Habermas, Jürgen, 20
habitus, 40–41
Hagan, John, 275
Hagan, John, et al., 10, 26, 174–75
Hagan, John and Bill McCarthy: *Mean Streets*, 187, 188
Hague war crimes tribunal, 291
Hallowell, Gerald, 141
Hankivsky, Olena, et al., 88
harm reduction strategies, 162, 327, 328, 404
Hartman, Phil, 84
hate crimes, 127, 227, 310, 404
Health Canada, 45, 143, 157; Alcohol and Drug Prevention Publications, 166
Health Inequities in Canada (Hankivsky et al.), 88
hegemony, 298
Here's the Deal: Don't Touch Me (Mandel), 71
Hess, Nicole H. and Edward H. Hagen, 348
heteronormativity, 104–5, 117
heterosexism, 117, 118
Hickie, Ian, 76
hidden injuries of social class, 224, 404
Highway of Heroes, 289
Hildebrandt, Martin, 44
Hill, Grant, 115
Himel, Susan, 130
hippies, 47
Hirschi, Travis, 173–74; *Causes of Delinquency*, 10; general theory of crime, 12; social bond theory, 10–11
History of Sexuality, The (Foucault), 126
Hitler, Adolf, xiv, 270
HIV/AIDS, 128, 227
Hoarders, 78
Hobsbawm, Eric, 283
hockey: violence in, 221
Hoeschmann, Michael, 176
Hoffman, Martin L., 12
Hollis, Brenda, 271
Holocaust, xiv, 26, 293, 294, 323
Home-Based Intervention Program (HBI), 95
home invasions, 212
homeless people: mental illness and, 83; victimization of, 311–12; youth, 187–89
homicide, 210, 227; Aboriginal people and, 316–17; in Canada, *204*, 204, 210, 230; domestic, 203; poverty and inequality and, 224; rates in selected countries, *206*, *230*; spousal, 217, 218; by youth, 184
homophobia, 115, 117, 404
homosexuality, 104, 130, 318; communities and cultures, 114–16; in DSM, 90; in films, 118; functionalism and, 120; health consequences of, 128; "passing" and, 105; prevalence of, 105–6, 114; social consequences of, 127; in sports, 115; tolerance for, 105
homosociality, 118, 404
Hong Kong: fashion and, 42
honour (respect): violence and, 207, 208, 214, 224
honour killings, 203, 208, 404
Hood, Robin, 283
Horkheimer, Max, 20–21
Horwitz , Allan, 68
Hosser, Daniela, et al., 344
hot spots, 307–9, 404
Housing Matters BC, 188
How I Met Your Mother: Barney Stinson in, 254
Huebner, Beth M. and Regan Gustafson, 394
human rights, 208

human trafficking, 325–26, 404
Hunting Humans (Leyton), 223
Hurd Clarke, Laura and Meredith Griffin, 35
Huxley, Aldous, 149; *Brave New World*, 359

identity theft, 262; consequences of, 260; media and, 254; types of, *259*
immigrants: children of, 22; drug use by, 156; juvenile delinquency and, 198; mental illness and, 88; organized crime and, 237; risk of victimization, 310
Imperial Tobacco, 144, 145
impression management, 239, 252–53
imprisonment, 349–50, 370, 378–83, 397; consequences for families and children, 394; costs of, 384, 396; economic consequences of, 395–96; effect of, 379; employment and income, 393–94; in films, 392–93; guilt and, 344; health consequences of, 395; inequality and, 394; in television programs, 393; in US, 380–81
imprisonment rates: in Canada, 378, 382, 383; racial minorities and, 383; for selected countries, *378*, 378; in US, 380
incapacitation, 369
incest, 211
India: organized crime in, 251
induction, 12
inequality: feelings of guilt and, 345; gender, 24; imprisonment and, 394; violence and, 224
informal control. *See* social control
information: crime and, 264; "institutions of", 298
information technology (IT), 264
in loco parentis, 171
Innes, Pamela, 348
innovation, 8, 38, 255, 336–37
insider trading, 239
Insite (Vancouver), 17–18, 162
institutional completeness, 114, 284, 404–5
institutions, 5, 361; competition between, 22–23; lack of confidence in, 226, 229, 239; total, 39, 83, 95, 290, 308, 379, 392, 409
interculturalism, 62
International Coalition for Drug Awareness, 69
International Crime Victimization Survey (ICVS), 244, 314
International Criminal Court, 293, 294
Internationale, The, 287
International Federation of the Phonographic Industry, 263
International Labour Organization (ILO), 326; Convention on the Worst of Forms of Child Labour (Convention 182), 130
International Monetary Fund (IMF), 240
Internet, 288; advertising, 360; crime and, 265; pornography and, 111; sexual harassment and, 177; victimization and, 306
intersectionality, 25
intoxication: social role of, 137–39; *see also* alcohol; drugs
involvement, 10, 174, 405
Iraq War, 292, 297, 298
Ireland: corporal punishment in, 354
Irish Republican Army (IRA), 277, 285
Islamic tradition: dress in, 41, 62
Italy: fashion in, 41; organized crime in, 250, 251
I Want to Live! (film), 392

Janus, Mark David, et al., 189
Jennex, Ramona, 308
Johnson, Lyndon, 160
Johnson, Paul, 147
journalism, 298
Ju/'hoansi (!Kung), 336
Juristat, 184, 185, 196, 198, 217, 244, 245, 258–59
justice system: costs of, 228

Kangasvuo, Jenny, 119
Kant, Immanuel, 368
Karp, David, 86
Katz, E. and P.F. Lazarsfeld, 341
Kelly, Maura: "Should 'fatties' get a room? (Even on TV)", 51
Kelly, Thomas M., et al., 389
Kennedy, Florence, 292
Kenny, Paul, 147
Khmer Rouge, 284
Kibby, Marjorie D., 349
Kinsey, Alfred, 104–5, 121
Kirby, Michael, 75
Kirilow, Ashley, 257
knowledge: Foucault on, 27
Koch, Jerome, Alden Roberts, Myrna Armstrong, and Donna Owen, 45
Ku Klux Klan, 377

labelling theory, 13–14, 16, 28, 87, 152, 405; drug and alcohol abuse and, 155; juvenile delinquency and, 191–92; mental illness and, 86–87; non-violent crime and, 256; social policy and, 13–14
landmines, 295
Laporte, Pierre, 203, 280
Laumann, Edward O., et al., 103
law enforcement, 21, 22; gendering of, 25; Turk on, 23
League for Socialist Action (LSA), 284

Leeder, Jesica Ann, 258
legal aid, 382
legalization, 405; of marijuana, 162–64
legislation: drug, 140–41, 161; sex-offender, 17; sexual assault and, 208–9
leisure activities, 41
leisure class, 60, 405
Lemert, Edwin, 16
Lepine, Marc, 203
Lewis, Sinclair: *Elmer Gantry*, 359
Leyton, Elliott: *Hunting Humans*, 223
Lieberman, Joe, 190
lies, 7
life expectancy, Canadian, 173
lifestyle theory, 310–11; homeless people and, 311; sex workers and, 315
Lim, K.-L., et al., 93
Lindner, Evelin Gerda, 208
literature: protest and, 286; social control in, 359
love withdrawal, 12
Lowenthal, Leo, 20
low-interest mortgage meltdown, 239
lust murders, 129
lynching, 377
Lyon Mackenzie, William, 282

Macmillan, Ross and Rosemary Gartner, 218
Madness and Unreason (Foucault), 88–90
Madoff, Bernie, 252, 253
male gaze, 59, 405
Malleus Maleficarum, 320–21
Mandel, Howie, 71–72; *Here's the Deal: Don't Touch Me*, 71
mania, 74, 75
Mao Zedong, 284
Marcuse, Herbert, 20, 126
"marginal men," 8
marijuana, 140, 147–49, 162; Becker on, 16; community of users, 151; culture, 153; decriminalization and legalization debate, 162–64; as gateway drug, 148; media depictions of, 153; situation factors in use of, 138; use by racial minorities and poor people, 156
marital infidelity, 103–4; estimates of, 121
Martinez, Bob, 190
Marx, Karl, xv, 343
Marx, Karl and Friedrich Engels, 290
Marxism, 20; revolution and, 290
masculinity: drinking and, 138; militarism and, 290; risk-taking and, 198; violence and, 138, 207
Mask (film), 38, 66
Masoch, Count von, 112
masochism, sexual, 112, 119
Matza, David: *Delinquency and Drift*, 171
McLloyd, V.C. and J. Smith, 356
McVeigh, Timothy, 296
Mead, George Herbert, 13, 29, 335
Mean Streets (Hagan and McCarthy), 187, 188
media: adolescent risk-taking and, 181; appearance and, 38, 63; in Canada, 360; conflict and, 289; fear of crime and, 261–62; homicide in, 204; human trafficking and, 326; male risk-taking and, 198; moral panics and, 136, 140, 342; pornography and, 111; portrayal of drug addicts, 136; sexual deviance and, 118–19; substance abuse and, 136, 140, 153; victimization and, 324–25; violent crime and, 220–21
Meldrim, Harmon, 104
men: anti-homosexuality among, 118; collective guilt and, 345; crime and, 265; ideal appearance, 36–37; obesity and, 50–51; public drinking by, 140; sexual assault and, 225; sexual assault of, 291; spousal violence and, 219; street crime and, 248; use of coercive control, 218–19; as victims of domestic violence, 217–18; violence and, 207; warfare and, 290
men, young: automobile accidents and, 178, 313; risk-taking and, 173; violence and, 213, 214
mental illness, 68–69, 74–83, 96, 405; anxiety disorders, 78; costs of, 93; critical theories and, 87–90; definition, 68; diagnosis of, 94; early history of, 69; economic consequences of, 92–93; education and, 93–94; Foucault on, 88–89; functionalism and, 86; homelessness and, 83, 312; impact of, 73; likelihood of, 73, *74*; Marxist approach to, 87; media depictions of, 84–85; modern approach to, 69; mood disorders, 74–77; moral treatment advocates, 69; neighbourhoods and, 88; pharmaceutical companies profiting from, 93; postmodern approaches to, 88–90; poverty reduction and, 94; prevalence amongst prison inmates, 90, *91*; prevalence rates, 71–73; public opinion of, 69, 70, 71; schizophrenia, 70–71, 77–78; sick role, 68; social consequences of, 90–92; social factors in, 69; social inequality and, 87–88; as socially structured, 96; social policy implications of, 93–96; stereotypes of, 96; stigma and, 68, 72, 86, 86–87, 91–92, 94; suicide, 78–83, 94–95; symbolic interactionism and, 86–87; symptoms of, 68, 96; treatment and non-compliance, 85–86; work and, 92, 93
mentally ill people, 74–83; communities and subcultures of, 83–84; deinstitutionalization of, 14,

83, 84, 87, 95–96, 384, 403; hospitals and asylums for, 69; social support networks, 85; in US prisons, 395
Merrick, David, 38
Merton, Robert, 8–9, 29, 126, 255; on anomie, 38, 54–55, 155, 158–59, 255, 280, 336; on city politics, 272; on norms of science, 322; strain theory of, 21
"Me So Horny" by 2 Live Crew, 190
message framing, 342
metropolitanism, 7
military forces, 290, 294–95
Milligan, S., 182–83
Mills, C. Wright, xv
minorities, ethnic and racial: imprisonment rates, 383; risk of victimization, 310; on television, 39
Miron, Anca M., et al., 345
Miron, Jeffret and Katherine Waldock, 161
money: future of, 264–65; laundering, 237, 240, 247, 259, 263
Montreal massacre, 203
mood disorders, 74–77, 92
Mood Disorder Society of Canada, 78
Moor, A., 314
Moore, Barrington, 281
moral entrepreneurs, 136, 405
moral panics, 19, 136, 405; about addiction, 136; media and, 136, 342; stages of, 136–37
Morgan, Laurie A. and Karin A. Martin, 349
Mothers Against Drunk Driving (MADD), 167, 178
motor vehicle theft, 245; youth and, 184
Mullen, Kenneth and Richard Hammersley, 151
Murphy, Emily: *The Black Candle*, 140–41
music: protest, 286; illegal file-sharing, 262–63
Mustaine, Elizabeth Erhardt and Richard Tewksbury, 306

Naranjo, C.A. and K.E. Bremner, 145
Nash, Steve, 115
National College Women Sexual Violence Study (US), 225
National Crime Victimization Survey, 225
National Institutes of Health, 50
nationalism, 322–23
National Longitudinal Survey of Children and Youth, 226, 395
National Opinion Research Center (NORC), 103, 121
National Parole Board, 383, 387, 388, 389, 399
National Population Health Survey (1996–7), 93
national security: threat and, 340
National Security Strategy of the United States (NSSUS), 340
nation-states, 361; "rule of law" in, 205–6
Nazism, 15, 294
Neapolitan Camorra, 15
neighbourhoods: crime and deviance and, 6; drug-use and, 152–53; fear of crime and, 261; inner-city, 6–7, 214; mental illness and, 88; schizophrenia and, 70–71; youth crime and, 198
Netherlands, the: drug use in, 150, 164
neutralization, techniques of, 253, 409
neutralization theory, 345, 405
New Democratic Party (NDP), 282
Nicholson, Rob, 129
nicotine addiction, 142–44, 160, 165; *see also* smoking
Nightingale, Florence, 69
Nineteen Eighty-Four (Orwell), 359
Nofziger, Stacey, 310–11
non-violent crime, 235–36; critical theories, 256–57; feminist approaches to, 257; functionalism and, 255–56; future trends in, 263–65; media depictions of, 254; public costs of, 258; relative deprivation and, 255; social consequences of, 259–60; social policy implications of, 263; symbolic interactionism and, 256; types and varieties of, 236–45; *see also* business crime; corporate crime; organized crime; street crime
Norgaard, Kari Marie, 345
normality, 29, 121; of crime, 5; versus abnormality, 90; postmodernism and, 26
"Normality of Crime, The" (Durkheim), 305
Norman, Ruth Trexler, 342
Nova Scotia Parents Against Bullying, 308
nuclear weapons, 295
nursing, 69
Nutt, David, 163

obesity, 48–49, 50–53; main factors affecting, 52–53; media and, 38; rates in major Canadian CMAs, *53*; social policy implications of, 61–62; stigma of, 51–52; transportation patterns and rates of, *54*
obsessive-compulsive disorder (OCD), 71–72, 78, 84
October Crisis, 203, 280
offenders: total population in Canada, *388*
offences: drug, 148, *148*, 158, *158*, 183; impaired driving, 184–85; police-reported, *122*; prostitution-related, 110; sexual, 122, 123; status, 193, 408; traffic, x, 184–85
Oklahoma City bombings, 296
Olsen, Marvin, 337, 339
One Flew Over the Cuckoo's Nest (film), 99–100, 392
Ontario Court of Appeal: prostitution decision, 129

Ontario Student Drug Use and Health Survey (OSDUHS), 172, 185
On-to-Ottawa, 299
Oosterhoff, Pauline, et al., 291
organized crime, 205, 235, 237–39, 247, 265, 405; in failed states, 250; friendship and kinship links, 250; global scope of, 259; intersection of legitimate and illegitimate business, 249; key conditions of, 250; mafia-enforced extortions, 251; social consequences of, 259–60
Orwell, George: *Nineteen Eighty-Four*, 359
Ost, Suzanne, 111
ostracism, 349–51
other: generalized, 335
othering, 340–41, 346, 405–6
O'Toole, Roger, 283–84
Ottawa Treaty, 295
Outsiders (Becker), 152
Overeaters Anonymous, 147

pain: as deterrent, 352; *see also* corporal punishment
Palestine: murder of girls and women, 208
Panic and Indifference (Giffen et al.), 140
Panopticon, 26, 27, 84
pansexuality, 105
paraphilia, 102, 111, 406; criminal, 113, 129; health consequences of, 128–29
parenting: adolescent risk-taking and, 180–81; authoritarian, 11; authoritative, 11–12, 180; discipline, 12; parental control, 11–12; permissive, 11, 12; unengaged, 11–12; use of corporal punishment, 354, 355, 356
parents: children of imprisoned, 394; "good," 11
Paris riots, 277, 282
Park, Robert, 8; "Cultural Conflict and the Marginal Man," 8
Parker, Gordon, 76
parole, 386–89; breaches of, 389; in Canada, 387–88; outcomes of day, *387*
partialism, 112
particularism, in government decision-making, 271–72
partner swapping, 130
"passing," 57; homosexuality and, 105
passion, crimes of, 222, 402
patriarchy, 24, 25, 123, 125, 208, 406; violence and, 220
patriotism, 322
patronage, 250, 270, 272, 406
patron-client networks, 250
peacemaking circles, 391–92
pedophilia, 106, 112; social consequences of, 127–28; victims of, 128–29
peers: adolescent risk-taking and, 180–81, 198
penalties: diversionary, 389, 403
penitentiaries, 368; costs of, 372; *see also* prisons
Pepler, D., D. Jiang, W. Craig, and J. Connolly, 307–08
Perreault, Samuel, 316
persuasion, 341–42; advertising and, 346; anti-smoking and, 342
pharmaceutical companies, 93, 127
Philadelphia (film), 118, 330
physical assault, 210; *see also* violent crimes
Piaget, Jean, 14
Pickton, Robert, 203, 315
Pinel, Philippe, 69
Pinker, Stephen, 205; *The Better Angels of Our Nature*, 203
piracy, 250; music and movie files, 262–63
plastic surgery, 62–63
play: three stages of, 14
plea bargaining, 382
pleasure: Foucault on, 126
police: crimes recorded by, xiii, xvi; non-violent crime, 263; racial profiling and, 246; relationship with criminals, 249; riots and, 276; use of Tasers, 277–78
political corruption, 270, 406
political crimes, 270; corruption, 270–73; critical theories, 289–91; economic consequences of, 296–97; environmental consequences of, 294–95; feminist approaches to, 290–91; functionalism and, 288; health consequences of, 295–96; media depictions of, 286–88; rebellion, 281–82; revolution, 280–81; riots and collective protests, 276–77; social consequences of, 292–94; social policy implications, 298–99; symbolic interactionism and, 288–89; torture, 277–78; treason, 273–76, 281; violent political protest, 279–80
politics: of reputation, 362; separation from religion, 323, 324; women in, 291
polyamorous relationships, 105
poly-victimization, 216–17
popular culture: violent crime in, 220–21; *see also* media
population aging: crime rates and, 213, 263–64
populist movements, 282, 406
pornification, 119
pornography, 110–11, 130; child, 111, 130; torture, 325
Porter, Joey, 115
postmodern approaches, 26–27, 29; to sexual deviance, 125–27
post-traumatic stress disorder (PTSD), 70, 91, 227, 296, 406; child abuse and, 215; prostitutes and, 128
Poulsen, Joan Rose, 350
poverty: criminalization of, 247; culture of, 199, 246, 402; drug and alcohol abuse and, 158–59; mental

illness and, 94; prostitution and, 123; violence and, 224; youth crime and, 198
power: Dahrendorf on, 22–23; Foucault on, 27; sexual deviance and, 122–23; victimization and, 309; war and, 289
power assertion, 12
power-control theory, 174, 406
Presentation of Self in Everyday Life, The (Goffman), 56
prevention, 368; *see also* deterrence
Prince Edward Island: temperance legislation in, 141
prison: Foucault on, 27
prisonization, 379, 406; secondary, 394
prisons, 351, 378; as hot spots, 308–9; illegal-drug users in, 160–61; mentally ill people in, 90–91; *see also* imprisonment
probation, 384–86; breach of order, 385–86; officers, 384, 385
procedures, surgical and non-surgical: top five, *59*
Prohibition: in Canada, 141; in US, 22, 141, 144, 155, 237
Pronger, Chris, 115
propaganda, 298
property crime, 244–45; declining rates of ordinary, *243*; rates for Canada and provinces, *245*
Proposition 8, 360
prostitutes, 108, 109; in public debate, 109, 110; three classes of, 107; as victims, 110
prostitution, 106–10; child, 127; crime and, 108; decriminalization of, 129–30, 315, 316; economic inequality and, 129, 130; entry by choice, 109; feminist approaches to, 124; functionalism and, 120; health consequences of, 128; laws around, 129–30; mental health consequences of, 128; persistence of, 107–8; social consequences of, 127; street-level, 108; street youth and, 187; symbolic interactionism and, 122
protest: collective, 276–77; movements, xv, 276–77, 282, 286, 299; political, 274, 279–80, 406
Protestantism: sobriety and, 140
Prus, Robert and Scott Grills, 15
psychoactive substances, 75, 136, 406; *see also* drugs
Psychopathia Sexualis (Ellis), 104
public engagement and participation, 299
public opinion: dominant ideology and, 298; threat and, 341
punishment, 367, 369–71; capital, 28, 370, 371–74, 374–78, 397; community supervision, 370, 371, 383–84, 402; corporal, 195, 351–58, 361, 370; costs of, 228; cruel and unusual, 370; definition of, 367, 390; fines and penalties, 370, 389–90; Foucault on, 379; goals of, 367–69; Kant on, 368; legal framework in Canada, 370; media depictions of, 392–93; probation, 384–86; restorative justice, 369, 397, 390–92, 407; social policy implications of, 396–97; types and characteristics of, 371–92; *see also* imprisonment
Punishment and Modern Society (Garland), 381
punk culture, 63; appearance, 46–47; differential association theory and, 55; music, 46

Quebec: drug legislation in, 161; temperance legislation in, 141
queer community, 114–16
Queercore filmmaking movement, 118
queer theory, 114, 406
Quinney, Richard, 23

race: capital punishment in US and, 377; depiction in media, 39
racial profiling, 246
racism, 246
Rahman, Omar Abdel, 279
rape: acquaintance, 211; "classic," 211; collective, 291, 402; definition of, 211; marital, 211; spousal, 208; statutory, 211; victim precipitation theory and, 313; as war crime, 291; women's risk of, 309–10
rape trauma syndrome, 227
rational choice theories, 27–28; deviance and, 15
rational-legal society, 321
Ravi, Dharun, 349
Rawson, Arnold, 312
reality: postmodernism and, 26; selective interpretation of, 345–46
reasonable accommodation, 62
rebellion (adaptation to anomie), 8, 38, 255, 280
rebellion (political crime), 270, 281–82, 406
Rebellions of 1837, 281
recidivism, 379–80, 406; in Canada, 380; youth crime and, 196
refugees: camps, 351; public opinion of, 340
rehabilitation, 368–69, 379, 406; probation and, 385
Rehm, Jürgen et al. , 145; *The Costs of Substance Abuse in Canada*, 156
Reiss, Albert, 120
religion, 324, 328; civil, 323; expressive versus repressive, 140; extremism, 323; versus science, 322; secret societies and, 285; separation from politics, 323, 324; as source of control and deviance, 320–24
Renner, Michael, 295
repression, 336
repressive justice, 373–74, 390, 406–7
restitutive justice, 374, 397, 407; Durkheim on, 390, 391
restorative justice, 369, 390–92, 397, 407; community–offender reconciliation, 391–92; key practices of,

390; victim–offender reconciliation, 391; victims and victimization and, 391
retreatism, 8, 159, 255, 407
retribution, 368, 407
revolution, 280–81, 290; "of the saints", 282; social class and outcome of, 281; social consequences of, 292; world, 284, 409
revolutionary communities, 283–84
revolving door, 379, 407; *see also* recidivism
Reynald, Danielle M., 306–07
Rice, Christopher, 146
Richard Riot, 276
Riel, Louis, 282
riots, 276–77
risk assessment, process of, *243*
risk management: probation and, 385
risk-taking: adolescent, 177–80, 180–81, 196; class-based conflict and, 192; developmental course of, 173–74
ritualism, 8, 38, 255, 407
robbery, 211–12; elderly people and, 310; victimization by, 307
Rohrbaugh, Joanna Bunker, 220
romantic love, 102–3, 407
Rotermann, Michelle, 179
Rothmans Benson & Hedges, 145
routine activity theory, 306–10, 407; capable guardianship, 306–7; homeless people and, 312; hot spots and, 307–9; sex workers and, 315; suitable targets, 309
Royal Canadian Mounted Police (RCMP), 201, 262, 263
Ruddell, Rick, 378
rule-benders, ordinary, 304
"rule of law," 205–6
Rules of the Sociological Method (Durkheim), 319
Rummel, R.J., 293
Russell, Bertrand, 3
Russia: corruption in, 272
Rutten, Rosanne, 343
Rwanda, civil war in, 295, 296–97

Sade, Marquis de, 112
sadism, sexual, 112
sado-masochistic communities and cultures, 113–14
Sampson, Robert J. and John H. Laub, 10
la sape, 42
Sapers, Howard, 395
Sartor Resartus (Carlyle), 39
Sato, Akihiko, 155
schizophrenia, 74, 77–78; impact of, 77–78; links to neighbourhood, 70–71; mortality and, 78; stigma of, 77
Schnittker, Jason and Andrea John, 395
schools: "Afrocentric," 194; corporal punishment in, 354; health promotion in, 61–62; as hot spots, 307–8, 311; juvenile delinquency and, 198; residential, 298, 327
school uniforms, 41
Schroeder, Jonathan E., 59
Schur, Edwin M.: *Crimes without Victims*, 318, 329
science, 328; norms of, 322; postmodernism and, 26; versus religion, 322
Scripps Research Institute, 147
secrecy: Simmel on, 7, 285
Secretary (film), 119
secret societies, 7, 285
secularism, 321
secularization, 323, 407
self: development of, 14; looking glass, 16; symbolic interactionism and, 13, 14, 16
self-control, 12–13, 222
Sellin, Thorsten, 21–22
Sennett, Richard and Jonathan Cobb, 224
sentencing: conditional, 385; in Criminal Code of Canada, 370; mandatory, 161
serial killers, 223
sex: extramarital, 121, 130; physical disability and, 126–27; premarital, 106, 108, 117, 130; survival, 187; young people, 179
sex-offending, 17
sex trade: functioning of, 107–9; international, 109–10; social inequality and, *123*
sex traffic, 109–10, 127, 130
sexual abuse: runaway youths and, 189; shame and, 343; suicide attempts by victims of, 227
sexual assault, 211; Aboriginal people and, 317; consequences of, 227; by family or acquaintances, *124*, 209; feminist approaches to, 224–25; gender and, 209, 211; rates of, *124*, *125*, 209; by spouses, 208; three levels of, 208–9, 211; victim precipitation theory and, 313; victims of, 227
Sexual Assault Investigation Team, Criminal International Tribunal for the former Yugoslavia (UCTY), 278
sexual deviance: acceptance of, 130; critical theories and, 122–27; dimensions of, 106, 120; feminist approaches to, 123–25; functionalism and, 119–20; health consequences of, 128; heteronormativity and, 104–5; history and public reactions, 105–6; marital infidelity, 103–4; media depictions of, 118–19; other forms of, 111–16; pornography, 110–11; postmodern approaches to, 125–27; prostitution, 106–10; public opinion and, 120; social

consequences of, 127–28; social inequality and, 122–23; social policy implications of, 129–30; symbolic interactionism and, 120–22
sexual gaze, 112, 407
sexual harassment, 125; rates of, *125*
sexual liberation, 103, 108
sexually deviant communities, 114
sexually transmitted diseases (STDs), 124, 128, 178, 179
sexual orientation: in Canada, *116*; Kinsey on, 105
sexual property, 125, 407
sexual violence, 124, 208; in warfare, 291
sex work, 110; *see also* prostitutes; prostitution
Shafia, Mohammad, 203
shame, 342–44
Shawshank Redemption, The (film), 393, 400
Sheldon, William, 49
shell shock, 69–70; *see also* post-traumatic shock disorder (PTSD)
SHOP (School Health Opportunities and Progress), 194
"Should 'fatties' get a room? (Even on TV)" (Kelly), 51
sick role, 68
SIECUS (Sexuality Information and Education Council of the United States), 194
Silfver, Mia, 343
Simmel, Georg, 7, 60; on fashion, 43; on secrecy, 7; on secret societies, 285
Simon, Jeffrey, 285
Simpson, Wallis, 48
Simpsons, The (television program), 191, 254
Skocpol, Theda, 281
slavery, 377
"slut" protests, 40
Smith, Tom W., 103, 105
smoking (cigarette): gender and, 156–57; health consequences of, 159–60; reduction in Canada, *143*; risks associated with, 145
smoking industry, 144
SNAP (outpatient program for suicide attempters), 95
soccer riots, 276
social bonds, 10; conformity and, 174; theory, 10–11, 407
social change: Durkheim on, 5
social cohesion, 154, 407–08
social constructionism, 4, 155, 408
social control, 335–37, 360–62; bureaucratization and, 339; economic consequences of, 360; informal versus formal, 361, 361–62; media depictions of, 359; non-violent crime and, 255; procedures for organizational survival, 339; rewards and, 337; social management, 338, 339; social sanctioning, 338–39; theories, 9, 15
social control strategies, 339–58; corporal punishment, 351–58; exclusion/ostracism, 349–51; gossip, 346–49; guilt, 344–46; persuasion, 341–42; shame, 342–44; threat, 340–41
Social Credit Party, 282
social disorganization theory, 6, 9, 10, 408; crime and, 186; drug and alcohol abuse and, 154; juvenile delinquency and, 191; non-violent crime and, 255–56; violence and, 213
social ecology, 6
social exclusion, 3, 408
social inequality, 29; mental illness and, 87–88; sexual deviance and, 122–23; suicide and, 80–83
social integration, 261, 348
social interaction, 4
socialization, 14–15, 29; development of self and, 16; non-violent crime and, 256
social legitimating, 16
social networks, 10
social norms, 335, 408; appearance and, 342
social order, x, xiii; conflict and, 21; deviance as indicator of, xi; play and, 14
social organization, 337–38
social problems: social construction of, 17–18
social recognition, 16
social rewards, 337–39
social structure, xi; *see also* social order
social ties, 277, 408
societalization, 323–24
socio-economic development, 361
socio-economic status: fatness and thinness and, 48–49, 52
sociological approaches. *See* critical theories; functionalism; symbolic interactionism
sociological imagination, xv
sociological method, 80
"Sociology of Prostitution, The" (Davis), 107–8
Socrates, 319
Somalia: piracy in, 250
somatotypes, 49
Sorel, Georges, 223–24
SOS (Secular Organizations for Sobriety), 161
spanking, 354, 355; *see also* corporal punishment
Specialized Emergency Room Care, 95
"spice" products, 163
SSRIS, 190
stalking, 125, 203, 212–13, 408
Standing Committee on Justice and Human Rights (Mann, 2008), 145–46

Statistics Canada, 148, 158, 182, 183, 184, 193, 213, 215, 258, 265, 310, 386; *Canadian Violence against Women Survey*, 218; on property crimes, 244–45
status markers, 42
statutory release, 388; breaches of, 389
Steiger, Howard, 51
stereotypes: of mental illness, 94, 96
Stewart, Kristen, 324
Stigma (Goffman), 57, 252–53
stigma/stigmatization, 58, 91, 408; anxiety disorders and, 78; discredited/discreditable features, 56; Goffman on, 56, 57; mental illness and, 68, 72, 86, 86–87, 91–92, 94; schizophrenia and, 77
Stouffer, Sam, 324
strain theory, 8, 21, 408; *see also* anomie
strategic culture, 288
Street Corner Society (Whyte), 186, 191, 249
street crime, 244–45, 248–49, 265, 408
strong reciprocity, 335–36
structural functionalism. *See* functionalism
subcultures, 7
subjects: versus authorities, 23
substance abuse: activities and characteristics of, 144–51; demographics of, 139; factors affecting, 138–39; history and public reactions, 139–44; media depictions of, 153; schizophrenia and, 78; social costs of, 156; *see also* alcohol abuse; drug abuse
Suicide (Durkheim), 5–6, 80, 320
suicide, 71, 74, 78–83; bullying and, 308; contagion, 79; Durkheim on, 5–6, 9, 78–79, 80, 86, 320; egoistic, altruistic, and anomic, 80; family-based care and, 94–95; family dysfunction and, 83; gender and, 79; mood disorders and, 77; rates, 81–82; schizophrenia and, 78; sexual abuse and, 227; social disruption and, 79; social inequality and, 80–83; veterans, 296
suitable targets, 309
suite crime, 239, 408; *see also* business crime
sumptuary laws, 42–43
Super Bowl, 322–23
Supreme Court: Insite case, 18; prostitution debate, 129
surveillance: Foucault on, 27, 59, 84
Sutherland, Edwin, 14–15, 22, 239, 248; *White-Collar Crime*, 240–41
Sweden: corporal punishment in, *358*
swingers, 114
Sykes, Gresham M. and David Matza, 345
symbolic crusade, 155, 408–9
symbolic interactionism, 4, 13–19, 29, 409; appearance issues and, 55–58; construction of social problems, 16–19; drug and alcohol abuse and, 155; eating disorders and, 57–58; ethnographic studies in, 13; juvenile delinquency and, 191–92; mental illness and, 86–87; non-violent crime and, 256; political crimes and, 288–89; secondary deviance and, 57; on self, 13, 14; sexual deviance and, 120–22; on socialization, 14; social policy implications of, 28; stigmatization and, 58; violent crime and, 222–23

Takahashi, Yoshiko, 391
Tarde, Gabriel, 15
Tasers: used by police, 277–78
taste: appearance and, 40
tattooing, 44–46, 63; health consequences of, 61; public views of, 45; removal, 61; sexual activity and, 45–46; women and, 45
tax cheating, 235, 236, 262; media and, 254
Taylor, Charles, 270, 271
Taylor-Butts, Andrea, 183
technology, 263; *see also* e-crime/cybercrime; Internet
teenagers: alcohol and substance use and, 139; smoking and, 145
television programs: anxiety disorders in, 78; business crime in, 254; crime in, 237; homosexuality in, 118–19; imprisonment in, 393; juvenile delinquency in, 191; marijuana use in, 153; overweight people in, 38, 51; political crimes in, 286–88; protest in, 286; race in, 39; social control in, 359; substance abuse in, 153; victimization in, 325; violent crime in, 220
temperance movement, 141, 156; *see also* Prohibition
terrorism, 270, 409; costs of, 297; definition of, 285; health consequences of, 295–96; sense of threat, 340; state-sponsored, 285–86
terrorists, 277, 279, 289; communities, 284, 285–86
theft, from a car, 244–45
Theory of the Leisure Class (Veblen), 42
Thrasher, Frederick, 185–86
threat, 340–41; environmental, 341; national security and, 340; othering and, 340–41; sense of, 340
Ticket of Leave Act, 386
tobacco: social role of, 157; use of, 144–45; *see also* smoking
Tomatis, Alfred, 77
Toronto: homeless adolescents in, 188; racial profiling in, 247
torture, 277–78
total institutions, 409; degradation in, 379; Goffman on, 39, 83, 379, 392; as hot spots, 308; mental hospitals as, 83, 95; military as, 290; uniform appearance in, 39
totalitarianism, 294

"tough on crime", 229, 380
Trafficking in Persons Report, 325
Trainspotting (film), 133, 153
Transparency International, 272, 273, 301
treason, 273–76, 281
Trocmé, Nico and David Wolfe, 216
Trudeau, Pierre Elliot, 117, 280
truth: postmodernism and, 26; problem of finding, 25
truth and reconciliation commissions, 298, 390–91; residential schools, 298
Tucker, J.S., et al., 149
Turk, Austin, 22, 23
Turner, H. and P. Muller, 356

underclass, 161, 193, 409
unemployment rates: Aboriginal people and, 317; young people and, 173
United Nations Outreach Program on the Rwanda Genocide, 296
United States: Prohibition in, 141–42, 144, 155, 237; punishment in, 371; use of torture, 277; war on drugs in, 160–61
United States Holocaust Memorial Museum, 297
University of Frankfurt, Institute of Social Research, 20
US National Survey of Adolescents, 310–11
usurpation, 20

Valley of the Dolls (film), 153
van Beest, I. and K.D. Williams, 350
Vancouver: Downtown Eastside, 315; 2011 riots, 276; street prostitution in, 110
Veblen, Thorstein, 60, 43; *Theory of the Leisure Class*, 42
veterans, 292, 296
victim blaming, 313
victimization, 304, 409; as cause of mental illness, 91; child abuse and, 215; consequences of, 326; deviant place theory, 311; lifestyle theory, 310–11; media depictions of, 324–25; of mentally ill people, 90, 91; problem of, 25; rates in selected countries, *314*; restorative justice and, 391; routine activity theory, 306–10; sex workers and, 315; social policy implications of, 326–27; women and, 24
victim precipitation theory, 312–14
victims: of bullying, 175, 177; of conscience, 304–5, 319–20; of crime, 304, 305; crimes without, 304, 318; gender and, 25; of non-crime, 304; reports from, xiii, xvi; of violent crime, 226–27
victims rights movement, 18–19, 380
Villaume, Alfred, 377
violence, 203–4; in action films, 221; alcohol and, 138; causes of, 206; climate of, 226; against colonizer, 287; communities and subcultures of, 213–14; demographics of, 230; family, 214–20, 225–26; gender and, 207; in hockey, 221; honour or respect and, 207–8, 214, 224; interpersonal, 207, 405; intimate partner, 217–20, 405; legitimate use of, 205, 206; organized crime and, 237; pimp-related, 108; political, 293–94, 296; rationalizations for, 222; same-sex couples and, 220; sexual, 124, 208, 291; social disorganization theory and, 213; subculture of, 214, 408; against women, 124; in the workplace, 307
violent crime, 203–7; costs of, 228; critical theories and, 223–25; decline in, 205–6, 210; defining, 209–13; economic consequences of, 228; fatal outcomes of, 227; feminist approaches, 224–25; functionalism and, 221–22; history and public reactions, 207–9; homicide and physical assault, 210; media depictions of, 220–21; mental health consequences of, 226–27; non-fatal outcomes of, 227–28; physical health consequences of, 227–28; power and, 224; rates of, 204–5, *205*; robbery, 211–12; sexual assault, 211; social and psychological consequences of, 225–26; social policy implications of, 228–29; stalking, 212–13; symbolic interactionism and, 222–23; victims of, 226–27, *309*
violent predators, 213, 409
Virk, Reena, 391
virtual communities, 265
Visher, Christy, et al., 393
voyeurism, 112, 409
vulnerability: physical and social, 261

Walkerton, Ont., 224
Wallace, Marjorie, 76
Walzer, Michael J., 282
war, 270, 278–79; changes in, 278–79; civil, 270; deaths in, 278, *279*, 295; destruction of cultural heritage, 292; economic cost of, 292; economic mobilization of, 288; functionalism and, 288; given positive spin, 289; health consequences of, 295–96; injuries from, 295–96; language and, 289; military establishment and, 290; power and, 289; property damage and, 292; rape in, 291; scientific and technological innovations, 288; stereotyping of enemies, 289
war crimes, 293, 294
War Measures Act, 280
"war on drugs," 142, 160–61, 380, 394, 409
"war on terror," 323
war system, 278, 290
Watson, Scott D., 340
Weber, Max, xv, 20, 140; on bureaucracy, 270–71; conflict analysis, 20; rational-legal society, 321

Welts, Rick, 115
Werner, Cynthia, 124–25
Werther effect, 79, 409
West Indian community: juvenile delinquency and, 194
What's Eating Gilbert Grape (film), 38–39
What's Love Got To Do With It? (film), 221
whistle-blowers, 241–44
white-collar crime, 239, 241, 248, 409; consequences of, 259–60; penalties of, 248; social consequences of, 260; *see also* business crime; corporate crime
Whitty, M.T., 104
Whyte, William Foote: *Street Corner Society*, 185, 186, 191, 249
Wiessner, Polly, 336
Wilson, Terence, 147
Wilson, J.Q. and G.L. Keeling, 255–56
Winickoff, Jonathan, 144
Winnipeg General Strike, 276, 282, 299
witch craze, 320–21
Wittfogel, Karl, 20
Wolfgang, Marvin and F. Ferracuti, 214
women: abductions and, 124–25; accusations of witchcraft, 320–21; aging and, 35; alcohol abuse and, 157; appearance and, 49, 58–59; appearance norms and, 35–36; "comfort", 291; criminality and, 193, 225; domestic violence, 218; dysthymia and, 75; eating disorders and, 49–50; in gangs, 193; gossip and, 348; homeless, 312; ideal (appearance), 36–37; imprisonment and, 394; mental illness and, 73, 92; in military, 290; non-violent crime and, 257; in politics, 291; pornography and, 111; as property, 207, 208; in prostitution, 107, 110; public drinking, 140; religious repression and persecution, 320; sexual assault and, 211, 225, 313–14; smoking and, 156–57; spousal violence and, 219–20; stalking and, 213; suicide and, 79; tattoos and, 45; victimization of, 24, 309, 310; victim precipitation theory and, 313–14; as victims of sexual crime, 124; violence against, 124
workplaces: as hot spots, 307; violence in, 307
World Health Organization (WHO), 78, 92; Mental Health Division, 99; Substance Abuse, 167
World Values Survey, 272
World War I, 295; mental illness and, 69–70
World War II, 69, 279, 291, 292, 295; homosexual subculture and, 114–15
Wortley, Scot and Julian Tanner, 247
Wretched of the Earth, The (Fanon), 286, 287

Xu, Jianhua, 307

Yakuza, 44
Young Offenders Act, 13; *see also* Youth Criminal Justice Act (YCJA)
youth: alcohol and, 139–40; anti-social tendencies in, 171; binge drinking and, 178; breach of probation and, 386; challenges facing, 173; drinking and driving, 178–79; drugs and, 181, 183; failure in school, 179–80; homelessness and, 187–89; homicide by, 184; movements, 186, 409; recreational programs, 196; risk of victimization, 310; runaway, 189–90; sexual assault and, 209; smoking and, 143; street, 187–89; tattoos and piercings and, 45; unsafe sex and, 179; violent offences and, 183
youth court: declines in caseload, *182*; multiple charge cases in, *184*; ten common offences, *183*
youth crime: decrease in, 184; impaired driving and traffic offences, 184–85; motor vehicle theft, 184; neighbourhoods and, 198; poverty and, 198; recidivism and, 196
Youth Crime Victimization Survey (2002), 247
Youth Criminal Justice Act (YCJA), 184, 196–97, 370; changes with Bill C-10, 197–98; custody and supervision order, 196–97; Intensive Support and Supervision Program, 197

Zadro, Lisa, et al., 350
Zimmerman, E., 280
Zoroastrian penal law, 373